ROBERT W. FOGEL
University of Chicago
Graduate School of Business
1101 East 58th Street
Chicago, Illinois 60637
USA

12.13.00

Beyond Shocks:

What Causes Business Cycles?

Contents

Foreword Cathy E. Minehan	ix
Beyond Shocks: What Causes Business Cycles? An Overview Jeffrey C. Fuhrer and Scott Schuh	1
Summing Up on Business Cycles: Opening Address Paul A. Samuelson	33
The Causes of American Business Cycles: An Essay in Economic Historiography Peter Temin	37
Discussion Christina D. Romer	60
Historical Evidence on Business Cycles: The International Experience U. Michael Bergman, Michael D. Bordo, and Lars Jonung	65
Discussion Richard N. Cooper	114

The Role of Interest Rate Policy in the Generation and Propagation of Business Cycles: What Has Changed Since the '30s? 121
Christopher A. Sims

Discussion
Lawrence J. Christiano 161
Benjamin M. Friedman 171

Financial Markets and Business Cycles: Lessons from Around the World. A Panel Discussion

After Asia: New Directions for the International Financial System 177
Rudiger Dornbusch

Financial Shocks and Business Cycles: Lessons from Outside the United States 187
Maurice Obstfeld

Market Mechanisms for Avoiding the Next Currency Crash: Lessons from Asia 194
Avinash Persaud

Technology and Business Cycles: How Well Do Standard Models Explain the Facts? 207
Susanto Basu

Discussion
Mark Bils 256
Thomas F. Cooley 264

Job Reallocation and the Business Cycle: New Facts for an Old Debate 271
Scott Schuh and Robert K. Triest

Discussion
Ricardo J. Caballero 338
Steven J. Davis 349

POLICY IMPLICATIONS: A PANEL DISCUSSION

The New Financial World: Policy Shortcomings and
Remedies   359
Henry Kaufman

A View of Recessions, from the Automotive Industry   371
Martin B. Zimmerman

Emerging Economies and the Business Cycle   377
Agustin G. Carstens

The Effects of International Policy   383
Michael Mussa

About the Authors   389

Conference Participants   395

Foreword

Over the past several years we at the Federal Reserve Bank of Boston have used our annual economic conference to focus our own research, the research of other experts, and the thoughts of conference participants on issues related to economic growth and prosperity in this country and elsewhere. To that end, recently we have looked at technological change, and at changes in saving and investment—particularly as they might be encouraged by Social Security reform—as critical elements in long-run growth. This year we consider the short run—that undefined but vital period of time over which monetary policy can affect economic fluctuations. As Keynes quipped, "In the long run we are all dead." Policymakers need to worry about the short run, and about how a combination of short runs can produce the optimal long run that has been the focus of some of our recent conferences.

The topic of our forty-second annual economic conference is one of the most important but perplexing issues in all of economics: What causes business cycles? Like many others, I have been asking this question more and more, lately. Several recent events—the aging economic expansion, financial crises in Asia, warning signs on the inflation front, and the surprising suggestion that we have conquered the business cycle—are putting increasing pressure on us to provide answers. As we have puzzled over this here at the Bank, we have realized that modern macroeconomics has trouble answering this question because of its widespread reliance on random, exogenous "shocks" as the cause of short-run economic fluctuations, or business cycles.

Business cycle theory suggests that unanticipated good or bad "shocks" occur periodically and create fluctuations around a long-run trend. Monetary and fiscal policy then must act to smooth the fluctuations. But I think most of us can agree that shocks are a less than fully satisfying explanation of the business cycle. What economic behavior lies behind these shocks? What causes consumers to alternate between spending sprees and retrenchment? Why is investment spending so volatile, and what causes businesses to suddenly lay off large numbers of workers at a time, or even close down altogether? Do monetary and fiscal policies contribute to economic fluctuations?

Our inability to pin down the source of some of the most important events in economic history seems to me a gaping hole in the intellectual underpinnings of modern macroeconomics. More important, can the economic behavior behind shocks be identified, so that policymakers can anticipate an unsustainable boom, or an approaching downturn, before it happens rather than after? The ability to do that obviously relates to our biggest challenge of late, which has been trying to foresee anything that will upset the enviable success our economy currently enjoys.

My hope is that this conference has produced the beginnings of understandable, *economic* explanations of the sources of cyclical fluctuations—explanations that not only are more satisfying intellectually, but also are more *practical* for policymakers. I also hope that study of the papers and discussions will stimulate further research into the contentious issues raised and explored here.

December 1998

Cathy E. Minehan
President and Chief Executive Officer
Federal Reserve Bank of Boston

BEYOND SHOCKS: WHAT CAUSES BUSINESS CYCLES? AN OVERVIEW

Jeffrey C. Fuhrer and Scott Schuh*

In the summer of 1997, when the Federal Reserve Bank of Boston selected the topic for its forty-second annual economic conference, many pundits were asking: "Is the business cycle dead, or at least permanently dampened?" By the time the Bank's conference convened in June 1998, the same pundits queried: "What caused the massive recessions in Asia?" and "Can the United States remain 'an oasis of prosperity,' as Fed Chairman Alan Greenspan termed it, while economies worldwide are under siege from financial crises?" How quickly things change!

Beyond Shocks: What Causes Business Cycles? turned out to be a particularly timely conference. Of course, the answers to the pundits' questions are inextricably tied to an underlying fundamental question: What makes economies rise and fall? To determine whether the business cycle is dead, one must first determine whether economic fluctuations arise from the decisions of governments, financial market participants, and businesses, or simply from unexpected events (that is, "shocks"). To determine why Asian economies plunged into severe recession, it is necessary to understand how external pressures on vulnerable financial markets can lead to a sudden collapse, with severe consequences for nonfinancial sectors. And to determine whether the robust economic expansion in the United States will continue, it is necessary to evaluate how a slew of adverse economic factors, financial and real, could interact to end it.

So, what caused the Asian crisis, the recessions of the 1970s and 1980s, and even the Great Depression? According to many modern

---

*Vice President and Economist, and Economist, Federal Reserve Bank of Boston. The authors thank Lynn Browne for helpful comments on this summary.

macroeconomists, shocks did. This unsatisfying answer lies at the heart of a currently popular framework for analyzing business cycle fluctuations. This framework assumes that the macroeconomy usually obeys simple behavioral relationships but is occasionally disrupted by large "shocks," which force it temporarily away from these relationships and into recession. The behavioral relationships then guide the orderly recovery of the economy back to full employment, where the economy remains until another significant shock upsets it.

Attributing fluctuations to shocks—movements in important economic variables that occur for reasons we do not understand—means we can never predict recessions. Thus, a key goal of the conference was to try to identify *economic* causes of business cycles, rather than attributing cycles to "shocks." The greater the proportion of fluctuations we can classify as the observable and explainable product of purposeful economic decisions, the better chance we have of understanding, predicting, and avoiding recessions.

Several themes emerged during the conference. One was the concept of "vulnerability." It was especially prominent in discussions of the recent Asian crises and bears on the distinction between shocks and systematic economic behavior. Rudiger Dornbusch perhaps put it best in the following analogy. Consider the collapse of a building during an earthquake. While the proximate cause of the collapse was the earthquake, the underlying cause may better be attributed to poor construction techniques. Because of its structural defects, the building was going to collapse when the right "shock" came along. So it goes with financial and real economic collapses, Dornbusch and many others would argue.

While it will always be difficult to anticipate the particular event that precipitates a collapse, it is important to constantly assess the vulnerability of financial, product, and labor markets to potential shocks. Macroeconomists and forecasters tend to focus primarily on the overall health of the economy as measured by aggregate demand or by the unemployment rate; they may be able to improve their economic models by incorporating vulnerability. Likewise, policymakers should be vigilant against vulnerability. To do so, they will need to develop new tools. In Asia, for example, policymakers should have had a better assessment of the ability of the financial system to absorb shocks to currency valuations.

Developing such an assessment would likely have been hampered, many conference participants pointed out, by the inability to obtain key data on the debt portfolios of financial institutions, the performance of bank loans, and the exposure of the country as a whole to exchange rate risk. Proposals abounded for more accessible banking data and new indexes of risk exposure. Although little agreement was reached on exactly what information would be most useful, most agreed that policymakers and investors need new and more timely measures to adequately assess the vulnerability of economies to severe disruptions.

A second theme of the conference discussion was the role of systematic monetary policy in causing and preventing business cycles. Many have blamed the bulk of recessions on monetary policy. But as pointed out by Peter Temin, Christina Romer, and Christopher Sims, in assigning blame, it is important first to distinguish the systematic response of monetary policy to existing conditions from policy regime shifts and exogenous policy shocks. To take a leading example, did the Fed cause the Great Depression by raising domestic interest rates to maintain the gold standard, or was the outflow of gold from the United States following Great Britain's abandonment of the gold standard the cause, and the response of the Fed a "business as usual" response to that triggering event? Such questions are very difficult to answer, but a careful attempt to do so must be made if we are to understand the role of monetary policy in cycles.

Most participants agreed that the Fed played a significant role in causing many of the recessions of the past century, largely in the pursuit of its goal of long-run price stability. The degree to which monetary policy did or could moderate the effects of cyclical downturns was less clear. Many pointed to the apparent diminution of the amplitude of business cycles in the postwar period as evidence of the Fed's ability to lessen the severity of contractions.

Interestingly, Sims's more formal analysis of this question raised doubts that the systematic component of monetary policy either causes fluctuations or can offset them, at least through interest rate movements. Using econometric substitution of modern interest rate policy back into the Great Depression era, Sims found that modern policy would have had little effect on employment or prices. While this finding met with a good deal of skepticism from participants, one skeptic who tried to prove Sims wrong—discussant Lawrence Christiano—reported that he could not. In any case, the suggestion that conventional interest rate policy is limited in its ability to offset major recessions is thought-provoking. Of course, the limitations of interest rate policy do not preclude alternative policies, such as deposit insurance and acting as lender of last resort in financial crises. These policies may be at least as important as interest rate policy.

A third conference theme was the importance of a deeper understanding of the contribution of changes in the efficiency and structure of production to business cycle fluctuations. Recently, some macroeconomists have advanced the idea that shocks to these supply-side or "real" factors cause many, if not most, of the ups and downs in the economy. This idea contrasts sharply with the traditional macroeconomic notion that changes in aggregate demand cause most fluctuations, and the two views generate quite different policy implications.

Two real shocks were evaluated. One is a shock to the technological efficiency of firms' production of goods and services. Technological changes are very positively correlated with output and business cycles, a relationship that has led many observers to conclude that technology shocks cause fluctuations. Susanto Basu, however, demonstrates that more detailed and sophisticated estimates of technological change substantially reduce, if not completely eliminate, the correlation between technology shocks and the business cycle. He also shows how modern macroeconomic models, especially those that rely primarily on technology shocks, have difficulty fitting the data. Proponents of technology-oriented models were predictably skeptical of his results.

The second real shock is a change in the desired distribution or allocation of economic resources across firms, industries, and regions. Restructuring involves the costly and time-consuming reallocation of factors of production, especially workers, between firms, industries, and regions through the processes of job creation and destruction. It also typically involves lower output, higher unemployment, and often even recessions. In fact, job reallocation and job destruction rise sharply during recessions, leading some to surmise that shocks to the process of reallocation itself may be responsible for recessions and should therefore be taken into consideration by macroeconomic models. Scott Schuh and Robert Triest discover strong correlations between job reallocation and the primary determinants of how jobs are allocated across firms and industries: prices, productivity, and investment. Correlations between these determinants and job reallocation suggest that it is not mysterious allocative shocks that cause business cycles, but significant changes in observable economic variables.

Together, the two studies of real shocks reaffirm the fact that the production and employment behavior of firms is subject to substantial variation over the business cycle, but they deepen doubts that the variation is due to real shocks. Instead, the correlations between output and simple measures of real shock reflect the failure of conventional analyses to incorporate a sufficiently detailed specification of production and market structure. As more and more of firms' behavior is accounted for in macroeconomic models, less and less scope remains for real shocks to generate business cycles. However, much is still to be learned about business cycles from the behavior of factor utilization, investment, prices, productivity, and the like.

SUMMING UP ON BUSINESS CYCLES

Paul Samuelson's opening address begins with the question "Is the business cycle dead?" While the macroeconomy appears to have stabilized over the past 50 years, perhaps owing to successful countercyclical macropolicy, Samuelson sees no evidence of a trend toward the elimination of business cycle fluctuations. He notes that after most periods of extended expansion, especially those accompanied by outstanding performance in asset markets, suggestions of a "new era" of recession-proof prosperity have arisen, and they have been received "with increasing credulity" as the expansion rolls on. Acknowledging this historical association between healthy economies and booming asset markets, Samuelson takes a more realistic view, stressing also the intertwined histories of business cycle downturns and bubbles and crashes in asset markets.

Samuelson cites Victor Zarnowitz's recent observation that in the seven decades between 1870 and World War II, the United States suffered six major depressions. In the past 50 years, we have had no declines of comparable severity. Samuelson attributes this improved performance to changes in "policy ideology, away from laissez-faire and toward attempted countercyclical macropolicy." But despite the gains in policy's management of the economy, Samuelson sees no "convergence towards the disappearance of non-Pareto-optimal fluctuations. We are not on a path to Nirvana." The scope for improved performance arising from better government policies appears marginal today.

So pronounced fluctuations in production, prices, and employment are here to stay, despite the best efforts of policymakers. But why? In the end, Samuelson argues, fluctuations are usually the product of two factors. First, on the upside, asset price bubbles will always be with us, because individuals have no incentives to eliminate "macromarket inefficiency." While we have made tremendous progress toward "microefficiency"—making individual financial markets more efficient through the widespread use of options and other derivatives, for example—little evidence can be found, either in economic history or in economic theory, that "macromarket inefficiency is trending toward extinction." One can make money by correcting any apparent mispricing of a particular security, but one cannot make money attempting to correct apparent macro inefficiencies in the general level of stock market prices.

Economists and financial market participants simply have no theory that can predict when a bubble will end. As a result, an individual investor will be perfectly rational in participating in a bubble, as he will make money from the bubble so long as it continues, which could be indefinitely. As Samuelson puts it, "You don't die of old age. You die of hardening of the arteries, of all the things which are actuarially ... associated with the process. But that's not the way it is with macro inefficiency." Bubbles go on until they stop, and no one has ever been able to predict when that will be.

Downturns can develop from the asset markets themselves, and they can develop quite quickly. Because asset prices are based on the "prudent ex ante expectations" of market participants, swings in market expectations can produce large and rapid swings in asset prices, causing massive revaluation of asset-holders' wealth. This was in part the cause of the ongoing Asian crisis, according to Samuelson. Market participants reasonably reassessed the valuation of investments (and therefore currencies) in Asia and quickly altered the direction of capital flow, precipitating a currency and banking crisis there.

Given the lack of private incentive to restrain the stimulative effects of this "oldest business cycle mechanism," we come to the second factor that contributes to business cycle fluctuations: government policy. Samuelson noted that he has often said, "When the next recession arrives, you will find written on its bottom, 'Made in Washington.'" This is not, as he points out, because the Fed is a sadistic organization. Rather, "if the central bank and fiscal authorities did not step on the brakes of an overexuberant economy *now*, they might well have to overdo that later." When persistent macromarket inefficiencies threaten both employment and price stability and private incentives fail to encourage financial markets back into line, only policymakers can take the systemic view necessary to guide the economy back into balance.

THE CAUSES OF AMERICAN BUSINESS CYCLES

Peter Temin examines the causes of U.S. business cycles over the past century. In developing his taxonomy of causes, Temin points out three inherent problems with the effort. First, the idea of a "cause" is fraught with ambiguity. In part, this ambiguity arises from the difficulty in distinguishing the endogenous, or "normal response" component of government policies and private actions, from the exogenous, or out-of-the-ordinary actions of private and public agents. In Temin's view, only exogenous events should be seen as causal. He uses oil prices and the 1973-75 recession to illustrate the dilemma: Was the recession following the oil shock "caused" by the oil shock, or by the monetary policy response to the oil shock? The imputation of causes depends on one's model of economic history, and particularly on the degree to which one makes behavior endogenous or exogenous.

Second, the Great Depression should be treated as a unique event. As Temin notes, output lost during this enormous downturn was almost one-half of the sum of output lost in all other downturns in the past century. The body of writing on the Great Depression is larger than that on all other business cycles combined. Consideration of the causes of the Great Depression provides useful lessons about the causes of the less prominent cycles of the past century. For example, it seems implausible that a single "shock" in 1929 pushed the U.S. economy into massive depression. Instead, Temin argues, the Great Depression was likely the result of a sequence of contractionary influences. Prominent among these were the fear that the hyperinflationary pressures in Eastern Europe following the First World War would spread to the United States, the adoption by industrialized countries of the relatively inflexible gold standard in response to these pressures, and the breakdown of banking and legal systems. The Great Depression was really a sequence of smaller recessions large and persistent enough, given policy responses, to throw the world into depression.

Third, Temin cautions that his assignment of causes relies on the existing literature on the subject. The literature on recessions other than the Great Depression is quite sparse, with earlier recessions receiving considerably less attention than more recent ones. And within this limited set of sources, most authors focus on the *transmission* of cycles, rather than on the causes. Finally, most of the available sources do not highlight expectations and do not clearly distinguish anticipated from unanticipated changes.

Temin classifies the reported causes of recessions as either domestic or foreign, and either real or monetary. Changes in the relative prices of assets, both real and financial, are classified as real phenomena. Temin finds that the preponderance of cycles in the past century may be attributed to domestic causes, with the split between real and monetary causes roughly equal for the entire period. Monetary causes of recessions were more prevalent in the pre-World War I period than during the post-World War II period, however.

Temin focuses on the larger downturns. The cause of the Great Depression of 1931 is classified in Temin's taxonomy as a foreign monetary phenomenon. The action of the Fed to maintain the gold value of the dollar by raising interest rates was to behave as a "traditional and responsible central banker" or, in other words, to follow a normal and expected endogenous policy course. Thus, the Fed's behavior cannot be viewed as an exogenous cause of the Great Depression, in Temin's view. The search for causes then reverts to the question of what produced this monetary policy response. Temin suggests that U.S. monetary policy was responding to the external gold drain that arose from Britain's departure from the gold standard, which threatened to weaken the dollar. The Fed's reaction in increasing interest rates, and the bank panics and failures that followed, were endogenous responses to the gold drain.

In assessing the causes of the four largest downturns of the century—the Great Depression, and the recessions of 1920, 1929, and 1937—Temin concludes first that no single cause explains all four downturns. Three of the four possible causes in Temin's taxonomy appear as causes of the downturns. Second, three of the four recessions appear to be responses to domestic shocks. Most often, we cannot blame our downturns on foreign causes.

Taking all of the cycles studied into consideration, Temin offers the following conclusions: (1) "It is not possible to identify a single type of instability as the source of American business cycles." Thus, Dornbusch's statement, "None of the U.S. expansions of the past 40 years died in bed of old age; every one was murdered by the Federal Reserve," is not supported by Temin's analysis. (2) Domestic real shocks—ranging from inventory adjustments to changes in expectations—were the most frequent source of fluctuations. (3) Other than the two oil shocks of 1973 and 1979, foreign real shocks were not an important source of U.S. cycles. (4) Monetary shocks have decreased in importance over time. (5) When measured by the loss of output, domestic sources have loomed larger than foreign sources; real sources have caused about the same losses as monetary sources.

Christina Romer takes issue both with Temin's classification scheme and with his interpretation of the literature on the causes of recessions. She suggests that an improved classification scheme and a different reading of the literature would yield a more critical role for domestic monetary shocks, particularly in the inter- and postwar periods.

Romer suggests that Temin's methodology is biased toward finding very few monetary causes of recessions. Whereas Temin classifies most Fed behavior as a fairly typical response to prevailing conditions and therefore not the ultimate cause of the recession, Romer would prefer a more practical classification of monetary policy actions. If the monetary policy action was the inevitable or highly likely result of a trigger, then we should consider the policy action endogenous and therefore not a cause. If, however, "a conscious choice was made" or if "alternative policies were ... discussed at the time," then the policy should be considered at least partly exogenous, and monetary policy should get some blame for the recession.

Romer shows that, using this criterion, many more of the twentieth-century recessions have an important monetary policy aspect. Monetary factors would likely be given an important causal role in the 1931 recession, for example, as "reasonable men *at the time* were urging the Fed to intervene" in the face of financial panics. Thus, the choice not to intervene but to raise the discount rate was not inevitable or even most likely. Romer also questions the extent of the constraint imposed by the gold standard, as U.S. gold reserves in 1931 were probably adequate to have allowed the Fed to pursue expansionary open market operations while maintaining the gold value of the dollar, as in fact it did in 1932.

Turning to the 1973 recession, for which Temin ascribes no monetary role, Romer argues that the central bank was not simply acting as "a respectable central bank [that] resists inflation," and therefore responding only as expected. Romer points out that the decision to tighten in 1974 was not a foregone conclusion but rather a conscious choice, as "the economy was already in a downturn and many were calling for loosening." Thus, "monetary policy and the oil shock share responsibility for the 1973 recession."

Romer also challenges Temin's attribution of the 1957 and 1969 recessions to declines in government spending. She points out that the high-employment budget surplus actually *falls* throughout the late 1950s, suggesting a net stimulative impulse from the federal government for the

1957 recession. For both recessions, Romer asserts that the Federal Reserve made a conscious decision to tighten in order to reduce inflation.

As Romer sees it, "the key change has not been from monetary to real shocks or vice versa, but from random shocks from various sources to governmental shocks." Since the Second World War, the government has been more effective at counteracting most shocks, accounting for the diminished frequency of cycles. However, the combination of a tendency toward overexpansion and a few large supply shocks caused inflation to get out of hand. In sum, Romer would agree with the thrust of Dornbusch's statement, which is that monetary policy has played a vital role in postwar recessions. She might re-cast the role of the Fed, however, as "more like a doctor imposing a painful cure on a patient with an illness than a murderer."

THE INTERNATIONAL EXPERIENCE

Michael Bergman, Michael Bordo, and **Lars Jonung** examine the broad cyclical properties of GDP, using a newly compiled data set of annual observations for a sample of "advanced" countries. Their data set spans the years 1873 to 1995. The authors show that the duration of business cycles (the calendar time from peak to peak or trough to trough) has been fairly similar across countries and fairly stable over time. The average duration rose from about four years in the pre-World War I period to about five and one-half years during the interwar period, falling back to just under five years in the period following World War II. The most severe recessions appear to have occurred prior to 1946, and the magnitude of all fluctuations in GDP seems to have decreased in the postwar period.

Formal statistical tests of diminished cyclical fluctuations in the postwar period generally confirm the visual evidence. This observation has often been interpreted as evidence that countercyclical policy has been more effective in the postwar period. However, an alternative explanation is that the increased integration of the world economy serves to mitigate the negative influence of any one country's disruptions on other countries.

Conventional wisdom holds that downswings are sharper and "steeper," whereas upswings are more gradual. Bergman, Bordo, and Jonung test this proposition and find that, for the United States, upswings are indeed more gradual than downswings. The evidence for other countries is more mixed, however, with most exhibiting this asymmetry prior to World War II but only a minority displaying asymmetry in the postwar period.

The authors then attempt to determine the extent to which different components of GDP—including consumption, investment, government expenditures and revenues, exports, and imports—account for its cyclical volatility. For virtually all countries and time periods, all components of GDP except consumption generally are more volatile than GDP. This finding is consistent with the presence of a consumption-smoothing motive, that is, the desire of consumers to maintain a relatively smooth stream of consumption over time in the face of volatility in their income and wealth.

The authors find that larger countries experience deeper recessions; the average decline in GDP below trend is larger for large countries than for small, open European countries. For most countries, the downturn in GDP during a recession is accounted for by declines in consumption, investment, and net exports.

Finally, Bergman, Bordo, and Jonung consider the patterns of international co-movement of output and prices in their data. They find that the correlations among real output in the 13 countries have increased over time, suggesting a more integrated world economy and possibly a stronger coherence of the business cycle across countries. During the gold standard, real GDP for most countries exhibited little or no correlation with real GDP in other countries. During the interwar period, U.S. GDP was significantly correlated with seven other countries, but corresponding correlations between other countries were not evident. The authors suggest that this correlation arises from the role of the United States as the "epicenter" of the Great Depression. Output linkages among European countries strengthened considerably in the postwar period, perhaps the result in part of the establishment of the European common market and in part of the common influence of the oil shocks in the 1970s.

Price levels appear to be much more consistently correlated across countries. Like output, price levels have become increasingly correlated over time, perhaps consistent with "increased global integration of goods markets," the authors suggest.

Richard Cooper offers a different perspective on Bergman, Bordo, and Jonung's conclusion that "the cyclical pattern . . . appears to remain surprisingly stable across time, regimes, and countries" and on the broad question of the international origin and transmission of the business cycle. He examines years in which the raw data for real GDP declined, for a set of nine countries during the periods 1873 to 1913 and 1957 to 1994. Cooper prefers this approach, as the authors' results may depend on the filtering and detrending methods that they used in constructing their data.

The conclusions that he draws for the earlier period are as follows: First, "most downturns are domestic in origin, and are not powerfully transmitted to the other important trading nations." Second, if one were interested in international transmission, one would focus on 1876, a year in which the Continent and Canada experienced declines in GDP, and on 1879 and 1908, years in which several countries experienced output declines. Third, Belgium exhibits only one downturn during these periods, a suspicious finding given the 12 downturns in neighboring Netherlands and 14 in France. As a result, Cooper calls into question the reliability of the annual data for any of these countries prior to 1914.

For the period 1957 to 1994, Cooper notes that the few recessions have been concentrated in five years: 1958, 1975, 1981-82, and 1993. This suggests strong international transmission, in contrast to the earlier period. All of the recessions in the United States were accompanied by recessions elsewhere. The greater coherence may be attributed to the importance of the oil price shocks in these recessions, Cooper notes.

Cooper goes on to question the detrending method used by Bergman and his coauthors. Only 60 percent of their recessions match NBER reference dates. The issue of appropriate filtering is important when considering the welfare implications of business cycles, Cooper suggests. A departure of output below its (rising) trend may imply relatively little lost income or underutilized resources, whereas an absolute decline in output would almost surely entail significant welfare losses.

Cooper outlines a number of broad changes in industrial economies that would lead one to question Bergman, Bordo, and Jonung's conclusion about the stability of the business cycle over long spans of time. He suggests that "the most dramatic by far . . . is the reduction in the fraction of the labor force required for food production." The decline in this number from about one-half in 1880 to below 5 percent by 1995 for all of these countries is likely to have altered the dynamics of the business cycle significantly, according to Cooper. Other important secular changes include the increased participation of women in the paid work force, the growth in the importance of government expenditures, and major technological innovations, including electricity, automobiles, and aircraft. "A relatively unchanged economic cycle that survived these dramatic secular changes in modern economies would be robust indeed," Cooper suggests.

INTEREST RATE POLICY AND BUSINESS CYCLES

Christopher Sims examines one of the most contentious questions in macroeconomics: the role of monetary policy in twentieth-century business cycles. Sims points out that one cannot determine the influence of monetary policy simply from observed changes in interest rates and output. The observation that a rise in interest rates precedes each postwar recession does not show that policy-induced interest rate movements *caused* the recession. If, for example, rapid expansion of private demand for credit systematically causes all interest rates to rise near the end of an expansion, this rise in interest rates should not be interpreted as the cause of a subsequent slowdown; it is a consequence of previous strong demand. Because such "eyeball" interpretations of the data can lead to confusion about the role of monetary policy, Sims advocates examining the interactions among many economic variables in order to obtain a clear picture of the role of any one of them in economic fluctuations.

Sims employs a methodology that allows each of six variables (industrial production, consumer prices, currency, a monetary aggregate, the discount rate, and commodity prices) to respond to lags of the other variables, and to the contemporaneous values of *some* of the other variables. The restrictions on the contemporaneous interactions among variables reflect common-sense notions about policy, goods market, and financial market behavior. Monetary policy-induced interest rate changes affect prices, output, and monetary aggregates only with a one-month lag; monetary policy responds to output and prices only with a lag, reflecting data availability; and commodity prices respond to everything contemporaneously, reflecting their auction-market, flexible nature.

This simple model is estimated on monthly data for the postwar years 1948 to 1997. Sims uses the model to show that most of the variation in the Fed's discount rate represents systematic policy responses rather than unanticipated shifts in policy. The discount rate responds primarily to movements in production, commodity prices, and M1. These three determinants of interest rate movements in turn cause the largest increases in CPI inflation, suggesting that the Fed responds to these as signals of future inflationary pressures.

When Sims estimates this same model on the interwar period from 1919 to 1939, he finds similarities but also some important differences in monetary policy responses and influences. One key difference is that the effect of interest rate changes in the early period is roughly double the effect in the later period. On the other hand, monetary policy in the early period appears to be more accommodative toward unanticipated increases in output, raising the discount rate less in response to output and thereby allowing greater inflation in commodity and in final goods prices. Interestingly, the model shows that when depositors' worries caused a rush into currency in the interwar period, the Fed typically *raised* the discount rate, accelerating the shrinkage of money.

This first set of exercises establishes that the systematic responses of policy to output and prices represent the dominant source of interest rate fluctuations in Sims's model, and that these interest rate movements are likely the most important source of policy's effects on the rest of the economy. Noting that economic fluctuations have been smaller in the postwar period, Sims proposes using his model to answer a key question: whether better systematic monetary policy is responsible for the improved economic performance of the postwar period.

To answer this question, Sims transplants the estimated monetary policy equation for one period into the other period, then observes the estimated behavior of output, prices, and monetary aggregates under this counterfactual monetary regime. The results from these exercises are remarkable. In the first variant, the (estimated average) policy judgment of Burns, Volcker, and Greenspan is imposed on the 1920s and 1930s. Overall, Sims finds the outcomes—particularly the Great Depression—would have been little changed by this more responsive postwar policy. The drop in production from 1929 to 1933 is "completely unaffected by the altered monetary policy." Postwar policy would have made the 1920-21 and 1929-33 deflations less severe, but not by much. The upheaval of the 1920s and 1930s would have been the same, even if modern monetary policymakers had been at the reins. Sims notes that his methodology leaves the banking runs, panics, and currency speculations that plagued the Depression era as unexplained non-monetary shocks. To the extent that a persistent commitment to monetary ease would have alleviated such disruptions, the drop in output might have been less severe, he suggests.

The effects of substituting interwar monetary policy into the postwar economy are qualitatively the same. Even though the discount rate responds much more slowly to the postwar economic fluctuations, resulting in a markedly different interest rate pattern, the influence of this altered policy on industrial production and consumer prices is quite small at business cycle frequencies. The implications for output and inflation at longer horizons are what one would expect with a more accommodative policy: Output and inflation both rise higher in the 1970s, resulting in a larger recession in the 1980s, although Sims is careful to point out that these findings may well be statistically unreliable. Overall, he reaches the startling conclusion that "the size and timing of postwar U.S. recessions had little to do with either shocks to monetary policy or its systematic component."

Lawrence Christiano focuses on Sims's surprising conclusion that monetary policy played little or no role in the Great Depression. He disagrees with the methodology that Sims uses to reach this conclusion, but upon employing what he considers a superior method, he confirms Sims's results.

One criticism of Sims's methodology revolves around the assumption that private agents behaved the same in the postwar period after the creation of the Federal Deposit Insurance Corporation (FDIC) as they did during the interwar period prior to the FDIC. Christiano suggests that the frequency with which interwar depositors converted deposits to currency at the slightest sign of bad news, in contrast to the virtual absence of such bank runs in the postwar period, suggests that the presence of the FDIC fundamentally changed private agents' behavior. In particular, they may have viewed the commitment of Federal Reserve policy to maintain banking system liquidity quite differently in the postwar period, and in a way that cannot be captured by the simple "reaction functions" or interest rate equations in Sims's analysis.

The more important flaw in Sims's analysis, according to Christiano, is the characterization of the postwar monetary policy rule. Under this rule, after all, the Fed would have *contracted* the money supply by 30 percent in the 1930s. Christiano cannot conceive of a sensible policymaker who would pursue a contractionary monetary policy during a widely recognized, worldwide depression. So Christiano proposes instead to use a monetary policy equation that keeps money (M1) from falling during the episode.

Using this more plausible counterfactual policy in Sims's model for the interwar period, Christiano finds that a stable M1 path for the early 1930s would have prevented the dramatic price declines that actually occurred. Surprisingly, however, even under the more realistic policy response, which implies a more realistic path of money growth, "the basic course of the Great Depression would not have been much different," as shown by the similarity between the path of output in Christiano's simulation and the actual path of output.

Benjamin Friedman is also skeptical of the empirical results developed in Sims's paper, stating: "If the model he presents has succeeded in identifying Federal Reserve actions and measuring their economic effects, these findings should force us to reconsider many aspects of economics and economic policy." Friedman finds troubling Sims's result that postwar monetary policy would not have significantly altered the course of the Great Depression, and he views as even more problematic the finding that Depression-era monetary policy would have worked just the same in the postwar period as did actual policy. Friedman notes that the general price level was approximately the same at the onset of World War II as at the onset of the Civil War, while prices since that time have risen approximately tenfold. That the monetary policy that delivered the interwar *de*flation is the same one that delivered the "historically unprecedented phenomenon of a half century of sustained *in*flation" would make inflation, even over periods of several decades, never and nowhere a monetary phenomenon.

Friedman suggests that Sims's model delivers its surprising results because it fails to adequately identify the Fed's monetary policy actions or the effects of those actions on the macroeconomy. If so, then the model's "implied irrelevance of monetary policy" for the postwar inflation translates further into irrelevance for assessing monetary policy's role in causing or cushioning business cycles. One indication that Sims's postwar policy rule does not accurately represent Fed actions, Friedman argues, is the difference between the Sims model's policy prescriptions for the Depression era and John Taylor's policy rule prescriptions for the same period. Friedman finds that Taylor's rule would imply nominal interest rates "an order of magnitude more negative than what Sims reports," casting some doubt on how well Sims's policy rule reflects all of postwar Fed behavior.

Finally, Friedman notes that the assumption that Fed policy can be characterized by one unchanging rule over the entire postwar period is implausible. He asks, "Are we really to equate Paul Volcker's tough stance against inflation with the see-no-evil regime of Arthur Burns?" While Friedman recognizes that Sims tests for a shift in monetary policy in 1979, Sims does so by testing for a shift in all 279 of his model's parameters. Friedman notes that Sims could have more narrowly focused this test to detect only shifts in the parameters that summarize monetary policy.

FINANCIAL MARKETS AND BUSINESS CYCLES: LESSONS FROM AROUND THE WORLD

A panel composed of **Rudiger Dornbusch**, **Maurice Obstfeld**, and **Avinash Persaud** analyzed recent financial market crises, most notably the turmoil in Asia, and drew lessons on how to reduce the likelihood and severity of future crises. Generally speaking, the panelists agreed more on why the crises occurred than on what should be done to prevent future crises.

Dornbusch believes that recent financial crises in Asia, Russia, and Mexico differed from most preceding crises because they centered on capital markets rather than on the balance of payments. Both types of crises often are associated with currency crises as well, but the vulnerability or risk imposed on an economy by a capital market crisis is fundamentally different. He explains that financial systems experiencing a capital market crisis exhibit five characteristics: (1) borrowing short and lending long generates a *mismatching of maturities* between liabilities and assets; (2) borrowing in foreign currency units and lending in domestic currency units generates a *mismatching of denominations*; (3) borrowing to carry assets exposed to large fluctuations in price generates *market risk*; (4) high risk exposure throughout a country generates a *national credit risk*; and (5) the central bank is weakened by *gambling away foreign exchange reserves*.

According to Dornbusch, the capital market crisis in Asia made the regional economy vulnerable, or at risk, to adverse external factors. And two such factors happened. First, "Japan went into the tank." Just as the Japanese economy was starting to show signs of emerging from several years of sluggish growth, the Japanese government tightened fiscal policy and the economy slumped again. This time the weakened economy exposed underlying banking problems that exacerbated the situation so much that the Japanese economy eventually began to contract. Because Japan is the largest economy in the region and the leader in regional export and import markets, the Japanese slump put stress on the foreign trade structure of the entire region, which is characterized by extensive export and import linkages.

A second adverse factor was the sharp depreciation of the yen vis-à-vis the U.S. dollar, "leaving the dollar peggers high and dry." Asian economies that were dependent on robust exports to Japan but had pegged their currencies to the dollar suddenly found their exports priced too high, in yen terms. Export demand fell sharply among Asian trading partners, and almost overnight domestic economies throughout the region began experiencing severe contractions. Together these adverse external factors turned vulnerable economies into collapsing economies. Thus, Dornbusch attributes the Asian economic downturn to a confluence of capital market vulnerability and adverse external factors.

Obstfeld also believes that the primary source of economic vulnerability in recent financial crises was capital markets, but he emphasizes shifts in expectations as the central factor driving the economic fluctuations. He notes that "exogenous fluctuations in capital flows have become a dominant business cycle shock" for developing countries in the modern era, and that similar financial crises were quite common prior to World War II.

Obstfeld describes two main types of crises—exchange rate (currency) crises, and national solvency crises—and explains that although they can occur separately, they often "interact in explosive ways." The main linkage between them is self-fulfilling expectations. An economy with a weak and vulnerable capital market can avoid crisis so long as there is no expectation of one. But when expectations change, the desirable but tenuous equilibrium will give way abruptly to a crisis. A sudden new expectation of currency depreciation can start the process rolling, once speculators perceive the threat that public debt will be paid through inflation. He cites Indonesia as an example of this phenomenon.

In Persaud's view, moral hazard and inadequate oversight were key factors in generating the underlying capital market vulnerability. "Moral hazard [induced by International Monetary Fund bailouts] . . . probably played a role in the exponential rise in foreign bank lending to Emerging Asia," and "crony capitalism" may have further "impaired the proper allocation of resources." Furthermore, Asia's economic success was "unbalanced" in the sense that lending went toward overinvestment that was concentrated in a limited number of sectors. Inadequate supervision and unreliable information about this worsening capital situation allowed the rise in risky lending and overinvestment to go unchecked until it was too late.

Persaud also cites the weakened Japanese economy and depreciating yen as important factors, but he identifies the collapse of the Thai baht on July 2, 1997 as the "trigger" that set off the Asian crisis. The effect of this trigger was amplified as investors suddenly realized new or mispriced risks in the region and greatly reduced their "appetites for risk"; this led to widespread and simultaneous capital outflows from the region.

A key factor contributing to this capital flight, says Persaud, was the sudden discovery that domestic corporate investment positions were highly concentrated. When the crisis emerged, heavyweight investors in the region discovered that their peers were also deeply vested in the same small number of collapsing Asian economies. Thus, these influential investors not only wanted to get out of Asia because of the inherent financial problems, they also wanted to get out first, because they knew that a massive capital outflow would dramatically reduce asset prices in the region.

The panelists generally agreed that unwise economic decisions had promoted an environment of vulnerability, and that Japan's economic weakness and other events turned a precarious situation into turmoil. However, their recommendations about how to respond to the current crisis, and how to prevent future crises, were notably different.

Dornbusch believes that the key to preventing future capital market crises is to control financial risk. He proposes using model-based value-at-risk ratings and disseminating "right thinking" within the international financial community regarding controlling and pricing such risk. Controlling capital flows themselves, however, is not appropriate. He advocates International Monetary Fund (IMF) inspections of financial market conditions during country consultations, but he is doubtful the IMF will become sufficiently forward-looking and preemptive, because IMF member countries will resist such changes. For this reason, he particularly opposes an Asian IMF. Dornbusch advocates moving toward regional currencies like the euro. Regarding the appropriate response to current developments, Dornbusch is adamant that tight money policies are required to restore financial stability; debt restructuring can be negotiated later. Fiscal policy is not a viable tool because of the fiscal deterioration associated with the recent crises.

Obstfeld asserts that "policy must counteract the severe capital-account shocks by creating a new expectational climate" that will restore confidence in these economies. He sees no economic prescription for this change "short of infeasibly extensive official financial support from abroad." In contrast to Dornbusch, Obstfeld concludes that fiscal expansion is the least risky policy prescription, particularly in Japan. Monetary expansion in Japan might also help, but it carries the risk of further yen devaluation and is insufficient until Japan resolves its banking problems. He ends by warning that monetary tightening now by the Federal Reserve and the new European Central Bank to fight domestic inflation "would be an error of perhaps historic proportions."

Persaud highlights the need to develop policies that "work with financial markets and not against them." He views many actual and proposed policies as counterproductive. Capital controls intended to curb outflows would implicitly curb much-needed inflows. Looking to the IMF for faster and more lucrative assistance is also unwise. He doubts that the IMF loans can keep pace with the magnitude of required private capital flows, and in any case further IMF assistance worsens the moral hazard problem.

Instead, Persaud wants an international financial system that permits countries access to an international pool of foreign exchange reserves if—and only if—they meet certain "selectivity criteria" intended to reflect sound and prudent financial operations. The criteria, which must be "public, clear, and transparent," would consider the extent of external debt, the productivity of capital inflows, the competitiveness of exchange rates, the soundness of government finances, and the openness of governance. Countries or financial institutions that do not meet these criteria should be allowed to fail. Indeed, Persaud believes that selective assistance is a critical requirement for eliminating moral hazard.

TECHNOLOGY AND BUSINESS CYCLES

Susanto Basu tackles another of the most contentious questions among modern macroeconomists: Do fluctuations in technological change or productivity growth actually cause business cycle fluctuations? Some prominent neoclassical macroeconomists assert not only that the answer is yes, but that technology change is the *primary* determinant of such fluctuations. This assertion is contested by macroeconomists like Basu who adhere to the Keynesian tradition of emphasizing fluctuations in aggregate demand as the primary contributor to business cycles. Because these two views of the sources of business cycles lead to radically different macroeconomic models and prescriptions for government policy, resolution of this debate is critical.

Basu argues that neoclassical economists have misinterpreted the link between technological change and business cycles by misusing the standard measure of technological change: the Solow residual, named after M.I.T. economist Robert Solow. Solow's methodology is simple: measure the growth of output; subtract the appropriately weighted growth of all observable inputs such as labor, capital, and materials; and the difference, or residual, is an estimate of unobserved technological change. Economists use this sensible but indirect measure because they do not have direct data measures of technological change.

Thus far, most attempts to construct Solow residuals with conventional data on inputs yield a measure that is positively correlated with output, giving rise to the claim that technological changes cause business cycles. But Basu argues the Solow residual was only intended to estimate the long-run impact of technology on the economy, not the cyclical impact. He notes that Solow warned long ago that his measure would be spuriously correlated with output and the business cycle because firms adjust to fluctuations in demand by varying the rates at which they utilize capital and labor.

Basu has developed a new measure of technological change that adjusts for features that could lead to an excessively positive correlation between technological change and output. Basu's methodology, developed in earlier research with John Fernald and Miles Kimball (henceforth the BFK technology measure), adjusts for four factors: (1) variable utilization of capital and labor; (2) variable worker effort; (3) imperfect competition and other special advantages firms may have in production; and (4) different characteristics of firms across industries. In other words, it adjusts for many of the demand-side features Solow was concerned about. The BFK methodology requires relatively few controversial restrictions or assumptions; indeed, previous measures of technological change are special cases of it.

The salient and distinguishing feature of the new BFK technology measure is that it is essentially uncorrelated with output and the business cycle. Unlike the Solow residual, which is positively correlated with output and the business cycle, it exhibits no simple statistical evidence of causing business cycle fluctuations. Moreover, the BFK measure is much less variable than the Solow residual. Together, these features reduce, if not eliminate, the likelihood that unexpected technological changes cause business cycles. Basu shows that this conclusion holds up in simple statistical models of the production process.

Another potentially important characteristic exhibited by the BFK technology measure is that it suggests what all workers fear: that technological improvements reduce employment. At least initially, the BFK measure is very negatively correlated with factor inputs, such as labor and factor utilization. In other words, when firms improve their technical efficiency by installing the latest and greatest machines, they are able to produce the same output with fewer inputs, so they reduce costs by cutting their work force rather than reducing their prices and producing more. Only much later, as profits rise, do they expand their output and hire workers. This interpretation of the data stands in stark contrast to interpretations based on the conventional Solow residual, in which employment and other factor inputs rise with technological improvements.

In the second part of his investigation, Basu uses his technology measure to evaluate whether the dynamic properties of two state-of-the-art macroeconomic models match the postwar data. One is the real business cycle (RBC) model, which features technological change as the main source of business cycle fluctuations. It also assumes complete, competitive markets with fully adjustable prices. The other model is basically similar but introduces slowly adjusting or "sticky" prices. Sticky prices are a common feature of macroeconomic models that emphasize fluctuations in aggregate demand as the main source of business cycles.

The result of Basu's evaluation is quite discouraging for state-of-the-art macroeconomic models. He finds that neither the RBC nor the sticky price model generally fits the data very well. The RBC model, in particular, does not match the dynamic properties of the data, and it cannot reproduce the essentially zero correlation that exists between the BFK technological change and output or the negative correlation between factor inputs and output. These models also fail to reflect the generally sluggish response of output changes in the economy. Basu reports that the sticky price model is qualitatively better because it approximately reproduces these two correlations, although it does not do so well. The prognosis for these models becomes even bleaker when he evaluates the models with both technological change and various specifications of monetary policy.

Basu concludes that the defining cyclical feature of technological change is a short-run reduction in inputs and factor utilization, and that business cycle models face the challenge of reproducing that feature. At present, standard RBC and sticky price models cannot do the job, and variable factor utilization does not impart enough rigidity to generate sufficient sluggishness. He projects that the sticky-price models, modified to include other sources of rigidities, "show some promise of being able to match the data, but clearly have a long way to go."

Mark Bils questions whether Basu's technology measure adjusts *too much* for the positive correlation between factor utilization and output. He hypothesizes that the proportions of capital and labor used in production are likely to be fixed in the very short run. Thus, when capital utilization rises slightly, labor hours will rise in equal proportion. If so, total factor productivity should be positively correlated with output but labor productivity should be approximately uncorrelated with output. Bils finds exactly these correlations in data on detailed manufacturing industries. Because the BFK methodology infers movements in capital utilization from movements in materials prices, and because materials prices are more positively correlated with output than labor costs, Bils believes the BFK measure makes capital utilization more positively correlated with output than labor utilization is.

Other aspects of Basu's methodology make Bils skeptical of the results. He doubts that labor quality (effort) is positively correlated with output, as in the BFK measure, because there is evidence that workers hired during expansions are paid less and therefore of lower quality. Moreover, he thinks the relationship between effort and hours will vary depending on the stickiness of wages and the type of shock. Bils also argues that factor utilization will vary more if shocks are transitory rather than permanent. Basu's methodology relies more on variables associated with transitory shocks, so it may yield estimates of utilization that are too positively correlated with output.

Finally, Bils assesses the plausibility of price stickiness in two empirical exercises. One exercise is based on the theory that if prices are sticky, then firms with significant inventory holdings should be less likely to reduce inputs and output when technology increases, because they can inventory unsold output. He reports evidence that "labor hours are much less likely to decline for industries that hold significant inventories," but points out that this evidence does not conclusively determine the actual flexibility of prices. So in a second exercise he provides more direct evidence from models of relative prices. Prices are significantly negatively correlated with current total factor and labor productivity but not with past productivity, a relation Bils interprets as evidence that prices are not sticky.

Thomas Cooley is also cautious about interpreting Basu's results as evidence against the idea that technological change is an important source of business cycle fluctuations. Like Bils, Cooley has reservations about the methodology underlying the BFK technology measure, although he embraces Basu's finding that firms do not enjoy market power from technological advantages in production. In particular, he notes that the correlation of the BFK technology measure with output is sensitive to the exact form of the econometric methodology used to construct the measure and to the identifying assumptions of the modeling framework.

However, granting the validity of Basu's results, Cooley directs his critique at the logic of Basu's inferences about the implications for macroeconomic models. First, he questions Basu's conclusion that the results necessarily rule out RBC-type models. He argues that RBC models no longer rely on artificially sluggish technology shocks to obtain sluggish output responses. Sluggishness can arise from factor utilization as well as financial market imperfections, differences among firms, and other features. As for the RBC model's inability to generate a negative correlation between technology and factor inputs, he suspects that this result is not robust.

Cooley also questions whether the evidence should lead one to conclude that prices are sticky. Basu provides no direct evidence of sticky prices, and economic theory does not make clear predictions about the direction in which capital and labor should respond to technology changes. The response will depend, among other things, on the nature of the technology change, market structure, and the sensitivity of demand to prices. This point calls into question Basu's assertion that he does not need to consider the behavior of profits and product markets.

Cooley thinks Basu's results suggest that technological change is embodied in new capital investment—a characteristic absent from the BFK methodology. With technology embodied in capital, the short-run responses of output and factor inputs to technological change are different from those of a standard RBC model and are capable of yielding the patterns Basu finds in the data. Moreover, in this case the nature of depreciation matters for interpreting the effects of cyclical factor utilization.

Job Reallocation and the Business Cycle

Scott Schuh and **Robert Triest** investigate the idea that business cycles might be caused by the shuffling of jobs as firms restructure the way they do business. New data produced during the past decade show that firms are continuously changing. Some expand and create jobs while others contract and destroy jobs. The pace of change is rapid; one in 10 jobs is newly created and one in 10 jobs newly destroyed in manufacturing each year. The sources of these ups and downs of particular firms include product demand and innovation, prices and wages, regional economic conditions, technological change, and other factors idiosyncratic to each firm, rather than factors common across all firms. Job creation and destruction together represent job reallocation, a measure of job turnover or churning in the economy.

Traditionally, macroeconomists looking at the labor market have ignored job reallocation and have focused solely on total employment growth (or the total unemployment rate). However, Schuh and Triest point out that a given rate of employment growth can occur with either low or high rates of job reallocation. More important, the intensity of job reallocation has significant consequences for unemployment, wage growth, and productivity growth.

For example, if changes alter the desired distribution of jobs across firms, industries, and regions, job reallocation must intensify to keep productive efficiency high. More intense reallocation usually means higher job destruction that forces many workers into unemployment. These unemployed workers lose any skills they had that were unique to their previous job (such as knowledge of firm operating procedures), have a hard time finding a comparable new job, and stay unemployed longer. Eventually they may have to accept a job entailing sizable reductions in their wages. Such issues are linked inherently to the determination of aggregate unemployment, wage growth, and productivity.

Schuh and Triest point out that job reallocation and the pace of restructuring rise markedly during recessions. Traditional macroeconomic models cannot explain why because they do not incorporate the phenomenon of job reallocation. But in light of the potentially negative economic consequences of job reallocation, it is important to know whether an identifiable connection exists between reallocation and business cycles, and whether the correlation between them is of no consequence and can continue to be ignored.

Schuh and Triest ask the following fundamental question: Does job reallocation cause business cycles, or do business cycles cause job reallocation? Evidence on job reallocation has sparked an interest in building theoretical models capable of explaining the observed patterns in the data, and they classify these theories into two types. One type stresses the role of factors that primarily determine the desired allocation of economic resources, such as workers, across firms. The other type stresses the role of aggregate factors, such as monetary policy, that primarily determine the overall level of economic activity. Both types of theories aim to explain why job reallocation rises during recessions. Yet both types of theories tend to rely on vaguely defined aggregate and allocative "shocks" rather than observable variables.

Schuh and Triest argue that these theories do not and cannot answer their fundamental question, for two reasons. First, although the two-way classification of factors may be conceptually sensible, in practice the definitions of allocative and aggregate factors become hopelessly muddled. Second, these theories have little to say about what *causes* business cycles—that is, *why* they occur—because they focus more on *how* they occur.

Schuh and Triest present results from three empirical exercises that extend research by Schuh with Steven Davis and John Haltiwanger on job creation, destruction, and reallocation (henceforth referred to as DHS). One exercise analyzes the behavior of job reallocation during the 1990s using newly available data. A second exercise attempts to learn what kinds of plants destroy and reallocate jobs and how, in hope of discovering clues about the causes of recessions. The third exercise looks for evidence of causal relationships between job reallocation, the fundamental determinants of reallocation, and the business cycle. Each of these exercises uses data from the U.S. Bureau of the Census on individual manufacturing plants (the Longitudinal Research Database (LRD)).

The new data show that the 1990-91 recession was much less severe in manufacturing than preceding recessions, as evidenced by a relatively modest decline in employment. Nevertheless, job destruction and job reallocation both increased in a manner similar to that in previous recessions. The ensuing expansion was unusual in that job destruction and reallocation remained above average, rather than declining quickly after the recession. In addition, job creation experienced two large surges that were *not* preceded by surges in job destruction, as creation surges typically are. The authors interpret these surges as evidence of favorable allocative shocks, in contrast to the unfavorable allocative shocks of the 1970s and 1980s.

Regarding the nature of job creation and destruction, Schuh and Triest take a deeper look at two areas: (1) the magnitude, permanence, concentration, and cyclicality of job flows; and (2) the differences in job flows between larger, older, and higher-wage plants (henceforth, simply "large") and smaller, younger, lower-wage plants (henceforth, simply "small"). Previous DHS research concluded that job flows are large, permanent, and concentrated in a minority of plants with large employment changes. Also, large plants account for most of the increases in job destruction and reallocation during recessions. Together these DHS findings suggest that during recessions only a small fraction of really large plants experience really large and permanent rates of job destruction, and thus they imply that the cause of job destruction and recessions is related to large plants.

The Schuh and Triest findings significantly refine this DHS view. They find that small plants tend to have much higher rates of job creation and destruction than large plants, and that high rates of job creation and destruction—especially plant start-ups and shutdowns—are much more likely to be permanent. Thus, even though large plants account for most of the increase in job destruction during recessions, these large-plant job destruction rates are likely to be much smaller in percentage terms and less permanent. In fact, Schuh and Triest find that almost one-half of all jobs destroyed by plants experiencing relatively mild contractions are ultimately restored within five years. In other words, all plants are adversely affected by recessions but large plants appear to be more resilient than small plants, which expand and contract more dramatically and permanently.

Finally, Schuh and Triest uncover some evidence that suggests allocative factors cause business cycles. Their evidence is based on the premise that there are observable determinants of the allocation of jobs across firms, industries, and regions—prices, productivity, and investment—and that changes in those determinants cause job reallocation to increase, which in turn causes recessions. One key finding is that when relative prices and productivity growth across detailed industries change dramatically, job destruction and job reallocation also increase dramatically shortly afterward. Another key finding is that increases in job reallocation generally are *not* associated with increases in trend productivity and investment growth, as some recent theoretical models seem to imply.

Ricardo Caballero regards some of the Schuh-Triest results as "potentially promising," but he challenges two fundamental tenets. He questions the central premise that job reallocation is countercyclical, and he doubts that reallocation shocks actually cause fluctuations. In addition, he objects to the authors' characterization and testing of theories of job reallocation.

Caballero contends that the term "job reallocation" is a misnomer. He does not dispute the fact that Schuh and Triest's measure of job reallocation is countercyclical. However, he argues that the main feature of job reallocation over time is a significant fluctuation in total job destruction that is unconnected with the process of total job creation. Thus, while individual jobs are destroyed and created at the plant level, thereby generating worker reallocation, it is what he calls a "dynamic fallacy of composition" to infer that a link exists between total job destruction and creation that could be characterized as total job "reallocation." Put another way, job "reallocation" would be higher if job destruction rose now and fell later while job creation stayed constant, but it would not be true in this case that job losers were reallocated to new jobs.

Caballero cites evidence from his own research that the surge in total job destruction during recessions is more than offset by a decline in destruction during the subsequent expansion. He calls this latter effect "chill," where job destruction falls below the rate associated with the "normal" underlying level of job turnover in the economy. He argues that it is important to understand that this chill can arise from market imperfections and produce technological sclerosis as a result of insufficient turnover. This argument contrasts with theories earlier this century that suggested that all job turnover is healthy for the economy.

Caballero believes "it is a large leap to claim that reallocation shocks are a substantial *source* of business cycles, at least in the United States," although he thinks they might be important elsewhere such as Eastern Europe, for example. He argues that plausible statistical models show that reallocation shocks are "substantially" less important than aggregate shocks, at least for net employment growth. He also demonstrates that such models can produce confusion about the relative importance of job reallocation, and asks whether the "fragile decomposition" of shocks as aggregate versus allocative is worthwhile, compared to focusing on observable shocks such as prices or interest rates.

In general, Caballero thinks it is a mistake at this point to focus on trying to discover whether or not reallocation shocks cause business cycles. Instead, effort should be directed toward the less debatable issue of whether "the churn [ongoing processes of creation and destruction] has a significant effect on the economy at *business cycle* frequencies."

Steven Davis shares the ambition of Schuh and Triest to develop new evidence on the connection between job reallocation and the business cycle. Indeed, he devotes a significant portion of his comments to explaining why this endeavor is important. But Davis, too, challenges the claim that reallocation activity is countercyclical, and he argues further that total job reallocation is inappropriate for this analysis. He also suggests a more effective methodology for summarizing the relationship between job flows and plant characteristics.

Davis provides a detailed description of the dynamic nature of job and worker flows and then advances several reasons why it is important to study these flows. First, "the extent to which the reallocation and matching process operates smoothly determines ... the difference between successful and unsuccessful economic performance," with European unemployment serving as a prime example. Second, successful conduct of policy requires accounting for the reallocation and matching process. Third, recent modeling of reallocation frictions and heterogeneity makes it evident that aggregate shocks have allocative consequences, and shocks to factor demand can drive fluctuations in economic aggregates. Fourth, "models with reallocation frictions also help to address some well-recognized shortcomings in prevailing theories of the business cycle."

Davis believes that Schuh and Triest err in treating gross job reallocation "as equivalent to the intensity of reallocation activity." His criticism is that gross job reallocation does not account for the fact that movements in job creation and destruction merely may be achieving changes in total employment instead of reflecting a fundamental reallocation of labor across plants. Davis argues that the amount of job reallocation in excess of the change in total employment is a more suitable measure of reallocation intensity. He reports evidence that, unlike total job reallocation, excess job reallocation is uncorrelated with the business cycle.

POLICY IMPLICATIONS

In the closing session, leading economists from the public and private sectors discussed the implications for government policies of the conference's analysis of the causes of recessions. Panelists focused especially on the important role of vulnerability in setting the stage for unanticipated or adverse events. Each argued that governments should implement policies to reduce the economy's vulnerability and exposure to risk, provide more and accurate information to private agents about the extent of risk, and—if necessary—aid the recovery of economies that plunge into crises.

Henry Kaufman believes that sweeping structural changes to financial markets in recent years have significantly altered the linkages between financial markets and the real economy. Among the developments he identifies are securitization, derivatives, globalization, and leveraged investing. Several themes pervade his analysis. First, global financial markets are becoming increasingly sophisticated and complete. Second, this maturation process increasingly makes financing available to borrowers who would not have been able to obtain it previously. Third, and a consequence of the first two points, financial markets are becoming increasingly volatile, as risk-taking becomes easier while accurate risk assessment becomes more difficult. Altogether, these changes increase the likelihood that financial market turbulence will make economies more vulnerable to shocks and recessions.

Kaufman believes the changes increase the difficulty and reduce the efficacy of monetary policy. Monetary policy is more difficult because traditional monetary factors—monetary aggregates, debt aggregates, and the like—have become less reliable indicators of the stance of monetary policy and the state of money markets. Monetary policy is less effective because increased availability and easier acquisition of credit mean that short-term interest rates must increase more to achieve the same real response. Furthermore, increased volatility in asset prices (wealth) leads to greater volatility in aggregate economic behavior. Thus, he argues, the Federal Reserve should take asset price developments explicitly into account in formulating monetary policy.

Internationally, Kaufman sees a need for increased supervision of financial markets. Paradoxically, he notes, when financial markets become deregulated and "freewheeling," the need for more accurate, timely, and complete information increases, particularly about the risks in which financial entities are engaging. He decries the poor job of oversight and information gathering done by official institutions thus far and proposes several reforms. In particular, he recommends a new body he calls a Board of Overseers of Major Institutions and Markets, which would set a code of conduct, supervise risk-taking, and harmonize capital requirements.

Kaufman also favors reforms to two international economic organizations. First, the IMF should be reorganized to specialize in a narrower set of core functions. The new IMF would continue to facilitate lending to countries in financial distress and to press for reform in government policies in these countries. But it would also be charged with rating the creditworthiness of countries, by assessing economic and financial conditions, reviewing extant government policies, and demanding remedial action where needed. Kaufman also argues that the G-7 must be restructured to account for the European Monetary Union and its euro currency.

Martin Zimmerman provides perspective from one of the largest and most cyclical components of the U.S. economy: the automobile industry. He explains how the auto industry, specifically Ford Motor Company, views the unfolding of a recession—how consumers postpone their car purchases, how auto makers respond to weakening sales, and how interest rate policy is an important determinant of the economic fortunes of the auto industry. But ultimately he argues against the central theme of the conference. That is, Zimmerman believes it is impossible to go "Beyond Shocks."

The economy is always subject to shocks, according to Zimmerman. For the auto industry, a shock is anything that causes consumers to suddenly alter their normal plans to purchase new cars. Zimmerman tells the story of how the 1990-91 recession unfolded. As late as June 1990, economic forecasters were predicting confidently that there would be no recession, only a slowdown. But Iraq's invasion of Kuwait and the U.S. military response caused a precipitous drop in consumer confidence and sales of cars to consumers. The shock of the Kuwait invasion, like all shocks, by definition was not forecastable, says Zimmerman (an assessment that was not well-received by his employers, he adds wryly).

Although shocks are pervasive, the central question is whether the shocks will tip the economy over into recession. Here, he asserts that not all shocks do, in fact, trigger recessions. The economy must already be vulnerable when the shocks hit. Absent this vulnerability, the economy may be able to withstand shocks. Likewise, absent shocks, vulnerability may never result in a recession.

What is the role of policy in a world of vulnerability and inevitable shocks? Zimmerman notes that every precipitous drop in auto sales has been associated with an increase in interest rates, so he tends to associate monetary tightening with the emergence of economic vulnerability (weak growth). But because not every increase in interest rates was followed by a recession, he surmises that a shock is required to turn vulnerability into recession. He asserts that monetary policy cannot prevent shocks because they are inherently unpredictable. Instead, policy should minimize vulnerability of the economy.

Agustin Carstens contributes a view of recessions and policy from the perspective of emerging economies such as Mexico. He identifies five characteristics of business cycles in emerging economies that distinguish them from business cycles in industrialized economies. First, business cycles in emerging countries are closely synchronized with the fortunes of industrialized countries: "When the United States gets a cold, Mexico gets pneumonia." Second, business cycles are more volatile in emerging economies. Third, emerging economies are susceptible to additional sources of volatility, such as terms of trade fluctuations. Fourth, and more recently, increasing globalization of markets has encouraged massive capitals flows into emerging countries like Mexico. But these capital flows are very unstable, so emerging countries can experience sudden and massive capital outflows that devastate their economies. Finally, emerging economies have to deal with exchange-rate regimes and their failures.

These characteristics force emerging economies to adopt very different policies to deal with business cycles. Industrialized countries, as leaders of the world economic engine, follow policies designed to manage aggregate demand so as to achieve low inflation and full employment. Such policies are countercyclical. In contrast, emerging countries follow policies designed to avoid or mitigate economic crises that break out there, often because industrialized countries are slumping and reducing their demand for emerging country exports. One essential goal of these policies is to reestablish the credibility of emerging economies, especially the credibility of their currencies and financial markets. Often this means reestablishing the credibility of governments that have made bad policy decisions. These types of policies, then, are usually procyclical.

Carstens offers four specific policy recommendations for emerging economies to help them to reduce vulnerability and follow a more stable path. First, they must reduce their vulnerability to changes in the international prices of exports, by adopting more open trade and investment regimes. Second, they should allow market determination of interest and exchange rates so these rates can accomplish their purpose of absorbing shocks. Third, they must ensure the robustness of their financial institutions to macroeconomic fluctuations. Fourth, they should push forward with structural changes in order to achieve central bank autonomy, privatization of production, labor market flexibility, and reduced dependence on foreign saving. In each case, more complex policies are required beyond the traditional demand management schemes followed by industrialized countries, Carstens notes.

Michael Mussa, as a leading official at the International Monetary Fund, offered an informed, practical—and oftentimes contrarian—view of the conference papers, the conventional wisdom about the ongoing global economic crises, and recent criticisms of international policy responses to the crises.

Mussa infers from Sims's paper that systematic monetary policy *does* have a significant, positive effect on the real economy, despite Sims's claim to the contrary. He says Sims understates the effect of monetary policy, citing Sims's own results showing that industrial output would have been nearly one-fifth higher if the Fed had followed modern monetary policies during the Great Depression. He also points out that Sims omits the positive role monetary policy can play in avoiding banking and financial panics by subsidizing and reforming weak banks, and by reassuring depositors that their accounts were safe. Had Sims accounted for this, and for the fact that fiscal policy should have been more aggressive, one-half to three-quarters of the impact of the Great Depression could have been avoided.

Mussa finds the two long historical analyses of business cycles to be inherently valuable. He particularly agrees with Temin's premise that recessions "have a multiplicity of causes," although he doubts that it is possible—or useful—to try to quantitatively separate causes into different categories of influence. Like Romer, Mussa believes that Temin underestimates the contribution of monetary policy to recessions. However, Mussa is cautious about the quality of older economic data and what we can reliably infer from them, particularly data for countries other than the United States.

Regarding the paper by Schuh and Triest on labor reallocation and business cycles, Mussa is "skeptical that labor reallocation is itself an independent cause of most U.S. business cycles." He suggests that the authors focus more on the relationship between labor reallocation and the NAIRU (non-accelerating-inflation rate of unemployment). Regarding the central issue addressed in Basu's paper, Mussa believes that "the notion that adverse downward movements in total technology cause recessions [because workers don't work as hard] is just plain silly. This is the theory according to which the 1930s should be known not as the Great Depression but as the Great Vacation."

Mussa then turned to a discussion of current economic developments and the appropriateness of policy. On the domestic economy, Mussa likens recent monetary policy performance to the movie, "As Good As It Gets." Aside from some minor quibbles, Mussa judges U.S.

monetary policy management during the last decade to be "remarkable" by any standard. But he notes that it has been "very good management with very good luck." Moreover, he warns, to say that monetary policy has been as good as it gets implies that monetary policy is better than it is normally expected to be—in other words, it is likely to get worse, not better. Ultimately, the monetary authority cannot avoid all recessions; it can only be expected to avoid "big" ones.

On the international situation, Mussa likens catastrophic economic events such as the Great Depression and the current worldwide financial crisis to the movie "Titanic." What caused the Titanic to sink, he asks? Perhaps an exogenous shock (the iceberg), he quips. But it was more than that. Errors in the design and operation of the ship, inadequate preparation for the sinking, and other factors all contributed. In the same way, the current financial crisis has many complex causes and contributing factors.

However, reasons Mussa, the *real* tragedy of the Titanic was not that it sank and 1,500 lives were lost, but that *800 of the Titanic passengers were saved that day*! Clearly this policy mistake discouraged shipbuilders from spending money on improving designs and shipping lines from bearing the cost of conducting safe navigation of future cruises across the Atlantic. The Titanic rescue demonstrated that entrepreneurs in the shipping industry didn't need to worry about safety—they knew that the government would be there to save them from their imprudence!

Mussa employs this tongue-in-cheek argumentation to rebut those who argue that moral hazard problems should prevent the international community from responding to the current financial crisis. Despite moral hazard problems, saving 800 Titanic passengers *was* the right thing to do. And despite clear moral hazard problems, Mussa says the IMF attempts to rescue Korea and other besieged economies *is* the right thing to do. He argues that IMF support is not a gift but a loan, and that the IMF's earlier financial support of Mexico has been validated by Mexico's successful servicing of IMF debt.

Conclusion

In the end, most participants agreed that the business cycle is *not* dead but is likely here to stay. No one championed the ideas that a "new," recession-proof economy has emerged, that unanticipated adverse economic events have stopped buffeting the economy, or that government policy has become so adroit that it can offset every dip in the aggregate economy. If anything, the mere mention of these ideas drew disdainful remarks, and even served as "proof" that the ideas were without merit. Indeed, the general premise among participants was that the right question was *when*, not *if*, the next recession occurs, what will have caused it? The consensus answer is the cause is likely to be not one but many things, with government policy and vulnerability playing important—but still not fully understood—roles.

Most participants also agreed that policymakers in a world continually subject to business cycles should adopt certain goals to improve their ability to deal with fluctuations. First, policymakers must learn how to recognize and address the economy's vulnerability to disruptions and unanticipated events. Second, policy institutions should conduct and support research that shows the contribution of deliberate actions of economic agents to economic fluctuations. Finally, and most important, policymakers should understand that they cannot prevent every recession, but they should concentrate their efforts on averting The Big Ones, such as the Great Depression.

Summing Up on Business Cycles: Opening Address

Paul A. Samuelson*

Is the business cycle dead? Or should the question be, "Was *the* business cycle ever alive?" After most periods of extended expansion, particularly if they also happen to be eras of bubbly capital gains, talk about a "New Era" geysers up and, what is more important, such talk is received with increasing credulity.

In my lifetime I have seen the soda fountain come into, and go out of, the American drug store. So too with the university course in business cycles. At the beginning of my teaching career, we had no courses in macroeconomics as such, but we always did have a basic course in Money and Banking. And to supplement that there was sure to be a course called Business Cycles. I used as textbook for that course Wesley Mitchell's 1927 survey of business cycles à la National Bureau of Economic Research, also Alvin Hansen's *Business-Cycle Theory* of the same year. But superseding them came Gottfried Haberler's 1937 *Prosperity and Depression*, whose pages presented the embalmed bones of pre-*General Theory* orthodoxy: monetary theories of the cycle; overinvestment theories; underconsumption theories; exogenous theories such as sunspots, as well as endogenous theories like those that combined the acceleration principle and the multiplier.

My Harvard teacher Joseph Schumpeter's 1939 two-volume treatise is almost a parody of eclecticism: It described short cycles under the Kitchin-Crum terminology; then the good old business cycle of allegedly eight to ten years' periodicity was labeled Juglar cycles; and of course there were also the long waves of Kondratieff and the Sunday newspaper supplements. But that was not the whole of it. In between Juglars and

---

*Institute Professor Emeritus at the Massachusetts Institute of Technology.

Kondratieffs came Kuznets's intermediate cycles in construction and immigration, with an alleged approximate periodicity of 18 to 20 years. The tortured epicycles of pre-Copernicus Ptolemaic astronomy had nothing on Schumpeter.

I can sum up by stating that, if you mean by a business cycle a periodic oscillation like the swing of a pendulum or the orbit of a planet, then in economics no business cycle ever did exist. But a common pulse in various time series, within time and also cross-sectionally, was just perceptible in the data. Procrustes stretched his short victims to fit an inflexible bed and also compressed his tall ones to force a fit. Similarly, Mitchell at his wits' end and with the help of Arthur Burns defined *reference cycles*, which had average characteristics in their beginning, middle, and end, and much ingenuity was spent in relating *specific* cycles to them.

All these post-1800 cycles were what we would call Main Street ups and downs in production, price levels, and unemployment. Before 1800—and persisting ever since—economic science and mythology already knew *financial crises*—manias, bubbles, and crashes cum bank failures: Seventeenth century Dutch tulips and eighteenth century South Sea Bubbles or John Law experiments provide examples. Gold discoveries and wartime inflations cannot legitimately be ruled off limits for economists' analysis. I descend to such a banality only to remind New-Classical Rational-Expectationists how implausible is any assertion about the impotence of policy actions to affect *real* variables rather than aggregate price levels. I will return to this oldest economic mechanism of bubbles and crashes.

ARE THINGS DIFFERENT IN "THE AGE AFTER KEYNES"?

It is a scientific sin not to notice *likenesses* that are there in the empirical data. An equal sin is not to notice *differences and changes*. In the two-thirds of a century since 1933, the business cycle "ain't been what it used to be." Let me quote from Victor Zarnowitz's well-titled NBER Working Paper 6367 of 1998, "Has the Business Cycle Been *Abolished*?" (my italics):

> [In the seven decades after 1870] six major depressions occurred in the United States.... No declines of comparable severity have been observed in the last half-century following the depressed 1930's and World War II.

Even when we take into account Christina Romer's revisionist upward adjustments to old-time recessions, I believe this Zarnowitz generalization testifies to an important truth: longer postwar expansions and shorter recessions. Eschewing the naive attribution of this change solely to Keynes's *General Theory*, I agree with the innuendo that changed policy ideology, away from *laissez faire* and toward countercyclical macro policy, helps explain the better macro performance of real GDPs in the final half of the twentieth century.

But I discern neither in the historical data, nor in the cogent advances in economists' models, any convergence toward the disappearance of non-Pareto-optimal fluctuations. Indeed, our success has risen just so far, and probably the mixed-market economies of North America and Europe are essentially marking time as far as further trend rates of "*fine* and *gross* tuning" are concerned. That is a personal judgment or guess.

Therapeutic successes have not come without costs. The age of subdued booms and busts—before America's labor force surprised us with a new flexibility and a new tolerance for accepting *mediocre* jobs—all this had happened, until the last 15 years at least, in an age of somewhat rising price levels. And in many a newspaper column I have had to write sentences such as the following:

> When the *next* recession arrives you will find written on its bottom "Made in Washington," just as was the case with the *last* one. This is not because the Fed is a sadist or an ignoramus; nor it is because the bedrooms in the White House are occupied by politicians eager to lose elections. Rather it is like the fact that hospitals are where most people die: If the central bank and fiscal authorities did not step on the brakes of an overexuberant economy *now*, they might well have to overdo that later. There is never a guarantee that intelligent and feasible policies can be discovered which will lead to perpetual soft landings at high employment and a steady price level.

The phoenix of *real* business cycles has been whistled up anew. But it has not come from the ashes of a wrongly discarded real business cycle methodology. That, like herpes, has always been with us.

What is new, and a little foolish, is the concept of a Pareto-optimal real business cycle, like the one *not* in the history books, where at one time in 1929 folks everywhere developed a desire to substitute intertemporally leisure off the job for good paychecks.

I have published a number of papers on real business cycles. Many of them can well take place *at an unchanged price level*, even though they all concomitantly involve fluctuations in outputs that ex ante and ex post the citizenry find regretful.

I am not here to preach a sermon. But wild horses cannot keep me from saying this:

> Implied in the previous paragraph is a critique of the notion that a good independent central bank can optimally concern itself only with inflation.

You should not believe that the know-all and end-all ethically is concern only for the price level, or that pragmatically that is a correct procedure to follow. Right now, when the honeymoon U.S. economy may be showing few signs of accelerating inflation, there could well be a case for tightening interest rates a bit in order to *prolong* the average level of U.S. prosperity. Waiting until you see the whites of the eyes of wage- and commodity-price inflation could be, from the standpoint of optimal stochastic control activity, a wait too long.

Of course, one will qualify any such advice to take into account what a Fed rise in the short-term interest rate might do to Asian slumps and to Wall Street quasi-bubbles. This brings me to my closing irony.

The pre-1800 pattern of commercial panics had to be a case of NON MACRO-EFFICIENCY of markets. We've come a long way, baby, in two hundred years toward *micro* efficiency of markets: Black-Scholes option pricing, indexing of portfolio diversification, and so forth. But there is no persuasive evidence, either from economic history or avant garde theorizing, that MACRO MARKET INEFFICIENCY is trending toward extinction: The future can well witness the oldest business cycle mechanism, the South Sea Bubble, and that kind of thing. We have no theory of the putative duration of a bubble. It can always go as long again as it has already gone. You cannot make money on correcting macro inefficiencies in the price level of the stock market.

The International Monetary Fund and its critics, and the statesmen of Asia, find precious few answers in the Mitchell and Hansen and Haberler taxonomies of Main Street business cycles—or for that matter few answers in the post-*General Theory* literature—to those current dilemmas and spectres that now haunt all the economies of the globe.

After I delivered this lecture, a high Federal Reserve official asked for clarification as to whether the business cycle is after all still alive. So let me make clear that, like the below-median poor, economic instability we have always with us.

THE CAUSES OF AMERICAN BUSINESS CYCLES: AN ESSAY IN ECONOMIC HISTORIOGRAPHY

Peter Temin[*]

This paper surveys American business cycles over the past century. Its task is to identify the causes of these cycles; other papers in this collection address the nature of policy responses to these causes. This paper can be seen as a test to discriminate between two views of the American economy. The first is expressed in a characteristically vivid statement by Dornbusch, who proclaimed recently: "None of the U.S. expansions of the past 40 years died in bed of old age; every one was murdered by the Federal Reserve" (Dornbusch 1997). This stark view can be contrasted with its opposite in the recent literature: "[N]one of the popular candidates for observable shocks robustly accounts for the bulk of business-cycle fluctuations in output" (Cochrane 1994, p. 358).

I expand the time period to consider the past century, but it is easy to distinguish the past 40 years, that is, the period since World War II. A survey of business cycle causes over an entire century runs into several problems, of which three seem noteworthy. First, it is not at all clear what "cause" means in this context. Second, the Great Depression was such a large cycle that it cannot be seen as just another data point. Third, the survey relies on the existing literature on business cycles, which is why I have entitled it an essay in economic historiography. The paper proceeds by discussing each of these problems in turn, then turning to the data, and finally drawing some conclusions from the preceding efforts.

---

[*]Elisha Gray II Professor of Economics, Massachusetts Institute of Technology. The author would like to thank Caroline Richards for research assistance. All errors remain the author's alone.

BUSINESS CYCLES: DEFINITION AND ANALYSIS

The cause of a business cycle typically is taken to be a shock or innovation to a relationship in the economy. Myriad relationships operate in a complex economy like ours, and some way needs to be found to impose order on the analysis of shocks. Order typically is imposed by abstracting from the actual economy to an abstract model. A more operational definition of cause, therefore, is a shock to a relationship in a macroeconomic model. It follows that shocks may be specific to models, which differ both in their level of detail and in their basic assumptions.

With differing levels of inclusiveness, one person's shock may be another's movement of an endogenous variable. Government actions are a case in point. Variation in government purchasing is taken to be exogenous in many economic models, and it is eligible as a business cycle cause in these models. But the growth of political economy has led people to endogenize government actions. Only deviations from the rule then would be admissible as a shock. Brown (1956) long ago looked for Keynesian stimuli during the Great Depression. He sanitized government spending to eliminate automatic stabilizers, that is, variations due to the state of the economy, to find the high-employment surplus. Keynesian stimuli then were changes in his calculated budget, not the actual budget. As Brown recognized half a century ago, the stimulus—or shock—was specific to the specification of the normal budgetary rule, that is, to the correction used.

Actions by the Federal Reserve fall into the same category. The Fed tries to respond to economic conditions. Are Fed actions endogenous or exogenous? Various authors have tried to endogenize the Fed. Wheelock (1991) and Toma (1997) have modeled the Fed in the interwar period. Taylor and others have proposed monetary policy rules to analyze Fed behavior since the Second World War (Taylor 1993a, 1993b). A typical policy rule indicates that the Fed raises interest rates when inflation rises and when the economy is operating above its trend level. Such Fed actions would be considered endogenous in a model that treated the Fed symmetrically with Brown's treatment of the budget.

An example may make this distinction clear. OPEC countries raised the price of oil sharply following the Yom Kippur War in the fall of 1973. Prices began to rise in the United States as a result, and the Fed sharply restricted monetary growth. A recession followed that Paul Samuelson quipped had "Made in Washington" stamped on its bottom. Was the recession "caused" by the oil shock or by monetary policy?

The answer to this question depends on the model. If we are using a model that regards Fed actions as exogenous (perhaps because we are searching for policies that can insulate the American economy from external shocks), then the Fed is the appropriate cause. If we are instead using a model that endogenizes the Fed (looking for sources of instability in the U.S. or world economy), then the oil shock is the obvious candidate. Causes, in other words, do not have independent existences. They are functions of the models being used and the questions being asked. They are exogenous events whose identification is endogenous to intellectual inquiry.

Christiano, Eichenbaum, and Evans (1998) survey monetary shocks. They are interested in the response of the economy to exogenous shocks. But they recognize that the very identification of these shocks is specific to the model being used. They survey, for example, the narrative approach used by Romer and Romer (1989) to identify exogenous shocks coming from the Fed. Christiano, Eichenbaum, and Evans argue that even these shocks are specific to the implicit model underlying Romer and Romer's narrative.

This ambiguity is present within any class of similar economic models, but further ambiguities come from the variety of theories that support macro models. Real business cycle theories find technology shocks to be the source of fluctuations. Demand shocks like Fed actions and oil price rises do not figure in these models. Technology shocks, however defined, are the underlying causes of fluctuations in income. If one is agnostic about which model is most accurate and useful, then the very idea of cause is ill-defined. Cochrane (1994) started from this unstructured position, employing a sequence of progressively more tightly specified VARs to indicate what kinds of shocks cause business cycles. He concluded that technology shocks were not an important source of variation in output. This is less ideological than it seems; as noted above, Cochrane concluded that no single class of exogenous shock—from either supply or demand—was the main source of business cycles.

If time-series analysis shows variety rather than uniformity of shocks, another approach may be more useful. I propose here to use a historical account. I examine American business cycles over the last century to inquire into their causes. Because this paper will be followed by others on policies, I interpret "cause" to mean the shock that initiates a downturn, trying to identify the source of instability rather than policy responses that may have aggravated the contraction. The Federal Reserve and the national government are endogenous. This view is consistent with Dornbusch's implicit framework, since murder is a willful deviation from normal behavior. In the 1970s, the oil shock is the identified villain, not the Fed.

This approach differs from that of Romer and Romer (1989). They looked for monetary shocks in the postwar period, "to identify episodes when there were large shifts in monetary policy or in the behavior of the monetary sector that were not driven by developments on the real side of the economy" (p. 122). But they implemented this search by looking for "times when concern about the current level of inflation led the Federal

Table 1
A Two-by-Two Classification of the Causes of Business Cycles

	Domestic	Foreign
Real	DR	FR
Monetary	DM	FM

Source: See the text.

Reserve to attempt to induce a recession" (p. 134). The problem with their approach, for my paper, is whether a monetary contraction in response to inflation is a shift in policy or simply policy itself. I interpret most actions by the Fed to reduce inflation as the job of the Fed and therefore endogenous. The Fed's response to the first oil shock in 1973 did not represent a break with previous Fed policy. I therefore classify the Fed's contractionary actions as endogenous and attribute the recession to the oil price shock.

I work with an elementary open-economy model: an augmented IS-LM model or Mundell-Fleming model. The model distinguishes domestic and foreign shocks as well as real and monetary shocks. The model recognizes demand shocks far more easily than supply shocks, which appear as shifts in the aggregate supply curve and are classified as real shocks. This level of abstraction and general orientation of underlying assumptions about the economy is typical of the historical literature on business cycles in the United States. This simple two-by-two classification is shown in Table 1.

Mention of the Fed brings up the second problem that must be cleared away. The Great Depression was the largest contraction in our history. It dwarfs all other contractions in the past century. Output lost in the Depression was almost one-half of the sum of output lost in all downturns during the past century (Romer 1994, p. 604). If one is interested in minimizing losses from forgone income, it may make more sense to explain the Great Depression than to worry about other, smaller fluctuations in output. Policies that avoid similar catastrophes may be more important than policies that fine-tune the economy.

The literature on the Great Depression also is larger than the literature on all other business cycles combined. The Great Depression has stood as a challenge to economists since the severity of the Depression became clear. Keynes (1936) was an important response to this challenge, but not the only one. Generations of macroeconomists have attempted to incorporate this massive fluctuation into their theories. Only recently, as prosperity appears more and more permanent, has explaining the Depression become part of history rather than economics. Historians, however, distrust current visions of a New Era that are so reminiscent of the 1920s—pride goes before a fall. We cannot afford to ignore or belittle the Great Depression.

This paper is concerned with shocks. Was the Great Depression due to a larger shock than all others? Was the economy simply unlucky in the 1930s? Should we be keeping our eyes open for similar dreadful shocks in the future? I have argued that the shock that produced the Great Depression was the First World War (Temin 1989). It surely is good advice to avoid world wars—and not just for the economic consequences of the subsequent peace.

But the story is not so simple. The Second World War was an even bigger shock to the world economy than the First. This can be seen easily by comparing the maximum share of national output devoted to the war effort in the two wars. The United States devoted 45 percent of its output to the war effort at the high point of expenditures in World War II, compared to only 13 percent at the similar point in World War I. For Britain, the maximum shares of output in the two wars were 57 percent in World War II and 38 percent in World War I. For Germany, the country most heavily involved in both wars, the comparable numbers are 76 percent and 53 percent. In addition to devoting a great share of production to war in the second global conflict, these countries also maintained high war expenditures longer (Feinstein, Temin, and Toniolo 1997, p. 189).

Yet the larger shock of World War II was not followed by the same economic strains as the interwar period. Economic (and political) policies were very different in the aftermath of the two world wars. The United Nations, the International Monetary Fund, and the World Bank were all planned while the second great war was still going on. It became apparent by 1947 that even these new institutions were not going to be sufficient to guarantee economic—and therefore political—stability in Europe. President Truman, in one of the great actions of an international leader in our century, then extended aid to Europe in the form of the Marshall Plan. The First World War followed the economically tranquil Victorian and Edwardian periods; there was no expectation and no preparation for the forces unleashed by the war. The Second World War, by contrast, followed the Russian Revolution, the Great Depression, and the Nazi domination of Europe. Policymakers had ample warning—if they cared to learn from history—that the world economy would not heal itself from the injury of the war quickly or smoothly without help.

Current thought attributes the Great Depression to the inability of interwar policymakers to deal with the shock of the First World War. Their solution to the immediate postwar chaos represented by hyperinflations in Eastern Europe was to revive the gold standard. But this solution froze the major industrial economies into insupportable positions and allowed little flexibility to deal with strain. The inability of policymakers to abandon the gold standard then produced the Great Depression (Temin 1989; Eichengreen 1992; Bernanke 1995).

Sins of omission can be just as harmful as sins of commission, but they are not exogenous shocks. Of course, if a behavioral equation predicts a change in policy that did not take place, then one can attribute the inaction to a negative shock to this relation. But the Depression was marked by governments and central banks acting in character, doing what they had been doing before even though conditions had changed. Historians of the Fed have been more struck by the consistency of its policies during the slide into the Great Depression than by its innovations. Wheelock (1991, p. 115) concluded, for example, "[I]f member-bank borrowing was low, as it was in the early 1930s, the Fed bought few securities because it appeared that the proximate objective of purchase—monetary ease—had already been achieved. The Fed seems to have employed this strategy consistently from 1924 to 1933."

In keeping with the resolution to the first problem described above, I focus on the shocks that precipitated the contraction in the early 1930s. We need to remember that these shocks only had the effects attributed to them because of the context in which they came. Context here means both the strains on the international economy that derived from the world war and the policy rules that dictated national policies in the United States and other countries. These factors are critical to an understanding of the Great Depression, but they are put to one side here.

There is an additional complication. It is hard to think that a single shock in the late 1920s, however large, could have plunged the United States and the world into the Great Depression. In addition, economists and historians have been unable to find a shock in the late 1920s that seems to be anywhere near large enough to have had this effect, even in the interwar context that magnified the effects of economic shocks. This corresponds with our understanding of the economy. A century or more of evidence shows that the economy generally functions at close to full employment. The combinations of shocks and policies that characterize the economy keep productive resources generally employed. It follows that a single shock, even in the unfavorable interwar environment, was unlikely to have led to the Great Depression.

Friedman and Schwartz (1963) distinguished two stages in the Great Depression, and writers since then have followed their lead. Perhaps two shocks occurred that together knocked the economy out of this normal equilibrium. I recall studying a model of this sort by James Duesenberry when I was a graduate student and just before he became Chairman of the Board of the Federal Reserve Bank of Boston. He started from a simple accelerator-type model where both output and capital were functions of the previous year's output and capital. The rate of growth of income in such a model depends linearly on the capital-output ratio, while the rate of growth of capital is a hyperbolic function of the same ratio. It follows that the two relations intersect twice or not at all. If twice, then the intersection at the higher rate of growth (and lower capital-output ratio) is stable, and the intersection at a lower rate of growth is unstable. A small shock lands the economy between the two equilibria, returning it to the high-growth point. Multiple shocks—or a single larger shock—could push the economy below the lower equilibrium. In that case, the economy would continue to decline and not return quickly to its high-growth equilibrium (Duesenberry 1958, pp. 203–8).

Just such a framework appears to fit the need here, brought up to date with appropriate bells and whistles. As just noted, no spectacular shock occurred in the late 1920s to drive the economy far from its high-growth, near-full-employment equilibrium. Instead, there was a sequence of shocks that drove the economy ever further from this equilibrium. The Great Depression should be thought of as a sequence of two (or more) recessions coming on top of one another. A recession starting in 1931 contracted the economy from its already depressed state. It required only the addition of a breakdown of the banking and legal systems, as described in Bernanke (1983) and Field (1992), to make the sequence of recessions large and durable enough to add up to the Great Depression.

The general literature on business cycles has made great strides since Duesenberry wrote his book. Progress may be seen in myriad journal articles and in any macro text where various mechanisms that might lead to recessions are described. Theoretical arguments are tested for fluctuations in general by sophisticated time-series techniques which generally confirm their validity. This literature, however, shies away from discussion of any specific business cycle. The accompanying text often refers to a recession or two, but as illustration rather than as the subject of careful analysis. The causes of interest here show up as errors, shocks, and innovations in these abstract models. In Cochrane's (1994) analysis, for example, it is hard to discover even what period the data are from.

It is possible to map statistical errors into historical events (Temin 1969, 1976). But one can do this exercise only relative to a specific model. Different models clearly give different residuals. If the goal is to find events that can be represented by the residuals, it may be possible to find events to explain one set of residuals as easily as another. But the variety of models extant today makes that kind of exercise unrealistic as a way to identify causes for multiple cycles.

As a result of the focus on general explanations, the literature on specific cycles is surprisingly sparse. Only occasionally do economists turn their attention to the explanation of a single downturn. The literature on earlier recessions, not surprisingly, is even more sketchy than the literature on recent ones. An inquiry that looks for specific shocks therefore is condemned to mine a narrow seam of literature. This raises the third problem mentioned at the start: This essay draws on the existing literature, with all of its shortcomings. For example, it is no accident that Friedman and Schwartz (1963) found monetary causes to be important.

Similarly, R.A. Gordon (1961) found real causes to dominate. This turns out not to be a problem because most authors, including these, focused on the transmission of cycles, the endogenous factors that turned shocks into cycles, rather than the exogenous shocks themselves. The more serious problem is the short shrift often given to the shocks.

Another characteristic of the narrative literature is its age. Almost all of it, including the sources I have just cited, was written before rational expectations became central to macroeconomics and before technology shocks were recognized as possibilities. The narratives do not highlight expectations, and they generally do not distinguish between anticipated and unanticipated changes in any careful way. That is not to say the historical authors were innocent babes in the woods. They were sophisticated observers, and they were aware of the various influences that have been modeled in the past two or three decades. But without a formal model, these authors were imprecise in their identification of shocks to the American economy.

The lack of attention in the recent economics literature to specific business cycles is curious. It could reflect the difficulty of assigning causes to any single cycle. Economists differ on such large downturns as the Great Depression and smaller ones like 1990. But controversy generally has encouraged contributions, not discouraged them. The lack may be a reflection of disinterest in history among economists. In this case, only the latest recession is of interest, and only for a short while. With the exception of macroeconomic texts which need illustrations, this hypothesis is consistent with the observations. The lack also may be a reflection of economic methodology in which general structures are more important than individual events. This methodological bias of course supports the ideological stance of the previous hypothesis.

I do not aim to disentangle this knot. I only want to set the stage for my historiographic exercise. Given the scarcity of sources, however, I could not resist speculating on the source of this scantiness.

Business Cycles of the Past Century

The first task in collecting data is to define the population to be studied. I use Romer's (1994) dates for business cycles. She dated cycles by the previous peak and utilized a consistent algorithm to find cycles in industrial production before and after World War II. The algorithm has two steps. First, cumulate "lost" industrial production between a peak and the subsequent attainment of this peak level of production, where lost production is the difference between the actual production in any month and the previous peak level. Second, classify periods where the cumulative loss exceeds 0.421 as recessions. This filter is designed to omit minor fluctuations in output; the cutoff value is the loss in the smallest postwar NBER reference cycle. Like Romer, I focus on the contractionary phase of cycles.

I restrict the sample further to include only the century 1890 to 1990, albeit including the recession of 1990. I also decompose the Great Depression into two recessions, in 1929 and 1931, respectively. I distribute the cumulative loss of output during the Great Depression between them as one-third and two-thirds. This division shows that the recession of 1929 would have been the deepest of the century even without the following economic collapse. But the bulk of the loss is attributed to the Great Depression itself.

There were eight cycles in each of three periods—1890 to World War I, from then to the end of World War II, and from then to 1990—with one more in 1990. The four largest cycles were all in the middle period, in the interwar years. In other words, even without the Great Depression, the cumulative loss in production was far higher between the world wars than in comparable years either before or after. Business cycles clearly did not vanish after World War II, but they were less frequent than before World War I. The three periods have the same number of cycles despite their varying length.

I searched the economic history literature for discussions of these cycles. Only a few sources were found, since individual cycles generally have not been a concern of economic historians or economists generally—as noted above. The Great Depression of course is a notable exception to this general pattern. The causes of cycles then were classified in the simple two-by-two matrix shown in Table 1: domestic or foreign, real or monetary.

Table 2 shows the causes listed in the literature for each cycle of the past century except 1916, the second smallest downturn, for which no sources could be found. Also listed in Table 2 are the losses of industrial production (in months of production) from Romer (1994, Table 7) to show the relative sizes of the different cycles. I was able to select a single dominant cause for all the cycles except one (1981). Given the diversity of causes represented in Table 2, adding subsidiary causes for individual cycles only reinforces the conclusion that shocks are diverse.

I classify shocks by the loss of output in the subsequent recession, but I do not want to suggest that there was a tight correspondence between the size of the shock and the size of the subsequent economic decline. Some economic institutions and policies transmitted and even augmented shocks more than others. But that is not the topic of this essay. I therefore ignore the transmission of economic shocks and focus only on their origins.

Consider first the differences between the columns of Table 2. There is a preponderance of domestic causes. Cycles in the interwar period were mainly domestic, although the largest (1931) was international. Weighted by number of cycles, the interwar period was insulated from

Table 2
Causes of Business Cycles in the United States

Peak	Production Loss (months)	Domestic Real	Foreign Real	Domestic Monetary	Foreign Monetary
1893	2.60			•	
1896	1.36			•	
1900	.80				•
1903	1.16	•			
1907	3.04				•
1910	1.53	•			
1914	.75				•
1918	.71	•			
1920	6.64			•	
1923	1.89	•			
1927	.68	•			
1929	10.40	•			
1931	20.78				•
1937	5.79			•	
1939	.65				•
1948	1.17	•			
1953	1.20	•			
1957	1.39	•			
1960	.92			•	
1969	.99	•			
1973	2.47		•		
1980	.42		•		
1981	1.68		•	•	
1990	.93	•			

Source: See the text and Table 1. Production loss taken from Romer (1994). The loss is the cumulative reduction during a recession in the level of industrial production from its peak value, between the peak and the subsequent attainment of this peak level of production.

the world. Weighted by lost production, the interwar period was more vulnerable to international shocks than the years either before or after the wars.

Consider now the rows of Table 2. There are roughly the same number of real and monetary causes, slightly more real. My convention has been to regard a change in the price of real assets, whether oil or equities, as real. Another classification might yield somewhat different results, but I doubt if the conclusion of a roughly equal number of monetary and real shocks would change. The trend is toward real causes, particularly if the period before the First World War is compared with the period after the Second.

To go beyond these general conclusions requires a deeper level of analysis. I turn to the literature on individual cycles. They are discussed in order of their size, to give the largest cycles pride of place. Not surprisingly, the largest cycles also have been the subject of the most sustained inquiry, and it is possible to say more about them than about cycles at random.

The Four Largest Cycles

The largest cycle by far in Table 2 is 1931, the downturn that started in the midst of an already depressed economy. This cycle, it should be recalled, is not derived from Romer's (1994) algorithm. Her cycles are dated from the previous peak. This cycle acquired much of its power from coming on top of an earlier contraction. In her classification, this "cycle" is the second part of the cycle beginning in 1929, a true peak of economic activity. The negative shock explains how a recession was turned into a depression. This shock may well have been the most potent single shock of the last century—measured by its effects as transmitted through endogenous policies—and it deserves to be classified as its own cycle.

The contraction starting in 1931 has been laid squarely at the door of the Fed. Friedman and Schwartz argued forcefully for this position 35 years ago. In their dramatic words: "On October 9, the Reserve Bank of New York raised its rediscount rate to 2½ per cent and on October 16, to 3½ per cent—the sharpest rise within so brief a period in the whole history of the System, before or since" (Friedman and Schwartz, 1963, p. 317). This sharp rise followed a gradual decline in the discount rate from its peak of 6 percent in 1929 to its low of 1.5 percent in April 1931. The Fed's actions then more than doubled the discount rate in two weeks—like raising the discount rate today by 5 or 6 percentage points. This should be contrasted with stock market jitters today on the rumor of a possible one-quarter percentage point rise. Friedman and Schwartz continued that the Fed's action "intensified internal financial difficulties and was accompanied by a spectacular increase in bank failures and runs on banks."

Friedman and Schwartz characteristically did not say that the Federal Reserve's action *caused* the bank failures and runs on banks, only that the Fed's action "was accompanied by a spectacular increase in bank failures and runs on banks." We, however, can bite the bullet and say what Friedman and Schwartz presumably intended and have been quoted for over 30 years as saying, namely, the Fed's dramatic increase in the discount rate sent the already depressed economy into a tailspin. For Friedman and Schwartz and for countless others, it was the Fed's mistaken policy that was the cause of the Great Depression.

As explained above, the model within which shocks are defined in this paper includes an endogenous Federal Reserve. Only if the Fed acted out of character, or failed to act when it normally would have, can Fed action or inaction be classified as a shock to the economy. In this case, the

Fed was acting in character. The problem was that the Fed acted totally traditionally and predictably under stress, not that it deviated from any existing norm.

Friedman and Schwartz also noted, "The Fed reacted vigorously and promptly to the external drain, as it had not to the previous internal drain" (p. 317). In other words, the Fed did its job in response to an external drain, while it had not done so in response to an internal drain. Several other authors have argued that the Fed's inaction was business as usual. The Fed read low interest rates and the lack of member-bank borrowing as monetary ease (Wheelock 1991; Toma 1997). Its action in October 1931 was in character as well. The Fed acted "vigorously and promptly" to preserve the gold value of the dollar.

It was the inability of central banks and political leaders to free themselves from this inflexible monetary arrangement that led them to undertake contractionary actions as the economy declined. The Great Depression was the inevitable result of sustained and cumulative deflationary policies in almost all the major industrial countries (Temin 1989). This view has received ample support from econometric analyses of the world depression and has become widely held (Eichengreen and Sachs 1985; Bernanke 1995).

Friedman and Schwartz, although they saw the Great Depression as a primarily American affair, agreed with this characterization of the Fed's action in October 1931. Their detailed discussion of the decision to raise the discount rate so dramatically reveals that the Fed was concerned overwhelmingly with the preservation of the dollar. None of the directors of the New York Reserve Bank thought that the Fed was doing anything other than being a traditional and responsible central banker. Friedman and Schwartz reported also that the Fed's decision was widely supported throughout the American financial community (Friedman and Schwartz 1963, pp. 380–84). More recently, Romer (1993, p. 26) concurred, characterizing the Fed as having a "slavish adherence to the gold standard."

Romer (1993), like most other economists, also cites the sequence of banking panics first emphasized by Friedman and Schwartz (1963) as intensifying the Great Depression. There is no doubt that banking panics are bad for economic activity. But were the banking panics of the early 1930s a cause of the 1931 cycle? There is first the problem of definition, whether bank runs should be thought of as exogenous shocks that precipitate economic decline or whether they are part of the transmission mechanism by which economies can contract. More important is the question whether banking panics would have continued if the Fed in October 1931 had expanded instead of contracting. Commentators from Friedman and Schwartz to the present have asserted that they would not. Grossman (1994) found that the only variable consistently associated with the presence of banking crises was adherence to the gold standard. Bank failures and Fed policy were both endogenous. The external gold drain was the exogenous cause of the 1931 cycle in America.

What then was the cause that led to the Fed's action? It was the external gold drain that followed Britain's departure from gold in September 1931. The British action was in turn a result of the German financial crisis in July 1931. Hot money was moving around the industrial world, speculating against currencies that looked increasingly weak as other currencies failed (Eichengreen 1992; Eichengreen and Temin 1997). The sequence of speculative attacks, loss of reserves, and devaluation or currency controls in a sequence of countries in 1931 differed from the parallel sequence in 1997 only by being European and American instead of Asian.

The cause of the cycle beginning in 1931, then, was foreign monetary, FM. It has been entered as such in Table 2. Because this cycle is an outlier, the way it is treated in any quantitative analysis determines the importance of international monetary shocks in precipitating American cycles.

Turning to the second largest cycle, 1929, the consensus among economic historians is that the shock was domestic, and agreement that it was real is growing. I argued for a real shock 20 years ago in the form of an autonomous fall in consumption from 1929 to 1930 (Temin 1976). Some authors have claimed that consumption did not fall unusually, but others have confirmed that it did (Mayer 1980; Hall 1986; Lebergott 1996). It has been explained in part as a result of the stock-market crash, which increased both consumers' leverage and their uncertainty (Mishkin 1978; Romer 1990).

A new paper provides a stronger explanation for this fiscal shock. Olney (1998) argues that the structure of consumer credit made consumption highly volatile at this moment in history. If a consumer defaulted on an automobile loan, to take the most important form of consumer credit, he or she did not retain any equity in the automobile used as security. Consumers therefore cut back consumption in an effort to retain their equity in their new cars. A dramatic fall in consumption was the result.

The exogenous fall in consumption in 1930 has been transformed into an endogenous fall in consumption by the research just cited. Being endogenous, it does not qualify as a cause of the cycle. We must move further back in the chain of causation. Two events of 1929 appear to have precipitated the sharp fall in consumption: the stock-market crash in October 1929, and the decline in industrial production which began in mid 1929. While these events are not satisfactorily explained, they have been regarded as bubbles, whose end is indeed exogenous (De Long and Shleifer 1991; Rappoport and White 1993). And since they involve the real economy, they are classified here as domestic real shocks.

This view is opposed by studies that document the slow growth of the money supply in 1928 and 1929 and the high interest rates that accompanied the stock market boom (Friedman and Schwartz 1963; Field

1984; Hamilton 1987). But Romer (1993, p. 29) observed that the slowdown in monetary growth was not large by historical standards and that real interest rates fell after the stock market crash. She concluded, "The source of this sharp decline is almost surely not contractionary monetary policy." In addition, this literature contains little discussion about whether the Fed was acting in or out of character in the late 1920s. The implicit assumption appears to be that the Fed was acting in its traditional fashion. If so, then for this reason also, the rate of growth of the money supply does not qualify as a shock to the economy. I therefore list 1929 in Table 2 as resulting from a domestic real shock, DR.

The next two largest cycles, 1920 and 1937, are best considered together. They were the other large cycles of the interwar years, and they have been discussed together in the literature. For both of them, as for 1929, there is agreement that the shock was domestic. And for both of them, there is disagreement about whether the shock was fiscal or monetary. The fiscal shock in 1920 was the cancellation of many war contracts when the Armistice ended the First World War. The fiscal shock in 1937 was the budget contraction after payment of the second soldiers' bonus in 1936. The monetary shock in 1920 was a contraction by the Fed, facing its first postwar test. The monetary shock in 1937 was the rise in the reserve ratio mandated by the Fed in order to sop up the tremendous rise in unborrowed reserves among member banks. The Fed apparently thought it was in a liquidity trap and that these excess reserves were the sign of a perfectly elastic supply of money.

Romer (1992) tested these explanations against each other. She used a simple reduced-form model in which income this year responds to fiscal and monetary shocks last year. The coefficients on fiscal and monetary shocks were unknown coefficients to be determined by the data. She constructed two equations with two unknowns by inserting values in the reduced form for 1920 and 1937. Solving, she found that the coefficient on fiscal shocks was essentially zero; monetary shocks were the cause of both cycles. It is easy to criticize this simple model, but it is hard with the limited available data to improve upon it. I accept Romer's conclusion and cite domestic monetary, DM, shocks for 1920 and 1937.

This treatment of 1920 is faithful to the literature, but it may not approach the ultimate cause of this cycle. It was the end of the war that led to all of these domestic actions. If the domestic actions were endogenous, then the cause of the cycle was the cessation of hostilities, which produced a negative international fiscal shock. This was the view of an early Keynesian analysis of this cycle, performed during the Second World War to predict if there would be a repetition after that war (Samuelson 1943). Romer (1988) took a different approach to the end of the war. She argued that "a positive supply shock in 1921" came from accumulated stocks of raw materials during the war. They appeared in the United States only after the release of shipping capacity from wartime controls and use. But Romer argued in her later paper that this was only a negligible part of the cause of the 1920 cycle (Romer 1992, p. 764).

This abbreviated survey of the literature on the four largest cycles of the past century shows several aspects of the literature. First, no single type of shock was responsible for them all. Three out of the four possible kinds of shocks distinguished in Table 1 are represented as causes of the four largest cycles of the century. This is a very strong conclusion. If one rejects the results of recent scholarship and reverses the causes of the contested cycles in 1920, 1929, and 1937, the conclusion still stands. And people who wish to remain agnostic and cite multiple causes for these cycles obviously preserve the conclusion of many different kinds of shocks.

Second, three out of four cycles were responses to domestic shocks. While instability in the international economy was capable of wreaking havoc at home, most often cycles originated in domestic disturbances. Third, the evidence adduced by economists and economic historians to identify the shocks causing these cycles ranges from formal models to informal narratives, with various quantitative and qualitative explorations in the middle. It is possible that we find so many different causes because we use so many different lenses to view the world. This is a persistent problem, but the correlation between the research method used and the conclusion reached does not appear to be good.

The Remaining Cycles

I turn now to a survey of the other cycles of the past century. I provide briefer narratives of the next 10 cycles, ordered by production lost. This list includes all but one of the cycles for which the cumulative loss exceeded one month of industrial production. The remaining 10 smaller recessions are surveyed in an Appendix. This division has no economic content. I want to expose enough narratives to show their varied nature, but not enough to bore my audience excessively. And we have better stories about larger cycles.

The cycle of 1907 started in the European money market. Problems in Europe had led to restriction by the Bank of England and the Reichsbank. The Bank of England additionally looked with disfavor on bills financing trade with America—as the Old Lady of Threadneedle Street had done before, most notably in 1836 (Temin 1969). The resultant monetary stringency in the United States was enough to generate a cycle, but it was augmented by a domestic banking panic. The banking panic in turn led banks to suspend payments, that is, to refuse to change bills into specie at par (Sprague 1910).

Friedman and Schwartz regarded the suspension of payments as another cause of the cycle. They argued that the suspension turned a mild contraction into a severe one (Friedman and Schwartz 1963, p. 163). De Long and Summers (1986) argued to the contrary that the financial panic was contained by the suspension, reducing its effects on production. Both sets of authors agree that the domestic expectations changed in response to the foreign stimulus. The expectations were endogenous, leaving only the foreign monetary cause.

The cycle of 1893 also was involved with international finance, but its origin appears firmly domestic. The Sherman Silver Purchase Act of 1890 set the stage for a possible American devaluation in the form of shifting from a gold to a silver standard. Silver had decreased in price in the course of the preceding two decades as new discoveries and technology vastly increased the supply of that metal. Cleveland's election in 1892 made this possibility into a probability, and a run on the dollar occurred in 1893. Interest rates rose as people rushed to sell government bonds, and banks suspended payment, as they would do again in 1907. The decade of the 1890s was marked by many dislocations in the economy, but the cycle of 1893 was caused by flirting with devaluation (Calomiris 1993; Fels 1959; Hoffman 1970).

The next largest cycle was 80 years later in 1973. There can be no doubt that the cause of this cycle was the quadrupling of oil prices by OPEC. This oil shock was clearly apparent at the time and has been the object of countless studies since. Many commentators at the time and later as well argued that Fed was excessively aggressive in its attempt to limit the resulting inflation (R.J. Gordon 1980; Zarnowitz 1992). This policy choice—poor policy from the point of view of industrial production—was the reason Samuelson regarded the Fed as the villain in this cycle. From the point of view of this paper, in which central bank actions are endogenous if in character, the Fed's action must be regarded as the inevitable result of an inflationary shock. A respectable central bank resists inflation, just as it resisted devaluation in 1931. The cause of this cycle then was foreign real, FR.

The 1923 cycle, with the next largest loss of production, followed hard on the heels of the 1920 cycle. Recovery was rapid, and the boom led to bottlenecks, inflation, rising interest rates, and expectations of another recession (R.A. Gordon 1961, p. 423). Even though this was a large cycle, it came in the middle of sustained expansion of production and has received little attention. To the extent that this cycle reflected strains in the preceding expansion, it must be judged to have been caused by domestic real causes.

It is clear where this review of the intermediate-sized individual cycles is going. The first four cycles in this extended review are listed as the result of four different kinds of shocks. All of the types of shocks distinguished in Table 1 are represented. As with the larger interwar cycles, no single kind of shock has been the origin of American cycles.

The 1981 cycle clearly was caused by the second oil shock, just as the 1973 cycle was caused by the first. But the rise in oil prices and the beginning of the downturn were separated by an election that confirmed the hard-line monetary policy undertaken by the Fed under President Carter. Paul Volcker was appointed by Carter, and his fiercely contractionary, "monetarist" policies led both to Carter's disgrace and defeat at the polls and then to President Reagan's apotheosis and subsequent great victory in his reelection. Since this was a departure from Fed policy during the 1970s, it must be regarded as a cause of the 1981 cycle (De Long 1998). This cycle then had two causes: foreign real and domestic monetary.

Not much is known about the cycle of 1910. Although relatively large, it was not accompanied by a breakdown of the financial system. It consequently did not receive much contemporary attention and has not been the focus of subsequent research. Friedman and Schwartz (1963, p. 174) commented that a drop in wholesale prices contributed to the recession, and I classify the shock as domestic real as a result.

The cycle of 1957 was caused by a decline in federal government expenditures as the federal debt neared its legal limit. The Eisenhower Administration made the decision not to ask for an increase in this limit, presumably in the interests of fiscal responsibility. Defense expenditures had been high in the first half of 1957, and the decline in the second half was large. Both durable and nondurable investment decreased, and production fell (Brown 1960; Freeman 1960; R.A. Gordon 1961; R.J. Gordon 1980, Moore 1959; Osborne 1958). Although monetary policy during the 1950s has been criticized as unnecessarily restrictive (Romer and Romer 1989), a real shock was the cause of this cycle.

Moving back half a century, the cycle of 1896 appears in the literature as a coda to the cycle of 1893, much as the cycle of 1923 is seen as a continuation of the process begun in the cycle of 1920. Uncertainty about the exchange rates was increased by the Democratic Party's nomination of Bryan for President. He proclaimed in ringing words at the convention, "You shall not crucify mankind upon a cross of gold." This was not calculated to calm the financial markets. As with 1893, the cause must be seen as domestic monetary. The threat was to the exchange rate, but it came from within the United States, not from foreign sources.

Returning again to the 1950s, the cycle of 1953 followed the end of the Korean War. It was caused by the decrease in government spending that resulted from the sharp cutback in military activity (Brown 1960; Freeman 1960; R.A. Gordon 1961; R.J. Gordon 1980; Zarnowitz 1992). This cycle therefore was like that of 1920 in having its cause in the fiscal shock of peace. It differed from 1920 in coming directly after the war and not having an intermediate boom. The more direct link between the end of hostilities and a cycle in 1953 may reflect the smaller size of the preceding war.

The cycle of 1948 also resembled that of 1920 in following a war. The parallel appears more direct than for 1953 because the war was far larger and because the downturn followed an immediate postwar boom. But

Table 3
Causes of American Business Cycles, 1890 to 1990

	Domestic Real	Foreign Real	Domestic Monetary	Foreign Monetary
Number of Cycles	11	2.5	5.5	5
Months of Lost Production	22.05	3.73	18.15	26.02

Source: Table 2.

while the cycle of 1920 was one of the largest of the past century, that of 1948 was quite small. Commentators have regarded the contraction as an inventory recession (Freeman 1960; R.J. Gordon 1980; Hamberg 1952). The economic scene in Europe after the war was ever-changing, but the realignment of European currency values in 1948 was accomplished without turmoil in the international financial markets.

As with the four largest cycles, there is variety to spare in the causes of these 10 cycles. All four types of causes are listed, although a foreign monetary cause was important in only one cycle, 1907. In fact, monetary causes of any sort are not prominent in this intermediate tier of cycles. Real causes outnumber monetary ones by two to one. Foreign real shocks were confined to the period after World War II for these intermediate-sized cycles.

This is a good place to end this review of individual cycles. The literature on smaller cycles lacks the intensity of the discussion of larger fluctuations. Consequently it is harder to discriminate among the suggested causes advanced by different authors. The Appendix contains short narratives of the 10 smallest cycles of the past century, omitting 1916 about which no information could be found. All four types of causes were represented among these smaller cycles, although domestic real and foreign monetary shocks were most numerous. There were slightly more real than monetary causes, and more domestic than foreign causes, as with larger cycles. Smaller cycles do not appear to have different causes than larger cycles.

Summary and Conclusions

The results of this study are summarized in Table 3. The first row shows the unweighted distribution of shocks over the past century, where each cycle is counted as one observation. The second row weights the cycles by the loss of production shown in Table 2 to show the months of production lost in cycles started by different causes. (In both rows, the cycle of 1981 with its dual cause is divided in two.)

As noted above in examining subsamples, all four types of causes played a role in American cycles of the past century. It is not possible to identify a single type of instability as the source of American business cycles. This is true for the century as a whole, for each subperiod, and for each size class. The dominant conclusion of this inquiry is that sources of instability are not homogeneous. The literature on American business cycles provides no basis for Dornbusch's stark indictment of the Fed. Instead, this informal survey supports the results of Cochrane's (1994) time-series tests on postwar data.

Domestic real shocks were the most numerous, simply counting cycles (as in the first row of Table 3). These shocks ranged from inventory adjustments to the changes in expectations that led to the dramatic fall in consumption in 1930. Even though they are grouped together in this classification, domestic real shocks were themselves quite diverse. Nonetheless, this conclusion may be surprising. The anti-Fed view is not even supported as an approximation.

Foreign real shocks were not an important source of American instability, with the exception of the two oil shocks. The oil shocks represent a new kind of instability for the American economy. It is unlikely that this change is due simply to the growing importance of international trade. It appears to come also from increased concentration in various markets that allow dramatic price changes to take place. But we have had only two oil shocks, which is not enough to test hypotheses. We do not know if more such shocks will occur or whether OPEC will turn out to be a transitory source of instability.

Monetary shocks, both domestic and foreign, appear to have decreased over time. The difference between this conclusion and the opposite view represented by Dornbusch's statement may come from the model I am using, in which the Fed is endogenous. If the Fed "caused" a downturn by responding to some other shock, then I regard the other shock as the cause, while someone regarding the Fed as exogenous might classify the Fed's action as the shock. But this interpretation may not be true to Dornbusch's intent. His use of the term, "murdered," suggests exogenous acts by the Fed. I did not find evidence that they were important in the period since World War II.

This comparison has taken all cycles to be equal. It is instructive to ask whether large cycles were caused by different shocks than small cycles. The narratives of cycles suggested this was not the case; the second row of Table 3 takes another look. Foreign monetary shocks emerge as the most important type of shock, measured by the amount of production lost. The contrast between the weighted and unweighted sums is due to the great size of the 1931 cycle. This downturn, which dwarfs all others of the past century, accounts for 21 of the 26 months of production lost as a result of foreign monetary shocks. If the Great Depression is seen as a special case, then the weighted and unweighted sums provide more similar pictures.

With the exception of the Great Depression, domestic shocks were much more important in the past century than foreign shocks. Aside from the Great Depression, foreign monetary shocks led to very small losses in output. And foreign real shocks led to even less. The view of the American economy that sees it as largely independent of the rest of the world gets abundant confirmation in the record of the past century—leaving the Great Depression to one side.

The losses due to real and monetary shocks are surprisingly similar. As noted above in the narratives, each kind of shock caused both large and small cycles. There appears to have been little bias in their incidence. Real shocks were slightly more important, as suggested by the unweighted sum. This conclusion appears stronger for the postwar years than for the century as a whole. For the past 40 years, production lost in business cycles has been caused more by real shocks than monetary ones. For only one, small cycle—the most recent—was the real shock possibly a productivity shock.

Finally, I reiterate that this has been an exercise in historiography. I have examined the secondary literature on business cycles in America over the past century and found the patterns exhibited here. The conventional call for more research is particularly apt here. Macroeconomic theory has developed in many directions since most of the research surveyed here was performed. The history of American business cycles offers a fertile field for empirical research.

Appendix

This appendix contains short narratives of the smallest 10 cycles of the past century, omitting 1916 about which no information could be found. This is not a discontinuity; the literature on small cycles often approaches zero. The cycles are discussed chronologically on the grounds that the range of size—from one-half to one month's production lost—is too small to be interesting. Chronological order also preserves some continuity in economic conditions as the narrative progresses.

1900: This small cycle was caused by a mild monetary stringency following the start of the Boer War (Friedman and Schwartz 1963, p. 148). Its cause is FM.

1903: This "rich man's panic" followed the great merger wave at the turn of the century. No specific cause for the cycle has been identified in the literature. I judge it to have resulted from a readjustment of equity prices after the enthusiasm of the merger wave had cooled a bit. This shift of expectations about the real economy makes the cause DR.

1914: This cycle followed the outbreak of the First World War. As usual, there was a brief panic that raised interest rates and led to a contraction of economic activity. The cause is FM.

1918: This cycle was caused by the decline in spending at the conclusion of World War I (R.A. Gordon 1961). It was the immediate effect of the war's end, limited in scope and followed by a brief boom and then the larger cycle of 1920. The cause of this cycle is a reduction in domestic spending, DR, even though this spending was related to the United States' activities in Europe. The cycle was not a response to a fall in the demand for exports.

1927: This cycle is attributed to the Ford Motor Company shutdown in 1927 for a model change (R.A. Gordon 1961, p. 424). This is not supported by anything more than temporal correspondence. Nonetheless, in the absence of other causes, I classify this cause as DR.

1939: Like those of 1900 and 1914, this cycle was the result of financial stringency caused by panic at the beginning of a war. The cause is FM.

1960: This cycle took place during the Eisenhower tight budgetary regime. While some people have regarded the budget surplus as a cause of contraction, the surplus was planned—in conjunction with expansionary monetary policy—as a stimulus to private investment. The cause of the contraction was "the drastic tightening of money that occurred in 1959–60" (R.J. Gordon 1980, p. 131). The cause is DM.

1969: Like 1918's, this cycle was caused by the decline in government spending attending the end—or at least the winding down—of the Vietnam War (R.J. Gordon 1980, p. 145; Zarnowitz 1992, p. 114). The cause is DR.

1980: This cycle is the smallest downturn classified as a cycle. It is a precursor of the larger cycle in 1981; no separate cause for it is noted in the literature. The following cycle, starting in 1981, is rightly attributed in part to Volcker's influence; this one, simply the result of the oil shock, FR.

1990: Blanchard (1993) and Hall (1993) said that this cycle was due to an exogenous fall in consumption—like 1929. Cochrane (1994) objected that consumption is endogenous; the consumption fall must have been caused by a change in expectations. Blanchard labeled these expectations "animal spirits," and both he and Hall referred to the invasion of Kuwait as a shock that discouraged consumption. Hansen and Prescott (1993) claimed a technology shock as the cause of the recession. Without resolving this disagreement, I classify the cause as DR.

References

Bernanke, Ben. 1983. "Nonmonetary Effects of the Financial Crisis in the Propagation of the Great Depression." *The American Economic Review*, 73 (June), pp. 257–76.

———. 1995. "The Macroeconomics of the Great Depression: A Comparative Approach." *Journal of Money, Credit and Banking*, 27, pp. 1–28.

Blanchard, Olivier J. 1993. "Consumption and the Recession of 1990–91." *The American Economic Review*, 83 (May), pp. 270–74.

Brown, E. Cary. 1956. "Fiscal Policy in the Thirties: A Reappraisal." *The American Economic Review*, 46 (December), pp. 857–79.

———. 1960. "Federal Fiscal Policy and the Postwar Period." In Ralph E. Freeman, ed., *Postwar Economic Trends in the United States*, pp. 141–88. New York: Harper.

Calomiris, Charles W. 1993. "Greenback Resumption and Silver Risk: The Economics and Politics of Monetary Regime Change in the United States, 1862–1900." In Michael D. Bordo and Forrest Capie, eds., *Monetary Regime Transformations*, pp. 86–132. Cambridge: Cambridge University Press.

Christiano, Lawrence J., Martin Eichenbaum, and Charles Evans. 1998. "Monetary Policy Shocks: What Have We Learned and to What End?" NBER Working Paper No. 6400.

Cochrane, John H. 1994. "Shocks." *Carnegie Conference Series on Public Policy*, 41, pp. 295–364.

De Long, J. Bradford. 1998. "Fiscal Policy in the Shadow of the Great Depression." In Michael D. Bordo, Claudia Goldin, and Eugene N. White, eds., *The Defining Moment: The Great Depression and the American Economy in the Twentieth Century*. Chicago: University of Chicago Press.

De Long, J. Bradford and Andrei Shleifer. 1991. "The Stock Market Bubble of 1929: Evidence from Closed-end Mutual Funds." *Journal of Economic History*, 51 (September), pp. 675–700.

De Long, J. Bradford and Lawrence Summers. 1986. "The Changing Cyclical Variability of Economic Activity in the United States." In Robert J. Gordon, ed., *The American Business Cycle: Continuity and Change*, pp. 679–734. Chicago: University of Chicago Press.

Dornbusch, Rudiger. 1997. "How Real Is U.S. Prosperity?" Column reprinted in *World Economic Laboratory Columns*, Massachusetts Institute of Technology, December.

Duesenberry, James S. 1958. *Business Cycles and Economic Growth*. New York: McGraw-Hill.

Eichengreen, Barry. 1992. *Golden Fetters: The Gold Standard and the Great Depression*. New York: Oxford University Press.

Eichengreen, Barry and Jeffrey Sachs. 1985. "Exchange Rates and Economic Recovery in the 1930s." *Journal of Economic History*, 45 (December), pp. 925–46.

Eichengreen, Barry and Peter Temin. 1997. *The Gold Standard and the Great Depression*. Cambridge, MA: NBER Working Paper No. 6060. June.

Feinstein, Charles, Peter Temin, and Gianni Toniolo. 1997. *The European Economy Between the Wars*. Oxford: Oxford University Press.

Fels, Rendigs. 1959. *American Business Cycles, 1865–1897*. Chapel Hill, NC: University of North Carolina.

Field, Alexander J. 1984. "Asset Exchange and the Transaction Demand for Money, 1919–29." *The American Economic Review*, 74 (March), pp. 43–59.

———. 1992. "Uncontrolled Land Development and the Duration of the Depression in the United States." *Journal of Economic History*, 52 (December), pp. 785–805.

Freeman, Ralph E. 1960. "Postwar Monetary Policy." In Ralph E. Freeman, ed., *Postwar Economic Trends in the United States*, pp. 53–90. New York: Harper.

Friedman, Milton, and Anna J. Schwartz. 1963. *A Monetary History of the United States, 1867–1960*. Princeton, NJ: Princeton University Press.

Gordon, Robert A. 1961. *Business Fluctuations*. Second Edition. New York: Harper and Row.

Gordon, Robert J. 1980. "Postwar Macroeconomics: The Evolution of Events and Ideas." In Martin Feldstein, ed., *The American Economy in Transition*, pp. 101–82. Chicago: University of Chicago Press.

Grossman, Richard S. 1994. "The Shoe That Didn't Drop: Explaining Banking Stability During the Great Depression." *Journal of Economic History*, 54 (September), pp. 654–82.

Hall, Robert E. 1986. "The Role of Consumption in Economic Fluctuations." In Robert J. Gordon, ed., *The American Business Cycle: Continuity and Change*, pp. 237–66. Chicago: University of Chicago Press.

_____. 1993. "Macro Theory and the Recession of 1990–91," *The American Economic Review*, 83 (May), pp. 275–79.
Hamberg, D. 1952. "The Recession of 1948–49 in the United States." *Economic Journal*, vol. 62 (March), pp. 1–14.
Hamilton, James D. 1987. "Monetary Factors in the Great Depression," *Journal of Monetary Economics*, 19 (March), pp. 145–69.
Hansen, Gary D. and Edward C. Prescott. 1993. "Did Technology Shocks Cause the 1990–1991 Recession?" *The American Economic Review*, 83 (May), pp. 280–86.
Hoffman, Charles. 1970. *The Depression of the Nineties*. Westwood, CT: Greenwood Publishing Co.
Keynes, John Maynard. [1936] 1964. *The General Theory of Employment, Interest, and Money*. New York: Harcourt, Brace & World.
Lebergott, Stanley. 1996. *Consumer Expenditures: New Measures and Old Motives*. Princeton, NJ: Princeton University Press.
Mayer, Thomas. 1980. "Consumption in the Great Depression." *Journal of Political Economy*, 86 (February), pp. 139–45.
Mishkin, Frederic S. 1978. "The Household Balance Sheet and the Great Depression." *Journal of Economic History*, 38 (December), pp. 918–37.
Moore, Geoffrey H. 1959. "The 1957–58 Business Contraction: New Model or Old?" *The American Economic Review*, 49 (May), pp. 292–308.
Olney, Martha L. 1998. Forthcoming. "Avoiding Default: The Role of Credit in the Consumption Collapse of 1930." *Quarterly Journal of Economics*.
Osborne, Harlow D. 1958. "National Income and Product—A Review of the 1957–58 Decline and Recovery." *Survey of Current Business*, 38 (November), pp. 9–17.
Rappoport, Peter, and Eugene N. White. 1993. "Was There a Bubble in the 1929 Stock Market?" *Journal of Economic History*, 53 (September), pp. 549–74.
Romer, Christina D. 1988. "World War I and the Postwar Depression: A Reinterpretation Based on Alternative Estimates of GNP." *Journal of Monetary Economics*, 22 (July), pp. 91–115.
_____. 1990. "The Great Crash and the Onset of the Great Depression." *Quarterly Journal of Economics*, 105 (August), pp. 597–624.
_____. 1992. "What Ended the Great Depression?" *Journal of Economic History*, 52 (December), pp. 757–84.
_____. 1993. "The Nation in Depression." *Journal of Economic Perspectives*, 7 (Spring) pp. 19–39.
_____. 1994. "Remeasuring Business Cycles." *Journal of Economic History*, 54 (September), pp. 573–609.
Romer, Christina D. and David H. Romer. 1989. "Does Monetary Policy Matter? A New Test in the Spirit of Friedman and Schwartz." In *NBER Macroeconomics Annual 4*, pp. 121–70. Cambridge, MA: The MIT Press.
Samuelson, Paul A. 1943. "Full Employment after the War." In S. E. Harris, ed., *Postwar Economic Problems*, pp. 27–53. New York: McGraw-Hill.
Sprague, O. M. W. 1910. *History of Crises under the National Banking System*. Washington, DC: Government Printing Office.
Taylor, John B. 1993a. *Macroeconomic Policy in a World Economy*. New York: W.W. Norton.
_____. 1993b. "Discretion versus Policy Rules in Practice." *Carnegie Conference Series on Public Policy* 39, pp. 195–214.
Temin, Peter. 1969. *The Jacksonian Economy*. New York: W.W. Norton.
_____. 1976. *Did Monetary Forces Cause the Great Depression?* New York: W.W. Norton.
_____. 1989. *Lessons from the Great Depression*. Cambridge, MA: The MIT Press.
Toma, Mark. 1997. *Competition and Monopoly in the Federal Reserve System, 1914–1951*. New York: Cambridge University Press.
Wheelock, David C. 1991. *The Strategy and Consistency of Federal Reserve Monetary Policy: 1924–1933*. New York: Cambridge University Press.
Zarnowitz, Victor. 1992. *Business Cycles: Theory, History, Indicators, and Forecasting*. Chicago: University of Chicago Press.

Discussion

Christina D. Romer*

Peter Temin has written a first-rate paper on the causes of American business cycles since 1890. It is careful, analytically serious, and exceedingly provocative. But, I suspect that he knows I am likely to disagree with much of what he says.

The task that Temin was given by the organizers was a daunting one—to summarize a century of American macroeconomic history in a 30-page paper. Temin, I think rightly, chose not to blaze new empirical ground, but rather to synthesize the existing literature. I strongly agree with his view that we can learn a great deal from reading what many sensible people have to say about the causes of recessions in the past. Indeed, I will go further and suggest that we can learn more from an "essay in economic historiography" than from running simple, unstructured regressions that ignore the nuances of causes and structural changes.

Temin took as his job to identify the conventional wisdom and then to classify the cause of each recession into one of four categories—domestic and foreign monetary shocks and domestic and foreign real shocks. (Since he lumps into real shocks everything from oil price shocks to drops in consumer confidence, it would be more accurate to describe his categories as monetary shocks and nonmonetary shocks.) His conclusion is that cycles over the last century have not been caused by a single predominant factor—indeed, the most striking feature of recessions is the diversity of their causes. Domestic factors have been more important than foreign, though not dramatically so. To the extent that a change has

---

*Class of 1957–Garth B. Wilson Professor of Economics, University of California, Berkeley.

occurred over time, it is away from monetary factors and toward real factors.

Given Temin's research strategy, there are two ways one could disagree with him. First, one could argue with his classification scheme. Second, one could argue with his portrayal of the conventional wisdom. Alas, I plan to do both. I will suggest that a more sensible classification scheme and a broader reading of the conventional wisdom indicate a crucial role for domestic monetary shocks, at least in the interwar and postwar eras.

With his classification scheme, Temin chooses to treat most policy changes as endogenous. Even in recessions where tight monetary policy is conventionally thought to be the proximate cause of the downturn, Temin looks instead at what caused the tight policy. Only a change in the Federal Reserve's usual behavior is classified as a monetary shock.

This focus on ultimate causes, I think, takes an overly narrow view of what constitutes the monetary regime. Because Fed behavior is invariably triggered by something, and because there is almost always some continuity in Fed behavior, it comes dangerously close to assuming that monetary policy shocks never cause recessions. Let me give you an extreme example that may illustrate the danger of Temin's classification scheme. Suppose that the Fed's "usual behavior" includes cutting the money supply in half every time the American League wins the World Series. Temin would attribute the recession that likely follows an American League victory to a real shock rather than to a monetary one, because the Fed has not deviated from its normal behavior. And yet, a more monetary-policy-caused recession is hard to imagine.

A more reasonable alternative involves asking whether the monetary change was the inevitable, or even just the likely, result of the trigger, or whether a genuine choice was involved. If a conscious choice was made to respond in a certain way or if alternative policies were understood and discussed at the time, then monetary policy should share at least some of the blame for the recession.

Following this criterion would lead one to classify the cause of many twentieth-century recessions quite differently than Temin does. Most important, it would change the way one views the deepening phase of the Great Depression (the 1931 recession in Temin's classification scheme). Temin attributes this recession solely to an international shock; he argues that in failing to respond to the financial panics the Federal Reserve was simply following its usual behavior. However, the fact that the Federal Reserve had been set up largely to prevent or contain panics and that reasonable men *at the time* were urging the Fed to intervene, suggests to me that the Fed's behavior was not purely endogenous or predetermined. While the gold standard no doubt constrained the Fed's behavior at some point in the Depression, the size of the U.S. gold reserves in 1930 and early 1931 makes it very likely that the Fed could have responded aggressively to at least the first two waves of banking panics. Indeed, the fact that the Fed was able to engage in very expansionary open market operations for several months in the spring of 1932 without an overwhelming gold drain casts doubt even on the view that the gold standard prevented a serious response after a devaluation mentality became prevalent in 1931. Therefore, to the extent that the financial collapse was a major factor in the acceleration of the real decline between 1930 and 1933, domestic monetary factors must be given some role, if not the central role, in this, the worst depression in U.S. history.

I believe that Temin's narrow rule also leads him astray in classifying several postwar recessions. Consider the 1973 recession. Temin says that monetary policy need be given no role because it was simply responding to the inflation caused by the oil price shock and "a respectable central bank resists inflation." First, I think one could argue with this somewhat cavalier description of usual Fed operating procedures; throughout the late 1960s and early 1970s the Fed showed itself to be quite willing to tolerate inflation. Therefore, there may have been a deviation from usual Fed behavior, and thus a domestic monetary shock, even in the Temin sense. More important, even if the Fed did usually fight inflation, the decision to contract substantially in 1974, when the economy was already in a downturn and many were calling for loosening, was still far from inevitable or even particularly likely. The Fed almost surely made the right decision to fight inflation in this case, but it most definitely made a decision and should be given both blame for the recession that followed and credit for restraining inflation. Finally, one has to mention the evidence that expansionary monetary policy bears much of the responsibility for the inflation of the early 1970s. Both De Long (1997) and Taylor (1998) point out that inflation was already very high and rising before the first oil shock in 1973. Thus, to the extent that the Fed was responding to inflation of its own creation, it is especially hard to absolve it of all blame for this recession.

What is surely true is that monetary policy and the oil shock share responsibility for the 1973 recession, just as Temin says they do for the 1981 recession. Indeed, I would suggest that monetary policy shares the blame for many of the postwar recessions that Temin attributes to nonmonetary factors. I think that Temin's view of policy, together with a limited view of the conventional wisdom, leads him to miss this crucial fact.

Let me give just a few examples. Temin attributes the recessions of both 1957 and 1969 to a decline in government spending—a domestic real shock in his classification scheme. And yet, the decline in the high-employment surplus preceding both recessions was actually quite small. Indeed, in the case of 1957 it is almost impossible to discern in the data: With the exception of a small, temporary rise in the first quarter of 1958, the ratio of the high-employment surplus to GDP fell nearly continuously from 1956 to the start of 1959. In both cases, however, I believe the conventional wisdom attributes the decline, at least partially, to tight monetary policy. I know that it is the view expressed in at least one of the papers cited by Temin (my paper with David Romer (1989)). Before both downturns the Federal Reserve made a conscious decision to tighten in order to reduce inflation, and in both instances this decision was reflected in higher real interest rates. While Temin does not mention these tightenings, I suspect that he has dismissed them as "business as usual" at the Fed. However, in both cases alternative polices were certainly considered and urged; nothing made the decisions inevitable or even very likely. Therefore, a more reasonable classification scheme would have to give domestic monetary factors at least part of the blame for these contractions.

If Temin adopted a somewhat less narrow definition of monetary policy shocks and considered multiple causes, his findings would be very different, especially for the postwar era. Monetary shocks not only played a role in 1957, 1969, and 1973, as I have argued, and in 1981 as Temin notes, but also played a role in 1948, 1980, and 1990. Thus, there is a crucial common link in postwar recessions: Monetary policy was one of the top two factors in nearly every postwar downturn.

This key role of postwar monetary shocks lies behind my own view of the fundamental change that has occurred in the cause of recessions over time. The key change has not been from monetary shocks to real shocks or vice versa, but from random shocks from various sources to governmental shocks. Before World War I, recessions were, as Temin suggests, generated by a wide range of monetary and nonmonetary shocks arising from the private sector—or, at least, not arising from conscious decisions by the government. By the end of World War II, the government had learned how to counteract most shocks and did so quite effectively. However, because of a tendency toward overexpansion and the increasing prevalence of supply shocks, inflation periodically got out of hand. In response, the Federal Reserve (and to a lesser degree the fiscal authority) has had to generate recessions to curb inflation.

It is this move toward government-caused (and controlled) recessions that accounts for an important change in the distribution of cycles over time. Cycles have become less frequent in the postwar era because the government is counteracting many shocks. Cycles have also become more concentrated in the moderate range because monetary policy and fiscal policy now eliminate small random recessions and prevent collapses such as the Great Depression. Postwar cycles have been of moderate size because that is what it takes to reduce inflation.

I like this view of the change in the cause of cycles over time not only because it strikes me as fundamentally right, but because it suggests that we do not have to choose between the two polar views identified by Temin. Both the no-single-shock and the only-monetary-shock stories are right for the appropriate eras. Temin is correct that in the prewar era recessions had a variety of causes, most of them unrelated to government actions. The view summarized by Dornbusch is correct for the postwar era: Policy, especially monetary policy, has played the crucial role. I might not have used Dornbusch's dramatic language—the Fed has acted more like a doctor imposing a painful cure on a patient with an illness than like a murderer—but the result in terms of recessions has been the same.

References

De Long, J. Bradford. 1997. "America's Peacetime Inflation: The 1970s." In Christina D. Romer and David H. Romer, eds. *Reducing Inflation*, pp. 247–76. Chicago, IL: University of Chicago Press for NBER.

Friedman, Milton, and Anna J. Schwartz. 1963. *A Monetary History of the United States, 1867–1960*. Princeton, NJ: Princeton University Press for NBER.

Romer, Christina D. and David H. Romer. 1989. "Does Monetary Policy Matter? A New Test in the Spirit of Friedman and Schwartz." *NBER Macroeconomics Annual* 4, pp. 121–70.

Taylor, John B. 1998. "An Historical Analysis of Monetary Policy Rules." Manuscript, Stanford University.

Historical Evidence on Business Cycles: The International Experience

U. Michael Bergman, Michael D. Bordo, and Lars Jonung*

This paper adopts a historical perspective to examine the characteristics of business cycle fluctuations within and across a large set of countries. Following the classical work by Burns and Mitchell (1946), we define business cycles as recurrent, but not necessarily periodic, fluctuations in economic activities with a duration of two to eight years. According to them, business cycles are characterized by their average duration and amplitude and the co-movement of economic activities. Our objective is to document regularities of these cyclical movements both across countries and across time.

Most recent empirical work within this strand of research has dealt with the American record; see, for example, Lucas (1977), Kydland and Prescott (1990), and Stock and Watson (1998). A number of recent studies have made international comparisons of business cycles, among others Sheffrin (1988), Baxter and Stockman (1989) and Backus and Kehoe (1992), or they have dealt with the record of countries other than the United States, among others Englund, Persson and Svensson (1992).[1] Our study focusing on many countries, including the United States, should be looked upon as fitting into this tradition of comparative international research on the business cycle. The issues we address in this paper concern, first, the behavior of cycles within countries ("country-specific"

---

*Bergman is Associate Professor of Economics, Lund University, Sweden; Bordo is Professor of Economics at Rutgers University; Jonung is Professor at the Stockholm School of Economics. The authors thank Richard Cooper and Christina Romer for helpful comments. They also thank Pontus Hansson, Jesper Hansson, and Antu Murshid for data assistance.

[1] Also see Zarnowitz (1992) for earlier international cyclical comparisons.

cycles); second, the sources of business cycles; and third, the interaction between business cycles across countries (the "international business cycle").

The approach we take in this paper is an empirical one, not guided directly by any one theory of the business cycle, although we are cognizant that meaningful empirical work is always driven by theory. Business cycle theory has evolved from an emphasis on the cycle as an independent, well-identified entity earlier in the century, to the Keynesian approach in the 1940s and 1950s emphasizing exogenous fluctuations in aggregate demand, to the monetarist approach of the 1960s and 1970s stressing the role of monetary shocks, to the recent real business cycle approach close to the classical view, stressing technology shocks, and the new-Keynesian emphasis on sticky prices and menu costs.[2]

Our approach also complements the traditional narrative approach to the study of business cycles, best exemplified in Thorp (1926) and Gayer, Rostow, and Schwartz (1953). In this approach contemporary press and periodical literature and similar sources are culled to give a picture of what contemporary opinion viewed as both a chronicle of business events and a list of causal factors. To follow such an approach is a gigantic task, beyond the limits of an essay. Instead, we present a bird's eye view of central features of the cyclical experience of advanced countries. We search for a number of empirical regularities as suggested by past and contemporary business cycle research.

We pay special attention to monetary regimes, more specifically to the institutions determining monetary arrangements within the economy as well as between economies. We focus on three distinct regimes: the classical gold standard era, the interwar period, and the post-World War II period, which we split into the Bretton Woods period and the post-Bretton Woods period.[3] The following 13 "advanced" countries are included in our sample: the United States, the United Kingdom, Germany, France, Japan, Italy, Canada, Belgium, the Netherlands, Denmark, Finland, Norway, and Sweden. The European experience is emphasized, partly by choice and partly because of data limitations.

Our empirical work extends the earlier literature in several directions. First, we examine a broader set of countries than did Backus and Kehoe (1992), who studied 10 countries. We have also extended their historical data backward and forward in time.

Second, we apply the Baxter-King (1995) band-pass filter to extract all variations of a variable at business cycle frequencies. We use the data extracted in this way to perform empirical tests of the hypothesis that the

---

[2] See Zarnowitz (1992, ch. 2).
[3] The rationale for this chronology is spelled out in Bordo and Jonung (1997) and Bordo and Schwartz (1998).

volatility of business cycle fluctuations has been dampened during the post-World War II period, compared to the classical gold standard era. We reconsider this hypothesis and perform empirical tests allowing us to examine this issue both for each country individually and for all 13 countries in our sample.

Third, we apply the band-pass filter to the components of national expenditures to determine whether their cyclical patterns are similar across cycles. We also use a panel data regression to ascertain the extent to which various expenditure components predict recessions.[4]

Fourth, we present evidence on common cyclical movements between countries. We observe patterns of the interrelationships between countries under different monetary regimes that reflect the growth and interdependence of markets and changing patterns of economic performance among countries.

The paper is organized in the following manner. The first section briefly discusses the relationship between monetary regimes and the business cycle. The next section seeks to document regularities (the amplitude and the asymmetry) of country-specific business cycles measured by band-pass-filtered GDP during the three major monetary regimes. In the third section we explore some issues concerning the co-movement of country-specific national income and the expenditure components — consumption, investment, government expenditures and revenues, exports and imports — as well as the money supply and the price level. We also extract expenditure components during recessions, to explore whether these can account for shortfalls in real GDP. The fourth section then examines some aspects of the international business cycle experience. The main question posed in this section is whether we can identify common cyclical patterns across groups of countries. The final section summarizes the paper.

MONETARY REGIMES AND THE BUSINESS CYCLE

Demarcating the data by monetary regimes, we believe, is a fruitful approach for an empirical study such as ours, as different cyclical patterns may emerge within as well as between countries under different monetary regimes. Traditional theory posits that a convertible regime, such as the classical gold standard that prevailed from around 1880 until the outbreak of World War I, is characterized by a set of self-regulating market forces that tend to ensure long-run price level stability. These forces operated through the mechanism commonly described by the classical commodity theory of money (Bordo 1984). According to that

---

[4] It was not possible to amass the data required to analyze the impact on the business cycle of technology shocks, the variable emphasized by the real business cycle approach.

theory, changes in gold production will eventually offset any inflationary or deflationary price level movements. The problem, however, is that unexpected shocks to the supply or demand for gold can have significant short-run effects on the price level and on real output, in the face of nominal rigidities.

In an international convertible regime, pegging nations' currencies to the fixed price of gold provides a stable nominal anchor to the international monetary system. Such stability, however, comes at the expense of exposure to foreign shocks, which can produce volatile output and employment. Adherence to the international convertible regime also implies a loss of monetary and fiscal independence, since under such a regime the authorities' prime commitment is to maintain convertibility of their currencies into the precious metal, and not to stabilize the domestic economy.

In a fiat money regime, in theory, monetary authorities could use open market operations, or other policy tools, to avoid the types of shocks that may jar the price level and real activity under a specie standard and hence provide both short-run and long-run nominal stability. Such a regime also allows greater fiscal policy autonomy. In addition to giving the authorities policy independence, adhering to a flexible exchange rate fiat regime provides insulation against foreign shocks.[5]

As in a convertible regime, countries following fiat money regimes can adhere to fixed exchange rates with each other. The key advantage of doing so is avoidance of the transaction costs of exchange in international trade. However, a fixed-rate system based on fiat money does not provide the stable nominal anchor of the specie convertibility regime unless all the members define their currencies in terms of the currency of one dominant country (for example, the United States under Bretton Woods or Germany in the European Monetary System), which in turn follows a rule that requires it to maintain price stability.

Finally, in a fiat money, flexible-rate regime, the absence of the nominal anchor of the fixed price of specie opens up the possibility that monetary authorities could use the printing press to engineer high inflation in order to satisfy the political goals of the government, for example, its fiscal demands or demands to maintain full employment.

---

[5] Theoretical developments in recent years have complicated the simple distinction between fixed and floating exchange rates. In the presence of capital mobility, currency substitution, policy reactions, and policy interdependence, floating rates do not necessarily provide complete insulation from either real or monetary shocks (Bordo and Schwartz 1989). Moreover, according to recent real business cycle approaches, there may be no relationship between the international monetary regime and the transmission of real shocks (Baxter and Stockman 1989).

The Classical Gold Standard

Under the pre-World War I classical gold standard, where nations' money supplies were determined by their monetary gold stocks, the business cycle was strongly influenced by shocks to the gold market, such as gold discoveries and changes in the demand for gold as new countries adopted the standard. Monetary and fiscal policies had a limited role in this era.

Central banks were supposed to follow the "rules of the game" and accommodate gold flows. Although violations were common, and monetary authorities on occasion sterilized gold flows and geared their policies to domestic objectives such as smoothing interest rates and possibly offsetting cyclical disturbances, in addition to serving as a lender of last resort to provide adequate liquidity to allay banking panics, the violations were never serious enough to force any of the advanced countries to abandon gold convertibility (Bordo 1998). The only situation when expansionary monetary policy was deliberately used was in the case of a major war, when convertibility would be temporarily suspended and government expenditures financed by the issue of inconvertible notes (Bordo and Kydland 1995). Fiscal policy also had a very limited role in this period. Debt-financed government expenditures were temporarily expanded during wartime as a form of tax smoothing (Bordo and Jonung 1997).

Financial crises (banking panics) were important sources of cyclical disturbances under the gold standard. They occurred regularly in England as part of the upper turning point of the business cycle in the years before 1866, after which the Bank of England learned to act as a lender of last resort. Similar experiences occurred on the Continent. In the United States, which did not have an effective lender of last resort and had a unit banking system unable to diversify portfolios in the face of shocks to various regions, banking panics were an important source, if not an aggravating factor, of the business cycle.

Finally, the pre-1914 era was considerably less industrialized than the subsequent years in most of the countries in our sample. Hence shocks to the agricultural sector such as harvest failures constituted important sources of disturbances. These country-specific shocks were in turn transmitted between countries via the fixed exchange rate linkages of most countries adhering to gold parity. They were transmitted via the current account and via capital flows in an era absent controls. Despite the presence of business cycles, the era was one of rapid growth and relative stability compared to the interwar years. Many attribute its success to the fact that it was dominated (in terms of trade flows and cyclical fluctuations) by the United Kingdom, which generally followed very stable financial policies.

The Interwar Period

The interwar period was a mixed regime of floating in the beginning, convertibility in the middle, and managed floating with extensive capital and exchange controls at the end. The early years were characterized by chaotic monetary and fiscal conditions on the continent of Europe and floating exchange rates in most countries. The attempt to restore gold convertibility after the war was responsible for a very serious worldwide recession between 1919 and 1921.

The restored gold exchange standard from 1925 to 1931 reintroduced many of the attributes of the classical gold standard including the conduit of international business cycle transmission via the monetary standard (Fisher 1935; Choudhri and Kochin 1980). It also suffered from fatal flaws that both made it more fragile and imposed deflationary pressure on world monetary gold stocks (Bordo and Eichengreen 1998).[6] The most serious problem of that era, and a key cause of the Great Depression, was the pursuit of pro-gold contractionary policies by the United States and France. The Great Depression originated in the United States but was transmitted abroad by the gold standard. Only when the links with gold were cut did recovery take place.[7]

Although the interwar period was by far the most unstable in our comparison, the 1920s were characterized by relative stability. Many attribute this experience to the effective use of monetary policy in the United States (Friedman and Schwartz 1963a) and central bank cooperation (Eichengreen 1992). The considerable instability that followed in the 1930s is attributed by these authors to the failure of Federal Reserve policy and the breakdown of cooperation.

The Postwar Period: Bretton Woods

The Bretton Woods System was designed to incorporate the perceived lessons of the monetary turmoil of the interwar period. Bretton Woods was the last global convertible regime.

The Articles of Agreement signed at Bretton Woods, New Hampshire, in 1944 represented a compromise between American and British

---

[6] The fatal flaws included: the adjustment problem, with asymmetric adjustment between deficit countries (Britain) and surplus countries (France and the United States); the failure by countries to follow the rules of the gold standard game (for example, both the U.S. and France sterilized gold flows); the liquidity problem (inadequate gold supplies, the wholesale substitution of key currencies for gold as international reserves leading to a convertibility crisis when countries subsequently tried to convert the key currencies back into gold); and the confidence problem, leading to sudden shifts among key currencies and between key currencies and gold (Bordo 1993; Eichengreen 1992).

[7] An alternative explanation for the Great Depression focuses on real factors: structural and demographic adjustments to the upheavals of World War I (Temin 1989).

plans. They combined the flexibility and freedom for policymakers of a floating-rate system, which the British representatives wanted, with the nominal stability of the gold standard rule emphasized by the United States. The system established was one of pegged exchange rates, but members could alter their parities in the face of a fundamental disequilibrium. Members were encouraged to use domestic stabilization policy to offset temporary disturbances. Thus, the Agreement explicitly made room for discretionary monetary and fiscal policies, whose use was minimal at best under the classical gold standard. These policies would be effective because of the presence of capital controls. The International Monetary Fund was to provide temporary liquidity assistance and to oversee the operation of the system.

The era was characterized by rapid growth, especially in Europe and Japan, and few serious recessions. The international transmission of cyclical disturbances was muted by capital controls and domestic financial policies. As was Britain under the gold standard, the United States was the dominant country of the Bretton Woods era, and Bretton Woods became a gold dollar standard. The system eventually broke down because of fatal flaws similar to those of the gold exchange standard and because the United States followed inappropriate policies for the center country (Bordo 1993).

The Postwar Period: The Managed Float

The move to a managed, floating exchange rate regime in the 1970s gave greater independence to monetary and fiscal policies. This was exhibited in higher money growth rates, rising fiscal deficits, and high debt-to-GDP ratios (Bordo and Jonung 1997). Most countries followed full employment policies in this period and exploited the Phillips curve trade-off to high inflation. The oil shocks of the 1970s were important aggravating factors (see Daniel 1997). Many believe that they precipitated serious recessions, which were transmitted between countries despite the policy independence afforded by floating rates. In this period, return to greater capital mobility made the world more close-knit and also may have more closely interconnected the business cycle. The high inflation period of the 1970s was followed by disinflation in the 1980s and 1990s and a return to more stable monetary and fiscal policies in the mid 1990s (Bordo and Jonung 1997).

To conclude, it has proved fruitful to adopt a monetary regime perspective to examine long-run patterns. Monetary regimes are an important determinant of the long-run behavior of nominal variables such as the money stock, the price level, and nominal interest rates. There is no clear-cut relationship between monetary regimes and the long-run behavior of real variables, however.

Here we focus instead on the relationship between monetary regimes and the short-run behavior of the economy, as a priori reasons suggest that the regime may influence cyclical behavior as well. However, we are aware that any cyclical differences found across regimes may be due to a host of factors. Various structural changes may be at work, such as the decline of agriculture and the industrial sector, and the rise of the service sector, the public sector, and the welfare state in a large number of countries in our sample. These structural developments may have exerted an influence on the characteristics of the business cycle.

PROPERTIES OF COUNTRY-SPECIFIC BUSINESS CYCLES

In this section we examine the business cycle properties of real GDP. We examine and compare the data for three different monetary regimes: the classical gold standard era 1873 to 1913, the interwar period 1920 to 1938, and the postwar period 1948 to 1995. The latter period is also split into the Bretton Woods period 1948 to 1972, and the post-Bretton Woods period 1973 to 1995. The data sources are listed in Appendix A.

Prior to our empirical analysis, we must extract the cyclical component from the macroeconomic time series. Recently, Baxter and King (1995) have developed a band-pass filter that isolates cyclical components of economic time series. This filter can be designed to isolate cyclical components of the data with durations conforming to the Burns-Mitchell definition of the business cycle, that is, cycles with durations between two and eight years.[8] We use a third-order, two-sided filter following Baxter and King (1995) that produces cyclical components with lengths between two and eight years. When applying this filter, we lose three observations at both ends of our sample. Initial conditions for the filter are actual observations on GDP for the three years preceding 1876 and projections of GDP from 1995 until 1998 based on fourth-order, univariate autoregressive models.[9]

The NBER chronology has long been a common starting point for business cycle analysis. To evaluate our band-pass filter technique we compare the NBER chronology for the United States with our estimated cyclical component, in Figure 1. This figure demonstrates a striking resemblance between NBER peaks and troughs and peaks and troughs estimated by the band-pass filter. Our filter detected 22 out of 26 troughs indicated by the NBER chronology since 1885. In 15 cases, our filter correctly dates the troughs, and we miss four troughs by plus/minus one

---

[8] Baxter and King (1995) compare the properties of cyclical components of U.S. GNP generated by different detrending techniques and find that the band-pass filter usually is superior to other filters in isolating cyclical variation within certain frequency bands.

[9] Stock and Watson (1998) also use univariate autoregressive models to construct predicted values used as initial conditions.

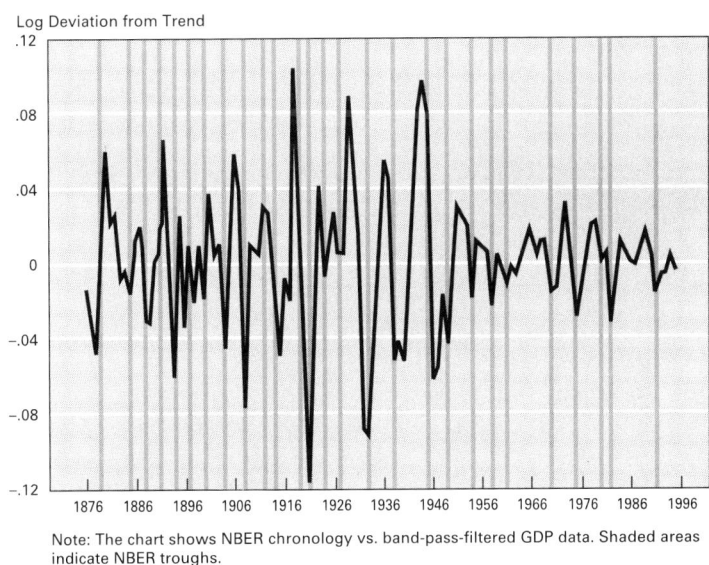

**Figure 1
U.S. Business Cycle: Cyclical Components of GDP**

Note: The chart shows NBER chronology vs. band-pass-filtered GDP data. Shaded areas indicate NBER troughs.

year. Three troughs cannot be dated correctly by our filter. This result supports the findings in Stock and Watson (1998), who also apply the band-pass filter to U.S. real GDP. Our interpretation is that the band-pass filter produces a good measure of the U.S. business cycle, as it conforms quite closely to the NBER chronology. Therefore, we apply this filter for our 13 countries to both national income and the components of national income. Plots of band-pass-filtered real GDP for the other 12 countries are shown in Appendix B.

Table 1 displays the average length (in years) of business cycles using band-pass-filtered data for the three monetary regimes. The number of cycles identified is given in parentheses. A comparison across regimes indicates that the typical business cycle lasted on average 3.8 years in the 13 countries in our sample for the classical gold standard period. In this period, cycles ranged from 2.9 years in Italy to 4.7 years in Sweden. The duration increased to 5.4 years on average during the interwar years and then fell back to 4.8 years in the postwar period. We suggest that the business cycle has been a fairly regular empirical phenomenon across time and that the duration is similar across our sample of countries.

Table 1
Average Length of Business Cycles under Different Monetary Regimes

Period	United States	United Kingdom	Germany	France	Canada	Italy	Japan
Gold Standard	4.1 (9)	3.5 (10)	4.0 (10)	4.2 (9)	3.4 (11)	2.9 (12)	4.0 (6)
Interwar	6.3 (3)	6.0 (3)	5.2 (4)	6.5 (2)	4.5 (4)	3.2 (5)	4.0 (5)
Postwar	5.5 (8)	5.6 (8)	4.8 (9)	4.3 (9)	5.1 (9)	4.8 (8)	4.8 (8)

	Belgium	Netherlands	Denmark	Finland	Norway	Sweden	All Countries
Gold Standard	3.7 (10)	3.4 (11)	3.8 (10)	3.8 (8)	3.9 (8)	4.7 (7)	3.8
Interwar	8.3 (3)	5.5 (2)	4.2 (4)	6.3 (3)	4.8 (4)	5.0 (4)	5.4
Postwar	4.1 (9)	5.1 (7)	4.6 (8)	5.8 (8)	3.6 (11)	4.8 (8)	4.8

Note: Gold standard is the period 1873–1913, interwar is 1920–38, and postwar is 1948–95. The numbers in the table refer to the average length in years of estimated cycles peak-to-peak (or trough-to-trough) that fall in each regime. The number of cycles is shown in parentheses.

Mild versus Serious Recessions

One theme in the literature on the business cycle states that severe downturns are of a different character from mild recessions (Burns and Mitchell 1946; Friedman and Schwartz 1963b). According to this view, the severe recessions that occurred before World War II were commonly associated with financial crises. As can be seen from Figure 1 and the graphs in Appendix B, severe recessions generally occurred before 1946. In the case of the United States and a few other countries, these recessions were associated with financial crises (Bordo 1986).

A striking feature of Figure 1 and the graphs in Appendix B is the lower amplitude displayed for the postwar period. However, disregarding the severe recessions in these graphs, volatility seems to have remained fairly constant over time. Next we perform empirical tests of the hypothesis that the business cycle has been dampened.

Has the Business Cycle Been Dampened?

A recent controversy concerns whether the volatility of the business cycle has been reduced, comparing the post-World War II period with the pre-World War II period. Many have argued that the evidence that business cycles have been dampened since World War II reflects the institution and successful application of stabilization policies including automatic stabilizers (DeLong and Summers 1986; Zarnowitz 1992). However, Romer (1989) disputes the basic evidence for the United States. Her reworking of Kuznets' national income series leads to the conclusion that there is little difference in cyclical amplitude between the pre- and post-World War II eras. The counterargument for the U.S. case is provided by Balke and Gordon (1989). International evidence that generally supports the traditional view has been provided by Sheffrin (1988), Backus and Kehoe (1992), and others. Bergman and Jonung (1993), however, do not find strong support for a dampening of the Swedish business cycle.

To provide evidence on this issue for the 13 countries in our sample, we measure the amplitude of the business cycle as the variance of band-pass-filtered real GDP. Our empirical analysis extends previous studies. Besides using band-pass-filtered data, we examine a larger set of countries than in previous studies. Sheffrin (1988) covers six European countries, whereas Backus and Kehoe (1992) cover 10 countries. In addition to testing whether the variance of the business cycle is invariant to monetary regimes for each country separately, we also test to see whether volatility has changed simultaneously across all 13 countries.

According to the standard deviations in Table 2 for the band-pass-filtered data (the cyclical component of GDP), volatility was considerably higher during the interwar years than during the pre-World War I gold standard and the post-World War II periods. This result confirms the conclusions from earlier studies showing that the interwar years displayed relatively high volatility.[10] There is consensus on this point. The deflation and depression of the early 1920s and the Great Depression of the 1930s brought havoc to the world economy in these years.

Table 2 also throws light on the issue of the possible dampening of the business cycle over time when comparing the classical gold standard era with the post-World War II period. The point estimates of volatility displayed in Table 2 are lower during the later period for 10 out of 13 countries. Figure 2 plots standard deviations of the cyclical component taken from Table 2 for two subperiods, pre-World War I and post-World War II. It shows that the point estimates of volatility are lower during the post-World War II period for all countries except Belgium, Norway, and Denmark.

To construct a formal test of the hypothesis that volatility measured by the variance of the band-pass-filtered GDP declined over time, we set up a Seemingly Unrelated Regression (SUR) system with 13 equations where the dependent variable is the variance of the bandpass filtered GDP and the independent variables are two dummy variables. The first dummy has the value one for the classical gold standard period and zero otherwise, whereas the second dummy takes on the value zero for the gold standard period and one otherwise. In this setup, each coefficient on the two dummy variables is a measure of the variance of the business cycle under each regime.

To test whether the variance is constant for each country separately

---

[10] See for example, Backus and Kehoe (1992, p. 873).

Table 2
Volatility and Skewness of Band-Pass-Filtered Real GDP during Different Monetary Regimes

Country	Entire Period 1876–1995		Gold Standard 1876–1913		Interwar 1920–38		Postwar 1948–95		Bretton Woods 1948–72		Post-Bretton Woods 1973–95	
	Stand. Dev.	Skewness	Stand. Dev.	Skewness	Stand. Dev.	Skewness	Stand. Dev.	Skewness	Stand. Dev.	Skewness	Stand. Dev.	Skewness
United States	.035	−.018	.032	−.145	.053	−.459	.016	−.435	.016	−.494	.016	−.378
United Kingdom	.022	−.205	.020	−.300	.029	−.700	.014	.628	.011	−.194	.017	.724
Germany	.054	−1.530	.024	.491	.077	−1.471	.019	−.057	.019	−.909	.020	.719
France	.044	−1.581	.024	−.803	.037	−.380	.010	.201	.011	.379	.010	−.178
Canada	.032	−.437	.031	−.237	.051	−.588	.015	−.335	.015	−.212	.015	−.498
Italy	.042	−5.092	.020	−.141	.025	.194	.012	.104	.012	.387	.012	−.132
Japan	.050	−2.078	.023	.541	.037	.272	.015	.353	.018	.012	.012	1.424
Belgium	.029	−2.392	.009	1.587	.025	−.208	.011	.043	.010	−.323	.012	.239
Netherlands	.049	−3.440	.030	−.158	.020	−.137	.017	.361	.022	.212	.010	−.512
Denmark	.038	2.208	.011	−.406	.024	.640	.015	−.149	.016	−.154	.013	−.187
Finland	.030	−1.853	.022	−.075	.027	−.390	.020	.034	.017	−.669	.022	.350
Norway	.036	−3.440	.011	−.099	.032	.470	.012	.322	.013	.554	.012	−.004
Sweden	.018	.151	.015	−.008	.025	.351	.011	−.213	.010	.797	.012	−.823

Figure 2
Standard Deviation of Cyclical Components during the Classical Gold Standard (1876 to 1913) and Post-World War II Periods (1948 to 1995)

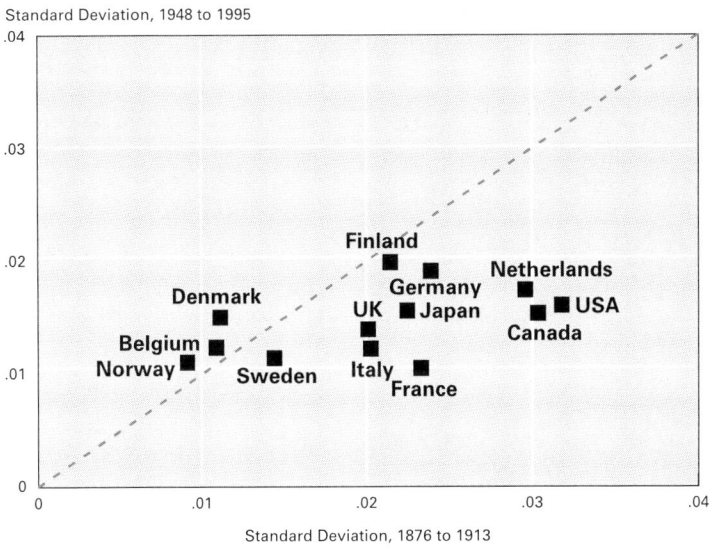

and also test the joint hypothesis that the variance is constant for all countries simultaneously, we use Wald tests. The results from these tests are summarized in Table 3. Judging from the p-values in this table, this hypothesis can often be rejected for each country by itself, that is, we reject constant variance in six out of 13 cases. Most notable is the fact that we cannot reject constant variance for Sweden, the country most associated with an active stabilization policy, but we can reject the null for the United States. A joint test covering all countries also rejects this hypothesis at very low significance levels. Thus, although the evidence is not overwhelming, the business cycle does appear to have changed its amplitude when this hypothesis is tested simultaneously for all these countries.

Empirical evidence of lower volatility in the postwar data has often been interpreted as resulting from successful stabilization policies. One alternative interpretation is that the international business cycle has been diversified such that developments in one core country no longer influence all other countries. For example, the United Kingdom dominated the world economy prior to the World War I period, and mistakes of the Bank of England could initiate severe recessions not only in the domestic economy but also in its trading partners (see Levy-Leboyer

Table 3
Wald Tests of the Hypothesis That the Variance of the Cyclical Component of Real GDP Is Constant across the Classical Gold Standard and the Postwar Periods.

	United States	United Kingdom	Germany	France	Canada	Italy	Japan
Wald test	14.749	2.384	1.773	6.397	10.036	11.417	5.734
p-value	.000	.122	.183	.011	.002	.001	.017
	Belgium	Netherlands	Denmark	Finland	Norway	Sweden	All 13 countries
Wald test	.342	7.437	3.390	.340	1.151	2.024	74.379
p-value	.559	.006	.560	.560	.283	.155	.000

Note: All tests are based on SUR regressions of the variance of band-pass-filtered GDP for each country on two dummy variables, where the first dummy takes on the value 1 for the classical gold standard (1888–1913) period and 0 otherwise (1948–95), whereas the second dummy takes on the value 0 for the classical gold standard period and 1 otherwise. The Wald tests are χ^2 distributed with 1 degree of freedom for the country tests and 13 degrees of freedom for the joint test.

1982). The increased integration of the world economy would limit negative influences from dominating economies, thus reducing the amplitude of the business cycle, a pattern consistent with the plots in both Figure 1 and Appendix B, as well as the empirical described tests above.

Other explanations include structural changes in the economy linked to the rise of the service sector and the public sector (both less cyclical than the primary and secondary sectors) and the incidence of smaller macroeconomic disturbances after World War II than during the classical gold standard era (see Zarnowitz 1992).

Is the Business Cycle Symmetrical?

The symmetry of the business cycle has been an issue for a long time. Mitchell (1927) and Keynes (1936), among others, were of the opinion that the business cycle was asymmetrical, the upswing being longer and more gradual than the downswing. A large number of empirical studies have dealt with tests of asymmetry without reaching a consensus; see, for example, Neftçi (1984), DeLong and Summers (1986), Falk (1986), Hamilton (1989), Stock (1987), and Bergman and Jonung (1992).

Here, using band-pass-filtered data, we present evidence on this unsettled issue using estimates of the skewness of the cyclical component. If the business cycle is symmetric, skewness would be zero. A negative skewness indicates that upturns are longer than downturns.

Table 2, reporting the skewness of the cyclical component of GDP, reveals that the business cycle is negatively skewed for a majority of the countries in our sample (including the major countries) during the classical gold standard period (10 out of 13 countries) and to some extent during the interwar years (eight out of 13 countries). However, during the post-World War II period only five out of 13 countries display negative skewness. Splitting this postwar period into a Bretton Woods period and a post-Bretton Woods period, we note that skewness has become more pronounced in the latter period. The U.S. business cycle remains asymmetrical across all regimes, whereas for all other countries the sign for skewness varies across regimes. These results suggest that the business cycle is still asymmetrical.

COUNTRY-SPECIFIC CO-MOVEMENTS

Cross-Correlations

In the table in Appendix C, we study the cyclical behavior of the components of national income, the money supply, and the price level, and their relation to the cyclical component of real GDP. All variables are filtered through the bandpass filter. The eight variables we consider are consumption, investment, government expenditures and revenues, exports, imports, the money stock, and consumer prices. The first column of the Appendix C Table reports the volatility ratio, measured as the ratio of the standard deviation of each of the eight different variables to the standard deviation of national income. A ratio greater than one implies that this variable has greater volatility than does real output.

Looking first at the expenditure components, a clear result emerges. All expenditure components, with the exception of consumption, are more volatile than output. The volatility ratio is greater than one for all countries and for all regimes with a single exception, the Netherlands during the gold standard period. The ratio for investment is in all countries in the range between 2 and 5, with the exception of Italy during the gold standard and interwar periods. The volatility ratio for the other components is as a rule within the same range as for investment. The volatility ratios for exports and imports are generally larger for the small European countries like Belgium, the Netherlands, Denmark, Finland, Norway, and Sweden than for larger countries like the United States and Germany.

The volatility ratio of consumption is close to one, and in 14 out of 25 cases below one. We regard this as indicating consumption smoothing over the business cycle — aside from the fact that consumption is the major component of national income, which implies that its volatility should be similar to that of national income.[11]

The variability of the money stock is greater than the variability of output for all countries and for all regimes with the following exceptions:

---

[11] These results are in line with those of Backus and Kehoe (1992) where comparable.

the United States, the United Kingdom, and Italy during the gold standard period and Canada, Denmark, and Norway during the interwar period. We also note that money stock variability has remained higher than output variability during the post-World War II period.

Turning to consumer prices, the Appendix C Table reveals that the U.S. price level is less variable than is output for all regimes. The same holds for Germany except during the interwar years. Consumer prices are more variable than output for Japan, the United Kingdom, France, and Italy, except during the gold standard era, and for the small European countries, with the exception of the Netherlands during the gold standard and the post-Bretton Woods periods.

The next three columns (columns 2 to 4) show the cross-correlations of each variable with national income at a one-period lead and lag, as well as the contemporaneous correlations. These columns reveal, first of all, that most of the significant correlations are registered for simultaneous observations. The business cycle is in this sense a phenomenon that occurs at the same time for most of the expenditure components. There is no clear-cut pattern across countries or across regimes.

Consumption and investment are strongly procyclical, according to the Appendix C Table. The same holds for exports and imports, in particular for imports. The volume of imports, as expected, seems to be determined by domestic activity. Exports are less frequently significantly correlated with domestic output, consistent with the common view that foreign demand is driving exports. This result suggests that cyclical activity across countries is not perfectly correlated; otherwise, exports would more frequently display a significant simultaneous correlation with output.[12]

Government expenditures and revenues do not display any clear-cut pattern, being neither procyclical nor countercyclical. The level of significance is low for most observations. Concerning leads and lags, the Appendix C Table shows no clear pattern either across countries or across regimes.

The correlation between money and output — where significant — is always positive for all countries and all regimes, except for the Netherlands during the gold standard era and Belgium during the post-Bretton Woods period. The United States is an exception in the sense that money and output are significantly and positively correlated for all three major regimes and of particular interest, in that the largest correlations are for the interwar period, as found in earlier studies such as Friedman and Schwartz (1963b). Other countries show no clear pattern. The same conclusions hold for money leading and lagging output by one year.

---

[12] This issue could be explored by a breakdown of exports on a country-by-country basis — a task that is beyond this paper.

Consumer prices and output are negatively related in 14 cases and positively related in three cases (with the United States before World War II the most notable), counting only significant correlations. The correlation is always negative during the post-World War II period. The price level thus tends to be countercyclical — a result found in other studies as well.

The lead and lag patterns can also be analyzed using regression analysis. For example, we can compare the R^2 from a regression of real GDP (y) on lags of real GDP and consumption (x) with the R^2 from the same regression but excluding lags of consumption. The difference between these two R^2 values, $R^2(y.x)$, then represents the additional explanatory power of lags of consumption for real GDP. Similarly, we can reverse the variables to illustrate the explanatory power of lagged real GDP for consumption, $R^2(x.y)$. These tests correspond to standard block-exogeneity tests (or Granger-causality tests) within vector autoregressive systems. A high relative $R^2(y.x)$ from these regressions does not imply causality, however. The tests only indicate that including the x-component in the information set increases our ability to predict the y-variable one period ahead.

Columns 5 and 6 in the Appendix C Table report the marginal R^2 from these regressions using two lags. A high $R^2(y.x)$ in column 5 implies that the addition of lags of the x-variable increases the prediction of real GDP, thus the x-variable leads real GDP. Similarly, a high relative $R^2(x.y)$ in column 6 indicates that lags of real GDP increase the ability to predict the x-variable, implying that the x-variable lags real GDP.

A few cases show large relative improvements for the R^2, but in most cases the percentage increase is below 20 percent. This result confirms our previous finding that most of the cyclical co-movement occurs for simultaneous observations and that there is no clear-cut pattern across countries and regimes.

Looking more closely at the empirical results, we find that the leads and lags relationship between cyclical components of consumption and the business cycle remains fairly stable over time for the nine countries for which data are available. Consumption leads the business cycle for about half the sample of countries in all monetary regimes. During the postwar period, for example, consumption leads output in the G–7 countries, with the exceptions of France and Italy, but it lags the business cycle in the small open European countries.

A similar pattern is also observed for investment. In all small European countries except Norway, investment lags the business cycle, whereas it leads the business cycle in the G–7 countries except the United Kingdom and Germany. Comparing the relationship between investment and output across monetary regimes reveals that investment tends to lag the business cycle more often during the postwar period than in earlier periods.

This tendency is also evident for government expenditures. The cyclical component of government expenditures lags output in four out of 13 countries during the gold standard period and in seven out of 13 countries during the postwar period.

The money stock leads the business cycle in six out of 13 countries during the gold standard period, in nine out of 13 countries during the interwar period, and in 10 out of 13 countries during the postwar period. The money stock also tends to lag the business cycle in the small open European countries, but it leads output in the G–7 countries. A similar pattern is evident for the price level.

The annual pre-World War I data used to generate the results in the Appendix C Table and Table 4 may have significant deficiencies, making the empirical results less than completely reliable, as discussed in Romer (1989). In addition, the use of annual data suppresses potential lead and lag relationships more evident in high-frequency data. For these reasons, it is useful to compare our results (for the postwar period, when comparable higher-frequency data are available) with results using quarterly data.

Stock and Watson (1998) employ the same empirical approach as we do, but use quarterly data. They find empirical results remarkably similar to the ones reported in the Appendix C Table. For example, they also find that consumption, investment, and imports are strongly procyclical, whereas consumer prices are countercyclical, and that all these variables lead the business cycle (by two quarters in Stock and Watson and by one year in our study). Money is procyclical with a lead of one or two years when using our annual data, whereas using quarterly data, Stock and Watson find that the money stock is procyclical with a lead of two quarters. Thus, the historical U.S. data we use in our study exhibit similar behavior to quarterly data, which we believe buttresses our findings. Whether the same holds for the other countries is a subject for further research.

The Behavior of Economic Aggregates during Recessions

The cross-correlations examined in the previous section provide information on the co-movements of economic aggregates and real GDP over both upturns and downturns. To explore the behavior of these aggregates during recessions, we pick out data for the trough years for all countries in our sample. The dates for the troughs are selected from the band-pass-filtered real GDP data shown in Figure 1 and in Appendix B. As mentioned earlier, the cyclical components represent deviations from trend and are measured in percents.

In Table 4, we report the average deviation from trend of band-pass-filtered real GDP, the components of national income and the nominal money stock. The first column reports the number of troughs identified in

Table 4
Average Deviation from Trend of Real GDP, the Components of National Income, and the Nominal Money Stock during Recessions

Country	Number of Recession Troughs	Y	C	I	G	T	X	M	M2
United States	22	−3.8	−1.9	−7.1	−2.9	−3.8	−3.5	−6.4	−2.2
United Kingdom	22	−2.6	−.4	−1.1	−2.3	−.8	−2.7	−4.3	−.3
Germany	25	−4.9	−.5	−7.7	3.1	.1	−2.4	−6.0	−.4
France	24	−3.4	−.2	−1.0	−1.4	−3.3	−5.7	−12.0	−.1
Canada	24	−3.5	−2.8	−4.1	−.8	−2.7	−4.9	−5.7	−.9
Italy	27	−3.2	−1.8	−8.9	1.1	−.9	−1.3	−2.7	−.4
Japan	23	−3.7	−1.2	−.5	2.5	.8	−.2	2.1	−.7
Belgium	23	−2.3		−5.8	−1.3	−.8	−3.3	−3.0	−1.0
Netherlands	23	−4.2		−2.8	1.2	−7.4	−4.9	−5.9	−1.2
Denmark	27	−2.8		−5.3	2.3	−1.9	−3.5	−6.9	.4
Finland	24	−2.9		−1.8	.4	−5.1	−16.8	−15.4	−1.9
Norway	27	−2.2	.2	−3.6	−1.3	−.8	−7.2	−3.4	.3
Sweden	23	−1.8	−1.4	−5.0	5.8	1.5	−4.7	−4.4	1.0

Note: Y = real GDP, C = private consumption, I = gross fixed capital formation, G = government expenditures, T = government revenues, X = exports, M = imports, and M2 = money stock.

the sample for each country and the second column shows the average deviation of real GDP from its trend during recessions. From this column, we observe that recessions tend to be deeper in large countries compared to the small open European countries. The average deviation from trend in the United States, Germany, France, Canada, and Italy is considerably higher than the average of the four Nordic countries and Belgium.

The deviations from trend of real GDP can be compared to deviations from trend of the components of national income, that is, private consumption (C), gross fixed capital formation (I), government expenditures (G), government revenues (T), exports (X) and imports (M). Consider, for example, the behavior of economic aggregates in the United States during recessions. The average deviation of real GDP from trend is -3.8 percent. From Table 4, we note that both capital formation, which was on average 7.1 percent below trend, and foreign trade (exports and imports) represent large fractions of the downturns in the U.S. economy, whereas private consumption and government expenditures represent only a minor proportion.

Similar results hold for other countries, in particular for Germany, Canada, Belgium, Denmark, Norway, and Sweden, even if the relative importance of these three economic aggregates differs. In France, the Netherlands, and Finland, foreign trade and government revenues represent the major part of the shortfall in real GDP. For example, for the Netherlands government revenues were 7.4 percent below trend, whereas real GDP was 4.2 percent below trend.

Table 5
Effects of Bandpass-Filtered Economic Aggregates on Real GDP during Recessions.
Pooled panel data regression

C	I	G	T	X	M	M2	R^2	Durbin Watson
.282	.072	.022	−.033	.075	−.003	.009	.803	1.871
(3.473)	(4.871)	(1.224)	(−1.203)	(3.288)	(−.146)	(.388)		

Note: The regression coefficients are OLS estimates, and the standard errors in their t-statistics shown below each coefficient are corrected for heteroscedasticity. The number of observations is 174. The regression also includes country dummies. The corresponding parameters are all statistically different from zero at conventional significance levels and are not reported to save space. See Table 4 for definitions of aggregates. Belgium, Denmark, Finland, and Norway are excluded from the data set for private consumption.

The last column of Table 4 shows the average shortfall of the money stock during recessions. From this column, we find that the nominal money stock only represents a minor share of the troughs in real GDP except for the United States, where the nominal money stock was 2.2 percent below trend during recessions.

Another way to characterize the behavior of the economic aggregates during recessions is to stack the data for our sample of countries and formulate a regression model to study the effects of deviations from trend of economic aggregates on deviations from trend of real GDP. The OLS estimates of this pooled regression are shown in Table 5. We constrain all parameters to be equal across the 13 countries. We also include country dummies in the regression to capture potential differences in units.

Since we lack data on private consumption for four countries (Belgium, Denmark, Finland, Norway), we exclude them from the data set. The estimates of the parameters associated with the dummy variables are not reported in Table 5. However, they are all statistically different from zero at conventional significance levels. According to the estimates in Table 5, three expenditure components, private consumption, investment, and exports, are statistically significant at the 5 percent level. This conclusion is consistent with the averages presented in Table 4 and implies that deviations of real GDP from trend can be allocated to these three economic aggregates. Three measures of economic policy, government expenditures and revenues and the money stock, are not significant in this regression and account only for small fractions of the shortfalls in real GDP during troughs, as is also the case in Table 4.

The fact that the money stock is not significant in these regressions may reflect the pooling of small open economies with larger, less open ones like the United States, and the pooling across fixed and flexible exchange rate regimes. Under fixed exchange rates, which covered much of the period investigated in the regression, one would not expect domestic monetary factors to be significant determinants of recessions for small open economies except indirectly via the balance of payments, whereas with larger, less open economies they could have significant effects. Under flexible exchange rates, monetary factors could have significant effects even for small open economies.

Although these results suggest that recessions are strongly associated with sharp declines in consumption, investment, and exports, we cannot infer causality from them. Cyclical declines in the various expenditure components may be due to factors not explicitly included in our analysis, such as productivity shocks. Thus, like the recent study by Cochrane (1994) for the postwar United States, the cross-country evidence over a century of data does not suggest a single cause of recessions.

INTERNATIONAL CO-MOVEMENTS OF OUTPUT AND PRICES

In this section we examine the co-movements of band-pass-filtered real GDP and price levels between countries. We retain the regime division used in the previous section.

Co-movements of Real Output

In Table 6 we report contemporaneous correlations of output for the 13 countries. A major impression from this table is that the correlations tend to increase over time. Most of the significant correlations are reported from the post-Bretton Woods period. We view this as indicating an increase in integration of the world economy in the past 20 years. Table 6 also reveals that the correlation between the United States and Canada has been high during all regimes for concomitant changes.[13]

Under the gold standard, U.K. output was significantly and positively correlated with output for only one country — Japan. The corresponding number for the post-Bretton Woods period is six. A similar picture emerges for Germany. The lack of apparent real output correlation under the gold standard in an era of high mobility in both good and factors of production is a puzzle. It may reflect the quality of the data. However, our results are consistent with earlier empirical evidence. See, for example, Baxter and Stockman (1989).

In the interwar period, significant correlations are observed between the United States and seven other countries. Such correlation is not found for any other country. These results seem consistent with the view that the United States was the epicenter of the Great Depression.

---

[13] We also calculated correlations across countries for leads and lags up to two years. These calculations, not reported here, but available from the authors on request, generally suggest no significant patterns. Most of the international co-movements seem to take place concurrently.

Table 6
International Contemporaneous Output Links, Band-Pass-Filtered Real GDP

		UK	Germany	France	Canada	Italy	Japan	Belgium	Netherlands	Denmark	Finland	Norway	Sweden
United States	prewar	.151	−.140	.063	.510	.340	−.278	.318	.109	.140	−.090	.134	.051
	interwar	.644	.003	.412	.839	.295	−.191	.312	.396	.499	.360	.425	.584
	postwar	.473	.276	.143	.721	.124	.377	.190	−.138	.156	.136	.177	−.037
	Bretton Woods	.138	.329	−.064	.645	−.205	.331	.090	−.412	−.141	.010	.065	−.181
	post-Bretton Woods	.744	.224	.427	.812	.487	.465	.285	.533	.586	.249	.321	.098
United Kingdom	prewar		−.201	.245	.039	.165	.333	.170	.345	.146	−.015	−.100	.020
	interwar		.140	.273	.681	.331	.584	−.020	.059	.241	.247	.276	.301
	postwar		.223	.468	.299	.251	.163	.279	.272	.498	.466	.085	.385
	Bretton Woods		.494	.381	−.090	−.058	−.076	.274	.357	.416	.377	.136	.550
	post-Bretton Woods		.057	.590	.587	.470	.431	.280	.300	.628	.516	.057	.298
Germany	prewar			.259	−.016	.108	−.114	.424	.117	.088	.326	−.066	.368
	interwar			.152	.148	−.009	.478	.063	.442	−.568	.293	−.023	.278
	postwar			.350	.087	.266	.470	.523	.397	.320	.124	.233	.237
	Bretton Woods			.319	.192	−.016	.408	.500	.352	.257	.607	.196	.527
	post-Bretton Woods			.389	−.017	.536	.587	.552	.594	.407	−.249	.274	−.005
France	prewar				.257	.366	−.085	.450	.260	−.160	.153	.095	.091
	interwar				.380	.214	.290	.610	.373	.399	.512	.639	.282
	postwar				.111	.435	.154	.589	.454	.275	.520	−.025	.434
	Bretton Woods				−.042	.144	−.091	.443	.426	.212	.509	.119	.505
	post-Bretton Woods				.327	.785	.604	.777	.582	.375	.559	−.228	.374
Canada	prewar					.126	−.280	.316	.004	−.149	−.043	.259	.125
	interwar					.380	−.028	.301	.452	.415	.547	.505	.592
	postwar					.109	.151	.206	−.035	.015	.176	.104	.105
	Bretton Woods					−.264	.076	.128	−.242	−.227	−.191	−.094	−.216
	post-Bretton Woods					.516	.280	.274	.496	.361	.494	.354	.405
Italy	prewar						−.175	.105	−.078	.458	.330	.071	.043
	interwar						−.229	.162	.039	.072	.260	.236	−.002
	postwar						.441	.504	.485	.220	.317	.292	.308
	Bretton Woods						.408	.141	.418	.044	.084	.338	.101
	post-Bretton Woods						.515	.836	.749	.450	.506	.241	.485

HISTORICAL EVIDENCE ON BUSINESS CYCLES 87

Table 6 continued
International Contemporaneous Output Links, Band-Pass-Filtered Real GDP

		UK	Germany	France	Canada	Italy	Japan	Belgium	Netherlands	Denmark	Finland	Norway	Sweden
Japan	prewar							-.154	-.158	.074	-.089	-.344	-.073
	interwar							.419	.338	-.386	.356	-.133	-.130
	postwar							.482	.208	.083	.288	.186	.055
	Bretton Woods							.479	.137	-.067	.343	.382	-.014
	post-Bretton Woods							.528	.465	.375	.255	-.146	.149
Belgium	prewar								.247	.099	.414	.142	.229
	interwar								.602	.228	.502	.524	.338
	postwar								.506	.109	.551	.192	.443
	Bretton Woods								.511	-.044	.747	.379	.471
	post-Bretton Woods								.682	.294	.412	.010	.425
Netherlands	prewar									-.282	.051	-.114	.248
	interwar									-.097	.391	.364	.425
	postwar									.430	.322	.437	.369
	Bretton Woods									.420	.442	.460	.432
	post-Bretton Woods									.511	.235	.451	.371
Denmark	prewar										.356	-.191	.140
	interwar										.128	.401	.317
	postwar										.120	.348	.259
	Bretton Woods										.122	.231	.351
	post-Bretton Woods										.126	.523	.168
Finland	prewar											.121	.460
	interwar											.459	.427
	postwar											.105	.652
	Bretton Woods											.362	.492
	post-Bretton Woods											-.124	.761
Norway	prewar												.294
	interwar												.603
	postwar												.087
	Bretton Woods												-.033
	post-Bretton Woods												.205

Note: Bold numbers denote correlations statistically significant at the 5 percent level using Newey-West optimal bandwidth standard errors.

Table 7
International Contemporaneous Price Level Linkages, Band-Pass-Filtered Price Levels

		UK	Germany	France	Canada	Italy	Japan	Belgium	Netherlands	Denmark	Finland	Norway	Sweden
United States	prewar	.396	.097	−.265	.451	.405	.339	.013	−.121	.020	.1148	.113	.157
	interwar	**.649**	−.148	.323	**.950**	.428	.161	.403	.443	.190	**.335**	.211	.460
	postwar	**.657**	**.554**	**.578**	**.752**	**.607**	**.422**	**.489**	**.313**	**.444**	**.413**	**.242**	**.521**
	Bretton Woods	**.664**	**.668**	**.650**	**.819**	**.624**	**.500**	**.761**	**.289**	.275	**.441**	.246	**.584**
	post-Bretton Woods	**.663**	**.443**	**.690**	**.695**	**.588**	**.516**	.252	.359	**.712**	**.426**	.243	**.470**
United Kingdom	prewar		**.591**	.172	**.621**	.077	.221	**.383**	**.421**	.240	**.489**	**.557**	**.480**
	interwar		−.696	**.355**	**.646**	**.543**	**.515**	.384	**.625**	**.359**	**.525**	**.609**	**.918**
	postwar		**.454**	**.392**	**.599**	**.690**	.236	**.625**	**.455**	**.459**	**.519**	**.408**	**.623**
	Bretton Woods		**.747**	.455	**.654**	**.728**	.202	**.756**	**.382**	**.575**	**.418**	.535	**.778**
	post-Bretton Woods		.284	**.608**	**.609**	**.716**	**.550**	**.572**	**.629**	**.453**	**.785**	.407	**.620**
Germany	prewar			.275	.283	.231	.105	**.551**	**.403**	**.509**	**.508**	**.580**	**.607**
	interwar			−.159	−.108	−.197	−.323	−.171	−.412	−.424	−.056	−.708	−.766
	postwar			**.495**	**.541**	**.652**	**.393**	**.682**	**.375**	**.419**	**.299**	**.274**	**.634**
	Bretton Woods			**.514**	**.596**	**.772**	**.425**	**.786**	.211	**.387**	.253	.269	**.768**
	post-Bretton Woods			**.576**	**.437**	**.459**	**.429**	**.542**	**.752**	**.401**	**.398**	.195	.306
France	prewar				−.068	.064	−.402	**.400**	.172	.256	.152	**.316**	.113
	interwar				**.404**	**.607**	.089	**.626**	**.382**	−.361	.115	−.026	.152
	postwar				**.643**	**.536**	**.569**	**.461**	**.270**	.239	**.408**	.107	**.348**
	Bretton Woods				**.661**	**.449**	**.564**	**.428**	.186	.121	.335	.025	.300
	post-Bretton Woods				**.789**	**.931**	**.604**	**.750**	**.657**	**.819**	**.751**	**.533**	**.590**
Canada	prewar					.002	.248	.265	.110	.115	.236	.273	.144
	interwar					**.448**	.210	**.500**	**.492**	.139	**.371**	.129	**.456**
	postwar					**.693**	**.319**	**.671**	**.571**	**.621**	**.658**	**.450**	**.584**
	Bretton Woods					**.682**	**.320**	**.831**	**.625**	**.561**	**.690**	**.349**	**.588**
	post-Bretton Woods					**.694**	**.479**	**.491**	**.484**	**.745**	**.636**	**.670**	**.588**
Italy	prewar						**.296**	.179	.046	.273	.152	.261	.236
	interwar						.207	.153	.131	−.175	.224	**.333**	**.362**
	postwar						**.393**	**.798**	**.517**	**.603**	**.563**	**.425**	**.639**
	Bretton Woods						**.381**	**.829**	**.418**	**.523**	**.442**	**.377**	**.618**
	post-Bretton Woods						**.634**	**.762**	**.696**	**.758**	**.824**	**.531**	**.674**

Table 7 continued
International Contemporaneous Price Level Linkages, Band-Pass-Filtered Price Levels

		UK	Germany	France	Canada	Italy	Japan	Belgium	Netherlands	Denmark	Finland	Norway	Sweden
Japan	prewar							-.105	-.241	-.169	-.136	.161	.014
	interwar							.199	**.708**	**.607**	**.807**	**.425**	**.442**
	postwar							**.294**	.032	-.046	.145	-.414	.009
	Bretton Woods							.238	-.077	-.167	.040	-.538	-.079
	post-Bretton Woods							**.660**	**.591**	**.603**	**.719**	.247	**.414**
Belgium	prewar								.252	**.417**	.265	**.508**	**.315**
	interwar								**.468**	-.120	.349	-.184	.276
	postwar								**.661**	**.488**	**.677**	**.468**	**.637**
	Bretton Woods								**.595**	**.502**	**.627**	**.504**	**.761**
	post-Bretton Woods								**.804**	**.453**	**.843**	**.428**	**.482**
Netherlands	prewar									**.513**	**.622**	.253	**.406**
	interwar									**.428**	**.624**	**.335**	**.611**
	postwar									**.403**	**.685**	**.414**	**.420**
	Bretton Woods									.386	**.666**	**.410**	**.370**
	post-Bretton Woods									**.394**	**.731**	.386	**.509**
Denmark	prewar										**.578**	**.591**	**.635**
	interwar										**.458**	**.734**	**.338**
	postwar										**.526**	**.540**	**.550**
	Bretton Woods										**.506**	**.527**	**.587**
	post-Bretton Woods										**.579**	**.526**	**.434**
Finland	prewar											**.475**	**.714**
	interwar											.259	.432
	postwar											**.404**	**.442**
	Bretton Woods											**.340**	**.359**
	post-Bretton Woods											**.596**	**.641**
Norway	prewar												**.747**
	interwar												**.591**
	postwar												**.628**
	Bretton Woods												**.734**
	post-Bretton Woods												.334

Note: Bold numbers denote correlations statistically significant at the 5 percent level using Newey-West optimal bandwidth standard errors.

Linkages between European countries have become more prevalent in the postwar period. The Netherlands is a nice illustration of this. Dutch output was not significantly correlated with output of any other country prior to 1914. During the post-Bretton Woods period, the correlation between Dutch output and that of 10 other countries turned significant.

The high and significant correlation between countries' output during the post-Bretton Woods period within a trade bloc consisting of Germany, France, Italy, Belgium, the Netherlands, and Denmark most likely demonstrates the establishment of a common market in Europe. It is tempting to speculate about this pattern as a prerequisite for a future European Monetary Union. Indeed, five of these six countries are identified by Bayoumi and Eichengreen (1993) as core European Union countries suitable for forming a monetary union. The more frequent incidence of significant international co-movements during the post-Bretton Woods period may also be due to large common shocks hitting in particular Europe, for example, OPEC I and OPEC II.

Co-movements of Price Levels

In Table 7 we report contemporaneous international price level correlations across the five time periods. The main impression of Table 7 compared to Table 6 covering international output correlations is the higher frequency of significant correlations. The incidence has also — as in Table 6 — increased over time. For example, the U.S. price level was correlated with only two countries during the gold standard era but with nine during the post-Bretton Woods period. In a similar way, Canadian prices were significantly correlated with prices in four countries under the gold standard. During the post-Bretton Woods period this number rose to 12, covering all countries in our sample. In the postwar period German prices are linked significantly to the prices of all other countries in our sample. These results, we believe, are consistent with evidence of increased global integration of goods markets in recent decades.

However, in contrast to the historical trend of increasing intercountry correlations over time, U.K. prices during the gold standard era were significantly correlated with prices in eight other countries. This pattern is most likely due to the central position held by Great Britain prior to 1914. Germany, another major economic power, also displayed significant correlations with many smaller European countries during the gold standard period. This evidence, we believe, is consistent with the operation of the 'law of one price' under the gold standard and the integration of global goods and factor markets before 1914 (see McCloskey and Zecher 1976, 1984; O'Rourke and Williamson 1998).

SUMMARY

This paper has examined business cycle fluctuations in a large sample of countries using more than a century of observations and adopting a monetary regime perspective. Our sifting through the empirical evidence suggests a number of conclusions bearing on current business cycle research. Among them, we would like to emphasize the following.

First, concerning the properties of country-specific business cycles, our evidence suggests that both the amplitude and the symmetry of cycles have changed over time. Echoing the conventional view, the interwar period is found to be more volatile than the classical gold standard era and the post-World War II period. In addition, the post-World War II period is marginally less volatile than the gold standard period. Formal empirical tests do not reject the hypothesis that the amplitude was equal during the classical gold standard and postwar periods for the majority of the countries in our sample. However, in testing whether the amplitude was constant in all countries simultaneously in these two periods, this hypothesis was strongly rejected. In our opinion, what may have caused the decline in volatility is an open question. The decline could be due to a host of structural changes, the conduct of stabilization policies, the construction of the data used, and so on.

Second, concerning the relationship between cycles in real GDP and in the expenditure components, we find a clear pro-cyclical pattern for consumption, investment, exports, and imports across all countries and all monetary regimes. The variability of investment, exports, and imports is higher than that of real GDP for all countries and periods. Consumption and real GDP display roughly the same variability. There is no clear cyclical pattern across countries and across regimes in the correlation between real GDP and government expenditures and revenues.

For the money stock we find evidence for a number of countries of a positive correlation with output, and evidence that the money stock leads the business cycle. It is of interest to note that for the United States, the largest correlations are for the interwar period. This result is consistent with the view attributing the Great Depression to inept Federal Reserve policy (Friedman and Schwartz 1963a). Also, with the key exception of the United States during the pre-World War II period, the price level is found to be pro-cyclical.

Third, it is striking that nearly all significant cyclical co-movements occur for concomitant observations. This pattern roughly holds for all countries and across all regimes, making it difficult to find lead and lag structures with our approach based on annual data.

Fourth, examining the behavior of cyclical variation during recessions, we find that the major proportion of the decline in real GDP can be accounted for by declines in three expenditure components, consumption, investment, and exports. According to our analysis, neither government expenditures and revenues nor the money stock significantly contribute to the recessions, as measured with our technique. However, the lack of significance of the money stock may reflect the pooling of open and closed economies across fixed and flexible exchange rate regimes. We did not possess sufficient data for our 13 countries to determine whether technology shocks, a variable stressed by recent approaches, could be a possible significant determinant of recessions.

Fifth, the cyclical co-movements for real GDP and prices across countries suggest growing international linkages over time. They also suggest global integration, which began under the gold standard, and significant linkages between the United States and many other countries during the unstable interwar period.

Finally, it is tempting to speculate about the influence on the business cycle from technological changes, structural shifts of the economy, the rise of stabilization policies, and the public sector, as well as other long-run developments. We do not rule out the possibility that such features may have influenced the business cycle, but when they are taken together we do not see any clear pattern over time supporting any single "structural" interpretation. There is one major exception, however. We find a rise in the frequency of significant cyclical co-movements across countries. This pattern is consistent with the view that international economic integration has increased over time.

In our opinion, the cyclical pattern in a number of respects thus appears to remain surprisingly stable across time, regimes, and countries — ignoring any potential measurement error due to low-quality data and the like. We do not want to claim that "all cycles are alike," only that the business cycle is always and everywhere apparent in a broad sense and that we see no serious signs that this will not hold in the future as well.

Appendix A: Data Sources

Belgium

Real national income. 1880–1920: Not available. 1921–39: GNP, E. Buyst (1997), "New GNP Estimates for the Belgian Economy During the Interwar Period," *Review of Income and Wealth*, vol. 43, pp. 357–375, table 4. 1940–47: Not available. 1948: NNP, Mitchell (1992). 1949–53: GDP, Mitchell (1992), 1954–94: GDP, *International Financial Statistics (IFS)*, series 99B.P. 1995: *OECD Economic Outlook.*

Prices. 1880–1948. CPI, Mitchell (1992), except 1914–20 and 1941–46: Not available. 1949–95: CPI, *IFS*, series 64.

Money stock. 1880–1971: M1, Statistical Appendix in J. Delbeke (1988), *Geld en Bankkrediet in Belgie, 1877–1983*, Klasse der Letteren, Jaargang 50, Nr. 129, Brussel: Koninklijke Academie voor Wetenschappen, Letteren en Schone Kunsten van Belgie, table 1.2, column 7 and table 1.3, column 9, except 1914–19 and 1941–46: Not available. 1972–95: Money, *IFS*, series 34.

HISTORICAL EVIDENCE ON BUSINESS CYCLES 93

Central government expenditures and revenues. 1880–1969: Mitchell (1978), except 1913–19 and 1940: not available. 1970–94: *IFS,* series 82 and 81. (Note: Change of definition in 1970.)
Exports. 1880–1988: Mitchell (1992), except 1901 and 1915–1918: not available. 1989–1996: *OECD National Accounts. Main aggregates* (1998), Volume I.
Imports. 1880–1988: Mitchell (1992), except 1901 and 1915–1918: not available. 1989–1996: *OECD National Accounts. Main Aggregates* (1998), Volume I.
Consumption. Not available.

Canada

Real national income. 1880–1926: GNP, M. C. Urquhart (1986), "New Estimates of Gross National Product, Canada, 1870–1926: Some Implications for Canadian Development" in S. L. Engerman and R. E. Gallman (eds.), *Long-Term Factors in American Economic Growth,* pp. 9–94, *Studies in Income and Wealth,* Vol. 51, NBER, Chicago: The University of Chicago Press, table 2.9. 1927–48: GNP, Mitchell (1993). 1949–95: GDP, *IFS,* series 99B.R.
Prices. 1880–1914: Interurban–Intertemporal CPI, R. C. Allen (1990), *Real Income in the English Speaking World,* University of British Columbia Press. 1915–48: CPI, Urquhart and Buckley (1965). 1949–95: CPI, *IFS,* series 64.
Money stock. 1880–1948: M2, definition and sources are given in Bordo and Jonung (1987), pp. 154–55. 1949–95: Money plus quasi-money, *IFS,* series 35L.
Central government expenditures and revenues. 1880–1947: Mitchell (1993). 1948–94: *IFS,* series 82 and 81.
Exports. 1880–1988: Mitchell (1992) (Note: change of definition in 1959). 1989–1996: *OECD National Accounts. Main Aggregates (1998),* Volume I.
Imports. 1880–1988: Mitchell (1992) (Note: change of definition in 1959). 1989–1996: *OECD National Accounts. Main Aggregates (1998),* Volume I.
Consumption. 1926–1987: Liesner, T. (1989): *One Hundred Years of Economic Statistics,* The Economist Publications Ltd., London. 1988–1996: *OECD National Accounts. Main Aggregates* (1998), Volume I.

Denmark

Real national income. 1880–1950: GDP, Mitchell (1992). 1951–95: GDP, *IFS,* series 99 B.P.
Prices. 1880–1949: CPI, Mitchell (1992). 1950–95: CPI, *IFS,* series 64.
Money stock. 1880–1971: Borgernes Likviditet (M2), N. Kjærgård (1991), *Økonomisk vækst: En økonometrisk analyse af Denmark 1870–1981,* Copenhagen: Jurist- og Økonomforbundets Forlag, pp. 582–83, table 3, series AM. 1972–95: Money plus quasi-money, *IFS,* series 35 L.
Central government expenditures and revenues: 1880–1947: Mitchell (1992). 1948–95: *IFS,* series 82 and 81.
Exports. 1880–1988: Mitchell (1992). 1989–1996: *OECD National Accounts. Main Aggregates* (1998), Volume I.
Imports. 1880–1988: Mitchell (1992). 1989–1996: *OECD National Accounts, Main Aggregates* (1998), Volume I.
Consumption. Not available.

Finland

Real national income. 1880–1980: GDP, Statistical Appendix in R. Hjerppe (1989), *The Finnish Economy 1860–1985, Growth and Structural Change,* Bank of Finland, Helsinki: Government Printing Centre, table 1. 1981–95: GDP, *IFS,* series 99B.P.
Prices. 1880–1980: Cost-of-living index, Hjerppe (1989), table 13. 1981–95: CPI, *IFS,* series 64.
Money stock. 1880–1971: M2, T. Haavisto (1992), *Money and Economic Activity in Finland 1866–1985,* Ph.D. thesis, Lund Economic Studies number 48, Lund University, average of end-of-month figures in table 4A.2. 1972–95: Money plus quasi-money, *IFS,* series 35L.
Central government expenditures and revenues. 1880–81: Not available. 1882–1948: Mitchell (1992). 1949–94: *IFS,* series 82 and 81.
Exports. 1880–1988: Mitchell (1992). 1989–1996: *OECD National Accounts. Main Aggregates* (1998), Volume I.

Imports. 1880–1988: Mitchell (1992). 1989–1996: *OECD National Accounts, Main Aggregates* (1998), Volume I.
Consumption. Not available.

France

Real national income. 1880–1950: GDP, Mitchell (1992), except 1914–20 and 1939–50: GDP, A. Maddison (1995), *Monitoring the World Economy 1820–1992,* OECD, table C-16a. 1951–95: GDP, *IFS,* series 99B.R.
Prices. 1880–1949: CPI, Mitchell (1992). 1950–95: CPI, *IFS,* series 64.
Money stock. 1880–1897: M1, Saint-Marc (1983). 1898–1977: M2, J.-P. Patat and M. Lutfalla (1990), *A Monetary History of France in the Twentieth Century,* London: Macmillan, tables 1.4, A2, A3 and A5. 1978–95: M2, *IFS,* series 38NB.
Central government expenditures and revenues. 1880–1949: Mitchell (1992). 1950–95: *IFS,* series 82 and 81.
Exports. 1880–1988: Mitchell (1992). 1989–1996: *OECD National Accounts. Main Aggregates* (1998), Volume I.
Imports. 1880–1988: Mitchell (1992). 1989–1996: *OECD National Accounts, Main Aggregates* (1998), Volume I.
Imports. 1880–1988: Mitchell (1992). 1989–1996: *OECD National Accounts, Main Aggregates* (1998), Volume I.
Consumption. 1949–1897: Liesner, T. (1989); 1988–1996: *OECD National Accounts. Main Aggregates* (1998), Volume I.

Germany

Real national income. 1880–1979: NNP, Sommariva and Tullio (1987), pp. 226–28. 1980–95: GDP, *IFS,* series 99B.R. (Unified Germany from 1991.)
Prices. 1880–1949: CPI, Sommariva and Tullio (1986), pp. 231–34. 1950–95: CPI, *IFS,* series 64.
Money stock. 1880–1913: M2, Data underlying M. D. Bordo (1986), "Financial Crises, Banking Crises, Stock Market Crashes and the Money Supply: Some International Evidence" in F. Capie and G. Wood (eds.), *Financial Crises and the World Banking System,* London: Macmillan. 1914–25: Not available. 1926–38: M2, Deutsche Bundesbank (1976), *Deutsches Geld und Bankwesen in Zahlen 1876–1975,* Frankfurt am Main: Fritz Knapp Gmbh, pp. 14 and 18. 1939–49: Not available. 1950–71: M2, Deutsche Bundesbank, *Monthly reports* (various issues). 1972–95: Money plus quasi-money, *IFS,* series 35L.
Central government expenditures and revenues. 1880–1951: Mitchell (1992), except 1922–23 and 1935–49: Not available. 1952–95: *IFS,* series 82 and 81. Note: Change of definition in 1970.
Exports. 1880–1988: Mitchell (1992), except 1914–1919 and 1944–1947: not available. 1989–1996: *OECD National Accounts. Main Aggregates* (1998), Volume I.
Imports. 1880–1988: Mitchell (1992), except 1914–1919 and 1944–1947: not available. 1989–1996: *OECD National Accounts, Main Aggregates* (1998), Volume I.
Consumption. 1885–1987: Liesner, T. (1989), except 1914–1924 and 1940–1947: not available. 1988–1996: *OECD National Accounts. Main Aggregates* (1998), Volume I. Note: change of definition in 1960.

Italy

Real national income. 1880–1951: GNP, Mitchell (1992). 1952–60: GDP, Mitchell (1992). 1961–67: GDP, IMF (1997), *International Financial Statistics Yearbook 1997,* Washington D.C., series 99B.R.
Prices. 1880–1948: CPI, Statistical Appendix in M. Fratianni and F. Spinelli (1991), *Storia Monetaria d'Italia,* Milan: Arnoldo Mondadori Editor, pp. 66–71, series CLI. 1949–95: CPI, *IFS,* series 64.
Money stock. 1880–1980: M3, Fratianni and Spinelli (1991), pp. 48–51, series U1+U2+D. 1981–95: M2, IMF (1997), series 38N.

Central government expenditures and revenues. 1880–1949: Mitchell (1992). 1950–91: *IFS*, series 82 and 81.
Exports. 1880–1988: Mitchell (1992), except 1943–1946: not available. 1989–1996: *OECD National Accounts. Main Aggregates* (1998), Volume I.
Imports. 1880–1988: Mitchell (1992), except 1943–1946: not available. 1989–1996: *OECD National Accounts, Main Aggregates* (1998), Volume I.
Consumption. 1885–1987: Liesner, T. (1989). 1988–1996: *OECD National Accounts. Main Aggregates* (1998), Volume I. Note: change of definition 1960.

Japan

Real national income. 1880–84: Not available. 1885–1929: GNP, B. R. Mitchell (1991). 1930–56: GDP, Mitchell (1991), except 1945 and 1952: GDP, Maddison (1995), table C-16a. 1957–95: GDP, *IFS*, series 99B.R.
Prices. 1880–1922: WPI, Mitchell (1991). 1923–48: CPI, Mitchell (1991). 1949–95: CPI, *IFS*, series 64.
Money stock. 1880–1971: M1, data supplied by the Bank of Japan. 1972–95: Money, *IFS*, series 34B.
Central government expenditures and revenues. 1880–1954: Mitchell (1991). 1955–93: *IFS*, series 82 and 81. (Note: changes of definitions in 1955 and 1976.)
Exports. 1880–1988: Mitchell (1991), except 1944–45: not available. 1989–1996: *OECD National Accounts. Main Aggregates* (1998), Volume I.
Imports. 1880–1988: Mitchell (1991), except 1994–45: not available. 1989–1996: *OECD National Accounts, Main Aggregates* (1998), Volume I.
Consumption. 1885–1929: Backus, D. and P. Kehoe (1992). 1930–1987: Liesner, T. (1989), except 1945: not available. 1988–1996: *OECD National Accounts. Main Aggregates* (1998), Volume I.

Netherlands

Real national income. 1880–1960: GDP, A. Maddison (1995) table C-16a. 1961–95: GDP, *IFS*, series 99B.R.
Prices. 1880–1949: CPI, Mitchell (1992). 1950–95: CPI, *IFS*, series 64.
Money stock. 1880–1990: Currency, data supplied by Mr W. F. Vanthood at De Nederlandsche Bank. 1901–71: M2, Central Bureau voor de Statistiek (1976), *75 Jaar Statistiek van Nederland.* 1972–985: Money, *IFS*, series 34.
Central government expenditures and revenues. 1880–1899: Not available. 1900–1948: Mitchell (1992). 1949–95: *IFS*, series 82 and 81. Note: change of definition in 1973.
Exports. 1880–1988: Mitchell (1992), except 1944–1946: not available. 1989–1996: *OECD National Accounts. Main Aggregates* (1998), Volume I.
Imports. 1880–1988: Mitchell (1992), except 1944–1946: not available. 1989–1996: *OECD National Accounts, Main Aggregates* (1998), Volume I.
Consumption. Not available.

Norway

Real national income. 1880–1949: GDP, Mitchell (1992), except 1940–46: Data supplied by J. T. Klovland. 1950–95: GDP, *IFS*, series 99B.P.
Prices. 1880–1948: CPI, Statistisk sentralbyrå (1994), *Historisk statistikk 1994,* Oslo. 1949–95: CPI, *IFS*, series 64.
Money stock. 1880–1971: M2, J. T. Klovland (1978), *Quantitative Studies in the Monetary History of Norway,* Ph.D. thesis, Bergen: Norwegian School of Economics and Business Administration. 1972–95: Broad money (M2), *IFS*, series 38N.
Central government expenditures and revenues. 1880–1953: Mitchell (1992). 1954–94: *IFS*, series 82 and 81.
Exports. 1880–1988: Mitchell (1992). 1989–1996: *OECD National Accounts. Main Aggregates (1998), Volume I.*
Imports. 1880–1988: Mitchell (1992). 19891996: *OECD National Accounts, Main Aggregates* 1998), Volume I.

Consumption. 1880–1987: Backus, D. and P. Kehoe (1992) except 1941–1946: not available. 1988–1996: *OECD National Accounts. Main Aggregates* (1998), Volume I.

Sweden

Real national income. 1880–1950: GDP, O. Krantz and C-A. Nilsson (1975), *Swedish National Product; 1861–1970: New Aspects on Methods and Measurements*, Lund: C.W.K. Glerup/Liber Läromedel, table .1 and table 1:2, columns 2 + 4 (GDP at factor cost plus indirect taxes and customs duties deflated by the implicit GDO-deflator at factor cost). 1951–95: GDP, Statistics Sweden (1996), *Statistiska Meddelanden SM 9601 N10*, table 1

Prices. 1880–1948: CPI, Statistiska Centralbyrån (1996), *Statistiska Meddelanden P15 SM9501*, p. 22. 1949–95: CPI, *IFS*, series 64.

Money stock. 1880–1971: Money stock (M2), L. Jonung (1975), *Studies in the Monetary History of Sweden*, Ph.D. thesis, Los Angeles: UCLA, Appendix A, table A-1, column (5). 1972–95: Broad money (M3), *IFS*, series 38N.

Central government expenditures and revenues. 1880: Not available. 1881–1947: Mitchell (1992). 1948–95: *IFS*, series 82 and 81. (Note: Change of definition in 1966.)

Exports. 1880–1988: Mitchell (1992). 1989–1996: *OECD National Accounts. Main Aggregates* (1998), Volume I.

Imports. 1880–1988: Mitchell (1992). 1989–1996: *OECD National Accounts, Aggregates* (1998), Volume I.

Consumption. 1880–1884: Krantz and Nilsson (1975). 1885–1987: Liesner, T. (1989) 1988–1996: *OECD National Accounts. Main aggregates* (1998), Volume I.

United Kingdom

Real national income. 1880–1948 GDP, B. R. Mitchell (1988), pp. 831–835. 1949–95: GDP, *IFS*, series 99B.R

Prices. 1880–1948: Feinstein's retail price series, F. Capie and A. Webber (1985), *A Monetary History of the United Kingdom, Volume 1*, London: George Allen and Unwin, table III, column 12. 1949–95: CPI, *IFS*, series 64.

Money stock growth. 1880–1966: Net money Supply (M2), Sheppard (1971), table A.3.3, column 6. 1967–95: Money plus quasi-money, *IFS*, series 35L.

Central government expenditures and revenues. 1880–1947: Mitchell (1992). 1948–95: *IFS*, series 82 and 81.

Exports. 1880–1988: Mitchell (1992), except 1813: not available; includes Eire up to and including 1920. 1989–1996: *OECD National Accounts. Main Aggregates* (1998), Volume I.

Imports. 1880–1988: Mitchell (1992), except 1813: not available; includes Eire up to and including 1920. 1989–1996: *OECD National Accounts. Main Aggregates* (1998), Volume I.

Consumption. 1885–1987: Liesner, T. (1989). 1988–1996: *OECD National Accounts. Main Aggregates* (1998), Volume I; includes Eire up to and including 1920.

United States

Real national income. 1880–1948 GNP, N. S. Balke and R. J. Gordon (1989), Appendix B, Historical data in R. J. Gordon (ed.) *The American Business Cycle, Continuity and Change*, Chicago: The University of Chicago Press, pp. 781–83. 1949–95: GDP, *IFS*, series 99B.R.

Prices. 1880–1948: CPI, U.S. Bureau of the Census, 1975. *Historical Statistics of the United States: Colonial Times to 1970*, series E135. 1949–95: CPI, *IFS*, series 64.

Money stock. 1880–1971: M2, Balke and Gordon (1989), pp. 784–86. 1972–95: Money plus quasi-money, *IFS*, series 35L.

Central government expenditures and revenues. 1880–1958: Mitchell (1993). 1959–95: *IFS*, series 82 and 81.

Exports. 1880–1988: Mitchell (1992). 1989–1996: *OECD National Accounts. Main Aggregates* (1998), Volume I.

Imports. 1880–1988: Mitchell (1992). 1989–1996: *OECD National Accounts. Main Aggregates* (1998), Volume I.

Consumption. 1989–1987: Liesner, T. (1989). 1988–1996: *OECD National Accounts. Main Aggregates* (1998), Volume I.

Appendix B
Band-Pass-Filtered GDP Data for 12 Countries

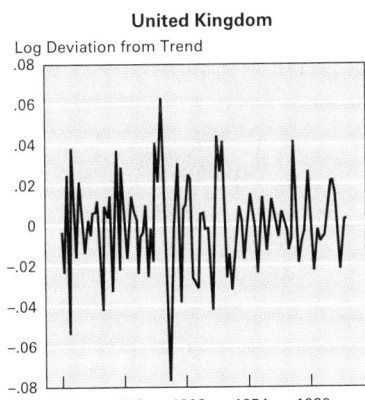

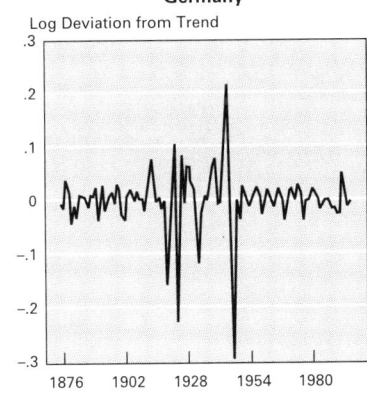

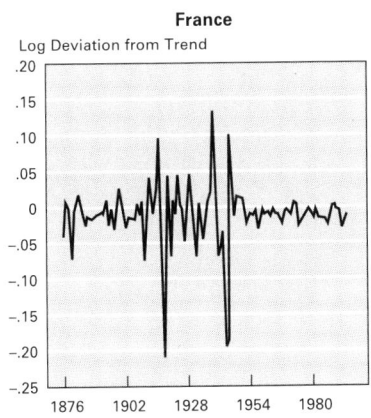

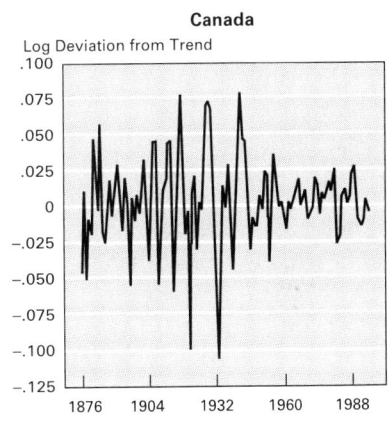

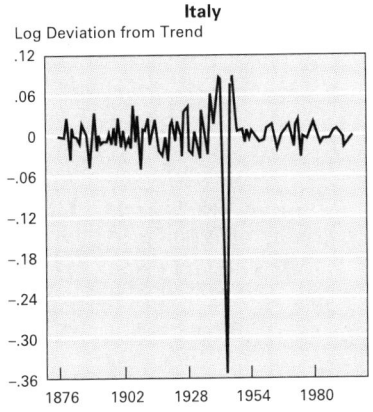

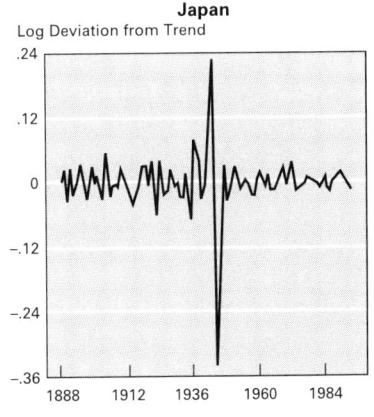

Appendix B, continued
Band-Pass-Filtered GDP Data for 12 Countries

Belgium
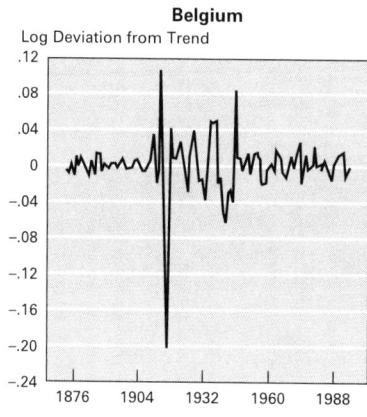

Netherlands
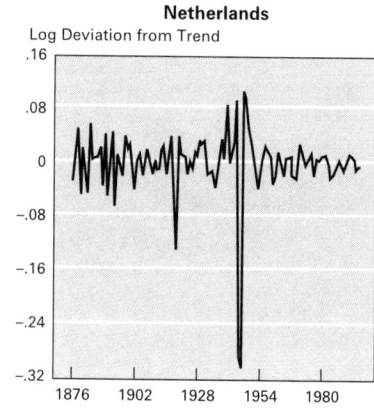

Denmark
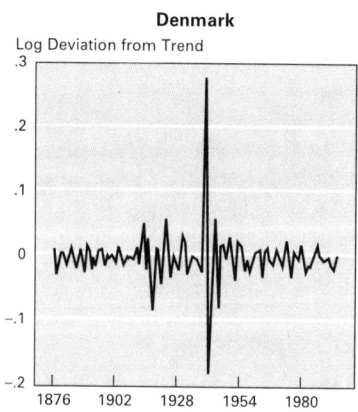

Finland
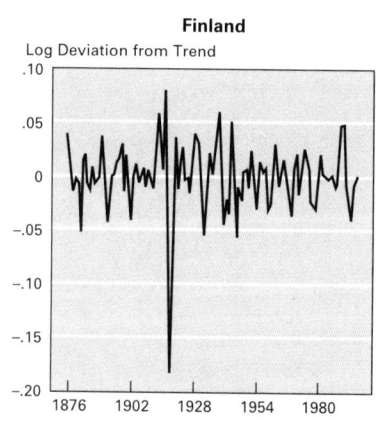

Norway
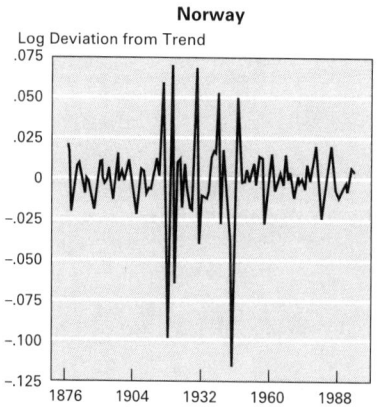

Sweden
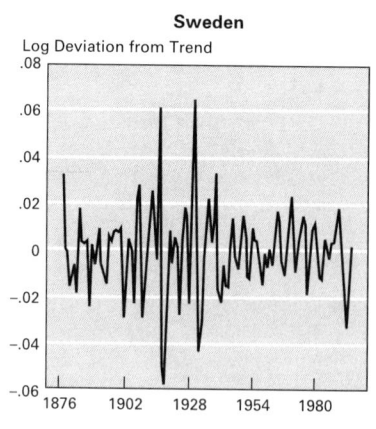

Appendix C
Cross-Correlations of Band-Pass-Filtered Real GDP with Expenditure Components, Money Stock and Prices

	United States					
	(1) Vol. ratio	(2) j = −1	(3) j = 0	(4) j = +1	(5) R²(y,x)	(6) R²(x,y)
Consumption						
Gold Standard	.748	−.320	**.478**	.149	.039	.144
Interwar	1.210	.488	**.912**	**.541**	.196	.106
Postwar	.626	−.218	**.553**	.127	.249	.085
Bretton Woods	.735	−.306	**.555**	.090	.295	.226
Post-Bretton Woods	.443	.030	**.598**	.163	.070	.002
Investment						
Gold Standard	2.385	−.091	**.817**	−.069	.004	.050
Interwar	3.578	.503	**.918**	**.460**	.179	.202
Postwar	2.979	−.046	**.601**	.040	.153	.141
Bretton Woods	2.975	−.230	.345	**−.332**	.191	.377
Post-Bretton Woods	2.988	.142	**.913**	**.376**	.027	.087
Government Expenditures						
Gold Standard	1.872	.063	−.162	−.078	.131	.017
Interwar	1.648	.113	.187	−.318	.002	.173
Postwar	3.577	.062	.064	.331	.037	.186
Bretton Woods	4.610	.159	**.221**	**.575**	.014	.363
Post-Bretton Woods	1.468	−.199	**−.525**	−.287	.064	.141
Government Revenues						
Gold Standard	1.779	−.241	.294	**.404**	.064	.184
Interwar	2.690	**.423**	**.605**	**.456**	.060	.254
Postwar	2.968	**−.432**	**.367**	**.754**	.337	.108
Bretton Woods	3.647	**−.398**	**.428**	**.828**	.499	.092
Post-Bretton Woods	1.799	**−.532**	.279	**.702**	.216	.349
Exports						
Gold Standard	1.736	.187	.251	.167	.115	.044
Interwar	2.303	**.579**	**.671**	**.215**	.138	.014
Postwar	4.156	**−.390**	.352	**.587**	.320	.195
Bretton Woods	4.334	**−.278**	**.450**	**.638**	.346	.334
Post-Bretton Woods	3.778	**−.441**	.214	**.515**	.188	.040
Imports						
Gold Standard	2.104	−.228	**.438**	**.238**	.010	.055
Interwar	2.680	**.557**	**.877**	**.152**	.112	.329
Postwar	3.605	.025	**.657**	.188	.091	.046
Bretton Woods	3.538	.189	**.738**	−.101	.135	.032
Post-Bretton Woods	3.645	−.109	**.561**	**.526**	.030	.358
Money Stock						
Gold Standard	.798	.043	**.658**	−.102	.062	.213
Interwar	1.134	**.373**	**.840**	**.633**	.177	.046
Postwar	1.214	.269	**.266**	−.069	.151	.023
Bretton Woods	1.320	.041	**.311**	−.004	.282	.156
Post-Bretton Woods	1.043	.310	.194	−.227	.092	.010
Consumer Prices						
Gold Standard	.375	**−.426**	.107	**.571**	.072	.214
Interwar	.550	**.361**	**.781**	**.626**	.039	.140
Postwar	.970	**−.645**	**−.391**	**.226**	.320	.028
Bretton Woods	.959	**−.586**	−.210	**.398**	.277	.140
Post-Bretton Woods	.983	**−.663**	**−.610**	**.100**	.270	.045

Note: Bold numbers denote statistically significant correlations at the 5 percent level using Newey-West optimal bandwidth standard errors.

Column 5 shows the difference between the R² from regressions of y (the business cycle) on two lags of x (the candidate series) and y, and the R² from regressions of y on two lags of y, whereas Column 6 shows the relative R² when x and y are reversed.

Appendix C continued
Cross-Correlations of Band-Pass-Filtered Real GDP with Expenditure Components, Money Stock and Prices

	United Kingdom					
	(1) Vol. ratio	(2) j = −1	(3) j = 0	(4) j = +1	(5) $R^2(y,x)$	(6) $R^2(x,y)$
Consumption						
Gold Standard	.485	**−.288**	**.715**	−.073	.064	.087
Interwar	.539	−.302	.309	.580	.199	.089
Postwar	1.106	**.450**	**.742**	.120	.097	.020
Bretton Woods	1.003	**.583**	**.606**	−.293	.117	.231
Post-Bretton Woods	1.150	.390	**.796**	**.345**	.092	.023
Investment						
Gold Standard	2.240	.107	**.413**	−.065	.071	.082
Interwar	2.310	**−.421**	.029	.329	.121	.151
Postwar	2.896	.264	**.706**	**.330**	.016	.110
Bretton Woods	2.592	.091	**.529**	.104	.094	.267
Post-Bretton Woods	3.026	.434	**.788**	**.436**	.054	.006
Government Expenditures						
Gold Standard	7.072	.033	**.142**	.323	.120	.038
Interwar	2.674	.115	.190	.208	.121	.067
Postwar	2.992	**−.304**	**−.535**	**−.125**	.001	.195
Bretton Woods	4.024	−.023	−.251	−.047	.083	.125
Post-Bretton Woods	2.309	**−.538**	**−.841**	**−.291**	.155	.218
Government Revenues						
Gold Standard	3.378	−.003	.180	.336	.101	.170
Interwar	2.444	**−.711**	**−.398**	**.218**	.338	.004
Postwar	2.443	**−.342**	**−.511**	.040	.009	.131
Bretton Woods	2.875	−.068	**−.427**	−.077	.023	.111
Post-Bretton Woods	2.219	**−.408**	**−.583**	.064	.032	.082
Exports						
Gold Standard	2.663	−.164	.254	.222	.039	.049
Interwar	4.590	−.198	.281	**.352**	.042	.099
Postwar	3.055	−.206	**.294**	**.330**	.066	.183
Bretton Woods	4.321	**−.364**	−.205	.319	.213	.077
Post-Bretton Woods	2.286	.142	**.403**	**.369**	.044	.301
Imports						
Gold Standard	1.556	−.112	.341	.218	.012	.021
Interwar	3.436	−.136	**.437**	**.662**	.035	.451
Postwar	4.800	−.166	**.548**	**.427**	.068	.217
Bretton Woods	6.441	−.281	**.511**	.367	.139	.133
Post-Bretton Woods	3.824	.129	**.602**	**.513**	.040	.364
Money Stock						
Gold Standard	.855	−.040	**.374**	**.595**	.223	.168
Interwar	1.134	−.475	−.343	−.201	.192	.137
Postwar	4.181	.308	.265	.087	.078	.003
Bretton Woods	3.006	**.699**	.099	−.341	.210	.201
Post-Bretton Woods	4.580	.239	.310	.228	.052	.040
Consumer Prices						
Gold Standard	.866	.287	−.096	.221	.069	.170
Interwar	1.743	**−.600**	−.387	**.216**	.171	.368
Postwar	1.436	**−.428**	**−.645**	−.066	.060	.092
Bretton Woods	1.278	**−.357**	**−.505**	**.286**	.132	.036
Post-Bretton Woods	1.487	**−.406**	**−.729**	−.289	.067	.120

Note: Bold numbers denote statistically significant correlations at the 5 percent level using Newey-West optimal bandwidth standard errors.

Column 5 shows the difference between the R^2 from regressions of y (the business cycle) on two lags of x (the candidate series) and y, and the R^2 from regressions of y on two lags of y, whereas Column 6 shows the relative R^2 when x and y are reversed.

HISTORICAL EVIDENCE ON BUSINESS CYCLES

Appendix C continued
Cross-Correlations of Band-Pass-Filtered Real GDP with Expenditure Components, Money Stock and Prices

	Germany					
	(1) Vol. ratio	(2) j = −1	(3) j = 0	(4) j = +1	(5) $R^2(y,x)$	(6) $R^2(x,y)$
Consumption						
Gold Standard	.591	.031	**.567**	−.029	.066	.021
Interwar	.564	.248	**.744**	.898	.005	.401
Postwar	.687	.187	**.656**	**.415**	.102	.047
Bretton Woods	.818	**−.191**	**.566**	**.638**	.109	.179
Post-Bretton Woods	.577	**.488**	**.759**	.215	.349	.008
Investment						
Gold Standard	5.476	.073	**.821**	−.072	.149	.023
Interwar	—	—	—	—	—	—
Postwar	2.813	**.401**	**.798**	−.078	.000	.010
Bretton Woods	3.368	**.363**	**.953**	.028	−.022	.037
Post-Bretton Woods	2.456	**.427**	**.705**	−.170	.069	.031
Government Expenditures						
Gold Standard	5.286	**−.688**	**−.617**	−.321	.462	.039
Interwar	—	—	—	—	—	—
Postwar	4.029	**−.261**	.034	**.444**	.009	.164
Bretton Woods	6.120	−.333	−.053	.497	.008	.233
Post-Bretton Woods	1.534	**−.328**	.282	**.596**	.030	.098
Government Revenues						
Gold Standard	2.042	−.059	−.258	−.010	.014	.002
Interwar	1.616	**.351**	**.856**	**.535**	.447	.355
Postwar	3.439	−.095	.273	**.486**	.280	.232
Bretton Woods	4.740	−.086	**.249**	**.542**	.556	.345
Post-Bretton Woods	1.302	−.268	**.545**	**.662**	.070	.381
Exports						
Gold Standard	2.049	−.106	**.389**	−.030	.017	.023
Interwar	1.280	−.239	.080	**.663**	.242	.314
Postwar	3.245	−.012	**.437**	.077	.099	.198
Bretton Woods	4.318	.008	.412	.154	.157	.294
Post-Bretton Woods	2.157	.019	**.523**	.023	.144	.110
Imports						
Gold Standard	2.141	.036	**.343**	.154	.076	.026
Interwar	1.584	**.249**	**.825**	.185	.360	.127
Postwar	3.045	.097	**.674**	.088	.036	.043
Bretton Woods	3.721	.093	**.835**	**.243**	.151	.106
Post-Bretton Woods	2.473	.141	**.534**	−.041	.110	.067
Money Stock						
Gold Standard	1.693	.096	−.113	.186	.041	.082
Interwar	—	—	—	—	—	—
Postwar	1.312	**.518**	.019	−.245	.153	.017
Bretton Woods	1.722	**.468**	−.037	**−.588**	.058	.202
Post-Bretton Woods	.931	**.664**	.078	.130	.454	.114
Consumer Prices						
Gold Standard	.748	.050	−.402	−.166	.044	.024
Interwar	61.638	**−.105**	**−.721**	.505	.033	.134
Postwar	.779	**−.460**	**−.294**	.402	.188	.282
Bretton Woods	.993	**−.538**	**−.349**	.551	.297	.520
Post-Bretton Woods	.482	−.330	−.231	.244	.054	.064

Note: Bold numbers denote statistically significant correlations at the 5 percent level using Newey-West optimal bandwidth standard errors.

Column 5 shows the difference between the R^2 from regressions of y (the business cycle) on two lags of x (the candidate series) and y, and the R^2 from regressions of y on two lags of y, whereas Column 6 shows the relative R^2 when x and y are reversed.

Appendix C continued
Cross-Correlations of Band-Pass-Filtered Real GDP with Expenditure Components, Money Stock and Prices

	France					
	(1) Vol. ratio	(2) j = −1	(3) j = 0	(4) j = +1	(5) R²(y,x)	(6) R²(x,y)
Consumption						
Gold Standard	—	—	—	—	—	—
Interwar	—	—	—	—	—	—
Postwar	.972	.025	**.461**	.134	−.025	.078
Bretton Woods	1.291	**−.505**	.232	**.342**	.195	.045
Post-Bretton Woods	.730	**.532**	**.726**	−.114	.204	.063
Investment						
Gold Standard	—	—	—	—	—	—
Interwar	—	—	—	—	—	—
Postwar	3.828	.240	**.537**	**.360**	.050	.043
Bretton Woods	3.661	.039	.060	**.412**	.040	.341
Post-Bretton Woods	3.952	**.325**	**.796**	**.338**	.080	.049
Government Expenditures						
Gold Standard	3.510	**−.333**	**−.373**	−.337	.093	.003
Interwar	2.981	**−.164**	**.564**	.051	.297	.145
Postwar	6.020	.005	.042	.336	.115	.113
Bretton Woods	7.674	−.037	.091	**.418**	.154	.191
Post-Bretton Woods	1.825	**−.401**	**−.203**	.139	.085	.288
Government Revenues						
Gold Standard	1.071	**.356**	**.546**	.250	.251	.059
Interwar	2.708	−.137	**.646**	.197	.063	.093
Postwar	4.866	.246	.248	.114	.046	.114
Bretton Woods	6.086	.271	.232	.124	.061	.129
Post-Bretton Woods	2.064	−.153	**.459**	.158	.068	.046
Exports						
Gold Standard	2.832	.071	**.304**	.377	.141	.279
Interwar	3.032	.028	**.734**	**.497**	.097	.075
Postwar	5.630	.249	**.751**	.349	.005	.048
Bretton Woods	6.414	**.448**	**.834**	.386	.014	.032
Post-Bretton Woods	4.236	−.081	**.607**	**.285**	.119	.107
Imports						
Gold Standard	3.595	.450	.243	−.089	.197	.015
Interwar	2.665	.181	**.727**	**.224**	.157	.018
Postwar	5.590	−.156	**.607**	**.339**	.262	.265
Bretton Woods	5.229	−.099	**.620**	**.454**	.303	.364
Post-Bretton Woods	6.101	−.166	**.607**	**.212**	.218	.182
Money Stock						
Gold Standard	1.134	.000	−.220	−.129	.029	.018
Interwar	1.624	.070	−.104	.093	.160	.035
Postwar	2.090	.242	.363	**.257**	.030	.006
Bretton Woods	2.028	.177	.485	**.403**	.001	.124
Post-Bretton Woods	2.191	.317	.199	.092	.097	.236
Consumer Prices						
Gold Standard	.501	.186	−.002	−.488	.023	.300
Interwar	1.741	−.276	.322	.257	.038	.018
Postwar	2.311	.077	.064	.262	.107	.122
Bretton Woods	2.759	.344	.241	.363	.228	.209
Post-Bretton Woods	1.421	**−.495**	**−.448**	.072	.231	.065

Note: Bold numbers denote statistically significant correlations at the 5 percent level using Newey-West optimal bandwidth standard errors.

Column 5 shows the difference between the R^2 from regressions of y (the business cycle) on two lags of x (the candidate series) and y, and the R^2 from regressions of y on two lags of y, whereas Column 6 shows the relative R^2 when x and y are reversed.

Appendix C continued
Cross-Correlations of Band-Pass-Filtered Real GDP with Expenditure Components, Money Stock and Prices

	Canada					
	(1) Vol. ratio	(2) j = −1	(3) j = 0	(4) j = +1	(5) $R^2(y,x)$	(6) $R^2(x,y)$
Consumption						
Gold Standard	1.331	.338	**.664**	.141	.119	.009
Interwar	1.125	**.434**	**.891**	**.624**	.248	.274
Postwar	.838	−.137	**.406**	**.290**	.100	.027
Bretton Woods	.890	−.040	.471	.207	.122	.031
Post-Bretton Woods	.734	−.184	.306	.377	.100	.127
Investment						
Gold Standard	3.442	.210	**.601**	.286	.046	.077
Interwar	3.580	**.242**	**.874**	**.741**	.257	.282
Postwar	3.078	−.143	**.561**	**.502**	.068	.011
Bretton Woods	3.231	−.150	.520	**.400**	.054	.095
Post-Bretton Woods	2.915	−.075	**.615**	**.608**	.098	.070
Government Expenditures						
Gold Standard	2.787	**−.405**	−.160	.131	.137	.311
Interwar	1.359	−.275	.108	.021	.065	.071
Postwar	2.932	.134	.114	.126	.124	.014
Bretton Woods	3.611	.332	.281	.082	.318	.002
Post-Bretton Woods	1.827	**−.285**	−.273	.191	.097	.032
Government Revenues						
Gold Standard	2.034	−.080	**.294**	.215	.233	.094
Interwar	1.453	**.632**	**.661**	**.110**	.098	.050
Postwar	3.439	−.055	**.433**	.152	.048	.000
Bretton Woods	4.122	.144	**.533**	.042	.041	.027
Post-Bretton Woods	2.412	−.425	.267	**.352**	.243	.098
Exports						
Gold Standard	2.125	**−.326**	−.019	**−.219**	.126	.167
Interwar	2.191	**.750**	**.657**	.024	.197	.016
Postwar	2.941	**.241**	**.666**	.126	.022	.022
Bretton Woods	2.436	.249	**.627**	.112	.077	.044
Post-Bretton Woods	3.411	.290	**.710**	.143	.003	.114
Imports						
Gold Standard	2.472	−.092	**.529**	.132	.376	.106
Interwar	2.415	**.579**	**.912**	**.354**	.037	.058
Postwar	3.769	.169	**.730**	.154	.008	.036
Bretton Woods	3.257	**.136**	**.750**	.137	.013	.114
Post-Bretton Woods	4.258	.227	**.721**	.162	.012	.001
Money Stock						
Gold Standard	1.056	**.539**	.323	−.169	.240	.070
Interwar	.551	**.836**	**.808**	**.368**	.398	.030
Postwar	1.551	−.115	.085	.175	.054	.053
Bretton Woods	1.407	**.402**	−.143	−.084	.208	.106
Post-Bretton Woods	1.647	−.536	.277	**.397**	.433	.086
Consumer Prices						
Gold Standard	.839	.502	−.148	.041	.197	.060
Interwar	.524	**.329**	**.783**	**.674**	.031	.159
Postwar	.980	−.319	**−.310**	.150	.034	.026
Bretton Woods	1.089	−.015	−.075	**.258**	.012	.062
Post-Bretton Woods	.842	**−.665**	**−.675**	−.047	.339	.083

Note: Bold numbers denote statistically significant correlations at the 5 percent level using Newey-West optimal bandwidth standard errors.

Column 5 shows the difference between the R^2 from regressions of y (the business cycle) on two lags of x (the candidate series) and y, and the R^2 from regressions of y on two lags of y, whereas Column 6 shows the relative R^2 when x and y are reversed.

Appendix C continued
Cross-Correlations of Band-Pass-Filtered Real GDP with Expenditure Components, Money Stock and Prices

	Italy					
	(1) Vol. ratio	(2) j = −1	(3) j = 0	(4) j = +1	(5) R²(y,x)	(6) R²(x,y)
Consumption						
Gold Standard	.573	.093	**.602**	−.092	.294	.162
Interwar	1.148	−.004	**.389**	−.311	.055	.124
Postwar	1.180	.064	**.785**	**.382**	.067	.141
Bretton Woods	1.304	.112	**.742**	.478	.035	.244
Post-Bretton Woods	1.040	.037	**.847**	.426	.175	.080
Investment						
Gold Standard	9.431	−.197	**.661**	−.211	.073	.025
Interwar	7.272	−.255	.594	−.106	.144	.088
Postwar	4.038	.248	**.871**	**.565**	−.071	−.362
Bretton Woods	4.212	.144	.204	−.003	.058	.000
Post-Bretton Woods	—	—	—	—	—	—
Government Expenditures						
Gold Standard	5.999	.235	−.094	−.027	.042	.024
Interwar	8.268	.106	**−.309**	.237	.021	.040
Postwar	4.498	−.300	**−.656**	**−.230**	.385	.687
Bretton Woods	7.684	−.022	.339	.075	.037	.239
Post-Bretton Woods	4.498	−.300	−.656	−.230	.075	.584
Government Revenues						
Gold Standard	5.329	.146	.039	−.062	.030	.024
Interwar	1.468	.228	−.249	−.072	.026	.309
Postwar	3.403	**−.386**	.025	.206	.186	.053
Bretton Woods	3.116	**−.289**	.233	.251	.241	.082
Post-Bretton Woods	3.592	**−.394**	−.101	.081	.159	.088
Exports						
Gold Standard	2.324	.087	−.001	−.084	.049	.010
Interwar	4.548	.230	−.063	.011	.062	.417
Postwar	5.805	.290	**.316**	−.259	.073	.052
Bretton Woods	5.824	.154	**.312**	−.034	.100	.047
Post-Bretton Woods	5.728	**.486**	**.321**	**−.326**	.216	.051
Imports						
Gold Standard	2.578	**.494**	.014	−.061	.260	.001
Interwar	6.229	.280	.064	−.111	.057	.437
Postwar	6.494	−.137	**.587**	.149	.100	.039
Bretton Woods	7.301	.115	**.473**	**.278**	.047	.085
Post-Bretton Woods	5.798	−.289	**.698**	.074	.317	.030
Money Stock						
Gold Standard	.813	−.103	−.030	−.170	.085	.177
Interwar	1.137	−.168	.001	**.645**	.062	.439
Postwar	1.810	**.447**	.122	−.217	.201	.041
Bretton Woods	1.694	**.420**	.183	−.204	.179	.037
Post-Bretton Woods	1.801	**.548**	.084	−.213	.205	.018
Consumer Prices						
Gold Standard	.575	**.343**	**.164**	**−.168**	.223	.057
Interwar	1.609	**−.420**	−.011	**.409**	.106	.061
Postwar	1.767	**−.557**	**−.218**	**.176**	.288	.034
Bretton Woods	1.966	**−.468**	−.100	.081	.204	.035
Post-Bretton Woods	1.574	**−.605**	**−.331**	.121	.430	.059

Note: Bold numbers denote statistically significant correlations at the 5 percent level using Newey-West optimal bandwidth standard errors.

Column 5 shows the difference between the R^2 from regressions of y (the business cycle) on two lags of x (the candidate series) and y, and the R^2 from regressions of y on two lags of y, whereas Column 6 shows the relative R^2 when x and y are reversed.

HISTORICAL EVIDENCE ON BUSINESS CYCLES

Appendix C continued
Cross-Correlations of Band-Pass-Filtered Real GDP with Expenditure Components, Money Stock and Prices

	Japan					
	(1) Vol. ratio	(2) j = −1	(3) j = 0	(4) j = +1	(5) R²(y,x)	(6) R²(x,y)
Consumption						
Gold Standard	1.093	−.021	**.479**	**−.329**	.095	.140
Interwar	.647	.118	**.853**	−.060	.015	.049
Postwar	.917	.011	**.571**	**.419**	.234	.116
Bretton Woods	.864	−.177	**.455**	.489	.292	.148
Post-Bretton Woods	1.018	**.258**	**.780**	.175	.006	.077
Investment						
Gold Standard	3.660	−.099	−.197	.220	.119	.104
Interwar	5.047	.042	.285	.089	.037	.005
Postwar	3.673	−.046	**.447**	**.433**	.218	.177
Bretton Woods	4.025	.006	.370	**.362**	.223	.237
Post-Bretton Woods	2.803	.114	**.706**	**.620**	.031	.063
Government Expenditures						
Gold Standard	6.088	−.151	−.160	−.088	.063	.076
Interwar	1.852	.290	.056	−.166	.014	.001
Postwar	7.821	−.126	−.348	−.031	.126	.028
Bretton Woods	8.873	−.146	−.365	.088	.237	.076
Post-Bretton Woods	4.851	−.145	−.324	−.339	.057	.256
Government Revenues						
Gold Standard	6.578	−.141	−.119	−.067	.081	.015
Interwar	1.582	**.449**	**.269**	−.249	.058	.035
Postwar	8.714	−.122	−.184	.189	.092	.063
Bretton Woods	9.830	−.111	−.239	.229	.155	.095
Post-Bretton Woods	5.588	−.233	.006	.178	.039	.037
Exports						
Gold Standard	3.899	−.094	**.301**	**−.426**	.060	.075
Interwar	2.768	−.262	**.427**	.013	.017	.267
Postwar	7.007	.101	−.190	−.323	.227	.048
Bretton Woods	7.589	.205	**−.245**	−.524	.277	.030
Post-Bretton Woods	5.121	−.166	−.009	**.367**	.022	.078
Imports						
Gold Standard	3.999	.195	−.228	.246	.158	.076
Interwar	2.236	.397	**.342**	**−.472**	.156	.581
Postwar	8.417	−.002	.062	.033	.209	.133
Bretton Woods	7.861	.132	−.031	−.232	.240	.462
Post-Bretton Woods	9.391	.006	.238	**.441**	.014	.068
Money Stock						
Gold Standard	4.939	−.349	.118	**.453**	.072	.050
Interwar	1.362	−.121	.020	.059	.059	.002
Postwar	2.923	−.039	**.244**	.275	.203	.021
Bretton Woods	3.202	−.246	.207	.334	.355	.034
Post-Bretton Woods	2.226	−.068	.362	−.057	.168	.015
Consumer Prices						
Gold Standard	1.387	.025	−.261	.238	.061	.085
Interwar	1.052	−.137	.275	.290	.032	.068
Postwar	2.975	−.359	**−.432**	.114	.282	.161
Bretton Woods	3.428	−.321	**−.431**	.194	.323	.204
Post-Bretton Woods	1.650	−.300	**−.525**	.146	.090	.129

Note: Bold numbers denote statistically significant correlations at the 5 percent level using Newey-West optimal bandwidth standard errors.

Column 5 shows the difference between the R² from regressions of y (the business cycle) on two lags of x (the candidate series) and y, and the R² from regressions of y on two lags of y, whereas Column 6 shows the relative R² when x and y are reversed.

Appendix C continued
Cross-Correlations of Band-Pass-Filtered Real GDP with Expenditure Components, Money Stock and Prices

	Belgium					
	(1) Vol. ratio	(2) j = −1	(3) j = 0	(4) j = +1	(5) $R^2(y,x)$	(6) $R^2(x,y)$
Consumption						
Gold Standard	—	—	—	—	—	—
Interwar	—	—	—	—	—	—
Postwar	—	—	—	—	—	—
Bretton Woods	—	—	—	—	—	—
Post-Bretton Woods	—	—	—	—	—	—
Investment						
Gold Standard	—	—	—	—	—	—
Interwar	—	—	—	—	—	—
Postwar	5.152	.062	**.592**	−.003	.020	.026
Bretton Woods	4.697	.149	**.497**	.094	.028	.097
Post-Bretton Woods	5.494	.069	**.655**	−.065	.071	.060
Government Expenditures						
Gold Standard	10.063	−.107	.060	**.230**	.016	.081
Interwar	5.409	−.307	.257	.318	.098	.214
Postwar	4.141	**−.287**	−.077	.183	.071	.017
Bretton Woods	10.854	−.106	.135	.071	.049	.647
Post-Bretton Woods	1.622	−.185	−.390	.200	.028	.160
Government Revenues						
Gold Standard	2.495	.087	**.310**	.220	.048	.038
Interwar	3.121	**.597**	**.430**	−.121	.463	.380
Postwar	3.963	−.258	**.203**	.293	.070	.071
Bretton Woods	6.436	−.256	**.396**	.403	.194	.439
Post-Bretton Woods	1.281	−.269	−.107	.064	.134	.099
Exports						
Gold Standard	9.763	**.362**	.202	.011	.157	.001
Interwar	4.047	**.576**	**.755**	.219	.280	.270
Postwar	5.214	.102	**.691**	.057	.137	.021
Bretton Woods	6.757	.249	**.680**	.071	.248	.085
Post-Bretton Woods	3.696	−.054	**.785**	.055	.051	.001
Imports						
Gold Standard	8.522	.357	−.073	.266	.182	.184
Interwar	4.539	**.642**	**.862**	**.273**	.340	.257
Postwar	4.401	.039	**.738**	**.148**	.098	.033
Bretton Woods	4.768	**.359**	**.702**	.133	.316	.137
Post-Bretton Woods	4.140	−.144	**.774**	.157	.117	.018
Money Stock						
Gold Standard	4.799	−.068	**.471**	**.354**	.087	.157
Interwar	3.000	**.463**	.393	−.031	.145	.002
Postwar	1.841	.097	−.196	.096	.044	.036
Bretton Woods	1.796	−.065	.110	**.373**	.163	.201
Post-Bretton Woods	1.847	.134	**−.458**	−.091	.107	.044
Consumer Prices						
Gold Standard	5.694	**−.477**	.259	**.340**	.195	.077
Interwar	2.055	.286	.269	.117	.043	.027
Postwar	1.319	**−.412**	−.159	.084	.222	.072
Bretton Woods	1.359	**−.362**	.085	**.101**	.321	.101
Post-Bretton Woods	1.249	**−.421**	**−.408**	.046	.289	.027

Note: Bold numbers denote statistically significant correlations at the 5 percent level using Newey-West optimal bandwidth standard errors.

Column 5 shows the difference between the R^2 from regressions of y (the business cycle) on two lags of x (the candidate series) and y, and the R^2 from regressions of y on two lags of y, whereas Column 6 shows the relative R^2 when x and y are reversed.

Appendix C continued
Cross-Correlations of Band-Pass-Filtered Real GDP with Expenditure Components, Money Stock and Prices

	Netherlands					
	(1) Vol. ratio	(2) j = −1	(3) j = 0	(4) j = +1	(5) R²(y,x)	(6) R²(x,y)
Consumption						
Gold Standard	—	—	—	—	—	—
Interwar	—	—	—	—	—	—
Postwar	—	—	—	—	—	—
Bretton Woods	—	—	—	—	—	—
Post-Bretton Woods	—	—	—	—	—	—
Investment						
Gold Standard	—	—	—	—	—	—
Interwar	—	—	—	—	—	—
Postwar	3.300	**.313**	**.567**	**.133**	−.011	.049
Bretton Woods	2.934	.168	**.589**	.162	−.045	.127
Post-Bretton Woods	4.271	**.669**	**.546**	.087	.348	.080
Government Expenditures						
Gold Standard	4.328	**−.519**	**−.665**	−.106	.144	.033
Interwar	3.784	**−.374**	−.189	−.184	.087	.021
Postwar	3.107	−.092	−.135	−.041	.001	.083
Bretton Woods	2.580	.108	.024	−.217	.065	.083
Post-Bretton Woods	3.420	.048	.079	.280	.162	.121
Government Revenues						
Gold Standard	.811	**−.327**	.114	−.209	.225	.264
Interwar	3.112	.280	**.501**	**.492**	.010	.403
Postwar	3.014	**−.223**	−.116	−.011	.019	.006
Bretton Woods	4.131	.217	.280	−.283	.082	.143
Post-Bretton Woods	4.137	.071	**.259**	**.400**	.208	.155
Exports						
Gold Standard	2.119	**.376**	.011	.159	.274	.042
Interwar	5.999	.256	**.651**	**.642**	.014	.186
Postwar	2.976	−.009	**.411**	.139	.107	.006
Bretton Woods	2.023	.012	.432	.298	.211	.010
Post-Bretton Woods	5.302	.008	**.493**	−.055	.070	.041
Imports						
Gold Standard	2.118	**.612**	.000	.142	.296	.113
Interwar	6.160	.114	**.595**	**.664**	.042	.191
Postwar	3.595	−.150	**.455**	**.434**	.165	.055
Bretton Woods	3.183	−.234	**.425**	**.616**	.261	.104
Post-Bretton Woods	4.933	.083	**.569**	.005	.043	.027
Money Stock						
Gold Standard	1.440	.105	**−.277**	−.094	.000	.011
Interwar	2.481	−.265	.113	.493	.164	.337
Postwar	1.815	**.460**	−.076	−.211	.329	.026
Bretton Woods	1.539	**.497**	.004	−.239	.313	.024
Post-Bretton Woods	2.639	**.454**	−.262	−.193	.488	.191
Consumer Prices						
Gold Standard	.790	**−.400**	.140	−.132	.135	.208
Interwar	1.933	.165	.222	**.363**	.003	.518
Postwar	.906	**−.518**	**−.242**	.106	.232	.023
Bretton Woods	.857	**−.595**	**−.225**	.179	.285	.051
Post-Bretton Woods	1.058	**−.288**	**−.289**	−.128	.080	.004

Note: Bold numbers denote statistically significant correlations at the 5 percent level using Newey-West optimal bandwidth standard errors.

Column 5 shows the difference between the R^2 from regressions of y (the business cycle) on two lags of x (the candidate series) and y, and the R^2 from regressions of y on two lags of y, whereas Column 6 shows the relative R^2 when x and y are reversed.

Appendix C continued
Cross-Correlations of Band-Pass-Filtered Real GDP with Expenditure Components, Money Stock and Prices

	Denmark					
	(1) Vol. ratio	(2) j = −1	(3) j = 0	(4) j = +1	(5) $R^2(y,x)$	(6) $R^2(x,y)$
Consumption						
Gold Standard	—	—	—	—	—	—
Interwar	—	—	—	—	—	—
Postwar	—	—	—	—	—	—
Bretton Woods	—	—	—	—	—	—
Post-Bretton Woods	—	—	—	—	—	—
Investment						
Gold Standard	4.165	−.326	.045	.333	.061	.012
Interwar	5.009	.062	**.798**	.137	−.051	.021
Postwar	4.589	.018	**.872**	−.032	.037	.081
Bretton Woods	3.980	−.086	**.875**	**−.228**	.022	.097
Post-Bretton Woods	5.470	.127	**.893**	.142	.138	.138
Government Expenditures						
Gold Standard	11.204	−.045	−.065	**.142**	.057	.032
Interwar	1.887	.111	−.238	.152	.086	.056
Postwar	2.878	.026	**−.387**	−.001	.154	.029
Bretton Woods	3.295	.026	−.322	.208	.146	.133
Post-Bretton Woods	1.972	−.020	**−.613**	−.442	.216	.129
Government Revenues						
Gold Standard	4.174	−.147	−.002	.152	.086	.015
Interwar	2.172	−.112	**.517**	−.297	.025	.056
Postwar	2.948	−.043	−.019	.270	.225	.163
Bretton Woods	3.481	−.096	**−.184**	.223	.221	.194
Post-Bretton Woods	1.683	.023	**.553**	**.447**	.207	.113
Exports						
Gold Standard	3.514	.013	**.464**	.025	.088	.006
Interwar	3.672	.170	**.430**	.065	.151	.031
Postwar	2.276	−.219	.138	.217	.009	.055
Bretton Woods	2.180	−.153	.225	.309	.012	.077
Post-Bretton Woods	2.423	−.317	.002	.057	.085	.049
Imports						
Gold Standard	4.689	−.162	−.034	.113	.018	.002
Interwar	3.961	.107	**.577**	.086	.098	.025
Postwar	3.601	**−.406**	**.478**	.254	.140	.058
Bretton Woods	3.632	**−.436**	**.468**	.341	.071	.071
Post-Bretton Woods	3.549	−.224	**.499**	.077	.245	.028
Money Stock						
Gold Standard	2.538	−.076	.234	.091	.005	.006
Interwar	.994	**.539**	**.637**	−.065	.175	.059
Postwar	2.098	**.398**	−.037	−.229	.101	.094
Bretton Woods	1.213	**.509**	−.079	**−.319**	.101	.156
Post-Bretton Woods	3.018	**.607**	−.010	−.190	.156	.081
Consumer Prices						
Gold Standard	2.112	**−.150**	−.161	.207	.005	.147
Interwar	1.921	.170	.033	.122	.183	.035
Postwar	1.031	**−.286**	**−.614**	−.071	.243	.032
Bretton Woods	1.089	−.226	**−.618**	−.035	.249	.031
Post-Bretton Woods	.840	−.223	**−.658**	−.044	.301	.025

Note: Bold numbers denote statistically significant correlations at the 5 percent level using Newey-West optimal bandwidth standard errors.

Column 5 shows the difference between the R^2 from regressions of y (the business cycle) on two lags of x (the candidate series) and y, and the R^2 from regressions of y on two lags of y, whereas Column 6 shows the relative R^2 when x and y are reversed.

HISTORICAL EVIDENCE ON BUSINESS CYCLES

Appendix C continued
Cross-Correlations of Band-Pass-Filtered Real GDP with Expenditure Components, Money Stock and Prices

	Finland					
	(1) Vol. ratio	(2) j = −1	(3) j = 0	(4) j = +1	(5) R²(y,x)	(6) R²(x,y)
Consumption						
Gold Standard	—	—	—	—	—	—
Interwar	—	—	—	—	—	—
Postwar	—	—	—	—	—	—
Bretton Woods	—	—	—	—	—	—
Post-Bretton Woods	—	—	—	—	—	—
Investment						
Gold Standard	3.103	.076	**.390**	**.271**	.137	.131
Interwar	3.460	**.538**	**.750**	**.375**	.120	.131
Postwar	3.722	.149	**.824**	**.529**	.000	.045
Bretton Woods	3.230	−.205	**.717**	**.386**	.012	.013
Post-Bretton Woods	4.004	**.341**	**.886**	**.606**	.019	.146
Government Expenditures						
Gold Standard	5.192	−.354	−.011	.240	.146	.021
Interwar	4.690	−.118	.098	.331	.089	.194
Postwar	2.443	**−.251**	.044	.068	.074	.142
Bretton Woods	3.485	−.203	**.256**	−.035	.087	.109
Post-Bretton Woods	1.379	**−.492**	−.290	.257	.034	.417
Government Revenues						
Gold Standard	2.402	−.265	−.182	**.132**	.026	.027
Interwar	3.829	.048	**.626**	**.608**	.120	.151
Postwar	2.348	−.028	**.367**	.181	.046	.010
Bretton Woods	3.207	−.064	**.310**	−.099	.074	.056
Post-Bretton Woods	1.559	.009	.495	**.539**	.019	.126
Exports						
Gold Standard	4.090	**.436**	**.568**	.001	.188	.022
Interwar	5.988	.261	**.574**	.241	.082	.023
Postwar	4.539	.207	**.424**	**−.182**	.005	.095
Bretton Woods	6.419	.051	**.542**	−.169	.009	.041
Post-Bretton Woods	2.743	**.517**	**.341**	−.243	.010	.417
Imports						
Gold Standard	3.209	**.301**	**.600**	.200	.088	.054
Interwar	5.155	**.396**	**.752**	**.360**	.001	.046
Postwar	4.793	.091	**.642**	.161	.023	.024
Bretton Woods	6.433	−.085	**.711**	.143	.016	.009
Post-Bretton Woods	3.358	**.378**	**.632**	.204	.015	.092
Money Stock						
Gold Standard	1.926	**.149**	.273	**.399**	.091	.064
Interwar	1.423	−.004	.293	**.532**	.093	.262
Postwar	4.399	.270	.283	−.017	.020	.036
Bretton Woods	6.584	.128	.217	−.233	.033	.082
Post-Bretton Woods	1.904	**.407**	**.583**	**.593**	.026	.060
Consumer Prices						
Gold Standard	1.527	−.296	**−.429**	.158	.165	.132
Interwar	1.144	.270	.044	.399	.225	.180
Postwar	1.647	−.199	−.132	.047	.054	.095
Bretton Woods	2.449	.003	−.100	−.137	.062	.113
Post-Bretton Woods	.787	**−.607**	−.253	**.387**	.049	.033

Note: Bold numbers denote statistically significant correlations at the 5 percent level using Newey-West optimal bandwidth standard errors.

Column 5 shows the difference between the R² from regressions of y (the business cycle) on two lags of x (the candidate series) and y, and the R² from regressions of y on two lags of y, whereas Column 6 shows the relative R² when x and y are reversed.

Appendix C continued
Cross-Correlations of Band-Pass-Filtered Real GDP with Expenditure Components, Money Stock and Prices

			Norway			
	(1) Vol. ratio	(2) j = −1	(3) j = 0	(4) j = +1	(5) $R^2(y,x)$	(6) $R^2(x,y)$
Consumption						
Gold Standard	1.224	−.342	.050	**.566**	.051	.307
Interwar	.570	−.111	.150	**.873**	.129	.605
Postwar	2.716	−.032	.233	.239	.026	.104
Bretton Woods	3.227	.027	.162	.046	.034	.055
Post-Bretton Woods	2.214	−.106	**.326**	.473	.008	.177
Investment						
Gold Standard	4.486	.300	**.537**	.194	.118	.026
Interwar	—	—	—	—	—	—
Postwar	5.351	**−.181**	**.090**	**.179**	.074	.024
Bretton Woods	4.908	−.107	.099	.111	.256	.011
Post-Bretton Woods	5.673	−.246	.082	.227	.030	.044
Government Expenditures						
Gold Standard	6.498	.018	.296	.125	.062	.113
Interwar	1.751	.030	**.178**	**.192**	.071	.317
Postwar	3.954	−.010	.003	−.001	.001	.005
Bretton Woods	5.536	**.205**	.073	−.028	.082	.009
Post-Bretton Woods	1.532	**−.485**	−.219	.057	.093	.047
Government Revenues						
Gold Standard	6.747	−.136	.310	**.321**	.047	.192
Interwar	2.382	−.181	**.332**	**.208**	.006	.170
Postwar	4.489	−.118	.115	**.113**	.015	.038
Bretton Woods	5.871	−.023	.108	.045	.028	.044
Post-Bretton Woods	2.735	−.267	.145	.270	.090	.029
Exports						
Gold Standard	4.899	.230	.108	**−.486**	.020	.169
Interwar	3.573	**.295**	**.675**	**−.425**	.094	.122
Postwar	6.483	.035	.278	−.152	.018	.045
Bretton Woods	7.158	−.114	.429	.020	.037	.057
Post-Bretton Woods	5.874	.171	.131	−.327	.021	.159
Imports						
Gold Standard	4.309	**.336**	.345	−.046	.078	.016
Interwar	3.423	.241	**.539**	**.471**	.382	.119
Postwar	4.397	−.028	**.364**	.250	.011	.071
Bretton Woods	4.138	−.070	.295	.111	.002	.038
Post-Bretton Woods	4.587	−.032	**.414**	.355	.010	.143
Money Stock						
Gold Standard	1.819	.112	.298	**.460**	.122	.244
Interwar	.648	**−.486**	.022	**.633**	.277	.356
Postwar	2.212	.062	**.256**	.119	.017	.097
Bretton Woods	2.535	.141	**.144**	−.071	.066	.090
Post-Bretton Woods	1.794	.063	**.398**	**.340**	.043	.267
Consumer Prices						
Gold Standard	1.969	.261	.236	**.484**	.161	.222
Interwar	1.373	−.072	.173	−.104	.079	.050
Postwar	1.528	**−.257**	−.346	−.022	.089	.003
Bretton Woods	1.848	−.081	−.158	.038	.070	.015
Post-Bretton Woods	1.191	**−.515**	**−.609**	−.084	.125	.005

Note: Bold numbers denote statistically significant correlations at the 5 percent level using Newey-West optimal bandwidth standard errors.

Column 5 shows the difference between the R^2 from regressions of y (the business cycle) on two lags of x (the candidate series) and y, and the R^2 from regressions of y on two lags of y, whereas Column 6 shows the relative R^2 when x and y are reversed.

Appendix C continued
Cross-Correlations of Band-Pass-Filtered Real GDP with Expenditure Components, Money Stock and Prices

	Sweden					
	(1) Vol. ratio	(2) j = −1	(3) j = 0	(4) j = +1	(5) R²(y,x)	(6) R²(x,y)
Consumption						
Gold Standard	1.353	−.081	**.599**	.069	.224	.049
Interwar	1.275	−.084	**.712**	**.468**	.102	.057
Postwar	.994	.124	**.511**	.242	.012	.029
Bretton Woods	1.005	.253	**.497**	−.073	.014	.035
Post-Bretton Woods	.985	.031	**.523**	**.448**	.023	.125
Investment						
Gold Standard	5.349	−.032	**.588**	**.161**	.087	.134
Interwar	3.468	**.384**	**.883**	.098	.129	.088
Postwar	4.818	.154	**.573**	**.377**	.014	.192
Bretton Woods	4.359	−.003	.236	.230	.126	.196
Post-Bretton Woods	5.125	.249	**.785**	**.482**	.050	.098
Government Expenditures						
Gold Standard	1.815	−.368	−.182	−.046	.168	.022
Interwar	6.963	.279	−.095	−.127	.088	.052
Postwar	3.498	−.160	**−.519**	−.223	.049	.115
Bretton Woods	4.719	.013	**−.560**	**−.404**	.015	.167
Post-Bretton Woods	2.172	**−.497**	**−.555**	−.032	.189	.172
Government Revenues						
Gold Standard	3.412	.125	**.532**	.045	.014	.030
Interwar	7.523	.294	−.006	−.003	.095	.028
Postwar	4.546	**−.292**	−.246	.194	.013	.140
Bretton Woods	5.813	−.228	**−.620**	−.096	.028	.169
Post-Bretton Woods	3.322	−.406	.209	**.544**	.087	.105
Exports						
Gold Standard	3.724	**.262**	**.455**	.037	.064	.114
Interwar	5.384	.316	.472	−.022	.128	.053
Postwar	5.835	.121	**.456**	.131	.006	.071
Bretton Woods	7.014	−.293	**.408**	.444	.038	.031
Post-Bretton Woods	4.795	**.581**	**.526**	−.182	.050	.353
Imports						
Gold Standard	3.032	.291	**.592**	−.003	.085	.052
Interwar	6.546	.063	.273	**.269**	.020	.026
Postwar	6.881	.065	**.437**	.213	.005	.085
Bretton Woods	8.115	−.330	.362	.447	.017	.019
Post-Bretton Woods	5.796	**.475**	**.529**	−.040	.027	.323
Money Stock						
Gold Standard	1.476	**−.406**	−.070	**.254**	.302	.011
Interwar	1.359	−.134	.145	**.292**	.054	.039
Postwar	5.948	.179	−.115	−.273	.009	.096
Bretton Woods	8.370	.215	−.281	**−.409**	.009	.099
Post-Bretton Woods	2.949	.259	.186	.025	.023	.013
Consumer Prices						
Gold Standard	1.465	−.160	.248	**.264**	.163	.002
Interwar	1.900	.165	.113	.039	.005	.006
Postwar	1.615	**−.527**	**−.410**	**.276**	.064	.061
Bretton Woods	2.033	**−.552**	**−.530**	**.269**	.110	.052
Post-Bretton Woods	1.201	**−.540**	−.298	.298	.194	.112

Note: Bold numbers denote statistically significant correlations at the 5 percent level using Newey-West optimal bandwidth standard errors.

Column 5 shows the difference between the R^2 from regressions of y (the business cycle) on two lags of x (the candidate series) and y, and the R^2 from regressions of y on two lags of y, whereas Column 6 shows the relative R^2 when x and y are reversed.

References

Backus, D. and P. Kehoe. 1992. "International Evidence on the Historical Properties of Business Cycles." *The American Economic Review*, 82, pp. 864–88.

Balke, N. and R. Gordon. 1989. "The Estimation of Prewar Gross National Product: Methodology and New Evidence." *Journal of Political Economy*, 97, pp. 38–92.

Baxter, M. and R. King. 1995. "Measuring Business Cycles: Approximate Band-Pass Filters For Economic Time Series." NBER Working Paper No. 5022.

Baxter, M. and A. C. Stockman. 1989. "Business Cycles and the Exchange-Rate Regime: Some International Evidence." *Journal of Monetary Economics*, 23, pp. 377–400.

Bayoumi, T. and B. Eichengreen. 1993. "Shocking Aspects of European Monetary Unification." In F. Torres and F. Giavazzi, eds., *Adjustment and Growth in the European Monetary Union*. Cambridge: Cambridge University Press.

Bergman, M. and L. Jonung. 1992. "Is the Norwegian Business Cycle Asymmetric?" Chapter 8 in K. Velupillai, ed., *Nonlinearities, Disequilibria and Simulation*. London: Macmillan.

———. 1993. "The Business Cycle Has Not Been Dampened: The Case of Sweden and the United States 1873-1988." *Scandinavian Economic History Review*, 41, pp. 18–36.

Bordo, M. D. 1984. "The Gold Standard: The Traditional Approach." In M. D. Bordo and A. J. Schwartz, eds., *A Retrospective on the Classical Gold Standard, 1821–1931*. Chicago: University of Chicago Press.

———. 1986. "Financial Crises, Stock Market Crashes and the Money Supply: Some International Evidence: 1870–1933." In F. H. Capie and G. Wood eds., *Financial Crises and the World Banking System*. London: Macmillan.

———. 1993. "The Gold Standard, Bretton Woods and Other Monetary Regimes: An Historical Appraisal." In *Dimensions of Monetary Policy: Essays in Honor of Anatole B. Balbach*. Federal Reserve Bank of St. Louis *Review*, Special Issue, April–May.

———. 1998. "The Gold Standard and Related Regimes: Introduction to the Collection." Chapter 1 of *Essays on the Gold Standard and Related Regimes*. New York: Cambridge University Press.

Bordo, M. D. and B. Eichengreen. 1998. "The Rise and Fall of a Barbarous Relic: The Role of Gold in the International Monetary System." NBER Working Paper No. 6436.

Bordo, M. D. and L. Jonung. 1987. *The Long-Run Behavior of the Income Velocity of Circulation: The International Evidence*. Cambridge: Cambridge University Press.

———. 1997. "A Return to the Convertibility Principle? Monetary and Fiscal Regimes in Historical Perspective. The International Evidence." Manuscript prepared for the International Economic Association conference in Trento, Italy, September 4–7, 1997.

Bordo, M. D. and F. E. Kydland. 1995. "The Gold Standard As a Rule: An Essay in Exploration." *Explorations in Economic History*, 32, pp. 423–64.

Bordo, M. D. and A. J. Schwartz. 1989. "Transmission of Real and Monetary Disturbances under Fixed and Floating Rates." In J. A. Dorn and W. A. Niskanen, eds., *Dollars, Deficits and Trade*. Boston, MA: Kluwer.

———. 1998. "Monetary Policy Regimes and Economic Performance: The Historical Record." In J. Taylor and M. Woodford, eds., *Handbook of Macroeconomics*, forthcoming.

Burns, A. and W. Mitchell. 1946. *Measuring Business Cycles*. New York: National Bureau of Economic Research.

Choudhri, E. U. and Kochin, L. A. 1980. "The Exchange Rate and the International Transmission of Business Cycle Disturbances: Some Evidence from the Great Depression." *Journal of Money, Credit, and Banking*, 12, pp. 565–74.

Cochrane, J. H. 1994. "Shocks." *Carnegie Rochester Conference Series on Public Policy*, 41, pp. 295–364.

Daniel, B. 1997. "International Interdependence of National Growth Rates: A Structural Trends Analysis." *Journal of Monetary Economics*, 40, pp. 73–96.

DeLong, J. and L. Summers. 1986. "The Changing Cyclical Variability of Economic Activity in the United States." Chapter 12 in R. Gordon, ed., *The American Business Cycle. Continuity and Change*. Chicago: NBER.

Eichengreen, B. 1992. *Golden Fetters: The Gold Standard and the Great Depression, 1919–1939*. New York: Oxford University Press.

Englund, P., M. Persson, and L.E.O. Svensson. 1992. "The Swedish Business Cycles: 1861–1988." *Journal of Monetary Economics*, 30, pp. 343–71.

Falk, B. 1986. "Further Evidence on the Asymmetric Behavior of Economic Time Series over the Business Cycle." *Journal of Political Economy*, 94, pp. 1096–1109.

Fisher, I. 1935. "Are Booms and Depressions Transmitted Internationally through Monetary Standards?" *Bulletin of the International Statistical Institute*, 28, pp. 1–29.

Friedman, M. and A. J. Schwartz. 1963a. *A Monetary History of the United States, 1867–1960*. Princeton, NJ: Princeton University Press.

———. 1963b. "Money and Business Cycles." *Review of Economics and Statistics*, 45, pp. 32–64.

———. 1982. *Monetary Trends in the United States and the United Kingdom*. Chicago: NBER.

Gayer, A., W. W. Rostow, and A. J. Schwartz. 1953. *The Growth and Fluctuation of the British Economy 1790–1850*. Oxford: Clarendon Press.

Hamilton, J. D. 1989. "A New Approach to the Economic Analysis of Nonstationary Time Series and the Business Cycle." *Econometrica*, 57, pp. 357–84.

Keynes, J. M. 1936. *The General Theory of Employment, Interest, and Money*. London: Macmillan.

Kydland, F. E. and E. C. Prescott. 1990. "Business Cycles: Real Facts and a Monetary Myth." Federal Reserve Bank of Minneapolis *Quarterly Review*, 14, pp. 3–18.

Levy-Leboyer, M. 1982. "Central Banking and Foreign Trade: The Anglo-American Cycle in the 1830's." In C. P. Kindleberger and J. P. Laffargue, eds., *Financial Crises: Theory, History and Policy*. New York: Cambridge University Press.

Lucas, R. 1977. "Understanding Business Cycles." In K. Brunner and A. Meltzer, eds., *Stabilization of the Domestic and International Economy*. *Carnegie-Rochester Conference Series*, 5, pp. 7–29.

McCloskey, D. N. and J. R. Zecher. 1976. "How the Gold Standard Worked, 1880–1913." In J. A. Frenkel and H. G. Johnson, eds., *The Monetary Approach to the Balance of Payments*. Toronto: University of Toronto Press.

———. 1984. "The Success of Purchasing Power Parity: Historical Evidence and Its Implications for Macroeconomics." In M. D. Bordo and A. J. Schwartz, eds., *A Retrospective on the Classical Gold Standard, 1821–1931*. Chicago: University of Chicago Press.

Mitchell, B. R. 1978. *European Historical Statistics, 1750–1970*. London: Macmillan.

———. 1988. *British Historical Statistics*. Cambridge: Cambridge University Press.

———. 1991. *International Historical Statistics: Asia*. New York: Stockton Press.

———. 1992. *International Historical Statistics: Europe 1750–1988*. London: Macmillan.

———. 1993. *International Historical Statistics: The Americas 1750–1988*. New York: Stockton Press.

Mitchell, W. C. 1927. *Business Cycles: The Problem and Its Setting*. New York: NBER.

Neftçi, S. N. 1984. "Are Economic Time Series Asymmetric over the Business Cycle?" *Journal of Political Economy*, 92, pp. 307–28.

O'Rourke, K. H. and Williamson, J. G. 1998. *Globalization and History: The Evolution of 19th Century Atlantic Economy*. Cambridge, MA: The MIT Press.

Romer, C. 1989. "The Prewar Business Cycle Reconsidered: New Estimates of GNP, 1869–1908." *Journal of Political Economy*, 97, pp. 1–37.

Saint-Marc, Michelle. 1983. *Histoire Monetaire de la France, 1880–1980*. Paris: Presses Universitaire de la France.

Sheffrin, S. 1988. "Have Economic Fluctuations Been Dampened? A Look at the Evidence Outside the United States." *Journal of Monetary Economics*, 21, pp. 73–83.

Sheppard, D. K. 1971. *The Growth and Role of U.K. Financial Institutions, 1880–1967*. London: Methuen.

Sommariva, A., and Tullio, G. 1986. German *Macroeconomic History, 1880–1979*. Basingstoke, U.K.: Macmillan.

Stock, J. H. 1987. "Measuring Business Cycle Time." *Journal of Political Economy*, 95, pp. 1240–61.

Stock, J. H. and M. W. Watson. 1998. "Business Cycle Fluctuations in U.S. Macroeconomic Time Series." NBER Working Paper No. 6528.

Temin, P. 1989. *Lessons from the Great Depression*. Lionel Robbins Lectures. Cambridge, MA: The MIT Press.

Thorp, W. L. 1926. *Business Annals*. NBER, New York.

Zarnowitz, V. 1992. *Business Cycles. Theory, History, Indicators, and Forecasting*. Chicago: University of Chicago Press.

DISCUSSION

Richard N. Cooper*

This paper by Michael Bergman, Michael Bordo, and Lars Jonung presents a number of statistics on annual fluctuations in economic activity drawn from 13 countries over the period 1873 to 1995. It first transforms the raw estimates on GDP, its various components, money supply, and consumer price indices by calculating the cyclic component around trends, using a Baxter-King band-pass filter. It then calculates, under four different monetary regimes covering the periods 1876 to 1913, 1920 to 1938, 1948 to 1972, and 1973 to 1995, variances and correlation coefficients for the transformed data, both within and between countries. Several generalizations emerge from these calculations, generalizations that are comfortably confirming of the conventional wisdom about business cycles. These generalizations are usefully summarized in the concluding section of the paper, and need not be repeated here. Rather, I will offer some remarks on the tasks the authors performed and their conclusion that "the cyclical pattern ... appears to remain surprisingly stable across time, regimes, and countries" and then on the broader question of international origins and transmission of the business cycle.

As a backdrop to my comments on the authors' calculations, I provide Tables 1 and 2, which show the years in which economic activity (as measured by real GDP) actually turned down in nine countries during the periods 1873 to 1913 and 1957 to 1994. The data are taken from Angus Maddison (1995, Table B-10).

Table 1, covering the gold standard era, shows only nine years (1882, 1887, 1898–99, 1905–07, 1911–12) of 41 in which at least one country of the nine did not experience a downturn. Second, only in 1908 did as many as

---

*Maurits C. Boas Professor of International Economics, Harvard University.

Table 1
Downturns in Real GDP, 1873 to 1913

	USA	Canada	UK	Germany	Netherlands	Belgium	France	Italy	Sweden
1873					X		X		
1874	X							X	
1875		X				X			X
1876		X		X	X		X	X	
1877				X					X
1878		X					X		X
1879		X		X	X		X		X
1880					X				
1881						X		X	
1882									
1883								X	
1884						X	X		
1885		X	X				X		X
1886									X
1887									
1888	X				X			X	
1889								X	
1890					X				
1891				X				X	
1892		X	X					X	
1893	X	X			X				
1894	X							X	
1895		X					X		
1896	X	X							
1897							X	X	
1898									
1899									
1900		X			X		X		
1901			X		X		X		X
1902							X	X	X
1903			X						
1904	X				X				
1905									
1906									
1907									
1908	X	X	X		X		X		X
1909									X
1910							X	X	
1911									
1912									
1913							X		

Source: Angus Maddison, 1995, *Monitoring the World Economy 1820–1992*. Table B-10, "GDP Indices for 17 Advanced Capitalist Countries," pp. 148–51. Organisation for Economic Cooperation and Development, Paris.

six countries experience a downturn, while five turned down in 1876 and again in 1879. Third, Belgium experienced only one downturn during the entire 41-year period, while France experienced 14 downturns and Italy and the Netherlands each experienced 12.

These observations on the untransformed data suggest several conclusions. First, most downturns are domestic in origin and are not powerfully transmitted to the other important trading nations. In particular, downturns in the world's leading trading country, Britain, are not notably reflected (as downturns) in its industrial trading partners, either contemporaneously or with a lag, with the possible exceptions of 1879, 1892–93, 1908, and, arguably, 1900–01.

Second, someone especially interested in international transmission would concentrate on 1876, which affected the Continental countries (and, oddly, Canada), on 1879, and on 1908, which affected mainly the maritime nations.

Third, the single downturn for Belgium is not believable, given the 12 downturns in the Netherlands and 14 in France. (Belgium did not experience exceptional growth during this period, its rate of 2.0 percent a year being the slowest after France, the United Kingdom, and Sweden.) That raises the question—a general one—about how good the annual real GDP data are for any of the countries in the pre-1914 period. Most of them, to be sure, reflect painstaking work by economic historians, but often on the basis of fragmentary data, much drawn from censuses taken much less frequently than annually, so that annual data involve heavy imputation from relatively few annual time series, or interpolations. In either case, an analysis of annual fluctuations of such data should be suspect.

Table 2 records downturns in real GDP in the nine countries for the period 1957 to 1994 (the decade 1948–1956 is blank except for the United Kingdom and Belgium in 1952 and the United States and Canada in 1954). Two points are noteworthy about Table 2, especially in contrast to Table 1. First, over the 48 years there have been few recessions (defined as a decline in real GDP from one calendar year to another) since the 1940s, with the United Kingdom at a maximum of seven and Sweden with six, three of which were contiguous (that is, one long recession). Second, the recessions for most countries have been concentrated in the years 1958, 1975, 1981–82, and 1993, suggesting strong international transmission. In particular, all the recessions in the United States, the world's leading economy and trading nation, were accompanied by recessions elsewhere. Of course, two (1975, 1981) and arguably three (1991) of the recessions were associated with major price shocks from the world petroleum market, with their simultaneous price-increasing and contractionary effects. "Stagflation" resulted from the inflationary impulse from the world's single most important commodity input, from the initial contrac-

Table 2
Downturns in Real GDP, 1957 to 1994

	USA	Canada	UK	Germany	Netherlands	Belgium	France	Italy	Sweden
1957									
1958	X		X		X	X			
1959									
1960									
1961									
1962									
1963									
1964									
1965									
1966									
1967				X					
1968									
1969									
1970									
1971									
1972									
1973									
1974	X		X						
1975	X		X	X	X	X	X	X	
1976									
1977									X
1978									
1979									
1980			X						
1981			X		X	X			X
1982	X	X		X	X				
1983									
1984									
1985									
1986									X
1987									
1988									
1989									
1990		X							
1991	X	X	X						X
1992			X						X
1993				X		X	X	X	X
1994									

Source: See Table 1.

tionary impact of the price increase, and from the anti-inflationary policy reactions in the major countries.

The authors are careful to point out that their correlations do not imply causation. Indeed, my impression is that it was agreed long ago that the causal dynamics of business cycles could not be discerned by inspecting annual data, however carefully. Quarterly and preferably monthly data are needed. And inventories, excluded from consideration, historically have played a crucial role in both booms and busts.

The data in the paper are de-trended, but we are not told how the trends are calculated. Implicitly recessions are defined as downward deviations from trend, whether or not GDP actually declined—that is, to include what is sometimes called a growth recession. The authors persuade themselves that their technique is satisfactory since for the United States it tracks the recessions as carefully and judgmentally defined by the NBER. But in fact the filtered data correctly date only 15 of the 26 recessions since 1885, that is, less than 60 percent. I do not consider that a good fit. Moreover, it is hardly surprising that cycles are pervasive with a technique that searches for periodicity of two to eight years around long-term trends.

Whether recessions should be defined as downward deviations from some (which?) trend or as absolute downturns, as in Tables 1 and 2, depends on the underlying purpose of the analysis. For studying the internal causal dynamics of business cycles, at least sharp upward or downward deviations from trend probably offer useful information although, as noted above, quarterly or monthly data are necessary for such analysis. From the point of view of human welfare and hence policy, however, more often than not there is a major difference between a downward deviation from a rapidly rising GDP and an absolute downturn. The latter implies unutilized capital and labor, hence wasted resources, and the hardships that may accompany lost income. Downward deviation from a rising trend need not imply any of these, and often does not. So what is the justification here for transforming the data, to isolate their cyclical components?

I turn now to some broader observations on the changes in industrial economies that have occurred over the past century and a quarter. The most dramatic by far, in my judgment, is the reduction in the fraction of the labor force required for food production. In 1880 this was around one-half in the United States, France, and Germany, and over half in Italy (but already down to 13 percent in Britain). By 1995 it was below 5 percent in almost all the countries covered (7 percent in Italy and Finland, 2.8 percent in the United States). The share of agricultural income dropped by almost as much. The share of manufacturing employment first rose dramatically over this period, then has declined sharply since the 1960s. It is difficult to believe that changes of these magnitudes have not affected the dynamics of the business cycle significantly.

Another major secular change concerns the role of women in paid employment. Women on farms work hard and long, in ways that may not be measured in GDP. Increased female participation in paid employment implies that measured GDP has grown more rapidly than the real output of goods and services. Since much of the unmeasured production undoubtedly was directly consumed, the ratio of measured consumption to measured production is understated in earlier decades; and the variability of measured consumption perhaps exaggerates true variability in earlier years.

A third secular change concerns growth in the importance of government expenditure. This was typically 5 percent of GDP around 1900 (10 percent in France). By 1995 it was around 20 percent of GDP in most industrial countries, and over 40 percent if transfer payments are added to government purchases of goods and services (somewhat lower in the United States and Japan). Insofar as such expenditures and transfers are not subject to the forces of the business cycle or, as in the case of unemployment compensation, may be countercyclical, business cycles should have lower variability, all else equal, in the late twentieth century than in the late nineteenth century. On the other hand, sharp changes in government expenditure, as in the several dramatic increases and declines in defense spending that took place in the United States over the period 1949 to 1995, could be a source of greater variability than was the case in the nineteenth century. Some cross-country comparisons of large movements in government expenditures might be fruitful.

A relatively unchanged economic cycle that survived these dramatic secular changes in modern economies would be robust indeed. If it exists, might it be an endogenous consequence of lags between perceived new demand for investment and sales from the product of that investment?

Finally, the world has experienced from time to time major investment-enhancing technological innovations, such as the introduction of electricity, automobiles, and civil aircraft, each of which required large investments in infrastructure as well as in products. These innovations were introduced in quantity into different countries at markedly different times, and that would provide another potential source for inter-country differences in cyclical timing.

In sum, I find the Bergman, Bordo, and Jonung results interesting but not compelling. My taste runs to more detailed and precise examination of the common and interlinked factors in those time periods where there seems to be some direct connection between downturns (or exceptional booms) in different countries.

THE ROLE OF INTEREST RATE POLICY IN THE GENERATION AND PROPAGATION OF BUSINESS CYCLES: WHAT HAS CHANGED SINCE THE '30S?

Christopher A. Sims*

Governments have two broad classes of macroeconomic impact. One has to do with the way government liabilities, including cash, interact with other traded assets in the financial system. The other has to do with government absorption and production of real resources through non-neutral taxation and provision of government goods and services like roads, schooling, and public health measures. Some evidence suggests that fluctuations in the latter class of impact are important,[1] and it can be shown theoretically that the effects could be substantial and are hard to pin down quantitatively on the basis of a priori reasoning.[2] Policy discussion and the macroeconomic literature may have overemphasized the former, financial class of impacts.

Nonetheless, this paper focuses on the financial impact. It presents empirical evidence, similar to much that has appeared previously using time series statistical modeling, that only a small portion of business cycle variation in the United States since 1948 can be attributed to fluctuations in monetary policy. Though this conclusion is not universally accepted, it is far from new. This paper therefore goes on to consider two additional possible ways of demonstrating important effects of monetary policy. It expands the usual time frame of the literature, extending its model to the interwar period, and it examines the behavior of the model with counterfactual variations in the equation describing policy behavior.

The paper presents evidence that the same methods of identifying the effects of monetary policy that have proved useful in the analysis of

---
*Henry Ford II Professor of Economics, Yale University.
[1] See Garcia-Mila (1987).
[2] See Baxter and King (1993).

postwar U.S. data can be applied to interwar data, where they show responses of the private sector to monetary policy shifts to have been quite similar then to what they are now. The fact that these methods prove robust in most respects across such widely varying historical circumstances provides additional support for their reliability in both periods.

The nature of private sector disturbances was different in these two periods, however, and the nature of monetary policy response to shocks also differed. During the interwar period, shocks that implied expected future price changes were not quickly met by countervailing monetary policy. Also, during the interwar period, disturbances that resulted in a flow out of bank deposits into currency were important. Such disturbances were met with interest rate increases, which might have exacerbated their effects on the banking system. Experimentation with counterfactual specifications of policy behavior suggests that in both periods, prices could have been kept more stable by a different monetary policy, but that there was only modest room for reducing cyclical fluctuations in output by modifying monetary policy.

Can we conclude that monetary policy has had little to do with the improved stability of economic activity in the postwar period? Only if we construe monetary policy narrowly, as the normal tightening and loosening of credit conditions associated with interest rate changes. Periods of financial crisis or "liquidity crunch" are treated by the modeling methods used here as surprises originating outside the policy process, but this is true only in a narrow sense. Beliefs of the public about the adequacy of bank supervisory regulation, and about the central bank's commitment to and capacity to act as lender of last resort and prevent the kind of accelerating inflation or deflation that ends in crisis, are determined by some aspects of monetary policy and institutions, although not by the month-to-month or year-to-year management of interest rate policy via open market operations.[3]

It is in this latter aspect of monetary policy, its provision of a stable base for financial markets, that it is most fundamentally entangled with fiscal policy. The paper invokes the recently articulated fiscal theory of the price level, which may provide some insight into the sources of policy difficulties in the Great Depression and in recent international banking, monetary, and fiscal crises. This line of thinking also suggests reasons for the observed greater postwar financial stability in the United States, and cautions concerning future developments in the U.S. and international monetary systems.

---

[3] Bernanke (1983) has argued for the importance of "non-monetary" financial mechanisms of propagation in the Great Depression. The results in this paper confirm his and, indeed, suggest less importance for interest rate and reserve policy than his discussion.

Although it is not essential to understanding this paper's empirical evidence, it may be worth recognizing here that the paper uses a somewhat different vocabulary and point of view than does much macroeconomic policy discussion. We are not dividing the influences of government into "aggregate demand" and "aggregate supply" components, as would the viewpoint of standard Keynesian hydraulics. Expectations of future monetary and fiscal policy can influence current inflationary pressures without changing current real flows of expenditures. In contrast with standard monetarist views, we are treating monetary and fiscal policy symmetrically, emphasizing the point that the price level, the ratio at which government nominal liabilities trade for real commodities, depends on the valuation of the entire portfolio of government assets. The fundamental determinants of the price level do not depend on whether reserve requirements are eliminated or whether privately issued interest-bearing money replaces currency. And of course the entire focus of interest in the paper is on the possible inadequacy of a viewpoint, like that of simple real business cycle theory, which ignores the financial impact of the government on macroeconomic fluctuations.

This "fiscal theory of the price level," or FTPL, point of view has been articulated in a growing stream of recent papers; for example, Ben-Habib, Schmidt-Grohe, and Uribe (1998); Cochrane (1988); Leeper (1991); Woodford (1994 and 1995); Sims (1994 and 1997). While some of this literature has emphasized the possibility of seeing inflation as determined primarily or entirely by fiscal policy, the theory implies that with stable fiscal policy of a certain plausible form, interest rate policy conducted through open market operations can be the main source of government-generated fluctuations in inflationary and deflationary pressures, just as it is in conventional macroeconomic theory. This paper's empirical work pursues this possibility. The distinctive FTPL point of view emerges mainly in the discussion of explanations outside the models estimated, for the behavior the models uncover.

Monetary Policy and the Business Cycle

The reason the importance of monetary policy to cyclical fluctuations remains an unsettled issue is that observed data can offer no simple resolution of it. The money stock, bank reserves, and interest rates reflect events in financial markets, which in turn are sensitive to every kind of important (and possibly also unimportant) influence on the economy. So while these variables are the main levers of monetary policy, we can reach misleading conclusions by simply plotting or regressing measures of economic activity on these "policy variables." Early monetarist empirical research largely did just that, invoking an assumption that the money stock was properly regarded as determined by policy, with response of the money stock to disturbances originating in the private sector less important than independent variation in monetary policy.[4] A plot of interest rates against output over the postwar period shows that interest rate rises preceded each recession. Some economists have taken the view that this leaves no room for doubt or subtlety: Monetary policy must have produced the recessions. But as it has become standard to use multivariate methods of time series analysis to characterize and interpret the data on interest rates, money stock, and business activity, it has become clear that simple bivariate interpretations of the data are misleading. In fact, the most likely interpretation of the data gives independent variation in monetary policy a modest role.

The literature that has reached this conclusion, concentrating mainly on postwar U.S. data, is by now extensive. It has been surveyed recently in Leeper, Sims, and Zha (1996). Rather than repeat that summary, this paper begins by encapsulating the results of the literature in a representative model. The model is constructed with an eye to allowing its extension, with minimal need to change data definitions, to the interwar period. We consider the joint behavior of six monthly time series that can be collected in more or less comparable form for both postwar and interwar periods: industrial production (IP), consumer price index (CPI), currency in circulation (Currency), currency plus demand deposits (M1), Federal Reserve discount rate (Discount), and a commodity price index (Pcomm).[5] All variables are measured in natural log units except the discount rate, which is measured in percentage points.

The use of the discount rate as the interest rate variable does not match most of the literature. Since the persuasive article of Bernanke and Blinder (1992), the most widely used interest rate in studies of monetary policy has been the federal funds rate. However, the federal funds market did not exist at the beginning of the postwar period. The discount window played a more important role at the beginning of the interwar period than it has since, and the discount rate is probably widely regarded as a lagging reflection of monetary policy in recent years. Other interest rates, in particular the 4- to 6-month commercial paper rate, are available over the full period of interest. However, spreads between private and government interest rates were more variable in the interwar period than they have been recently, and the degree to which monetary policy deliberately controlled private short rates was probably lower in

---

[4] Milton Friedman wrote in 1958, "Changes in the money stock are a consequence as well as an independent cause of changes in income and prices, though once they occur they will in their turn produce still further effects on income and prices. This consideration blurs the relation between money and prices but does not reverse it. For there is much evidence...that even during business cycles the money stock plays a largely independent role" (Friedman 1958).

[5] Some of these series required splicing of data from more than one source, so the reader is advised at some point to look at the Appendix describing the data in more detail.

the interwar period. Most of the calculations reported in this paper were carried out both with the 4- to 6-month commercial paper rate and with the discount rate. It is perhaps surprising that the results for the postwar period turn out to be qualitatively unaffected by which rate is used. The fit of the model for variables other than the interest rate is slightly better in the postwar period with the commercial paper rate, but the statistics testing the stability of the model across the postwar sample are slightly better for the version with the discount rate. In the interwar model, use of the commercial paper rate produces estimates that imply a brief, small, but statistically significant positive response of IP to a monetary contraction before the response turns negative. This no doubt reflects some inaccuracy in the identification of the model, and it leads to small anomalies in plots of results. It is for these reasons that the presentation concentrates on results with the discount rate.

The notation for the model is

$$A(L)y(t) = C + \epsilon(t), \tag{1}$$

where y is the $n \times 1$ column vector of variables in the model, A is a polynomial in the lag operator L with $n \times n$ matrix coefficients A_i on the L^i, C is a vector of constants, and ϵ is a vector of random disturbances, serially uncorrelated, uncorrelated with ys dated earlier, and with the correlation matrix the identity. This notation is a little different from that most common in the literature, in that it normalizes none of the coefficients in A_0 to one, and correspondingly normalizes the variances of the disturbances ϵ to one. Models with different A polynomials that have the same values of the reduced-form coefficient polynomial $B(L) = A_0^{-1}A(L)$ and the same value of the reduced-form residual covariance matrix $\Sigma = A_0'A_0$ imply the same distribution for the data.

The model follows the existing literature in assuming a delay of at least one month in the impact of interest rate changes on the private sector behavior that determines a block of variables including IP and CPI. The contemporaneous correlation of interest rate changes with economic activity tends to be positive; this assumption rules out the possibility that this positive correlation might arise from a positive effect of monetary contraction on business activity. The assumption is justified by the argument that the behavior of individual consumers, workers, and businessmen that determines industrial production and final goods prices does not involve continuous, sharp, finely calculated responses to market signals. This is to some extent due to technologically determined inertia, but probably more importantly to the lack of sufficient computational capacity on the part of individuals to make such continuous readjustments. Short-term fluctuations in money market rates are not an important day-to-day influence on most nonfinancial economic decisions, not because people cannot look up the federal funds rate in the newspaper or because it would be very difficult or expensive to react, but because people have too much else of greater personal importance absorbing their attention.[6]

The model differs from most previous literature, and follows Leeper, Sims, and Zha (1996) in including the money stock, and in this model also currency, in the block of variables determined within the sluggish sector. The usual money demand or liquidity preference relation is derived as an arbitrage relation connecting returns on bonds to the implicit yield on money balances. The derivation does not imply any lag in the relation. In treating currency and money this way, therefore, we are precluding a conventional money demand equation with no lags. However, the same reasoning that justifies assuming sluggishness in the reaction of IP and CPI to financial market signals implies that we should expect similar delay in the reaction of individuals and businesses to financial signals that imply they should deliberately change holdings of cash and demand deposits. Such holdings can of course react instantly to changes in flows of income and expenditure—to the same disturbances, in other words, that act on IP and CPI. Other models in the literature have produced reasonable results allowing for a money demand equation that includes a contemporaneous interest rate term. But it is difficult to justify a claim that disturbances to the aspects of private behavior that determine the money demand arbitrage relation should be unrelated to other shocks to private sector behavior. If money demand shocks are related to other shocks to private behavior, then the appearance of the interest rate in "money demand" must make it appear in all equations of the sluggish block, and this undermines identification.

An identifying restriction that is particularly important in extending the model to the interwar years is that the behavior of the Federal Reserve does not react within the month to IP or CPI. This does not mean that the Federal Reserve is assumed not to care about these variables. It simply reflects the fact that information on these variables is not available within the month. The specification does allow reaction by the Fed to these variables with a month's delay, and it allows contemporaneous reaction of the Fed to currency and M1, which the Fed monitors via its regulatory role, and to Pcomm, which reflects publicly known prices in continuously functioning auction markets.

The pattern of restrictions we have discussed can be displayed in the matrix shown here as Table 1. In this table, Xs represent unconstrained coefficients in A_0, 0s represent coefficients constrained on the basis of behavioral reasoning, as given above, and −s represent coefficients

---

[6] In Sims (1998a), I develop an argument that we should expect all reactions of individuals to external signals to behave, to a linear approximation, like relations that involve both lags (apparent inertia) and idiosyncratic random errors.

Table 1
Identifying Restrictions

Equations	Variables					
	IP	CPI	Currency	M1	Discount	Pcomm
IP	X	—	—	—	0	0
CPI	X	X	—	—	0	0
Currency	X	X	X	—	0	0
M1	X	X	X	X	0	0
Policy	0	0	X	X	X	X
Pcomm	X	X	X	X	X	X

constrained to zero as normalizations. Note that the first four equations, represented by the first four rows of the table, are distinguished only by normalizing restrictions. They do not have distinct behavioral interpretations. Only the block of four equations, representing sluggish components of private sector behavior, has an interpretation. The last row represents the reaction of commodity prices, in continuously clearing markets, to all current information.

The restricted matrix is almost, but not quite, in triangular form. Furthermore, it has only 20, not 21 free coefficients, meaning that the A polynomial has one less coefficient than the unrestricted reduced form model. Iterative methods are therefore required to estimate the model, but they can be executed quickly and reliably.[7]

POSTWAR RESULTS

The Patterns of Response to Policy and of Policy

When this model, with the order of A (the number of lags) set to seven, is estimated over the full 1948:8 to 1997:10 sample period, the result implies the pattern of responses to behavioral disturbances displayed in Figure 1. Each small graph shows the pattern of response of the variable that labels its row to the disturbance that labels its column. The center line is the estimated response itself, and the upper and lower lines

---

[7] The estimation also uses stochastic prior information, rather than ad hoc setting to zero of insignificant coefficients, to control the bad effects of estimating so many free coefficients at once. The methods are based on ideas in Sims and Zha (1998a), although here they can be implemented entirely with "dummy observations," making the calculations simpler than those described in that article.

Figure 1
Responses to Identified Shocks, 1948:8 to 1997:10

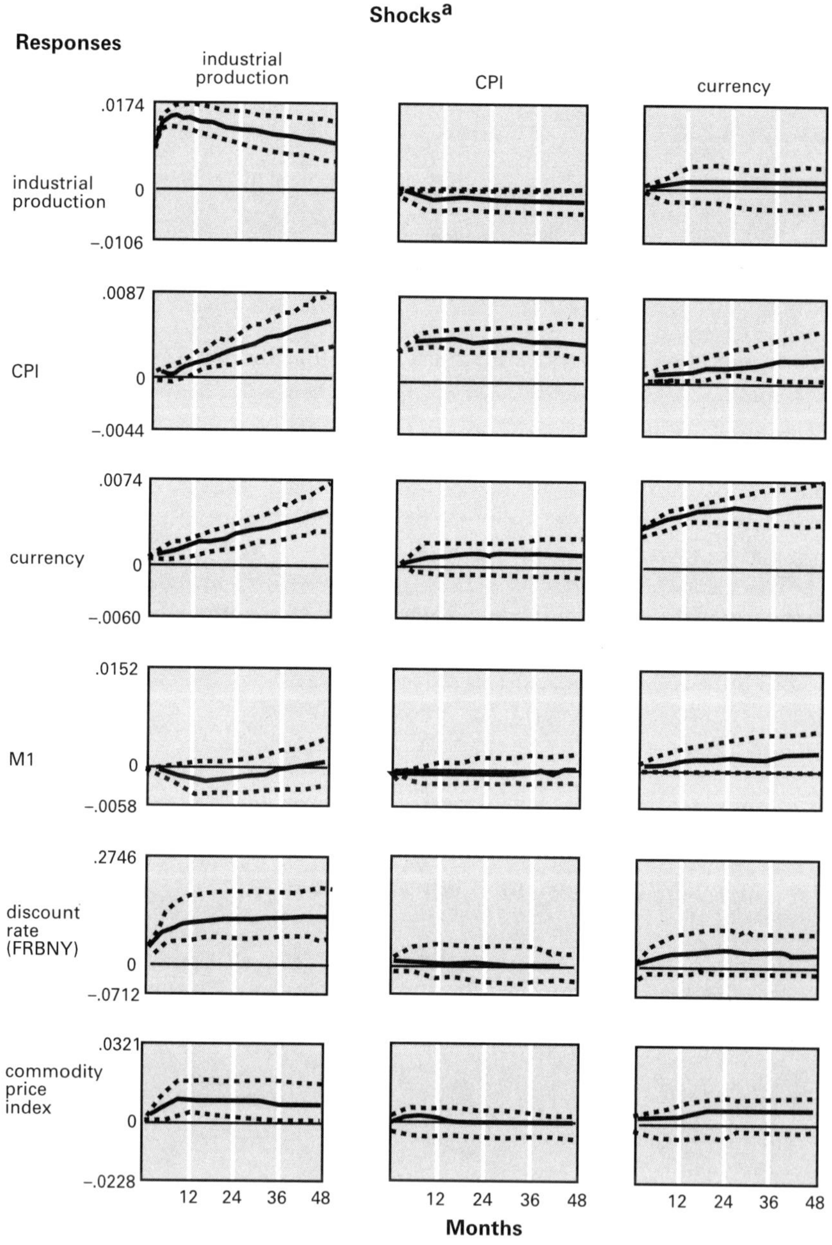

Shocks[a]

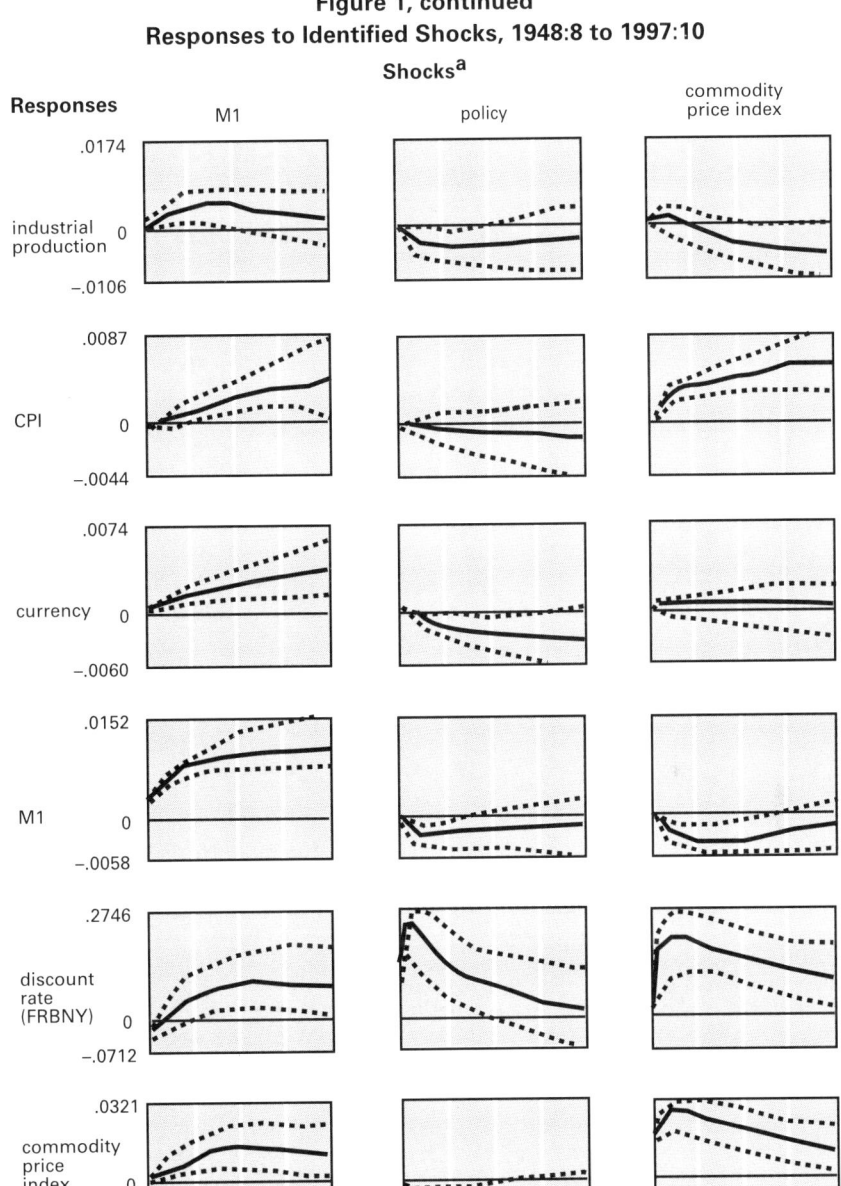

**Figure 1, continued
Responses to Identified Shocks, 1948:8 to 1997:10**

a Each shock represents a 1-standard-deviation disturbance in the corresponding equation, with the equations defined by the rows of Table 1.
Note: See the text and the Data Appendix for descriptions of the series. All variables are measured in natural log units except the discount rate, which is measured in percentage points. Upper and lower lines in each graph define 90 percent probability bands for the responses.

define a 90 percent probability band for the responses.[8] The column labeled "policy" shows the response of the rest of the economy to a typical (one-standard-deviation) disturbance in the policy equation. It displays a pattern of responses that is familiar from the previous literature. Interest rates rise and then slowly begin drifting back toward the mean. Currency and M1 both fall and remain low. Commodity prices and CPI both decline, with the decline in CPI small and delayed, while that in Pcomm is substantial and immediate. IP falls and returns very slowly toward trend. The error bands show that there is substantial uncertainty about the magnitude of the responses to policy, and in the case of the CPI response, even about the sign of it.

Looking across a single row in the figure, the relative sizes of the plotted responses show the relative importance of the sources of disturbance labeled in the columns in generating variation in the variable labeled in the row. We see from the discount rate row that policy shocks produce the largest impact on the interest rate, but that others, particularly the Pcomm shock, the IP shock, and the M1 shock, are cumulatively more important in generating interest rate variation. That is, though policy disturbances account for a substantial fraction of variation in interest rates, particularly in the short run, most variation in them is generated by systematic responses to disturbances originating outside the policy equations. Furthermore, the system implies a distinctly active response of policy to disturbances that imply inflationary pressure. The three non-policy shocks that imply interest rate increases also are the three that imply the largest increases in expected future CPI inflation and in current and expected future Pcomm levels.[9] In the case of Pcomm shocks, the rise in interest rates is sufficient to produce a decline in the money stock in the face of the inflationary pressure, and in the case of IP shocks, the interest rate rise is sufficient to hold the money stock essentially constant in the face of a rise in output and prices. The M1 shock does not show such a strong restrictive response to inflationary pressure. Interest rates rise, but only with a delay, and M1 rises substantially. This looks like what might be expected if monetary policy partially accommodated an expansionary disturbance originating elsewhere, for example, in an increased current or expected future fiscal deficit.

---

[8] The bands are computed as Bayesian posterior probability bands, using the approach described in Sims and Zha (1998b), except that the Monte Carlo simulations used the adaptive Metropolis-Hastings algorithm described in Sims (1998b). The bands were constructed from a 500-element subsample of 5,000 iterations of the simulation algorithm, which had an effective sample size of about 500.

[9] CPI shocks, which do not generate a strong interest rate response, account for a substantial part of variation in the level of CPI but they move the level in a single step, without implying much expected future inflation.

Stability of Behavior Over Time Within the Postwar Period

The rhetoric of monetary policy debate has certainly changed over the 1948–97 period. Attempts to model the behavior of monetary authorities over this period (including the attempt represented by this paper's model) can find statistically significant changes in behavior. The Lucas critique has conditioned many macroeconomists to think in terms of "regime shifts" as the only internally consistent way to think about improving policy, and hence to look for them statistically.[10] Why then does this paper present results from a fixed-coefficients linear model fit to the entire 1948–97 period?

Several arguments favor sticking with a fixed model for the period.

- Tests for shifts in regime based on conventional significance levels are inconsistent, in the technical econometric sense. This is not a strong argument here, since we do not actually believe in a literally fixed model. Nonetheless, the problem is symptomatic of a broader problem with conventional tests—in large samples, they will reject the hypothesis of parameter constancy even in cases where the parameter changes detected are trivially small.
- Shifts in policy rule of modest size, sustained over only a few quarters or years, may have been quite non-random from the point of view of some participants in the policy process at the time, or from the point of view of ex post statistical analysis, while still having been perceived as unpredictable randomness from the point of view of economic agents.
- As always in statistical modeling, we face a trade-off of bias versus precision. The more complex a scheme of variation in policy behavior parameters we allow for, the less precise can be our estimates of that scheme. We may be sure that a fixed model is not the absolute truth, while believing that nonetheless its bias is small enough that we would obtain worse results with a model that allowed for shifts in policy behavior.
- Using statistical criteria that explicitly gauge the trade-off of bias with precision and overcome the inconsistency problem in conventional statistical tests, we conclude that models that allow no change in parameters are preferred.

The quantitative evidence is as follows: Comparing the fit of a single model fit to 1948–97 with that of two separate models, in which all parameters, including the residual covariance matrices, are fit to the separate periods 1948:8 to 1979:6 and 1979:7 to 1997:10, twice the

---

[10] Macroeconomists who think this way are mistaken. See the section below, "What about the Lucas Critique?"

difference in log likelihoods (a statistic we will here call S) is 849.3379. The difference in numbers of free parameters is 279. Conventional statistical tests, based on asymptotic theory and using a 5 percent significance level, would certainly reject the null hypothesis of no change in parameters. The Akaike criterion, which aims at improving forecast performance but does not overcome the inconsistency of conventional tests, rejects for S exceeding twice the degrees of freedom, which would here be a threshold of 558. The most widely used consistent model selection criterion is the Schwarz criterion, which compares S to degrees of freedom times log of sample size; here it leads to a threshold of 1780, so that the fixed model is strongly favored. Another consistent criterion, which favors smaller models less strongly than Schwarz's, is the Hannan-Quinn criterion. It compares S to the degrees of freedom times twice log(log(sample size)) and here leads to a threshold of 1034, again strongly favoring the fixed model.[11]

That consistent model-selection criteria favor a fixed model is all the more remarkable given that the tests allow for changes in disturbance variance as well as changes in the coefficients themselves. Monetary policy from late 1979 through 1982 was announced as allowing for increased variation in interest rates, and the variance of changes in interest rates, including the discount rate, was indeed much higher in this period than in the rest of the postwar period. But this in itself does not imply a change in the shape of any of the responses plotted in Figure 1. In fact, it could be accounted for simply by increasing the variance of the disturbance to the monetary policy equation (which would imply increasing the relative size of the policy column of Figure 1 during this period, without changing its shape or that of other columns). If we allow for a change in the variance of the policy equation disturbance in this period, while otherwise holding model parameters fixed, it is likely that we would account for most of the evidence of parameter change in the data without requiring any alteration of our conclusions on the shapes of policy responses.

It might be supposed that, since the 1979–82 period was so clearly unusual, it would be better to simply omit those years in fitting the model

---

[11] For more discussion of these criteria, see, for example, Lütkepohl (1991, section 4.3). In constructing these statistics, the model was estimated in reduced form and the stochastic prior information used in constructing the estimated responses was not used. Because of the tendency of models estimated without use of stochastic prior information to be biased toward stationarity and to imply excessively accurate long-run predictions from sample initial conditions, testing for sample breaks this way is problematic. However, use of prior information would probably reduce, not increase, evidence of differences across subsamples. If data on the commercial paper rate replace data on the discount rate, the twice-log-likelihood-difference statistic becomes 969, which still gives the same conclusion by both the Schwarz and the Hannan-Quinn criteria, though it is somewhat less strongly in favor of the fixed model than are the results with the discount rate.

and to make our checks for parameter stability omitting those years as well. But these years, precisely because they showed so much variability in interest rates, provide strong evidence on the effects of monetary policy. Omitting them substantially increases the uncertainty in estimates of the model. The best procedure would be to weight the observations for the policy equation lower in this period, in proportion to the higher variance of the period, while still using all the data, but we proceed with estimates that simply use the full sample without weighting.

INTERWAR RESULTS

Applying the same set of identifying restrictions to the interwar period 1919:8 to 1939:12, we find the responses displayed in Figure 2. The column corresponding to the effects of policy disturbances is qualitatively very similar to that in Figure 1. Note, though, that the scale on the output, CPI, and currency rows is more than double the scale on the corresponding rows for the postwar Figure 1. Because this period is shorter, the error bands are somewhat wider than for Figure 1.

Output shocks in the interwar period educed a much more accommodative response of monetary policy than did the smaller corresponding shocks in the postwar period. In the later period, a typical-sized output shock of about 1.5 percent generated an increase in the discount rate within a year of about 13 basis points. This was enough to keep M1 from increasing at all, and to keep the rise in commodity prices to about 1.3 percent. A corresponding shock in the interwar period raised output by 3.8 percent within the year, yet produced a rise in the discount rate of less than 5 basis points. This was reflected in M1's expanding with output, by about 1 percent, and in greater inflation, measured both by commodity prices and especially by the CPI.[12]

An especially interesting difference between the periods shows up in the currency shock column. Interwar currency shocks moved currency and M1 strongly in opposite directions, and the discount rate followed currency, not M1. Periods when people converted bank deposits to cash, corresponding to periods with positive currency shocks, reflected worries about the solvency and liquidity of the banking system. It is noteworthy that interwar monetary policy apparently accelerated the shrinkage in money by tightening—raising the discount rate—as deposits were draining out of the banking system.

To disturbances other than currency shocks, responses of the discount rate were generally smaller and more delayed in the interwar

---

[12] Bear in mind that this is a linear model, so it makes no distinction between increases and decreases. In the interwar period, monetary accommodation was of course often accommodation of recession and deflation, not of growth and inflation.

134   Christopher A. Sims

**Figure 2
Responses to Identified Shocks, 1919:8 to 1939:12**

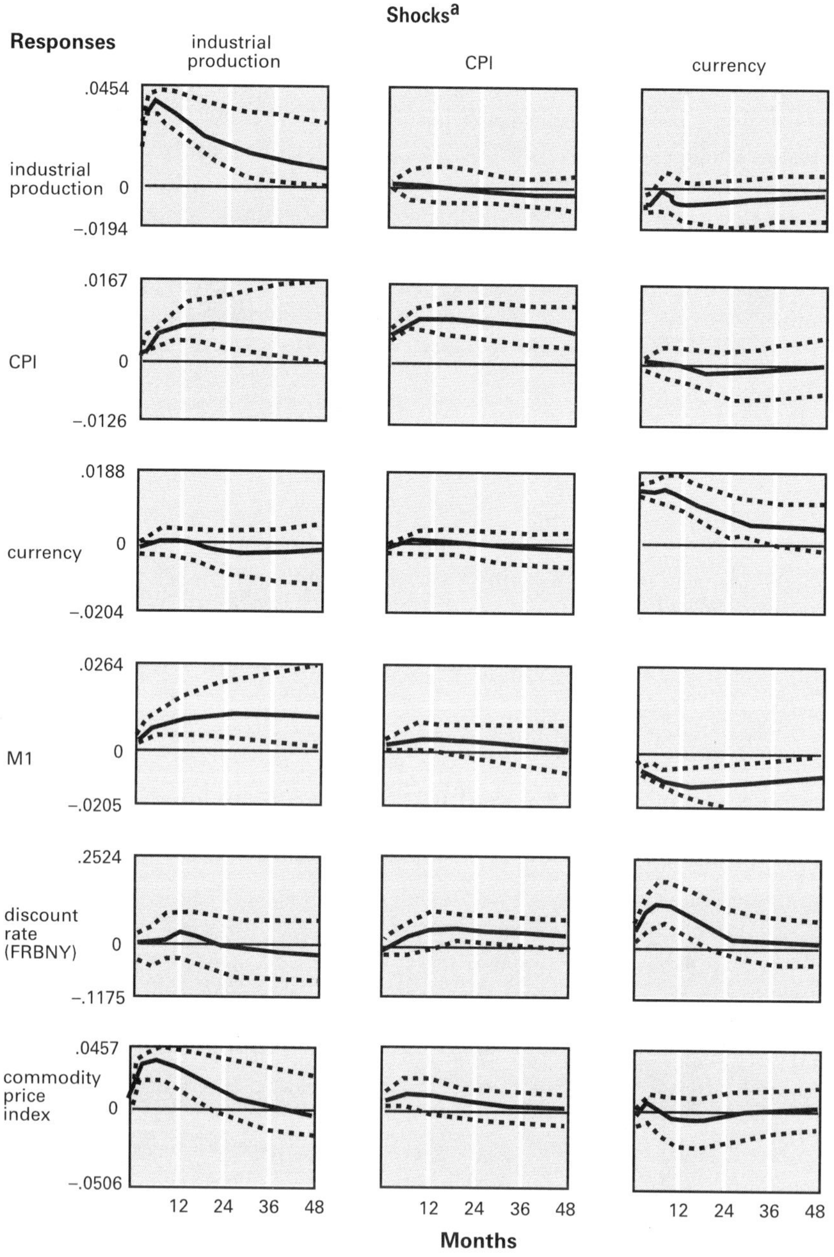

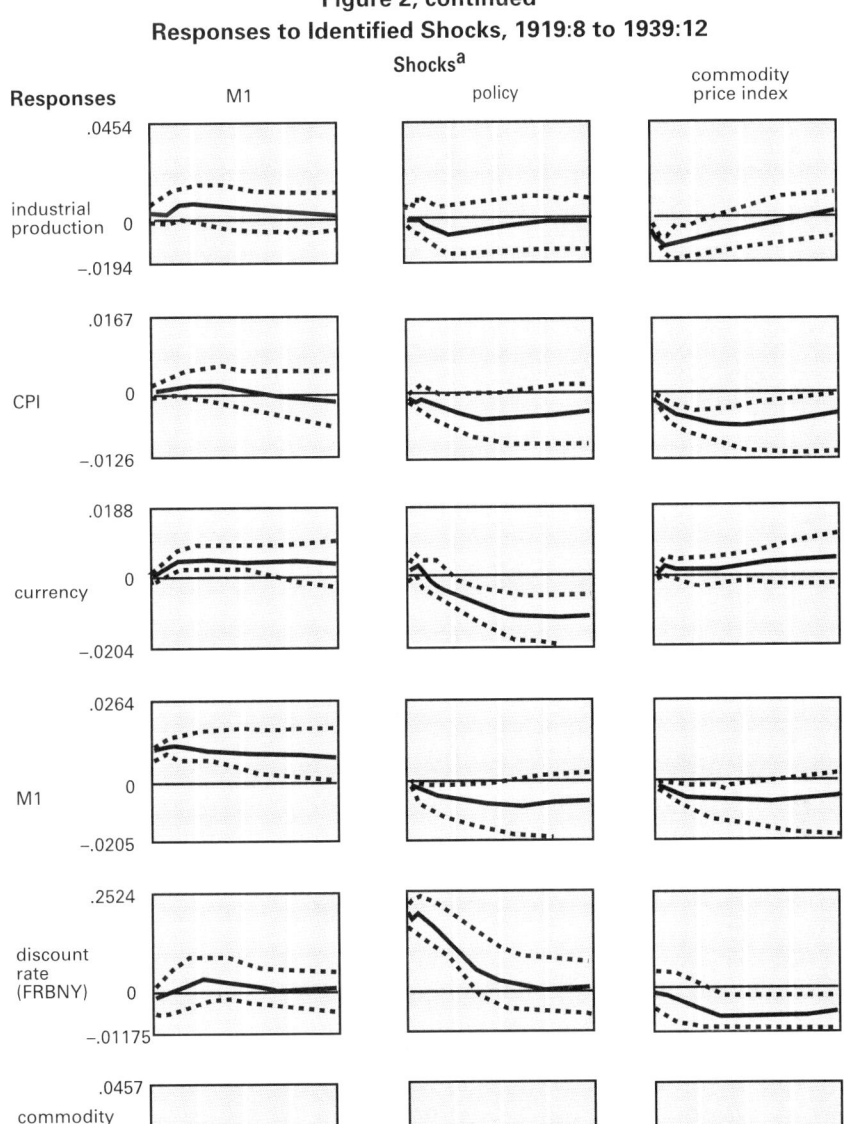

Figure 2, continued
Responses to Identified Shocks, 1919:8 to 1939:12

[a] Each shock represents a 1-standard-deviation disturbance in the corresponding equation, with the equations defined by the rows of Table 1.
Note: See the text and the Data Appendix for descriptions of the series. All variables are measured in natural log units except the discount rate, which is measured in percentage points. Upper and lower lines in each graph define 90 percent probability bands for the responses.

Table 2
48-Month Horizon Variance Decomposition, 1948–79

	IP	CPI	Currency	M1	Policy	Pcomm
IP	79%	1%	1%	5%	6%	8%
CPI	20%	21%	4%	19%	1%	35%
Currency	19%	1%	53%	14%	13%	1%
M1	1%	0%	5%	83%	3%	8%
Discount	26%	0%	3%	11%	22%	37%
Pcomm	13%	1%	1%	17%	19%	50%

Note: Numbers may not add to 100 because of rounding.

period, despite the large sizes of the shocks as measured by their effects on other variables.

THE CONTRIBUTION OF MONETARY POLICY TO FLUCTUATIONS

We can see directly from Figures 1 and 2 that the proportion of variability in IP in either period that is accounted for by disturbances in monetary policy is estimated as small. This follows from the fact that in the first row of the figures, all responses are much smaller in magnitude than the responses to IP shocks themselves. We can summarize what can be seen from the figures by allocating to the sources of disturbance the variance of forecast errors in all variables over the four years displayed in the figures. These allocations are summarized in Table 2 and Table 3. Each row of these tables sums to 100 percent, and shows where variation in the variable labeling the row originated during the period. Industrial production is accounted for mainly by its own disturbances in both periods. The discount rate is accounted for more by responses to variables other than policy than by policy disturbances in the postwar data, but the reverse is true in the interwar data.

Table 3
48-Month Horizon Variance Decomposition, 1919–39

	IP	CPI	Currency	M1	Policy	Pcomm
IP	83%	1%	4%	3%	3%	7%
CPI	30%	41%	0%	1%	10%	17%
Currency	3%	0%	44%	7%	43%	2%
M1	29%	1%	23%	26%	11%	9%
Discount	1%	9%	20%	2%	53%	15%
Pcomm	30%	4%	1%	1%	8%	57%

Note: Numbers may not add to 100 because of rounding.

Results like this do not of course directly imply that monetary policy is unimportant to cyclical fluctuations. They imply only that unpredictable variation in monetary policy has been unimportant. It could be true that monetary policy has been highly systematic and predictable, yet also that it could have greatly changed the pattern of fluctuations if it had taken a different course. We can use this model to gain some insight into how the economy's behavior might have differed, had monetary policy been systematically different. Indeed, we have seen that there are notable differences in the way the discount rate responded to the state of the economy in the interwar and in the postwar periods. The differences are largely in the direction that most economists would agree improves monetary policy: In the postwar period, interest rates rise more quickly and sharply in response to disturbances that predict inflationary pressure, and there is less tendency for the discount rate to rise when the public starts to substitute cash for deposits. At the same time, fluctuations have been smaller in the postwar period. Maybe the changes in the systematic behavior of monetary policy have been responsible for some of the improvement.

The modeling framework used here allows us to answer this question directly. We do so by excising the monetary policy equation of the system, the fifth row of the set of dynamic equations displayed in (1), from the model of one period, transplanting it into the model for the other period as a replacement for the original policy equation of that model, and observing how the resulting chimera behaves.[13]

Replaying the Great Depression with Postwar Monetary Policy

Consider first the outcome of sending an average of Arthur Burns, Paul Volcker, and the like back in time, to manage the Federal Reserve System in the '20s and '30s. The impulse responses of the grafted system are displayed in Figure 3, alongside the originally estimated responses for the 1919–39 period.

Changing the policy equation has a noticeable, if not large, effect. CPI and M1 respond less to IP shocks and to commodity price shocks with the postwar policy, while currency responds more. However, the effect on IP's responses to shocks is very small. IP shocks have a slightly less persistent effect on IP with the postwar policy. Perhaps surprisingly, the postwar policy behavior raises interest rates following an interwar currency shock, just as did the actual interwar policy. The increase in

---

[13] In doing this, we are subject to the "Lucas critique." The reflex reaction of many economists that this makes such exercises internally contradictory or misleading is mistaken. We take up this point at more length below. In the meantime, the reader is urged to proceed to see how interesting the results are before assessing whether they must be dismissed on doctrinal grounds.

138   Christopher A. Sims

**Figure 3
Responses: 1919 to 1939 Model, Actual and Counterfactual
Shocks**[a]

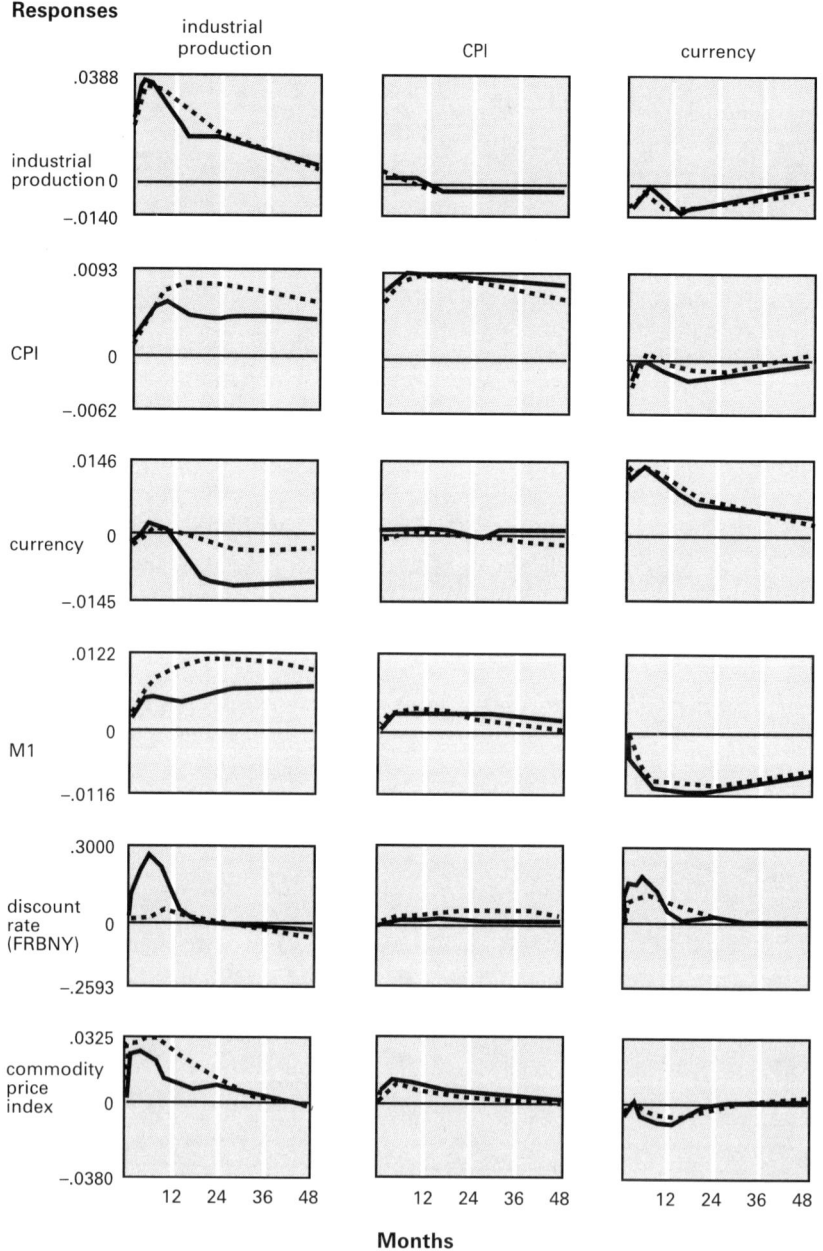

THE ROLE OF INTEREST RATE POLICY 139

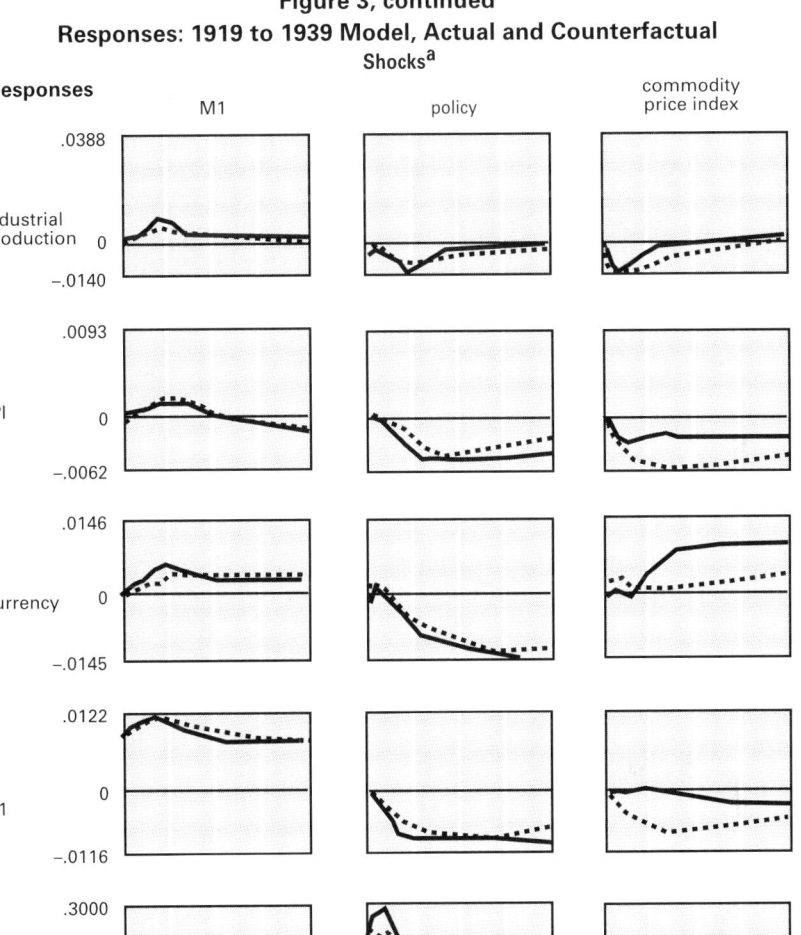

Figure 3, continued
Responses: 1919 to 1939 Model, Actual and Counterfactual Shocks[a]

[a] Each shock represents a 1-standard-deviation disturbance in the corresponding equation, with the equations defined by the rows of Table 1.
Note: The solid lines use the 1948-97 policy reaction function in the 1919-39 model, while the dotted lines match Figure 2, the original estimated responses for the 1919-39 model.

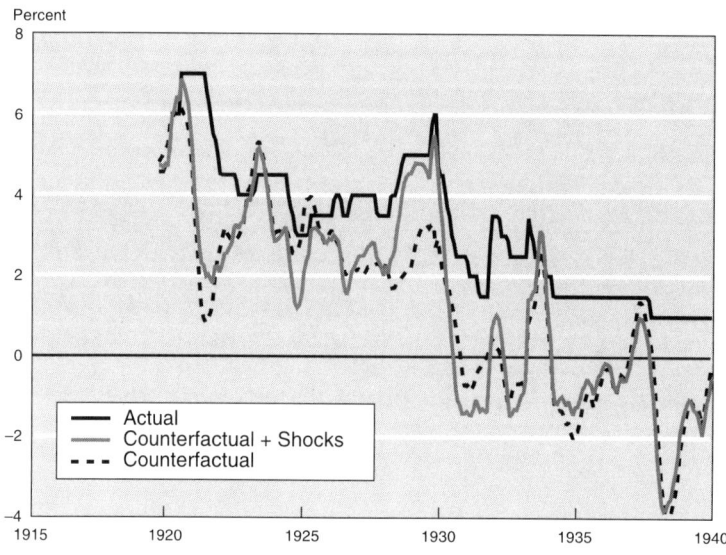

**Figure 4
Interwar Discount Rate, Actual and Counterfactual**

discount rate following this shock is less persistent than it was in the actual interwar data, but this does little to dampen the outflow of deposits as currency increases.

What would have been the historical outcome if these responses had characterized actual interwar monetary policy? We can answer that question by feeding the actual historical initial conditions and shocks through our 1919–39 "chimerical VAR." Because the variables in the system are in some cases indexes whose base years do not match across the two periods, the constant term in the policy equation requires adjustment, and there is no unique best way to choose the adjustment. The results we present choose the constant so that when current and lagged values of all variables are set at their means over the 1919:1–7 initial conditions period, the policy equation has a zero residual. This leads to simulations in which, as in Figure 4, the discount rate becomes negative after 1930. By choosing a somewhat higher constant term, the counterfactual discount rate can be kept positive. We present the results with the discount rate going negative because with the higher constant term, and thus tighter monetary policy, the differences between actual and counterfactual IP paths are smaller. Since the differences are remarkably small even when the non-negativity bound is ignored, we show these results to underline the model's implications for the limitations of monetary policy in counteracting the forces that generated the Great

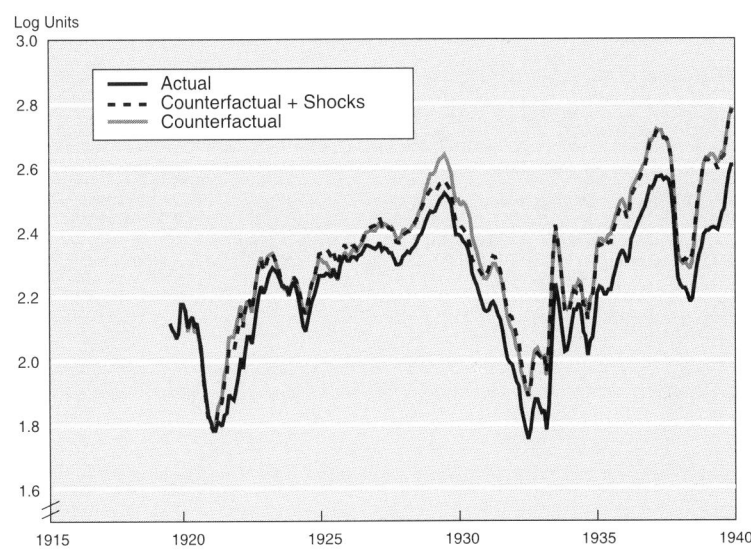

**Figure 5
Interwar Industrial Production, Actual and Counterfactual**

Depression. Each of the Figures 4 through 9 shows three lines—actual data, simulated data using the postwar policy behavior function and no disturbances, and simulated data using the postwar policy behavior function with the disturbances from the original 1919–39 policy behavior function.

With postwar policy, the discount rate would have dropped sharply during the 1920–21 recession, and the model implies that this would have somewhat accelerated the recovery of production and sharply curtailed the associated decline in the price level and the money stock. The discount rate would have dropped more sharply during 1929 and 1930 at the onset of the Depression, according to the simulation that includes policy disturbances, and by about the same amount as the actual discount rate decline according to the simulation without policy disturbances. The simulations imply, adjusted for the fact that interest rates cannot in fact be made negative, that discount rates would have been at approximately zero throughout the 1930–39 period. Note, though, that the rise in rates in September 1931, associated with Britain's departure from the gold standard, is partially reproduced in the results without policy shocks. The rise is not so great, and starts earlier, but it is still there.

Figure 5 shows that the (infeasibly) greater ease of the simulated monetary policy is implied to have increased the level of output at the end of 1939 by about 18 percent compared to the actual outcome, adding

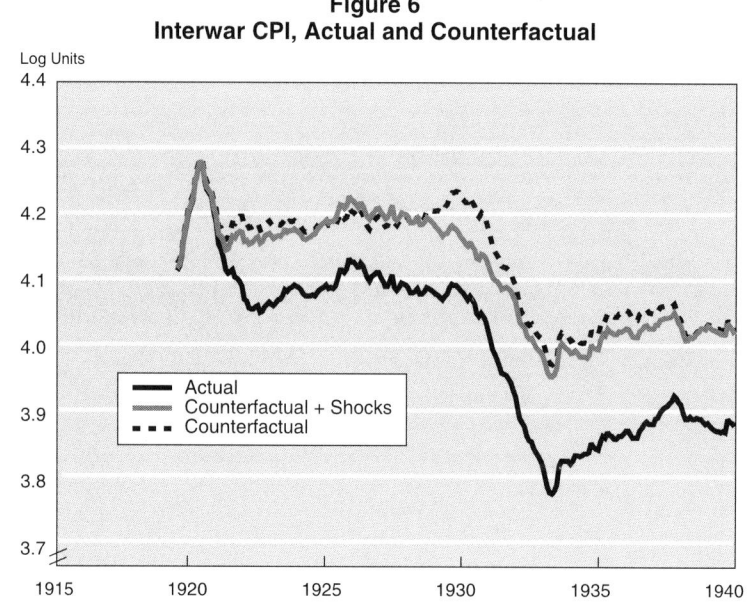

**Figure 6
Interwar CPI, Actual and Counterfactual**

about 1.2 percent per year to the mean growth rate over the 1924–39 period. However, it should be borne in mind that the statistical accuracy of the model deteriorates at long horizons. Thus, this effect on the long-term growth rate is very uncertain, with a zero effect quite possibly within a reasonable error band. When we consider the effects of the postwar policy on the cyclical movements within the period, we see very modest changes in the path of IP. The drop in IP from 1929 to 1933 is completely unaffected by the altered monetary policy. Recovery from 1933 to 1937, the renewed recession thereafter, and the recovery again through 1939, all reappear in roughly the same form and magnitude despite the altered monetary policy.

The postwar policy would have cut short the 1920–21 deflation, and it would have moderated the decline in CPI between 1929 and 1933, as can be seen from Figure 6. In the 1929–33 period the CPI decline would have been about 20 to 25 percent, instead of 30 percent. Figure 9 (below) shows that the 1920–21 decline in commodity prices would, like that in the CPI, have been cut short by postwar monetary policy. But after that period, the postwar monetary policy makes little difference to the time path of interwar commodity prices. Currency and money supply growth would have been substantially greater, as can be seen from Figure 7 and Figure 8, but the cyclical pattern of the movements in these two simulated series remains close to that of the series' actual paths.

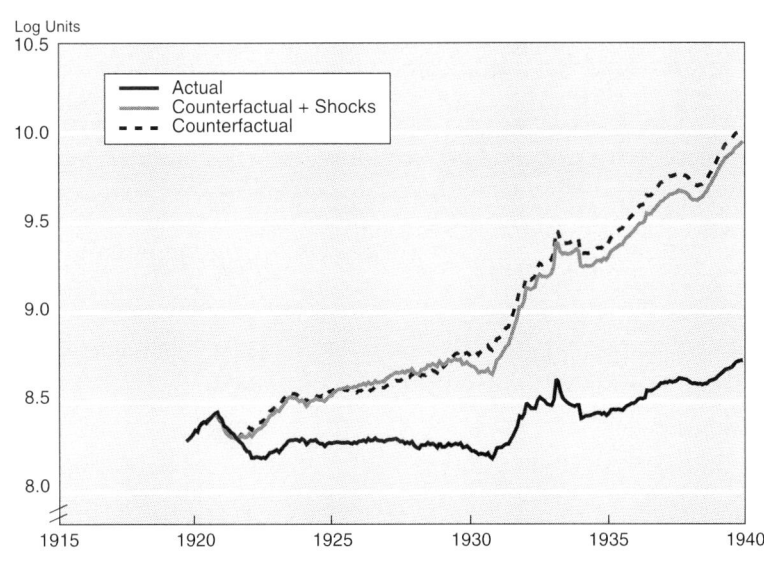

**Figure 7
Interwar Currency, Actual and Counterfactual**

The results taken together imply that postwar policy reactions would have reproduced much of the cyclical pattern in interest rates and money stock that actually occurred. Postwar policy reactions might well have led to a less restrictive monetary policy on average over the period (as in our simulations), but greater policy ease would have had only modest effects on the path of prices and even more modest effects on the path of output, despite substantial effects on the long-term growth rates of money and currency.

These results, it must be remembered, treat all disturbances that arise from crises of confidence in the banking system or speculative pressure on gold reserves as non-policy disturbances. Bernanke (1983) has pointed out that bankruptcy and bank failure seem to have played a role in the propagation of the Great Depression beyond what can be accounted for by their effects on the money stock. The calculations here suggest that movements in interest rates and the quantity of money in themselves may have been rather unimportant, but they leave Bernanke's arguments in full force. In fact, it might well be argued that if monetary policy had succeeded in expanding currency and deposits as rapidly as is assumed in this paper's counterfactual simulation of the interwar period, at least some of the bank failures of the '30s might have been avoided. Large-scale bankruptcies and bank failures do not occur in ordinary times, so to a linear model they appear as external disturbances, but they might in fact have been dampened by a persistent commitment to monetary ease.

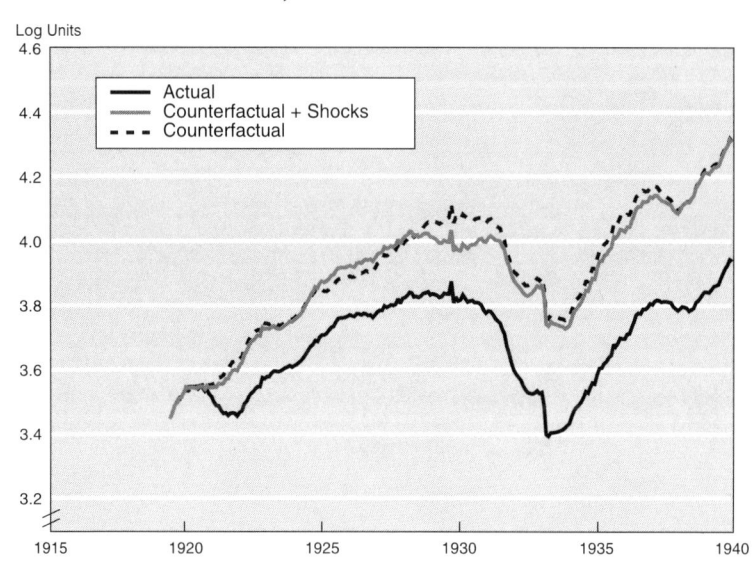

**Figure 8
Interwar M1, Actual and Counterfactual**

But would a policy of ease of the sort simulated here have been feasible? And would it have been monetary policy? The simulations show that to inflate the growth of money would have required pushing the discount rate down to about zero. Furthermore, it would have required convincing banks to expand. When interest rates on the securities it buys in open market operations have reached zero, a central bank's open market operations cease having any effect on the private sector's overall portfolio: They simply replace one non-interest-bearing government liability with another. Banks were holding large amounts of reserves at this time. It seems unlikely that they would have made much of a distinction between holding non-interest-bearing deposits with the Federal Reserve System and holding non-interest-bearing government securities.

To affect bank behavior, the Federal Reserve would have had to open the discount window, and to do so systematically. That is, it would have had to offer to discount bank loans at an attractive rate and to do so in a way that would attract banks to the discount window on a large scale. It is true today that discounting of bank assets by government agencies, when carried out on a case-by-case basis and subject to a determination of "need," cannot attract large-scale use by banks because it becomes a signal of financial distress. This was true also, and probably to an even greater extent because of the widespread concern about bank solvency,

Figure 9
Interwar Commodity Prices, Actual and Counterfactual

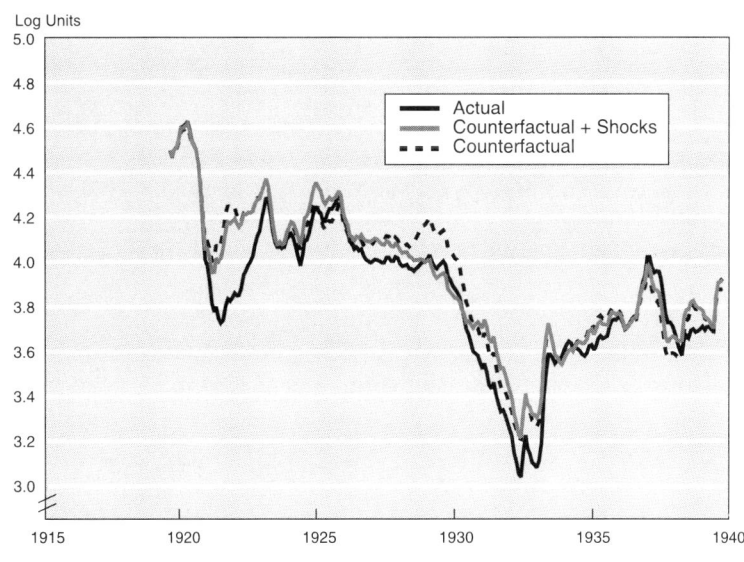

during the Great Depression.[14] We have seen that in fact the tendency was to increase the discount rate in the face of disturbances that tended to increase currency and shrink deposits. This behavior, I would argue, is not a simple mistake, but arises naturally when the central bank is reluctant to or legally forbidden to take on essentially fiscal commitments. Open market operations in short-term government securities denominated in dollars have no appreciable effects on the risk characteristics of the central bank's portfolio. Acquisition of rediscounted private sector loans at a time when the economy is declining and concern about bankruptcy is widespread is in this respect quite different, and was certainly understood to be different at the time of the Great Depression. At least potentially, it presents a substantial risk of losses. To undertake such risk without undermining confidence in the central bank itself, the central bank must have fiscal backing. That is, it must be understood that, were there to be substantial losses on the private assets being acquired, the central bank would be kept solvent by government budgetary action.[15]

---

[14] See Friedman and Schwartz (1963, p. 325), for example.

[15] The recent international monetary crises have brought this point sharply into relief in some cases. For example, in the 1994 peso collapse in Mexico, the central bank discounted a large quantity of bank debt that proved to be bad. In 1998, there is a political struggle over

That in a deflationary crisis the line between monetary and fiscal policy blurs is not an accident, but a reflection of a general principle. Starting with Leeper (1991), the literature on the fiscal theory of the price level has brought out the interdependence of monetary and fiscal policy regimes in guaranteeing a unique price level. One combination of regimes, labeled "active money, passive fiscal" by Leeper and "active money, Ricardian fiscal" by Woodford, involves a commitment by the monetary authority to raise nominal interest rates by enough to raise real interest rates when inflation rises, accompanied by a commitment by the fiscal authority to increase primary surpluses via taxation or expenditure reduction by more than enough to cover the increased interest expense implied by the rise in nominal rates. In such a pairing of regimes, the price level is determined by monetary policy, in the sense that stochastic shocks to the monetary policy rule have a direct impact on prices, while stochastic shocks to the fiscal rule have no effect on prices. It seems that this kind of pairing of regimes characterizes most advanced economies most of the time.

However, as Ben-Habib, Schmidt-Grohe, and Uribe (1998) have recently emphasized, this pairing of regimes does not deliver global uniqueness of the price level. The commitment by monetary authorities to raise rates when inflation advances must be matched by a corresponding commitment to lower them when inflation recedes, and to lower them further when inflation is replaced by deflation. So long as one component of the government debt is non-interest-bearing currency, it will not be possible to make nominal interest rates negative. But this means that if events force the monetary authority, following its "active" rule, into near-zero-interest-rate territory, it must eventually lose its ability to move rates in the same direction as inflation and by enough to lower real rates as inflation declines. The passive or Ricardian fiscal policy that couples with an active monetary policy to deliver a determinate price level becomes a source of indeterminacy in circumstances where the monetary authority has lost the ability to respond strongly to changes in inflation with changes in interest rates. Determinacy of the price level when monetary policy is forced to leave the nominal rate fixed requires a fiscal commitment to keep the real primary surplus insensitive to changes in the real value of outstanding government debt. If all interest rates, including long rates, fell to zero, this would mean no more than that the budget surplus should not increase with deflation. But long rates are

---

the fiscal measures needed to cover this transaction, and the delay in resolving it is causing continued difficulties for the banking system. This seems to have been an instance where the central bank acted on the assumption that it had fiscal backing, the fiscal backing has since come into doubt, and the result is that the original effect of increasing confidence in the banking system is being partially unraveled. (See *Business Week*, June 22, 1998, p. 62.)

likely to remain positive even if short rates are driven near to zero.[16] The required fiscal commitment then is that the conventional deficit should increase with deflation by more than enough to offset any rise in the real value of interest expenditures due to deflation. Putting the matter more broadly, in a deflationary crisis the problem is that government liabilities in general are too attractive relative to private sources of wealth. Countering the deflation requires policy action that decreases the expected return on government liabilities. Budget deficits, or reduced surpluses, if perceived as a permanent change in fiscal policy, can accomplish this. Open market operations in government securities cannot.

A related exercise was undertaken by McCallum (1990). He concludes that a monetary base rule could have largely eliminated the Great Depression. The difference in results comes from several sources. He deliberately refrains from modeling prices and real output separately, concentrating entirely on whether nominal GNP could have been kept stable. The model estimated in this paper implies stronger influence of monetary policy on prices than on output for the interwar period. McCallum also uses a model with simple dynamics and strong a priori restrictions. Most important, his model includes no recognition of the fact that monetary policy reacts to the state of the economy, and that this should affect the interpretation of estimated regression equations.

Replaying Postwar History with Interwar Monetary Policy

The interwar period involved such large cyclical disturbances that the relatively modest effect of changing the monetary policy rule on the implied outcomes for that period may not be representative of the effect of changing policy rules in more stable periods. It is therefore interesting to reverse the experiment of the previous section, replacing postwar monetary policy with interwar policy in the postwar model.

Figure 10 shows the effect of the change on responses to disturbance. The change in the way the discount rate responds to non-policy disturbance is substantial. IP, M1, and Pcomm disturbances, all of which imply future inflation, produce interest rate responses of the same sign with the interwar function as with the postwar reaction function, and after several years the responses achieve similar magnitudes, but the postwar responses are much quicker. This difference has noticeable effects on the responses of commodity prices to the same shocks, with commodity prices responding less under the postwar policy. However, IP and CPI

---

[16] Yields on 12-year government bonds averaged 3.6 percent in 1929 and did not fall below 2 percent from then through 1939. See Board of Governors of the Federal Reserve System (1943, Table 130).

Figure 10
Responses to Identified Shocks, Postwar, Actual and Counterfactual Shocks[a]

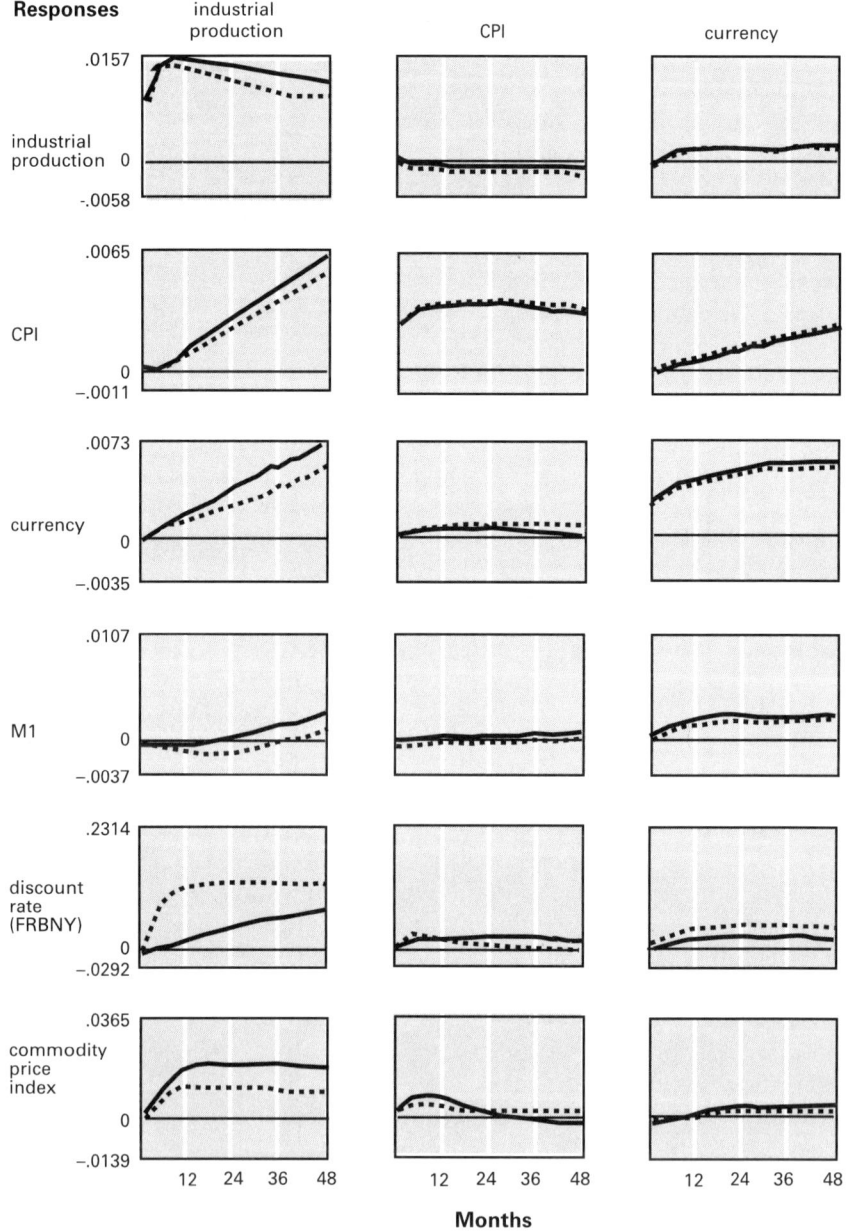

Figure 10, continued
Responses to Identified Shocks, Postwar, Actual and Counterfactual

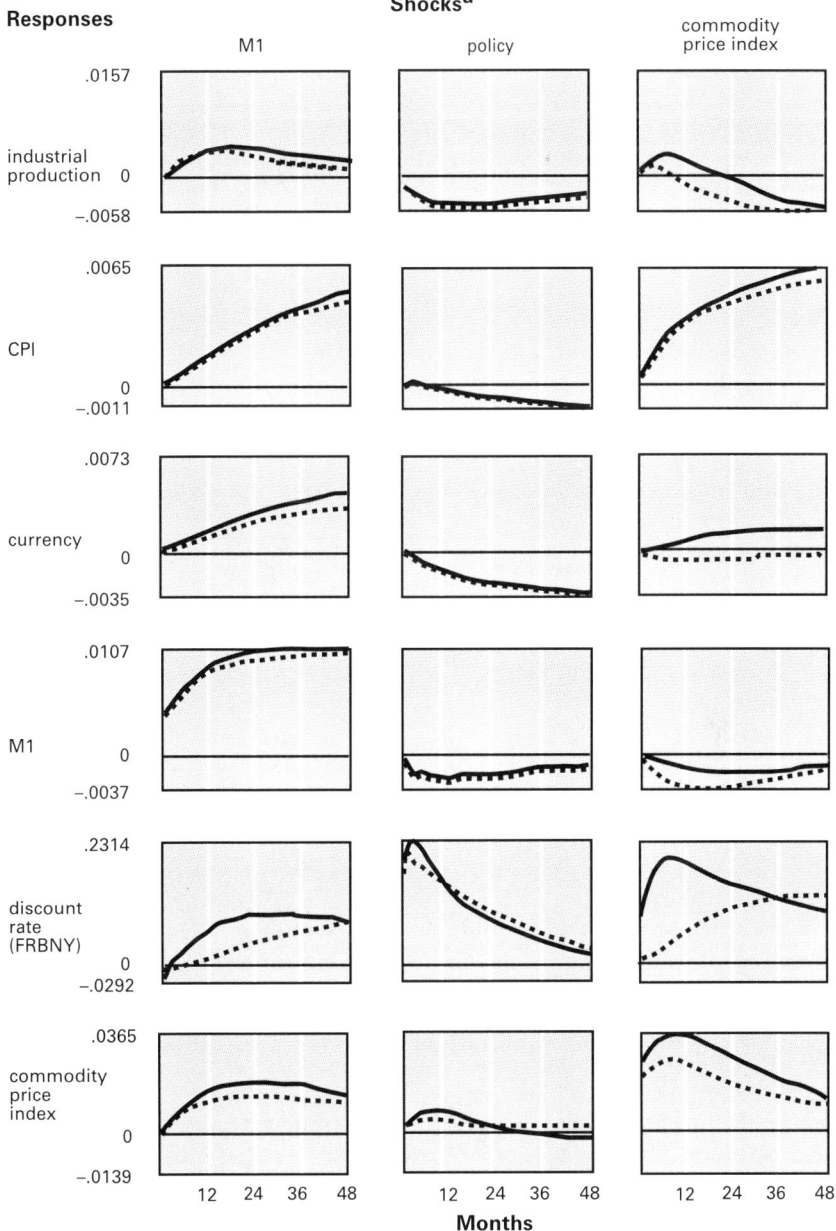

[a] Each shock represents a 1-standard-deviation disturbance in the corresponding equation, with the equations defined by the rows of Table 1.
Note: The solid lines use the 1919-39 policy reaction function in the 1948-97 model, while the dotted lines match Figure 1, the original estimated responses for the 1948-97 period.

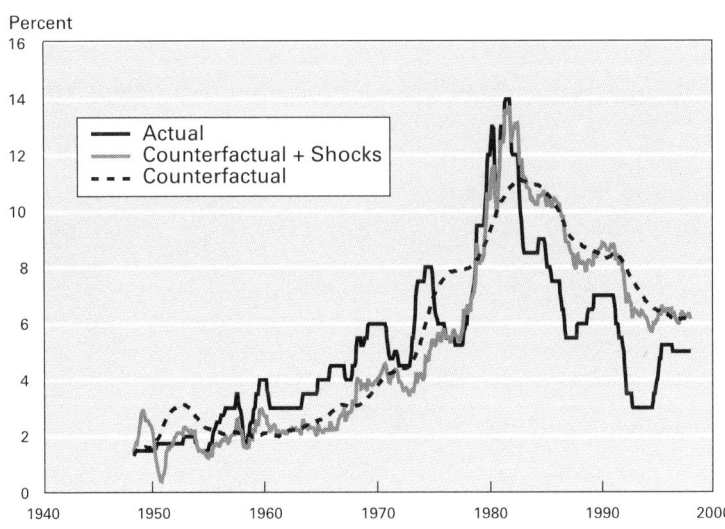

**Figure 11
Postwar Discount Rate, Actual and Counterfactual**

respond in much the same way with either policy rule. There is an effect, with CPI inflation and IP responses less under the postwar policy, but the effect is quite small.

If we rerun postwar history with the interwar reaction function, we find in Figure 11, as would be expected from the impulse responses, notable differences in the history of the discount rate. The counterfactual discount rate is lower in the '60s and the first part of the '70s than the actual rate, then rises faster than the actual discount rate. The simulation without policy shocks has the rate rising earlier in the '70s than the actual path, but then not rising quite as high in the early '80s. When policy shocks are added, the rise of rates from the late '70s to the early '80s is reproduced almost exactly, in timing and magnitude. The interwar policy rule keeps rates high notably longer than did the actual path of policy.

In Figure 12 we see that the earlier rise of rates in the '70s in the no-policy-shock simulation produces a sharper temporary reversal of commodity price inflation, so that by the early '80s commodity prices are on almost the same track in the no-policy-shock path as in the policy-shock counterfactual path, despite the less pronounced peak in rates under the former path.

Figures 13 and 14 show, perhaps surprisingly given the small differences in responses to shocks in Figure 10, that the difference in

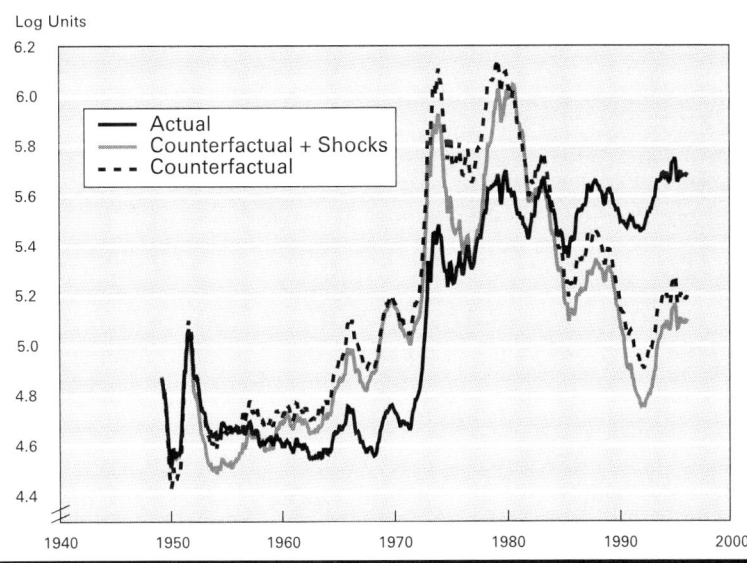

Figure 12
Postwar Commodity Prices, Actual and Counterfactual

policy has noticeable effects on the time paths of CPI inflation and IP. The low interest rates through the early '70s under the interwar policy produce greater CPI inflation, and this is accompanied by higher output growth. The higher inflation eventually requires interest rates just as high under the interwar as under the postwar policy, however, and as these bring inflation down, they also slow output growth. The recession of the early '80s is larger under the interwar policy, and the growth rate of IP remains generally lower under the interwar policy until the early '90s.

There is some plausibility to this analysis of how outcomes might have differed with a monetary policy that, like the interwar policy, responded less promptly to inflationary and deflationary pressure, but the statistical caveats mentioned earlier bear repeating here. The effects on CPI and IP are visible on a time scale of five or 10 years for the most part. This is why they are more visible on the plots of simulated history than they are on the impulse response graphs, which cover only four years. But responses at longer time horizons are less reliably estimated, so the differences found, while interesting, may be statistically unreliable.

At business cycle frequencies, IP fluctuations are very similar for all three lines plotted in Figure 14. It seems likely that the NBER business cycle chronologies would have looked quite similar with any of these paths. Putting the matter another way, the size and timing of the postwar

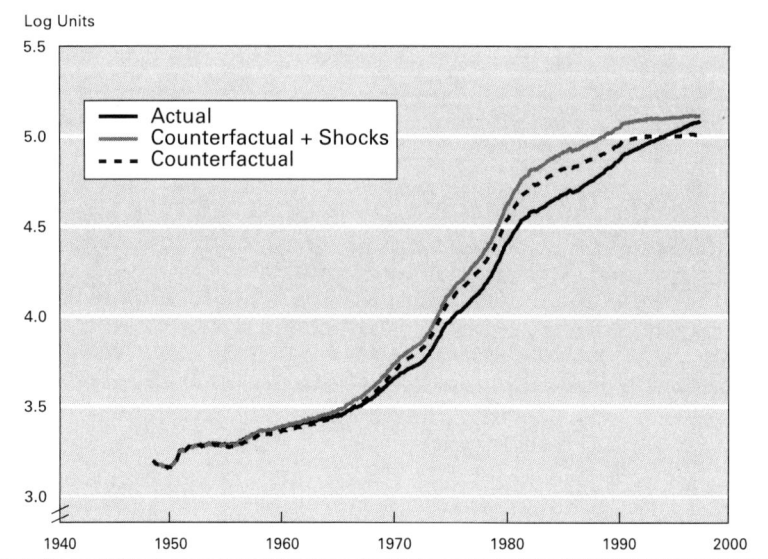

Figure 13
Postwar CPI, Actual and Counterfactual

U.S. recessions had little to do with either shocks to monetary policy or its systematic component.

It also seems clear from the simulations that postwar monetary policy is not as much different from interwar policy as might have been imagined. Estimates of policy responses to inflationary and banking system pressures obtained from data on the '20s and '30s reproduce the qualitative features of postwar monetary policy responses. They also trace the history of interest rate rises during the accelerating inflation of the '70s much as they occurred in fact.

WHAT ABOUT THE LUCAS CRITIQUE?[17]

The analytical framework of this paper is one in which all policy actions, hypothetical or historical, are regarded as realizations of random variables. The task of econometric model identification is that of constructing a model that contains a component describing how the conditional distribution of economic outcomes varies as the random variables

---

[17] The first part of this section reviews long-standing philosophical disputes on which I have stated my views many times before. It is only because my views on these issues seem still to be controversial in some quarters, and perhaps incompletely understood, that I review them here.

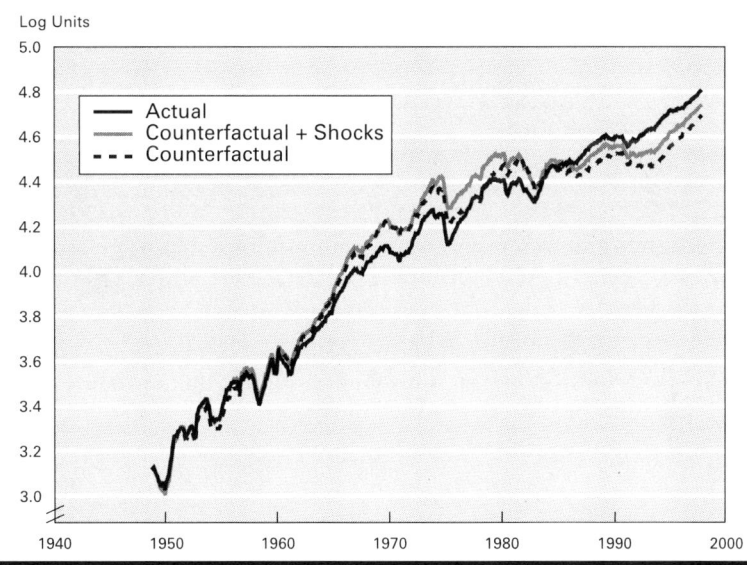

**Figure 14
Postwar Industrial Production, Actual and Counterfactual**

characterizing policy take on different possible values. Our modeling approach does this, and it is therefore legitimate to use it to discuss counterfactual history or to project the future of the economy under various policy choices as a guide to policy formulation. There is no other approach to policy evaluation that recognizes the existence of uncertainty and that is internally consistent.

The Lucas critique of econometric policy evaluation can be formulated in a variety of ways. At its most straightforward, it points out that in a stochastic model that explicitly models the dynamics of expectations formation, evaluating changes in policy rule as if they could be made permanently, while leaving expectations formation dynamics unchanged, is a mistake. This version of the critique clearly does not apply to this paper's analysis, as the models being used contain no explicit expectations-formation dynamics. Another version of the critique makes it a warning about the potential importance of a particular type of nonlinearity. Every applied economist understands that the linear (or otherwise mathematically simple) models we use are approximations valid over a certain range. The conventional version of this point is that it is dangerous to extrapolate results from a linear regression to independent variable values much larger or smaller than those actually observed in the sample. Lucas's analysis made clear that in dynamic macroeconomic models the absolute size of changes in random variables being conditioned on in

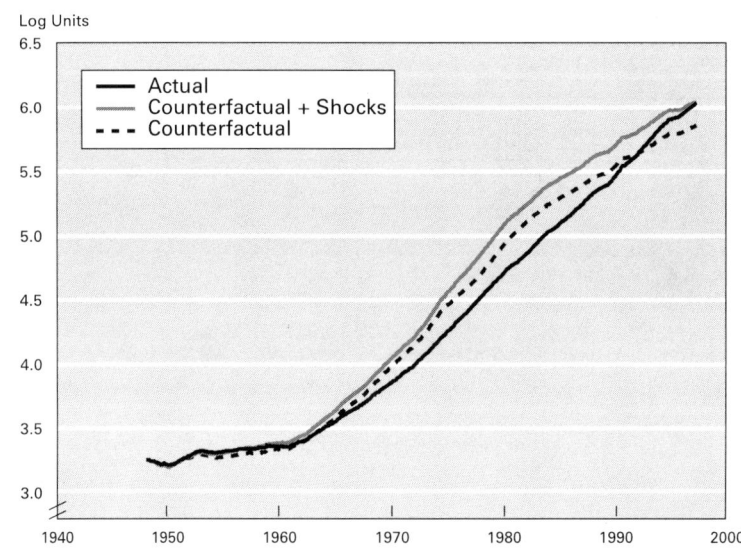

Figure 15
Postwar Currency, Actual and Counterfactual

making projections is not the only worry. Sequences of values for conditioning random variables that are historically unprecedented in their serial correlation properties—like persistently high or low money growth rates or interest rates—might make models run astray even when they are not outside the range of historical experience in absolute size. This version of the critique does apply to this paper's analysis, and we need to consider it.

A third version of the critique makes it into a philosophical puzzle akin to Zeno's paradox. Policy properly understood, from this viewpoint, is the policy rule. Since without changing the rule we will not change the stochastic process describing the economy, no intervention that leaves the rule intact produces any real change. Hence discussion of policy by economists should be limited to discussion of changes in policy rule. As a corollary, changes in policy will always have to be accompanied by an analysis of how the change in rule affects private behavior via expectations formation. But once we recognize that the parameters of the rule can change, and that a rational public is aware that they can change, then we must also recognize that the particular values of the parameters of the rule that are chosen are realizations of random variables, for which the public, assuming rational behavior, knows the true probability distribution. We are then back at square one; changes in the parameters of the

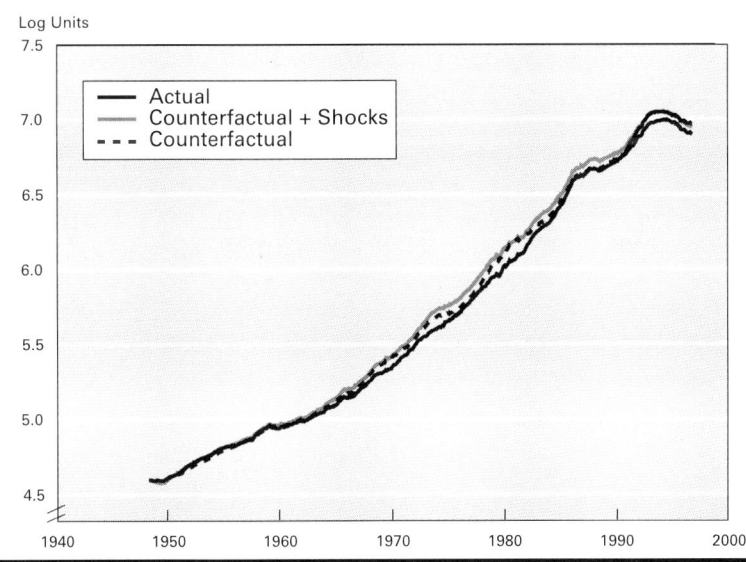

**Figure 16
Postwar M1, Actual and Counterfactual**

rule itself are mere realizations of random variables, generating no real change in the probability distribution of the economy.[18]

The fallacy in this third version is its assumption that change in policy that does not change the probability distribution of economic outcomes is trivial. Two economies whose probability distributions are the same may have very different actual realized histories. If the probability model is non-stationary or nearly so, as are most economic models, they may even have different histories when averaged over time.

Our attention then focuses on version 2 above. Are we conditioning on variations in policy so great that it is implausible that the public would view them as realizations of a fixed probability law for policy behavior? If we had found drastically different behavior of the economy as we switched policy rules, this would be a strong caveat to the results. But we found differences that were for the most part quite modest. Of course, if actual policy followed either of the no-policy-shock rules, the public would quickly discover the perfectly fitting regression equation that

---

[18] A clear exposition of this viewpoint, bringing out its nihilistic implications for the possibility of internally consistent policy evaluation, is in Sargent (1984). That paper also contains an articulation of another position, even more nihilistic (that policymakers are always behaving optimally), that Sargent incorrectly (but apologetically) attributes to me. My own views on this are articulated at more length in Sims (1987).

determines policy reactions and build it into their expectations. This would lead to much more certainty about monetary policy than there is in fact. In this sense, our simulation of these rules is unrealistic, as it ignores the reduction of uncertainty about monetary policy that they would entail. But clearly we are thinking of these simulations as representative of similar rules that still contain error terms. We display them only to give some insight into how much of historical policy behavior is attributed to the historical pattern of realized random policy disturbances.

Also, we have already made the point that an important nonlinearity is probably lurking in the interwar results that could be seen as a version of the Lucas critique idea: A policy that succeeded in expanding bank deposits as rapidly as our counterfactual interwar policy would probably have had to entail increasing confidence in bank liquidity and solvency. It might well therefore have eliminated or reduced some of the financial crisis shocks that the model treats as unrelated to monetary policy.

But on the whole, it appears that these considerations are only one of many reasons to be somewhat cautious about these results, not a reason for ignoring them. The postwar simulations do involve persistent differences from historical patterns in rates of monetary expansion and price inflation. If the historical pattern had shown extremely stable inflation around a fixed mean, this would be strong reason for concern. Historical dynamics might then have reflected a public that has a strong tendency to forecast rapid mean-reversion in inflation. But historical postwar U.S. experience shows a complicated pattern of near-non-stationary drift in inflation rates. Actual rational expectations-formation therefore must have involved recognition that the inflation rate can drift, and our simulated counterfactual patterns of drift are not far outside the range of actual experience.

The identifying assumptions we have used in deriving our model are certainly legitimately subject to dispute, and altering those assumptions might alter results. These are much stronger reasons for questioning the results than the Lucas critique, which is after all just one particular line of attack on a model's identifying assumptions. In this case, it seems that other identifying assumptions would provide a better place to start.

Conclusion

The assigned topic of this paper was the role of government as a source of business cycles. We began by limiting attention to the role of budgetary and monetary policy in generating business cycles. We have developed a way of looking at historical data that allows us to consider both whether erratic variation in monetary policy has been an important source of fluctuations and whether systematic patterns of response of monetary policy to the private sector have been important in shaping business cycle fluctuations. The conclusion of our analysis is that even during the Great Depression, the role of interest rate policy in generating or propagating cycles was modest. The systematic component of monetary policy has been remarkably stable, not only within the postwar period, but between the interwar and postwar periods. Changes in the systematic component of monetary policy of the magnitude seen between these two periods would not have greatly changed historical business cycle chronologies, though they would probably have changed the postwar history of inflation. And random fluctuations in monetary policy also do not have effects large enough to substantially alter the economy's business cycle chronology.

Analysis of the limitations of monetary policy during the '30s, as interest rates approached a zero lower bound, and consideration of the importance of disturbances related to financial crises, suggest routes by which government actions outside the bounds of normal interest rate policy could have had substantial effects, not modeled in this approach.

The overall conclusion might be that the aim of good monetary policy should be to make monetary policy unimportant to the business cycle, and that postwar U.S. monetary policy has largely succeeded in this respect.

Data Appendix

I. Interwar

Except for IP, the series are from the National Bureau of Economic Research (NBER) macro history database, which is accessible at
www.nber.org/databases/macrohistory/data/04/.

- IP: Federal Reserve code B50001

Industrial Production, total index, seasonally adjusted, from the Federal Reserve Board. Accessible at http://www.bog.frb.fed.us/releases/G17/iphist/ip1ahist.sa

- CPI: NBER series 04128

Consumer Price Index, All Items, U.S. Bureau of Labor Statistics
Units: 1957–1959 = 100
Seasonal adjustment: None
Source: BLS Release, "Consumer Price Index—U.S.: All Items, 1913–1960," Series A.
Notes: Prior to 1953, this series was called the "index of cost of living." Data have been converted to the average 1957–59 base by BLS. Prior to September 1940, only fuel and food components were monthly; all other components were priced at intervals of 3, 4, and 6 months. (See *Survey of Current Business,* May 1941; also *Monthly Labor Review,* August 1940, and BLS *Bulletin* nos. 699 (1941) and 966 (1949) for detailed information.) The early segment of this series represents monthly interpolations by the U.S. Department of Commerce.

- Currency: NBER series 14125

Currency Held by the Public, Seasonally Adjusted
Units: millions of dollars
Seasonal adjustment: Seasonally adjusted by source
Source: Friedman and Schwartz, *Monetary Statistics of the United States* (NBER 1970), Table 27, Column 3, pp. 402–15.
Notes: Data represent vault cash of all banks subtracted from currency in circulation outside the Treasury and Federal Reserve Banks. Data are for the Wednesday nearest the end of the month.

- M1: NBER series 14144

Money Stock, Commercial Banks plus Currency Held by the Public, Seasonally Adjusted
Units: billions of dollars
Seasonal Adjustment: Seasonally adjusted by NBER
Source: Data are computed by NBER from the sum of series 14125 (currency held by the public) and series 14145 (demand deposits adjusted and time deposits all commercial banks). See Friedman and Schwartz, *Monetary Statistics of the United States* (NBER 1970).
Notes: Data are for the Wednesday nearest the end of the month.

- Discount Rate: NBER series 13009

Discount Rates, Federal Reserve Bank of New York
Units: Percent
Seasonal Adjustment: None
Source: Federal Reserve Board, data for 1914–1921: "Discount Rates of Federal Reserve Banks, 1914–1921," 1922. Data for 1922–1969: *Annual Reports* for 1931–1942; *Federal Reserve Bulletin,* successive issues.
Notes: Data are computed by NBER by taking simple averages of rates for commercial, agricultural, and livestock paper, and weighting them by the number of days each rate was in force. Data are for all classes and maturities of discount.

- Commodity Prices: NBER series 04202

Units: 1947–1949 = 100
Seasonal adjustment: None
Source: Ruth P. Mack, "Inflation and Quasi-Elective Changes in Costs," *The Review of Economics and Statistics,* August 1959.
Notes: Series discontinued after January 1957.

II. Postwar
All series except M1 (in part) were drawn from Citibase.

- IP: Citibase series name IP.
Industrial Production: total index (1992=100, SA)

- CPI: Citibase series name PUNEW
CPI-U: all items (82–84=100, SA)

- Currency: Citibase series name FMSCU.
Money Stock: currency held by the public (bil$,SA)

- M1: Citibase series name FM1, spliced together with the NBER historical M1 series cited above. The Citibase M1 series starts in 1959:1. The earlier data were scaled to match the modern series in 1959:1. Citibase title: Money Stock: M1 (currency, travelers checks, demand deposits, other checkable deposits) (bil$,SA)

- Discount Rate: Citibase series name FYGD.
Discount Rate, Federal Reserve Bank of New York (% per annum)

- Commodity Prices: Citibase series name PSCCOM.
Spot Market Price Index: BLS & CRB: all commodities (1967=100, NSA)

References

Baxter, M. and R.G. King. 1993. "Fiscal Policy in General Equilibrium." *The American Economic Review*, 83 (June), pp. 315–34.

Ben-Habib, Jess, Stephanie Schmidt-Grohe, and Martin Uribe. 1998. "Monetary Policy and Multiple Equilibria." New York University discussion paper available at *http://www.econ.nyu.edu/user/benhabib/research.htm*.

Bernanke, Ben. 1983. "Nonmonetary Effects of the Financial Crisis in the Propagation of the Great Depression." *The American Economic Review*, 73, pp. 257–76.

Bernanke, Ben and Alan Blinder. 1992 "The Federal Funds Rate and the Channels of Monetary Transmission." *The American Economic Review*, 82, pp. 901–21.

Board of Governors of the Federal Reserve System. 1943. *Banking and Monetary Statistics, 1914–1941*. Washington, DC.

Cochrane, John H. 1988. "A Cashless View of U.S. Inflation." Presented in March at the NBER Macroeconomics Annual Conference.

Friedman, Milton. 1958. "The Supply of Money and Changes in Prices and Output." In *The Relationship of Prices to Economic Stability and Growth*, 85th Congress, 2nd Session, Joint Economic Committee Print. Washington DC: Government Printing Office. Reprinted in Friedman 1969, pp. 171–87.

_____. 1969. *The Optimum Quantity of Money and Other Essays*. Chicago: Aldine Publishing Company.

Friedman, Milton and Anna Schwartz. 1963. *A Monetary History of the United States 1867–1960*. Princeton, NJ: Princeton University Press.

Garcia-Mila, Teresa. 1987. *Government Purchases and Real Output: Empirical Evidence and an Equilibrium Model with Government Capital*. University of Minnesota Ph.D. thesis.

Leeper, Eric M. 1991. "Equilibria under 'Active' and 'Passive' Monetary and Fiscal Policies." *Journal of Monetary Economics*, 27 (February), pp. 129–47.

Leeper, Eric M., C.A. Sims, and Tao Zha. 1996. "What Does Monetary Policy Do?" *Brookings Papers on Economic Activity*, 1996:2, pp. 1–63.

Lütkepohl, Helmut. 1991. *Introduction to Multivariate Time Series Analysis*. New York: Springer-Verlag.

McCallum, Bennett T. 1990. "Could a Monetary Base Rule Have Prevented the Great Depression?" *Journal of Monetary Economics*, 26(1), August, pp. 3–26.

Sargent, Thomas J. 1984. "Autoregressions, Expectations, and Advice." *The American Economic Review Papers and Proceedings*, 74 (May), pp. 408–15.

Sims, Christopher A. 1987. "A Rational Expectations Framework for Short-Run Policy

Analysis." In *New Approaches to Monetary Economics*, W. Barnett and K. Singleton, eds., pp. 293–310. Cambridge University Press. Also available at *http://www.econ.yale.edu/~sims*.

———. 1994. "A Simple Model for Study of the Determination of the Price Level and the Interaction of Monetary and Fiscal Policy." *Economic Theory*, 4, pp. 381–99.

———. 1997. "Fiscal Foundations of Price Stability in Open Economies." Presented at the July 1997 Far Eastern meetings of the Econometric Society. Available at *http://www.econ.yale.edu/~sims*.

———. 1998a. "Stickiness." Processed, Department of Economics, Yale University.

———. 1998b. "Adaptive Metropolis-Hastings Sampling." Processed, Yale University.

Sims, Christopher A. and Tao Zha. 1998a. "Bayesian Methods for Dynamic Multivariate Models." *International Economic Review,* forthcoming.

———. 1998b. "Error Bands for Impulse Responses." *Econometrica*, forthcoming.

Woodford, Michael. 1994. "Monetary Policy and Price Level Determinacy in a Cash-in-Advance Economy." *Economic Theory,* 4(3), pp. 345–80.

———. 1995. "Price Level Determinacy without Control of a Monetary Aggregate." NBER Working Paper No. 5204.

DISCUSSION

Lawrence J. Christiano*

Christopher Sims's paper sheds light on an important question: "Does monetary policy play an important role in business cycles?" For at least two reasons, many think the answer must be "Yes." First, a casual look at postwar data shows that short-term interest rates generally rise sharply just before a recession (Figure 1). Since short-term interest rates are thought to be controlled by the Fed, it seems only natural to conclude that the Fed is responsible for the run-up in rates and for the subsequent recessions.[1] Second, there is general agreement with the Friedman and Schwartz (1963) view that, although bad monetary policy may not have caused the Great Depression, it greatly exacerbated it. Those who find these and other reasons compelling will find Sims's paper very provocative. That is because he presents an empirical model which suggests that the role of monetary policy in business cycles may be negligible.

The most dramatic part of Sims's paper is his conclusion that monetary policy played little or no role in the Great Depression. This is the focus of my comment. I argue that Sims's method for reaching his conclusion is flawed. However, when I apply what I think is a superior method, I confirm Sims's result. Overall, Sims's paper represents a fascinating and thought-provoking challenge to those who believe that monetary policy plays an important role in business cycles.

It is useful to organize my discussion of Sims's paper around the notion of a monetary policy rule:

$$R_t = f(\Omega_t) + \varepsilon_t.$$

---

*Professor of Economics, Northwestern University.

[1] On three occasions, 1957, 1966, and 1984, the federal funds rate rose sharply and yet no recession followed. Still, in each case, growth in GDP slowed significantly afterward.

This breaks down the monetary authority's actions, R_t, into a part, f, that is systematically related to the state of the economy, Ω_t, and a part that is not, namely, the monetary policy shock, ε_t. In general, R_t would be a vector of all the variables that the monetary authority controls, and f specifies the authority's strategy for manipulating these variables in response to different contingencies as captured by Ω_t. In addition to an interest rate, these variables would include others, among them variables that might be used in an emergency, such as a bank panic. This might include suspension of convertibility from deposits to currency, buying up of the assets of a bank having liquidity problems, and so on. In this paper, Sims focuses his analysis by measuring monetary policy with a single variable, the discount rate. This is the interest rate paid by banks when they borrow from the Federal Reserve.

The paper breaks down the basic question of interest into two parts, corresponding to the two parts of the decomposition. The first part is "How much have monetary policy shocks contributed to business cycle fluctuations?" Sims concludes that the answer is "Very little." He finds that around 6 percent of postwar and interwar business fluctuations are due to monetary policy shocks. Sims has reached this conclusion in previous papers. I will not comment on this aspect of the analysis, since it is not what is new and interesting about this paper.[2]

The second question is "How much has the monetary policy rule contributed to business cycle fluctuations?" This is the really interesting question. It is also the difficult one. The question corresponds to the following counterfactual exercise: "If the monetary authority had adopted a different policy rule, would the business cycle have been very different?" Sims asks the question in the context of the postwar and interwar U.S. business cycle experiences. In both cases, his answer is a surprising "No." Although I disagree with the method that Sims uses to reach this conclusion, when I adopt what I think is a more reasonable alternative, I reach the same conclusion. In the following section, I explain Sims's approach and why I believe it is flawed. I then describe the results based on an alternative approach. The last section provides concluding remarks.

THE 1930S UNDER SIMS'S REPRESENTATION OF THE POSTWAR MONETARY POLICY RULE

The standard approach to assessing the impact of f is to undertake counterfactual experiments with alternative fs.[3] The classic example is

---

[2] For a survey of Sims's and other work on the importance of monetary policy shocks in business cycles, see Christiano, Eichenbaum, and Evans (1998).

[3] An alternative, "historical approach," has been used, too. An example of this is Taylor (1998), which compares U.S. economic performance under various different policy rules like

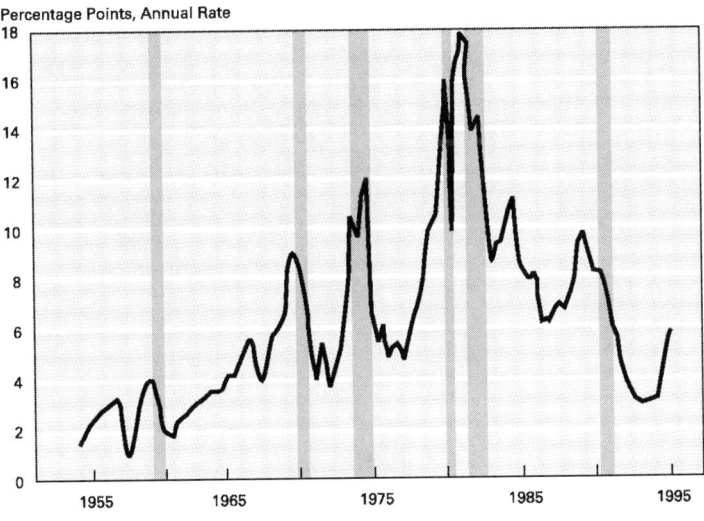

**Figure 1
Federal Funds Rate and NBER Recessions**

Friedman and Schwartz (1963). They conjecture that if the Fed had adopted the f in place in 1907, the Fed would have suspended convertibility from demand deposits to currency during the first wave of bank failures in 1930, and the Great Depression might not have been so "great."[4] Thus, they conclude that f matters a lot. The distinguishing characteristic of the Friedman and Schwartz approach is that the economic model being used for the analysis is not spelled out explicitly. In effect, the counterfactual experiment is run in their heads. What distin-

---

the gold standard, and the pre- and postwar Fed. Taylor interprets the differences in economic performance across these episodes as reflecting the effects of varying the monetary policy rule. Of course, this approach is not without its pitfalls. The implicit assumption, that the primary changes in the U.S. economy over this time centered on the monetary policy rule, is debatable.

[4] Friedman and Schwartz (p. 167) refer to the counterfactual approach as "conjectural history." They say (pp. 167–68): "If the 1907 banking system had been in operation in 1929, restriction of payments [for example, suspension of convertibility from demand deposits to currency] might have come in October 1929 when the stock market crashed . . . [the restriction] would have prevented the collapse of the banking system and the drastic fall in the stock of money that were destined to take place, and that certainly intensified the severity of the contraction, if they were not indeed the major factors converting it from a reasonably severe into a catastrophic contraction." Later (p. 313) they argue that there were signs in early 1931 that the economy was reviving. They say, " . . . if those tentative stirrings of revival had been reinforced by a vigorous expansion in the stock of money, they could have been converted into sustained recovery. But that was not to be."

guishes Sims's work is that, to a much greater extent, he does spell out the model used for the counterfactual analysis. An advantage of this is that if you disagree with the results, you have something concrete to point to and to argue about.[5]

The most surprising result in Sims's paper is his finding that monetary policy during the Great Depression did not matter. This result runs contrary to the conventional wisdom stemming at least from the analysis of Friedman and Schwartz mentioned above. According to that wisdom, the Fed may not have actually started the Great Depression. However, bad monetary policy is what converted it from what might have been a very severe recession into a major catastrophe.[6] Sims's model suggests that this conventional wisdom deserves rethinking.

To put Sims's counterfactual experiment as concretely as possible, he asks the following question:

> If we dropped Alan Greenspan into the United States of the 1920s and 1930s and made him Fed Chairman at the time, would the Great Depression have been averted or at least mitigated?

To answer this question, Sims estimates a model for the interwar U.S. economy and replaces the monetary policy equation with the one characterizing U.S. monetary policy in the postwar period. In making the policy change, he makes and defends the assumption that the equations characterizing the private economy are invariant to the change in policy rule.

A consequence of Sims's invariance assumption is that the private economy can essentially be modeled as a reduced form, a black box. A potential advantage of this approach, assuming the invariance assumption is correct, is robustness to the type of specification errors that can occur with a more structural approach. An important potential pitfall, of course, lies in the possibility that the invariance assumption is false. This is the possibility emphasized in the famous Lucas critique. A source of concern, in this regard, is that the comparison between inter- and postwar periods offers perhaps the most dramatic example of the Lucas critique. In particular, monetary policy in the postwar period, with the Federal Deposit Insurance Corporation as its backbone, left little reason to doubt that the Fed would work to guarantee the liquidity of the banking system. The interwar evidence clearly shows that the Fed was less committed to

---

[5] Other papers that do counterfactual experiments using an explicit model include Bordo, Choudri, and Schwartz (1995) and McCallum (1990). Both these papers find that alternative monetary policies could have made a big difference to the outcome of the Great Depression.

[6] For an argument that monetary policy may also have been one of the primary impulses underlying the Great Depression, see Hamilton (1987).

this at that time. This policy change from the interwar to the postwar period generated a sharp change in private agents' policy rules. In the early period, they were inclined, at the slightest sign of bad news, to rush to the bank to convert their deposits into currency. In the later period, essentially no runs took place.

The Lucas critique of the invariance assumption used by Sims, and Sims's rebuttal, have been clearly spelled out in the literature. Apart from the note of concern expressed in the previous paragraph, I will not dwell on this issue any further.

Surprisingly, Sims finds that the Great Depression would have unfolded roughly as it did, even if the postwar policy rule had been adopted. According to the calculations in the paper, with Alan Greenspan at the helm the Fed would have allowed M1 to fall by roughly 30 percent (see Sims's Figure 5), and output would have fallen roughly as it did. This is the basis for Sims's conclusion that monetary policy did not matter in the Great Depression.

The 1930s under a Different Representation of the Postwar Monetary Policy

I am skeptical that Sims has correctly captured the postwar policy rule. I am confident that Alan Greenspan would *not* have stood idly by and let M1 drop by 30 percent. Friedman and Schwartz's view, that allowing M1 to collapse in the 1930s was a massive blunder, is widely shared today. Just about *any* economist transported from the post-Friedman and Schwartz world into the 1930s would have fought hard to prevent the drop in M1. Surely, something must be wrong with Sims's representation of the postwar policy rule.

Technically, the reason that replacing the interwar policy rule with the postwar policy rule makes little difference is that the two rules are very similar. So, the demonstration that the Great Depression would have unfolded as it did, even with the postwar policy rule, is just a demonstration of continuity: A small change in one of the equations of Sims's model produces only a small change in the outcome. However, I do not believe that the analysis reported justifies the conclusion that policy did not matter in the Great Depression.

So, suppose Alan Greenspan had been parachuted into Washington in the 1930s. Why is Sims's estimated postwar policy rule unreliable as a guide to what Greenspan would have done? As noted above, monetary policy broadly conceived virtually eliminated bank panics from the postwar data set. As a result, the raw time series used to estimate the postwar policy rule does not carry any information about what the postwar Fed would have done, had a bank panic occurred. Mechanically, we can of course plug in any Ω_t we want into the estimated policy rule. But, there is no reason to have any confidence in the predictions of the estimated policy rule for Ω_ts very different from the sample used for estimation. And, the events of the 1930s were completely unlike anything that happened in the postwar period.

Still, to a first order of approximation, we *know* what the postwar Fed would have done in the 1930s: It would not have permitted the drastic fall in M1. So, I think a better way to address Sims's question is to imagine that a postwar policymaker transplanted to the 1930s would have acted to prevent the fall in M1. I implemented this policy, using Sims's model and using the type of methodology that he has advocated in this paper and elsewhere.[7] In particular, I assumed that all the non-policy shocks throughout the interwar period were as Sims estimated them to be. I also set the pre-August 1929 policy shocks to their estimated values. I then computed a sequence of policy shocks for the period August 1929 until December 1939 that would keep M1 on the same average growth path as the one M1 was on during the 1919–29 period.[8] Technical details appear in the Appendix.

The results are reported in Figures 2 and 3.[9] Figure 2a displays the policy shocks used in the counterfactual simulation. In this figure, the shocks labeled "actual" refer to the pre-August 1929 estimated policy shocks. The shocks labeled "counterfactual" refer to the counterfactual policy shocks used from August 1929 on, designed to keep average M1 growth roughly to what it was in the 1920s. The mean (standard deviation) of these shocks is 0.015 (0.18) and -0.082 (0.62) over the first and second periods, respectively.[10] Thus, the counterfactual policy shocks involve only a negligible reduction in mean relative to the 1920s. Primarily, they involve a threefold increase in standard deviation.

Figures 2b to 2f report actual data for the entire interwar sample, and they also exhibit the data for the counterfactual simulation. Note from Figure 2b that the counterfactual policy indeed does keep M1 in the 1930s roughly on the 1920s growth path. Figure 2c shows that this implies a very large increase in currency. Also, Figures 2d and 2e show that the counterfactual policy would have prevented the drastic decline in prices that occurred.

---

[7] I am very grateful to Sims for providing me with his model parameter values and his data, which I used in the analysis described below.

[8] Since, according to Sims's model, the money stock is not influenced within the month by a policy shock, the best that policy can do is influence the expected money supply starting in the next month. The assumption that the money stock is predetermined within the period relative to a policy shock is not unusual in the monetary policy literature. See, for example, Christiano, Eichenbaum, and Evans (1998).

[9] The data and mnemonics are as in Sims's paper.

[10] Figure 2a and these statistics refer to the policy shock as defined in the policy rule displayed above in the text. Thus, they refer to the fifth element of Sims's shock, ε_t, *after* division by the fifth diagonal element of his A_0. As a result, the shocks are expressed in units of the interest rate, which in turn is expressed in percentage points, at an annual rate.

Figure 2
Interwar Model Results with Counterfactual Policy Shocks
Designed to Prevent a Fall in M1

2a: Policy Shock
Percentage Points, Annual Rate

2b: M1
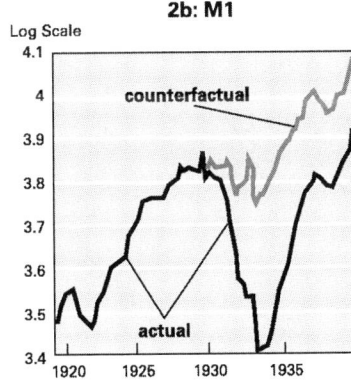
Log Scale

2c: Currency
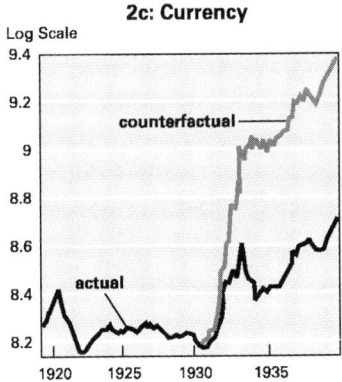
Log Scale

2d: CPI
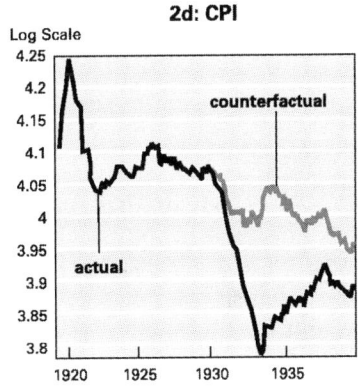
Log Scale

2e: Commodity Prices
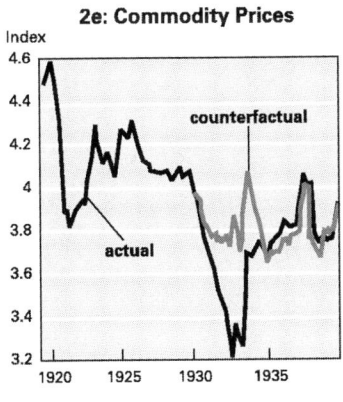
Index

2f: Discount Rate
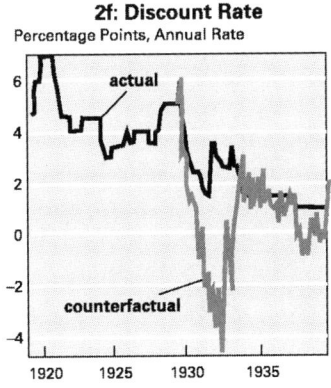
Percentage Points, Annual Rate

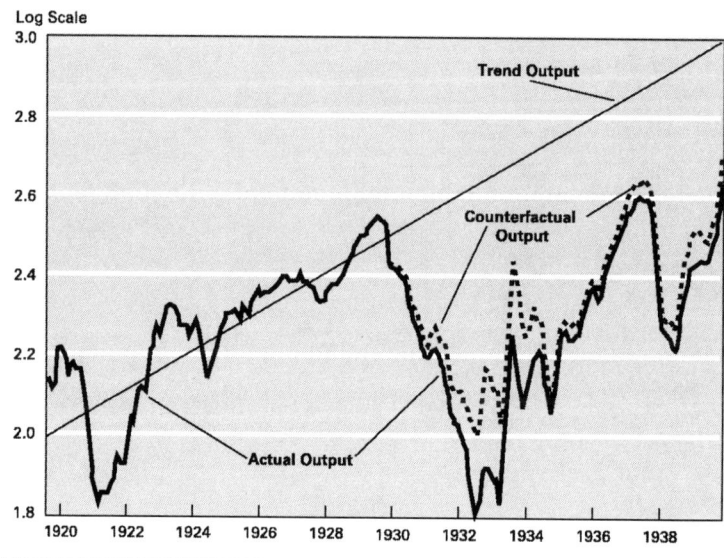

**Figure 3
Impact of the Counterfactual Simulation on Industrial Production**

Figure 2f shows that the discount rate is driven down relative to its historical value. In fact, the discount rate goes negative (as it does in Sims's own experiments). If the discount rate were a market rate, this would be impossible. With a negative interest rate of, say, −5 percent, lenders would require only 95 cents back for every dollar loaned. In this case, borrowers in effect receive a 5 cent gift with each one-dollar loan transaction. To make this gift as large as possible, borrowers would try and borrow as much as they could. No matter what supply was, demand would always be larger; no equilibrium could exist in a loan market with a negative rate of interest. But, the interest rate in Sims's model is not a market rate of interest. As noted above, it is the rate that the Fed charges on loans to banks. The "gift" associated with a negative discount rate is just a bank bailout. So, the counterfactual policy implies that the Fed bails out some of the member banks of the Federal Reserve System.

Figure 3 shows the impact of the counterfactual simulation on output. Surprisingly, even though the drastic fall in M1 was prevented under the counterfactual simulation, the basic course of the Great Depression would not have been much different, according to Sims's model.

Conclusion

The calculations reported here support Sims's basic conclusion: According to his model, monetary policy does not matter. His model

DISCUSSION

suggests that if M1 had been prevented from falling during the Great Depression, the calamitous fall in output would have occurred anyway. But, what about the other facts that suggest that money matters? For example, in the introduction to my remarks I cited the fact that high interest rates precede recessions. If the results implied by Sims's model hold up to further scrutiny, then nonmonetary explanations for these observations should be explored.[11]

Sims's results are so surprising, I suspect that most will find them unacceptable. I too am suspicious. But, the results have been produced using an explicit, quantitative model. For anyone who disagrees, Sims has presented something very concrete to shoot at.

Appendix: The Counterfactual Experiment

In this appendix I describe how I computed a sequence of monetary policy shocks that would have kept money growth in the 1930s roughly on its 1920s growth path. Let the vector of data be as in Sims's paper, that is,

$$Y_t = [\log(GDP_t), \log(CPI_t), \log(currency_t), \log(M1_t), \log(R_t), \log(Pcomm_t)],$$

where R_t is the discount rate and $Pcomm_t$ is an index of commodity prices. The vector autoregressive representation for Y_t is:

$$Y_t = B_0 + B_1 Y_{t-1} + B_2 Y_{t-2} + \ldots + B_7 Y_{t-7} + A_0^{-1} \varepsilon_t, \quad (A.1)$$

where ε_t is a 6 × 1 vector of shocks that is uncorrelated over time and has a variance-covariance matrix equal to the identity matrix. Also, A_0 and B_i, $i = 1, \ldots, 7$, are 6 × 6 matrices and B_0 is a 6 × 1 vector of constants estimated by Sims.[12] The monetary policy shock is the fifth element of ε_t. The identifying restrictions imposed by Sims on A_0 imply that all elements above the diagonal of A_0^{-1} are zero, except the (5,6) element, which is non-zero.

The estimation procedure implemented by Sims produces a sequence of fitted shocks, ε_t, for $t =$ January 1919 to $t =$ May 1939. When these and the initial observations on Y_t for the last seven months of 1918 are incorporated into (A.1), the simulated Y_ts for the period January 1919 to May 1939 reproduce the actual data exactly. The counterfactual experiment keeps the non-policy historical shocks unchanged at their historical values too. It keeps the pre-1929 values of the policy shocks at their historical values too. It simply replaces the post-December 1928 policy shocks by values that keep money growth roughly on the same growth path as it followed in the 1920s. That is, I compute a date t policy shock to keep $E_t \log(M1_{t+1}) - \log(M1_t)$ close to 0.0033 for $t =$ January 1929 to $t =$ May 1939.

The period t policy shock is computed as follows. The fifth element of ε_t is to be determined, while the others are determined by their historical values. Let $\tau = [0\ 0\ 0\ 1\ 0\ 0]$, and note that

$$\log(M1_t) = \tau(B_0 + B_1 Y_{t-1} + B_2 Y_{t-2} + \ldots + B_7 Y_{t-7} + A_0^{-1} \varepsilon_t).$$

---

[11] For initial steps in this direction, see Christiano and Fisher (1998) and Sims (1980).
[12] For an extensive review of the identification issues involved in inferring the B_is and A_0 from a sample of data, see Christiano, Eichenbaum, and Evans (1998).

Since the fifth element of ε_t does not enter this expression, $\log(M1_t)$ is well defined. Then,

$$0.0033 = E_t \log(M1_{t+1}) - \log(M1_t)$$

$$= \tau[B_0 + B_1B_0 + (B_1B_1 + B_2)Y_{t-1} + \ldots + (B_1B_6 + B_7)Y_{t-6}$$

$$+ B_1B_7Y_{t-7} + B_1A_0^{-1}\varepsilon_t] - \log(M1_t).$$

Given that $\log(M1_t)$ is determined, this represents one equation in the one unknown element of ε_t. Denote the policy shock generated by this computation, $\tilde{\varepsilon}_{5t}$. Denote the historical value of the policy shock by $\hat{\varepsilon}_{5t}$. I found that replacing $\hat{\varepsilon}_{5t}$ by $\tilde{\varepsilon}_{5t}$ resulted in counterfactual simulations in which all variables but $\log(M1_t)$ oscillated so wildly that the scales on the graphs had to be expressed in scientific notation. The results reported in the comment are instead based on replacing $\hat{\varepsilon}_{5t}$ by $0.7\hat{\varepsilon}_{5t} + 0.3\tilde{\varepsilon}_{5t}$. This completes the discussion of the computation of the period t policy shock. With ε_t in hand, Y_t may be computed using (A.1). I then proceed to compute ε_{t+1} and Y_{t+1}, and so on.

References

Bordo, Michael, Ehsan U. Choudri, and Anna J. Schwartz. 1995. "Could Stable Money Have Averted the Great Contraction?" *Economic Inquiry*, 33, no. 3, July, pp. 484–505.

Christiano, Lawrence J., Martin Eichenbaum, and Charles Evans. 1998. "Monetary Policy Shocks: What Have We Learned and to What End?" NBER Working Paper No. 6400. Forthcoming in Taylor and Woodford, eds., *Handbook of Macroeconomics*.

Christiano, Lawrence J. and Jonas D. M. Fisher. 1998. "Stock Market and Investment Good Prices: Implications for Macroeconomics." Manuscript, Federal Reserve Bank of Chicago.

Friedman, Milton and Anna Jacobson Schwartz. 1963. *A Monetary History of the United States, 1867–1960*. Princeton, NJ: Princeton University Press for National Bureau of Economic Research.

Hamilton, James D. 1987. "Monetary Factors in the Great Depression." *Journal of Monetary Economics*, 19, pp. 145–169.

King, Robert and Mark Watson. 1996. "Money, Prices, Interest Rates and the Business Cycle." *The Review of Economics and Statistics*, LXXVIII, no. 1, pp. 35–53.

McCallum, Bennett. 1990. "Could a Monetary Base Rule Have Prevented the Great Depression?" *Journal of Monetary Economics*, 26, pp. 3–26.

Sims, Christopher A. 1980. "International Evidence on Monetary Factors in Macroeconomic Fluctuations." Center for Economic Research Discussion Paper no. 80–137, Department of Economics, University of Minnesota, September.

Taylor, John B. 1998. "An Historical Analysis of Monetary Policy Rules." Paper prepared for the National Bureau of Economic Research Conference on Monetary Policy Rules, Islamorada, Florida, Jan. 15–17, 1998.

Discussion

Benjamin M. Friedman*

   In an important series of papers, now dating over more than a quarter-century, Christopher Sims has added to our understanding of U.S. macroeconomic behavior in general and the influence on macroeconomic activity of U.S. monetary policy in particular. The contribution made by these papers lies both in their specific empirical findings and in the methodologies they have developed, which other researchers (here I include myself) have widely adopted for their own purposes. Sims's paper in this volume nicely extends this line of work: Its methodology appears to be of broad applicability. The empirical results it presents are striking, indeed startling. And as is so often the case in Sims's papers, side comments scattered throughout the paper (including the footnotes) offer nuggets of wisdom on the epistemology of economics.
   That said, I am skeptical that the current paper delivers on its objective of clarifying the role played by Federal Reserve policy in either causing or cushioning U.S. business cycles. Sims's main conclusion here is that monetary policy is pretty much irrelevant to fluctuations in macroeconomic activity: that the departures from regular policy behavior that have occurred historically have had only small consequences and, further, that substituting one pattern of regular behavior for another would not have made much difference. If the model he presents has succeeded in identifying Federal Reserve actions and measuring their economic effects, these findings should force us to reconsider many aspects of economics and economic policy.
   The title of this conference is "Beyond Shocks." The methodology that Sims deploys in his paper honors the obvious intent of this title, in

---

*William Joseph Maier Professor of Political Economy, Harvard University.

that it goes beyond the conventional practice of most vector autoregression analyses applied to monetary policy (which in turn resonates all too well with the theoretical presumptions of modern rational expectations macroeconomics), which is to ignore the regular, systematic behavior of monetary policy and focus only on the "shocks" corresponding to irregular, nonsystematic central bank actions. Yes, Sims does examine here the historical sequence of monetary policy shocks that his model implies, and yes, he investigates how both real economic activity and prices respond to those policy shocks. But he also focuses on the way in which monetary policy has systematically tightened in response to real economic strength and inflation, or, alternatively, eased in response to economic weakness. And he tries to pin down the effects of this systematic policy behavior by asking what difference it would have made, for real output, prices, and so on, if one kind of systematic monetary policy had been substituted for another.

While I therefore applaud this aspect of Sims's methodology, in the end it is precisely this feature of his work here that, if correct, proves subversive of so much of what we think we know about economics in general and monetary policy in particular. Specifically, Sims estimates two different representations of systematic monetary policy behavior: one describing the postwar period (1948 to 1997) and the other describing the interwar period (1919 to 1939). The two clearly differ. But the heart of his conclusion that monetary policy does not much matter for business cycles is his finding that, to a first approximation, the Great Depression of the 1930s would still have occurred, even if the Federal Reserve in the interwar years had instead followed the far more proactive monetary policy it adopted after World War II (and, according to Sims, has pursued ever since). See in particular Sims's key Figure 5.

In light of the focus of this conference on business cycles, in the standard sense of fluctuations in production and employment, this emphasis on whether a different monetary policy could have prevented or at least cushioned the Great Depression is appropriate. But Sims also applies his methodology in the opposite direction—that is, looking to see what the *postwar* period would have been like if the Federal Reserve had simply carried on, for another half-century, under the same monetary policy as in the 1920s and 1930s. And here, unlike in his analysis of the Depression, Sims's model produces findings that practically every economist—and plenty of other readers too—will find deeply problematic.

As in much of the industrialized world, a major feature of the post-World War II experience in the United States has been the sustained rise in prices. Before World War II, prices sometimes rose but also sometimes fell, with no discernible trend over long periods of time. U.S. prices on the eve of World War II were, on average, approximately the same as on the eve of the Civil War (or, for that matter, the eve of the American Revolution, to the extent that the vast differences in economic circumstances admit direct comparisons). By contrast, prices have risen almost continuously since 1945. Over the past half century the American economy has, in effect, added a zero to the average price. The first-class letter that cost 3 cents in the early postwar years now costs over 30 cents.

Sims's most striking finding, I believe, is not that monetary policy had little to do with the interwar Depression but that it had little to do with the postwar inflation. During the interwar period prices fell dramatically. (See Sims's Figure 6.) Yet according to Sims, if the Federal Reserve in the postwar period had followed the same systematic monetary policy that delivered that interwar *de*flation, the postwar result would still have been the historically unprecedented phenomenon of a half century of sustained *in*flation. (See Sims's Figure 13.) One does not have to be a believer in the claim that "Money is everywhere and always a monetary phenomenon," or similarly misleading overstatements, to think that over periods as long as 20 years in one case and 50 years in the other, the trend rate of rise or fall of the price level is importantly influenced by monetary policy. Here it simply is not.

The most probable reason, I believe, is that Sims's model has not adequately identified the Federal Reserve's monetary policy actions, or their macroeconomic effects, or perhaps neither. If that is so, however, then the model's implied irrelevance of monetary policy for inflation is not all that is problematic. The implied irrelevance for business cycles, including not only questions about the Great Depression but also whether monetary policy has played a major role in either causing or cushioning the business recessions our economy has experienced in the postwar period, is invalid as well.

A close reading of the paper suggests that Sims is aware of these problems too. His reference to potentially important effects of "nonmonetary" aspects of central bank policy—for example, whether or not it is standard practice to rescue illiquid and/or insolvent banks, whether bank depositors are insured against whatever failures do occur, and so on—is a clear recognition that something of consequence may happen in the economy but not in his model. But even apart from such supernumerary aspects of central bank policy, it is also entirely possible that the model's estimated "policy" equation, relating the discount rate to output, prices, and money, does not adequately capture how monetary policy has historically behaved. (For example, the rule of thumb that John Taylor has proposed to describe Federal Reserve behavior during the Greenspan years would imply interest rates in the Depression an order of magnitude more negative than what Sims reports in his Figure 4 from applying to the Depression the rule that he estimates to represent the postwar period.) Correspondingly, it is also possible that the model's equations relating output and prices to the discount rate are likewise underestimates.

One straightforward way to check out this possibility would be to solve the model backward, to see what pattern of interest rates (since that is how Sims characterizes monetary policy) would have been necessary to achieve a given clearly counterfactual outcome. Most obviously, what pattern of interest rates does the model say the Federal Reserve would have to have implemented in order to hold prices (and, indirectly, money) to a flat rather than rising trend over the postwar period? Is this implied interest rate trajectory plausible? If so, then maybe the model is correct after all, and the Federal Reserve could have adopted a slightly different but nonetheless noninflationary monetary policy but just did not do so. But if the implied noninflationary interest rates are implausible, then instead of believing that a noninflationary policy path was somehow impossible in the postwar period, I would instead conclude that the model misrepresents monetary policy, or its effects, or both. (Carrying out an equivalent exercise for the interwar period, asking what monetary policy would have prevented the Depression, is less straightforward because even in Sims's own interwar simulations, the zero minimum on nominal interest rates is a problem. As he suggests, direct intervention to prevent bank failures, and other policy actions also not modeled at all here, would presumably have been necessary to arrest the early 1930s decline in real activity levels.)

I will conclude with a few shorter remarks about aspects of Sims's paper that also bear comment but are less central to his principal mission. First, Sims's treatment of systematic Federal Reserve policy in the postwar period as having followed one unchanging pattern throughout seems to me highly dubious. Are we really to equate Paul Volcker's tough stance against inflation with the see-no-evil regime of Arthur Burns? Or to think of Alan Greenspan as simply the reincarnation of G. William Miller? Sims does test for a shift in systematic monetary policy, at July 1979 (why not October?), but he does so by asking whether all 279 of his model's estimated parameters, from all six equations, remain unchanged. I did not understand why he did not focus his test more narrowly on the parameters of the one equation that he takes to represent monetary policy. After all, when he uses his model to investigate the effect of substituting one systematic monetary policy for another, it is only that one equation that he changes.

Second, Sims's appeal to the "fiscal theory of the price level" seems to me very much a red herring in the context of this paper. As recent papers by Michael Woodford and Willem Buiter help to make clear, the so-called fiscal theory of the price level amounts to invoking one pathology to rectify the problems created by another. In particular, as Bennett McCallum's work nicely demonstrated some time ago, when the central bank engages in a "pure interest rate peg" (like what the Federal Reserve was forced to follow in the early postwar years, before the 1951 Treasury–Federal Reserve Accord), the absence of any nominal anchor to monetary policy means that the price level is, in principle, undetermined. In practical terms, over time prices could do anything. The fiscal theory of the price level amounts to positing that the government can follow what is normally an infeasible budget trajectory (Woodford calls this a "non-Ricardian" trajectory), which somehow violates the usual intertemporal constraint requiring the government to raise taxes in the future to either service or pay off its debt outstanding as of any given time. As Woodford and others have shown, under the right conditions one consequence of this infeasible budget trajectory is to restore the determinacy of the price level, which the central bank had given up by pegging a nominal interest rate.

The opening that Sims exploits to introduce this bizarre confluence of pathologies here is the zero minimum on nominal interest rates: Once easy monetary policy pushes the short-term interest rate to zero, and keeps it there, the central bank has backed into a pure interest rate peg. Hence the price level becomes indeterminate. But once the interest rate on Treasury obligations is zero, in principle the government can sell whatever amount of securities it chooses without having to worry about needing tax revenues later on to service the (zero) interest payments as they come due, and a "non-Ricardian" fiscal trajectory, which is normally nonfeasible, becomes feasible in this case. Hence fiscal policy restores price determinacy.

A problem in all this, of course, is that once the Treasury starts selling securities in volume, the required interest rate will rise above zero unless the central bank buys them in—in which case we are back to the usual case of printing money. Moreover, as Sims points out, even during the Depression the interest rate on longer-term Treasury debt never came close to zero anyway. (A related issue is that I did not understand Sims's statement that the central bank's ability to carry out its lender-of-last-resort function depends on its access to direct budgetary support from the government. I agree that what is involved in acting as a lender of last resort is, ultimately, command over resources. But so long as the central bank can print money—in other words, create reserves on its own books—I do not see why direct support from the government's budget is necessary.)

Finally, Sims's nicely articulated rejection of what he calls the third version of the Lucas critique (including not only the discussion in his section "What About the Lucas Critique?" but also his well-put footnote 10) should be required reading for all students of macroeconomics. So should the philosophy he advances, in the first part of his paper, on the all-important subject of individual maximization. It is, in fact, far more subversive of currently fashionable practice than he lets on. Here, as in so much else, I say more power to him.

Financial Markets and Business Cycles: Lessons from Around the World. A Panel Discussion

After Asia: New Directions for the International Financial System

Rudiger Dornbusch*

In Mexico's massive earthquake, some years back, many of the splendid new buildings collapsed, burying and killing a large number of people in the debris. Without the earthquake they surely would not have crashed; in fact they had graced the skyline for years, monuments to their proud owners and builders. But examination revealed that the concrete had far too much sand and too little of the real stuff. Not surprisingly, under stress they gave way. That surely was not an accident—the building codes were there, and the inspectors stood by, collecting the payoffs for overlooking unsound construction. Just the same has been happening in cross-border finance. Emerging market balance sheets stand up in fair weather, but under stress they collapse. *Vulnerability* is the key word; *risk* is another way of looking at it. No two crises are quite alike, but they all have in common that without significant vulnerability, currency and financial collapse is very unlikely.

In the aftermath of every crisis, whether war or currency collapse, a soul-searching effort is made to build a better world. Just such an effort, short-lived and without leaving a trace, got under way after the Mexican debacle. Another is being conducted just now. Asia's collapse and Japan's implosion are the obvious triggers. This is a great occasion for bad ideas, or just impractical ones, to draw attention and gain respectability. Let us set out here where the crises come from and what is the most effective way of dealing with them, before we rush headlong down the wrong path.

In the past, balance-of-payments crises were predominantly current

---

*Ford Professor of Economics and International Management, Massachusetts Institute of Technology.

account crises and the story would go somewhat like this. A country had a large trade deficit from overvaluation or overexpansion or both. There was some debt service and not enough money around. Reserves would already have run off, new loans were not to be gotten. Sooner or later a devaluation and/or recession would rectify the situation, and as for habitual offenders, they would soon be back in the same situation. More often than not, the external deficit was just the counterpart of a budget deficit, happy twins of overspending. Invariably they would be supplemented with fixed rates to contain inflation and thus give the public a boon, too, by raising real wages in dollars. Social peace means high wages in dollars, big government, and full employment, while external balance means just that—you can pay your way. Obviously the two goals can come in conflict and reality, meaning the external constraint, always wins out, sooner or later. When it comes to the showdown, spending needs to be cut and wages in dollars have to fall, with austerity the answer.

More recent crises, starting with the early 1980s in Latin America, Mexico in 1994-95, and now Asia and Russia, are fundamentally different in that balance-sheet issues are entirely central to the fact and surely the propagation of the crisis. Moreover, they increasingly involve the private sector and not just public sector external debt, as in the 1980s debt crisis or in the case of Mexico. These crises have to do with an inability to roll over an existing debt, a liquidation scramble, and a resulting currency collapse.[1] Balance-sheet crises by their nature have far more leverage both in collapsing a country's financial structure and hence its economy and in spreading contamination. They are capital market crises. Capital market crises have more oomph once they happen; meltdown is the best description. Their resolution is also more complicated and certainly more costly.

Designing an international system that is less crisis-prone must address the central issue of capital market crises—unsound finance, which translates into national balance sheet vulnerability. It is naïve to believe that we can abolish crises altogether, but surely we must be able to do far better in limiting the fallout, once crises happen.

INTERPRETING THE ASIAN CRISIS

The Asian crisis is easily interpreted as a capital market crisis—not a crisis of capitalism, as Japanese officials like to argue. Central to that interpretation are several ingredients:

- In the balance sheets of the financial system and large corporations there was systematic mismatching of *maturities*. Emerging market

---

[1] The term liquidation scramble comes from the 1930s, when it was used in the context of the liquidity of the national balance sheet at a time of financial crisis.

banks and firms borrowed short, either because it was cheaper or because nobody was willing to lend to them at long maturities. On the asset side they used loans to fund long-term investments such as real estate development, corporate capital formation, or even infrastructure: not a good idea, to fund highways with overnight money! In referring to "loans," already we make the point implicitly that equity might have been a much better vehicle. The resulting vulnerability takes the form of liquidity risk—the sudden inability to roll over debts that moves companies and countries from sunny skies into the midst of a funding crisis.
- The second source of vulnerability was mismatching of *denominations*. Asia borrowed in dollars or yen to fund investments with payoffs in local currency. As a result, balance sheets were exposed to the risk of currency movements. A major currency depreciation would carry the risk of bankrupting a large part of the financial system or their loan customers. Mismatched denominations are like driving without car insurance: Every day there is no accident, it is money saved. But when an accident occurs, the absence of a currency hedge becomes disastrously expensive.
- The third source of vulnerability was *market risk*—borrowing to carry assets that are exposed to large fluctuations in their capital value: stocks, commodities, foreign exchange, or high-risk instruments such as Brady bonds. Korean financial institutions, for example, had taken a large position in Russian bonds and Brazilian Brady bonds. When their prices fell sharply, the balance sheets of the Koreans instantly had a huge hole.
- The next source of vulnerability was *national credit risk*. Because the various banks and companies collectively had assumed a large risk position, the national credit rating had been put at risk, with spillover effects to anyone in case of a liquidation scramble, both in terms of the capital value of their assets and their access to alternative sources of credit.

In a well-supervised financial system—say the United States or the United Kingdom today—all this could not have happened. But, of course, it is routine in Japan, Russia, or anywhere in Latin America. The negligent or deliberate lack of regulation, supervision, and transparency then comes in as an explanation for the fragile financial structure. This is further complicated by a key mistake on the part of central banks: gambling away the reserves. Central banks in both Thailand and Korea went out of their way to take gambles in forward markets until their reserves were gone; they went out of their way to cheat on the numbers. Any sense of sleaze or lack of transparency was certainly reinforced by the active cooperation of bureaucrats who have worked untiringly taking bribes, overlooking flagrant risk-taking, and adding to the vulnerability by misrepresenting central bank assets. All this would not be possible without active help from politicians. In this last sense, the Asian crisis is also a crisis of corrupt governments.

Of course, vulnerability alone is not enough to cause an accident. Something has to happen to bring the fragility into play. Here external factors play a role. It would be wrong to place the entire blame on mismanagement in the Asian economies themselves. Two critical complications came from the outside. But that is by way of explanation—vulnerability has to do with just such possibilities! First, Japan went into the tank, and the resulting deterioration in Asian economies' trade environment accounts for some of the problem. The shadow following over Asian investment opportunities added to the problem.

Second, and perhaps more important, the dollar/yen rate moved sharply, thereby leaving the dollar peggers high and dry. That, too, is only by way of explanation. The yen had been as strong as 80 ¥/$ only as recently as 1995 and as weak as 200 ¥/$ in the mid 1980s. The idea that the yen could depreciate was not a brand-new concept that risk-takers could be excused for overlooking. Those who enjoyed the stark yen overvaluation, with its resulting export competitiveness for dollar peggers, surely must have understood that the pendulum swings wide *both* ways.

The summary of factors can be customized to country experiences. How, for example, did the Philippines avoid meltdown? They came late to the game, took little of the external money, and hence had less of a balance-sheet problem and less of a meltdown—more nearly the old style of crisis. Or Malaysia, banking problems, yes, but much less of an external debt problem because financing took the form of direct investment. Or Korea, where the aggravation of circumstances lies in the dysfunctional corporate structure—debt-equity ratios of 500 percent plus for the chaebols, which control 50 percent of GDP.

If so much is made of vulnerability now, how come nothing had gone wrong in the past? The answer is that the vulnerability was of very recent vintage—three or four years and not more. Financial opening, and hence the very possibility of taking on big risks rather than just bad loans on balance sheets, is a matter of the past handful of years.

The typical scenario, following financial liberalization, is a lending boom funded by offshore borrowing under the cover of a fixed or at least very stable exchange rate. Then, once positions are in place, a disturbance comes on the horizon: Domestic investment, notably overdone, goes sour, and soon there is a conflict between keeping up the financing by high interest rates and keeping up the domestic institutions, banks and companies, by low interest rates. If the interest rates are cut, the currency crashes, and if they are raised, the banks and companies crash. In the end, both crash because individual foreign lenders understand that the situation is not viable; returns do not cover the risk, the herd is leaving, and they certainly do not want to be left holding an empty bag.

Vulnerability is in part an objective fact but, just as in the case of bank runs, in part it is in the eyes of the beholder. *Contamination* therefore is very much part of the play. If the unsustainability of banks or debts is obvious in one place, hard questions will immediately be asked of the next—Why not earlier? is an interesting question, but not relevant at this point. Safety first is the motto of investors when they smell a rat. Thus, one vulnerable economy tumbles after another. They did not have to, in some immutable statistical sense; it was just that they came under suspicion, and the rest is history. Countries that are not vulnerable will also be tested, but they can raise rates and defend their currency and that quickly becomes a losing game for investors, so that they call off the siege, at least until further notice.[2]

Note that neither current account deficits nor budget deficits nor even misaligned exchange rates were part of the balance-sheet-crisis story. In fact, the budget situation in most Asian economies was quite strong and while exchange rates collapsed, they certainly had not been crassly overvalued as measured by PPP comparisons. (At least that was the case in Asia, though not, of course, in Mexico.) If there was a sign of something amiss it was in the boom atmosphere that had gotten to construction, consumption, and luxury imports. It had all the experience of what in the late 1970s Argentines called *plata dulce.*

GOOD ANSWERS

The right answer for crisis avoidance is controlling risk. That is done routinely in the domestic financial system of the United Kingdom or the United States, where the supervisory authorities set and enforce capital standards as well as sophisticated risk measurement. The London authorities go further in imposing differentiated capital requirements for cross-border loans to regions where regulatory or supervisory standards are classified as lax. That is being serious about risk.

How could this be done at the international level? A modest ambition is to create a new culture that focuses on dissemination of the right thinking, learning from the present crisis to put in place more responsible balance sheets. A more ambitious scheme would make support in the case of "honest" accidents conditional on compliance with a tightly written and audited scheme.

The starting point of any discussion is that regulators and supervisors in most countries even today have no clue, nor for that purpose do

---

[2] What is said here of Asia is not the case, however, for Russia or Brazil, where budgets are unabashedly large.

rating agencies. The appropriate conceptual framework is *value at risk*—a model-driven estimate of the maximum risk for a particular balance sheet situation over a specified horizon. There are genuine issues of modeling, but no issue whatsoever in recognizing that this approach is the right one. Measures such as debt-to-exports never appear in it, but the ratio of foreign liabilities as a share of total liabilities, or the share that is short-dated, would be just as important as the variability of asset prices or the likelihood of an external shock that triggers contamination.

If authorities everywhere enforced a culture of risk-oriented evaluation of balance sheets, extreme situations such as those of Asia would just disappear or, at the worst, become a rare species. Perhaps it took a bad experience to understand that the issue is risk. And it is latent in a balance sheet rather than falling from heaven.

A more ambitious step, with an appropriate transition period, would be to actually use the regular International Monetary Fund (IMF) consultations as the inspection opportunity for the national balance sheet. Countries that want to have IMF support when in trouble would qualify only if they have, in fact, in the recent past been in compliance with an agreed risk control strategy. This procedure has three advantages. First and foremost, it institutionalizes risk analysis as part of the local supervisory process and as such creates the right culture. Second, it directly lowers risk levels worldwide, because countries will be eager to qualify for IMF support in case of honest accidents, which are still possible though less likely. Third, anyone who opts out and wants to run a national gambling house can do so. But it would be clear to financial markets that value at risk exceeds internationally acceptable thresholds and, as a result, financing will be hard to get and will be expensive. Hence the incentive for rogue countries to join the club.

There is nothing wild-eyed about this proposal, particularly if it includes a transition period in which countries can implement what each and every one of them should want to do with the greatest urgency. But that does not mean it will happen at the IMF. The IMF is owned and operated by its board, that is, by representatives of countries like Japan who have no concept of sound finance and no willingness to get there soon. The IMF and its board actively enjoy crisis situations, since they give bureaucrats the opportunity to wield power and expand the scope and mandate of their institution. The notion that anything preemptive is impractical is far too easily accepted. Accordingly, the immediate interest of what to do with a Russia commands the only attention, and how to get a less risky system some four or five years from now gets none.

IMF Programs

Another area of contention is what exactly the IMF should ask of countries on the operating table. In the course of the Asian crisis the IMF got a bad name, just as it already had in Latin America in the 1970s. In the past, the IMF had been demonized, and it is a bit surprising how it recovered its reputation or at least lost the stigma. Perhaps it was the success of Mexico with ultra-IMF policies.

Many, but most surprisingly World Bank chief economist Joseph Stiglitz, have been preaching liberation theology. Their message is simply this: The IMF is wrong, high interest rates in the process of stabilization are destructive of sound credit, and fiscal restraint is inappropriate since it adds to the recessionary forces. It is not quite clear what the stabilization is all about, if it is not tighter money and sounder public finances, however.

A key point is to separate debt restructuring, which is unpopular but maybe inevitable, from high interest rates. To restore financial stability, the first point is to put a floor under the currency. If everybody wants to get out because the risk-reward trade-off is too unfavorable, high interest rates are the way to change the equation. A successful stabilization without a hike in rates is like Hamlet without the Prince of Denmark. But that may well leave the issue of bad debts in banks and companies and, as a result, bankruptcy risks. The answer is twofold. First, you cannot make omelets without breaking some eggs. Second, debt write-offs may be inevitable; not raising rates is just a bad idea, not a solution.

Mexico, for example, fully implemented a stark U.S.-IMF program of tight money to stabilize the currency and restore confidence. It implemented a tight fiscal policy to restore public credit. Starting off in a near-meltdown situation, confidence returned and within a year the country was on the second leg of a V-shaped recovery. The high interest rate policy was far from easy, economically and politically, and partial debt relief was provided, at public expense, to various sectors. That pragmatic way of dealing with the high interest rate issue ought to be the example of separating debt issues (dead money) from the problem of reversing capital flight and stabilizing exchange rates. The IMF is unqualifiedly right in its insistence on high interest rates as the front end of stabilization.

The fiscal issue is in principle more complicated. If a country runs into a currency crisis but actually has no fiscal or debt problem to speak of, should the budget be tightened? The answer is surely no, that there is no reason to take extra pain. Of course, in practice that is not the case. In Asia the financial distress of banks and companies moved a very substantial liability into the budget. The result was a major prospective fiscal deterioration and a resulting need to make provision. Taking a 30-percent-of-GDP hit in public credit needs an offset in the budget to restore the confidence of investors. In fact, the less is done on the budget, the more will have to be done with interest rates. Thus, while in some cases the IMF may have been overzealous, it is doubtful that much of a mistake was made. Public finance has deteriorated massively; calling back mega projects at such a time is totally correct.

It must be confusing to finance ministers and central bankers around the world to see the World Bank shoot them in the back just as they try and stabilize their currencies. The World Bank's liberation theology is a very bad idea, one that makes everybody's task of stabilization even harder than it already is. If somewhere in the Washington institutions malpractice is to be found, it surely is at the World Bank.

But there is a more critical issue, one of prevention versus remedy. Part of crisis management is to change the way the game is played. Intelligent leadership uses the crisis situation not just to make the country function better. Surely, the IMF should go a step further than just shifting hundreds of billion dollars to the bailout front. Even more so in a systemic crisis, as is claimed for the Asian situation, improvements ought to be made in the way the system is run. Let the IMF's bailout function be supplemented by rigorous reporting and auditing of national balance sheets, so that the bailouts are more in line with acceptable moral hazard rather than, as in the case of Russia today, a flagrant in-your-face assertion of "too large to fail" by the client.

If IMF stabilization programs are right in basic design, an issue of calibration is always present, and so far the IMF has felt safe to err on the side of amputation without sedation—but there is no excuse for the IMF's long-standing disregard for risk management. The IMF, unlike the Bank for International Settlements in Basle, has paid no attention to balance sheets and their risks; it has been plain asleep at the wheel. It has indulged in lecturing about budget deficits and lack of commitment to low inflation, disregarding the far more explosive issue of mismanaged balance sheets. The Mexican crisis was not one of inflation or budget deficits, nor was the Asian crisis. There is no excuse for the disregard of risk management, the more so if the IMF is eagerly calling for more resources to enhance its role as a lender of last resort. To have a fiscal affairs department that explores the nooks and crannies of budgets but not to have a balance sheet department is stark mad. The U.S. Congress should refuse further IMF monies until an entire floor of the IMF building is devoted to balance sheet and risk management supervision, even if that means closing the cafeteria.

EXCHANGE RATE REGIMES[3]

Exchange rates played a crucial role in leveraging the Asian crisis. Accordingly, it stands to reason that we should reevaluate the lessons for

---

[3] For a further discussion, see R. Dornbusch and F. Giavazzi, "Hard Money and Sound Credit," on the author's website at http://www.mit.edu/~rudi.

exchange rate policy that come out of the experience of Mexico and Asia. For many countries in Eastern Europe and in Latin America, the answer is obvious: Forget about nationally managed monies, adopt the euro in Europe or the dollar in Latin America as the national money. The notion that central banks can successfully maintain fixed exchange rates, until further notice, is not supported by any evidence. The scheme just leads to mega bets on the currency and, in the end, the country sides with the loser and picks up the losses. Having no national currency (just like giving up the "national" airline) becomes totally plausible once we recognize that capital markets rather than current accounts dominate exchange rate issues.

If giving up the national money outright is not an acceptable answer, a currency board goes far in the same direction. It abolishes largely, though not fully, the question of credibility of the exchange rate. Such a system has functioned well in Argentina and Hong Kong. It cannot, of course, avoid the spillover of regional economic crises, but it can perfectly well avoid a collapse of the currency, which makes everything much worse. The counterargument, that currency boards or full dollarization sacrifice the lender of last resort function, is deeply misguided. National central banks can print money, and that is rarely the right answer to a banking crisis provoked by a loss of confidence in the country. Lender of last resort support can readily be rented, along with bank supervision, by requiring financial institutions to carry offshore guarantees. That is a system in line with modern capital markets; nationally managed currencies that are highly politicized are the stark opposite.

DENOUNCING SOME BAD ANSWERS

Among the bad ideas, we should single out some as particularly inadequate. If Goldman goes to the capital market to get more firepower, should not the IMF and the World Bank also get more ammunition? The first impulse is, of course, to provide more money. True, the world financial system today has far more firepower than ever before. Investors have deep pockets and countries cannot be expected to have the resources that can conceivably match what 100 short sellers (including central banks that join the attack, as indeed happens) can put on the table. But making available more rescue money, without anything else, is much the same as answering the plea for bigger and better arms for the police—it raises the quality of the shootouts.[4]

It is already the case that the resources used since Mexico exceed anything one might have imagined at the beginning of the 1990s, when

---

[4] See "Capital Controls: An Idea Whose Time Is Gone," on the author's website at http://www.mit.edu./~rudi.

the last debt default was still being worked off. As we come to the hard core "too large to fail" countries, Russia and Brazil—flagrant offenders both in fiscal probity and in risk management—the numbers become staggering and the violence done in terms of moral hazard unbounded. Would it not be a good idea to have a country like Russia do a forced restructuring of maturities, to make the point that what seems totally liquid to the lender in fact never is, in a crunch? That ought to help mismatching of maturities.

Another terrible idea is capital controls as an alternative to risk management. One might have sympathy with Chilean-style management of inflows, but one has to doubt that countries where inefficient or dishonest administration is the rule (unlike in sweet Chile!) can run a sensible system. More likely, it will be a festival of corruption.

An even worse idea, or a non-idea, is an Asian IMF. In the heat of the Thailand crisis, possibly as a very cynical move to push the U.S. Treasury and the IMF into lending and thus avoid a key contributing role for itself, Japan offered the idea of an Asian IMF, and it has kept that idea alive to this day. The Asian IMF would pool resources and do mutual surveillance in the region. Who can take this seriously? The lead country, Japan, is the most in need of a serious financial cleanup and the least able to exercise leadership, since it is totally stymied by its own problems. Who can see a Korean official telling an Indonesian that they need to pull their socks up and cannot be quite so corrupt? If this proposal had gone anywhere, it would have meant a festival of restrictions and circumvention and priorities for Japanese banks to get paid off ahead of the rest. Fortunately and rightly, China stayed away from the whole exercise and it flopped.[5]

---

[5] Flop it did, but it is not quite dead. The Japanese Ministry of Finance just released a report which, among many bad ideas, proposes once again regional IMFs and, of course, massive injection of financial support. See Ministry of Finance, "Lessons from the Asian Currency Crises—Risks Related to Short-Term Capital Movement and the '21st Century-Type' Currency Crisis." Tokyo, May 1998.

Financial Shocks and Business Cycles: Lessons from Outside the United States

Maurice Obstfeld*

Both history and contemporary experience are replete with episodes of financial crisis leading to major output contractions. Predecessors of the current Asian crisis can be found in the interwar period as well as under the pre-World War I gold standard, although U.S. experience post-World War II is free so far of a recession initiated by widespread credit-institution problems. In 1890, the Barings crisis not only threw Argentina into turmoil, but also spilled over to "emerging markets" as distant as Australia and Turkey. In the United States, financial panics leading to recession were a regular occurrence before 1914. And, of course, even after: In 1931, twin banking and currency crises in central Europe spread to the United States, to other industrial economies, and to developing countries, hammering real activity and provoking a wave of international debt defaults. The developing-country debt crisis of the 1980s led to a near-decade of lost growth in Latin America and elsewhere, while the 1994-95 Mexican peso crisis led to a short, sharp contraction there and to contagion effects elsewhere, notably in Argentina.

Indeed, it is fair to say that for developing economies, exogenous fluctuations in capital flows have once again become a dominant business cycle shock. They remain a potential problem in developed economies as well, although lessons learned in the Great Depression and the resulting institutional reforms have greatly blunted the threat.

---

*Class of 1958 Professor of Economics, University of California, Berkeley. The author thanks Jay Shambaugh for assistance, and the National Science Foundation for research support.

Capital Flows and Instability of Expectations

It is well accepted that credit markets can have multiple equilibria, so that exogenous shifts in expectations—"sunspots" if you will—can play a role, potentially an important role, in generating cyclical fluctuations. Diamond and Dybvig (1983) formalized the point that an illiquid credit institution could be viable if depositors had confidence in the value of its short-term obligations, but would fail if depositors coordinated instead on an equilibrium in which all attempted to withdraw their funds. Of course, long experience had strongly suggested the possibility as well!

In a purely domestic context, public policy has sought to limit such expectational instability through partial deposit insurance, lender of last resort support, accounting standards, capitalization requirements, and direct prudential supervision and regulation. The latter three ingredients serve to limit the moral hazard—on the part of depositors as well as deposit takers—that official guarantees induce. Even in developed countries, however, such safeguards have failed to stop financial malfeasance and failure—witness the costly U. S. savings and loan collapse. Nor have they always prevented contagious financial crises. The current predicament of Japan, whose economy shrank at an annual rate above 5 percent in the first quarter of this year, stems from a number of factors, all of which have been greatly amplified by widespread corruption and a weak financial system that has never recovered from the collapse of the late-1980s Japanese "bubble" economy.

Financial crises can bring into question the credit of entire countries as well, and here too there can be an element of self-fulfilling prophecy, as in a bank run. In this case, pure investor panic becomes an important driving force for the economy. In East Asia, the effects of recent crises have been dramatic. Countries in the region have moved rather abruptly from very rapid positive to negative growth rates. First quarter 1998 GDP was 1.8 percent below its level a year earlier in Malaysia, 3.8 percent below in South Korea, 6.2 percent below in Indonesia, and 2 percent below in Hong Kong (*The Economist*, July 18th-24th, 1998, p. 92).

The possibility of national financial collapse, sparked by a reversal of capital inflows, is inherently harder to contain than the problem of domestic financial stability. In the international setting, gaps and asymmetries in prudential regulation make evasion comparatively easy. Formal deposit insurance does not apply, accounting standards differ across countries, there is no clearly defined lender of last resort nor any universally accepted legal procedure for working out insolvency problems. (International cooperation to plug some of these holes has been on the docket of the Basle Committee of international bank regulators since the 1970s.) In addition, exchange-rate risk adds another big potential source of illiquidity or even insolvency.

In thinking about problems due to capital flow instability, it is useful to separate for analytical purposes two types of international crisis—exchange-rate or currency crises, and national solvency crises. The separation is artificial, in that the two types of crisis may occur simultaneously and interact, but I wish to consider them separately for the moment, and only then ask why they often occur together.

Exchange-Rate Crises

In the 1990s, foreign exchange crises have disrupted exchange markets in western Europe, eastern Europe, South Africa, Latin America, and, of course, East Asia. These recent crises have sharpened debate over two opposing views on the causes of crises. One claim is that otherwise successful economies have been victims of greedy market operators, usually foreign ones. This view is especially popular with government ministers in the afflicted countries. The opposing view is that such crises are largely home-grown, and that the global capital market is simply performing a needed role in disciplining imprudent government policies.

Early modern analytical thinking on exchange-rate crises, starting with Krugman's (1979) seminal article, tended to support the latter view. In Krugman's story, a government with a finite stock of foreign exchange reserves is simultaneously pegging the exchange rate and following an expansive fiscal policy inconsistent with the indefinite maintenance of the peg. Because the fiscal expenditures are financed by running down foreign reserves, an eventual currency collapse is inevitable. Krugman elegantly showed how that collapse would occur on a uniquely defined date, as the result of a sudden speculative attack that forces the authorities to relinquish the currency peg even though their reserves are positive beforehand. In this story, speculators are merely acting as they must to prevent the emergence of excess profit opportunities.

Recent thinking on crises would argue that this theory is not universally correct, although it does not support the idea, either, that currency crises can occur any time market whims dictate one. Instead, there may be extensive "grey areas" in which unwise policies make countries vulnerable to crises, but in which a crisis is not inevitable and might in fact not occur without the impetus of international capital outflows.

For example, a government with a large domestic-currency public debt of short maturity may be induced to devalue by very high short-term interest rates, which themselves reflect a rational expectation of devaluation. The government's motivation in devaluing is to debase its debt in real terms so as to limit future tax burdens. On the other hand, there can be a benign equilibrium in which markets do not expect devaluation, interest rates are low, and the government's pain therefore is not so great as to induce a devaluation (Obstfeld 1994). A jump from the second equilibrium to the first—due to an essentially exogenous shock to market expectations—generates a sudden crisis. The Russian crisis that erupted in the late spring of 1998 fits this model well, as does the recent attack on Brazil's currency.

This logic suggests that crises may contain a self-fulfilling element, just as bank runs do, which can generate multiple equilibria in international asset markets and render the timing of crises somewhat indeterminate. What we see in these cases is a sharp break from an essentially tranquil equilibrium to a crisis state, rather than a gradual deterioration in domestic interest rates and other market-based indicators. This view helps explain why capital markets can appear to impose too little discipline before the crisis arrives, and too harsh a discipline afterward.

CRISES OF NATIONAL SOLVENCY

Solvency crises, on the other hand, could occur even in a country that uses the U.S. dollar as its currency; the exchange rate channel is not central in theory, although it often has been in practice. If lenders refuse to roll over a country's maturing dollar debts, and if the country lacks the liquid resources—foreign reserves and credit lines—with which to meet its obligations, a crisis ensues. Here we have a pretty precise analogy with the case of a banking panic, since willing rollover would preclude panic, whereas a market fear that others will flee makes it optimal for each individual lender to flee as well. In the 1980s debt crisis, much developing-country debt was incurred by sovereign governments or guaranteed by them. In the 1990s, the borrowers have been private banks and corporations, but governments have felt compelled to back up at least the banks' debts so as to avoid domestic financial collapse. And government credit support of banks has in some cases been on-lent to their corporate customers so as to (temporarily) prop up the paper value of bank assets. Thus, the earlier example of a government funding crisis largely applies. Díaz Alejandro (1985), describing Chile's experience in the early 1980s, gave a classic account of the nationalization of supposedly private foreign debts.

HOW CURRENCY CRISES AND NATIONAL SOLVENCY INTERACT

The European countries that devalued in the 1992 Exchange Rate Mechanism (ERM) currency crises did not subsequently fall into solvency crises, which is why their forced devaluations did not impair growth (indeed, may have helped it). In other cases, however, exchange rate and solvency crises can interact in explosive ways. The attempt to assure fixed exchange rates (or a preannounced ceiling on exchange depreciation) can lead to the very vulnerabilities that raise the possibility of an international solvency crisis. When domestic banks and corporate borrowers are (over)confident of an exchange rate, they may borrow dollars or yen without adequately hedging against the risk that the domestic currency will be devalued, sharply raising the ratio of their domestic-currency liabilities to their assets. They may believe that even if a crisis occurs, the government's promise to peg the exchange rate represents an implicit promise that they will be bailed out in one way or another. Borrowers may face little risk of personal loss even if a bailout does not materialize, because they have little capital of their own at stake.

This problem has been especially severe in developing countries, where prudential regulation is looser, financial institutions are weaker, and even the government's credit may be questionable. When market sentiment turns against the exchange rate peg, the government is effectively forced to assume the short foreign-currency positions in some way—or else to allow a cascade of domestic bankruptcies. Since the government at the same time has used its foreign exchange reserves (in a vain attempt to peg the exchange rate), may have sold dollars extensively in forward markets as Thailand did prior to floating the baht in July 1997, and cannot borrow more in world credit markets, national default becomes imminent.

What potential macro adjustments ratify the expectations of depreciation that start the process rolling? It is essentially the threat that the government budget, now burdened with higher public debts and the debts of the private banking system, will be balanced through inflation. It is of course true that currency depreciation is bankrupting the domestic financial system and the government might prefer an equilibrium in which there is no depreciation and no inflation. But that is not the Nash equilibrium that characterizes a crisis. *Given* market expectations of depreciation, it still may be optimal for the government to inflate.[1]

Indonesia's severe crisis illustrates these mechanisms at work. In 1997 Indonesia had come down from its spectacular economic performance of earlier years, but still had a healthy rate of growth, a reasonable real exchange rate, and a current account deficit of manageable size. The country had a short-term external debt of 182 percent of GDP; but the figure had been nearly as large in 1995 (according to the Bank for International Settlements) and the country had avoided a crisis then. After the July 1997 Thai devaluation, however, the rupiah came under pressure and was cut loose to float.

Sharp depreciation in December 1997—part the result of increasingly evident regional problems, part the result of domestic financial panic reinforced by policy uncertainties—led to a massive deterioration in

---

[1] Of course, other mechanisms are driving such crises, as well. Because domestic interest rates rise, entities that finance long-term domestic lending with short-term domestic borrowing—for example, bank deposits—come under immediate pressure.

Figure 1
Changes in the Money Supply, Exchange Rate, and Price Level in Indonesia

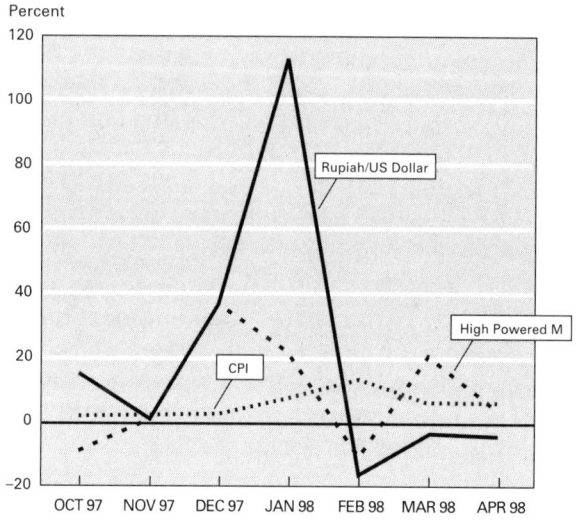

Source: Bank Indonesia and Datastream.

private sector balance sheets. Interest rates rose and the stock market collapsed. The government reacted by providing massive doses of liquidity in December and January, fueling further depreciation and, soon, sharply higher inflation (Figure 1). The new year also saw continuing runs on domestic banks, with the currency/M2 ratio rising from 16.6 in December to 21.8 in January. In effect, the government was buying up the private sector's negative net worth and financing the bailout through inflationary money creation. Of course, the collapse of the financial sector and the cessation of capital inflows have been accompanied by collapses in investment and in consumer durables purchases, and by difficulties for the export sector, which relies on trade credits.

It is hard to maintain that the Indonesian crisis was inevitable. Other of the regional crises, I would argue, also contain self-fulfilling elements to greater or lesser degrees. Hong Kong's ongoing problems offer a case in point. How can an economy as open as Hong Kong's gain economically from devaluing? Yet speculation has continued through 1998 and political support for maintaining the link to the U.S. dollar could erode in the face of rising unemployment.

CONTAINING THE CURRENT CRISIS

How should monetary and fiscal policies be managed in the current crisis? The stakes are extraordinarily high, but the easy answers are few—in effect, policy must counteract the severe capital-account shocks by creating a new expectational climate, and economics has little to say as to how this can be done short of infeasibly extensive official financial support from abroad. Fiscal expansion would seem to carry minimal risks, given the generally sound public finances of these countries in the past. It is especially needed in Japan, where a negative fiscal shock in 1997 has helped propel the economy downward. Japanese monetary expansion risks further yen depreciation and adverse competitive effects elsewhere in the region. But it would still give a welcome boost to world demand and might marginally help those who have borrowed in yen. The optimal response by Japan would be a policy mix of monetary and fiscal expansion with offsetting exchange rate effects.

Given the dollar and yen debts incurred in other Asian countries, monetary expansion by them risks throwing gasoline on the fire. However, it is unlikely that tight money policies alone will restore confidence in regional currencies until Japan, seemingly suffering from policy paralysis, gets its house in order. Moreover, the Federal Reserve and the new European Central Bank have an extraordinary power to worsen the situation by raising interest rates in pursuit of domestic inflation objectives. To do so now would be an error of perhaps historic proportions. The Fed, at least, seems to have recognized the danger.

References

Diamond, Douglas and Phillip Dybvig. 1983. "Bank Runs, Liquidity, and Deposit Insurance." *Journal of Political Economy* 91 (June), pp. 401–19.

Díaz Alejandro, Carlos F. 1985. "Goodbye Financial Repression, Hello Financial Crash." *Journal of Development Economics* 19 (September/October), pp. 1–24.

Krugman, Paul R. 1979. "A Model of Balance-of-Payments Crises." *Journal of Money, Credit and Banking* 11 (August), pp. 311–25.

Obstfeld, Maurice. 1994. "The Logic of Currency Crises." *Cahiers Economiques et Monétaires* 43, pp. 189–213.

Market Mechanisms for Avoiding the Next Currency Crash: Lessons from Asia

Avinash Persaud*

The international financial system is failing us. At times, financial markets disappear, financial contagion sweeps away exchange rate arrangements that are fundamentally supported, and currency crises have real, worldwide economic impact. Disturbingly, these episodes appear more frequent and more ferocious than before. The solution is not to curtail portfolio flows, which have the potential to deliver scarce investment to developing countries, or for the International Monetary Fund (IMF) to do more of the same, just more quickly and with more money. We must try to work with the financial markets and not against them. Countries that meet simple, transparent criteria should be eligible to draw support from a superfund of pooled foreign exchange reserves whenever they choose. Currency crashes should be selectively avoided, not ameliorated afterwards. Countries that do not meet the criteria should be offered technical assistance and development support, but not bailouts. The moral hazard associated with bailouts is already acting as an obstacle to reform in a number of economies.

Under Strain: The International Financial System

The international financial system is failing its constituents: There are periods of severe dislocation when some financial markets disappear, financial difficulty in one country sweeps contagiously across regions, and the resulting financial turmoil impairs economic growth, worldwide. These features of the international financial system were visible during the Asian currency turmoil, triggered by a collapse of the Thai baht in July 1997. In the midst of the Asian currency crisis, the currency options

---

*Global Head of Foreign Exchange & Commodity Research, J. P. Morgan Co., Inc.

Table 1
Currency Contagion

	Exchange Rates versus the Dollar		Percentage Fall	Inflation Rate May 97–May 98
	End-May 1998	End-May 1997		
Southeast Asia				
Indonesian rupiah[a]	10,500	2,443	76.7	33.3
Thai baht[a]	39.6	27.9	34.8	10.6
Malaysian ringitt	3.85	2.51	34.8	6.4
Philippine peso	26.4	39.1	32.4	10.1
Singapore dollar	1.67	1.43	14.4	2.5
North & Near Asia				
South Korean won[a]	1,413	893	36.8	8.5
Taiwan dollar	33.9	27.9	15.5	2.0
Indian rupee	41.4	35.8	13.5	8.6
Hong Kong dollar	7.75	7.74	.1	4.5
China yuan	8.28	8.29	−.1	1.8
Latin America				
Colombian peso	1,397	1,074	23.1	18.3
Mexican peso	8.88	7.91	10.9	17.3
Venezuelan bolivar	538	484	10.0	42.1
Brazilian real	1.15	1.07	7.0	4.6
Argentinian peso	1.00	1.00	.0	.6
Europe and Africa				
Hungarian florin	213	182	14.6	17.1
South African rand	5.16	4.47	13.3	7.4
Polish zloty	3.51	3.20	8.8	13.9
Russian rouble	6.16	5.77	6.3	11.1
Czech koruna	33.5	32.8	2.0	10.0

[a] Countries that received IMF assistance in 1997.

market of the Thai baht and Indonesian rupiah effectively ceased to exist for several days, and "onshore" and "offshore" exchange rates diverged sharply. Although countries in the region were proclaimed as enjoying the East-Asia growth miracle just a few months before, the collapse in the Thai baht on July 2 was followed in quick succession by crashes in the Philippine peso, Indonesian rupiah, Malaysian ringitt, and Korean won, along with considerable downward pressure—so far resisted—on the Hong Kong dollar, Russian rouble, and Brazilian real (Table 1).

The currency turmoil and related economic difficulties in the Asian region have had global impact. The crisis has led many forecasters to slash their forecasts for global GDP growth in 1998 by as much as 1 percentage point, from around 3 percent to around 2 percent. Concern over the economic ramifications of the developments in Asia has been cited by Chairman Greenspan of the Federal Reserve Board and Governor George of the Bank of England as one reason why their institutions have

Table 2
The Economist Commodity Price Index

	Percentage Change to End-May 1998 from	
	Last Month	Last Year
SDR Index	−2.9	−22.5
Dollar Index	−3.5	−25.4
Oil	−4.5	−28.6
Sterling Index	−1.6	−25.7

not sanctioned a tightening of monetary policy, despite strong domestic economic activity. This concern has also been reflected in strengthening bond markets and the dramatic weakening in commodity prices. Despite GDP growth in the first quarter of 1998 of over 4 percent, the U.S. 30-year bond is yielding less than 6 percent and *The Economist* All Items, SDR Commodity Index has lost 22.5 percent over the past 12 months (Table 2). In turn, this has accelerated weakness in commodity-linked currencies such as the South African rand, the Mexican peso, the Venezuelan bolivar, and the Australian, New Zealand, and Canadian dollars.

These far-reaching developments are not unique to the Asian currency crisis. They were also apparent, if for a shorter period, during the turmoil sparked by the devaluation of the Mexican peso in December 1994 and in the European Monetary System crises of September 1992 and July 1993. Disturbingly, periods of financial dislocation and contagion, leading to adverse economic impacts, appear to be more frequent and more ferocious than before.

A new measure of the instability of the international financial system can be obtained by looking at the rank correlation of short-term performance and long-term risk. Short-term performance is measured by the total return from borrowing dollars and depositing in a local currency over the past 20 days, and long-term risk is measured by the average outperformance of the spot rate versus its forward rate—a measure of the risk premium—over 100 of the past 120 months. We exclude the 20 most extreme values in order to arrive at a measure of the average risk premium over normal conditions.

Assuming that all of the information contained in the history of an exchange rate is already reflected in its level, we should not expect to see any strong relationship between today's performance of currencies and yesterday's risk premia. At any one time, we might expect to see roughly half of those countries with a high risk premium in the top half of the rank of performance and half in the bottom half. We would expect the coefficient of correlation between the rank of current performance and the rank of past risk to wander around the zero mark through time, only very rarely reaching above +0.7 or below −0.7 out of pure chance. Instead, we

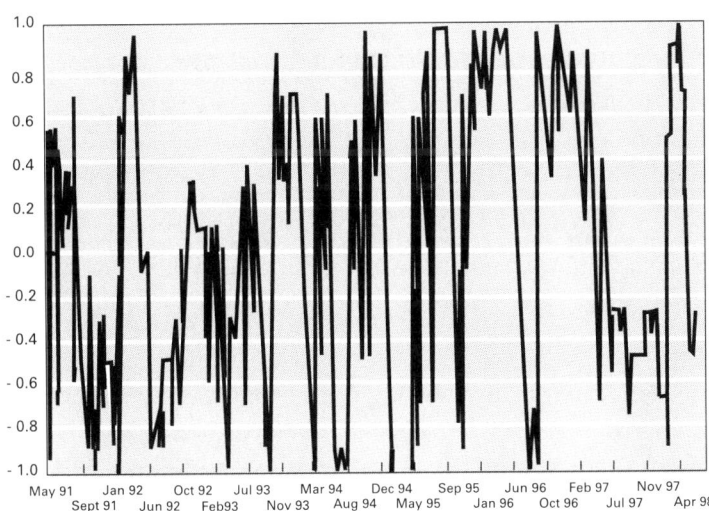

**Figure 1
J.P. Morgan Global Risk Appetite Index**

Source: J.P. Morgan Co., Inc., Global FX Research. The J. P. Morgan Global Risk Appetite Index is a correlation coefficient between two ranks: The first is the rank of foreign exchange performance over the past month; the second is the rank of long term risk, measured using the average monthly volatility of the trade-weighted exchange rate across the previous five years (up to one month ago to ensure no overlap in time with the first rank). When the Index is at +1 for instance, it implies that all the traditionally "risky" markets have been strengthening over the past month versus "safe" markets and doing so in the order of their "risk." We interpret this as an occasion of high investor risk appetite. See "Investors Shifting Appetite for Risk," A. Persaud, July 1996, J. P. Morgan.

observe that for 30 percent of the time over the past 10 years, the correlation coefficient is either above +0.7 or below −0.7 and it is, in fact, rarely close to the zero mark (see Figure 1).

What does this mean? It would appear that for 30 percent of the time, almost all "risky" currencies are outperforming "safe" currencies and are doing so in the order of their past risk premia, or almost all "risky" currencies are underperforming "safe" currencies and, again, are doing so in the order of their past risk premia. This behavior is best explained by investors switching from a general preference for risk worldwide to an aversion to risk. This pattern of currency performance suggests that "contagious behavior," where exchange rates are driven more by international financial developments than by domestic fundamentals, is not rare but is a regular feature of the international financial system, only brought to our attention when currency movements are large. Given that international financial developments are unlikely to coincide neatly with the demands of the domestic economy, this behavior could lead to severe resource misallocation over the long term and may represent one important obstacle to the narrowing of the gap between the developed and developing worlds.

What Is Wrong with Current Proposals?

In response to the Asian crisis, many are contemplating measures to curb portfolio flows or to put sand in the wheels of international finance. An old favorite, James Tobin's proposal for a tax that offsets a high interest rate differential, has rejoined the debate on how to reform the international financial system. Other variations of the Tobin Tax include a withholding tax that falls, the longer portfolio inflows stay in the country, in order to discourage short-term flows. It should be noted that levying a tax on capital flows is very difficult in practice.

But the real problem is that in erecting hurdles against portfolio outflows, we are implicitly erecting hurdles against inflows. When the freedom to exit a market is partially removed, investors are far more reluctant to enter in the first place. In the current environment of declining official assistance, curtailing portfolio flows into developing economies in an attempt to reduce the volatility of flows would be like cutting off your nose to spite your face. While inward portfolio investment does not always bring benefits, it does have the potential to accelerate investment and economic development. Certainly the likely dramatic decline in capital inflows to Emerging Asia, from $172 billion in 1997 to an estimated $99 billion in 1998, will be associated with a forecast decline of real GDP growth in the region from 6.4 percent in 1997 to 1.4 percent in 1998—despite the 30-odd percent turnaround in competitiveness.

Those who are reluctant to tamper too much with the free flow of portfolio money often look to the IMF to play a more aggressive role in supporting the international financial system. Instead of reforming the system, they want to reform the IMF to enable it to offer more speedy assistance, to extend larger loans, and to better anticipate currency crashes. Indeed, comparing the IMF's actions during the Asian crisis with its actions during the Mexican crisis of 1994–95 or the Latin American debt crisis of the mid 1980s, it is arguable that on this occasion they reacted more quickly, pledged larger loans than ever before, and successfully forestalled a sovereign default. However, more may be expected of the IMF than it can deliver or should deliver.

It is doubtful that the size of IMF loans could keep pace with the size of private capital flows. In the year before the Asian crisis, net capital flows to emerging economies grew by 15.5 percent to $310 billion (Table 3). At that rate of growth, IMF bailouts could become bigger and bigger while never being big enough. It should be remembered that even today, with the global fallout from the Asian turmoil as visible as could be, there is a lack of political consensus in favor of an enlargement of the IMF's

Table 3
Net Capital Inflows to Emerging Economies
Billions of U.S. Dollars

	1995	1996	1997
Total	262	310	208
Emerging Asia	147	172	99
Latin America	64	80	66
Emerging Europe and Africa	51	58	43
of which			
Net debt inflows	155	173	68
net short-term	60	48	−11
Net equity inflows	107	137	139
net portfolio	14	26	19

capital base. Moreover, it is by no means clear that quicker, bigger loans in the case of Asia helped. The exchange rates of the three countries aided by the IMF (Table 1) remain over 30 percent below their levels last year—over 70 percent in the case of Indonesia—and while a sovereign default has been avoided, portfolio inflows show little sign of returning. If this speedier, larger IMF assistance had not been forthcoming, would Asian economies be substantially worse off today? There are those who are unconvinced.

Further, large IMF bailouts raise a genuine problem of moral hazard: The more the financial markets are convinced that the IMF will offer sufficient funds to any large country to ensure the smooth functioning of the international financial system, the more private sector institutions will become reckless in their search for higher returns and, hence, the more the IMF will end up lending. At the extreme, the system will become self-defeating as creditor governments find the size of IMF bailouts politically impossible to support.

Moral hazard is not just a neat theoretical construct. It probably played a role in the exponential rise in foreign bank lending to Emerging Asia—a critical factor in the resulting turmoil. The more that banks saw other banks lending to Emerging Asia, the more they felt comfortable to lend more, in the knowledge that they would not all be allowed to fail (Table 4). Today the principal justification for the large inflows into Russian local currency debt over the past 12 months—despite a clearly unsustainable hole in the government's finances and a troublesome Duma—is the belief that Russia, with its nuclear arsenal, 150 million people, and strategic and economic links with the rest of Europe, is too important for the IMF to let fail. Given that the world is not in the mood to perpetually underwrite the Russian government, this belief will only serve to delay the eventual reform of domestic finances and to increase

Table 4
Bank for International Settlements—Reporting Banks' Net Claims on the Financial Sector in Asia
Billions of U.S. dollars, end of period

	1993	1994	1995	1996
South Korea	20.9	29.3	42.9	58.3
Indonesia	6.0	9.2	12.1	11.0
Malaysia	−5.6	2.4	2.9	4.1
Philippines	.4	.2	1.0	4.7
Thailand	22.2	39.5	69.9	77.4

the size of the eventual turmoil if reforms are not forthcoming soon and the rug is pulled from under Russia's fragile economy.

Both the curbing of international portfolio flows and the expansion of the IMF's role offer uncertain benefits and significant risks. To an extent, both of these approaches to avoiding the next currency crisis are designed to operate *against* the market. We need to think more about solutions that guide the market to better outcomes and help markets to become more immune to the contagious behaviour illustrated in Figure 1. A good starting point is an examination of what went wrong with the Asian economic miracle.

WHAT WENT WRONG IN ASIA: THE LESSONS

Undoubtedly, many factors contributed to the turmoil that erupted in Asia from July 2, 1997. For example, in terms of the market timing, the May 9 "crash" of the Czech koruna—a currency associated with a large current account deficit (6 percent in 1997)—may have turned the market's focus to Asia's large current account deficits. In terms of the longer-term causes, the political system will have played a part. If and where it existed, "crony capitalism" will have impaired the proper allocation of resources. However, listing all the causes of Asia's currency crisis runs the risk of losing sight of the key factors. Below we offer a stylized view of the key economic ills that set the crisis off.

In some ways, Asia was a victim of past, unbalanced success. A history of strong economic growth, low government deficits, high savings, and stable exchange rates encouraged the inflow of portfolio money and the buildup of short-term external debt. In 1996, Indonesia, for example, offered investors 13.3 percent interest rates—more than 7 percentage points above U.S. interest rates—and a monthly standard deviation of the dollar exchange rate of less than 0.5 percent, less than one-fifth the standard deviation of $/Yen (Table 5). These attractions were underpinned by a 7.8 percent growth in GDP, marginally down

Table 5
Exchange Rate Rigidity
Standard Deviation of Monthly Changes in U.S. Dollar Exchange Rate

	Jan 80–Dec 89	Jan 90–Jun 95	Jul 95–Jun 97
Japan	3.5	2.9	3.7
Germany	3.6	3.4	2.6
South Korea	.9	.6	1.2
Taiwan	1.1	1.0	1.1
Malaysia	1.3	1.4	.8
Singapore	1.7	1.1	.7
Indonesia	5.3	.2	.5
Thailand	1.9	.5	.4
Philippines	4.1	2.6	.3

from 8.2 percent in 1995, and a budget that was in balance in 1996 after a deficit of less than 1.0 percent in 1995. Except for large current account deficits, Asia looked very different from Mexico, and those current account deficits appeared less of a worry because they were being financed, not by overseas purchases of government debt, but by overseas purchases of private sector debt and equity (Table 6).

However, the shallowness of domestic markets meant that investment as a whole and the portfolio inflow in particular were concentrated into a few sectors which, before the crisis, showed strong signs of overinvestment. In the case of Thailand, for example, almost 90 percent of loans by overseas banks were to the financial sector (Table 7). The current account deficit increasingly was being financed by unproductive, short-term investment.

The absence of adequate supervision meant that the buildup of short-term external debt went unchecked and in many cases unmonitored. In the throes of the crisis, for example, the Korean government made substantial, upward revisions to its estimate of external debt. The

Table 6
The Fundamentals in 1997

	Current Account Balance Percent	Real GDP Growth Percent
Malaysia	−7.4	8.0
Indonesia	−5.0	7.0
Philippines	−4.1	5.1
Thailand	−3.5	.5
Korea	−1.9	5.5
Taiwan	1.8	6.8
Singapore	14.0	7.5

Table 7
Structure of Loans by BIS-Reporting Banks
Percent of Total Gross Liabilities, Mid 1996

	Indonesia	Malaysia	Philippines	Thailand
Total loans (US$ billions)	56.5	25.8	13.4	98.7
Maturity				
Less than one year (%)	60.3	49.4	27.2	69.0
Over one year (%)	35.5	38.2	72.8	27.3
Short-term loans (US$ billions)	34.1	12.8	3.6	68.1
Distribution by sector (%)				
Financial	38.8	62.8	70.1	85.9
Public sector	13.1	11.5	n.a.	3.8
Nonfinancial private	48.1	25.7	29.9	10.3

presence of large, short-term, external debt—large as a percent of GDP, exports, and reserves—and sizable current account deficits financed by increasingly unproductive, short-term portfolio investment, made the countries in the region very vulnerable to any economic shocks (Table 8). During 1996 and 1997, two external shocks came along.

The Japanese economy continued to perform poorly and Japanese interest rates now stood at close to zero. Between mid 1995 and mid 1997 the Japanese yen depreciated against the U.S. dollar by over 30 percent, from ¥80 to ¥115. By virtue of stable exchange rate arrangements versus the dollar, the yen depreciated by a similar amount versus Asian currencies, reducing the competitiveness of Asian goods in the important Japanese market and decreasing the attractiveness of East Asia as a production platform for Japanese producers. It is interesting to note that the three currencies to crash in Asia were those with the largest proportion of exports destined for Japan and the largest current account deficits before the crisis (Tables 6 and 9). The recent investment emphasis on electronics also hurt East Asia badly, given the plunge in semiconductor prices in 1996. In Malaysia, electronics as a proportion of total

Table 8
External Debt Indicators, End-1997 Estimates

	Debt/GDP (%)	Debt/Exports (%)	Short-Term Debt ($bn)	Foreign Exchange Reserves ($bn)
Indonesia	58	200	27	28
Korea	33	87	60	17
Thailand	61	126	32	29
Emerging Asia	31	89	237	353

Table 9
Share of Exports Going to Japan
Average over 1992–1996 (percent)

	Indonesia	29.6
	Philippines	16.5
	Thailand	16.9
	Korea	13.7
	Malaysia	12.8
	Taiwan	10.8
	Singapore	7.7
	India	7.6

exports more than doubled from 23.1 percent to 58.9 percent in just the four years from 1992 to 1996 (Table 10).

Contagion within Southeast Asia was powerful, for two reasons. First, these economies shared similar exports (electronics) and similar export destinations (Japan and the United States) and so a devaluation in one country caused a substantial worsening of competitiveness in another. But contagion ran along another route as well: shared investors. Investors in one country, observing a currency crisis next door, awoke to risks they had not fully priced; or, having lost money in one country, investors lost their appetite for risk. Both factors led them to leave the entire region, together and at the same time. This behavior determined the scale of the crisis. As investors ran for the exit, the resulting currency weakness caused short-term lenders to call in their loans, which led to further weakness as debtors sold local currency to pay back dollars at the same time. The cycle was vicious indeed. Were it not for these investor and debtor dynamics, some currencies would have fallen less and some might not have fallen at all.

NEW MECHANISMS TO AVOID THE NEXT CURRENCY CRASH: A BLUEPRINT

The power of financial contagion in deepening and spreading currency crises means that coming to the support of a country after its

Table 10
Electronics as a Percent of Total Exports

	1992	1996
Malaysia	23.1	58.9
Singapore	40.5	42.0
Philippines	20.0	40.0
South Korea	28.2	32.7
Thailand	24.2	29.0
Indonesia	.4	2.8

currency has crashed will not contain the resulting financial and economic difficulties locally and abroad, but will instead create moral hazard. The IMF's current focus is misplaced.

A better approach would be to selectively avoid currency crashes before they happen and selectively defend currencies from the contagion of a crash that has occurred elsewhere. The selectivity is necessary to avoid moral hazard. In those countries where a currency crash is allowed to occur, there should be no bailout of creditors, but technical assistance should be provided to help with the adjustment, and development assistance to ease economic hardships.

A small set of criteria should be developed under which, if a country meets all but one, say, it will be granted access to a large pool of reserves for the defense of its exchange rate. The criteria should lead to a selection of countries which have exchange rates that should be defended and can be defended. The criteria should be focused on ends rather than means, to give governments policy freedom and an incentive to develop effective policies that will achieve these ends. The precise criteria should be developed and monitored by regional development banks, but approved by the IMF. Setting the conditions at this level will allow the criteria to fit the different political and economic imperatives that operate in different regions.

The selection criteria could include the following:

(1) No excessive external debt.
    Target for the ratio of short-term debt plus amortization payments to foreign exchange reserves. (100%?)
(2) No unproductive capital inflows.
    Target for domestic rates of return, weighted by their exposure to portfolio inflow. (Perhaps calculated as an average of the past and countries around the world?)
(3) Competitive exchange rate.
    Target for the real exchange rate, weighted by the currency of trade and of trading competitors. (Not more than 10 percent above the five-year weighted exchange rate?)
(4) Sustainable domestic finances.
    Target for the government deficit as a percentage of GDP. (Less than 3 percent?)
(5) Open governance.
    Regular, extensive collection and reporting of key economic and financial data.

The reserve pool could be made up of a call on a proportion of the reserves of those countries eligible for assistance within a region and agreements to borrow from other central banks, the IMF, and private banks. If such a fund had been in existence at the beginning of 1997 and all the Asian countries met the selection criteria, and the call on their foreign exchange reserves was 50 percent, the Asian fund would have been in the region of $200–300 billion, an amount significantly greater than the entire net capital inflow into the region in 1996. The presence of such a fund would bring substantial credibility benefits to any country eligible to draw upon it.

The criteria should be public, clear, and transparent. This will allow the market to work with the authorities, not against them. Countries that meet the criteria would bask in the additional credibility of the fund and would attract the investment they require at reasonable rates—but not excessive investment, because that would raise the risk of the country losing its eligibility through falling rates of return (criterion 2) or an overvalued exchange rate (criterion 3). Indeed, a country experiencing strong inflows would have an incentive to broaden and deepen its financial markets to keep rates of return from falling. In similar vein, the criteria will represent a benchmark of good governance. Countries pursuing policies that will enable them to be eligible will be rewarded by the market, while those that are not may at times pay dearly.

It was hoped that credit-rating agencies would provide a similar, strong incentive for governments to pursue the right policies. This has not entirely happened because, if private credit-rating agencies made the credit-rating process totally transparent and public, they would find it hard to charge for their services. Second, an AAA rating does not guarantee anything, except that the next rating move is down. In this regard, the arrangements proposed here should be superior. The fund would be a public institution, and those administering it would lose nothing and gain much by making the selection process completely transparent. If eligibility carried the right to use a fund in excess of $200–300 billion, it would be a guarantee of substantial support.

References

American Express Bank (Amex). *Award Essays in International Finance*, 7, 1995.
Bank for International Settlements. *Annual Report*, 1996, 1997.
Bank for International Settlements. *International Banking Developments Quarterly*.
Bank for International Settlements/Organisation for Economic Cooperation and Development. *Statistics on External Indebtedness*.
Cline, William R. 1984. *International Debt: Systemic Risk and Policy Response*. Washington, DC: Institute for International Economics.
International Monetary Fund. *IMF, World Economic Outlook*, 1996, 1997.
International Monetary Fund. *International Capital Markets, Developments & Prospects*, 1996, 1997.
Kenen, Peter B., Francesco Papadia, and Fabrizio Saccomanni, eds. 1994. *The International Monetary System: Proceedings of a Conference Organized by the Banca d'Italia*. Cambridge: Cambridge University Press.
Morgan Guaranty Trust Company of New York, *World Financial Markets*, March 1998.
Williamson, John. 1982. *The Lending Policies of the International Monetary Fund*. Washington, DC: Institute for International Economics.
World Bank, *World Debt Tables*, 1996, 1997.

TECHNOLOGY AND BUSINESS CYCLES: HOW WELL DO STANDARD MODELS EXPLAIN THE FACTS?

Susanto Basu*

How well do current business-cycle models explain historical output fluctuations? Almost a decade has passed since Plosser (1989) claimed that a simple real-business-cycle (RBC) model could generate simulated output with a correlation of 0.87 with actual output over the period since the Korean War. A similar observation led Prescott (1986) to claim that theory is ahead of business-cycle measurement. This paper revisits Plosser's exercise, using some recent innovations in business-cycle theory and measurement. It uses estimates of technology change recently derived by Basu, Fernald, and Kimball (1998) (henceforth BFK) and finds that a simple RBC model calibrated with these shocks produces simulated output that is *negatively* correlated with actual output. A simple dynamic general-equilibrium (DGE) model with sticky prices does somewhat better: Its impulse response to a technology improvement is qualitatively similar to that found in the data, but quantitatively the results are only moderately satisfactory. A simulation of the sticky-price model using estimates of both technology and monetary policy shocks generates model output that has a correlation of about 0.30 with actual output. Thus, current business-cycle models cannot easily explain the observed facts—measurement seems to be ahead of theory once again.

My results differ from Plosser's mainly because of the new measure of technological change that I employ. The particular series used here was

---

*Associate Professor of Economics, University of Michigan. The author thanks Alejandro Micco for outstanding research assistance, Craig Burnside and Michael Kiley for supplying data and programs, and discussants Mark Bils and Tom Cooley for stimulating comments. He also thanks John Fernald and Miles Kimball, who collaborated on much of the research summarized here, and provided invaluable suggestions for this paper. Finally, the author is grateful to the National Science Foundation and the Alfred P. Sloan Foundation for financial support.

estimated by BFK, but it is similar to those derived by a number of recent researchers attempting to produce better measures of short-run technical change than the standard Solow residual (for example, Burnside, Eichenbaum, and Rebelo 1996; Gali 1998). This new series shows that short-run changes in output and, especially, inputs are negatively correlated with technology improvements. As is well known, the usual RBC model produces impulse responses for output and other variables that are strongly positively correlated with technical change. Thus, it is unsurprising that the RBC model cannot duplicate the co-movements between observed variables and the new measure of technical change.

This paper makes four points. First, it reviews the evidence suggesting that technical innovation has contractionary effects in the short run. BFK argue that a major reason for the strong positive correlation of the Solow residual with output is measurement error coming from variable capital and labor utilization. Second, the paper shows that a sticky-price model with variable capital utilization can do a reasonable job of matching very short-run movements in business-cycle variables following an improvement in technology, but it also finds that the model does not capture the medium-run dynamics. Third, the paper argues that variable utilization is not just a bias; it can be an important propagation mechanism for both technology and money shocks, amplifying and propagating the effects of small disturbances.[1] However, even with this new mechanism, nominal shocks do not have persistent effects. The basic problem appears to be the standard one in the sticky-price literature, the lack of sufficiently strong propagation mechanisms (real rigidities[2]) in addition to variable utilization. Fourth, however, the paper suggests that real rigidities that are strong enough to generate substantial endogenous price stickiness in response to nominal shocks may lead to implausibly large fluctuations in response to technology shocks. Thus, producing plausible sticky-price DGE models of business cycles may be even more complicated than hitherto believed.

The first part of the paper reviews the method that BFK use to purge the Solow residual of various nontechnological components. Plosser (1989) took the standard Solow productivity residual as his measure of short-run technical change. Since then, a huge body of work has searched for other explanations for the procyclicality of productivity. This literature has advanced four main explanations for procyclical productivity. First, as Plosser assumed, procyclical productivity may reflect procyclical technology. Second, widespread imperfect competition and increasing

---

[1] This point has also been made by Burnside and Eichenbaum (1996); Dotsey, King, and Wolman (1997); King and Rebelo (1997); and Wen (1997).

[2] The term is from Ball and Romer (1990). Kimball (1995) provides an insightful discussion of the relationship between the amplification of shocks in the static setting of Ball and Romer and their propagation over time in the setting of current DGE models.

returns may lead productivity to rise whenever inputs rise. Third, as already mentioned, utilization of inputs may vary over the cycle, in a way that is not properly captured by standard input measures. Fourth, reallocation of resources across uses with different marginal products may contribute to procyclicality. For example, if different industries have different degrees of market power, then inputs will generally have different marginal products in different uses. Then aggregate productivity growth is cyclical if sectors with higher markups have input growth that is more cyclical.[3]

BFK control for the three nontechnological components of measured productivity and derive technology change as a residual. Empirically, variations in utilization and cyclical reallocation seem the most important for generating the negative correlation between technology and inputs. Given these results, it is easy to confirm that the standard RBC model, even augmented with variable capital utilization, cannot duplicate the impulse responses observed in the data. This finding may seem perplexing given the recent claim of King and Rebelo (1997) that variable capital utilization can "resuscitate" the RBC model. In the third section of this paper, I discuss why my conclusions differ from theirs.

I then partially confirm the conjecture of BFK that a sticky-price model with variable utilization can reproduce the impulse responses estimated from the data. The intuition is straightforward. As a simple example, suppose the quantity theory governs the demand for money, so output is proportional to real balances. In the short run, if the supply of money is fixed and prices cannot adjust, then real balances and hence output are also fixed. Now suppose that a positive technology shock occurs. With improved technology, firms need less labor to produce this unchanged output. As a result, they lay off workers and reduce hours. Over time, however, as prices adjust, the underlying real-business-cycle dynamics take over, and output and inputs rise.

It turns out that a more sophisticated version of this model can reproduce the initial contractionary effect of a technology improvement quite well, predicting a small fall in output and a large fall in inputs. However, the period of price stickiness is so short—and the response of the monetary authority to the initial contraction is likely to be so expansionary—that the contraction is succeeded by a boom far more quickly in the model than in the data.

Since the empirical section of the paper implies that changes in factor utilization are very important, I then investigate the extent to which variable utilization can also act as an important propagation mechanism

---

[3] For examples of these four explanations, see, respectively, Cooley and Prescott (1995); Hall (1988, 1990); Basu (1996), Bils and Cho (1994), and Shapiro (1996); and Basu and Fernald (1997).

in a dynamic general-equilibrium (DGE) model. One advantage of this method of controlling for utilization (taken from Basu and Kimball 1997) is that it also provides estimates of some of the critical parameters governing changes in utilization. Dotsey, King, and Wolman (1997) use the Basu-Kimball results to calibrate a sticky-price DGE model, and they claim that a model with interest-inelastic money demand, infinitely elastic labor supply, and variable capital utilization can generate persistent output fluctuations in response to nominal shocks. However, their result does not appear to extend to the case considered in this paper, where nominal interest rates are governed by a plausible Fed reaction function and where the labor supply elasticity is more realistic. In this setting, I can generate persistence only by allowing utilization to be highly variable. But the fact that I want the sticky-price model to deliver sensible impulse responses to both technology and money shocks turns out to be a binding constraint: Highly variable utilization produces more persistent dynamics in response to money shocks, but implausibly large fluctuations in response to technology shocks. Thus, extending sticky-price models to consider technology shocks is important both for matching the data, which suggest that such shocks are important, and for developing the theory of how they affect the economy.

The paper is structured as follows. The first section reviews the BFK method for estimating technology change, and the next two sections summarize the data and some of the empirical results. These results establish the facts that we want to match. The fourth section presents simple DGE models with and without nominal price rigidity and discusses their calibration. Model results are then presented, and the final section offers conclusions.

The Empirical Model

The empirical model is based only on cost-minimization by firms and one weak assumption about consumer preferences. It is thus consistent with a wide class of models including—but not limited to—the models explored in the fourth section, "A DGE Model with Variable Capital Utilization." The strategy will be to derive a series of corrected residuals, using the methods of Basu and Kimball (1997) and Basu and Fernald (1997). These residuals were first constructed, and their properties discussed, in BFK. This section of the paper reviews their methods.[4]

The Basic Setup

I assume that each firm's production function for gross output takes the following form:

---

[4] The presentation in this section draws on Basu and Fernald (1998).

TECHNOLOGY AND BUSINESS CYCLES

$$Y = F(\tilde{K}, \tilde{L}, M, T) \tag{1.1}$$

The firm produces gross output, Y, using capital services $\tilde{K}$, labor services $\tilde{L}$, and intermediate inputs of materials and energy M. T indexes technology. T also includes the effects of any externalities that may exist. (For simplicity, time and firm subscripts are omitted.)

In principle, the services of labor and capital depend on both the raw quantities of these inputs (hours worked, and the capital stock) and the intensity with which they are used. Hence, labor services, $\tilde{L}$, depend on the number of employees, N, hours worked per employee, H, and the effort of each worker, E. Capital services depend on the capital stock, K, and the utilization of the capital stock, Z. Input services are therefore the following products:

$$\tilde{L} = EHN, \tag{1.2}$$
$$\tilde{K} = ZK$$

I generally assume that the capital stock and the number of employees are quasi-fixed, so that firms cannot change their levels costlessly. In the short run, firms can vary their inputs of capital and labor only by varying utilization.

I assume that the firm's production function F is (locally) homogeneous of arbitrary degree γ in total inputs. Constant returns corresponds to the case where γ equals one. Formally, we can write returns to scale in two useful, and equivalent, forms. First, returns to scale equal the sum of output elasticities:

$$\gamma = \frac{F_1 \tilde{K}}{Y} + \frac{F_2 \tilde{L}}{Y} + \frac{F_3 M}{Y}, \tag{1.3}$$

where F_j^i denotes the derivative of the production function with respect to the Jth element (that is, the marginal product of input J). Second, once we assume that firms minimize cost, we can denote the firm's cost function by $C(Y)$. (In general, the cost function also depends on the prices of the variable inputs and the quantities of any quasi-fixed inputs, although for simplicity I suppress those terms here.) The *local* degree of returns to scale equals the inverse of the elasticity of cost with respect to output (see Varian 1984, p. 68):

$$\gamma(Y) = \frac{C(Y)}{YC'(Y)} = \frac{C(Y)/Y}{C'(Y)} = \frac{AC}{MC}, \tag{1.4}$$

where AC equals average cost, and MC equals marginal cost. Note that increasing returns, for example, may reflect overhead costs or decreasing marginal cost; both imply that average cost exceeds marginal cost. If increasing returns take the form of overhead costs, then $\gamma(Y)$ is not a constant structural parameter, but depends on the level of output the firm produces. As production increases, returns to scale fall as the firm moves down its average cost curve.

As equation (1.4) shows, there is no necessary relationship between the degree of returns to scale and the slope of the marginal cost curve. Indeed, increasing returns is compatible with increasing marginal costs, as in the standard Chamberlinian model of imperfect competition. One can calibrate the slope of the marginal cost curve from the degree of returns to scale only by assuming no fixed costs. This point is an important one, because it is the slope of the marginal cost curve that determines the slopes of the factor demand functions, which in turn are critical for determining the results of DGE models, like the one in the fourth section, below. A number of studies have used estimates of the degree of returns to scale to calibrate the slope of marginal cost: This procedure is not legitimate.

Firms may charge a price P that is a markup, μ, over marginal cost. That is, $\mu = P/MC$. Returns to scale γ is a technical property of the production function, while the markup μ is essentially a behavioral parameter, depending on the firm's pricing decision. However, the following identity links the two parameters:

$$\gamma = \frac{C(Y)}{YC'(Y)} = \frac{P}{C'(Y)} \frac{C(Y)}{PY} = \mu(1 - s_\pi), \qquad (1.5)$$

where s_π is the share of pure economic profit in gross revenue. As long as pure economic profits are small (Rotemberg and Woodford 1995 provide a variety of evidence suggesting that profit rates are close to zero), equation (1.5) shows that μ approximately equals γ. Large markups, for example, require large increasing returns.

Given low estimated profits, equation (1.5) also shows that strongly diminishing returns (γ less than one) imply that firms consistently price output below marginal cost (μ less than one). Since pricing below marginal cost makes no economic sense, I conclude that firm-level returns to scale must either be constant or increasing. Note also that increasing returns *requires* that firms charge a markup, as long as firms do not make losses.

The Solow-Hall Approach

Solow's (1957) seminal contribution involves differentiating the production function and using the firm's first-order conditions for cost minimization. Solow assumed constant returns to scale and perfect competition, so the first-order conditions (discussed below) imply that output elasticities are observed in the data as factor shares in revenue. Hall (1988, 1990) builds on Solow's contribution, extending it to the case of increasing returns and imperfect competition. Under these conditions, output elasticities are not observed, since neither returns to scale nor markups are observed. However, Hall derives a simple regression equation, which he then estimates. This section extends Hall's approach by using gross-output data and taking account of variable factor utilization.

Taking the logarithm of the production function (1.1), and differentiating it totally, one gets

$$dy = \frac{F_1 ZK}{Y}(dk + dz) + \frac{F_2 EHN}{Y}(de + dh + dn) + \frac{F_3 M}{Y} dm + dt, \quad (1.6)$$

where lower-case letters represent logs. Without loss of generality, I have normalized to one the elasticity of output with respect to technology.

Suppose firms take the price of all J inputs, P_J, as given. They may have market power in output markets. If all factors are freely variable, then the first-order conditions for cost-minimization imply that:

$$PF_J = \mu P_J. \quad (1.7)$$

In other words, firms set the value of a factor's marginal product equal to a markup over the factor's input price. Equivalently, rearranging the equation by dividing through by μ, this condition says that firms equate each factor's marginal revenue product $((P/\mu)F_J)$ to the factor's price.

Equation (1.7) still holds in the case where some factors are quasi-fixed, as long as we define the input price of the quasi-fixed factors as the appropriate *shadow* price, or implicit rental rate. I return to this point in a later subsection, when I specify a more complicated dynamic cost-minimization problem. Note also that the price of capital, P_K, must be defined as the *rental price* (or shadow rental price) of capital. In particular, if the firm makes pure economic profits, these are generally paid to capital: These profits must be subtracted before computing the rental price. (Note that these profits are over and above the quasi-rents that can accrue to a fixed factor, which are incorporated into the rental price of capital.)

Using equation (1.7), we can write each output elasticity as the product of the markup multiplied by total expenditure on each input divided by total revenue. Thus, for example,

$$\frac{F_1 ZK}{Y} = \mu \frac{P_K K}{PY} \equiv \mu s_K. \quad (1.8)$$

(Note that the marginal product of capital is F_1Z, since the services from a machine depend on the rate at which it is being utilized.)

Substituting these expressions for the output elasticities into (1.6), we get the basic estimating equation for the markup:

$$dy = \mu[s_K(dk + dz) + s_L(dn + dh + de) + s_M dm] + dt$$

$$= \mu[s_K dk + s_L(dn + dh) + s_M dm] + \mu[s_K dz + s_L de] + dt \tag{1.9}$$

$$\equiv \mu dx + \mu du + dt,$$

where dx is a share-weighted average of conventional (observed) input growth, and du is a weighted average of unobserved variation in utilization and effort. Note that the shares are the total *cost* of each type of input divided by total *revenue*. Thus, the shares in dx sum to less than one if firms make pure profits.

The derivation so far is in the spirit of Hall (1990), generalized to include variable utilization. Hall, in turn, generalizes Solow (1957) to the case of imperfect competition. (Both Hall and Solow considered variable utilization, at least in principle.) Solow's derivation assumes perfect competition and constant returns, so μ equals one. Since there are no economic profits in that world, as shown by equation (1.5), capital's share can be taken as a residual.

Note that using equation (1.5), we can rewrite equation (1.9) in terms of returns to scale γ. In this case, the weights used to calculate weighted-average inputs dx are cost shares, which sum to one. Hall (1990) pioneered this latter approach, although no economic difference is found between thinking of the output elasticity of inputs in terms of the markup and thinking in terms of returns to scale, and the data requirements are the same in the two cases.

It is important to note that the derivation relies solely on cost minimization: Profit maximization is irrelevant. This is a large advantage, since we can ignore the firm's behavior in product markets, which may be very complex. For example, firms may sell output with sticky prices (as in the model in the fourth section, below), or engage in strategic interactions in a repeated-game setting, but the existence of such behavior does not affect the results.

Several practical issues need to be resolved before estimating equation (1.9). First, we must figure out the appropriate prices to use in calculating weights. With quasi-fixed inputs, the appropriate shadow price is not, in general, the observed factor price. Second, we must find suitable proxies for du. To address these practical issues, we next specify a cost-minimization problem that provides a framework for analysis.

A Dynamic Cost-Minimization Problem

Although the problem is relatively complicated, specifying a particular dynamic cost-minimization problem provides insight into several practical issues in attempting to estimate equation (1.9). In the subsection "Variable Utilization," below, it also provides proxies for unobserved utilization, as well as a method for estimating crucial parameters used to calibrate the models of the fourth section.

The firm is modeled as facing adjustment costs in both investment and hiring, so that both the amount of capital (number of machines and buildings), K, and employment (number of workers), N, are quasi-fixed. I model quasi-fixity for two reasons. First, I want to examine the effect of quasi-fixity per se on estimates of production-function parameters and firm behavior. Second, quasi-fixity is necessary for a meaningful model of variable factor utilization. Higher utilization must be more costly to the firm, otherwise factors would always be fully utilized. If increasing the rate of investment or hiring had no cost, firms would always keep utilization at its minimum level and vary inputs using only the extensive margin, hiring and firing workers and capital costlessly. Only if it is costly to adjust along the extensive margin is it sensible to adjust along the intensive margin, and pay the costs of higher utilization.[5]

While capital and labor have adjustment costs, I assume that the number of hours per week for each worker, H, can vary freely, with no adjustment cost. In addition, both capital and labor have freely variable utilization rates. For both capital and labor, the benefit of higher utilization is its multiplication of effective inputs. I assume two costs of increasing capital utilization, Z. First, capital depreciates faster because of extra wear and tear. Second, firms may have to pay a shift premium to compensate employees for working at night or at other undesirable times. I take Z to be a continuous variable for simplicity, although variations in the workday of capital (that is, the number of shifts) are perhaps the most plausible reason for variations in utilization. The variable-shifts model has had considerable empirical success in manufacturing data, where, for a short period of time, one can observe the number of shifts directly.[6] The cost of higher labor utilization, E, is a higher disutility on the part of

---

[5] One does not require *internal* adjustment costs to model variable factor utilization in an aggregative model (see, for example, Burnside and Eichenbaum 1996), since changes in input demand on the part of the representative firm change the aggregate real wage and interest rate, so in effect the concavity of the representative consumer's utility function acts as an adjustment cost that is *external* to the firm. However, if one wants to model the behavior of firms that vary utilization in response to idiosyncratic changes in technology or demand—obviously the case in the real world—then one is forced to posit the existence of internal adjustment costs in order to have a coherent model of variable factor utilization. (Both of these observations are found in Haavelmo's (1960) treatment of investment.)

[6] See, for example, Shapiro (1996).

workers that must be compensated with a higher wage. I allow for the possibility that this wage is unobserved from period to period, as might be the case if wage payments are governed by an implicit contract in a long-term relationship.

Consider the following cost-minimization problem for the representative firm of an industry:

$$\underset{Z,E,H,M,I,A}{\text{Min}} \ C(Y) = \int_0^\infty e^{-\int_0^s r d\tau} [WNG(H,E) + P_M M + WN\Psi(A/N) + P_I KJ(I/K)] \, ds \quad (1.10)$$

subject to

$$Y = F(ZK, EHN, M, T) \quad (1.11)$$

$$\dot{K} = I - \delta(Z)K \quad (1.12)$$

$$\dot{N} = A. \quad (1.13)$$

The production function and inputs are as before. In addition, I is gross investment, and A is hiring net of separations. $WG(H,E)$ is total compensation per worker, where W is the base wage (compensation may take the form of an implicit contract, and hence not be observed period-by-period); $WN\Psi(A/N)$ is the total cost of changing the number of employees; $P_I KJ(I/K)$ is the total cost of investment; P_M is the price of materials. $\delta(Z)$ is the variable rate of depreciation. I continue to omit time subscripts for clarity.

Using a perfect-foresight model amounts to making a certainty-equivalence approximation. But even departures from certainty equivalence should not disturb the key results, which rely only on intratemporal optimization conditions rather than intertemporal ones.

I assume that Ψ, J, and δ are convex, and make the appropriate technical assumptions on G in the spirit of convexity and normality.[7] It is also helpful to make some normalizations in relation to the normal or "steady-state" levels of the variables. Using an asterisk to denote these steady-state levels, let $\delta(Z^*) = \delta^*$, $J(\delta^*) = 0$, $J'(0) = 1$, $\Psi(0) = 0$. I also assume that the marginal employment adjustment cost is zero at a constant level of employment: $\Psi'(0) = 0$.

I solve the representative firm's problem using the standard current-

---

[7] The conditions on G are easiest to state in terms of the function Φ defined by $\ln G(H, E) = \Phi(\ln H, \ln E)$. Convex Φ guarantees a global optimum; assuming $\Phi_{11} > \Phi_{12}$ and $\Phi_{22} > \Phi_{12}$ ensures that optimal H and E move together.

value Hamiltonian, letting λ, q, and θ be the multipliers on constraints (1.11), (1.12), and (1.13) respectively. Using numerical subscripts for derivatives of the production function F with respect to its first, second, and third arguments, and literal subscripts for derivatives of the labor cost function G, the firm's six intratemporal first-order conditions for cost-minimization are:

Z: $\quad \lambda K\, F_1(ZK,\, EHN,\, M;\, T) = qK\delta'(Z)$ \hfill (1.14)

H: $\quad \lambda EN\, F_2(ZK,\, EHN,\, M;\, T) = WN\, G_H(H,\, E)$ \hfill (1.15)

E: $\quad \lambda HN\, F_2(ZK,\, EHN,\, M;\, T) = WN\, G_E(H,\, E)$ \hfill (1.16)

M: $\quad \lambda F_3(ZK,\, EHN,\, M;\, T) = P_M$ \hfill (1.17)

A: $\quad \theta = W\Psi'(A/N)$ \hfill (1.18)

I: $\quad q = P_I J'(I/K).$ \hfill (1.19)

The Euler equations for the capital stock and employment are:

$$\dot{q} = [r + \delta(Z)]q - \lambda Z F_1 + P_I[J(I/K) - (I/K)J'(I/K)] \quad (1.20)$$

$$\dot{\theta} = r\theta - \lambda EHF_2 + WG(H, E) + W[\Psi(A/N) - (A/N)\Psi'(A/N)]. \quad (1.21)$$

As the Lagrange multiplier associated with the level of output, λ can be interpreted as marginal cost. Since the firm internally values output at marginal cost, λF_1 is the marginal value product of effective capital input, λF_2 is the marginal value product of effective labor input, λF_3 is the marginal value product of materials input, and λF_4 is the marginal value product of energy input.[8] Using the definition that the markup, μ, equals the ratio of output price, P, to marginal cost, I rewrite λ as:

$$\lambda = C'(Y) = \frac{P}{\mu}. \quad (1.22)$$

Note that equation (1.22) is just a definition, not a theory determining the markup. The markup depends on the solution of the firm's more complex profit-maximization problem, which we do not need to specify at all.

Equations (1.20) and (1.21) implicitly define the shadow (rental) prices of labor and capital:

---

[8] For the standard static profit-maximization problem, of course, marginal cost equals marginal revenue, so these are also the marginal revenue products.

$$\lambda ZF_1 = [r + \delta(Z)]q - \dot{q} + P_I[J(I/K) - (I/K)J'(I/K)] \equiv P_K \qquad (1.20')$$

$$\lambda EHF_2 = r\theta - \dot{\theta} + WG(H, E) + W[\Psi(A/N) - (A/N)\Psi'(A/N)] \equiv P_L \qquad (1.21')$$

As usual, the firm equates the marginal value product of each input to its shadow price. Note that with these definitions of shadow prices, the atemporal first-order condition (1.7) is satisfied for all inputs. For some intuition, note that equation (1.20') is the standard first-order equation from a q-model of investment. In the absence of adjustment costs, the value of installed capital q equals the price of investment goods P_I, and the "price" of capital input is then just the standard Hall-Jorgenson rental cost of capital, $(r + \delta)P_I$. With investment adjustment costs, there is potentially an extra return to owning capital, through capital gains $\dot{q}$ (as well as extra terms that reflect the fact that investing today incurs additional adjustment costs, but produces the benefit of lowering adjustment costs in the future).

The intuition for labor in equation (1.21') is similar. Consider the case where labor can be adjusted freely, so that it is *not* quasi-fixed. Then adjustment costs ψ are always zero; so is the multiplier θ, since constraint (1.13) does not bind. In this case, as we expect, (1.21') says that the shadow price of labor input to the firm—the right side of (1.21')—just equals the (effort-adjusted) compensation $WG(H,E)$ received by the worker. Otherwise, the quasi-fixity implies that the shadow price of labor to a firm may differ from the compensation received by the worker.

Implementation in Discrete Time

I now turn to issues of estimation. Equations (1.6) and (1.9) hold exactly in continuous time, if the values of the output elasticities are adjusted continuously. In discrete time, if the elasticities are treated as time-invariant, then equation (1.6) is a first-order approximation (in logs) to any general production function. For a consistent first-order approximation, one should then treat equation (1.9) as representing small deviations from a steady-state growth path and evaluate derivatives of the production function at the steady-state values of the variables. Thus, to calculate the shares in equation (1.9), one should use steady-state prices and quantities and, hence, treat the shares as constant over time. The markup is then also taken as constant.

For example, in the first-order approach, we want the steady-state output elasticity for capital, up to the unknown scalar μ. Using asterisks to denote steady-state values, we use equations (1.19), (1.20'), and the normalizations to compute the steady-state output elasticity of capital:

TECHNOLOGY AND BUSINESS CYCLES

$$\frac{F_1^* U^* K^*}{Y^*} = \mu^* \frac{P_K^* K^*}{P^* Y^*} \equiv \mu^* \frac{(r^* + \delta^u) P_I^* K^*}{P^* Y^*}. \qquad (1.23)$$

Note that the steady-state user cost of capital is the frictionless Hall-Jorgenson (1967) rental price.[9] Since quasi-fixity matters only for the adjustment to the steady state, in the steady state $q = P_I$ and $\dot{q} = 0$. Operationally, I calculate the Hall-Jorgenson user cost for each period and take the time average of the resulting shares as an approximation to the steady-state share. I proceed analogously for the other inputs. In the final estimating equation for (1.9), I use logarithmic differences in place of output and input growth rates, and use steady-state shares for the weights.

Thus, I can construct the index of observable inputs, dx, and take the unknown μ^*, multiplying it as a parameter to be estimated. We can use a variety of approaches to control for the unobserved du; some of them are discussed in the next section. In any case, we have to use instruments that are orthogonal to the technology shock dt, since technology change is generally contemporaneously correlated with input use (observed or unobserved).[10]

Variable Utilization

Before we can estimate μ from equation (1.9), we need to settle on a method for dealing with changes in utilization, du. A priori reasoning—and comparisons between results that control for du and those that do not—argue that du is most likely positively correlated with dx; thus, ignoring it leads to an upward-biased estimate of μ^*. Three general methods have been proposed. First, one can try to observe du directly using, say, data on shift work. When possible this option is clearly the preferred one, but data availability often precludes its use.[11] Second, one can impose a priori restrictions on the production function.[12] Third, one

---

[9] In practice, one would also include various tax adjustments. We do so in the empirical work but omit them in the model to keep the exposition simple.

[10] Olley and Pakes (1996) propose an insightful alternative to the usual instrumental-variables estimation strategy; see Griliches and Mairesse (1995) for an excellent discussion. However, their procedure generally cannot be used when estimating structural parameters governing changes in utilization, because it relies on using investment as a proxy for changes in technology, dt. The method discussed in the next subsection uses investment as a proxy for the shadow value of installed capital; thus, we cannot use the Olley-Pakes procedure and identify all the structural parameters of the model.

[11] In the United States, shift-work data are available solely for manufacturing industries, and then only for a few years. The only data set on worker effort that we know of is the survey of British manufacturing firms used by Schor (1987).

[12] For example, Jorgenson and Griliches (1967) assume that the unobserved service flow of capital is proportional to electricity use. Burnside, Eichenbaum, and Rebelo (1996) have recently used this assumption to derive utilization-adjusted estimates of technology shocks.

can derive links between the unobserved du and observable variables using first-order conditions like equations (1.14) to (1.19). Both the second and third approaches imply links between the unobserved du and observable variables, which can be used to control for changes in utilization.

Bils and Cho (1994), Burnside and Eichenbaum (1996), and Basu and Kimball (1997) argue that one can also control for variable utilization using the relationships between observed and unobserved variables implied by first-order conditions like equations (1.14) to (1.19). The discussion here follows Basu and Kimball.

They begin by assuming a generalized Cobb-Douglas production function:

$$F(ZK, EHN, M; Z) = Z\Gamma((ZK)^{\alpha_K}(EHN)^{\alpha_L}M^{\alpha_M}), \qquad (1.24)$$

where Γ is a monotonically increasing function. In their case this assumption is not merely a first-order approximation, because they make use of the second-order properties of equation (1.24), particularly the fact that the output elasticities are constant. Although they argue that one can relax the Cobb-Douglas assumption, I shall maintain it throughout the discussion.

Equations (1.15) and (1.16) can be combined into an equation implicitly relating E and H:

$$\frac{HG_H(H,E)}{G(H,E)} = \frac{EG_E(H,E)}{G(H,E)}. \qquad (1.25)$$

The elasticity of labor costs with respect to H and E must be equal, because on the benefit side the elasticities of effective labor input with respect to H and E are equal. Given the assumptions on G, (1.25) implies a unique, upward-sloping E–H expansion path, so that we can write

$$E = E(H), \qquad E'(H) > 0. \qquad (1.26)$$

Equation (1.26) says that the unobservable intensity of labor utilization E can be expressed as a monotonically increasing function of the observed number of hours per worker, H.

Finding the marginal product of capital from (1.14), substituting into (1.8), and rearranging, we find that the level of capital utilization depends on the degree to which the current marginal value product of capital exceeds future marginal products:

$$Z\delta'(Z) = \lambda\gamma\alpha_K\frac{Y}{qK}. \qquad (1.27)$$

TECHNOLOGY AND BUSINESS CYCLES

Since fluctuations in marginal cost λ, returns to scale γ, and the marginal value of capital q are difficult to observe directly, we would like to express these factors in terms of other variables that are more readily observed.

The problem with trying to measure q directly is not just the difference between the marginal and average value of capital but also the noisiness of the asset prices one would use to gauge the average value of capital. Instead of trying to measure q directly, Basu and Kimball use equation (1.19) to express q as the price of investment goods times a function of I/K. (Note that Tobin's q is actually q/P_I in my notation.) Equation (1.19) can be inverted to say that I/K is a function of Tobin's q.

The first-order condition for materials usage (1.17) is the key to expressing the product $\lambda\gamma$ in terms of observables. Combining this equation with the expression for the marginal products of materials, we find

$$\lambda\gamma = \frac{P_M M}{\alpha_M Y}. \tag{1.28}$$

Thus, we can measure the marginal value product of capital as:

$$\lambda\gamma\alpha_K = \frac{\alpha_K}{\alpha_M}\frac{P_M M}{Y}. \tag{1.29}$$

Substituting the expression for the marginal revenue product of capital (equation 1.29) and the expression for q (equation (1.19) into (1.27) leads to the desired expression for capital utilization in terms of observed variables and the ratio α_K/α_M:

$$Z\delta'(Z) = \frac{\alpha_K}{\alpha_M}\frac{P_M M}{P_I K}\frac{1}{J'(I/K)}. \tag{1.30}$$

Define a number of elasticities in terms of steady-state values of different variables; let

$$\zeta \equiv \frac{H^* E'(H^*)}{E(H^*)},$$

$$\Delta \equiv \frac{Z^* \delta''(Z^*)}{\delta'(Z^*)},$$

and

$$j \equiv \frac{(I/K)^* J''((I/K)^*)}{J'((I/K)^*)} = \frac{\delta^* J''(\delta^*)}{J'(\delta^*)}.$$

Thus, from equation (1.26),

$$d \ln(EHN) = dn + dh + de = dn + (1 + \zeta)dh. \qquad (1.31)$$

With a constant α_K/α_M,[13] (1.31) implies

$$dz = \frac{1}{1 + \Delta}(dp_M + dm - dp_I - dk) - \frac{j}{1 + \Delta}(di - dk). \qquad (1.32)$$

Putting everything together, we have an estimating equation that controls for variable utilization:

$$dy = \mu^* dx + \mu^* \zeta s_L dh + \frac{\mu^*}{1 + \Delta} s_K (dp_M + dm - dp_I - dk)$$
$$- \frac{\mu^* j}{1 + \Delta} s_K (di - dk) + dt. \qquad (1.33)$$

This specification controls for both labor and capital utilization, without making special assumptions about separability or homotheticity. However, for this simple derivation, the Cobb-Douglas functional form is important. One payoff of the Basu-Kimball approach is that it allows one not only to control for variations in utilization, du, but also to estimate the key elasticities governing changes in Z and E, which will be used in the model simulations below.[14] The residual from this equation is a measure of technology change, cleansed of distortions coming from imperfect competition and variable utilization.

The Definition of Technology Change

How are the firm-level technology shocks defined (implicitly) by equation (1.33), related to aggregate technology shocks? Aggregate technology change is sometimes defined from a macro (top down) perspective, and sometimes from a micro (bottom up) perspective. A sensible macro definition is the change in final output (that is, $C + I +$

---

[13] This equation is where the Cobb-Douglas assumption matters; Basu and Kimball differentiate (1.31) assuming that α_K/α_M is a constant. Their theory allows for the fully general case where the ratio of the elasticities is a function of all four input quantities, but they argue that pursuing this approach would demand too much of the data and instruments.

[14] So far, we have abstracted from the existence of a shift premium. However, utilizing capital more intensively by running it for extra shifts may require paying workers on later shifts a higher base wage to compensate for the disutility of working at non-standard hours. Basu and Kimball extend the model above to incorporate a shift premium. They show that an estimating equation with the same three extra variables as (1.33) controls for utilization even in this extended model. Thus, the technology residuals and markup estimates are correct even in this more general framework. However, the parameters governing changes in utilization—particularly Δ—are no longer identified once the model is generalized to include a shift premium.

G + X − M), for given aggregate primary inputs. A sensible micro definition is an appropriately weighted average of firm-level technology change. With constant returns and perfect competition, these two perspectives are equivalent (Domar 1961; Hulten 1978). Rotemberg and Woodford (1995) show that equivalence also holds with imperfectly competitive product markets, under certain restrictive conditions: perfect factor markets, and all firms having identical separable gross-output production functions, charging prices that are the same markup over marginal cost, and always using intermediate inputs in fixed proportions to gross output.

If the Rotemberg-Woodford assumptions fail—if, for example, factor markets are imperfectly competitive or firms have different degrees of market power—then the two perspectives lead to different definitions; that is, aggregate technology from a macro perspective is not a weighted average of firm-level technology.[15] For example, suppose differences in markups or factor payments across firms lead the same factor to have a different social value for its marginal product in different uses. Then changes in the *distribution* of inputs can affect final output, even if firm-level technology and aggregate inputs are held constant. Conceptually, however, we may not want to count such variation as "technology change," since it can occur with no change in the technology available to any firm.

Now consider the following definition of technical change: the increase in aggregate output, holding fixed not only aggregate primary inputs, but also their distribution across firms and the materials/output ratio at each firm. Although this definition is close in spirit to the macro perspective, it also corresponds to a reasonable micro definition, since aggregate technology changes only if firm-level technology changes. Indexing firms by i, Basu and Fernald (1997) show that this measure of technical change equals:

$$dt = \sum_i w_i \frac{dt_i}{1 - \mu_i s_{Mi}}, \qquad (1.34)$$

where w_i is the firm's share of aggregate nominal value added:

$$w_i = \frac{P_i Y_i - P_{Mi} M_i}{\sum_i (P_i Y_i - P_{Mi} M_i)} \equiv \frac{P_i^V V_i}{P^V V}.$$

Conceptually, this measure first converts the gross-output technology shocks to a value-added basis by dividing through by $1 - \mu s_M$. (A

---

[15] Basu and Fernald (1997).

value-added basis is desirable because of the national accounts identity, which tells us that aggregate final expenditure equals aggregate value added.)[16] These value-added shocks are then weighted by the firm's share of aggregate value added.

Equation (1.34) defines a "micro" measure of technical change, since it changes only if firm-level production technology changes. However, it also nests the Rotemberg-Woodford definition of technology as a special case, and thus it correctly measures "macro" technical change under their conditions. This property is desirable, since the Rotemberg-Woodford assumptions are implicit or explicit in most dynamic general-equilibrium models with imperfect competition. I thus focus on definition (1.34) in constructing the aggregate technology series.

However, the measure defined in equation (1.34) has the disadvantage that it requires one to know (or estimate) the firm-level markups. Domar (1961) and Hulten (1978) propose a different definition of aggregate technology:

$$dt' = \sum_i w_i \frac{dt_i}{1 - s_{Mi}}. \qquad (1.35)$$

They show that equation (1.35) satisfies both the micro and macro definitions of technical change when there are constant returns and perfect competition: Note that (1.34) reduces to (1.35) when μ equals one everywhere.

With imperfect competition, the Domar-weighted measure shows how much increases in firm-level technical change increase final output, holding fixed both the aggregate quantities and the distributions of primary *and* intermediate inputs. This definition is unappealing, since it corresponds to a thought experiment where firms are not allowed to use more intermediate inputs even when they receive favorable technology shocks. However, it does have the advantage that it does not require knowledge of sectoral markups. BFK thus also use this measure of technical change to check the robustness of the primary measure, and they find that their results are unaffected by using one measure rather than the other.

We define changes in aggregate utilization as the contribution to

---

[16] Basu and Fernald (1997) discuss this conversion to value added at length. To understand why $(1 - \mu s_M)$ is the right denominator, consider the case where a firm uses materials in fixed proportion to output, and receives a gross-output technology innovation dt. The firm's output (which, for simplicity, we can assume is sold only for final demand) increases both because of the technology improvement and because of the productive contribution of the required additional materials. Since the marginal product of materials is μs_M, output increases by $dy = dt + \mu s_M dm$. Since $dm = dy$ (the materials/output ratio is fixed), this equation implies that the change in output is $dt/(1 - \mu s_M)$.

final output of changes in firm-level utilization. This, in turn, is a weighted average of firm-level utilization change du_i:

$$du = \sum_i w_i \frac{\mu_i du_i}{1 - \mu_i s_{Mi}} \qquad (1.36)$$

Note from equation (1.9) that $\mu_i du_i$ enters in a manner parallel to dt_i and hence (1.36) parallels (1.34).

DATA AND METHOD

The Data

I now construct a measure of "true" aggregate technology change, dt, and explore its properties. As discussed in the previous section, I estimate technology change at a disaggregated level, and then aggregate. The aggregate is the private U.S. economy, and the "firms" are 34 industries; for manufacturing, these industries correspond roughly to the 2-digit SIC level.

Each industry contains thousands or tens of thousands of firms, so it may seem odd to take industries as firms. Unfortunately, no firm-level data sets span the economy. In principle, I could focus on a subset of the economy, using the Longitudinal Research Database, say; however, narrowing the focus requires sacrificing a macroeconomic perspective, as well as panel length and data quality. By focusing on aggregates, the paper complements existing work that uses small subsets of the economy.

I use data compiled by Dale Jorgenson and Barbara Fraumeni on industry-level inputs and outputs. These data consist of a panel of 33 private industries (including 21 manufacturing industries) that cover the entire U.S. nonfarm private economy. These sectoral accounts seek to provide accounts that are, to the extent possible, consistent with the economic theory of production. Output is measured as gross output, and inputs are separated into capital, labor, energy, and materials. These data are available from 1947 to 1989; in the empirical work, however, I restrict my sample to 1950 to 1989, since the money shock instrument is not available for previous years. For a complete description of the data set, see Jorgenson, Gollop, and Fraumeni (1987).

I compute capital's share s_K for each industry by constructing a series for required payments to capital. I follow Hall and Jorgenson (1967) and Hall (1990), and estimate the user cost of capital R. For any type of capital, the required payment is then $RP_K K$, where $P_K K$ is the current-dollar value of the stock of this type of capital. In each sector, I use data on the current value of the 51 types of capital, plus land and inventories, distinguished by the U.S. Bureau of Economic Analysis in constructing the national product accounts. Hence, for each of these 53 assets, indexed by s, the user cost of capital is

$$R_s = (r + \delta_s) \frac{(1 - ITC_s - \tau d_s)}{(1 - \tau)}, \quad s = 1 \text{ to } 53. \qquad (2.1)$$

r is the required rate of return on capital (and on all other assets except money), and δ_s is the depreciation rate for assets of type s. ITC_s is the asset-specific investment tax credit, τ is the corporate tax rate, and d_s is the asset-specific present value of depreciation allowances. I follow Hall (1990) in assuming that the required return r equals the dividend yield on the S&P 500. Jorgenson and Yun (1991) provide data on ITC_s and d_s for each type of capital good. Given required payments to capital, computing s_K is straightforward.

For the empirical work, we need instruments that are uncorrelated with technology change. I use two of the Hall-Ramey instruments: the growth rate of the price of oil deflated by the GDP deflator and the growth rate of real government defense spending.[17] (I use the contemporaneous value and one lag of each instrument.) To these I add a version of the instruments used by Burnside (1996), quarterly Federal Reserve "policy shocks" from an identified VAR. I use the sum of the four quarterly policy shocks in year $t - 1$ as instruments for input growth in year t.[18]

Estimating Technology Change

To estimate "firm-level" technology change, I estimate equation (1.33) for each industry. Although I could estimate these equations separately for each industry (and indeed do so as a check on results), some parameters, particularly the utilization proxies, are then estimated

---

[17] We drop the third instrument, the political party of the President, because it appears to have little relevance in any industry. Burnside (1996) shows that the oil price instrument is generally quite relevant, and defense spending explains a sizable fraction of input changes in the durable-goods industries.

[18] The qualitative features of the results in the next section, "Empirical Results," appear robust to using different combinations and lags of the instruments. On a priori grounds, the set I choose seems preferable to alternatives—all of the variables have strong grounds for being included. In addition, the set chosen has the best overall fit (measured by mean and median F statistic) of the a priori plausible combinations considered. Of course, Hall, Rudebusch, and Wilcox (1996) argue that with weak instruments, one does not necessarily want to choose the instruments that happen to fit best in sample; for example, if the "true" relevance of all the instruments is equal, the ones that by chance fit best in sample are in fact those with the largest small sample bias. That case is probably not a major concern here, since the instrument set we choose fits well for all industry groupings; for example, it is the one we would choose based on a rule of, say, using the instruments that fit best in durables industries as instruments for nondurables industries, and vice versa.

rather imprecisely. To mitigate this problem, I combine industries into four groups, estimating equations that restrict the utilization parameters to be constant within industry groups. Thus, for each group we have

$$dy_i = c_i + \mu_i dx_i + adh_i + b(dp_{Mi} + dm_i - dp_{li} - dk_i) + c(di_i - dk_i) + dt_i. \quad (2.2)$$

The markup μ_i differs by industries within a group (Burnside (1996) emphasizes the importance of allowing this heterogeneity). The groups are durables manufacturing (11 industries); nondurables manufacturing (10); natural-resource extraction, such as mining and petroleum extraction (4); and all others, mainly services and utilities (8). To avoid the "transmission problem" of correlation between technology shocks and input use, I estimate each system using Three-Stage Least Squares, using the instruments noted above.

After estimating equation (2.2), the sum of the industry-specific constant $\hat{c}_i$ and residual $d\hat{t}_i$ measures technology change in the gross-output production function. Since I am ultimately interested in the aggregate effects of technology shocks, I take an appropriately weighted average of the firm-level estimates of technology change, using equation (1.34).

EMPIRICAL RESULTS

This section summarizes the properties of the "true" technology series; the results are taken from BFK. These results serve two purposes. First, they explain the properties of the technology series, which will be used as an input into the model simulations of the fifth section, "Simulation Results," below. Second, they allow us to compute impulse responses to technology improvements, which will serve as benchmarks for assessing the performance of the models.

Basic Correlations

Table 1 reports summary statistics for three series: (i) the Solow residual; (ii) a series that makes no utilization corrections, but corrects only for aggregation biases; and (iii) a "technology" measure based on equation (2.2). Note that the first measure uses aggregate data alone, whereas the other two are based on sectoral regression residuals, which are aggregated using equation (1.4).

The corrected series have about the same mean as the Solow residual. However, the variance is substantially smaller: The variance of the fully corrected series is less than one-third that of the Solow residual, so the standard deviation (shown in the second column) is only about 55 percent as large. The reported minimums show negative technical change in some periods, but the lower variance of the technology series implies

Table 1
Descriptive Statistics for Technology Residuals

	Mean	Standard Deviation	Minimum	Maximum
Solow Residual	.011	.022	−.044	.066
Technology Residual (No Utilization Correction)	.012	.016	−.034	.050
Technology Residual (Full Basu-Kimball (1997) Correction)	.013	.012	−.013	.032

that the probability of negative estimates is much lower. For example, the Solow residual is negative in 12 out of 40 years; the fully corrected residual is negative in only 5 out of 40 years.

The fully corrected series now are plotted against some familiar business-cycle variables. Figures 1 and 2 show how the estimated technology series differs dramatically from the usual Solow residual.

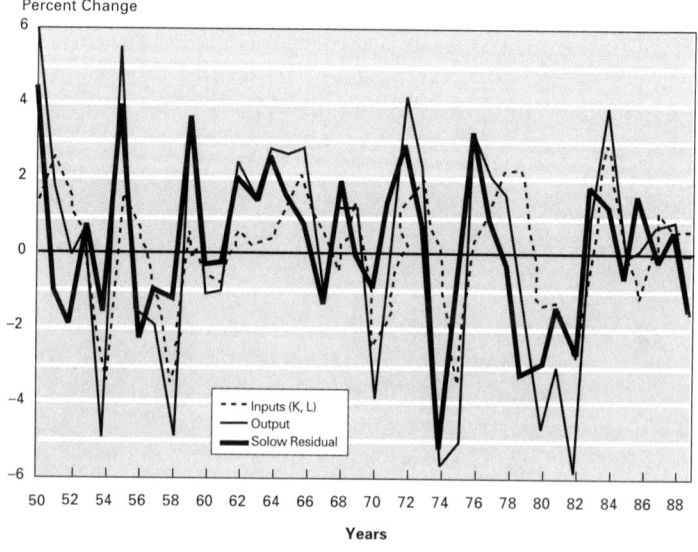

**Figure 1
Solow Residual, Input Growth, and Output Growth**

Note: All series are de-meaned.

Figure 2
Technology Residual, Solow Residual, Output and Input Growth

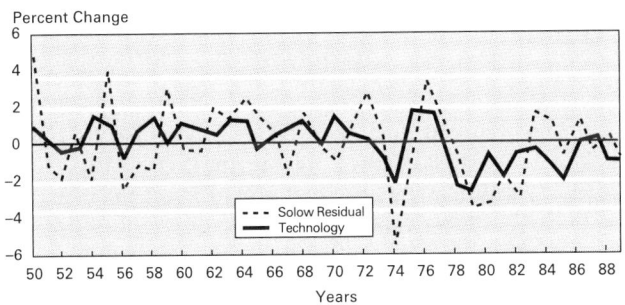

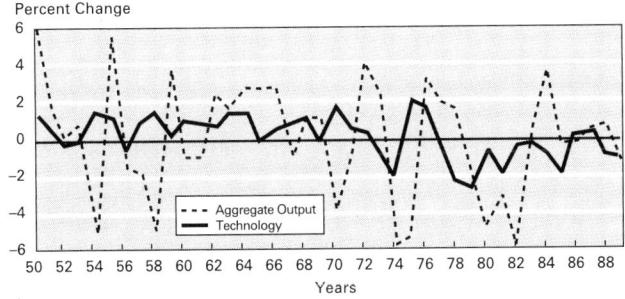

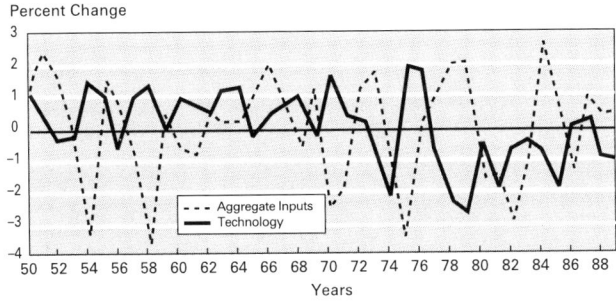

Note: The technology series is the fully adjusted residual. All series are de-meaned.

Figure 1 plots basic business-cycle data: the Solow residual dp, aggregate output growth dv, and aggregate primary input growth, dx^V. These three series clearly co-move positively, quite strongly so in the case of dp and

dv. (All variables are de-meaned; that is, the average has been removed from all series.)

Figure 2 plots the fully corrected technology series against these three variables. Comparing technical change to the standard Solow residual, the fluctuations in the technology series are significantly smaller than the fluctuations in the Solow residual, consistent with the intuition that much of the volatility of the Solow residual reflects nontechnological factors such as variable input utilization. In addition, some periods show a phase shift: The Solow residual follows technology change with a lag of one to two years. This phase shift reflects the utilization correction: In the estimates, high technology shocks are associated with low levels of utilization, which in turn reduce the Solow residual relative to the technology series. The phase shift, in particular, appears to reflect primarily movements in hours per worker, which generally increase one year after a technology improvement. The model of the first section of this paper says that an increase in hours per worker signals an increase in unobserved effort, which the Solow residual incorrectly interprets as positive technical change.

Aggregate value-added output growth (dv) is then plotted against the same technology series. The series less clearly move together contemporaneously. Again, the series appear to have a phase shift: Output co-moves with technology, lagged one to two years. This result is qualitatively consistent with the sticky-price model in the next section, where the contemporaneous correlation between technology shocks and output growth is ambiguous but is clearly positive with a lag.

Finally, Figure 2 plots the growth rate of primary inputs of capital and labor (dx^V) and the same technology series. These two series clearly co-move negatively over the entire sample period.

It is clear that the co-movements between technology and input and output are quite different from those found in the usual real-business-cycle (RBC) literature, where one takes the standard Solow residual dp as the measure of technology change.

Why do these results differ from those of King and Rebelo (1997), who argue that variable capital utilization can "resuscitate" the RBC model? The difference arises from the different techniques used to purify the Solow residual. King and Rebelo specify a particular dynamic general-equilibrium (DGE) model, and then feed in just the observed Solow residual as data. The model then decomposes the Solow residual into technical change and variations in utilization, where the change in utilization must be consistent with the rest of the model, given the implied technology shock. In some ways this method goes into too much depth, but in other ways it is insufficiently general. For example, King and Rebelo specify a full model in order to derive the responses of labor, investment, and other variables to a technology shock. But it is not necessary to specify the environment to this extent, since these variables

TECHNOLOGY AND BUSINESS CYCLES

can all be observed in the data. On the other hand, their model does not allow for capital and labor adjustment costs, imperfect competition, sticky prices, or the variable labor effort and composition effects that we find are empirically extremely important. It is important to realize that the model of the first section nests the King-Rebelo model as a special case—the fact that I get very different results implies that the data reject their model.

Impulse Responses to Technology Improvement

I now present impulse responses of the basic variables to a technology innovation, using bivariate VARs and studying the response of a series of variables to technology shocks. The variables examined are aggregate output growth (dv), aggregate input growth (dx^V), total hours worked ($dh + dn$), and the constructed series for utilization change, du, as defined in equation (1.36).

The VAR estimated is of the form

$$\mathbf{A}(\mathbf{L})\begin{bmatrix} dt \\ dj \end{bmatrix} = \begin{bmatrix} \varepsilon \\ \eta \end{bmatrix}, \quad (3.1)$$

where dj is one of the variables studied. For dt I use the fully corrected measure of technology change. I assume that it is exogenous, so I set $a_{12}(L) = 0$. In all other cases I use a lag length of 2 periods. All equations include constants. Note that I am identifying technology shocks just as before; I am not obtaining identification from assumptions imposed on the VAR, for example, the long-run neutrality assumptions of Blanchard and Quah (1989) or Gali (1998). The VAR is just a convenient way of presenting some of the results.[19]

Figure 3 shows the impulse responses to a technology improvement: the effects of a 1 percentage point technology improvement on the (log) levels of technology, output, inputs, manhours, and utilization. Along with the impulse responses are 95 percent confidence intervals, bootstrapped using the procedure in the RATS statistical package.[20]

Both output and inputs fall on impact; the fall in inputs is strongly significant, regardless of the type of input considered (manhours, utilization, or dx^V). The fall in output is not statistically significant.

Output grows strongly after the shock; the impulse response is

---

[19] I do not use cointegration techniques, because levels of output and input need not be cointegrated with technology. For example, changes in demographic structure (for example, the baby boom) or in immigration policy can cause permanent changes in the size of the labor force that are not related to technology.

[20] These confidence intervals treat dz as data, although dz is a generated variable. They do correct for the generated-regressor problem in ε given this assumption about dz.

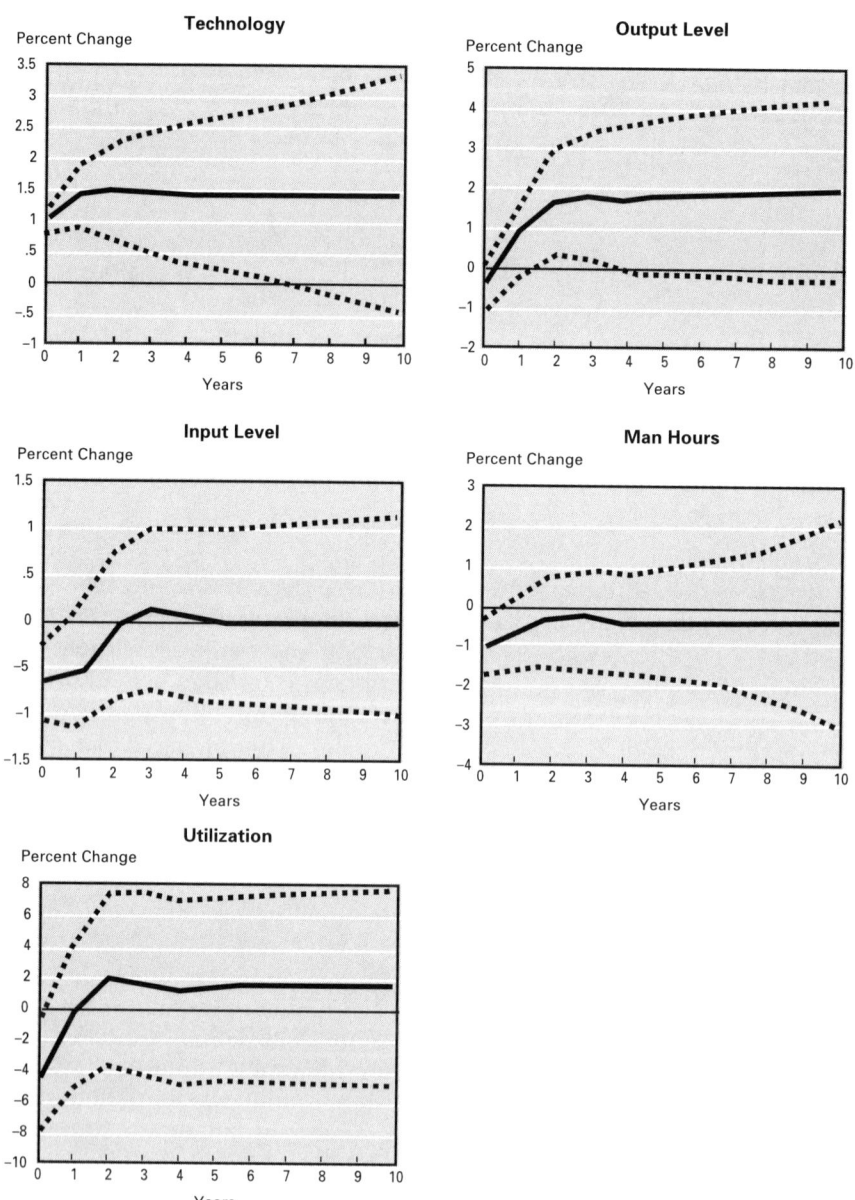

**Figure 3
Impulse Responses to Technology Improvement: Basic Variables**

Note: Impulse responses to a 1 percent age point improvement in technology. The technology series is the fully adjusted residual. Dotted lines show 95 percent confidence intervals, computed using RATS bootstrap method. Sample period is 1952 to 1989.

significantly different from zero with a two-year lag, and the point estimate shows output growing by about 1.8 percent. Inputs grow more slowly, but the standard errors of the estimates are large. For example, the point estimates say that dx^V falls 0.8 percent on impact, and then recovers to its pre-shock level (normalized to zero) in three years. However, at three years the 95 percent confidence interval runs from about 1 percent to -1 percent. The same is true of hours worked, except that the point estimate never recovers to its pre-shock value. On the other hand, the point estimates show utilization remaining above its pre-shock level indefinitely.

The finding that technology improvements reduce both output and input on impact seems problematic for standard flexible-price RBC models. This assertion will be documented below.

In a standard RBC model (for example, Cooley and Prescott 1995) with a capital share of 0.35, a 1.4 percent increase in Hicks-neutral technology (which is how I have normalized the series) should increase output by about 2.15 percent in the long run (computed as $1.4/(1 - 0.35)$), increase inputs (including capital) by about 0.75 percent in the long run, and leave manhours and utilization unchanged. The point estimate for the output response is fairly close to the predicted value. The point estimate for the input response is much lower, but the predicted value is well within the confidence interval. The same is true for utilization and hours worked.

A DGE Model with Variable Capital Utilization

This section lays out a simple sticky-price, dynamic general-equilibrium model with variable capital utilization and imperfect competition. It is representative of a number of models in the recent literature,[21] but the presentation follows Kiley (1998). The model nests a competitive flexible-price model with variable utilization and, of course, the standard RBC model with a fixed short-run supply of capital services. I do not treat variable labor effort, because in terms of model calibration the only effect of variable effort is to make the effective labor supply curve more elastic. Since I intend to follow the RBC literature and simply assume that effective labor supply is very elastic, variable labor effort is not included in the model.[22] However, variable capital utilization makes the model differ qualitatively from the standard RBC model, and this feature is discussed below. As in the empirical model of the first section of this

---

[21] For example, Kimball (1995); Chari, Kehoe, and McGrattan (1996); and Dotsey, King, and Wolman (1997).

[22] However, one can use the empirical evidence supporting the variable-effort hypothesis to rationalize the high short-run labor supply elasticity assumed below.

paper, the penalty for utilizing capital more intensively is that it wears out faster.

Consumers

The consumer side of the model is standard. An infinitely lived, representative consumer/worker supplies labor, rents capital, and owns the firms. The consumer maximizes the discounted value of expected utility, which is given by

$$E_t \sum_{i=0}^{\infty} \beta^i [(1 - \alpha) \log (C_{t+i}) + \alpha \log (1 - N_{t+i})], \quad (4.1)$$

subject to the usual series of budget constraints:

$$C_t + A_{t+1} = W_t N_t + (1 + r_t)A_t + \Pi_t.$$

C is consumption, A is the consumer's stock of assets (equal to the capital stock K in equilibrium), N is labor supply, r is the real interest rate on bonds (equal to the marginal revenue product of capital minus depreciation), W is the real wage, and Π is economic profit (if any).

Optimization implies that the consumer is indifferent between consumption and leisure at a point in time, and between consumption at two different times. Thus, in equilibrium,

$$\alpha(1 - N_t)^{-1} = (1 - \alpha)W_t C_t^{-1}, \quad (4.2)$$

and

$$\beta E_t \left[\left(\frac{C_t}{C_{t+1}} \right)(1 + r_{t+1}) \right] = 1.$$

Since no government consumption is included in this model, aggregate output equals the sum of consumption and investment:[23]

$$Y_t = C_t + I_t. \quad (4.3)$$

The Final Goods Sector

The final goods sector is competitive and has flexible prices. The production function for final goods output, Y, uses intermediate goods,

---

[23] Abusing notation slightly, I use Y to denote aggregate national output. In the empirical section above, Y represented gross output, while national output is, of course, real value added (which was called V in the first section).

TECHNOLOGY AND BUSINESS CYCLES

Y_i, as inputs to production. There is a continuum of such goods, indexed by $i \in [0, 1]$. Thus,

$$Y = \left[\int_0^1 Y_i^\theta \, di \right]^{1/\theta}, \qquad 0 < \theta \leq 1. \tag{4.4}$$

Note that final goods are produced with constant returns to scale. Let S_i denote the price of intermediate goods, Y_i. Then cost-minimization by the final goods firms implies constant elasticity of substitution demand functions of the form:

$$Y_i = Y \left(\frac{S_i}{P} \right)^{-1/(1-\theta)}, \tag{4.5}$$

where P is the ideal aggregate price index:

$$P = \left[\int_0^1 S_i^{\theta/(\theta-1)} \, di \right]^{(\theta-1)/\theta}.$$

Note that the monopoly markup resulting from this demand specification is constant at

$$\mu = \frac{1}{\theta}.$$

The Intermediate Goods Sector

The intermediate goods sector comprises a continuum of firms, each of which is a monopolist in the production of a single variety of good. Each firm has the production function:

$$Y_{it} = T_t (Z_{it} K_{it})^\alpha N_{it}^{1-\alpha} - \Phi, \tag{4.6}$$

where $\Phi \geq 0$ is a fixed cost of production (paid in units of output) and T is the level of technology. All firms have the same technology. Log technology change follows an autoregressive process:

$$\tilde{T}_t = \xi \tilde{T}_{t-1} + \omega_t. \tag{4.7}$$

If $\Phi > 0$, then firms produce with increasing returns to scale. Note, however, that increasing returns are not introduced by having diminishing marginal cost, a specification that is standard in the literature but has little empirical support. Here, marginal cost is independent of firm-level output. In this model, the steady-state degree of returns to scale is given by

$$\gamma^* = \frac{Y^* + \Phi}{Y^*}.$$

Since the increasing returns are internal to the firm, increasing returns require imperfect competition, for the reasons discussed above following equation (1.5).

The capital stock at each firm evolves according to

$$K_{i,t+1} = I_{it} + (1 - \delta(Z_{it}))K_{it}. \tag{4.8}$$

Note that unlike the empirical model, no adjustment costs for capital or employment are included. Excluding adjustment costs makes the model simpler, and also easier to compare to the existing literature.

In the sticky-price model, firms are required to set the same nominal price for two periods. Half the firms set prices in odd-numbered periods, and the other half in even-numbered periods. This specification, a variant of that introduced by Taylor (1980), is intended to capture price stickiness in a parsimonious fashion.[24] Firms set prices to maximize discounted profits. Let λ denote the firm's real marginal cost of production, as in the first section. Using a tilde (~) to denote log deviations from the steady state and assuming the one-period discount factor is approximately equal to 1, the log-linearized pricing equation is

$$\tilde{S}_{it} = \frac{1}{2} E_t [\tilde{P}_t + \tilde{\lambda}_{it} + \tilde{P}_{t+1} + \tilde{\lambda}_{i,t+1}]. \tag{4.9}$$

Not surprisingly, equation (4.9) shows that nominal prices are set as a markup over nominal marginal cost in the two periods. It is assumed that firms must meet all demand at the posted price; that is, rationing is ruled out. In equilibrium, all firms at time t set the same price S_t.

Note that by definition the (log) change in real marginal cost is the change in the relative price minus the change in the markup:

$$\tilde{\lambda}_{it} = (\tilde{P}_{it} - \tilde{P}_t) - \tilde{\mu}_{it}. \tag{4.10}$$

Finally, the price level is the average of prices set at t and $t - 1$:

$$\tilde{P}_t = \frac{1}{2}[\tilde{S}_t + \tilde{S}_{t-1}]. \tag{4.11}$$

---

[24] The other common variant is the Calvo/Rotemberg partial-adjustment model. Kiley (1997) compares the two specifications and argues that partial adjustment imposes a large amount of exogenous price stickiness in the case where prices are endogenously fairly flexible.

Money

Following Kiley (1998), money is introduced via an interest rate rule, where the monetary authority sets the nominal interest rate. Kiley (1998) discusses the advantages of this specification as opposed to an explicit model of money demand arising from either the presence of money in the utility function or a cash-in-advance constraint. Shocks to the interest rate rule occur, as in the empirical VAR literature. The log-linearized rule is:

$$\tilde{i}_{t+1} = \phi_y \tilde{Y}_t + \phi_p \Delta \tilde{P}_t + v_t, \qquad (4.12)$$

where

$$v_t = \rho v_{t-1} + \varepsilon_t$$

and ε is an iid shock.

Given the nominal interest rate, the real interest rate follows from the Fisher equation:

$$\tilde{r}_{t+1} = \tilde{i}_{t+1} - E_t \Delta \tilde{P}_{t+1}.$$

Implications

Here I discuss the implications of the major innovation in the model, variable capital utilization. First, note that the cost-minimization problem facing the intermediate-goods firms in this model is a simplified version of the problem discussed in the first section. Firms face the same decision regarding variable capital utilization, although there are no investment adjustment costs and no variations in labor effort. Thus, equation (1.27) applies directly. Log-linearizing (1.27) for the case of $q \equiv 1$ and using equation (4.10), we find the expression for optimal utilization:

$$\tilde{Z}_{it} = \frac{(\tilde{P}_{it} - \tilde{\mu}_{it}) + (1/\gamma^*)\tilde{Y}_{it} - \tilde{K}_{it}}{1 + \Delta}. \qquad (4.13)$$

As before, Δ is the elasticity of the *marginal* rate of depreciation with respect to utilization.

Substituting equation (4.13) into the log-linearized production function, we find:

$$\tilde{Y}_{it}\left(1 - \frac{\alpha}{1 + \Delta}\right) = \frac{\gamma^* \alpha \Delta}{1 + \Delta} \tilde{K}_{i,t-1} + \gamma^*(1 - \alpha)\tilde{N}_{it} + \frac{\gamma^* \alpha}{1 + \Delta}((\tilde{P}_{it} - \tilde{P}_t) - \tilde{\mu}_{it})$$
$$+ \gamma^* \tilde{T}_t. \qquad (4.14)$$

As King and Rebelo (1997) observe, one gains intuition about the effects of variable capital utilization by studying the limiting cases of equation

(4.14). First, suppose that $\Delta = \infty$. Then changes in capital utilization are so costly that utilization never changes, and (4.14) reduces to the familiar equation for log-linearized output growth with increasing returns:

$$\tilde{Y}_{it} = \gamma^* \alpha \tilde{K}_{i,t-1} + \gamma^*(1-\alpha)\tilde{N}_{it} + \gamma^* \tilde{T}_t.$$

Second, suppose that $\Delta = 0$, so that depreciation increases only linearly with utilization. Suppose we are in the perfectly competitive case, where $(\tilde{P}_{it} - \tilde{P}_t) - \tilde{\mu}_{it} \equiv 0$. Then the reduced-form production function is linear in labor input—thus, there is effectively no diminishing marginal product of labor, even in the short run, implying that marginal cost is less procyclical and the propagation mechanism for external shocks is stronger. Finally, in the imperfectly competitive case, note that a firm with countercyclical markups experiences larger changes in output if Δ is small. For example, if monetary policy is unexpectedly expansionary and all prices are sticky, the change in the relative price is zero but the change in the markup is negative.[25] This countercyclical markup has the expansionary effect of increasing the demand for all factors, including capital services. The resulting increase in utilization is larger if Δ is small.

Calibration

This subsection discusses the calibration of the RBC model with variable capital utilization, and the additional parameters needed to calibrate the sticky-price model. The calibration is done so that each model period corresponds to two quarters. Thus, in the sticky-price model, each firm keeps its price fixed for one year.

The RBC Model. The RBC model consists of the model above with one-period price setting (thus making prices perfectly flexible), perfect competition, and constant returns. Perfect competition requires $\theta = 1$; constant returns implies that $\Phi = 0$. With two exceptions, the remaining parameters are calibrated to equal those of the benchmark RBC model of Cooley and Prescott (1995, p. 22).[26] In particular, the critical intertemporal

---

[25] The markup falls because expansionary monetary policy necessarily raises marginal cost in this model. In other models, marginal cost might actually fall as output increases—for example, in the "sunspot" model of Farmer and Guo (1994). Markups might also be countercyclical in flexible-price models, for reasons advanced by Rotemberg and Woodford (1992) and Gali (1994).

[26] Since this model does not have steady-state growth, I set the investment share to match the data using equation (33) in Cooley and Prescott (1995). Thus, although the model has neither trend technology growth nor population growth, I use the values for those parameters found in Cooley and Prescott's table (1995, p. 22). The model would be quite consistent with steady-state growth with some modification that makes the degree of returns to scale stationary. One such change would be to have the size of fixed costs grow deterministically at the trend rate of growth of the economy, but there are also other possibilities. See Rotemberg and Woodford (1991, 1995).

elasticity of labor supply is calibrated to equal approximately 2.2 (somewhat lower than most of the RBC literature, though still higher than most of the micro estimates of this parameter).

The first exception is the variance of the innovation to technology. As noted above, I use the actual innovations to technology estimated using the BFK procedure.[27] However, since the estimated residuals are annual, I assume that the technology shock occurs in the first half of each year. The technology shock for the second half of the year is always zero. Since agents in the model always expect the technology innovation to equal zero, and the log-linearization eliminates higher-order responses to uncertainty such as precautionary saving, this procedure does not cause any obvious problems.

The second exception is the parameter Δ, which Cooley and Prescott (1995) do not need to calibrate since their model implicitly assumes $\Delta = \infty$. Burnside and Eichenbaum (1996) calibrate $\Delta = 0.56$, but they do so using a very restrictive functional form that implies

$$\Delta \equiv \frac{Z^* \delta''(Z^*)}{\delta'(Z^*)} = \frac{Z^* \delta'(Z^*)}{\delta(Z^*)} - 1 = \frac{r^*}{r^* + \delta(Z^*)}. \tag{4.15}$$

This method thus identifies Δ purely from a functional form assumption, which is clearly undesirable. Basu and Kimball (1997) discuss the shortcomings of this approach. They estimate Δ from an instrumental variables regression of equation (1.33) and find Δ approximately equal to 1, but with a large standard error (also about 1). I therefore use 1 as my benchmark value of Δ, but also experiment with other values.

Finally, the log-linearized capital accumulation equation also requires one to calibrate the elasticity of $\delta(Z^*)$. However, as equation (4.15) shows, this parameter can be calibrated from the steady-state real rate of interest (which in turn is a function of the discount rate β) and the steady-state depreciation rate, and does not require additional estimation.

The Sticky-Price Model. The real side of the sticky-price model is identical to that of the RBC model, with one exception: the degree of imperfect competition and markups. I follow a calibration that assumes zero economic profit in the steady state and thus equates the markup and the steady-state degree of returns to scale (see equation 1.5).[28] A variety of evidence indicates that the plausible degree of imperfect competition

---

[27] However, I do maintain the Cooley-Prescott calibration of 0.95 (quarterly) for the autoregressive parameter ξ. The point estimate for ξ is actually larger than 1, but one cannot reject the lower value at the 95 percent level. I thus maintain the Cooley-Prescott value for the model simulations, to allow easier comparison to the existing literature.

[28] Rotemberg and Woodford (1995) present a variety of evidence supporting the proposition that pure profit rates are close to zero.

and/or the degree of increasing returns is small.[29] Thus, I set $\gamma^* = \mu^* = 1.05$, implying that $\theta = 0.95$ and $\Phi/Y^* = 0.05$. Recall that this markup, already very small, is the markup on real value added. Assuming a material's share in production of 0.50, it implies that firms sell actual goods for about 2 percent higher than their marginal cost of production—a calibration well within the confidence interval of any recent estimate.

The sticky-price model also requires another set of parameters, relating to the nominal side of the model. Interpreting equation (4.12) as a policy rule, Taylor (1993) suggests that in the post-1987 period the Federal Reserve has followed a policy described by setting $\phi_y = 0.5$ and $\phi_p = 1.5$. These are the parameters I adopt as my baseline case, as does Kiley (1998). Since it is unlikely that the Fed has adhered to this rule over the 40 years of my sample period, the historical simulations based on this rule should be treated as suggestive. I also experiment with reinterpreting equation (4.12) as a standard LM curve, with an exogenous money supply, an income elasticity of money demand equal to 1, and an interest elasticity of money demand equal to -0.5.[30] The calibration implies $\phi_y = 2$ and $\phi_p = 2$. The steady-state inflation rate is assumed to be zero.

In all cases, the autoregressive parameter ρ is set to 0.50.[31] The impulses for the money supply rule are residuals from an assumed monetary policy reaction function, estimated by Burnside (1996).[32] They are residuals from an OLS regression of the 3-month T-bill rate on lags of itself and on current and lagged values of GDP growth, inflation, and commodity prices. The estimation is done at a quarterly frequency, so the shocks for the first period are the sum of the shocks in the first two quarters and the shocks for the second period are the sum of the shocks from the third and fourth quarters.

SIMULATION RESULTS

This section presents two sets of results: impulse responses to both technology and monetary policy shocks, and historical simulations, of the sort performed by Plosser (1989).

Impulse Responses

I first present results for the RBC model, the benchmark model described above, with variable capital utilization. The value of Δ is set to

---

[29] See, for example, Basu (1996), Burnside (1996), and Basu and Fernald (1997).
[30] In this case the equation gives the value of the nominal interest rate at time t, not $t + 1$.
[31] See Kiley (1998) for a discussion.
[32] I thank Craig Burnside for providing these data.

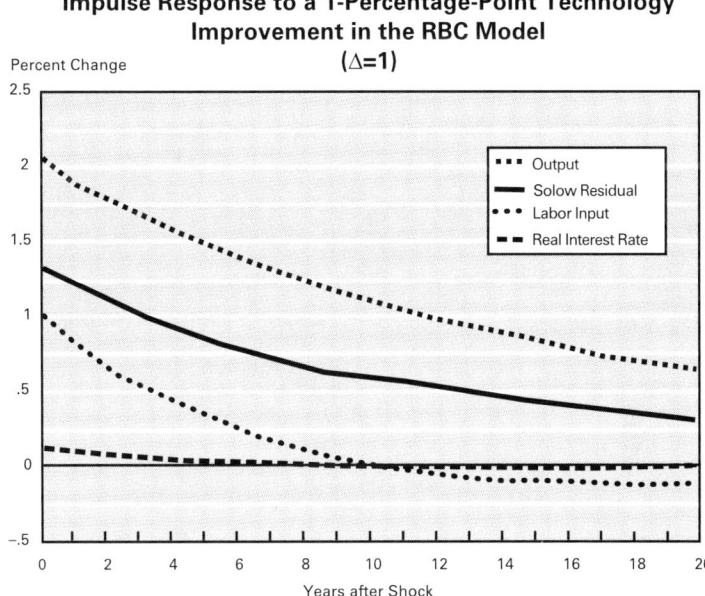

**Figure 4
Impulse Response to a 1-Percentage-Point Technology Improvement in the RBC Model
($\Delta=1$)**

the estimate of 1 in Basu and Kimball (1997). The series shown are the responses of output, labor hours, the real interest rate, and the Solow residual. The residual is calculated as it would be from the data—that is, changes in utilization show up as changes in the residual. Knowing the time path of technology, we can infer the time series for utilization.

Figure 4 gives the impulse response to a 1-percentage-point technology improvement in the RBC model. Output rises by about 2 percent on impact, and labor input by about 1 percent. Note that the Solow residual is higher than 1 on impact, showing that capital utilization increases in response to the technology improvement. Thus, as conjectured, variable utilization amplifies the effects of shocks.

But, as we know from a long line of work, the impulse responses of the RBC model are dramatically different from the empirical results presented in Figure 3. In the data, both output and labor input fall when technology improves, and reach their peak two or three years later. The model shows no fall on impact; all variables are at their peak at time zero.

We now turn to the sticky-price model, to see whether it can explain the observed impulse responses. Figure 5 presents the sticky-price version of the RBC model simulated above. The model has the bench-

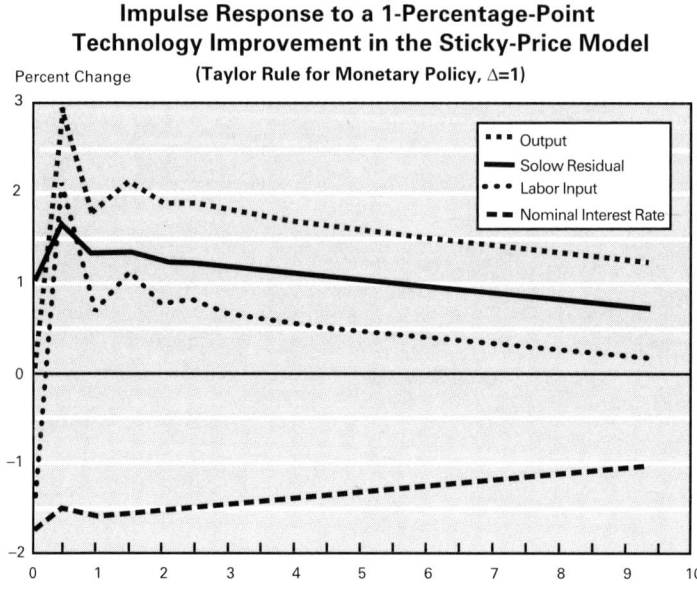

**Figure 5
Impulse Response to a 1-Percentage-Point
Technology Improvement in the Sticky-Price Model
(Taylor Rule for Monetary Policy, Δ=1)**

mark calibration, including $\Delta = 1$ and monetary policy as described by the Taylor rule. (The figures for the sticky-price model display the time path for the nominal interest rate, rather than the real interest rate.)

The results are mildly encouraging. Labor hours fall significantly on impact—about 1.5 percent, more than the point estimate from the data but well within the confidence interval. Output basically does not respond on impact, which is also quite consistent with the data. The Solow residual rises by less than 1 percent, showing that utilization must have fallen, as it does in the data. The model thus displays the strong negative co-movement between technology and inputs that is observed in Figure 3.

The major failure of the sticky-price model is its inability to explain the drawn-out contraction observed in the data. Output and inputs reach their peak just one period (six months) after the shock, when only half the firms have changed prices. They then fall somewhat, before converging smoothly to the steady state. The empirical results, however, have output and inputs reaching their peak about two or three years after the shock.[33]

---

[33] Part of this pattern may be changed by using the actual ARI(1,1) process for technology change that is observed in the data.

I now turn to the other major issue to be investigated, the importance of variable utilization as a propagation mechanism. I first study the effects of variable utilization on the impulse response for nominal shocks, and return to technology shocks after this detour. Figure 6 shows the effects of a 1-percentage-point increase in the nominal interest rate in the model just simulated. The experiment is to shock v_t in equation (4.12) by 1 percentage point, and then let the future path of the nominal interest rate be given by the autoregressive time path for v, as well as the endogenous monetary response dictated by the Taylor rule. The results in Figure 6 are not encouraging. Output falls by more than 1.5 percent in the period of the shock, as does labor input. The Solow residual falls as well, matching the co-movement between observed productivity and nominal shocks documented by Evans (1992). In this case, the majority of the fall is due to the reduction in utilization, though a small percentage can be attributed to the effects of increasing returns to scale in production. With increasing returns, productivity changes when inputs change, and in the same direction. Note that the Taylor rule dictates very expansionary monetary policy in response to the fall in output and inflation. Even though the exogenous component of monetary policy is still tight, the endogenous response is so large that the nominal interest rate falls to -0.56 percent.

However, the shock is not propagated over time. Indeed, output and inputs "overshoot" the steady state only one period after the shock, and converge quickly to the steady state in an oscillatory fashion. This result is puzzling given the encouraging findings of Dotsey, King, and Wolman (1997), who calibrate a similar model, with the same parameters governing variable utilization, and report moderate persistence eight quarters after a nominal shock. However, they assume that the monetary authority does not respond to an economic contraction by loosening monetary policy: The nominal interest rate in their model is derived from an LM specification for money demand. The behavior of the nominal interest rate in Figure 6 suggests that endogenous monetary policy is quite important. I thus change the calibration of this part of the model, in an effort to see how much of the difference in my results comes from the assumption of endogenous monetary policy. I replace the Taylor rule with an LM curve, assuming that the elasticity of money demand with respect to output is 1, and its elasticity with respect to the nominal interest rate is -0.5. (The latter figure is probably somewhat high given the empirical estimates in the literature.)

Figure 7 reports the results. The experiment is still a 1 percentage point increase in v, but now the nominal interest rate falls only -0.3 percentage points below its steady-state level the year after a shock. The effects of the increase in the interest rate are much smaller—output and inputs fall less than 0.5 percentage points—but this calibration avoids the overshooting result: The period after the shock, output and inputs are

Figures 6 and 7
Impulse Response to a Monetary Contraction[a]
in the Sticky-Price Model

Taylor Rule for Monetary Policy, Δ=1

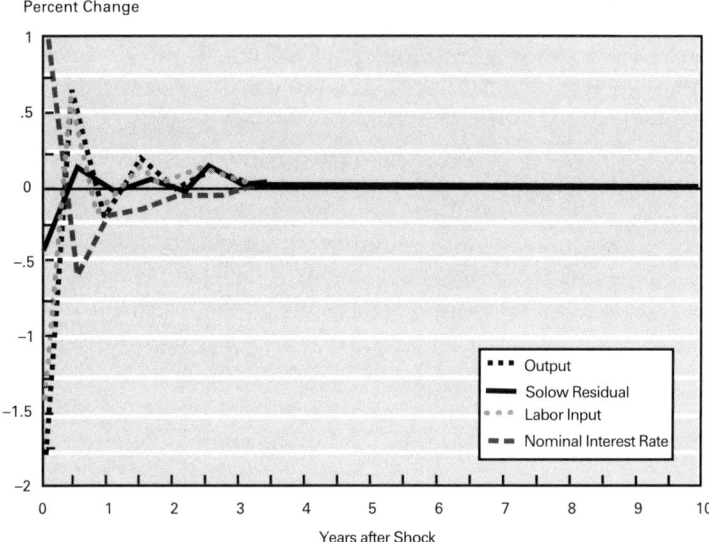

Exogenous Money, Δ=1

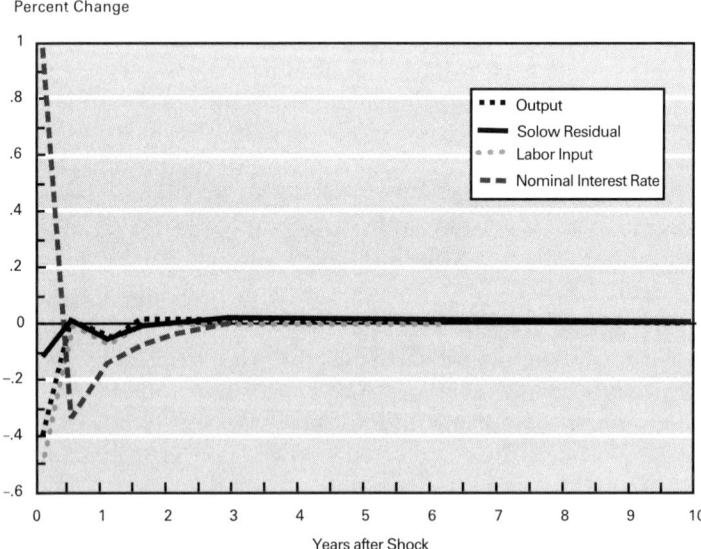

[a] 1-percentage-point increase in nominal interest rate.

back at the steady state, not significantly higher than their steady-state levels. I still do not reproduce the Dotsey et al. results, but I am using much higher values for the interest elasticity of money demand (they use zero) and the labor supply elasticity (which they assume is infinite).

However, as Kiley (1998) argues, it seems better to calibrate sticky-price models using Fed reaction functions rather than money demand equations that assume exogenous monetary policy.[34] First, an interest rate targeting function is clearly a more realistic description of how Fed policy now operates; the Fed definitely perceives the nominal interest rate as its policy instrument. Second, the results in Dotsey et al. and Chari, Kehoe, and McGrattan (1996) are sensitive to the assumed interest elasticity, which is a very poorly estimated parameter. The advantage of the reaction-function approach is that the money demand parameters are irrelevant for the results. Thus, the challenge is to reproduce the Dotsey et al. results, using the more realistic framework employed here.

One method is to follow Dotsey et al. and make labor supply infinitely elastic. This strategy seems problematic—the elasticity of 2 assumed here seems about as high as one can reasonably get, even with variable labor effort. The other way to make factor supply more elastic is to reduce the size of Δ. Since Δ is quite imprecisely estimated, it seems reasonable to experiment with values smaller than one.

Figure 8 reports the results for the limiting case of $\Delta = 0$, returning to the case where the nominal interest rate is set by the Taylor rule. The results seem encouraging; output and inputs fall by almost 2 percent and remain above their steady-state levels for a year. No overshooting occurs, as was the case for the same model with $\Delta = 1$ (shown in Figure 6).

However, there is still not enough persistence, relative to the results found in the empirical literature. Of course, this result may simply indicate still not enough "real rigidities" in the model. Ball and Romer (1990) point out the importance of real rigidities for generating substantial real effects of nominal shocks in static models with state-dependent pricing; Kimball (1995) confirms their results in a dynamic DGE model with time-dependent pricing. In the context of this model, the degree of real rigidity corresponds (inversely) to the assumed size of Δ, given the other calibration, particularly the intertemporal elasticity of labor supply. Thus, the answer may simply be that we need even more real rigidity than the minimum value of Δ allows. For example, countercyclical variation in the size of *desired* markups would help enormously, for reasons explained by Kimball (1995).

However, the fact that we now want sticky-price models to generate

---

[34] However, it is not clear that the Taylor rule is the best one. Orphanides (1997) argues that estimation using real-time data supports simple forward-looking rules over the Taylor rule.

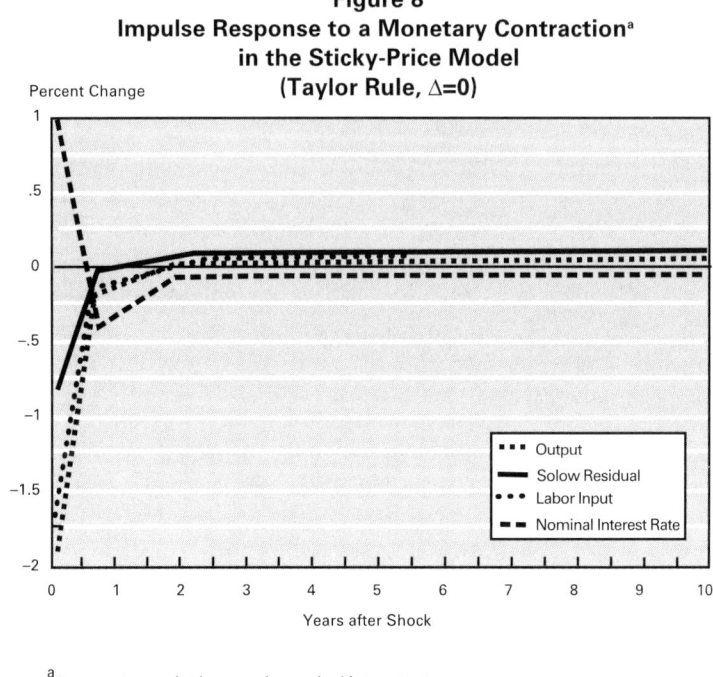

**Figure 8
Impulse Response to a Monetary Contraction[a]
in the Sticky-Price Model
(Taylor Rule, $\Delta=0$)**

[a] 1-percentage-point increase in nominal interest rate.

sensible impulse responses to technology shocks puts greater constraints on the search for real rigidities. To document this assertion, Figure 9 shows what happens in the sticky-price model with $\Delta = 0$ in response to a 1-percentage-point technology improvement. First, we see the expected fall in inputs and output, now almost 4 percent. Utilization falls so much that the Solow residual actually *falls* slightly in response to an *improvement* in technology! But then, in the first period after the shock, the model predicts enormous increases in output (almost 10 percent) and inputs (about 7 percent). These far exceed in magnitude any of the impulse responses observed in the data, at any lag. But, according to the fully adjusted technology residual, a 1-percentage-point or larger change in technology relative to its mean is not an uncommon event in the data—we find such changes in 17 of the 40 years of the sample. Thus, the $\Delta = 0$ model must be rejected for implying *too much* real rigidity to be consistent with the observed effects of technology—while at the same time it generates *too little* real rigidity to rationalize persistent real effects of money.

The reasons are not hard to understand. A nominal shock is fundamentally a weak shock, relying on price rigidity to have any real

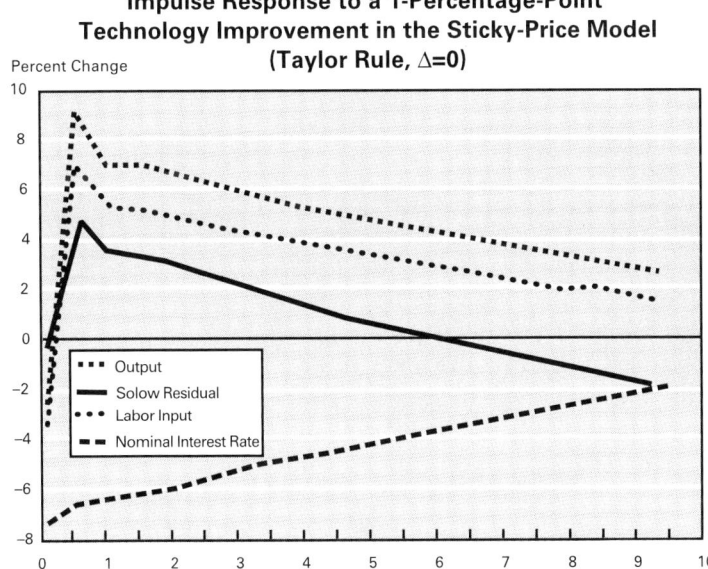

**Figure 9
Impulse Response to a 1-Percentage-Point
Technology Improvement in the Sticky-Price Model
(Taylor Rule, Δ=0)**

effects. For weak shocks to have large, persistent effects, the economy needs to be in a state of "near indeterminacy," depicted in the labor market as flat labor supply and demand curves lying almost on top of one another.[35] But technology shocks are large, real shocks. An economy that displays business-cycle-sized fluctuations in response to money shocks may well display implausibly large fluctuations in response to technology shocks—as Figures 8 and 9 show.

This result does not mean that the search for a sensible, integrated model of business cycles is hopeless. What it does imply is that we need "shock-dependent" real rigidities. For example, the implicit-collusion model of countercyclical markups[36] predicts that changes in the markup depend on the time path of output and interest rate responses to shocks. These paths are likely to differ in response to different shocks. Similarly, if leisure is durable, then labor supply will be more elastic in response to

---

[35] The phrase and interpretation are from Hall (1991). Kimball (1995) and Kiley (1998) discuss this issue in the context of sticky-price DGE models.
[36] Rotemberg and Woodford (1992, 1995).

temporary rather than to permanent changes in the demand for labor. If the effects of monetary shocks last only over the "short run," but the effects of technology shocks last over the "medium run," then the degree of real rigidity from flat labor supply may well be larger in the case of monetary shocks.

Historical Simulations

I now simulate the two benchmark models using historical shocks, and then compare the realizations with actual data for the years 1950 to 1989. The simulation for the RBC model is simple, since I need only choose a value for Δ (set equal to one) and feed in the estimated series of technology shocks. The sticky-price model simulation is much harder, since I also need to specify the form of the Fed's reaction function. For a historically accurate simulation, one would actually need to supply a variety of reaction functions, since it seems clear that the Fed has fundamentally changed its procedures several times over this sample period. However, I assume that the reaction function was given by the Taylor rule throughout, but the exogenous component of money was subject to the shocks estimated by Burnside's (1996) VAR. Thus, the simulation should be regarded more as an instructive exercise than a rigorous attempt to duplicate the historical record. I also maintain $\Delta = 1$ for this model.

The results for the RBC model are summarized in Table 2. The first panel shows basic standard deviations and correlations for the data. For the data, I use private output growth (a chain-weighted index of aggregate GDP minus government purchases); private consumption, investment, and hours worked; and the Solow residual for the private economy. The only surprises are the high correlation of consumption growth with output growth, which I find to be 0.92, and the high standard deviation of consumption, 1.81. Most studies using annual data put these figures at about 0.8 and 1.3. I speculate that the difference comes partly from the fact that I am using the new chain-weighted NIPA data and partly from my definition of output, which excludes government. On the other hand, I find that investment is somewhat less correlated with output than generally reported.

As one might have guessed from the impulse responses, the results are not kind to the RBC model. Since the volatility of the estimated technology shocks is much smaller than the volatility of the Solow residual series used by Plosser (1989), the model underpredicts the standard deviations of all the variables. All variables are too highly correlated with output, a standard result when only one shock is driving all fluctuations. Most problematically, the correlations of the simulated growth rates with the actual ones are mostly negative. The correlation between the actual and simulated output series is −0.21, and the

Table 2
Summary Statistics for Historical Simulation: RBC Model
($\Delta=1$)

A. Actual

	Standard Deviation	Correlation with Output	Correlation with Actual
$\Delta \log (Y)$	2.97	1.00	1.00
$\Delta \log (C)$	1.81	.92	1.00
$\Delta \log (I)$	10.51	.86	1.00
$\Delta \log (N)$	2.28	.80	1.00
$\Delta \log (SR)$	2.98	.98	1.00

B. Predicted

	Standard Deviation	Correlation with Output	Correlation with Actual
$\Delta \log (Y)$	2.30	1.00	−.21
$\Delta \log (C)$	.98	.94	.08
$\Delta \log (I)$	6.44	.99	−.41
$\Delta \log (N)$	1.16	.97	−.62
$\Delta \log (SR)$	1.48	1.00	−.12

correlation between the two labor series is −0.62. Time-series plots for the actual and generated series (in de-meaned growth rates) are shown in Figure 10.

Results for the sticky-price model are more encouraging (Table 3). Many of the standard deviations are much higher; in fact, the standard deviation of hours worked is almost 50 percent larger in the model than in the data. This result is not typical of DGE models, particularly ones with such low labor supply elasticities as the model used here. Hours are so volatile for two reasons. First, capital utilization is allowed to vary, reducing the rate at which the diminishing marginal product of labor sets in. Second, technology shocks produce a "whiplash" effect, first reducing then increasing hours above their steady-state level. The correlations with output are also reduced—implausibly so, in the case of consumption. (The main reason seems to be that consumption rises in response to a technology improvement, even though output falls on impact.) Most importantly, the correlations with the actual series are positive, albeit mildly so. For example, the output and hours correlations are both about 0.3.

This model seems promising, because two small modifications are likely to go a long way towards improving the summary statistics. The first is adding variable labor effort. I have argued that from a modeling standpoint variable effort is equivalent to a higher labor supply elasticity. Thus the labor series in the model should be regarded as the sum of observed (hours) and unobserved (effort) labor fluctuations in the model.

Figure 10
Historical Simulation: RBC Model
($\Delta=1$)

A. Output
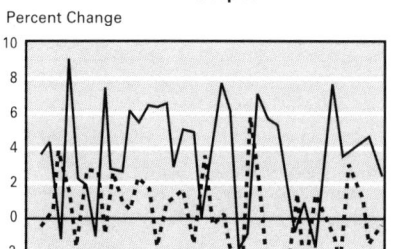

B. Consumption
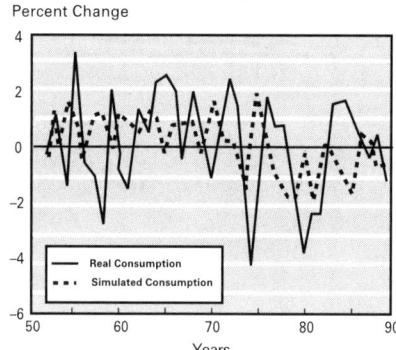

C. Investment
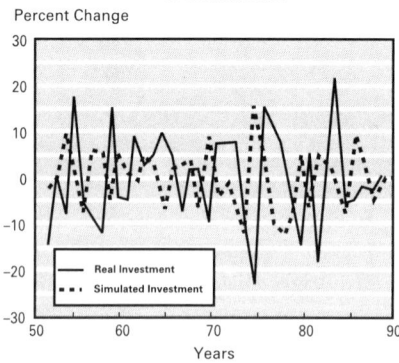

D. Hours Worked
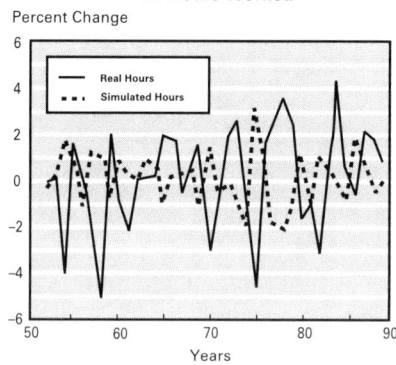

E. Solow Residual
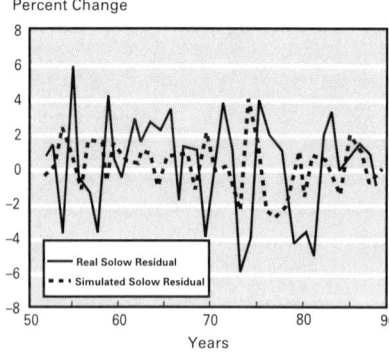

Table 3
Summary Statistics for Historical Simulation: Sticky-Price Model
(Taylor Rule, $\Delta = 1$)

A. Actual

	Standard Deviation	Correlation with Output	Correlation with Actual
$\Delta \log (Y)$	2.97	1.00	1.00
$\Delta \log (C)$	1.81	.92	1.00
$\Delta \log (I)$	10.51	.86	1.00
$\Delta \log (N)$	2.28	.80	1.00
$\Delta \log (SR)$	2.98	.98	1.00

B. Predicted

	Standard Deviation	Correlation with Output	Correlation with Actual
$\Delta \log (Y)$	2.59	1.00	.30
$\Delta \log (C)$	1.03	.35	.19
$\Delta \log (I)$	9.62	.95	.35
$\Delta \log (N)$	3.19	.84	.33
$\Delta \log (SR)$	1.29	.59	.12

But from an empirical standpoint, modeling unobserved effort would increase the standard deviation of the simulated Solow residual and its correlation with output, while reducing the standard deviation of hours—all desirable outcomes. Second, both the volatility of consumption and its correlation with output can probably be increased by modeling liquidity constraints. After all, most research on consumption strongly rejects the simple permanent-income model used in the DGE literature. Liquidity constraints might prevent the countercyclical behavior of consumption in response to technology improvements that is found in the model but not the data (see BFK).

However, the model is nowhere close to experiencing the sort of success that Plosser (1989) claimed for the RBC model. Inspecting the time-series plots in Figure 11 suggests that the reason is the lack of propagation discussed earlier. Panel A, which plots the two output series, shows that fluctuations do not seem as long-lived in the model as in the data, leading to the relatively poor fit between prediction and outcome. It may be possible to reduce this problem by adding more real rigidities to the model—but bearing in mind the caveat discussed above.

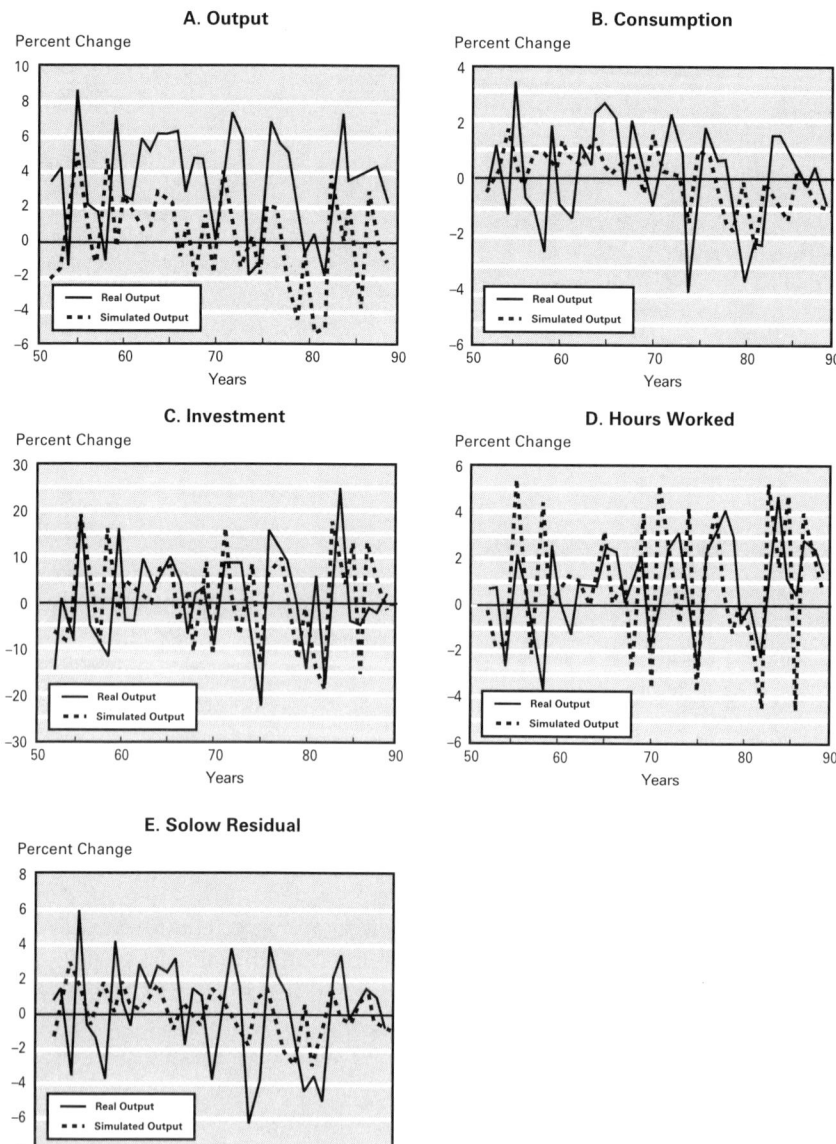

Figure 11
Historical Simulation: Sticky-Price Model
(Taylor Rule, $\Delta=1$)

CONCLUSION

The behavior of the economy in response to technology shocks is a challenge for business-cycle theory. Current empirical results show that when technology improves, inputs fall significantly in the short run and output is almost unchanged. The results in this paper show that benchmark models of the business cycle are unable to rationalize this behavior fully. Sticky-price models show some promise of being able to match the data, but they clearly have a long way to go.

Disappointingly, just adding a plausible amount of variable factor utilization to the sticky-price model does not impart enough real rigidity to match estimated impulse responses for either technology or money. In some ways, this result may not seem particularly discouraging. After all, variable utilization is only one of many possible real rigidities, and the others may pick up the slack. Variable capital utilization is different, however, in that it is solidly documented (for example, by Shapiro 1996, using firm-level data), and some of the parameters governing changes in utilization have been estimated. By contrast, many of the other mechanisms discussed in the literature—for example, kinked demand curves, sector-specific externalities, efficiency wages, or countercyclical target markups—remain more in the realm of wishful thinking.

Finally, while adding technology shocks to sticky-price models holds the promise of being able to explain the puzzling facts about the effects of technology on the economy, researchers now face the challenge of producing sensible impulse responses for two kinds of shocks using the same model. While this discipline is desirable, it makes an already difficult job even harder.

However, a second class of propagation mechanisms that has some solid empirical support has not been considered here. These are models where, as a result of frictions of some kind, cyclical changes in the composition of output serve to magnify the effects of shocks. And since different types of shocks lead to different output composition, this class of models has the potential to produce different degrees of real rigidities for technology shocks than for money shocks. However, research on calibrated multisector models with frictions is extremely demanding, both computationally and in terms of the effort needed to understand the workings of the model at a deep level. Some research is under way,[37] but it is too early to say whether these models will make a significant contribution to solving the problems identified here.

---

[37] See, for example, Horvath (1995), Basu, Fernald, and Horvath (1996), and Phelan and Trejos (1996).

References

Ball, Laurence and David Romer. 1990. "Real Rigidities and the Non-neutrality of Money." *Review of Economic Studies*, 57 (April), pp. 183–203.
Basu, Susanto. 1996. "Cyclical Productivity: Increasing Returns or Cyclical Utilization?" *Quarterly Journal of Economics*, 111 (August), pp. 719–51.
Basu, Susanto and John G. Fernald. 1997. "Aggregate Productivity and Aggregate Technology." International Finance Discussion Paper 593, Board of Governors of the Federal Reserve System.
———. 1998. "Why is Productivity Procyclical? Why Do We Care?" Forthcoming in NBER volume, *New Directions in Productivity Research*.
Basu, Susanto, John G. Fernald, and Michael T. K. Horvath. 1996. "Aggregate Production Function Failures." Manuscript.
Basu, Susanto, John G. Fernald, and Miles S. Kimball. 1998. "Are Technology Improvements Contractionary?" Manuscript.
Basu, Susanto and Miles S. Kimball. 1997. "Cyclical Productivity with Unobserved Input Variation." NBER Working Paper No. 5915.
Bils, Mark and Jang-Ok Cho. 1994. "Cyclical Factor Utilization." *Journal of Monetary Economics*, 33 (April), pp. 319–54.
Blanchard, Olivier and Daniel Quah. 1989. "The Dynamic Effects of Aggregate Demand and Supply Disturbances." *The American Economic Review*, 79, no. 4, pp. 654–73.
Burnside, Craig. 1996. "What Do Production Function Regressions Tell Us about Increasing Returns to Scale and Externalities?" *Journal of Monetary Economics*, 37 (April), pp. 177–201.
Burnside, Craig and Martin Eichenbaum. 1996. "Factor-Hoarding and the Propagation of Business-Cycle Shocks." *The American Economic Review*, 86, pp. 1154–74.
Burnside, Craig, Martin Eichenbaum, and Sergio Rebelo. 1996. "Sectoral Solow Residuals." *European Economic Review*, 40, pp. 861–69.
Chari, V. V., Patrick J. Kehoe, and Ellen R. McGrattan. 1996. "Sticky-Price Models of the Business Cycle: Can the Contract Multiplier Solve the Persistence Problem?" NBER Working Paper No. 5809.
Cooley, Thomas F. and Edward C. Prescott. 1995. "Economic Growth and Business Cycles." In Thomas F. Cooley, ed., *Frontiers of Business Cycle Research*. Princeton, NJ: Princeton University Press.
Domar, Evsey D. 1961. "On the Measurement of Technical Change." *Economic Journal*, 71 (December), pp. 710–29.
Dotsey, Michael, Robert G. King, and Alexander Wolman. 1997. "Menu Costs, Staggered Price Setting, and Elastic Factor Supply." Manuscript, June.
Evans, Charles L. 1992. "Productivity Shocks and Real Business Cycles." *Journal of Monetary Economics*, 29 (April), pp. 191–208.
Farmer, Robert and Guo, Jang-Ting. 1994. "Real Business Cycles and the Animal Spirits Hypothesis." *Journal of Economic Theory*, 63, pp. 42–72.
Gali, Jordi. 1994. "Monopolistic Competition, Business Cycles, and the Composition of Aggregate Demand." *Journal of Economic Theory*, 63, pp. 73–96.
———. 1998. "Technology, Employment, and the Business Cycle: Do Technology Shocks Explain Aggregate Fluctuations?" *The American Economic Review*, forthcoming.
Griliches, Zvi and Jacques Mairesse. 1995. "Production Functions: The Search for Identification." NBER Working Paper No. 5067.
Haavelmo, Trygve. 1960. *A Study in the Theory of Investment*. Chicago: Chicago University Press.
Hall, Alastair R., Glenn D. Rudebusch, and David W. Wilcox. 1996. "Judging Instrument Relevance in Instrumental Variables Estimation." *International Economic Review*, 37 (May), pp. 283–98.
Hall, Robert E. 1988. "The Relation Between Price and Marginal Cost in U.S. Industry." *Journal of Political Economy*, 96 (Oct.), pp. 921–47.
———. 1990. "Invariance Properties of Solow's Productivity Residual." In Peter Diamond, ed., *Growth, Productivity, Unemployment*. Cambridge, MA: The MIT Press.
———. 1991. "Labor Demand, Labor Supply, and Employment Volatility." In Olivier Blanchard and Stanley Fischer, eds., *NBER Macroeconomics Annual*.

Hall, Robert E. and Dale W. Jorgenson. 1967. "Tax Policy and Investment Behavior." *The American Economic Review*, 57 (June), pp. 391–414.

Horvath, Michael T. K. 1995. "Cyclicality and Sectoral Linkages: Aggregate Fluctuations from Independent Sectoral Shocks." Manuscript, Stanford University.

Hulten, Charles. 1978. "Growth Accounting with Intermediate Inputs." *Review of Economic Studies*, 45, pp. 511–18.

Jorgenson, Dale W., Frank Gollop, and Barbara Fraumeni. 1987. *Productivity and U.S. Economic Growth*. Cambridge, MA: Harvard University Press.

Jorgenson, Dale W. and Zvi Griliches. 1967. "The Explanation of Productivity Change." *Review of Economic Studies*, 34, pp. 249–83.

Jorgenson, Dale W. and Kun-Young Yun. 1991. *Tax Reform and the Cost of Capital*. Oxford: Oxford University Press.

Kiley, Michael T. 1997. "Partial Adjustment and Staggered Price Setting." Manuscript, Federal Reserve Board.

———. 1998. "Staggered Price Setting and Real Rigidities." Manuscript, Federal Reserve Board, February.

Kimball, Miles S. 1995. "The Quantitative Analytics of the Basic Neomonetarist Model." *Journal of Money, Credit, and Banking*, 27 (November), pp. 1241–77.

King, Robert G. and Sergio Rebelo. 1997. "Resuscitating Real Business Cycles." Manuscript, December.

Lilien, David M. 1982. "Sectoral Shifts and Cyclical Unemployment." *Journal of Political Economy*, 90 (August), pp. 777–93.

Olley, G. Steven, and Ariel Pakes. 1996. "The Dynamics of Productivity in the Telecommunications Equipment Industry." *Econometrica*, 64, pp. 1263–97.

Orphanides, Athanasios. 1997. "Monetary Policy Rules Based on Real-Time Data." Manuscript, Federal Reserve Board, December.

Phelan, Christopher and Alberto Trejos. 1996. "On the Aggregate Effects of Sectoral Reallocation." Manuscript, Northwestern University.

Plosser, Charles I. 1989. "Understanding Real Business Cycles." *Journal of Economic Perspectives*, 3 (Summer), pp. 51–77.

Prescott, Edward C. 1986. "Theory Ahead of Business Cycle Measurement." *Carnegie Rochester Conference Series on Public Policy*, 25 (Autumn), pp. 11–44.

Rotemberg, Julio J. and Michael Woodford. 1991. "Markups and the Business Cycle." *NBER Macroeconomics Annual*.

———. 1992. "Oligopolistic Pricing and the Effects of Aggregate Demand on Economic Activity." *Journal of Political Economy*, 100 (December), pp. 1153–1207.

———. 1995. "Dynamic General Equilibrium Models with Imperfectly Competitive Product Markets." In Thomas F. Cooley, ed., *Frontiers of Business Cycle Research*. Princeton, NJ: Princeton University Press.

Schor, Juliet B. 1987. "Does Work Intensity Respond to Macroeconomic Variables? Evidence from British Manufacturing, 1970–1986." Manuscript, Harvard University.

Shapiro, Matthew D. 1996. "Macroeconomic Implications of Variation in the Workweek of Capital." *Brookings Papers on Economic Activity*, (2), pp. 79–119.

Solow, Robert M. 1957. "Technological Change and the Aggregate Production Function." *Review of Economics and Statistics*, 39, pp. 312–20.

Taylor, John B. 1980. "Aggregate Dynamics and Staggered Contracts." *Journal of Political Economy*, 88 (February), pp. 1–23.

———. 1993. "Discretion versus Policy Rules in Practice." *Carnegie Rochester Conference Series on Public Policy*, 39 (December), pp. 195–214.

Varian, Hal. 1984. *Microeconomic Analysis*. New York: W. W. Norton.

Wen, Yi. 1997. "Capacity Utilization under Increasing Returns to Scale." Manuscript.

Discussion

Mark Bils*

Hall (1987) wrote, "Hardly any fact about the United States economy is better established than the procyclical behavior of productivity." But in Basu and Kimball (1997), Basu, Fernald, and Kimball (1998), and in this paper, Basu and his coauthors (from here on Basu) argue that, correctly measured, *technology shocks* are not procyclical. They are very negatively correlated with inputs, including hours of work, and largely uncorrelated with output.

A key element of Basu's papers is to instrument for cyclical fluctuations using variables arguably orthogonal to technology shocks. Papers by Gali (1998) and Kiley (1997) also conclude that technology shocks are very negatively correlated with inputs. But those authors identify technology shocks very differently, using structural restrictions on a VAR. It is interesting that these two sets of papers, with very different approaches, have similar results. Both sets of papers stress output-price stickiness as key to understanding the strong negative relationship between technology shocks and inputs.

I first review Basu's exercise, asking whether it perhaps adjusts too much for procyclical factor utilization. My primary objective, however, is to test the conclusions of Basu, Gali, and Kiley that the negative correlation they find between inputs and their technology shocks is support for sticky prices.

COUNTERCYCLICAL TECHNOLOGY SHOCKS

At least since Jorgenson and Griliches (1967), procyclical unmeasured utilization of factors has been viewed as part of the explanation for

---

*Associate Professor of Economics, University of Rochester.

Table 1
Correlations of TFP Growth and Productivity Growth with Growth in Output and Hours, Aggregate Data

	$\Delta Ln(Y)$	$\Delta Ln(N)$
$\Delta Ln(TFP)$	.81	.40
$\Delta Ln(Y/N)$	.56	.04

Note: Data are for the total private U.S. economy, annually for 1948 to 1994.
Source: U.S. Bureau of Labor Statistics.

procyclical productivity. Basu allows for procyclical capital utilization and procyclical labor effort. Most writers, including Jorgenson and Griliches (1967) and Shapiro (1993), have focused on capital utilization. Suppose, for the moment, that firms add to production by extending the workweek, say, by adding a sixth weekly workday on Saturday. This would seem to increase worker hours, utilized capital, and output all by one-fifth. Output per hour worked is unaffected. If we take this as a reference point, it suggests looking at output per hour worked (labor productivity) as a simple alternative measure of technology shocks.

Table 1 compares the cyclical behavior of total factor productivity (TFP) to that for labor productivity. The table gives correlations of TFP and labor productivity first with output, then with hours. The series are annual growth rates for aggregate (private sector) U.S. data for 1948 to 1994. Adopting labor productivity as a measure of technology eliminates the positive correlation of technology shocks with hours, but a strong positive correlation remains with output.

In addition to cyclical factor utilization, Basu also generalizes TFP accounting to allow for imperfect competition. His estimate of the gross markup, however, is essentially one (perfect competition), so the impact of imperfect competition is nil. Basu also employs disaggregated data to reduce biases from aggregating. Table 2 repeats the correlations reported in Table 1, but this time calculated for annual data from 1958 to 1994 for

Table 2
Correlations of TFP Growth and Productivity Growth with Growth in Output and Hours, 4-digit Manufacturing Data

	$\Delta Ln(Y)$	$\Delta Ln(N)$
$\Delta Ln(TFP)$	.61	.27
$\Delta Ln(Y/N)$	.63	−.05

Note: Data are for 450 U.S. manufacturing industries, annually for 1958 to 1994. As a result of calculating inventory accumulation and first differencing, observations are for 1960 to 1994.
Source: NBER Productivity Database.

450 4-digit manufacturing industries. These data are taken from the *NBER Productivity Database* and largely reflect information in the *Annual Surveys of Manufactures*. (Basu employs 2-digit data and incorporates information beyond manufacturing.) Comparing Tables 1 and 2, the correlation between output and labor productivity drops from .40 to .27, but remains very significantly positive. The correlation between hours and labor productivity is now negative ($-.05$), but much less so than for Basu's technology shock. I would conclude that Basu's most important adjustments to TFP reflect the allowances for procyclical factor utilization.

My reference point supposes that utilized capital moves one-for-one with hours. By assuming that production is Cobb-Douglas in materials as well as capital and labor, Basu treats capital input as moving like the cost of materials (subtracting movements in capital's shadow price). Materials costs vary much more cyclically than do labor costs. As a result, I believe Basu's series for utilized capital is considerably more procyclical than hours worked.

Also departing from my reference point, Basu has quality of labor input varying because of procyclical effort. How the quality of labor input varies cyclically is an open question. Bils and Cho (1994) and Basu cite evidence contained in Schor (1987) that effort measures for piece-rate workers in England vary positively with hours per worker. But these variations are relatively small. On the other hand, there is considerable evidence that the workers who are added to the work force in an expansion are considerably lower-paid (for example, from Solon, Barsky, and Parker 1994, by more than 30 percent), and presumably of lower quality. I would expect the effect of adding less able workers in booms to dominate any variations in effort, making quality of effort countercyclical.

Basu's series is based on a formal model, identifying assumptions, and estimation. So to attack Basu's results, ultimately one must confront his identification. Basu instruments for cyclical fluctuations using government spending, oil prices, and monetary variables. This maps out a predicted relationship between outputs and inputs under the presumption of a constant technology. Deviations from that relationship are then interpreted as technology shocks. I interpret Basu's findings as follows: Productivity is actually more positively correlated with instrumented changes in inputs than with all changes in inputs. This implies that Basu's residual measure of technology shocks must be negatively correlated with inputs. Basu interprets this as true technology shocks creating, given sticky prices, a fall in inputs.

But suppose that at a cyclical frequency technology shocks are fairly unimportant. Then movements in TFP largely reflect variations in the utilization or quality of inputs. If the variations in these inputs are more procyclical for the instrumented expansions than for expansions in hours more generally, this is sufficient to qualitatively generate Basu's findings.

Why might factor utilization vary more for some fluctuations, more exactly Basu's instrumented fluctuations, than for others? The instruments Basu uses, oil shocks and the like, are relatively transitory shocks. We would expect greater use of increased factor utilization for more transitory shocks. Furthermore, transitory fluctuations lead to smaller employment increases relative to hours per worker, and therefore less of a reduction in the average quality of worker.[1]

Second, Basu assumes a constant relation between effort and hours. Similarly, in Bils and Cho (1994) preferences are such that workers will simultaneously adjust leisure at home and leisure at work, resulting in a perfect correlation between hours per worker and effort per hour. But central to that result is a labor market in which wages are perfectly flexible, or firms and workers behave as though wages are perfectly flexible. Bils and Chang (1998) show that if wages are sticky, then effort goes up with hours for some shocks, but down for others. For example, a positive shock to government spending (one of Basu's instruments) should, under market clearing, result in a fall in the real wage. If rigidities prevent the real wage from falling, then effort rises to clear the market simultaneously with an increase in hours. By contrast, for a technology shock the market-clearing real wage should rise. If wage rigidity prevents this, then effort actually falls to clear the labor market simultaneously with an increase in hours.

Finally, and perhaps most important, if inputs are measured with error in the disaggregate data, then it is possible to find a stronger impact of inputs on output when one instruments with variables orthogonal to technology shocks, *even if true technology shocks are positively correlated with inputs*. This result is in fact expected if technology shocks are relatively unimportant.

INVENTORIES AND THE RESPONSE OF HOURS TO TECHNOLOGY SHOCKS

Why might inputs be negatively correlated with technology shocks? One possibility is that product demands are inelastic, at least in the short run. By contrast, Basu, as well as Gali (1998), Kiley (1997), and Basu, Fernald, and Kimball (1998), focus on sticky prices. The reasoning is straightforward. With a predetermined (sticky) price, sales are given. For given sales and output, a rise in productivity must reduce inputs.

Generally speaking, sales do not equal production. If firms produce

---

[1] Basu and Kimball (1997) attempt to correct for worker quality by using a quality-of-worker index constructed by Dale Jorgenson. But this index only adjusts for the observable traits of sex, education, and experience. It rationalizes only a small portion of the differences in earnings across workers found by Solon, Barsky, and Parker (1994) and others.

Table 3
Response of Hours to Labor Productivity

	$\Delta Ln(N)$	
$\Delta Ln(Y/N)$	−.096 (.0089)	−.267 (.047)
$\dfrac{\bar{I}}{S}$		−.047 (.012)
$\left(\dfrac{\bar{I}}{S}\right)\Delta Ln(Y/N)$		1.009 (.129)

Note: Data are for 450 U.S. manufacturing industries, 1958–1994; see Table 2. Standard errors are in parentheses. Regressions include time dummies.
Source: See Table 2.

to stock or hold nontrivial working inventories, then, in response to a favorable cost shock, firms can expand output relative to sales. They would do so to exploit any transitory nature of a productivity increase and also to increase inventory stocks up to higher anticipated levels of production and sales (for example, Kahn 1987). This suggests examining the response of inputs to technology shocks for industries where inventories are important separately from those where they are less important. Even under flexible prices we expect inputs to respond more to cost shocks if firms can inventory their output (for example, West 1991). But the role of inventories will be particularly important if prices are sticky.

Table 3 presents the response of labor hours to labor productivity. The variables again are in terms of annual growth rates and the data are for the 450 industries in the *NBER Productivity Database*. (The regression includes dummies for each of the time periods.) Looking at Column 1, an increase of 1 percentage point in labor productivity is associated with a fall in hours of about 0.10 percent, with a standard error of 0.0089 percent. (By comparison, a 1 percentage point increase in TFP is associated with an increase in hours of 0.37 percent, with a standard error of 0.012 percent.)

The second column of Table 3 adds two additional variables: the average ratio of inventories to sales for the industry for the period 1958 to 1994, and this ratio interacted with the growth rate in labor productivity. As predicted, labor hours are much less likely to decline for inventories that hold significant inventories. The interaction variable has a coefficient of 1.009 with a standard error of 0.129. For an industry with an inventory-sales ratio of 0.16, which is the mean across industries, this implies that hours fall by 0.105 percent for each percentage point increase in labor productivity. By contrast, for an industry with an inventory-sales

DISCUSSION

Table 4
Response of Prices to Labor Productivity

	ΔLn(P)	
$\Delta Ln(Y/N)$	−.199 (.0044)	−.238 (.011)
$\dfrac{\bar{I}}{S}$		.0097 (.0061)
$\left(\dfrac{\bar{I}}{S}\right)\Delta Ln(Y/N)$		.232 (.064)

Note: Data are for 450 U.S. manufacturing industries, 1958–1994; see Table 2.
Standard errors are in parentheses.
Regressions include time dummies.
Source: See Table 2.

ratio of 0.30, equaling two standard deviations above the mean, hours would actually rise slightly, by 0.033 percent.

As discussed just above, however, we should expect inventory holding to be associated with a more positive response of hours even if prices are completely flexible. So it is useful to examine price behavior more directly.

EVIDENCE ON STICKY PRICES

As I have stated, Basu in this paper, Basu, Fernald, and Kimball (1998), Gali (1998), and Kiley (1997) all attribute a negative correlation between technology shocks and inputs to sticky prices. Nevertheless, these papers do not directly examine how prices respond to their constructed technology shocks. Here I take a look at price responses for my simple measure of technology shocks, labor productivity.

The first column of Table 4 relates industry price changes, again for the *NBER Productivity Database*, to industry growth in labor productivity. The regression includes time dummies, so fluctuations in variables are judged relative to movements in manufacturing as a whole. A 1 percentage point increase in productivity is associated with a very significant fall in price of 0.20 percent (standard error 0.0044). For comparison, a 1 percentage point increase in measured TFP in an industry is associated with a price decrease of 0.40 percent (standard error 0.0057 percent). So prices do respond rather dramatically to these measures of productivity movements.

The second column of Table 4 again interacts growth in labor productivity with the industry's average ratio of inventories to sales. Flexible price models would suggest that firms cut price less in response

Table 5
Response of Prices to Productivity

		$\Delta Ln(P_t)$
$\Delta Ln(TFP_t)$	−.408 (.0059)	
$\Delta Ln(TFP_{t-1})$	−.038 (.0059)	
$\Delta Ln(Y_t/N_t)$		−.205 (.0045)
$\Delta Ln(Y_{t-1}/N_{t-1})$		−.031 (.0046)

Note: Data are for 450 U.S. manufacturing industries, 1958–1994; see Table 2. Standard errors are in parentheses. Regressions include time dummies.
Source: See Table 2.

to a technology shock if they can produce for inventory. By the reasoning in the previous section, the firm that produces to inventory exhibits a larger output response to the technology shock. If short-run marginal cost is upward-sloping, this leads to a higher marginal cost and a higher price. In fact, the interaction is significantly positive (coefficient of 0.232 with a standard error of 0.064), providing some support for the joint hypothesis of upward-sloping marginal cost and price flexibility.

Finally, Table 5 presents the industry relative price response to both this year's and last year's productivity growth. If prices are sticky, we should expect lagged productivity growth to enter significantly, as productivity shifts are clearly persistent. The first column measures productivity shifts by growth in TFP. The previous year's growth in TFP does enter statistically very significantly in reducing this year's price increase. The magnitude of the effect is not large, however, being a full order of magnitude smaller than the negative impact of current TFP growth. The second column measures productivity shifts by labor productivity, with results similar to those for TFP. Last year's growth in labor productivity does reduce this year's price increase, but the impact is less than one-sixth of that for current growth in labor productivity.

In Conclusion

To my knowledge, no one has shown that technology shocks, correcting in some reasonable manner for utilization, are positively correlated with inputs. On the other hand, we have no reason, outside of some questionable parameter choices by calibrators, to expect a priori that output will increase more than proportionately to a favorable technology shock. So I do not see it as puzzling that inputs might be negatively affected by improvements in technology.

Basu's clever efforts lead him to conclude not only that inputs are negatively correlated with technology shocks, but that the magnitude of this relation is *very large*. The magnitude is so large, in fact, that output is not positively correlated with technology shocks. I am more than willing to recognize a zero correlation between output and technology innovations as a startling puzzle. To calm myself (if not others) I have offered some reasons why Basu's approach might overly correct for procyclical factor utilization, thereby hiding a strong positive correlation between technology shocks and output.

I have also presented some tentative evidence on price rigidities, which Basu suggests may be the source of a weak relation between shocks to technology and output. I find that labor responds considerably more positively to productivity improvements if firms hold considerable inventories. This is potentially consistent with price rigidities. But more important, in my view, is the fact that industry prices fall substantially when productivity increases, suggesting a fairly limited role for sticky prices.

References

Basu, Susanto and Miles S. Kimball. 1997. "Cyclical Productivity with Unobserved Input Variation." Manuscript.

Basu, Susanto, John G. Fernald, and Miles S. Kimball. 1998. "Are Technology Improvements Contractionary?" Manuscript.

Bils, Mark and Yongsung Chang. 1998. "Wages and the Allocation of Hours and Effort." Manuscript.

Bils, Mark and Jang-Ok Cho. 1994. "Cyclical Factor Utilization." *Journal of Monetary Economics* 33 (April), pp. 319–54.

Gali, Jordi. 1998. "Technology, Employment, and the Business Cycle: Do Technology Shocks Explain Aggregate Fluctuations?" Forthcoming, *The American Economic Review*.

Hall, Robert E. 1987. "Productivity and the Business Cycle." *Carnegie-Rochester Conference Series on Public Policy* 27, pp. 421–44.

Jorgenson, Dale W. and Zvi Griliches. 1967. "The Explanation of Productivity Change." *Review of Economic Studies* 34, pp. 249–83.

Kahn, James A. 1987. "Inventories and the Volatility of Production." *The American Economic Review* 77, pp. 667–79.

Kiley, Michael. 1997. "Labor Productivity in U.S. Manufacturing: Does Sectoral Comovement Reflect Technology Shocks?" Manuscript.

Schor, Juliet B. 1987. "Does Work Intensity Respond to Macroeconomic Variables? Evidence from British Manufacturing, 1970–1986." Manuscript.

Shapiro, Matthew D. 1993. "Cyclical Productivity and the Workweek of Capital." *The American Economic Review* 83 (May), pp. 229–33.

Solon, Gary, Robert Barsky, and Jonathan Parker. 1994. "Measuring the Cyclicality of Real Wages: How Important Is Compositional Bias?" *Quarterly Journal of Economics* 109, pp. 1–25.

West, Kenneth. 1991. "The Sources of Fluctuations in Aggregate Inventories and GNP." *Quarterly Journal of Economics* 106, pp. 939–72.

DISCUSSION

Thomas F. Cooley*

In a much-cited paper, Edward C. Prescott (1986) argued that "technology shocks account for more than half the fluctuations (in real output) in the post-war period, with a best point estimate near 75%." This claim was based on simulating a very simple model economy founded on the Solow growth model but perturbed by shocks to technology whose properties mimic Solow residuals. Since that time, many authors have tried to refine this estimate by looking at more fully articulated dynamic general equilibrium models and at models with different features of the economic environment. Some have argued, on the basis of both empirical and quantitative evidence, that the Prescott claim overstates the contribution of technology shocks. Susanto Basu in this paper and a number of earlier papers has been working on a direct approach to measuring the true technology change in the Solow residuals. This is an ambitious agenda and Basu's results are interesting and a bit puzzling.

A useful way to think about the conventional wisdom on the importance of technology shocks is described in a paper by Rao Aiyagari (1994). He proposed a model-independent way to measure the contribution of technology shocks. It requires a standard specification of technology, then three critical assumptions: 1) perfect competition; 2) no external economies; 3) no measurement error. Under these assumptions, technology shocks should be able to account for three facts that characterize U.S. business cycles: 1) The correlation between productivity and the labor input is approximately zero. 2) The variability of the labor input relative to output is 0.86. 3) Labor's share of output is about 0.64. Given these assumptions, Aiyagari shows that *either* the contribution of technology

---

*Professor of Economics, University of Rochester.

DISCUSSION

shocks to fluctuations in output must be about 78 percent *or* some of these facts must be violated.

What happens when we alter the basic set of assumptions? We know the following:

- Introducing monopolistic competition lowers the contribution of technology shocks.
- Introducing economies of scale lowers the contribution of technology shocks.
- Introducing wage premiums can, but need not, lower the contribution of technology shocks.
- Introducing measurement error can lower the contribution of technology shocks.

To know how much these things matter for the contribution of technology shocks, we have to know something more about a number of elasticities and about measurement error. Absent compelling evidence that these things are important, Prescott's estimate seems pretty good.

Basu in this paper tries to address some of these issues directly by getting an empirical estimate of the size of technology shocks. He constructs a new series of aggregate technology change that controls for the following:

- imperfect competition,
- variable utilization of capital and labor, and
- aggregation bias.

Given this series, he investigates how well current business-cycle models can explain movements in business-cycle variables following an improvement in technology as measured by his technology change series, and how much they can explain historical output fluctuations. Lastly, he compares the performance of two business-cycle models, a standard real business cycle (RBC) model with variable factor utilization and a sticky-price model with variable factor utilization.

The empirical finding of the paper is quite striking. It suggests that technology changes have contractionary effects in the short run. This conclusion derives from the fact that the correlation between his corrected series of technological change and output growth is *low*, and from the finding that the correlation between his corrected series of technological change and input growth is *negative*.

Basu uses this series to show, via a quantitative exercise, that an RBC model with variable capital utilization cannot explain these findings. He also uses it to argue in favor of a sticky-price view of the world by showing that a model with sticky prices and variable capital utilization does a slightly better job.

THE ECONOMIC ENVIRONMENT

The basic assumption is that there are cost-minimizing firms with access to the production technology

$$Y = F(\tilde{K}, \tilde{L}, M, T), \quad \underbrace{\tilde{L}}_{\text{labor services}} = EHN, \quad \underbrace{\tilde{K}}_{\text{capital services}} = ZK \quad (1)$$

- K and N are quasi-fixed, but H, E, and Z can vary in the short run.
- M represents intermediate inputs and energy.
- T indexes technology.
- F is (locally) homogeneous of arbitrary degree γ.

$$\gamma = \frac{F_1 \tilde{K}}{Y} + \frac{F_2 \tilde{L}}{Y} + \frac{F_3 M}{Y} \quad (2)$$

This setup, with a bit of work, leads to the following estimating equation for the markup, based on totally differentiating the production function:

$$dy = \mu[s_K(dk + dz) + s_L(dn + dh + de) + s_m dm] + dt$$
$$= \mu[s_K dk + s_L(dn + dh) + s_M dm] + \mu[s_K dz + s_L de] + dt$$
$$= \mu \underbrace{dx}_{\substack{\text{share-weighted} \\ \text{average of observed input growth}}} + \mu du + dt \quad (3)$$

The problem in estimating this is to find some suitable proxies for the utilization term du. Here Basu exploits the results of several of his other papers. Basu and Kimball (1997) use the basic insight that a cost-minimizing firm operates on all margins simultaneously, both observed and unobserved, to show that increases in observed inputs can proxy for unobserved changes in utilization. Basu and Fernald (1997) argue that under a variety of conditions—for example, different industries having different degrees of market power—inputs may have different marginal products in different uses. Aggregate productivity growth depends on which sectors change input use over the business cycle. To get the "right" aggregate technology index, one should correct sectoral Solow residuals and then aggregate across sectors.

Why does an RBC model with variable capital utilization do a poor job? There are several reasons for procyclical productivity:

- procyclical technology,
- imperfect competition and increasing returns,
- cyclical factor utilization, and
- cyclical reallocation of resources with different marginal products.

Basu controls for these three nontechnological components of measured productivity and derives technology as a residual. Empirically, we know from his work and the work of others that increasing returns and imperfect competition are not likely to be important and that cyclical factor utilization and cyclical reallocation seem to be the most important factors generating the negative correlation between technology and inputs.

Basu argues that a sticky-price model seems to be more consistent with these findings, and the intuition is fairly simple. Suppose the quantity theory governs the demand for money. In the short run, if the supply of money is fixed and prices cannot adjust, real balances and output are fixed. In this setup, a positive technology shock will lead to *less* employment and hours, since firms need less labor to produce the fixed output, leading to the negative relationship between technology change and factor inputs.

How should we think about the findings of the paper? In discussing this I want to emphasize two issues. The first is whether we should be concerned about the apparent reduced importance of the technology shocks and the negative contemporaneous correlation with inputs. The second is whether this should lead you naturally to think about sticky price models.

First, I think we have moved a long way from the original real business cycle view of the world that relied on large, very volatile and persistent aggregate technology shocks to produce output fluctuations at the business cycle frequency. Burnside, Eichenbaum, and Rebelo (1995) and Burnside and Eichenbaum (1996) have shown that cyclical factor utilization is an important propagation mechanism for business cycle shocks. Other work models firm heterogeneity and firm financial decisions and finds these to be important and powerful sources of propagation for business cycle shocks (Cooley and Quadrini 1997; Bernanke, Gertler, and Gilchrist 1998). All of these things suggest that the size and persistence of technology shocks needed to generate fluctuations are greatly reduced. This does not address the finding that the technology residual is only weakly correlated with output, but that finding is very sensitive to the choice of instruments and to the identifying assumptions that the paper uses.

Should these findings lead you to think of this as evidence for sticky prices? As indicated above, the findings do fit the sticky-price framework to some extent, but there is no direct evidence to support this. Moreover, theory makes no clear prediction about whether labor or capital is likely to work more or less in response to technology improvements. Examples are abundant of improvements in technology due to changes in organization or work rules where output remains unchanged and inputs fall. Clearly, the nature of industry equilibrium, whether final demand is elastic or inelastic, may be important for this. The nature of the technology is also important. If technology is embodied in capital—a vintage capital world—improvements in technology can lead to reallocation of labor from older to newer vintages and employment can fall in the short run. This is a feature of the model in Campbell (1998).

I would be led in the direction of thinking that these results suggest that we may have the wrong model and that investment-specific technological change may be important. For example, Greenwood, Hercowitz, and Krusell (1998) simulate an economy where the only shock to the economy is investment-specific technology change of the form

$$k = (1 - \delta(h)k + iq.$$

Here depreciation is related to utilization; the term iq captures the technical change. They calibrate q using Gordon's (1990) price series. Unlike in standard RBC models, the technology shock here does not directly affect the production function in the current period. The current output is affected by the decline in marginal utilization cost of capital. Although equipment investment is only 7 percent of GNP, this transmission mechanism turns out to be important. Their findings suggest that this form of technological change is a source of about 30 percent of output fluctuations.

Considerations like this would imply a mis-specification in the empirical part of the analysis. It may be that, absent direct evidence of price rigidity, we should think about the implications of a vintage capital world. In vintage capital models, depreciation is typically economic rather than physical. If that is the case, then there is a danger of overstating the consequences of cyclical factor utilization. Moreover, in a vintage capital world with learning-by-doing, as in Cooley, Greenwood, and Yorukoglu (1997) or Greenwood and Yorukoglu (1996), technological change can be associated with contemporaneous output declines.

These are all reasons why I would be slow to argue that this evidence suggests technology shocks have little to do with business cycles. What is the alternative? Nevertheless, I think this is interesting work. It forces us to think hard about the nature of technology shocks; it adds to the body of persuasive evidence that suggests that increasing returns are not an important feature of the data and that cyclical factor utilization is important.

References

Aiyagari, S. Rao. 1994. "On the Contribution of Technology Shocks to Business Cycles." *Quarterly Review*, Federal Reserve Bank of Minneapolis, Winter, pp. 22–34.

Basu, Susanto and John Fernald. 1997. "Aggregate Productivity and Aggregate Technology." International Finance Discussion Paper 593, Board of Governors of the Federal Reserve System.

Basu, Susanto and Miles Kimball. 1997. "Cyclical Productivity with Unobserved Input Variation." NBER Working Paper No. 5915.

Bernanke, Ben, Mark Gertler, and Simon Gilchrist. 1998. "The Financial Accelerator in a Quantitative Business Cycle Framework." NBER Working Paper No. 6455, *Handbook of Macroeconomics*, forthcoming.

Burnside, Craig and Martin Eichenbaum. 1996. "Factor Hoarding and the Propagation of Business Shocks." *The American Economic Review*, 86, pp. 1154–74.

Burnside, Craig, Martin Eichenbaum, and Sergio Rebelo. 1995. "Capital Utilization and Returns to Scale." In B. Bernanke and J. Rotemberg, eds. *NBER Macroeconomics Annual 1995*. Cambridge, MA: The MIT Press.

Campbell, Jeffrey R. 1998. "Entry, Exit, Embodied Technology, and Business Cycles." *Review of Economic Dynamics*, 1, No. 2, pp. 371–408.

Cooley, Thomas F., Jeremy Greenwood, and Mehmet Yorukoglu. 1997. "The Replacement Problem." *Journal of Monetary Economics*, 40, 3, pp. 435–56.

Cooley, Thomas F. and Vincenzo Quadrini. 1997. "Monetary Policy and the Financial Decisions of Firms." Working Paper, University of Rochester.

Gordon, R. 1990. *The Measurement of Durable Goods Prices*. Chicago: University of Chicago Press.

Greenwood, Jeremy, Zvi Hercowitz, and Per Krusell. 1998. "The Role of Investment-Specific Technological Change in the Business Cycle." *European Economic Review*, forthcoming.

Greenwood, Jeremy and Mehmet Yorukoglu. 1997. "1974." *Carnegie-Rochester Series on Public Policy*, 46, pp. 49–95.

Prescott, Edward C. 1986. "Theory Ahead of Business Cycle Measurement." *Quarterly Review*, Federal Reserve Bank of Minneapolis, Fall, pp. 9–22.

JOB REALLOCATION AND THE BUSINESS CYCLE: NEW FACTS FOR AN OLD DEBATE

Scott Schuh and Robert K. Triest*

Can the reallocation of factors of production among firms and sectors, or the restructuring of production technology, cause business cycle fluctuations? Theoretically, the answer is unequivocally "yes." But *do* reallocation and restructuring actually cause fluctuations? The answer to this question—like most questions about economic causality—is much less clear. Indeed, determining whether or not reallocation and restructuring cause fluctuations is as fundamentally difficult as identifying supply and demand. The purpose of this paper is to examine the relationship between the business cycle and reallocation and restructuring, with a particular emphasis on trying to learn whether reallocation causes recessions. We conduct our investigation by briefly assessing existing evidence and theories of reallocation and restructuring, and then providing new evidence designed to improve our understanding of the relationship.

Held a generation ago, this conference probably would not have included a session devoted to understanding the role of reallocation and restructuring (henceforth, simply "reallocation") in business cycle fluctu-

---

*Economists, Federal Reserve Bank of Boston. The authors have benefited from comments by Hoyt Bleakley, Lynn Browne, Ricardo Caballero, Steven Davis, Jeff Fuhrer, and Michael Klein. Kevin Daly and Marie Willard provided excellent research assistance. Georgeanne DaCosta excellent typesetting assistance. We thank Joyce Cooper, Steven Davis, Tim Dunne, Lucia Foster, John Haltiwanger, and C.J. Krizan for providing data, documentation, and general data assistance. The research in this paper was conducted while the authors were Census Bureau research associates at the Boston Regional Data Center. Research results and conclusions expressed are those of the authors and do not necessarily indicate concurrence by the U.S. Bureau of the Census, the Federal Reserve Bank of Boston, or the Board of Governors of the Federal Reserve System. This paper has been screened to ensure that no confidential data are revealed.

ations. But during the 1970s and 1980s, the U.S. economy endured an intense period of reallocation associated with large, persistent energy price increases, increasing international trade, widespread deregulation, demographic changes from the Baby Boom, regional migration, sweeping financial market innovations, and shifts in the level and composition of government spending. It was also an economically painful period, with stubbornly high rates of inflation and unemployment, permanent job loss by high-wage experienced workers, plant closings and permanent "downsizing," slower real wage and trend productivity growth, and an increasing wage gap between skilled and unskilled workers. Traditional macroeconomic models at this time did not incorporate reallocation and thus were unable to explain many of these phenomena and the economic turmoil they generated.

Reflecting on this period, economists began investigating the role that reallocation among firms and sectors may have played in producing or amplifying the macroeconomic problems of the time. Initially, attention focused on two features: (1) heterogeneity and changes in the demographic characteristics of unemployed workers, and (2) dispersion in employment growth across highly aggregated sectors of the economy. The former was subsumed in calculations of the natural rate of unemployment and had little effect on the fundamental behavioral characteristics of macroeconomic models. The latter was dismissed initially as merely a by-product of heterogeneity in the cyclical sensitivity of sectors. Thus, the prevailing macroeconomic view continued to be that recessions were periods of temporarily low aggregate demand and that firms responded to this reduced demand by temporarily laying off workers, recalling them when government demand-management policies kicked in to raise aggregate demand. What prevented reallocation from being taken seriously as a factor in business cycle fluctuations was the lack of convincing empirical evidence.

Evidence of an important business cycle role for reallocation began unfolding in the late 1980s. Building on a limited base of earlier work, Steven Davis and John Haltiwanger (later joined by Scott Schuh) embarked on an extensive project of measuring the gross flows of jobs across U.S. manufacturing establishments using a unique, and particularly well-suited, new data base at the U.S. Bureau of the Census called the Longitudinal Research Database (LRD).[1] As summarized in their recent

---

[1] The research includes Davis and Haltiwanger (1990, 1992, 1995, 1998) and Davis, Haltiwanger, and Schuh (1990, 1996). Precursors include: the U.S. Bureau of Labor Statistics Manufacturing Turnover Data Base, Leonard (1987), Dunne, Roberts, and Samuelson (1989), and Blanchard and Diamond (1990). Other studies with U.S. data include: Troske (1993); Lane, Isaac, and Stevens (1994); Anderson and Meyer (1994); and Foote (1998). See Table 2.2 in Davis, Haltiwanger, and Schuh (1996) for references to international evidence on job flows.

book, Davis, Haltiwanger, and Schuh (1996), the extent of gross job flows is remarkable: One in five manufacturing jobs is either created or destroyed each year, on average. But these job flows are not the result of transitory, heterogeneous responses of plants to business cycle fluctuations. Rather, they reflect primarily *permanent* job creation and destruction that cause *permanent* relocation of workers to new jobs throughout the economy.

More important for the purpose of this paper is the cyclicality of the gross job flows. Not surprisingly, job destruction increases regularly and dramatically during recessions. The surprising result is that job creation does not decrease in recessions nearly as much as destruction increases—in fact, sometimes it even *increases* during recessions. Furthermore, sharp increases in job destruction are often followed by surges in job creation, as dislocated workers find new jobs elsewhere over time. Together, these job flow dynamics produce a strongly countercyclical rate of total job reallocation (the sum of creation and destruction). In other words, gross job reallocation increases during recessionary periods and decreases during expansionary periods. This reallocation of jobs often entails permanent displacement of workers across plants, destruction of human capital, and reduction in permanent income.

Many economists find these results intriguing on a variety of dimensions, but the most pertinent feature for macroeconomists is the surprising countercyclicality of permanent job reallocation. Why does permanent job reallocation rise during recessions? Traditional macroeconomic models are essentially silent about the heterogeneity of individual agents and firms and thus have difficulty explaining this phenomenon. Underlying economic churning—the rise and fall of particular firms, the employment and unemployment of particular individuals—is acknowledged to exist but viewed as benign for understanding macroeconomic fluctuations. To a first approximation, inflation, unemployment, and interest rates depend only on the level of aggregate demand in traditional macroeconomic models. Thus, traditional models must be modified and enhanced to incorporate and explain countercyclical reallocation.

In recent years, economists have begun proposing numerous theories to explain countercyclical job reallocation. Proposed theories must confront the following question: Does reallocation cause business cycles, or do business cycles cause reallocation? If the factors that determine the allocation of economic activity across plants and sectors change and induce costly, time-consuming reallocation, then aggregate economic activity will decline and reallocation will have caused the business cycle. Alternatively, if the economy experiences a business cycle slump and the slump leads plants and sectors to permanently destroy and create jobs, then the business cycle will have caused reallocation. More specifically, the countercyclical movements in job reallocation rates are initiated by sharp increases in job destruction prior to, and during, recessions. Thus, the theories must articulate what causal force(s) drive the increased job destruction, though they may also explain more generally the dynamic patterns of gross job creation and destruction that follow.

Broadly speaking, theories of countercyclical reallocation can be classified by how they answer these questions. One type stresses the role of *allocative* forces that induce reallocation across firms and sectors. Because reallocation is costly and time-consuming, aggregate demand declines. A second type stresses the role of *aggregate* forces that reduce aggregate activity, producing recessions. Either the reduction in aggregate activity directly increases (decreases) job destruction (creation), thereby setting off reallocation activity, or it indirectly induces reallocation activity by creating incentives to engage in such activity when the opportunity cost is low. Although most theories provide a role for both allocative and aggregate forces during recessions, the causal ordering of allocative and aggregate forces is usually a defining feature of the theories.

Despite the vast wealth of new empirical evidence on reallocation, and despite the technical and intellectual impressiveness of the new theories of countercyclical reallocation, no consensus has been reached on whether reallocation causes business cycle fluctuations. One key reason the issue is unresolved is its sheer complexity. What we know about reallocation is just the tip of the iceberg, and modern theories of reallocation model only a small fraction of what we know. Much like the fabled blind men trying to describe an elephant, most of our attempts to understand the complex process of reallocation have been just one piece of the puzzle at a time.

To gain a better understanding of countercyclical reallocation, prior empirical and theoretical analyses must be expanded, deepened, and corroborated along several dimensions. First, most analysis has relied on one-dimensional characteristics: industry, region, size, age, and the like. Much is yet to be learned from simultaneous disaggregation along multiple dimensions. Second, most of the analysis has focused solely on *job* reallocation. But firms choose labor simultaneously with other factors of production, and factor prices, productivity, and inventories also affect these choices. Jointly examining all aspects of production should improve our understanding of reallocation. Third, virtually all analysis has focused on the supply side. But demand factors, such as the level of demand, product innovation, product mix, market structure, and regional economic conditions, are also important determinants of reallocation. Finally, consideration of how expectations, uncertainty, and learning affect reallocation has been limited.

Our goal in this paper is to begin addressing a modest number of these issues. In the next two sections, we characterize the relationship between job reallocation and the business cycle with an updated review of the existing empirical evidence and a nontechnical summary of theories of countercyclical reallocation. In the remainder of the paper, we provide some new evidence, similar in style to that in Davis, Haltiwanger, and Schuh (1996), that provides a deeper understanding of this relationship and an overview of the research we intend to pursue. Although we do not formally test theories of countercyclical reallocation, we use them to formulate appropriate and interesting empirical exercises. Based on the evidence, we draw inferences about reallocation and business cycles, note potential implications for theories, and suggest areas for further investigation. Finally, we close with some new and up-to-date information about current job reallocation developments, and we hazard some guesses about the likelihood of future reallocation.

Although we do not conclusively resolve the question of causality, two general findings emerge that advance our understanding of job reallocation and business cycles. First, much of the cyclical fluctuation in gross job creation and destruction occurs in larger plants with relatively moderate employment growth that tends to be transitory, especially at medium-term horizons (up to five years). Unusually large employment growth rates, especially plant start-ups and shutdowns, are primarily small-plant phenomena and tend to be permanent, less cyclical, and to occur later in recessions than moderate, transitory job flows. Further, high rates of job flow rates occur primarily in plants that recently have been experiencing sharp employment contractions or expansions. Second, we discover that some of the key variables that should determine the allocation of factors of production across plants and sectors do in fact appear to be related to gross job flows, particularly to job destruction. Relative prices, productivity, and investment all exhibit suggestive time series correlations with the process of job reallocation that lead us to suspect that allocative driving forces may contribute significantly to business cycle fluctuations.

Facts about Job Reallocation and the Business Cycle

We begin with a brief review of job reallocation in U.S. manufacturing by summarizing the evidence from Davis, Haltiwanger, and Schuh (1996) (henceforth, "DHS") for the period 1972 to 1993, which includes new evidence on job reallocation during the latest recession. This section defines terminology, presents the data in graphical and tabular form, and restates the salient features of the data. Readers interested in more details may consult DHS.

Measurement of job reallocation begins at the plant level. The Longitudinal Research Database (LRD) contains employment data for about 50,000 to 70,000 plants each year. These plants are linked over time, and their employment change is measured each period. Plants whose employment increases are said to have created jobs; plants whose employment decreases are said to have destroyed jobs.[2] Gross job creation is the sum of employment gains at all plants with increasing employment, and gross job destruction is the sum of employment losses at all plants with decreasing employment. These gross job flows are expressed as rates relative to total employment. Gross job reallocation is the sum of gross job creation and destruction, and net employment (job) growth is the difference between gross job creation and destruction. The persistence of job flows is the fraction of jobs created (destroyed) that still (do not) exist in some future period (for example, one year later).

Four basic facts emerge from the gross job flow data, which are plotted and summarized in Figure 1 and Table 1. First, the gross flow rates are *large* at all times. Roughly one in 10 jobs is created, and one in 10 destroyed, each year on average in the annual data. The annualized flow rates are much larger for the quarterly data because of seasonal fluctuations, temporary layoffs, measurement error, and other transitory factors. These data reveal that a substantial fraction of employment—sometimes more than one-fourth—is involved in a continuous process of gross job reallocation, which can be costly and time-consuming. Even in periods of "full employment" at the ends of expansions, extensive job reallocation occurs.[3]

A second, more important fact for this paper, is that gross job reallocation is *countercyclical*. Countercyclical reallocation results from asymmetric cyclicality between job creation and destruction: Job destruction increases sharply in recessions but job creation decreases relatively little, or even increases, during recessions. One measure of this asymmetry—the ratio of variances of job destruction and creation, calculated from Table 1—shows that job destruction is 3½ times more volatile than job creation.[4] Some of the cyclical fluctuation in gross job reallocation is associated with big (and transitory) swings in net employment growth, and some is attributable to a lag between the initial occurrence of job destruction and subsequent job creation. But during a typical recession-

---

[2] Implicit in this definition is that a job is equated with employment, which neglects the fact that there may be unfilled jobs. Also, plant-level employment change is net of internal job flows. Plants create and destroy many jobs that are not measured by the LRD data, so employment change is the number of jobs created net of jobs destroyed. Further, a plant's net employment change does not fully reflect the actual amount of worker flows through jobs at the plant, because plants may hire and fire workers without changing the stock of jobs.

[3] Evidence on the large magnitude of gross job flows has been known for a long time. Although simultaneous and large rates of job creation and destruction motivate a reconsideration of some aspects of macroeconomic thinking, the magnitude may be irrelevant for business cycle analysis. Thus, in this paper, we are not concerned with explaining why job flows are large; rather, we focus on why they are correlated with the business cycle.

[4] The asymmetry between the variances of job destruction and creation appears to be unique to manufacturing. Ritter (1994) and Foote (1998) provide evidence that job creation varies about the same amount as job destruction in nonmanufacturing industries.

**Figure 1
Gross Job Flows in U.S. Manufacturing**

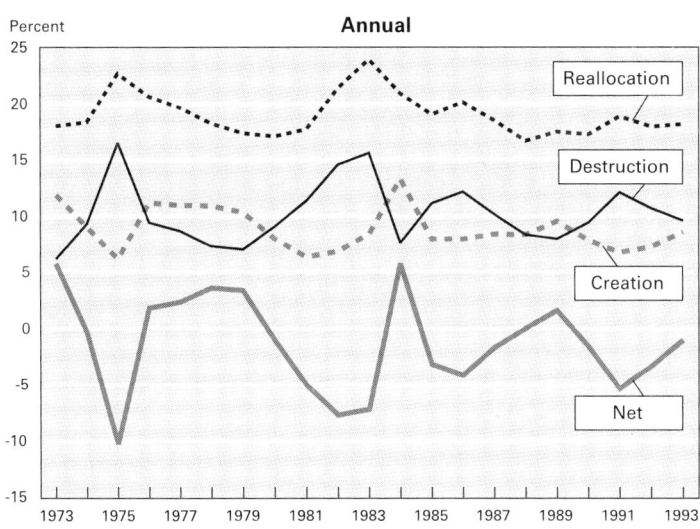
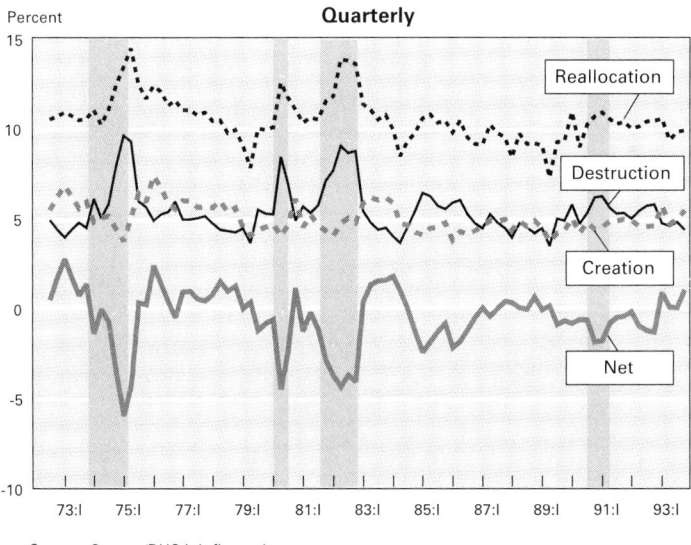

Source: Census/DHS job flows data.

Table 1
Gross Job Flows in U.S. Manufacturing: Summary Statistics

	Rates (%)							
	1972–93				1972–88			
	Annual		Quarterly		Annual		Quarterly	
	Avg.	S.D.[a]	Avg.	S.D.	Avg.	S.D.	Avg.	S.D.
Job Creation (C)	8.8	1.9	5.1	.8	9.1	2.1	5.2	.9
Job Destruction (D)	10.2	2.8	5.5	1.3	10.3	3.1	5.5	1.7
Job Reallocation (R)	19.0	1.9	10.6	1.3	19.4	2.1	10.7	1.6
Net Employment Growth (N)	−1.3	4.4	−.4	1.7	−1.1	4.8	−.3	2.1

	Quarterly Correlation Matrices					
	1972–93			1972–88		
	C	D	R	C	D	R
Destruction	−.29			−.36		
Reallocation	.68	.90		.71	.91	
Net Growth	.31	−.82	−.49	.22	−.83	−.53

[a]Standard deviation.
Source: Authors' calculations using the Census/DHS job flows data, and DHS (1996, Table 2.1).

ary period, which can last several years, the underlying trend rate at which jobs are permanently reallocated across plants, above and beyond net employment growth, increases. This surge in reallocation during recessions and the relative stability of job creation are surprising and intriguing features of the macroeconomy.

Two other basic facts help fill out the picture. One possible explanation for countercyclical reallocation is that the sharp increase in job destruction is merely the result of temporary layoffs, with workers being recalled to their jobs when aggregate demand rebounds. A third basic fact largely rules out this possibility—most job reallocation is *persistent*, or permanent. On average, about three-fourths of job destruction and one-half of job creation persist for two years, or twice the average length of a recession. A fourth basic fact addresses the unevenness of the job flows across plants. A common assumption in traditional macroeconomic models is that plants and industries rise and fall together. Already it can be seen from the high rates of job creation during recessions that this assumption is in trouble. But in addition, the plant-level data show that job flows are *concentrated* primarily in a relatively small number of plants that experience unusually large employment changes. Indeed, two-thirds of job creation and destruction occurs in plants that expand or contract employment by 25 percent or more per year.

In closing this section, let's look at the new gross job flow data containing the 1990–91 recession. Once again, job destruction and reallocation both increased. Actually, the increases occurred prior to the NBER-dated recession because manufacturing employment began contracting in 1989. Compared to earlier recessions, however, job destruction and job reallocation rose much less in the most recent recession, apparently because this recession was less severe, at least in manufacturing. Reallocation in this recession also remained high for an unusually long time. By the end of 1993, job destruction was still above its level five years earlier at the peak of manufacturing employment growth; during this period, job creation was rising steadily. Thus, while the rise in job reallocation was less dramatic, the cumulative amount of reallocation was substantial. More generally, Table 1 demonstrates that the data for 1989–93 do not change the basic time series properties of the earlier data for 1972–88.

BUSINESS CYCLE THEORIES WITH COUNTERCYCLICAL REALLOCATION

The surprising countercyclicality of job reallocation has sparked an interest in developing macroeconomic theories to explain this phenomenon. Prior to the LRD evidence, most multisectoral theoretical models were not designed to produce countercyclical job reallocation or asynchronous job creation and destruction.[5] Instead, sector-specific shocks generally were assumed to cancel out as the number of sectors increased, so that only an unusual—and, in the view of many, implausible—confluence of shocks could generate a large aggregate effect. The "sectoral shifts" literature provided empirical evidence of countercyclical dispersion in employment growth and argued that reallocation was a driving force behind aggregate economic fluctuations.[6] But formal models of countercyclical reallocation were lacking.

In recent years, new theoretical models have been developed in which job reallocation is an endogenous behavioral response to changes in the surrounding economic environment.[7] Broadly speaking, two types of theories have arisen that explain the cyclical properties of job creation

---

[5] Rigorous multisector general equilibrium models date back at least to Johnson (1962). More recently, part of the literature focuses on how allocative shocks generate unemployment due to costly and time-consuming search and worker reallocation, including Lucas and Prescott (1974), Hall (1979), Diamond (1981), Mortensen (1982), and Hamilton (1988). Other multisectoral general equilibrium models include Kydland and Prescott (1982), Long and Plosser (1983), Rogerson (1987), Hopenhayn and Rogerson (1993), and Greenwood, MacDonald, and Zhang (1996).

[6] This literature includes Lilien (1982), Black (1987), Loungani (1986), and Davis (1987), and many subsequent articles.

[7] A detailed and comprehensive technical review of these theories is beyond the scope of this paper. See Chapter 5 of DHS (1996), Davis and Haltiwanger (1998), and Hall (1998) for further reading and additional references.

and destruction. One type stresses the role of allocative driving forces in generating business cycle fluctuations and determines that job reallocation causes business cycles. The other type stresses the role of aggregate driving forces and determines that business cycles cause reallocation. In Hall's (1997a) business cycle classification terminology, job reallocation is an "impulse" in allocative theories and job reallocation is a "propagation" and/or "amplification" mechanism in aggregate theories.

Not wanting to lose this simple organizing thought, we must note that both types of theories acknowledge a contemporaneous role for the other driving force as well as intertemporal feedback between the driving forces. But the core issue for this paper is: Can allocative driving forces, by themselves, induce aggregate fluctuations large enough to generate business cycles, or do aggregate driving forces cause essentially all business cycles?

Defining Allocative and Aggregate Driving Forces

Much of the debate over whether allocative or aggregate driving forces cause business cycle fluctuations can be attributed to a fundamental ambiguity about what these forces are. Thus, before discussing alternative theories it is necessary to describe how we define terms and interpret the ambiguities in assessing the debate.

Simply put, aggregate driving forces are economic factors that initially affect firms or consumers in a similar direction and magnitude, whereas allocative driving forces are economic factors that initially affect firms or consumers in a dissimilar direction or magnitude. The most common aggregate driving forces are aggregate demand and aggregate productivity; similarly, the most common allocative driving forces are sectoral demand, sectoral productivity, and relative prices. Demand, measured by income, output, or employment, and relative prices are observable. Productivity, on the other hand, is unobservable and usually estimated as a Solow residual—a concept fraught with measurement difficulties, as illustrated by the Basu article in this volume, and ultimately unsatisfying conceptually.

Ambiguity about allocative versus aggregate driving forces arises in at least three ways. First, changes in aggregate driving forces often affect sectors differentially. A good example is the difference in the cyclical sensitivities of industries producing durable goods and nondurable goods. Another good example is monetary policy, where some firms and consumers are more adversely affected than others by rising interest rates and restricted credit. In these cases, the initial impact of the driving force seems to be both aggregate and allocative in nature.

Second, changes in aggregate demand typically are not spread evenly throughout the economy. A good example is government spending, a classic measure of aggregate demand in traditional macroeconomic models. Government programs, such as military purchases, often are targeted at narrow groups of industries, plants, and regions, as California and Massachusetts found out earlier this decade. Thus, this aggregate driving force seems to be initially allocative in nature, although the concomitant reduction in GDP is likely to affect all agents later as well.

Third, allocative forces such as relative prices appear to have aggregate implications as well. Oil price changes are a quintessential example of an allocative driving force that may not be purely allocative: Only oil producers experience the output price changes (allocative), but virtually every consumer and every other producer buys products or services based on oil (aggregate). Oil price changes also affect the aggregate price, at least in the short run. Exchange rates are another case. Not all industries and plants engage in international trade, but most consumers and plants purchase some foreign goods. Even monetary policy falls into this category, because it is still an open question whether all firms or consumers are adversely affected by interest rate increases.

This discussion suggests most driving forces have both an aggregate and an allocative nature. But most observers tend to view driving forces as being either aggregate or allocative, with the other serving as a means of amplifying and propagating the initial driving force. Empirically, it seems reasonable to conclude that both types of driving forces operate within the common frequencies of macroeconomic data (monthly, quarterly, and annual). Evaluating the nature of the driving force as frequency increases (daily, hourly), however, seems to point more often toward allocative factors as the initial driving force behind fluctuations.

Theories Based on Allocative Driving Forces

Theoretical models with allocative driving forces introduce heterogeneity in workers, plants, capital, products, and the like. Often plants are grouped by common characteristics, such as industry, which form a sector. The allocation of factors of production across plants and sectors is determined primarily by relative prices of goods and factors, relative productivity, and consumers' tastes and preferences for goods. Allocative driving forces cause a change in the desired allocation of factors across plants.

Multisectoral models in which allocative forces drive recessions usually focus on one particular driving force that disrupts the optimality of existing factor allocation. In Davis and Haltiwanger (1990), sectoral productivity shocks govern the exogenous evolutions of high- and low-productivity plants. Often sectoral productivity shocks are amplified and propagated by things such as nonconvexities and complementarities (Cooper and Haltiwanger 1993), sparse input-output structures (Horvath 1998b, 1998c), and uncertainty and learning (Horvath 1998a). In Hamilton (1988), oil price increases alter the efficient allocation of labor (as well as reducing aggregate real income).[8] Other observable allocative forces include real exchange rate fluctuations (Gourinchas 1998) and geographical movements (Blanchard and Katz 1992). Davis, Loungani, and Mahidhara (1997) examine reallocation across geographic regions driven by changes in oil prices and military spending. In all of these models, the driving forces induce desired reallocation across plants and sectors. Actual reallocation ultimately depends on the magnitude, timing, permanence, and uncertainty associated with the driving forces.

In a world without frictions, factor reallocation would occur instantly. But the real world is full of costly and time-consuming frictions that prevent factors from being instantly reassigned to the plant where they are most highly valued. Plants that become unprofitable due to allocative shocks may destroy jobs quickly, but the job creation process often takes more time. Construction of new structures, and delivery and installation of new equipment, may involve significant lead times. And matching displaced workers to the newly created job openings often requires workers and firms to acquire new information, retrain, or shift geographic location. All of these types of frictions typically involve forgone output and a reduction in aggregate activity.

Theories Based on Aggregate Driving Forces

Theoretical models based on aggregate driving forces generally take the aggregate force as a shock given from outside the model, and then focus on explaining how factor allocation changes in response to the shock. Although there are many rich explanations, three basic classes of models have emerged.

One class of models develops direct links between aggregate shocks and factor reallocation, specifically job creation and destruction. In Mortensen (1994) and Mortensen and Pissarides (1994), negative aggregate shocks destroy the profitability of worker-job matches relative to alternative productive opportunities, which must be found through search. In Caballero and Hammour (1994), aggregate shocks reduce the profitability of low-productivity jobs with old capital and cause them to shut down. Caballero and Hammour (1996, 1998) extend their framework to incorporate inefficiencies due to incomplete contracting, financial market imperfections, and suboptimal government policies that amplify and propagate the aggregate shock. Hall's (1997b) model also produces plant shutdowns based on reductions in the expected present value of profits tied to discount rate changes (monetary policy). And Garibaldi (1997) links monetary policy with job flows in a Mortensen-Pissarides

---

[8] Other articles focusing on the role of oil price shocks include Loungani (1986), Davis and Haltiwanger (1996, 1997), and Bresnahan and Ramey (1993).

framework. Through a variety of complex mechanisms, these models try to match the asymmetry between creation and destruction found in the job flow data.

A second class of models develops an indirect link between aggregate activity and factor reallocation. These models, exemplified by Davis and Haltiwanger (1990), Cooper and Haltiwanger (1993), and Hall (1991), embody a "reallocation timing hypothesis" (RTH). The RTH says that when the level of aggregate demand is low, as in a recession, the opportunity cost of reallocation—forgone output—is also low. Thus, while there is some steady underlying rate of reallocation in the economy, it is optimal to bunch reallocation into periods of low opportunity cost. This intertemporal substitution generates countercyclical reallocation.

The third class of models assumes the presence of microeconomic nonconvexities that produce discrete and infrequent employment adjustment from (S,s) or adjustment hazard-type policy rules. Examples include Bertola and Caballero (1990), Caballero and Engel (1993), Caballero, Engel, and Haltiwanger (1997), and Campbell and Fisher (1998). In these models, the likelihood of plant employment adjustment depends on the gap between actual and desired employment. Aggregate shocks represent small shifts in the average employment gaps but generate large employment changes by pushing some plants over the adjustment threshold. Although not always designed explicitly to explain countercyclical job reallocation, these models are able to produce a sharp spike in job destruction. Furthermore, they provide a nice accounting framework for evaluating the relative importance of aggregate versus allocative shocks. Caballero, Engel, and Haltiwanger (1997) find that aggregate shocks dominate.

Implications for Causality

So, do any of these theories tell us anything about what causes business cycles? Unfortunately, the answer is no. Generally speaking, neither allocative nor aggregate theories of countercyclical reallocation provide much guidance on what *causes* business cycles. Although the reasons differ, both types of theories fail to provide guidance largely because they do not really try to explain *why* business cycles occur. More often than not, fluctuations are assumed to be exogenous shocks—an increasingly tenuous strategy as more and more dimensions of the economy are being explained endogenously in macroeconomic models. Instead, these models address the relatively easier task of explaining *how* business cycles occur.

Theories based on aggregate driving forces do not explain what causes business cycles because they assume the preexistence of business cycles. These theories take as given negative aggregate demand or productivity shocks—that is, recessions—and then try to explain how reallocation occurs in response to the shock. Except for the distinction between aggregate demand and aggregate productivity, these theories really do not depend on the causes of the recession, and thus can treat them as ambiguous, exogenous forces. Nevertheless, the theories do provide some guidance about which broad empirical features might be observed in the data simultaneously with the job reallocation.

Theories based on allocative driving forces have the potential to be more specific about what causes business cycles, but thus far they have not been. One key reason is that they are based on the same kind of unobservable and unsatisfying exogenous productivity shocks on which aggregate theories are based. Another reason is that many of the more promising observable sources of allocative driving forces, such as relative prices, supply linkages, international factors, geographic factors, and product market factors, remain relatively unexplored. Many rich alternative supply-side explanations would arise from a more detailed look at production—a point that resonates with the Basu paper in this volume. Likewise, many demand-side explanations would arise from a more detailed look at the product market environment—we are unaware of any efforts in this regard. Lastly, advocates of allocative driving forces are still a minority, and multisectoral general equilibrium models are technically challenging.

NEW EVIDENCE ON THE NATURE OF GROSS JOB FLOWS

This section extends the work of DHS (1996) on the nature of plant-level job flows and presents new tabulations from the LRD. In the first subsection, we examine the cyclical properties of the concentration and persistence of gross job flows, and the relation of these two properties to plant size, in search of clues about what causes job flows, especially job destruction. In the second subsection, we examine the dependence of gross job flows on plants' recent employment growth, in an effort to better understand the nature of plant-level employment adjustment and the possibility that it is governed by nonconvexities.

The Cyclicality of Job Flows by Concentration, Persistence, and Size

In describing the nature of plant-level job flows, DHS (1996, pp. 146–49) paint a picture in which old, large plants play a central role in recessions. "Job flow dynamics in good times are dominated by the creation and destruction of jobs among relatively young and small plants.... During recessions, older and larger plants experience sharply higher job destruction rates, so that their contribution to the job and worker reallocation process rises. This time of intense job destruction by older and larger plants coincides with the rise in layoff unemployment,

Figure 2
Percentage of Total Manufacturing Jobs Destroyed, by Degree of Plant's Contraction

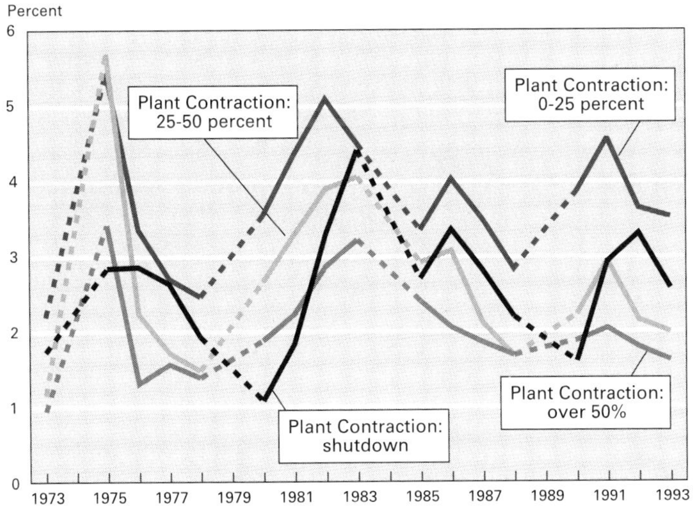

Note: Dotted lines represent interpolated numbers.
Source: Authors' computations from Longitudinal Research Database.

especially among prime-age workers." This subsection refines and sharpens these ideas.

Although an increase in the number of manufacturing plants undergoing large decreases in employment occurs in recessions, this is not primarily a phenomenon of plants closing. As Figure 2 shows, the percentage of jobs destroyed in plant shutdowns increases during recessions, but so does job destruction due to much more modest reductions in plants' employment.[9] The figure shows a strong countercyclical pattern to the job destruction at plants undergoing all four degrees of contraction. Job destruction in plant closings tends to appear somewhat later in recessions than does job destruction due to more modest degrees of contraction, however.

An interesting relationship exists between the size of a plant and the degree of its contraction: Small plants tend to destroy jobs in much more concentrated contractions than do large plants. This result is documented

---

[9] Because new panels were introduced in the Annual Survey of Manufactures (ASM) in 1974, 1979, 1984, and 1989, job destruction rates were not calculated for those years. The dashed lines in the figure interpolate between the adjacent years for which data are available.

in Figure 3, which shows the concentration of job destruction by plants' average level of employment (measured over all years in which the plant appears in the LRD) separately for recession and non-recession years.[10] About one-third of the job destruction in plants with less than 50 employees is due to plant shutdowns, while less than 15 percent of the job destruction in plants with more than 1,000 employees is due to shutdowns. Interestingly, for all four employment size classes shown in the figure, shutdowns account for a somewhat smaller proportion of job destruction in recession years than they do in non-recession years. Job destruction due to plant closings is countercyclical, but less so than job destruction due to employment reductions in continuing plants.

In general, larger plants exhibit a higher percentage of job destruction occurring in relatively modest employment contractions. Half of the jobs destroyed by plants in the largest employment size class were lost in employment reductions of 25 percent or less, while only 20 percent of the jobs destroyed by plants in the smallest employment size class were in this range.

These differences between the ways large and small plants destroy jobs are potentially quite important. Plant shutdowns may be determined by processes that are substantively different from those that produce more moderate reductions in a plant's staffing. One indication of this, shown in Table 2, is that the persistence of newly destroyed jobs increases with the degree of the plant's contraction.[11] Job destruction due to plant shutdowns is nearly always permanent, while about one-half of the jobs destroyed in contractions of less than 25 percent will be restored within five years.[12] Table 2 reveals that although the one-year persistence rates associated with employment reductions of any magnitude short of a full shutdown vary relatively little with the degree of the plant's contraction, the differences across the concentration classes increase as one examines persistence over longer time horizons.

The average persistence rates in Table 2 hide considerable and informative heterogeneity in plant-level persistence rates. We investigate the heterogeneity of persistence by plotting the distributions of plant-

---

[10] We define 1974–75, 1981–83, and 1990–91 as recession years, and other years in the 1973–93 period as non-recession years, when using annual data. However, our calculations exclude 1974, 1979, 1984, and 1989 because new ASM panels were introduced in those years.

[11] The persistence rates shown in Tables 2 and 3, and Figures 4 and 8, are based on tabulations from the LRD. Persistence rates were calculated in each year for plants that were included in the LRD sample for five years beyond that year (except in the case of plant closings, where closed plants are assumed to remain closed if they do not reappear in the LRD in a future year). The rates were then aggregated over plants and years, weighting each plant-year observation by the number of jobs destroyed or created times the sample weight.

[12] We extend the DHS persistence measure horizon from two to five years to see whether some of the "permanent" plant-level employment adjustment in the short run might be "transitory" in the medium term. Changing capital stocks, production technologies, and product lines could easily take more than two years.

Figure 3
Concentration of Job Destruction, by Size of Plant

Recession Years

Fewer than 50 Employees

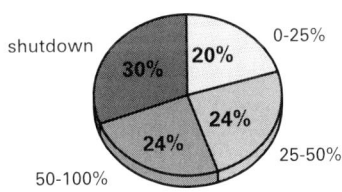

50 to 249 Employees

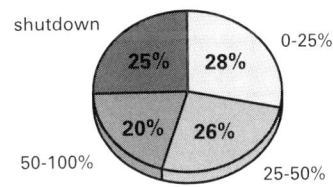

250 to 999 Employees

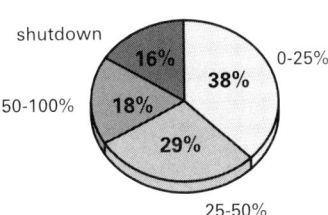

1000 or More Employees

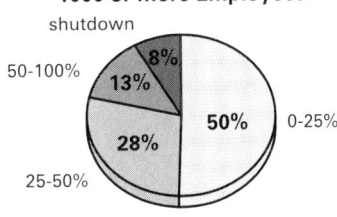

Non-Recession Years

Fewer than 50 Employees

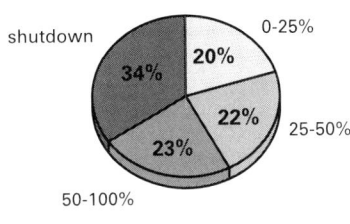

50 to 249 Employees

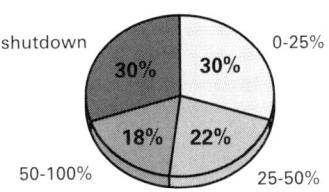

250 to 999 Employees

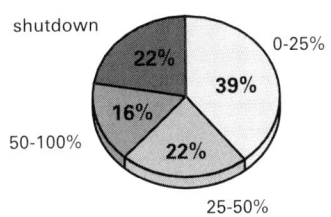

1000 or More Employees

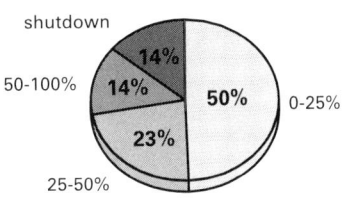

Source: Authors' computations from Longitudinal Research Database.

Table 2
Job Destruction Persistence Rates, by Degree of Plant's Contraction, 1973 to 1988
Percent

Plant Contraction	One-Year Horizon	Two-Year Horizon	Five-Year Horizon
0–25 Percent	75	64	51
25–50 Percent	79	69	58
Over 50 Percent	80	74	68
Shutdown	99	98	97

Source: Authors' calculations using Longitudinal Research Database.

level job destruction persistence rates in Figure 4. Because we are primarily interested in the extent to which job flows are permanent versus transitory, we focus on a very simple discrete distribution with three cells: permanent (85 to 100 percent), intermediate (15 to 85 percent), and transitory (0 to 15 percent).[13] Figure 4 shows that plant-level destruction persistence tends to be bimodal, with most mass clustered in the tails near 0 (transitory) and 100 (permanent), rather than being bell-shaped, with most mass concentrated near the mean persistence rate.[14] As the time horizon increases, the proportion of plants in the permanent range falls and the proportion in the transitory range increases. For example, among plants contracting less than 25 percent, 64 percent of job destruction is permanent and only 16 percent is transitory after one year. But after five years, only about 40 percent is permanent and another 40 percent is transitory. In future work, we plan to develop a better understanding of why some plants permanently destroy jobs and others temporarily destroy jobs.

The persistence of job destruction associated with moderate degrees of plant employment reductions (0 to 25 percent) follows an interesting pattern over the business cycle. As Figure 5 shows, one- and two-year persistence rates tend to increase just before a recession begins and then drop in the recession's final year. This suggests that the persistence of jobs lost in moderate plant contractions may be very sensitive to aggregate demand. A drop in aggregate demand will increase the persistence of job

---

[13] Because plants' persistence rates are weighted by the number of jobs destroyed in computing the distribution, the frequencies show the proportion of destroyed jobs located in plants with persistence rates in each of the three categories.

[14] The actual probability density function of persistence rates is determined by the driving process for plant-level employment growth rates, which we do not specify but know from the evidence in DHS is bell-shaped (though definitely not normal). A more detailed and careful treatment of this issue is clearly warranted but beyond the scope of this paper. However, we note that the observed bimodal distribution is markedly different from even a uniform distribution, in which we would expect to see 70 percent of persistence in the intermediate range (15 to 85 percent). In fact, however, a much smaller proportion of destruction falls in this range.

Figure 4
Distribution of Job Destruction Persistence Rates, by Degree of Plant's Contraction

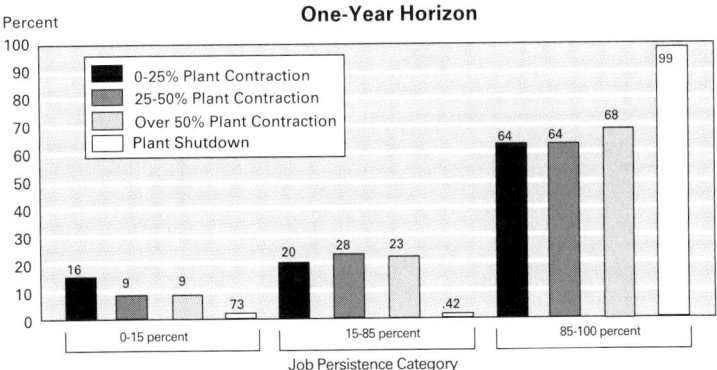

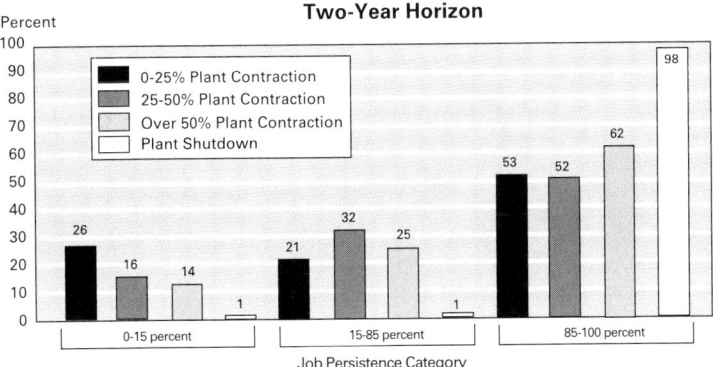

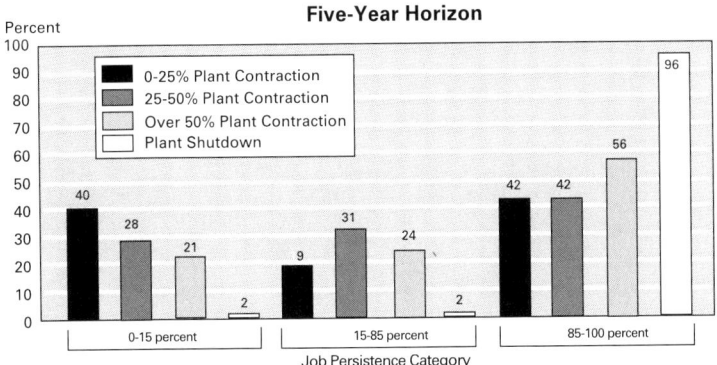

Source: Authors' computations from Longitudinal Research Database.

Figure 5
Persistence of Job Destruction, by Degree of Plant's Contraction

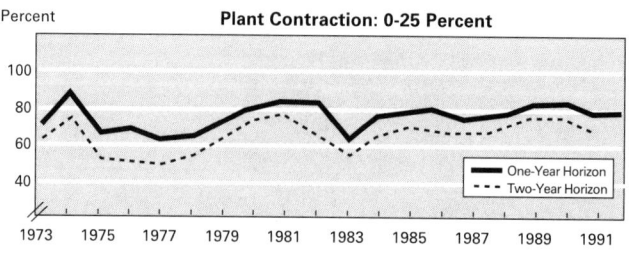

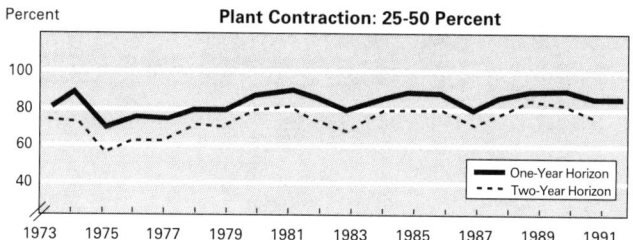

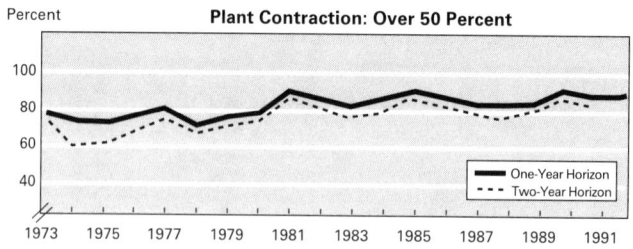

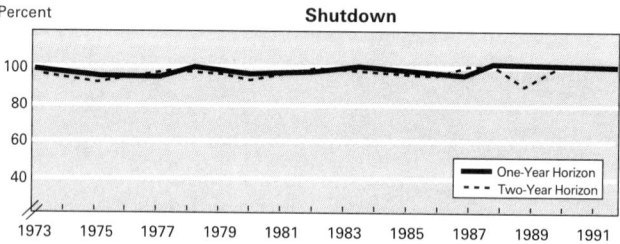

Source: Authors' computations from Longitudinal Research Database.

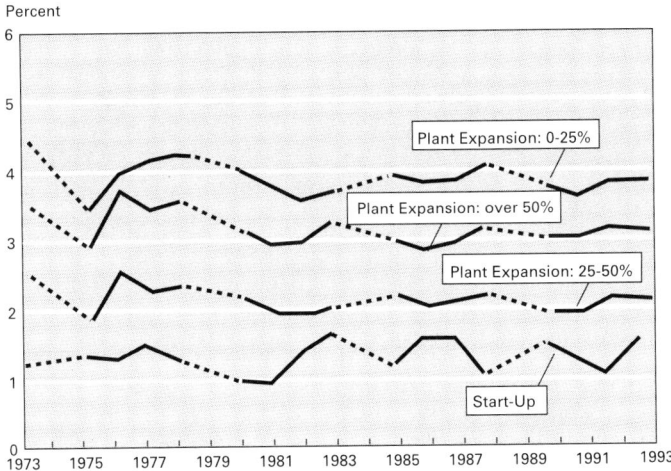

**Figure 6
Percentage of Total Manufacturing Jobs Created,
by Degree of Plant's Expansion**

Note: Dotted lines represent interpolated numbers.
Source: Authors' computations from Longitudinal Research Database.

destruction, while an increase in demand will make the job destruction more transitory. This pattern also shows up, although to a lesser degree, for jobs destroyed in plants contracting between 25 and 50 percent. For plants contracting over 50 percent, however, the main pattern seems to be an upward drift of persistence rates over time, and plant shutdowns are nearly always permanent in all years.

Turning to the job creation side of employment reallocation, Figure 6 shows the pattern over time of the percentage of total manufacturing jobs created each year, according to the degree of plant expansion. The first three concentration classes, existing plants, display job creation patterns that are very procyclical during the 1970s, but less so in the 1980s and 1990s. However, new plants (start-ups) follow a pattern that is acyclic or possibly even countercyclic. One possibility is that much of the job creation in the moderate expansion classes following a recession is due to the restoration of jobs temporarily destroyed during the recession. Recall that the persistence rates of job destruction are relatively low for moderate degrees of job destruction, and drop toward the end of recessions. This would lead one to expect an increase in job creation rates in the moderate expansion classes immediately following recessions.

As with job destruction, there are marked differences by plant size in the concentration of job creation. As Figure 7 shows, a much larger

Figure 7
Concentration of Job Creation, by Size of Plant

Recession Years

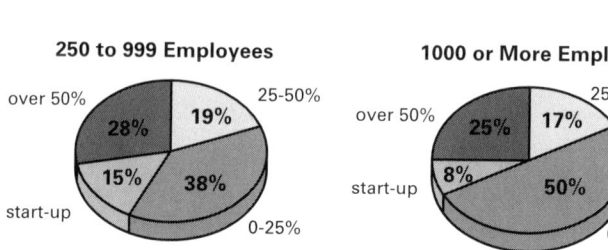

Non-Recession Years

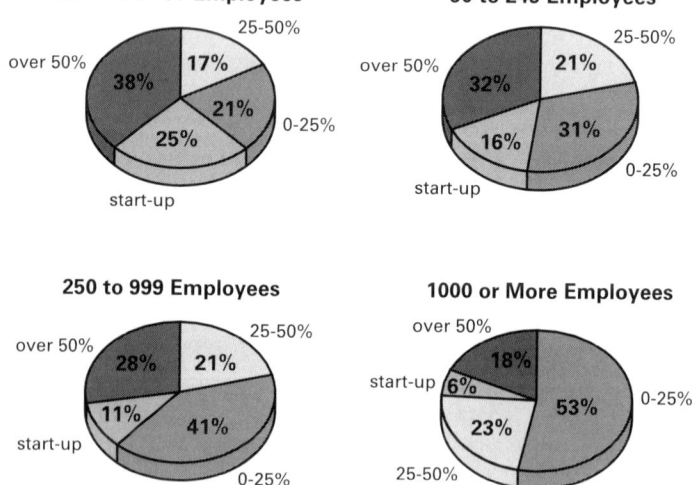

Source: Authors' computations from Longitudinal Research Database.

Table 3
Job Creation Persistence Rates, by Degree of Plant's Expansion, 1973 to 1988
Percent

Plant Expansion	One-Year Horizon	Two-Year Horizon	Five-Year Horizon
0–25 Percent	66	50	28
25–50 Percent	71	55	33
Over 50 Percent	72	59	39
Start-Up	74	62	44

Source: Authors' calculations using Longitudinal Research Database.

proportion of the jobs created by small plants is in start-ups or created through very high rates of expansion than is the case for large plants. These patterns are similar to those we documented earlier for the concentration of job destruction. Small plants tend to adjust employment through start-ups/shutdowns and truly massive percentage changes in their employment levels, while large plants tend to make smaller percentage adjustments both when expanding and when contracting. Also note that for large plants, the higher proportion of job creation through start-ups or very large (more than 50 percent) increases in employment is higher in recession years than in non-recession years. Recall that we found job destruction in large plants is more concentrated in shutdowns during non-recession years than during recessions. The job creation and destruction patterns together suggest that start-ups, shutdowns, and other massive employment changes in large plants may tend to be the result of long-run planning, while smaller percentage employment changes may be caused by fluctuations in product demand.

As with job destruction, the persistence of job creation increases with the degree of the plant's employment change (as shown in Table 3): Jobs created in start-ups are most persistent, while jobs created in expansions of less than 25 percent are least persistent. Like the job destruction persistence rates, job creation persistence rates tend to be concentrated in the tails of the distribution (as shown in Figure 8). Many fewer plants have persistence rates in the intermediate (15 to 85 percent) range than one would expect if the persistence rates were uniformly distributed. As the horizon over which persistence is measured increases from one to five years, the proportion of plants in the high persistence (85 percent or greater) category shrinks and the proportion in the low persistence category (less than 15 percent) increases; the proportion in the intermediate class remains relatively stable. Further research is needed to understand why some plants create long-lived jobs, while others increase their employment only temporarily.

Figure 9 shows that the persistence (at the one- and two-year horizons) of jobs created by plant start-ups is largely acyclic, but the

Figure 8
Distribution of Job Creation Persistence Rates, by Degree of Plant's Expansion

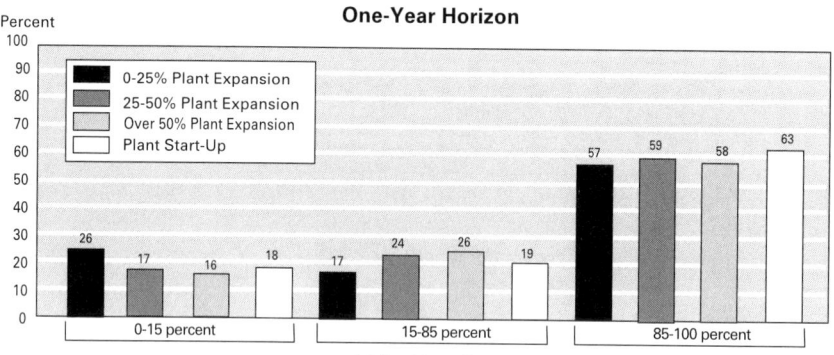

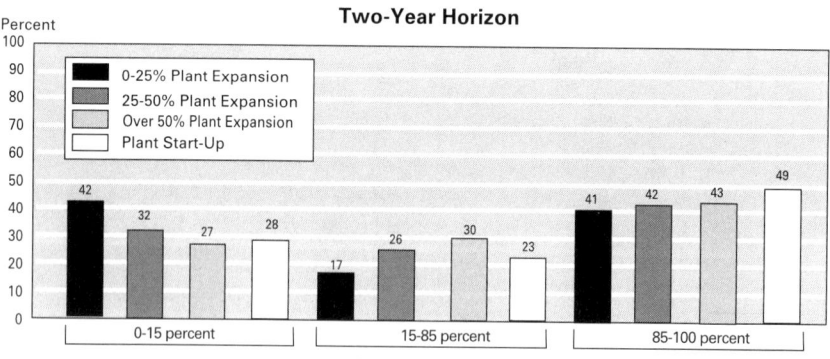

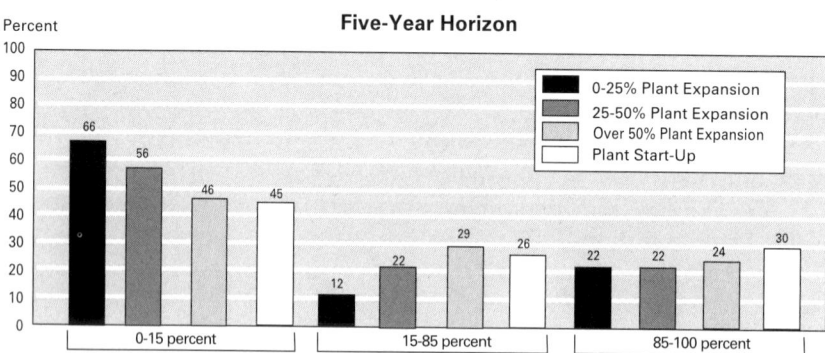

Source: Authors' computations from Longitudinal Research Database.

Figure 9
Persistence of Job Creation, by Degree of Plant's Expansion

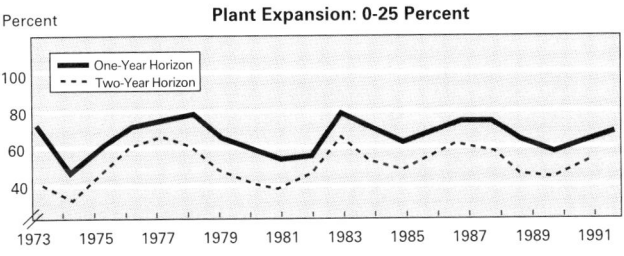
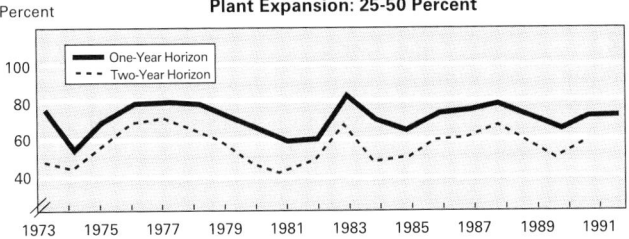
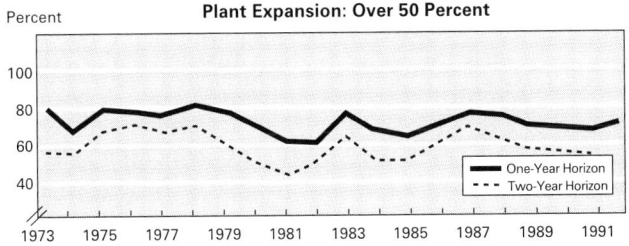
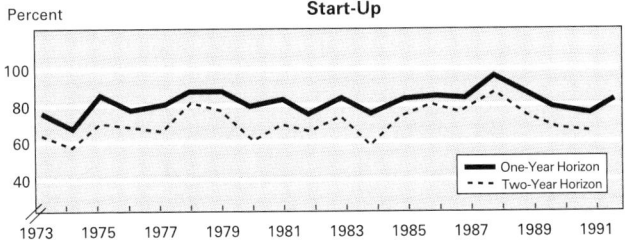

Source: Authors' computations from Longitudinal Research Database.

persistence rates of jobs created in moderate percentage expansions of plants' employment follow a pattern of decreasing early in a recession and then increasing before the recession ends. Jobs created relatively early in a recession seem to be at risk of being eliminated because the plant is contracting before the recession ends, while jobs created at the end of a recession are more likely to survive because of the more favorable demand conditions coming in future years.

Implications and Extensions. Putting together the facts on the concentration and persistence of job destruction yields a number of interesting enhancements to the basic DHS picture of plant job flows. Although larger plants exhibit a greater cyclical asymmetry between job creation and destruction, large plant job flows are likely to be much more moderate than small plant job flows. Small plant job flows are much more likely to be concentrated in shutdowns or massive contractions and expansions. Because higher job flow rates tend to be much more persistent, small plant job flows tend to be more permanent and large plant job flows more transitory. High job flow rates tend to be less cyclical than moderate job flow rates, and the predominance of large plant job flows (especially destruction) during recessions occurs in relatively moderate (less than 50 percent) contraction and expansion classes. Further, these moderate expansions and contractions are more likely to be transitory, especially in the medium term. To summarize, while large plants dominate movements in job flows during recessions, their flows are smaller and less persistent than inferred from DHS.

To the extent that small plants tend to be part of smaller firms than are large plants, the greater concentration of small plants' job flows in sharp expansions and contractions could be due to credit market imperfections. Large firms may reduce employment and output because of a transitory decrease in product demand or increase in costs, but in many cases they eventually resume operating at their previous level. Small firms may instead close down entirely under the same circumstances because of lack of credit and depletion of internal funds. The fact that job destruction due to plant closings tends to occur relatively late in recessions adds further credence to this hypothesis.

Small plants might also employ workers with less organization-specific human capital than workers in large plants. In this case, small plants might be more likely to close or permanently downsize owing to the smaller capital loss in dissolving existing worker-firm matches. Another possible explanation is that large plants are more diversified (or are parts of more diversified firms) than are small plants. A reallocative shock may prompt a large plant to temporarily decrease employment and output while it retools to produce new products, while a small plant might find that its optimal response to the shock is to shut down. Yet another possibility is that the differences in the ways in which small and large plants destroy jobs are partly due to differences in the distribution of plant sizes across industries. For example, large plants may be more likely to be part of cyclically sensitive durable goods industries than are small plants. Clearly, more research is needed in order to better understand the differences in the job destruction patterns of small and large plants.

Plant-Level Time Series Characteristics of Employment Growth

Aside from the facts that plant-level employment adjustments are often quite large and that flows of newly created and destroyed jobs tend to persist for at least two years, little is known about the plant-specific time series properties of employment growth. Much of the literature, such as Hammermesh (1989), Caballero and Engel (1993), and Caballero, Engel, and Haltiwanger (1997), views the large, persistent plant-level employment adjustment as arising from microeconomic nonconvexities that also cause adjustments to be infrequent. This view contrasts sharply with the standard macroeconomic treatment of employment being subject to adjustment costs that induce serial correlation and partial adjustment. The contrast of these two views motivates a deeper look at the plant-specific time series properties of employment growth.[15]

We conduct a simple exercise to obtain an approximate estimate of the historical time dependence in plant-level employment growth. Unfortunately, the short time series dimension of the LRD (at most 20 years, much less for most plants) inhibits direct estimation of plant-specific autocorrelation properties. Instead, for each plant we calculate the average employment growth rate during the prior two years and tabulate the gross job flows by eight prior employment growth categories, plus a missing category.[16] This latter group contains primarily plant start-ups and, in certain years, new panel entrants.

Table 4 reports gross job flow rates and shares by prior employment

---

[15] Without a formal model of the process of plant-level employment adjustment, it is impossible to know what the exact nature of employment time dependence is. If plant-level employment is stationary, microeconomic nonconvexities suggest that time dependence should be minimal and employment growth prior to large employment adjustments should be quite small (averaging close to zero). However, if plant-level employment contains a deterministic or stochastic trend, nonconvex employment adjustment could exhibit time dependence. But trending plant employment—especially upward trending—is hard to conceive without joint adjustment of capital (buildings and equipment). Abel and Eberly (1997) argue that nonconvexities in capital adjustment can cause large, infrequent employment adjustments even in the presence of convex labor adjustment. Cooper and Haltiwanger (1998) find that a model with a mix of convex and nonconvex employment adjustment fits the plant-level data best.

[16] Results are similar using the previous one, two, or three years of prior employment growth, but longer periods entail more missing values. Two years smooths out the "regression to the mean" behavior associated with transitory employment changes while providing a sense of the trend in employment growth and has fewer missing observations than three years.

Table 4
Gross Job Flows in U.S. Manufacturing, by Prior Employment Growth

Prior Growth[b]	Rates (%)				Shares (%)[a]		
	C	D	R	N	C	D	E
Recession years:							
−50% or less	66.3	18.8	85.1	47.4	2.0	.3	.2
−50% to −25%	14.7	19.9	34.6	−5.2	6.5	4.8	3.2
−25% to −10%	5.5	15.1	20.6	−9.6	6.6	9.4	8.3
−10% to 0%	3.5	11.8	15.4	−8.3	12.0	20.9	23.5
0% to 10%	3.7	10.1	13.8	−6.4	13.4	19.6	26.0
10% to 25%	5.3	12.9	18.2	−7.5	8.2	10.5	10.9
25% to 100%	7.6	19.1	26.7	−11.6	5.0	6.7	4.7
More than 100%	12.2	18.2	30.4	−5.9	7.1	7.5	6.2
Missing	25.9	14.3	40.3	11.6	38.8	20.1	17.0
Expansion years:							
−50% or less	62.2	20.6	82.7	41.6	1.8	.6	.3
−50% to −25%	17.8	16.7	34.5	1.1	7.3	5.9	3.7
−25% to −10%	8.8	10.4	19.2	−1.6	9.7	10.2	9.8
−10% to 0%	5.4	8.0	13.4	−2.6	15.9	22.1	26.0
0% to 10%	5.1	7.1	12.2	−2.0	14.9	18.9	25.5
10% to 25%	7.0	9.7	16.7	−2.6	9.7	11.9	12.0
25% to 100%	8.9	14.8	26.8	−5.9	5.6	8.4	5.5
More than 100%	14.3	16.6	30.9	−2.2	3.1	3.3	1.9
Missing	28.1	11.9	40.1	16.2	32.0	18.6	15.2

[a] Totals may not sum to 100 because of rounding.
[b] Prior employment growth rate classes represent the average plant-level total employment growth during the preceding two years.
Note: C = Job Creation, D = Job Destruction, R = Job Reallocation, N = Net Employment Growth, E = Employment.
Source: Authors' calculations using Longitudinal Research Database.

growth for recession and expansion years. The table reveals a clear U-shaped pattern between gross job flows and prior employment growth: Plants with higher absolute rates of prior employment growth have higher job flow rates. The pattern is slightly different between creation and destruction. Job creation rates are flatter in the moderate prior growth classes, then rise sharply in the higher absolute growth classes. Particularly notable is the enormous rate of job creation for plants that had been radically contracting (–50 percent or less). Job destruction rates are more V-shaped, and destruction is not notably higher in radically contracting plants.

The table also reveals a strong negative correlation between net employment growth and prior employment growth. Excluding the missing category, the net employment growth rate tends to decline as prior employment growth rises. Bearing in mind that total manufacturing employment and average plant employment size were declining on average in the LRD sample during this period, it is still quite interesting that only two extreme categories experienced above-average net employment growth. The missing category has strong net employment growth because it is dominated by plant start-ups (including first-time plant births), which tend to grow relatively rapidly in their early years—see especially the job creation rates. But the only other category with positive net employment growth is the most rapidly contracting plants. In fact, net employment growth for these plants is so large that it goes a long way toward eliminating the earlier decline.[17]

The last three columns of the table provide perspective on the importance of the variation in job flow rates across growth rate categories, by reporting the shares of job creation and destruction and employment. About half of all plants had very moderate prior employment growth (–10 percent to 10 percent). The shares of employment in the large (in absolute value) classes are considerably smaller, but these categories account for disproportionately high shares of job flows.

A final result from the table pertains to the cyclical pattern of time dependence. The U-shaped pattern of job flows is roughly the same in recession and expansion years, indicating that the result is not driven by business cycle effects. The U-shaped pattern in job destruction is much flatter across categories in recessions, but the pattern in job creation is somewhat deeper (except in the categories of very high absolute growth rates). Perhaps most striking is the cyclical change in the shares of job creation, destruction, and employment in the highest prior growth class (more than 100 percent), which all increase dramatically in recessions. Two kinds of plants may be in this category. Some plants might overexpand employment leading up to a recession, perhaps as a result of forecast errors, and destroy jobs when their expectations are updated. Other plants might be growing rapidly and, when their demand remains high during the recession, are encouraged to expand further. The relative acyclicality of job creation in startups shown earlier may also help explain this result, particularly if start-ups in larger plants are spread gradually over several years.

Implications and Extensions. The simple tabulations in this section imply that theories of employment adjustment must exhibit historical time dependence in gross job flow behavior to fit the data. Job flow rates are systematically related to prior employment growth, with higher job flow rates being associated with plants whose employment previously

---

[17] One possible explanation for the U-shaped pattern in rates is that it is driven by differences in plant size, age, average wage, and the like. Larger, older, higher-wage plants have markedly lower rates of gross job flows, on average, so if they tended to have smaller absolute prior employment growth rates as well, the plant characteristics would explain the pattern. However, calculations not reported here indicate that the same general U-shaped pattern appears across all size classes.

has been changing dramatically. Also, the more a plant's employment grew recently, the more likely it is to decline a lot currently. Theories based on convex adjustment exhibit time dependence inherently; theories based on nonconvex adjustment must introduce time dependence in a sensible way.

Combining the results on prior employment growth with the results in the previous subsection paints an interesting but complex picture of employment adjustment. Recall that most plant-level job flows, especially extreme expansions and contractions, are persistent. Consequently, high rates of creation and destruction will show up as high rates of employment expansion or contraction for the next two years. Thus, large employment adjustments appear to be a common, rather than unusual, feature for plants that exhibit high job flow rates. In other words, high job flow rates seem to come in batches or are an inherent feature of certain plants.

Consecutive large rates of annual job flows do not necessarily indicate plant employment is trending, though. The data show roughly equal evidence of four basic patterns of plant employment adjustment: (1) rapid expansion for two years, then rapid expansion for two more; (2) rapid expansion for two years, then rapid contraction for two years; (3) rapid contraction for two years, then rapid contraction for two more; and (4) rapid contraction for two years, then rapid expansion for two years.

What does this evidence suggest about convexity of employment adjustment? If plant employment is stationary, the time dependence favors convex adjustment. If plant employment is trending, cases (1) and (3) could reflect nonconvex adjustment because trending employment will hit upper and lower adjustment thresholds that induce large adjustments. This argument is made by Foote (1998), based on the fact that total manufacturing employment was trending downward during the LRD period. However, even the prior employment growth results in this section do not provide concrete evidence on the relationship between the employment trends of the specific plants that exhibited large employment adjustments. The real empirical challenge for theories of nonconvex employment adjustment are cases (2) and (4), where large positive and negative employment trends are suddenly reversed by high destruction and creation rates, respectively.

Large job flow rates that reverse large employment trends, such as high job destruction in rapidly expanding plants, suggest either a deliberate, large, and transitory employment adjustment, such as temporary layoffs or retooling, or employment adjustment associated with forecast errors, information surprises, and the like. Consecutive large employment adjustments in the same direction, such as high job destruction in rapidly contracting plants, indicates that large, permanent employment adjustments are spread out over several years. If so, this phenomenon may imply that marginal employment adjustment costs are rising, or perhaps that uncertainty and learning may slow the adjustment of employment to its desired level. Clearly more detailed investigation is required on these issues.

NEW EVIDENCE ON THE CONNECTION BETWEEN JOB REALLOCATION AND THE BUSINESS CYCLE

This section presents new empirical evidence on the connection between job reallocation and business cycles and the causal ordering between the two. The empirical exercises were designed to address some of the goals for expanding our understanding of job reallocation as described in the introduction. Although not formal tests of modern theories of reallocation, the exercises yield new evidence that is relevant for many of the theories. Analyses in this section are conducted at the industry and sectoral levels using Census/DHS gross job flows and related data.

Time Series Causality

A logical and simple first step is to look for evidence of standard time series causality between reallocation and business cycles. With the usual strong caveats about causality in mind, we conduct two types of exercises designed to detect allocative effects on reallocation. First, we look for differences in gross job flow behavior among sectors defined by plant characteristics. To keep the results manageable, plant characteristics are simplified into two-way classifications, such as large and small. Despite the high degree of parsimony, important differences emerge. The goal is to discover differences among plants in gross job flows that may yield clues about the causes of recessions. Second, we look for lead-lag relationships between sectoral job flows and aggregate activity that may reflect causality.

At this point, we want to temporarily narrow our focus to job destruction. Figure 10 plots the gross job flows for the entire postwar period (see Davis and Haltiwanger (1995) for data construction). A sharp increase in job destruction is a regular feature of every postwar recession, not just the LRD period. Although job creation is more variable prior to 1972, the asymmetry between destruction and creation variances, and the countercyclicality of total job reallocation, are evident in this period as well. Furthermore, the relatively modest decline in job creation during recessions is almost always followed by a surge in job creation. Thus, the tendency for job destruction to change more and earlier during recessionary periods than job creation suggests that whatever causes job destruction may be what causes recessions.

Table 5 reports cyclical characteristics of job destruction by plant-

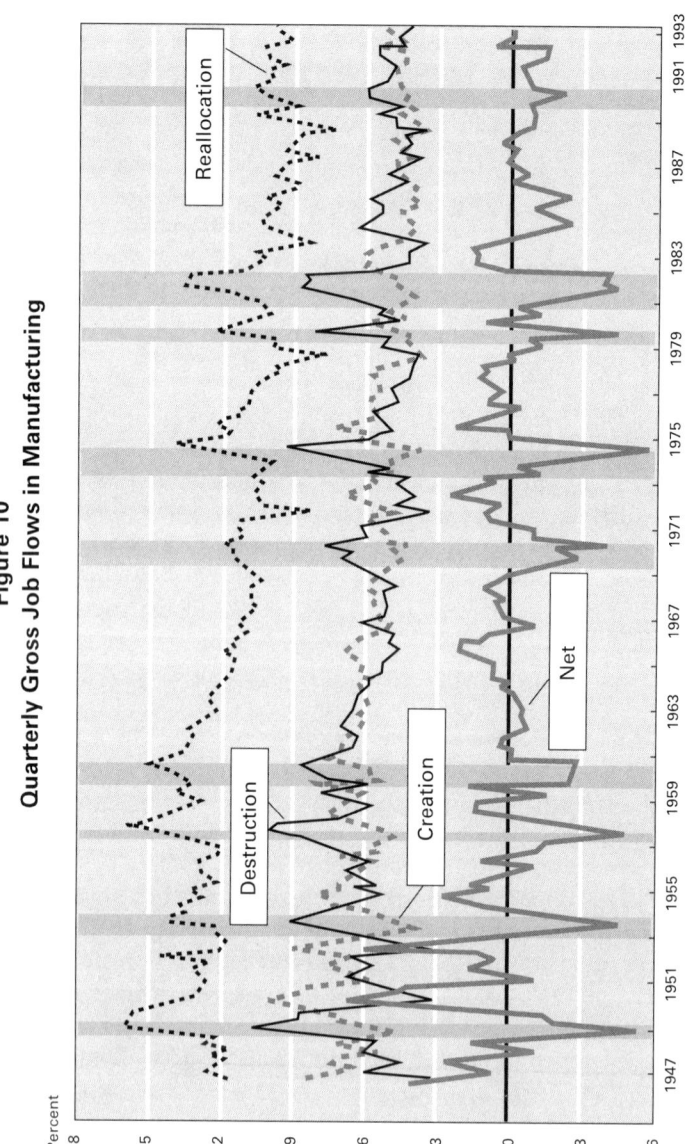

Figure 10
Quarterly Gross Job Flows in Manufacturing

Source: Census/DHS job flows data.

Table 5
Quarterly Characteristics of Job Destruction over the Business Cycle[a]

Plant classification	Variance Ratio[b]	Average Job Destruction in:		Business Cycle Change[c]		
		Expansions	Recessions	1975	1980	1982
Total Manufacturing	3.4	5.1	7.2	5.7	3.6	3.2
Nondurable Goods Industries	2.0	5.4	6.7	3.9	1.6	2.3
Durable Goods Industries	3.4	5.1	7.8	6.9	5.2	4.0
East Region	3.7	4.8	6.4	4.9	2.6	2.8
North Region	3.7	4.9	7.8	7.7	6.6	3.9
South Region	2.8	4.7	6.6	5.5	2.7	3.6
West Region	1.4	6.7	8.8	5.4	3.4	3.3
Small Plants	2.2	6.2	8.4	4.5	3.2	3.6
Large Plants	3.1	4.2	6.4	6.9	3.9	3.0
Young Plants	1.3	6.1	8.1	5.5	3.4	2.9
Old Plants	4.1	4.8	6.9	5.8	3.6	3.3
Specialized Plants	3.4	5.4	7.9	6.2	3.7	3.0
Diversified Plants	2.5	4.5	6.5	5.2	3.5	3.3
Low-Wage Plants	2.7	5.6	7.6	5.3	3.0	3.1
High-Wage Plants	3.8	4.2	6.8	6.2	4.7	3.9
Low Energy-Intensity Plants	3.3	5.0	7.0	4.9	3.5	3.0
High Energy-Intensity Plants	3.2	5.1	7.4	6.4	3.6	3.4
Low Capital-Intensity Plants	3.5	5.8	7.6	5.2	3.1	3.4
High Capital-Intensity Plants	3.3	4.4	6.8	6.1	4.2	3.4

[a] Based on quarterly data from 1972 to 1988.
[b] Ratio of the variance of job destruction to the variance of job creation.
[c] The increase in job destruction from the average value in the four quarters before the recession to the maximum value during the recession.
Source: Authors' calculations based on data from Davis and Haltiwanger (1996).

characteristic sectors. The table includes three types of statistics: the ratio of the variance of job destruction to the variance of job creation; the average levels of job destruction in expansions versus recessions; and the business cycle change in job destruction during recessions.[18] The variance ratios reveal considerable heterogeneity in the extent of countercyclical reallocation among plants—the larger the ratio, the greater the asymmetry between destruction and creation, and hence the more reallocation. Certain types of plants exhibit relatively high variance ratios and reallocation: durable goods, eastern and northern, large, old, high-wage, and

---

[18] The business cycle change in job destruction is the increase in destruction from the business cycle peak (average rate during the peak and previous three quarters) to the maximum value during the recession.

specialized. Ironically, plants with high variance ratios tend to have lower average rates of job destruction in both expansions and recessions. But during recessions, these types of plants experience larger increases in job destruction than their counterparts. To summarize, whatever causes recessions must account for the fact that these types of plants experience disproportionate increases in job destruction.

Table 5 shows that despite the asymmetry between creation and destruction rates, *all* types of plants experience substantial increases in job destruction rates during recessions. Business cycle changes in all sectors are broadly similar to total manufacturing, except for the industry sectors. On average, job destruction in durable goods industries rises twice as much as in nondurable goods industries, presumably because the demand for individual durable goods is inherently lumpy and more sensitive to credit conditions and the business cycle. Note that plants in durable goods industries also tend to be larger, older, higher-wage, and disproportionately located in the east and north. Together these facts beg the question: Do the plant characteristics arise because of industry differences (demand) or do industry differences arise because of plant production characteristics (supply)? Most theories of countercyclical reallocation are predicated on the latter, but the data hint at the former. However, the industrial differences may apply only to the transitory, rather than the permanent, component of destruction. More detailed disaggregation is needed to sort out these issues.

One can see further the similarity of job flows among sectors during recessions in Figure 11. Despite differences in relative variances, destruction (creation) rates clearly rise (fall) in all sectors during recessions. The magnitudes of change differ across sectors, but the time series patterns are remarkably similar. No sector averts the recession on either the creation or destruction margin. In contrast, Figure 12 plots gross job flow shares and highlights some important differences across sectors. The share of job destruction (creation) tends to rise (fall) during recessions for large and durable goods plants. One obvious potential explanation for this result is that these types of plants engage more in temporary layoffs. Another interesting difference, which is secular but timed around the 1981–82 recession, is a permanent increase in the share of job destruction and creation in old and, to a lesser extent, high-wage plants.

Two results stand out thus far. First, countercyclical reallocation prevails in all of the sectors. But, second, no clear sectoral differences arise to indicate that allocative driving forces hit some sectors but not others during recessions. Instead, the sectoral job flow characteristics resemble the early empirical results on dispersion in employment growth rates, where quantitative rather than qualitative differences could easily be explained by differing cyclical sensitivity of sectors to aggregate driving forces. However, these sectors are highly aggregated and may be masking clearer differences at more disaggregated levels. Finer sectoral classifications might identify sectoral differences that would more clearly suggest evidence of allocative driving forces. Based on the results so far, disaggregating by industry, interacted with plant characteristics, seems to be particularly promising for finding substantial sectoral differences.

Our second exercise looks for lead-lag relationships in the spirit of traditional econometric causality tests, as pioneered by Granger (1969) and Sims (1972). Consider first graphic evidence from the so-called butterfly plots in Figures 13a, 13b, and 13c for each of the three NBER official recessions during the 1972–88 period. The butterfly plots show sectoral job flows for one year before and after each business cycle peak (solid vertical line).[19] These plots are designed to detect cases where job destruction increases before recessions and hence might be said to have caused the recession. Similarly, these plots can detect lead-lag relationships between the sectoral rates of job destruction.

These plots show that destruction begins rising in virtually every sector prior to recessions. Although the spike in job destruction occurs after the recession begins, an unmistakable and substantial (often several percentage points) increase in job destruction occurs before all three recessions. Interestingly, job creation does not tend to change much before recessions except in 1981–82, when it declines a bit for some sectors. Note, however, that the plots also show that the leading nature of job destruction is generally similar across sectors. Except for a mild blip in job destruction in Figure 13c, there is no visual evidence of a lead-lag relationship between job flows within sectors.

To quantify this finding more rigorously, we estimated small-scale VAR models with job creation and destruction similar to those found in the literature.[20] These models impose structural restrictions designed to identify fundamental driving forces called allocative innovations and aggregate innovations. The relative importance of allocative versus aggregate driving forces is inferred from variance decompositions. A very disappointing common feature of these models is that estimates of this relative importance are highly sensitive to the identifying assumptions, and thus the models provide inconclusive estimates of the relative importance of allocative and aggregate driving forces.

Although our econometric models are similar, our focus is slightly different. Following Davis and Haltiwanger (1997), we model sectoral job flow rates together with an observable measure of aggregate activity—in

---

[19] Recall that NBER recession dating pertains to the entire U.S. economy, whereas the job flow data pertain only to manufacturing. Thus, if manufacturing activity tends to decline before nonmanufacturing in recessions, then job flows would spuriously lead the business cycle.

[20] This literature includes Blanchard and Diamond (1989, 1990), Davis and Haltiwanger (1996, 1997), Haltiwanger and Schuh (1998), and Campbell and Kuttner (1996).

Figure 11

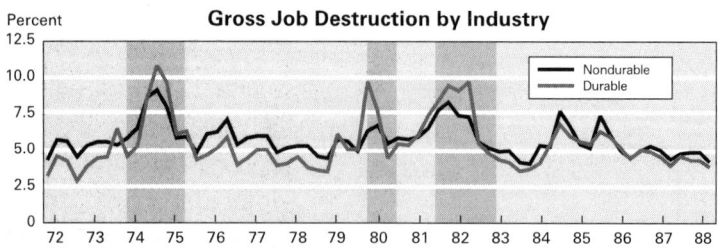

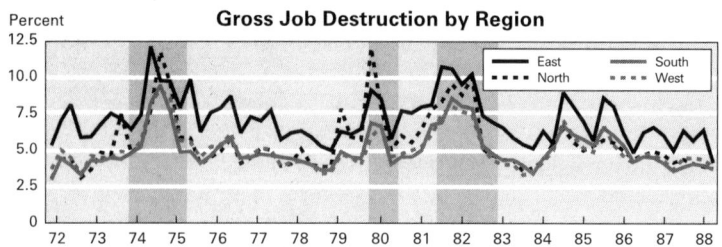

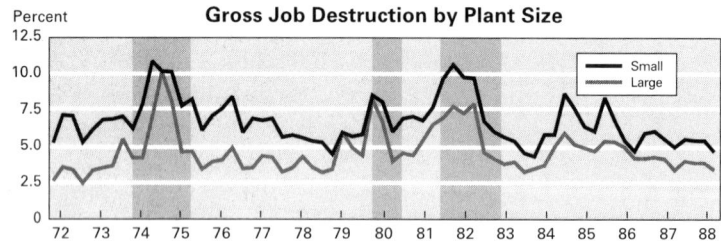

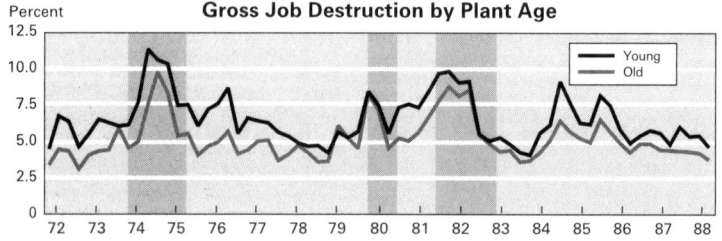

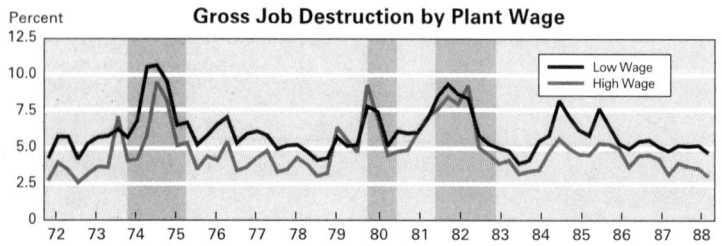

Source: Census / DHS job flows data.

JOB REALLOCATION AND THE BUSINESS CYCLE

Figure 11, continued

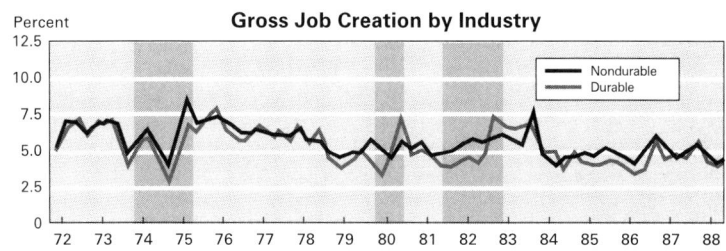

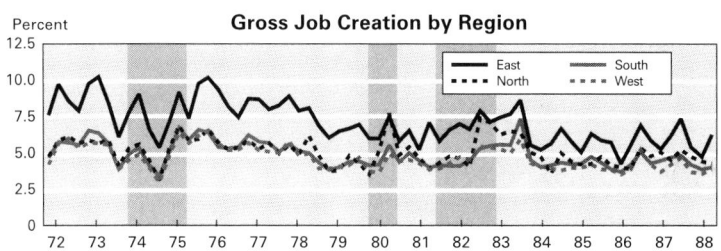

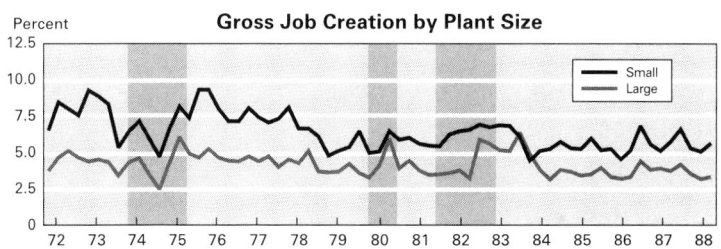

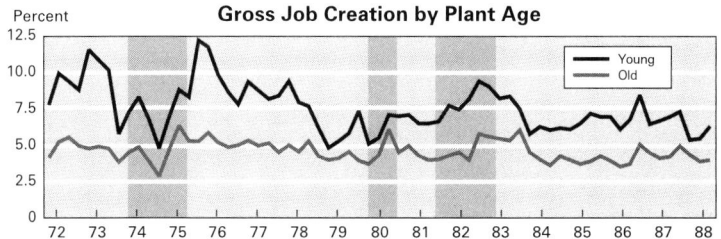

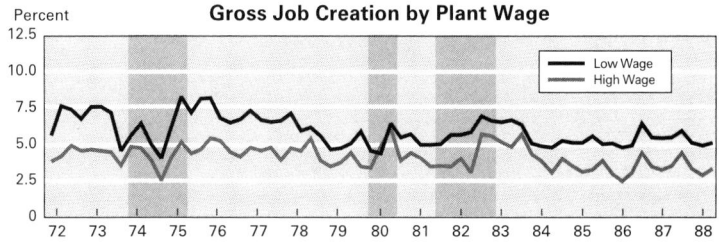

Source: Census / DHS job flows data.

Figure 12

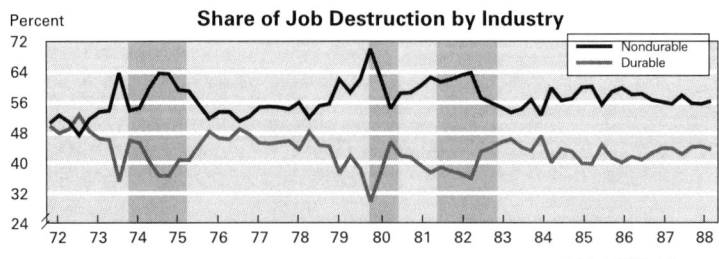

Share of Job Destruction by Industry

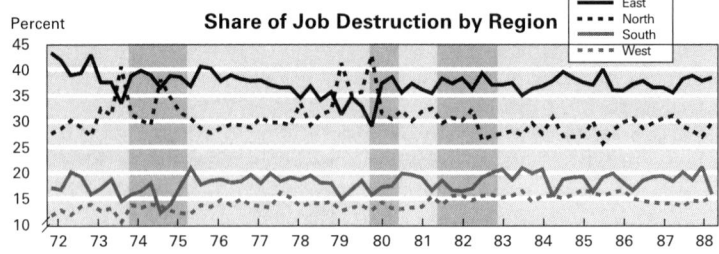

Share of Job Destruction by Region

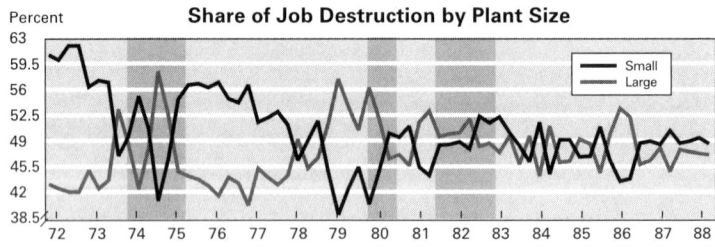

Share of Job Destruction by Plant Size

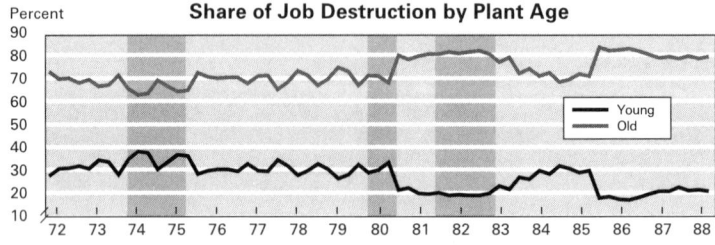

Share of Job Destruction by Plant Age

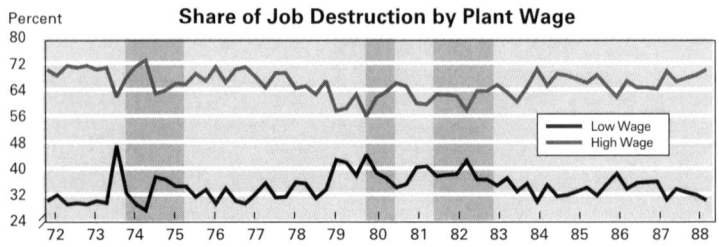

Share of Job Destruction by Plant Wage

Source: Census / DHS job flows data.

Figure 12, continued

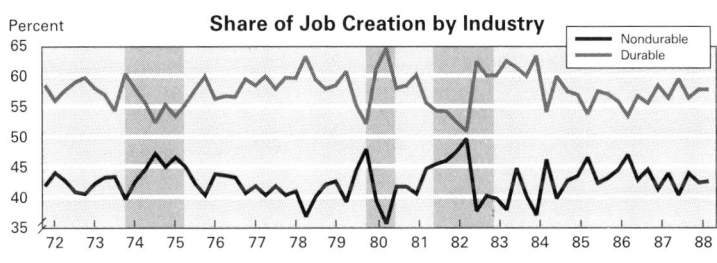

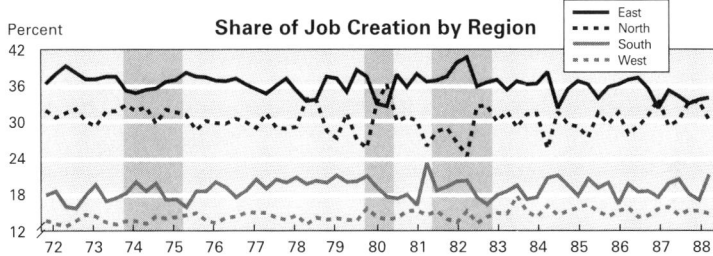

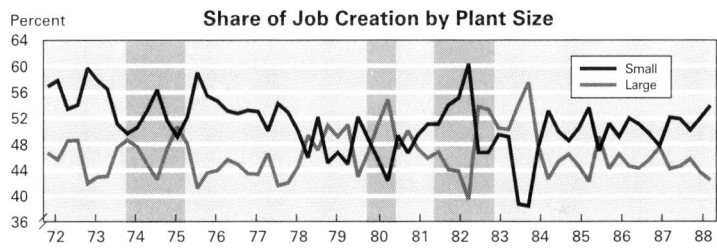

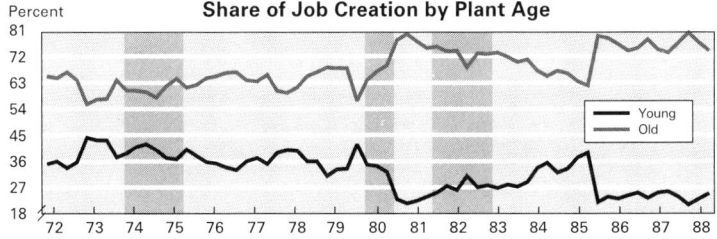

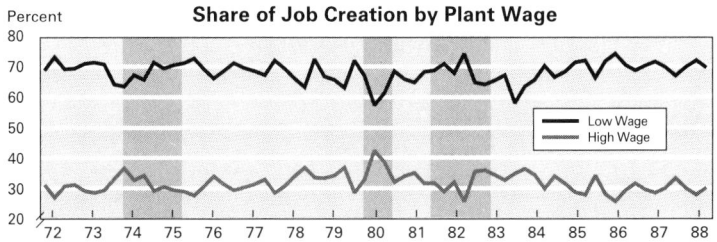

Source: Census / DHS job flows data.

Figure 13a
Sectoral Job Flows around 74:I Business Cycle Peak

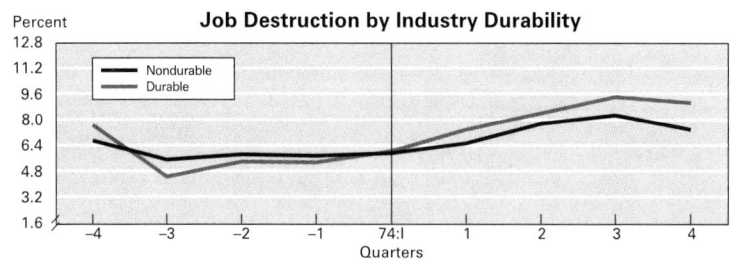
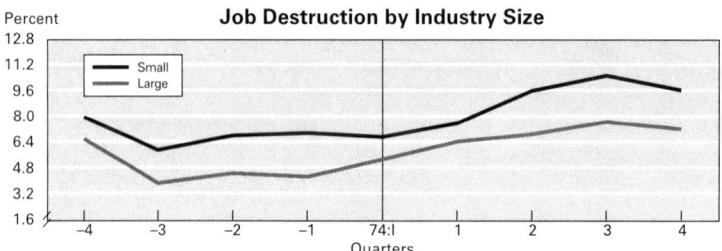
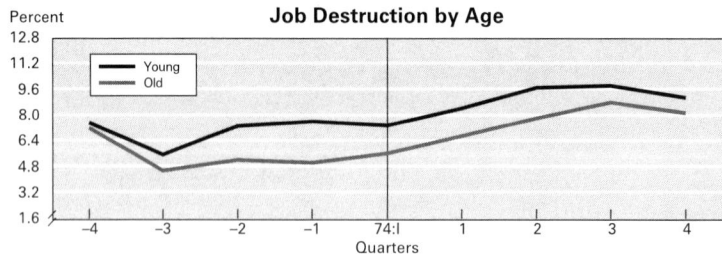
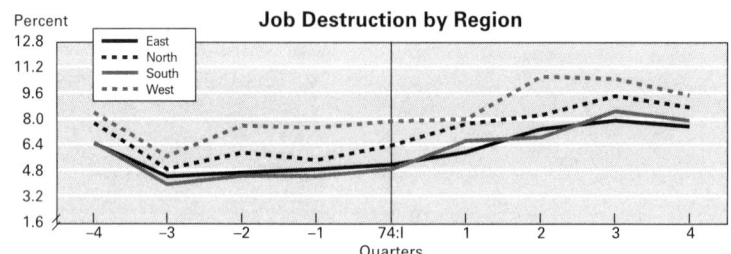
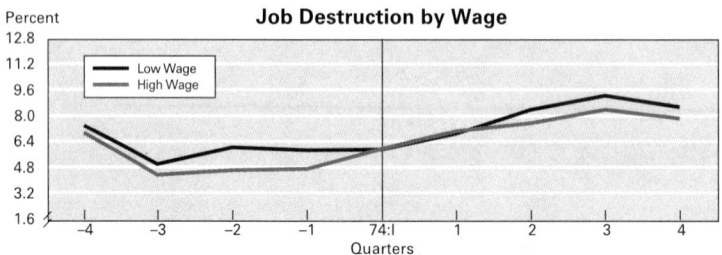

Source: Census / DHS job flows data.

JOB REALLOCATION AND THE BUSINESS CYCLE 311

Figure 13a, continued

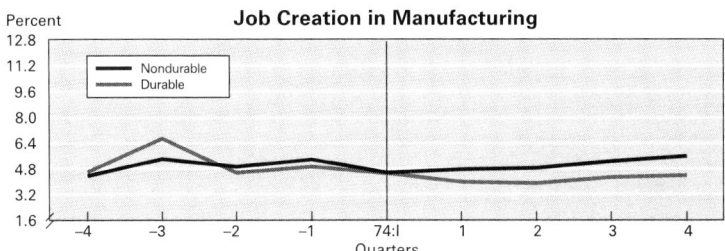

Job Creation in Manufacturing

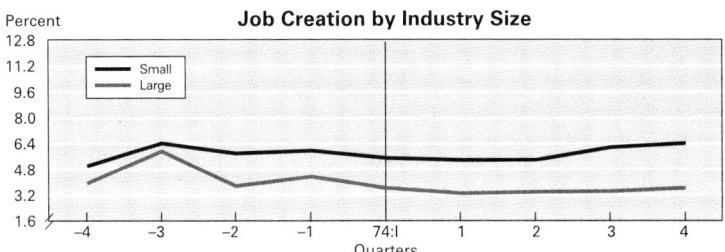

Job Creation by Industry Size

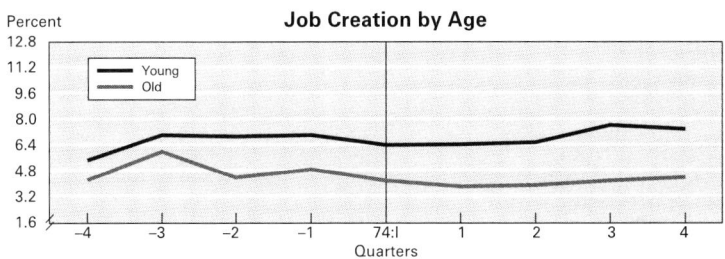

Job Creation by Age

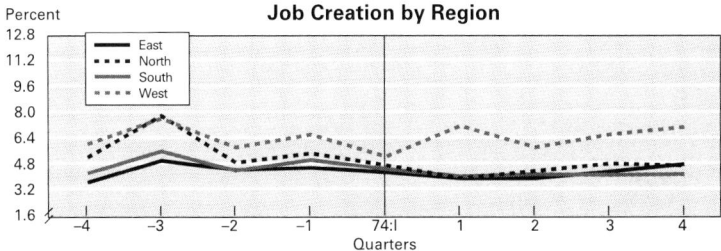

Job Creation by Region

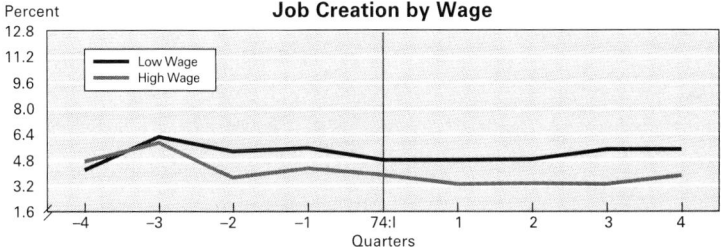

Job Creation by Wage

Source: Census / DHS job flows data.

Figure 13b
Sectoral Job Flows around 80:I Business Cycle Peak

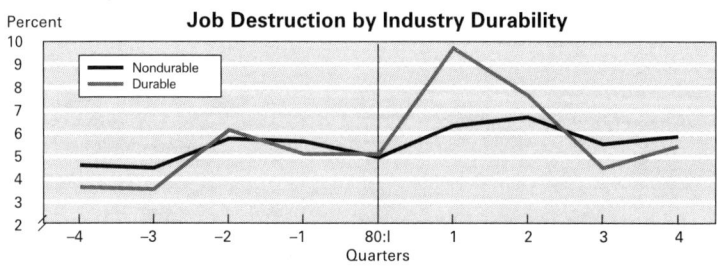

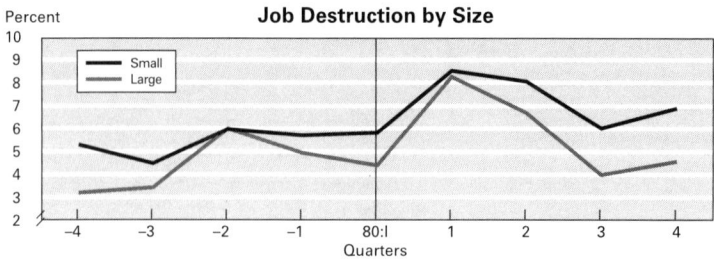

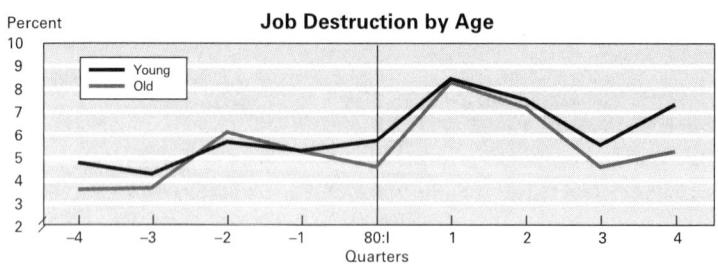

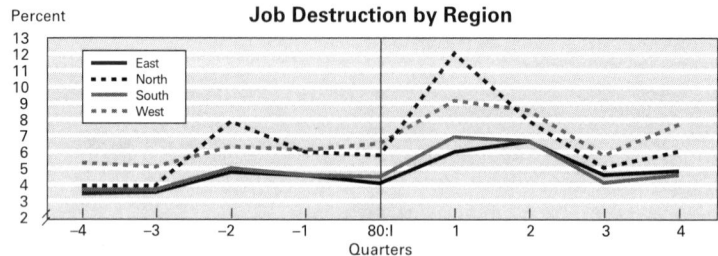

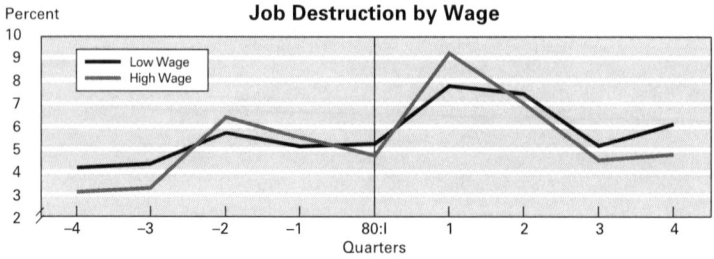

Source: Census / DHS job flows data.

JOB REALLOCATION AND THE BUSINESS CYCLE

Figure 13b, continued

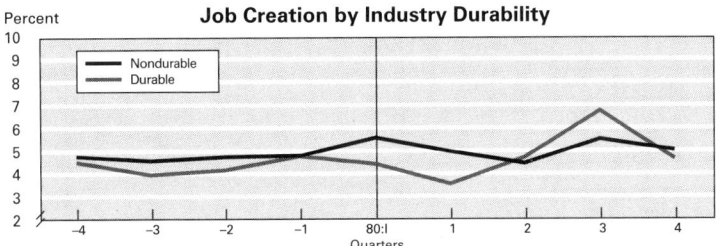

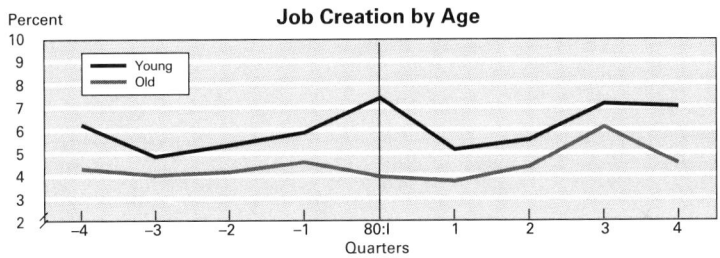

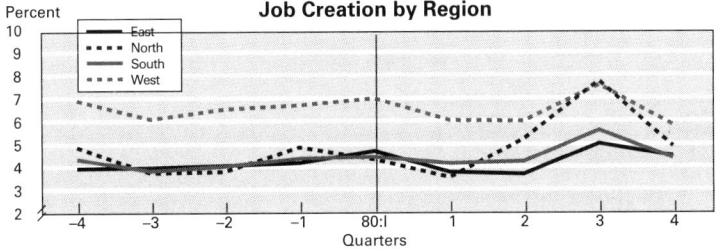

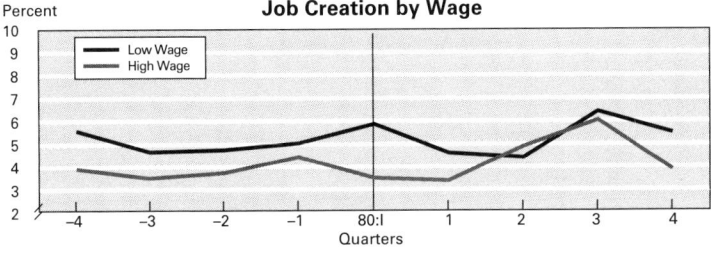

Source: Census / DHS job flows data.

Figure 13c
Sectoral Job Flows around 81:III Business Cycle Peak

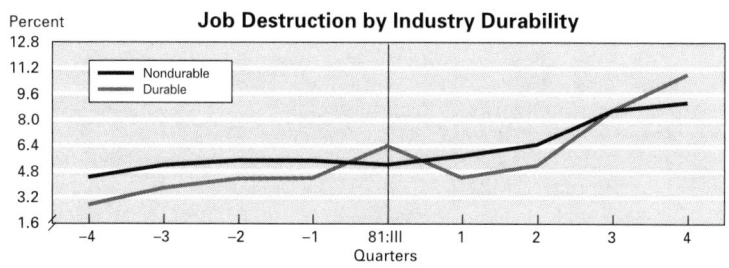

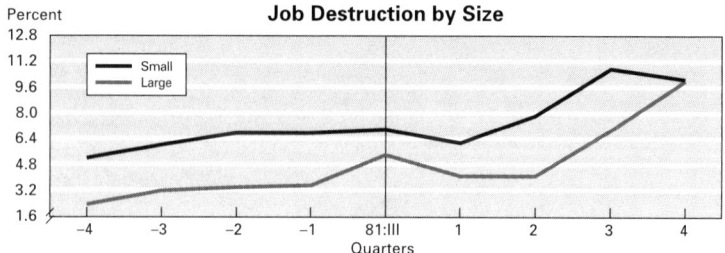

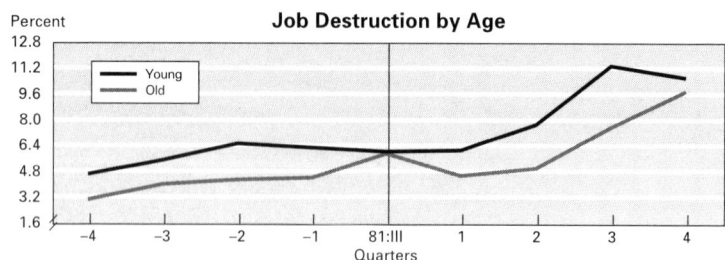

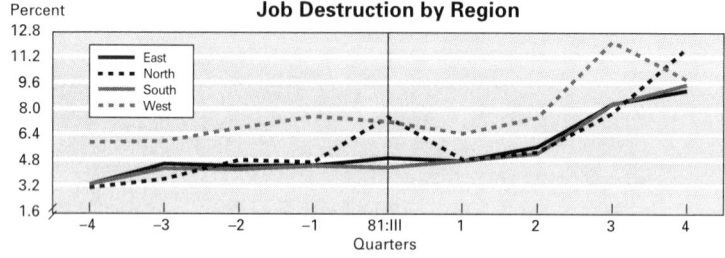

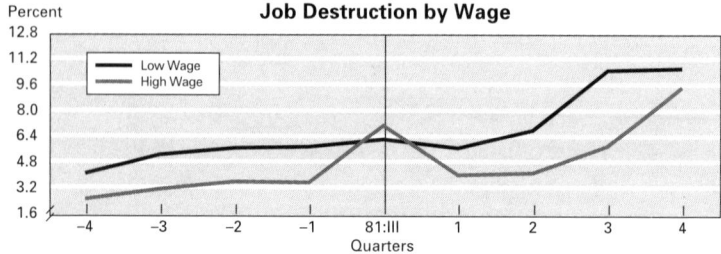

Source: Census / DHS job flows data.

JOB REALLOCATION AND THE BUSINESS CYCLE 315

Figure 13c, continued

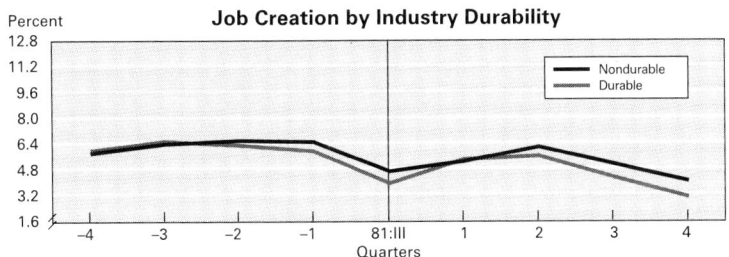

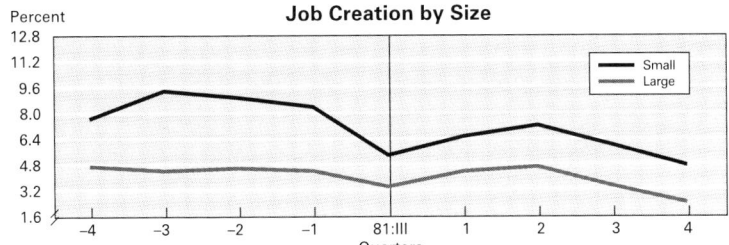

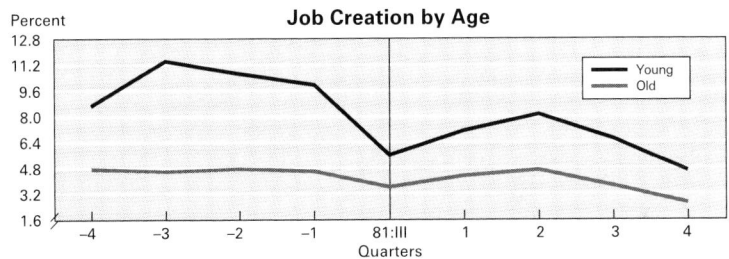

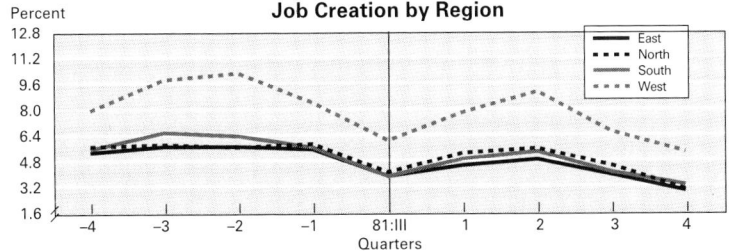

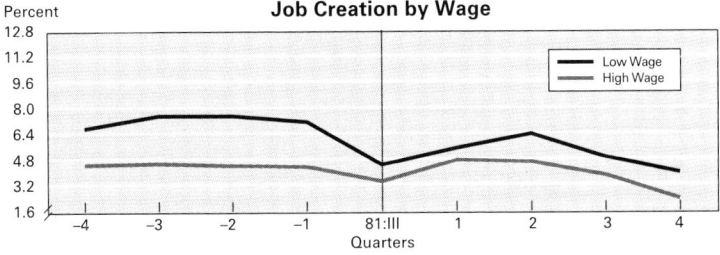

Source: Census / DHS job flows data.

Table 6
Causality Tests for Industrial Production (IP), Job Creation (C), and Job Destruction (D)[a]

Plant Classification	IP Equation			D Equation			C Equation		
	IP	C	D	IP	C	D	IP	C	D
Total Manufacturing	.32	.81	.05	.18	.57	.14	.95	.00	.08
Nondurable goods	.06	.57	.03	.04	.06	.00	.84	.00	.22
Durable goods	.37	.73	.06	.28	.94	.32	.88	.00	.03
East	.07	.51	.01	.04	.37	.00	.75	.00	.02
North	.18	.97	.52	.24	.99	.68	.45	.25	.01
South	.35	.74	.01	.45	.77	.00	.73	.00	.31
West	.07	.73	.01	.02	.00	.04	.34	.00	.06
Small	.12	.74	.02	.07	.04	.02	.91	.00	.30
Large	.32	.98	.11	.12	.81	.47	.84	.01	.03
Young	.15	.47	.01	.29	.11	.00	.75	.01	.02
Old	.37	.98	.13	.22	.88	.45	.64	.01	.04
Low-Wage	.27	.64	.01	.13	.14	.00	.72	.00	.17
High-Wage	.03	.92	.43	.04	.78	.84	.73	.00	.07
Specialized	.53	.21	.02	.37	.32	.05	.98	.00	.12
Diversified	.16	.63	.08	.08	.65	.23	.73	.00	.04

[a] Table entries are p-values from the hypothesis test that all lags of the variable (second row of headings) can be excluded from the equation (first row of headings).
Source: Authors' calculations using quarterly census/DHS job flows data for the period 1972 to 1988.

our case, growth of total manufacturing industrial production (IP).[21] But instead of trying to gauge the relative importance of contemporaneous allocative versus aggregate innovations, we simply examine what the VAR model lag structures imply about Granger-Sims causality. If IP growth causes job destruction, evidence accrues in favor of aggregate driving forces; if job destruction causes IP growth, evidence accrues in favor of allocative driving forces.

Table 6 reports the p-values from the causality tests. The third and fourth columns of numbers provide suggestive evidence that job destruction tends to cause IP growth. In all but four cases job destruction cannot

---

[21] We use manufacturing IP, rather than an economywide measure of aggregate activity such as GDP or unemployment, to prevent cyclical timing differences between manufacturing and nonmanufacturing from affecting the results. We use IP, rather than manufacturing net employment growth, to obtain a broader measure of economic activity. Two sensible extensions to the VARs are as follows: (1) include other aggregate variables, such as the federal funds rate and oil price growth, to account for the possibility that other aggregate variables cause job destruction and IP growth; (2) simultaneously include job flows from both sectors to examine intersectoral causality.

be excluded from the IP equation at the 10 percent level, and two of those cases are close (0.11 and 0.13). At the same time, IP lags are insignificant in most of the IP equations. In contrast, IP can be excluded from most sectoral job destruction equations, but job destruction generally cannot. In five sectors—durable goods, the south, young plants, low-wage plants, and specialized plants—the tests suggest destruction causes IP growth. In one sector—high-wage plants—the tests suggest that IP growth causes destruction. The remaining cases are statistically unclear.

Two other interesting conclusions emerge from these tests. First, lags of job creation are essentially irrelevant for either destruction or IP growth, though they are highly significant for creation itself. Only for nondurable goods, the west, and small plants does creation have any predictive power and that is only for destruction. Second, job destruction plays an important role in predicting job creation, while IP growth has no explanatory power for creation. Much more often than not, job destruction appears to cause job creation but not vice versa. To reiterate, aggregate activity tends to be irrelevant for predicting sectoral job flows, especially job creation.

Summarizing these causality tests without pushing them too hard, they offer modest evidence of allocative driving forces through lead-lag relationships. The data imply the following dynamic pattern. Job destruction in certain sectors reduces aggregate production. Both the decline in aggregate production and the allocative driving forces lead to job destruction in other sectors. Eventually, rising job destruction leads to higher subsequent job creation in most sectors.

This general pattern is difficult to reconcile with the view that an overall decline in aggregate activity causes an increase in job destruction. Also, the fact that job destruction in young, low-wage, specialized plants, rather than old, high-wage, diversified plants, leads IP growth is difficult to reconcile with vintage capital explanations of embodied technical change. Of course, these results could change significantly if an omitted aggregate driving force, such as monetary policy, leads sectoral job destruction. The results for young plants are somewhat suggestive of this, though one expects to see this causal pattern for small plants as a result of financial market imperfections, as argued by Gertler and Gilchrist (1994).[22]

Our investigation of time series causality between reallocation and business cycles yields two somewhat opposite conclusions. First, no sector clearly stands out as driving business cycles or recessions. Instead,

---

[22] The small-plant results may not be well-suited to testing for financial market imperfection effects because the small plant category includes small plants belonging to large companies, and the imperfections hypothesis is predicated on company-level financial conditions. Regressions on sectors defined by plant ownership type (single-plant companies versus multi-plant companies) and size would be more appropriate.

the cyclical experience is broadly similar for all types of plants, with differences in reallocation activity being primarily quantitative rather than qualitative in nature. These conclusions suggest that aggregate driving forces are at work. Second, the VAR models provide reasonably strong evidence that aggregate activity does not help predict sectoral job flow behavior, and modest evidence that sectoral job destruction helps predict aggregate activity. These causality results suggest that allocative driving forces are at work, although the VAR modeling and causality testing clearly require further development.

Reallocation, Investment, and Productivity

In this section, we examine the relationships among job reallocation, investment, and productivity growth. Two main factors motivate the investigation. First, as noted earlier, it is important to jointly consider decisions about all factors of production. Capital is an obvious factor to begin with given its relatively large share of output, plus the fact that it can affect job flows in different ways. Second, many reallocation theories based on cleansing, reorganizing, or other forms of "creative destruction" activities suggest that old, inefficient, and unproductive capital is destroyed and new, efficient, and productive capital is created. This idea implies that investment and productivity changes may be connected integrally to gross job flows, as workers matched with unproductive capital lose their jobs and productive new capital-worker matches are created. It also raises the general question of whether transitory declines in aggregate demand (recessions) are associated with permanent effects on productivity, presumably raising it. Productivity-enhancing creative destruction and embodied technological change could be internal to the plant, through restructuring, or internal to the industry, through shutdown, start-up, and other permanent reallocation across plants.

Direct evidence on the link between reallocation and productivity is limited, and most previous work has focused on the link at the plant level.[23] Baily, Bartelsman, and Haltiwanger (1996), for example, find that permanent job destruction in plants disproportionately accounts for the procyclicality of productivity. Other studies decompose industry productivity growth into the contributions of within-plant versus between-plant changes in productivity, including entry and exit. Several studies find that entry and exit of plants is a primary determinant of aggregate productivity growth, especially in the longer run. Foster, Haltiwanger,

---

[23] The relevant literature includes Dunne, Roberts, and Samuelson (1989); Baily, Hulten, and Campbell (1992); Dunne, Haltiwanger, and Troske (1996); Baily, Bartelsman, and Haltiwanger (1996); Olley and Pakes (1996); Liu and Tybout (1996); and Foster, Haltiwanger, and Krizan (1998).

and Krizan (1998) find that increases in nonproduction labor share are almost entirely driven by within-plant increases in the longer run. A serious drawback to these plant-level productivity studies, however, is the use of 4-digit industry deflators for output and input prices when there is likely to be tremendous heterogeneity in prices across plants.

In this section, we take a notably different approach to quantifying the relationship between job reallocation and productivity. First, we quantify the relationship between job reallocation and *trend*, rather than cyclical, productivity growth. This method is found in DHS (1996), which documents a jump in trend productivity growth in the steel industry after the massive job destruction during the 1981–82 recession (Figure 5.8, p. 117). One reason to consider trend growth is to mitigate the influence of capacity utilization. Another is that new investment may take several years to reach efficient operation and manifest itself in productivity. Second, we examine the relationship at the 4-digit industry level, rather than the plant level. The industry-level approach captures the cumulative effects of within-plant and between-plant productivity-enhancing reallocation. In addition, the price deflators required to construct quantities such as output and investment are industry-level prices. Thus, unlike the plant-level analyses, the industry analysis is immune to potential biases from heterogeneous plant-level prices.

The empirical exercise is as follows. For the three major recessionary periods in the sample, we sorted industries by the cumulative amount of industry reallocation during the recession. Then, for each quintile of industries, we calculated the changes in trend productivity growth (labor and total factor) and investment growth around recessions. Trend growth is measured as the average growth rate during an expansion, and is assumed to be able to change between expansions.[24] The key issue is to determine the extent to which cumulative reallocation in recessions is associated with increases in trend productivity and investment growth. If industries with the most cumulative reallocation during a recession also experience increased productivity and investment growth, in either absolute or relative terms, then the industries may be experiencing

---

[24] This exercise uses annual data from the Census/DHS job flows and the NBER Productivity Database described in Bartelsman and Gray (1996). Expansions are 1971–73, 1976–79, 1983–89, and 1992–94. The 1980 and 1981–82 recessions were combined because of their close proximity and relation. Cumulative industry reallocation is the sum of reallocation in all recession years, where reallocation is measured as the deviation from average industry reallocation during expansion years to control for cross-sectional variation in the level of reallocation (essentially a fixed effect). Labor productivity is real value added per production worker hour; total factor productivity (TFP) is preconstructed; and investment is total investment expenditures deflated by the investment deflator. Using average growth rates during expansions should uncover secular (trend), rather than cyclical, changes in productivity and investment. TFP growth for industry quintiles is the value-added weighted average of industry TFP growth.

Table 7
Productivity and Investment Growth around Recessions, by Cumulative Job Reallocation

Cumulative Job Reallocation (Percent)[a]	Productivity Growth (Percent)[b]						Investment Growth (Percent)[b]			
	Labor			Total Factor						
	Before	After	Chg.	Before	After	Chg.	Before	During	After	Change
1974–75 Recession										
Very low (<−3.4)	4.2	3.4	−.8	−.4	1.9	2.3	1.2	6.5	7.1	5.9
Low (−3.4 to 1.0)	4.4	1.3	−3.1	.2	.3	.1	12.7	−.9	13.1	.4
Average (1.0 to 5.9)	5.0	1.7	−3.3	.5	.7	.2	12.0	−8.0	6.7	−5.3
High (5.9 to 12.0)	1.1	.7	−.4	.8	1.3	.5	22.4	−19.0	10.4	−12.0
Very high (>12.0)	6.0	2.2	−3.8	1.7	2.8	1.1	22.7	−28.4	14.1	−8.6
1980–82 Recession										
Very low (<−3.7)	4.5	6.8	2.3	3.1	2.3	−.8	14.9	−2.7	6.1	−8.0
Low (−3.7 to 2.6)	1.9	3.5	1.6	1.0	.4	−.6	10.1	−2.0	6.5	−3.6
Average (2.6 to 9.1)	1.7	2.6	.9	1.5	.5	−1.0	11.2	−8.7	6.6	−4.6
High (9.1 to 18.2)	1.4	4.6	3.2	.9	1.4	.5	8.9	−15.9	5.9	−3.0
Very high (>18.2)	.6	3.3	2.7	.3	1.3	1.0	6.4	−22.8	3.3	−3.1
1990–91 Recession										
Very low (<−9.2)	4.2	9.9	5.7	1.0	5.5	4.5	2.8	−.1	8.2	5.4
Low (−9.2 to −5.2)	4.4	3.8	−.4	1.0	1.2	.2	4.3	−1.4	3.5	−.8
Average (−5.2 to −1.3)	3.1	1.9	−1.2	.9	.9	.0	8.9	−3.2	5.6	−3.3
High (−1.3 to 2.1)	4.5	5.7	1.2	1.8	2.8	1.0	6.0	−5.5	2.3	−3.7
Very high (>2.1)	4.2	2.9	−1.3	.7	.9	.2	5.4	−1.7	2.7	−2.7

[a] Cumulative reallocation is the sum of the rates of job reallocation in a 4-digit industry during the recession, where reallocation is measured at the deviation from mean industry reallocation during all expansion years.
[b] Annual average growth rates during the expansions before and after recessions.
Source: Authors' calculations using Census/DHS job flows data and the NBER Productivity Database for the period 1973 to 1994.

cleansing, reorganizing, or other forms of creative destruction. And, if so, it would then be appropriate to ask whether or not such creative destruction was the driving force behind the recession.

Table 7 reports the results. Total factor productivity (TFP) growth is the more pertinent measure for this exercise and yields the clearest results. In two of the three recessions (1974–75 and 1990–91), by far the greatest increase in trend productivity growth (column 6) occurred in industries with the *least* cumulative reallocation. In fact, productivity growth increased very little except in very low reallocation industries. In contrast, during the 1980–82 recessionary period, industries with the *most* cumulative reallocation experienced the largest increases in productivity growth. However, trend productivity growth did not increase much in any industry group after this recession, and the increase in very high reallocation industries was considerably smaller than the increase in very low reallocation industries around other recessions.

What accounts for these changes in trend productivity growth? The data suggest that investment growth likely played a key role. In all three recessions, industries with the largest increase in trend productivity growth also exhibited the largest increase in real investment growth. In the 1974–75 and 1990–91 recessions, industries with very low reallocation increased their investment growth markedly; the remaining industries actually reduced their investment growth collectively. In the 1980–82 recession, industries with very high reallocation showed the most improvement in investment (although investment in all industries declined, investment in very high reallocation industries declined the least). Not surprisingly, industries with the most reallocation exhibit the largest cyclical reductions in net employment growth and they also exhibit the largest cyclical reductions in investment growth. But these industries also exhibit the largest secular reductions in investment growth.

Figure 14 illustrates the basic point by plotting job creation and destruction in the very low and very high reallocation industries for each recession. The cleansing theories of Caballero and Hammour (1994, 1996), for example, postulate a sharp increase in job destruction followed by a lagged surge in job creation. Industries with very high reallocation exhibit precisely this postulated pattern in the first two recessions. However, these industries *reduced* their rates of investment—by 23 to 28 percent during the recessions and by 3 to 8 percent in trend—and did not generally see absolute or relative trend productivity growth rise much, if at all. In the third recession, this job flow pattern generally did not occur, at least not by 1993. In contrast, industries with very low reallocation, whose trend productivity growth often increased markedly, exhibit essentially acyclical job reallocation. The variances of job creation and destruction are about the same in each subsample (variance ratios of 1.0, 0.6, and 1.6, chronologically).

Table 7 also shows two other interesting developments related to the cross-sectional distributions of trend productivity and investment growth around recessions. First, the *levels* of cross-sectional trend productivity and investment growth were inversely related to the *changes* in trend growth. In other words, industries with relatively low trend growth before recessions tended to experience the largest increases in trend growth after recessions, and vice versa, *regardless of the amount of cumulative reallocation*. Second, dispersion in cross-sectional trend investment growth tended to decline dramatically after recessions. In other words, trend investment growth rates were quite different across industries before the recession but quite similar afterward. However, this feature was not observed generally in trend productivity growth.

Implications and Extensions. Industries experiencing unusually large bursts of job reallocation during recessions generally do *not* exhibit significant increases in trend productivity or investment growth. Instead, increases in productivity and investment tend to occur in industries with

Figure 14
Job Flows in High and Low Reallocation
Industries in Three Time Periods

Period around 1974-75 Recession

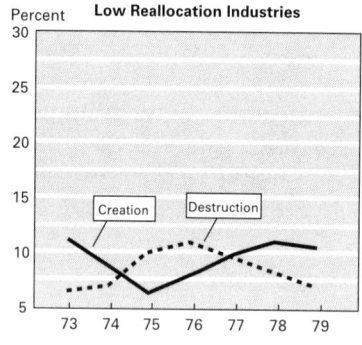
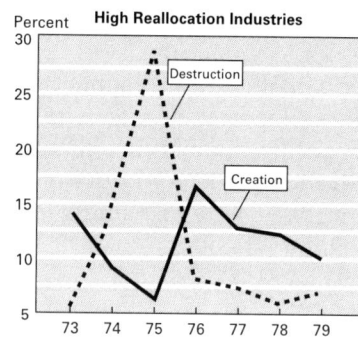

Period around 1980-83 Recessions

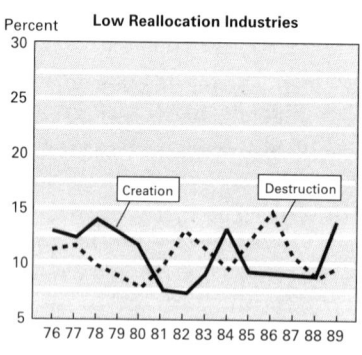
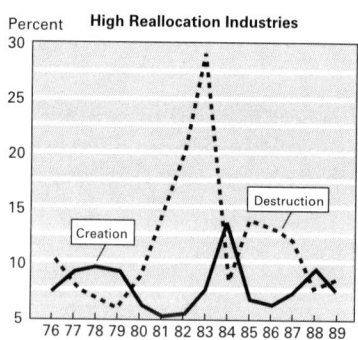

Period around 1990-91 Recession

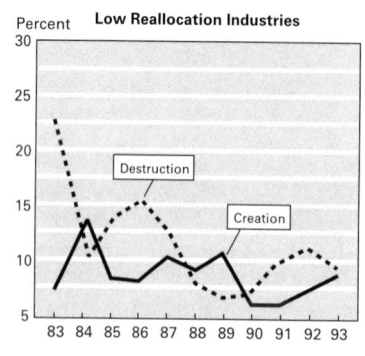
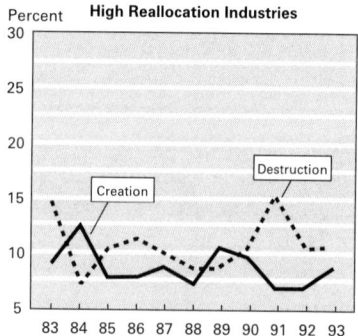

Source: Census/DHS job flows data.

very little job turnover and relatively low trend productivity and investment growth prior to the recession. The 1980-82 recessionary period shows some evidence for the conventional wisdom that this recession involved fundamental, productivity-enhancing restructuring. But the evidence is quite weak, and based on what we know about earlier postwar recessions, it appears that the 1980-82 recession was rather unusual in this regard.

This evidence on the connection between reallocation and trend productivity and investment growth does not conform well to theories that posit improvements in investment and productivity through creative destruction channels in either the short or long run. Whether the channel is through embodied technical change, intensified search and rematching, retooling, or some other mechanism, cleansing, reorganizing, and related theories imply some observable improvements in long-run productivity. Empirically, however, increased reallocation normally is not correlated with increased trend productivity and investment around recessions. Cyclical productivity fluctuations may be larger in the short run, but they are transitory and associated with fluctuations in utilization. Changes in the trend dominate over the long run.

Even if productivity improvements implied by creative destruction theories are very small, these theories have trouble explaining two main business cycle patterns observed in this data. First, trend productivity and investment growth often *fall* after bursts of job reallocation rather than rise, as predicted by the theories. It is possible, however, that the kinds of market inefficiencies stressed by Caballero and Hammour (1996, 1998), such as appropriability problems and financing constraints, could more than offset any productivity gains. But the second pattern is more problematic: Trend productivity and investment growth often rise substantially *without* any significant increase in reallocation. Thus, although these theories may explain how the process of reallocation works in *some* industries, they do not explain the connection among reallocation, investment, and productivity for the entire economy nor why the connection is linked to the business cycle. Because high reallocation industries normally do not exhibit observable productivity gains while low reallocation industries do, creative destruction theories do not appear to be complete explanations of business cycle fluctuations.

Our results suggest that understanding the role of investment—an old, familiar feature of recessions—is critical to understanding the nature and consequences of job reallocation. Investment appears to be a key determinant of productivity growth, but the bulk of investment growth does not always coincide with massive job reallocation over the business cycle or in the long run. Investment often is redirected toward industries that do not require major structural reallocation and that weather the storm of recession relatively well. For some reason, these industries also tend to have relatively low trend productivity and investment growth before the recession. These new facts are intriguing but puzzling, and certainly merit further consideration.

Sectoral Price and Productivity Dispersion

Early empirical efforts to identify allocative driving forces behind business cycles, such as Lilien (1982), focused on the sectoral dispersion in employment growth rates. Lilien found that dispersion in employment growth rates across sectors (defined as 1-digit industries) was countercyclical and helpful in explaining the time series behavior of the unemployment rate. Abraham and Katz (1986) disputed this finding by showing that heterogeneity in the cyclical response of industries to aggregate driving forces would produce sectoral growth rate dispersion as a consequence, rather than cause, of business cycles.

Loungani, Rush, and Tave (1990) and Loungani and Trehan (1997) contributed further evidence that allocative forces, termed "sectoral shifts," are important for business cycle fluctuations, using dispersion in stock prices. This measure is less susceptible to the Abraham-Katz criticism because, unlike employment dispersion, it appears to be econometrically exogenous: Stock price dispersion forecasts unemployment and output but not vice versa. Nevertheless, many observers remain unconvinced that allocative forces induce reallocation across sectors and cause business cycle fluctuations.

Even stock price dispersion may result from business cycles rather than cause them, though. If agents are rational, stock prices should equal the expected present value of future dividends. Thus, if firms' dividends fluctuate cyclically because of some link to aggregate activity, and firms' cyclical sensitivity is heterogeneous, then expected declines in aggregate activity will cause stock price dispersion as well. Empirically, stock price dispersion will lead employment dispersion because expectations and stock prices adjust quickly while real quantities, which may be subject to adjustment costs, change slowly. Thus the question remains: What causes dividends to fluctuate—the business cycle or firm- and sector-specific factors?

This section presents new evidence on allocative driving forces by examining two factors more likely to be a root *cause*, rather than *result*, of reallocation: relative prices and relative productivity. In a multisector general equilibrium model with fixed consumer preferences, relative prices and productivity are key determinants of firms' demand for factors of production and of consumers' demand for output.[25] Thus, changes in

---

[25] Determination of sectoral demand and production is complicated by numerous demand-side characteristics, such as differentiated products, imperfectly competitive industries, multi-product plants, corporate structure, and related issues. Size differentials among

relative prices and productivity should be key forces driving the reallocation of final demand and factors of production across sectors. The actual timing of the reallocation process (creation and destruction) will depend on the extent to which agents view the changes as permanent versus transitory, and on the relative flexibility of prices and productivity versus quantities. With uncertainty and real frictions, it seems reasonable to expect that the driving forces—changes in relative prices and productivity—precede the actual reallocation of quantities.

At least three types of relative prices determine the allocation of factors of production across sectors.[26] Output (finished goods) prices are a primary determinant of the relative level of demand for a sector's product, so relative output price changes will alter demand for output and factors of production across sectors. Input (raw) materials prices and investment prices are primary determinants of the mix of materials, capital, and other factors of production, so changes in relative materials and investment prices will change the mix of factors of production and demand for labor across sectors. Relative productivity, a key determinant of relative output prices, can also affect the demand for factors of production through many channels: relative output prices, investment, and so on. Cross-sectional changes in these relative prices and productivity should lead to reallocation of factors of production such as labor across sectors.

Figure 15 charts job destruction and dispersion in relative price changes and in total factor productivity (TFP) growth.[27] If sectoral relative prices and TFP growth converge to steady-state equilibrium cross-section distributions with a constant finite variance, dispersion would appear as a straight horizontal line in the figure. Actual dispersion reflects the extent to which sectoral rates deviate from that equilibrium. When dispersion increases, relative prices and productivity growth are changing across sectors. If the increase in dispersion is large enough and

---

plants or firms in industries raise questions about competitiveness, credit-market access, and scope for new technology. In short, the allocative role of relative prices and productivity is clearly more complex in practice.

[26] The term "sector" is used broadly enough to mean plants or group of plants with common characteristics, such as industry, geography, or any other observable plant characteristic.

[27] This exercise is also based on 4-digit industries and uses the Census/DHS job flows and NBER Productivity Database. Industry prices are the shipments deflators, materials price deflators, and investment price deflators from the NBER Productivity Database. Aggregate prices are the PPI for finished goods (shipments), PPI for crude materials (materials), and the GDP fixed-weight price index for nonresidential business fixed investment. Because the prices are indexes (all equal 100 in the base year), we cannot use dispersion in relative price *levels*; instead, our dispersion measures are the standard deviations of log *changes* of the relative prices. This approach is consistent with the relative price dispersion literature, typified by Debelle and Lamont (1997). TFP growth dispersion is the standard deviation of the gap between industry and manufacturing growth.

Figure 15
Job Destruction and Dispersion in Prices and Productivity across Industries

Real Shipments Price Changes

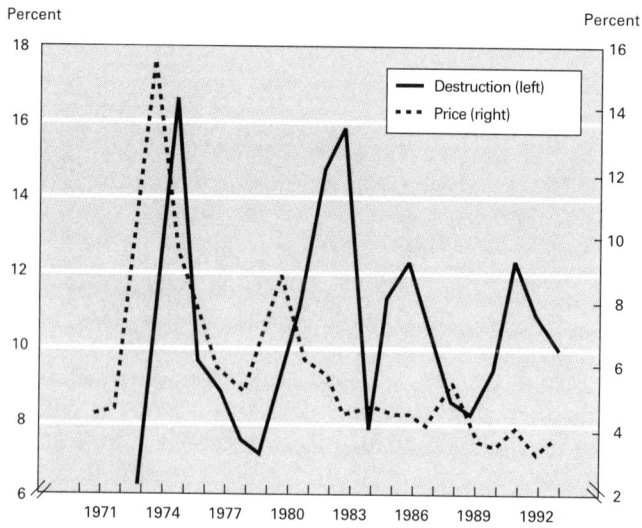

Real Materials Price Changes

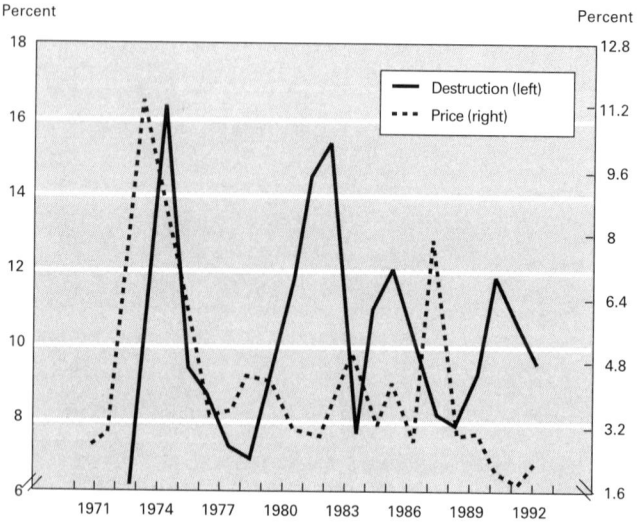

Source: Census/DHS job flows data.

Figure 15, continued

Real Investment Price Changes

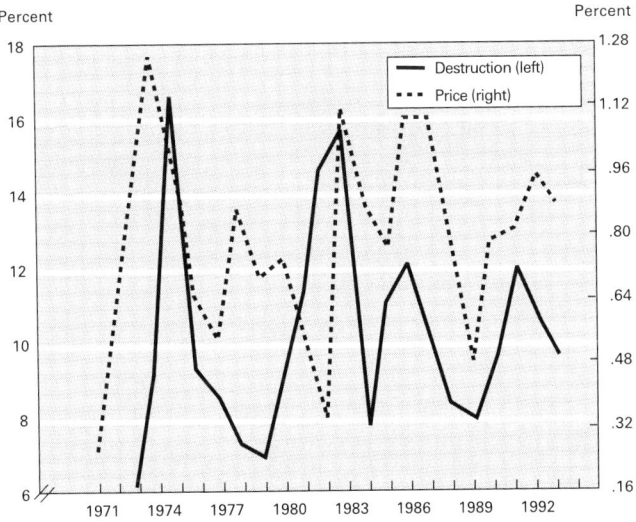

Growth Rates of Total Factor Productivity

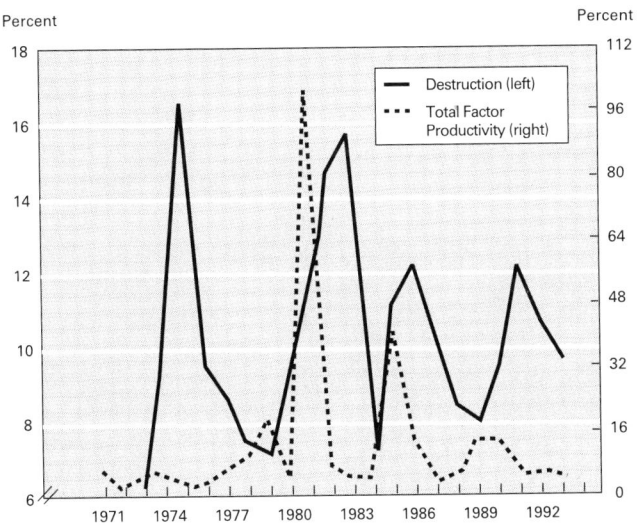

Source: Census/DHS job flows data.

permanent enough, it can cause permanent job destruction in adversely affected sectors and permanent job creation in positively affected sectors. The timing of job creation and destruction in response to the increased dispersion will depend on several factors. If productivity declines in one sector but is unchanged in another—an *unfavorable* sectoral driving force—job destruction is likely to precede creation. But if productivity increases in one sector and not the other—a *favorable* sectoral driving force—job creation may precede destruction. However, this latter scenario will depend on the availability of workers—unemployed and new labor force entrants—to fill the jobs.

Not surprisingly, recent decades have seen sharp increases in the dispersion of relative price changes and productivity growth. Perhaps surprising, however, is the timing: Dispersion increased sharply *prior* to each major increase in job destruction, which in turn was often followed by an increase in job creation. Cross-correlations (not reported) indicate that every dispersion measure leads job destruction by one or more years. This general pattern of increased dispersion, increased job destruction, and then increased job creation seems broadly consistent with the view that the U.S. economy suffered a series of persistent, unfavorable allocative driving forces during this period.

Prior to the 1974–75 recession, all price dispersion increased dramatically, and productivity dispersion rose somewhat too. In each case, dispersion peaked one year ahead of job destruction. Prior to the 1980–82 recessionary period, all four dispersion measures rose again but this time much earlier, with dispersion peaking as early as 1978 (relative investment price changes) and job destruction peaking in 1983. The increase in price dispersion was much smaller than in the previous recession, but the increase in productivity dispersion was much larger. Prior to the 1986 peak in destruction (not an official period of economywide recession), dispersion increased in all but the output price change measure. Prior to the 1990–91 recession, dispersion increased in all measures except investment price changes, which was contemporaneously correlated with destruction. The increase was especially evident in materials prices, corroborating the view that inflationary pressures during this time began "in the pipeline" of materials and supplies distribution.

Implications and Extensions. The data indicate that relative price change and relative productivity growth become significantly more dispersed prior to large increases in job destruction and hence prior to recessions. The leading nature of the dispersion is significant. Unlike employment growth dispersion, which is correlated contemporaneously with the business cycle, dispersion in relative prices and dispersion in TFP growth lead the business cycle. Hence, it is much less likely that the business cycle causes the dispersion in relative price changes and TFP growth. Unlike stock price dispersion, which is based on expectations of economic activity and appears to lead the business cycle for relatively short horizons, dispersion in relative price changes and TFP growth can lead the business cycle by several years. Whether such a long lead is reasonable depends on how quickly agents learn about the dispersion, its permanence, and the costliness of responses to the dispersion, such as the shutdown and start-up of new plants.

Although a picture can be worth a thousand words, the evidence presented here is merely suggestive and obviously does not establish causality from reallocation to business cycles. It does establish, however, that the variables most expected to determine the allocation of factors across sectors do change significantly prior to significant increases in job destruction and reallocation, and prior to decreases in aggregate economic activity. Note, however, that even if dispersion in relative price change or productivity growth induces reallocation and reallocation causes a reduction in aggregate economic activity, it would be incorrect, strictly speaking, to conclude that reallocation causes business cycles. Instead, relative prices and productivity would be the causes, or driving forces, behind business cycles. Of course, this conclusion leaves unanswered the question of what causes dispersion in relative price change and productivity growth.

In any event, the results in this section clearly motivate further investigation. The data suggest that models purporting to explain gross job flows at the plant or sector level should take relative prices and productivity into account. Furthermore, the models must also explain the significant lag between changes in the incentives to reallocate and the actual reallocation. It seems reasonable to suspect that expectations, learning, investment irreversibility, adjustment costs, and other frictions will be important components of successful models.

Our plan is to continue investigating these issues at the detailed industry and plant levels. The main unexplained issue is whether the dispersion is actually causing the fluctuations in gross job flows associated with deliberate reallocation. The only way to resolve this issue is to examine whether relative prices and productivity are important explanatory variables for the job flow behavior of particular plants and industries. Specifically, we need to know whether job destruction is occurring in plants and industries where relative prices (productivity) are rising (falling), and whether job creation is occurring where relative prices (productivity) are falling (rising). In future research, we plan to investigate this by estimating dynamic labor demand models with panel data econometric techniques using industry-level data bases and the Longitudinal Research Database (LRD).

THE OUTLOOK FOR JOB REALLOCATION AND BUSINESS CYCLES

Undoubtedly, the primary drawback to incorporating reallocation into macroeconomic models and government policymaking is the lack of broad and timely gross job flow data. The best U.S. data source is the LRD, but the LRD data are several years behind (currently five) at best and available only for manufacturing. Although the Census Bureau is making good progress on releasing data on a more timely basis and in acquiring nonmanufacturing data, timely release of economywide gross job flows is years away. The U.S. Bureau of Labor Statistics is also making good progress on producing up-to-date gross job flow data, but release of these data is not imminent either.

New Proxies for Gross Job Flow Data

Fortunately, two proxies for gross job flows are available on a timely basis. One is a measure of job flows between 4-digit industries, as reported in Ritter (1993, 1994) and Haltiwanger and Schuh (1995). Between-industry job flows exhibit cyclical characteristics strikingly similar to those exhibited by within-industry and total gross job flows. Between-industry job flows still require fairly large data base maintenance and manipulation, but they provide job flows estimates within a few months of the current period and they cover the entire nonfarm U.S. economy.

A second, and previously unexploited, proxy for gross job flows comes from the National Association of Purchasing Managers (NAPM). The NAPM publishes data reflecting the assessments of about 350 purchasing managers in manufacturing and some nonmanufacturing industries about the qualitative change (higher, lower, or the same) in economic activity at their companies. Diffusion indexes are used to summarize the net change in employment, as well as production, inventories, deliveries, prices, and other variables for all NAPM companies. Underlying the diffusion indexes are "gross flow" measures representing the fraction of companies with higher or lower activity. Using the NAPM employment data, job creation (destruction) is proxied by the percentage of companies with higher (lower) employment.

Two key differences arise between the NAPM job flows and the LRD job flows. First, the NAPM job flows reflect the number of companies with increasing or decreasing employment, rather than the number of jobs actually being created or destroyed. Thus, if jobs are being created or destroyed disproportionately by certain types of companies (as the LRD data indicate they are), the NAPM job flows may be substantially biased. Only if all firms were the same size and employment adjustments the same magnitude would the NAPM job flows exactly mirror the actual gross job flows. Second, the unit of observation is a plant in the LRD but a company in the NAPM. Thus the NAPM proxy is an interfirm job flow measure that will understate the interplant measure from the LRD, but nothing is known yet about the relative cyclicality of interplant and interfirm job flows.

Despite potential measurement drawbacks, the NAPM job flows are readily available each month and for a long period of history, so it is worth seeing whether the NAPM and LRD job flows are closely correlated. Figure 16 plots the NAPM and LRD gross job flow data. Despite some differences, the NAPM job flows do a pretty decent job of proxying for the LRD job flows. The quarterly correlations for the seasonally adjusted data are 0.61 for creation, 0.77 for destruction, and 0.53 for reallocation. Visual inspection suggests the correlations are high enough to gauge the general pattern of recent reallocation behavior.

The NAPM data paint a somewhat different picture of gross job flow dynamics during the current expansion. Job destruction and reallocation have declined steadily since the last recession, as they typically do during expansions, but they are significantly higher than at this point in previous expansions. A particularly notable difference arises between the LRD and NAPM job destruction rates since the last recession, with NAPM destruction becoming increasingly larger than LRD destruction. A possible explanation for this wedge between LRD and NAPM destruction is that the anecdotes and speculation about nonmanufacturing experiencing greater churning this decade may be true (recall that NAPM includes some nonmanufacturing companies). Another interesting difference about this expansion is that job creation surged twice, peaking in 1994 and 1998. Unlike previous creation surges, these did *not* come on the heels of a large surge in job destruction.

One possible interpretation of this creation-led employment expansion, which has coincided with a surprising plunge in the unemployment rate, is that the economy has been experiencing *favorable* allocative driving forces rather than unfavorable ones. Recall that in allocative theories of fluctuations, the timing of creation and destruction may depend on whether allocative forces raise productivity and profitability in some sectors or lower productivity and profitability in some sectors. In the former case, job creation would rise—provided the available stock of workers was sufficient. And apparently it was. Not only did many unemployed workers become employed, but labor force growth surged simultaneously with the surges in creation. So why did labor force growth surge? Answers to this question, which require detailed investigation beyond the scope of this paper, may provide a better understanding of the nature of recent reallocation.

Predictions for Reallocation and Recessions

Although current rates of job reallocation are moderate, the outlook for job reallocation is less sanguine. Absent a formal model, we cannot provide rigorous forecasts of reallocation. Nevertheless, based on the analysis in this paper, we can provide a judgmental view of the likelihood that job reallocation will play a role in future economic fluctuations.

Figure 16
Comparison of LRD and NAPM Gross Job Flows

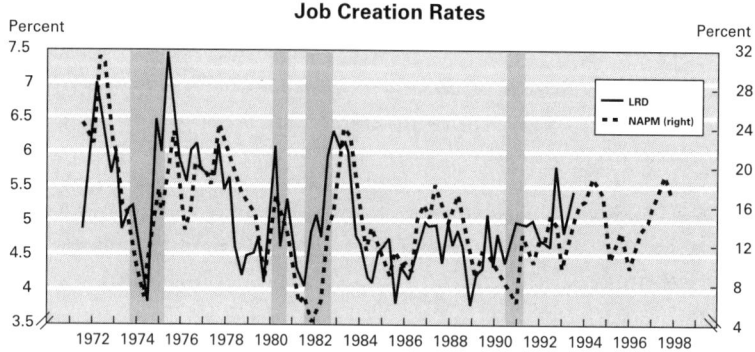

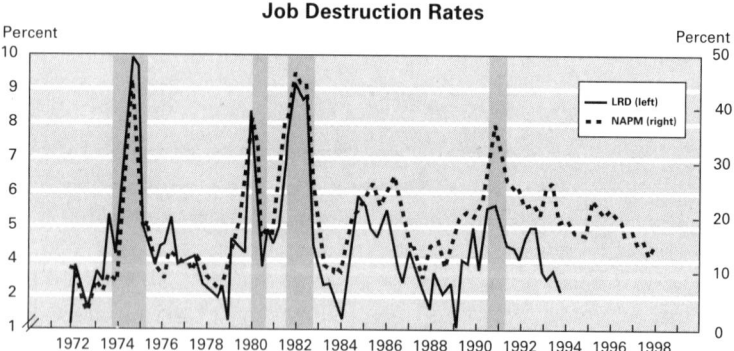

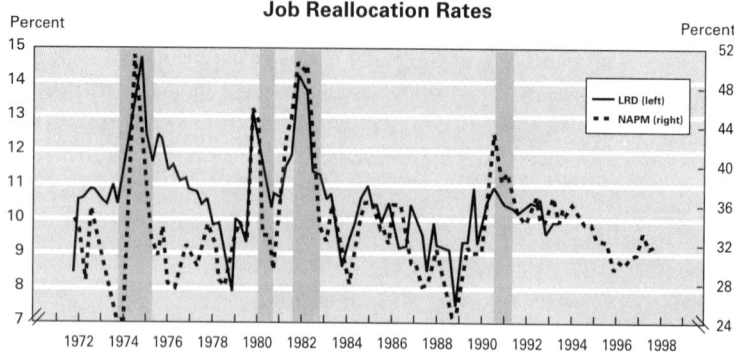

Source: Census Longitudinal Research Database and National Association of Purchasing Management.

Despite the relatively mild reallocation during the most recent recession, the propensity for reallocation to occur during recessions does not appear to have declined over the postwar period. Thus, it seems safe to predict that reallocation will rise again when the next recession occurs. Of course, if aggregate shocks cause business cycles and reallocation, then reallocation is irrelevant for predicting recessions, although the nature and extent of reallocation may be important for understanding the appropriate policy responses to the recession. But if reallocation causes business cycles, it is critical to be on the lookout for factors determining reallocation.

Several factors could induce job reallocation in the foreseeable future. Oil prices, now low and stable, always have the potential for disruptive increases. Regional conditions are currently quite evenly balanced throughout the country, but events could change that (although it is hard to predict what events). The Asian economic crisis could sow the seeds of reallocation in at least two ways. First, the violent swings in exchange rates affect the relative prices of goods imported from, and exported to, Asia. Furthermore, Asian demand for U.S. exports is already sagging along with Asia's output. Together, these developments directly affect plants and sectors that trade with Asia differentially from those that do not trade. Second, these direct effects, especially the price effects, are likely to indirectly impact plants that compete in the same industries with exporting and importing plants. Indeed, more generally, increasing globalization of the U.S. economy brings with it new dimensions for allocative driving forces.

Another source of potential reallocative activity is the considerable amount of retooling required in computer-intensive plants and sectors associated with the Year 2000 (Y2K) problem. Like the case of oil as a factor of production, the usage of computers in production is unevenly distributed across industries (see McGuckin and Stiroh 1998). Consequently, investment patterns and production disruptions—*if* they happen—will be quite uneven across industries. If work on this problem is spread out gradually, the reallocative activity may not cause fluctuations. But the point-in-time nature of the problem at least admits the possibility of significant trouble. Also, the recent humorous story about loads of personal pagers going down as a result of satellite trouble contains a serious strand as well. The increasing reliance on such high-tech devices in a wide range of telecommunications applications produces a vulnerability to concentrated problems. Recent government mandating of a changeover to high-definition TV falls into this category as well.

To summarize, we ask: Will the variables that induce high rates of job reallocation change again dramatically in the future? Probably. With the possible exception of monetary policy, which during the past 15 years may have become increasingly proficient in adjusting to economic conditions, nothing has occurred recently to lead us to believe that the factors determining reallocation have somehow become more stable or less likely to cause allocative fluctuations. Thus, proponents of the idea that reallocation causes business cycle fluctuations would almost surely agree that business cycles are *not* dead nor likely dampened. Instead, the relative calm since the early 1980s has been the result of relatively mild changes in the incentives to reallocate, incentives that generally cannot be controlled well by government policy. It is likely that, sooner or later, incentives to reallocate will arise and that the process of reallocation may cause or contribute to a recession.

References

Abel, Andrew B. and Janice C. Eberly. 1997. "The Mix and Scale of Factors with Irreversibility and Fixed Costs of Investment." NBER Working Paper No. 6148.
Abraham, Katharine G. and Lawrence F. Katz. 1986. "Cyclical Unemployment: Sectoral Shifts or Aggregate Disturbances?" *Journal of Political Economy*, 94(3), pp. 507–22.
Anderson, Patricia, M. and Bruce D. Meyer. 1994. "The Extent and Consequences of Job Turnover." *Brookings Papers on Economic Activity: Microeconomics*, pp. 177–236.
Baily, Martin Neil, Eric J. Bartelsman, and John Haltiwanger. 1996. "Labor Productivity: Structural Change and Cyclical Dynamics." NBER Working Paper No. 5503.
Baily, Martin Neil, Charles Hulten, and David Campbell. 1992. "Productivity Dynamics in Manufacturing Plants." *Brookings Papers on Economic Activity: Microeconomics*, pp. 187–249.
Bartelsman, Eric J. and Wayne Gray. 1996. "The NBER Manufacturing Productivity Database." NBER Technical Working Paper No. 205.
Bertola, Guiseppe and Ricardo J. Caballero. 1990. "Kinked Adjustment Costs and Aggregate Dynamics." In Olivier Blanchard and Stanley Fischer, eds., *NBER Macroeconomic Annual*. Cambridge, MA and London: The MIT Press.
Black, Fischer. 1987. *Business Cycles and Equilibrium*. New York and Oxford: Basil Blackwell.
Blanchard, Olivier and Peter Diamond. 1989. "The Beveridge Curve." *Brookings Papers on Economic Activity*, 1:1989, pp. 1–60.
_____. 1990. "The Cyclical Behavior of the Gross Flows of U.S. Workers." *Brookings Papers on Economic Activity*, 2:1990, pp. 85–143.
Blanchard, Olivier and Lawrence F. Katz. 1992. "Regional Evolutions." *Brookings Papers on Economic Activity*, 1, pp. 1–61.
Bresnahan, Timothy F. and Valerie A. Ramey. 1993. "Segment Shifts and Capacity Utilization in the U.S. Automobile Industry." *The American Economic Review*, 83(2), pp. 213–18.
Caballero, Ricardo J. and Eduardo M.R.A. Engel. 1993. "Microeconomic Adjustment Hazards and Aggregate Dynamics." *Quarterly Journal of Economics*, 108(2), pp. 359–83.
Caballero, Ricardo J., Eduardo M.R.A. Engel, and John C. Haltiwanger. 1995. "Plant-Level Adjustment and Aggregate Investment Dynamics." *Brookings Papers on Economic Activity*, 2:1995, pp. 1–39.
_____. 1997. "Aggregate Employment Dynamics: Building from Microeconomic Evidence." *The American Economic Review*, 87(1), pp. 115–37.
Caballero, Ricardo J. and Mohamad L. Hammour. 1994. "The Cleansing Effect of Recessions." *The American Economic Review*, 84(5), pp. 1350–68.
_____. 1996. "On the Timing and Efficiency of Creative Destruction." *Quarterly Journal of Economics*, 111(3), pp. 805–52.
_____. 1998. "Improper Churn: Social Costs and Macroeconomic Consequences." Unpublished paper.
Campbell, Jeffrey R. and Jonas D.M. Fisher. 1998. "Aggregate Employment Fluctuations with Microeconomic Asymmetries." Unpublished paper.
Campbell, Jeffrey R. and Kenneth Kuttner. 1996. "Macroeconomic Effects of Employment Reallocation." *Carnegie-Rochester Conference Series on Public Policy*, 44, pp. 87–116.

Cooper, Russell W. and John Haltiwanger. 1993. "The Aggregate Implications of Machine Replacement: Theory and Evidence." *The American Economic Review* 83(3), pp. 360–82.
____. 1998. "On the Nature of Adjustment Costs for Capital and Labor." Unpublished paper.
Davis, Steven J. 1987. "Fluctuations in the Pace of Labor Reallocation." *Carnegie-Rochester Conference Series on Public Policy* 27, pp. 335–402.
Davis, Steven J. and John Haltiwanger. 1990. "Gross Job Creation and Destruction: Microeconomic Evidence and Macroeconomic Implications." In Olivier Blanchard and Stanley Fisher, eds., *NBER Macroeconomics Annual*, pp. 123–68. Cambridge, MA and London: The MIT Press.
____. 1992. "Gross Job Creation, Gross Job Destruction, and Employment Reallocation." *Quarterly Journal of Economics*, 107(3), pp. 819–63
____. 1995. "Measuring Gross Worker and Job Flows." NBER Working Paper No. 5133.
____. 1996. "Driving Forces and Employment Fluctuations." NBER Working Paper No. 5775.
____. 1997. "Sectoral Job Creation and Destruction Responses to Oil Price Changes and Other Shocks." Unpublished paper.
____. 1998. "Gross Job Flows." In Orley Ashenfelter and David Card, eds., *Handbook of Labor Economics* (forthcoming).
Davis, Steven J., John C. Haltiwanger, and Scott Schuh. 1990. "Published versus sample statistics from the asm: Implications for the l & d." In *1990 Proceedings of the Business and Economic Statistics Section*, American Statistical Association, pp. 52–61.
____. 1996. *Job Creation and Destruction*. Cambridge, MA: The MIT Press.
Davis, Steven J., Prakash Loungani, and Ramamohan Mahidhara. 1997. "Regional Labor Fluctuations: Oil Shocks, Military Spending, and Other Driving Forces." Unpublished paper.
Debelle, Guy and Owen Lamont. 1997. "Relative Price Variability and Inflation: Evidence from U.S. Cities." *Journal of Political Economy*, 105(1), pp. 132–52.
Diamond, Peter. 1981. "Mobility Costs, Frictional Unemployment, and Efficiency." *Journal of Political Economy*, 89(4), pp. 798–812.
Dunne, Timothy, John Haltiwanger, and Kenneth R. Troske. 1996. "Technology and Jobs: Secular Changes and Cyclical Dynamics." NBER Working Paper No. 5656.
Dunne, Timothy, Mark Roberts, and Larry Samuelson. 1989. "The Growth and Failure of U.S. Manufacturing Plants." *Quarterly Journal of Economics*, 104(4), pp. 671–98.
Foote, Christopher L. 1998. "Trend Employment Growth and the Bunching of Job Creation and Destruction." *Quarterly Journal of Economics* (forthcoming).
Foster, Lucia, John Haltiwanger, and C.J. Krizan. 1998. "Aggregate Productivity Growth: Lessons from Microeconomic Evidence." Unpublished paper.
Garibaldi, Pietro. 1997. "The Asymmetric Effects of Monetary Policy on Job Creation and Destruction." *IMF Staff Papers*, 44(4), pp. 557–84.
Gertler, Mark and Simon Gilchrist. 1994. "Monetary Policy, Business Cycles, and the Behavior of Small Manufacturing Firms." *Quarterly Journal of Economics*, 109(2), pp. 309–40.
Gourinchas, Pierre-Olivier. 1998. "Exchange Rates, Job Creation and Destruction." In Olivier Blanchard and Stanley Fisher, eds., *NBER Macroeconomics Annual* (forthcoming).
Granger, C.W.J. 1969. "Investigating Causal Relations by Econometric Models and Cross-Spectral Models." *Econometrica*, 37, pp. 424–38.
Greenwood, Jeremy, Glenn M. MacDonald, and Guang-Jia Zhang. 1996. "The Cyclical Behavior of Job Creation and Job Destruction: A Sectoral Model." *Economic Theory*, 7(1), pp. 95–112.
Hall, Robert E. 1979. "A Theory of the Natural Unemployment Rate and the Duration of Employment." *Journal of Monetary Economics*, 5(2), pp. 153–69.
____. 1991. "Labor Demand, Labor Supply, and Employment Volatility." In Olivier Blanchard and Stanley Fisher, eds., *NBER Macroeconomics Annual*, pp. 17–47. Cambridge, MA and London: The MIT Press.
____. 1995. "Lost Jobs." *Brookings Papers on Economic Activity*, 1:1995, pp. 221–56.
____. 1997a. "Impulses, Amplification, and Persistence." In John Taylor and Michael Woodford, eds., *Handbook of Macroeconomics* (forthcoming).

_____. 1997b. "The Temporal Concentration of Job Destruction and Inventory Liquidation: A Theory of Recessions." Unpublished paper.
_____. 1998. "Labor Market Frictions and Employment Fluctuations." NBER Working Paper No. 6501.
Haltiwanger, John and Scott Schuh. 1998. "Macroeconomic Implications of the Relationship Between Plant and Industry Job Flows." Unpublished paper.
Hamermesh, Daniel S. 1989. "Labor Demand and the Structure of Adjustment Costs." *The American Economic Review*, 79(4), pp. 674–89.
Hamilton, James D. 1988. "A Neoclassical Model of Unemployment and the Business Cycle." *Journal of Political Economy*, 96(3), pp. 593–617.
Hopenhayn, Hugo and Richard Rogerson. 1993. "Job Turnover and Policy Evaluation: A General Equilibrium Analysis." *Journal of Political Economy*, 101(5), October, pp. 915–38.
Horvath, Michael. 1998a. "Business Cycles and the Failure of Marginal Firms." Unpublished paper.
_____. 1998b. "Cyclicality and Sectoral Linkages: Aggregate Fluctuations from Independent Sectoral Shocks." Unpublished paper.
_____. 1998c. "Sectoral Shocks and Aggregate Fluctuations." Unpublished paper.
Johnson, Harry. 1962. *The Two-Sector Model of General Equilibrium*. London: George Allen & Unwin Ltd.
Kydland, Finn and Edward Prescott. 1982. "Time to Build and Aggregate Fluctuations." *Econometrica*, 50, pp. 1345–70.
Lane, Julia, Alan Isaac, and David Stevens. 1994. "Job Flows, Worker Flows, and Churning." Centre for Economic Policy Research Discussion Paper No. 1125.
Leonard, Jonathan S. 1987. "In the Wrong Place at the Wrong Time: The Extent of Frictional and Structural Unemployment." In Kevin Lang and Jonathan Leonard, eds., *Unemployment & the Structure of Labor Markets*. New York: Basil Blackwell.
Lilien, David. 1982. "Sectoral Shifts and Cyclical Unemployment. *Journal of Political Economy*, 90(4), pp. 777–93.
Liu, Lili and James R. Tybout. 1996. "Productivity Growth in Chile and Colombia: The Role of Entry, Exit, and Learning." In Mark J. Roberts and James R. Tybout, eds., *Industrial Evolution in Developing Countries: Micro Patterns of Turnover, Productivity, and Market Structure*. New York: Oxford University Press.
Long, John B. and Charles Plosser. 1983. "Real Business Cycles." *Journal of Political Economy*, 91(1), pp. 39–69.
Loungani, Prakash. 1986. "Oil Price Shocks and the Dispersion Hypothesis." *The Review of Economics and Statistics*, 62(3), pp. 536–39.
Loungani, Prakash, Mark Rush, and William Tave. 1990. "Stock Market Dispersion and Unemployment." *Journal of Monetary Economics*, 25(3), pp. 367–88.
Loungani, Prakash and Bharat Trehan. 1997. "Explaining Unemployment: Sectoral vs. Aggregate Shocks." Federal Reserve Bank of San Francisco *Economic Review*, (1), pp. 3–15.
Lucas, Robert E., Jr. and Edward Prescott. 1974. "Equilibrium Search and Unemployment." *Journal of Economic Theory*, 7(2), pp. 188–209.
McGuckin, Robert H. and Kevin J. Stiroh. 1998. "Computers, Productivity, and Growth: Explaining the Computer Productivity Paradox." The Conference Board Economic Research Report 1213-98-RR.
Mortensen, Dale T. 1982. "The Matching Process as a Non-Cooperative Bargaining Game." In John McCall, ed., *The Economics of Information and Uncertainty*. Chicago: University of Chicago Press.
_____. 1994. "The Cyclical Behavior of Job and Worker Flows." *Journal of Economic Dynamics and Control*, 18(6), pp. 1121–42.
Mortensen, Dale T. and Christopher A. Pissarides. 1994. "Job Creation and Job Destruction in the Theory of Unemployment." *Review of Economic Studies*, 61(208), pp. 397–415.
Olley, G. Steven and Ariel Pakes. 1996. "The Dynamics of Productivity in the Telecommunications Equipment Industry." *Econometrica*, 64(6), pp. 1263–97.
Ritter, Joseph. 1993. "Measuring Labor Market Dynamics: Gross Flows of Workers and Jobs." Federal Reserve Bank of St. Louis *Review*, 75(6), pp. 39–57.
_____. 1994. "Job Creation and Destruction: The Dominance of Manufacturing." Federal Reserve Bank of St. Louis *Review*, 76(5), pp. 39–57.

Rogerson, Richard. 1987. "An Equilibrium Model of Sectoral Reallocation." *Journal of Political Economy*, 95(4), pp. 824–34.
Schumpeter, J.A. 1942. *Capitalism and Democracy*. New York: Harper and Brothers.
Sims, Christopher A. 1972. "Money, Income, and Causality." *The American Economic Review*, 62(4), pp. 540–52.
Troske, Kenneth. 1993. "The Dynamic Adjustment Process of Firm Entry and Exit in Manufacturing and Finance, Insurance and Real Estate." *Journal of Law and Economics*, 39(2), pp. 705–35.
Veracierto, Marcelo. 1998. "Plant-Level Irreversible Investment and Equilibrium Business Cycles." Federal Reserve Bank of Chicago *Working Paper* WP-98–1.

DISCUSSION

Ricardo J. Caballero*

Scott Schuh and Robert Triest have written a useful and interesting paper, collecting existing evidence on job flows and providing us with a few brand new facts to chew on. I wish to touch on some of the many good things in the paper, but it comes with the discussant's job description that I must focus on the parts of the paper that I view as more problematic.

Few economists would deny that an ongoing process of factor reallocation is essential to the economic growth and prosperity of a market economy. The field is more divided on whether or not the churn (that is, the ongoing processes of creation and destruction) has a significant effect on the economy at *business cycle* frequencies. But even if we accept its relevance to the business cycle, it is a large leap to claim that reallocation shocks are a substantial *source* of business cycles, at least in the United States.

Perhaps constrained by the *shocks* theme of the conference, Schuh and Triest chose to emphasize this last, most debatable claim in many passages of their paper, including the introduction. I suspect this is a mistake at this stage, when we still have plenty to learn about the two less controversial claims, and the intermediate one in particular. Indeed, many of the recent developments in the reallocation literature relate to the intermediate claim, that is, that the job reallocation process is important for business cycle considerations. Moreover, most of the survey and "testing" part of the paper is not about models that are based on reallocation shocks, but about the response of the churn to changes in business cycle conditions. I share their eagerness to go beyond this stage

---

*Professor of Economics, Massachusetts Institute of Technology.

and identify actual reallocation shocks; however, I also believe that with rare exceptions, which mostly do not apply to the modern United States, understanding the basic behavior of the reallocation process over the business cycle is a precondition to finding reliable "reallocation shocks."

Broadly, the paper has four ingredients: (i) A central supporting fact: "Job reallocation is strongly countercyclical; that is, job reallocation increases during recessions and decreases during expansions"; (ii) A central question: "Do reallocation and restructuring actually cause fluctuations?"; (iii) A brief taxonomy of theories of reallocation over the business cycle; and (iv) An organization of existing and new evidence. The latter has two main purposes: (a) to "test" the theories in (iii), and (b) to find traces of reallocation shocks.

I intend to focus my discussion on (i) and (ii), because I suspect that is where the interest of a broader audience lies, but I must say a few words about (iii) and (iv.a) before doing so. As for (iv.b), the evidence presented, as the authors acknowledge, is still quite preliminary and inconclusive. Among the new facts presented, however, I find the evidence in their section on relative prices quite interesting and potentially promising. Perhaps future versions of the paper, or follow-up papers, may reward us by focusing on this evidence more extensively.

Minor Quibbles

On Models of Reallocation

Under the heading "Theories Based on Aggregate Driving Forces," the authors discuss modern theories of reorganization over the business cycle. Their first group consists of "opportunity cost" stories, where recessions offer a chance to reorganize at low cost. The work of Hall (1991), Davis and Haltiwanger (1990), Cooper and Haltiwanger (1993) and Caballero and Hammour (1994, 1996, 1998) is all merged here. Although most of these theories are indeed opportunity cost-type stories, my work with Mohamad Hammour should not be included in this category. In our models, production units are "cleansed" not because recessions are times when it is relatively cheap to do so, but because it becomes privately too expensive to maintain the least (broadly defined) efficient units. This is an important conceptual difference. Moreover, one of the main messages of this line of research is that this cleansing is often *not* socially efficient. Rather than translating into useful and desirable reallocation, it often results in wasteful unemployment. This point hints at one of the issues I will raise later on: It seems odd to call a surge in destruction an increase in reallocation if it is not matched by a surge in creation. Yet the main measure of reallocation used in this paper does precisely that.

On Tests of Reallocation Models

One should never test a theory along dimensions the theory is not designed to explain.[1] The theories reviewed by Schuh and Triest are about job flows over the business cycle; they need an additional mechanism to generate an ongoing churn. It is a modeling tautology to argue that reallocation must move from worst to best units, once one considers all of the shadow values and rents faced by private agents. If the concern is not with the precise source of churn but with the cyclical behavior of job flows, then it seems perfectly fine to index the ranking of units by a catchall variable called productivity. But it seems less reasonable to accept or reject these theories on the basis of this reduced-form variable.

It does make sense, however, to explore what this reduced form variable is, in reality. Do agents respond to the right social shadow values? Are separations privately and/or socially efficient? Do spurious rents play an important role in the ranking of production units? Do rents and inefficiencies become worse during recessions? and so on. I suspect these are the questions the authors should be trying to address, and perhaps this section of the paper will eventually shed light on these important issues.

And it also makes sense to explore the relevance of the productivity dimension, as one of the ingredients determining the ranking of production units. In doing so, however, one needs to keep the following in mind: First, the productivity effects generated by "cleansing" models over the business cycle are an order of magnitude smaller than the fluctuations in productivity observed over the business cycle. As discussed in Caballero and Hammour (1994), labor hoarding and other traditional effects fully dominate cleansing mechanisms at high frequencies. Second, most of the evidence presented examines reallocation and productivity performance across sectors. In fact, cross-sectional comparisons require a multisector model as metric, and in such a model, even a purely neoclassical one, productivity is no longer a sufficient statistic. The correct variable to look at in this case is not productivity but revenue or profits. Recall Baumol's old explanation of factor reallocation from agriculture to manufacturing. If demands are sufficiently inelastic, then the sector with the *fastest* productivity growth will shed more labor in favor of lagging sectors. In equilibrium, relative price effects will dominate relative productivity effects. The same argument is used today to explain the ongoing reallocation from manufacturing to services.[2]

---

[1] Unless, of course, that dimension is crucial for the functioning of the model, which is not the case here, as the discussion in the main text contends.

[2] Moreover, using cross-sectional data without controlling for a series of individual effects may not be entirely appropriate.

Is Reallocation Strongly Countercyclical?

The main supporting fact of the paper represents a widely held view: "Job reallocation is strongly countercyclical, that is, job reallocation increases during recessions and decreases during expansions."

I am not sure the fact is indeed a fact.

I am a great admirer of the Davis-Haltiwanger and Davis-Haltiwanger-Schuh work on job flows; they have created a literature on their own and have fed the imagination of theorists with great force. But I have always disagreed with using the words "job reallocation" to describe the sum of job creation and destruction.[3] As they have so thoroughly documented, and as many others seem to be replicating all over the world, manufacturing job destruction rises dramatically during recessions, while job creation declines much more moderately. The sum, therefore, rises during recessions.

But why should a surge in job destruction be called an increase in job reallocation? I suspect that part of the answer to this question lies in what I would describe as a *"dynamic fallacy of composition."* If an individual loses a job, his or her employment status can only be recovered by the creation of another job.[4] Thus at the *microeconomic* level, an act of destruction must yield an act of creation along a reemployment path. The fallacy lies in the extension of this logic to the aggregate economy. A surge in *aggregate* destruction may be offset by a compensating decline in destruction later on. Such a process would maintain the stationarity of employment with no change in the aggregate rate of job creation; many other combinations are possible (see below). This lack of connection between an initial surge in aggregate destruction and the path of aggregate creation is fully consistent with the tight connection between creation and destruction at the microeconomic level, where jobs lost by specific individuals are recovered through the normal churn process.

In a recent paper (Caballero and Hammour 1998) we have explored this issue in some detail. We use the expression "turbulence" to refer to situations where cumulative destruction is positive after a full recession-recovery episode.[5] The opposite phenomenon, where cumulative destruction turns negative as the recession-recovery cycle is completed, we describe as "chill."

---

[3] Davis-Haltiwanger-Schuh define a measure they call "excess reallocation" as the difference between the sum of the flows and the absolute value of the net flow. This measure is less subject to my criticism below, but unfortunately the literature has chosen to focus more on the measure of job reallocation without the net correction.

[4] Leaving aside standard job reshuffling.

[5] Note that we could use cumulative creation instead of destruction, since they must be equal if employment is stationary. This is the case in post-1960s U.S. manufacturing.

In the least structural part of that paper, we estimate a fairly standard semi-structural VAR:

$$\begin{bmatrix} N \\ D \end{bmatrix} = A(L) \begin{bmatrix} \epsilon^a \\ \epsilon^r \end{bmatrix}$$

where $A(L) = A_0 + A_1 L + A_2 L + \ldots$, N and D are manufacturing employment and job destruction, respectively, and ϵ^a and ϵ^r represent i.i.d. innovations that correspond to aggregate and reallocation shocks, respectively. Besides normalizations, achieving identification requires two additional restrictions. For this purpose, we assumed that the two innovations are independent of each other, and that at impact a recessionary shock raises destruction and lowers creation. Based on Davis and Haltiwanger (1996), we set the relative size of the absolute response of destruction compared to creation to 1.6, which is roughly the value that maximizes the contribution of aggregate shocks to net employment fluctuations.

Figure 1 here reproduces Figure 5.3 in Caballero and Hammour (1998). The first column presents the impulse response to a recessionary shock that yields a cumulative effect on (minus) employment equivalent to the cumulative (economywide) unemployment generated during the 1974–75 recession.[6] The first two panels are rather familiar, and the bottom one contains our results on cumulative flows. After the familiar short-term turbulence, there is clear evidence of a chill. Bootstraps confirmed the statistical significance of this finding. It is this figure, together with a series of companion robustness experiments, that leads me to conjecture that the widespread view that job reallocation is countercyclical may be incorrect.

Why is this discussion of any interest to macroeconomists? Earlier in this century the "liquidationist" view of recessions had strong support. According to this argument, recessions are necessary to a healthy economy because they facilitate the reallocation of resources from least to most productive units. Although this view is much less prevalent today, I suspect that many see increased reallocation as the "silver lining" of recessions. I do not share this belief, at least for the United States. In the very short run, the observed turbulence is a mostly wasteful reallocation into unemployment or secondary jobs rather than into new opportunities. And after all is said and done, a recession-recovery cycle may yield *less* rather than *more* productivity-enhancing reallocation. In Caballero and Hammour (1998) we estimate that depressed cumulative reallocation may add as much as 30 to 40 percent to the "normal" unemployment costs of recessions.

---

[6] The impulse responses for job creation are obtained from the identity $\Delta N = H - D$.

Figure 1
Impulse Responses to a Recessionary Shock

(minus) Employment

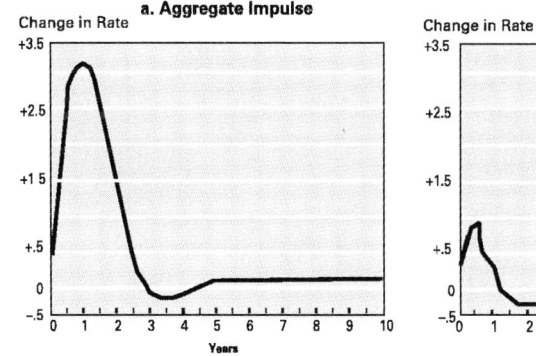
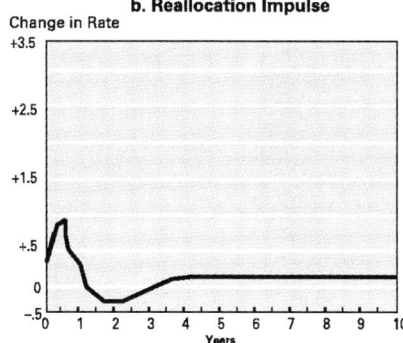

Job Creation and Destruction

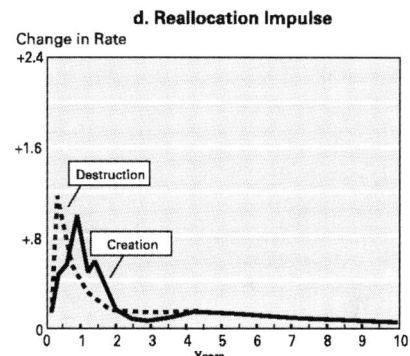

Cumulative Job Creation and Destruction

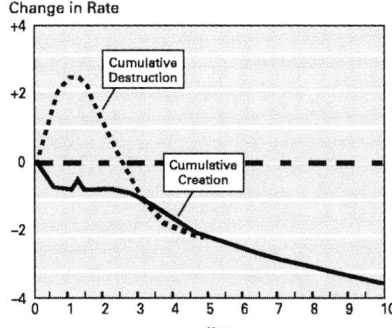
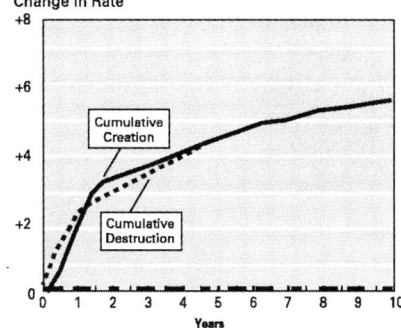

Source: Caballero and Hammour 1998, Figure 5.3.

Do Reallocation Shocks Actually Cause Fluctuations?

In Eastern Europe and other economies experiencing deep transformation of their productive structures, the answer to this question must be a clear yes. In the United States, on the other hand, the answer is much less clear.

The second column in Figure 1 has one possible answer. It shows the impulse response of (minus) employment, job flows, and cumulative flows to a reallocation shock of the same size (in terms of own standard deviations) as the aggregate shock. A comparison of panels (a) and (b) reveals that the contribution of reallocation shocks to net employment fluctuations is substantially less than that of aggregate shocks. Note, however, that this is not the case for *gross* flows and their accumulation, where reallocation shocks play an important role.[7]

Nonetheless, it is certainly possible that reallocation shocks may indeed be important to certain episodes of aggregate employment change. The unusual nature of the most recent recession may have been the result of a shift in the pattern of reallocation. Figures 2a and 2b, which show the shocks decompositions of the VAR presented above, reflect fairly large (relative to aggregate) reallocation shocks around the recession-recovery years. This result is also consistent with the persistent excess destruction during this episode highlighted by Schuh and Triest in their paper.

But more fundamentally, what are these reallocation shocks? Changes in the degree of job protection, or a dramatic departure from existing relative prices or business practices, qualify and have played important roles in many countries. But in the United States these shocks seem small enough that they may well come from modeling errors. Figure 3 presents the results of running the same VAR as in Figure 1, but using artificial data generated by a model with reasonable labor and financial market frictions subject to aggregate shocks only, calibrated to match a series of labor market features of the U.S. economy. Despite the fact that the true model was hit only by aggregate shocks, the VAR identified reallocation shocks that are comparable in magnitude and effects on aggregate employment to those found in the data.[8] I believe

---

[7] As detailed above, the identifying assumption made in the VAR results presented here corresponds to that which maximizes the relative contribution of aggregate shocks to net employment fluctuations, according to the careful study in Davis and Haltiwanger (1990). Thus, a more accurate characterization of the comparison of the two columns in Figure 1 is that it is possible to generate a configuration of parameters such that reallocation shocks are not very important for aggregate employment fluctuations.

[8] This experiment generates the right shape in the response of gross flows and their accumulation, but not enough amplitude. This is consistent with the finding in Caballero, Engel, and Haltiwanger (1997) where, using detailed microeconomic data, we reached the

**Figure 2
Shocks Decompositions of the Model**

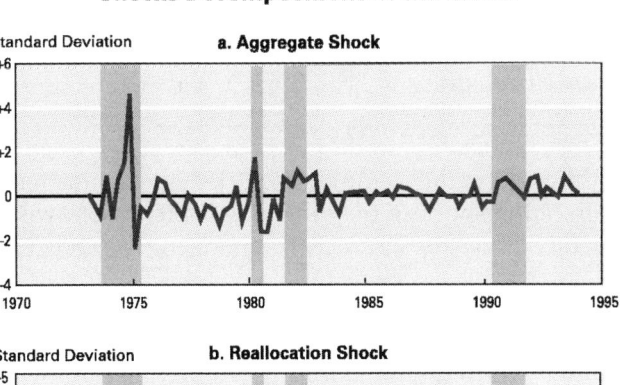

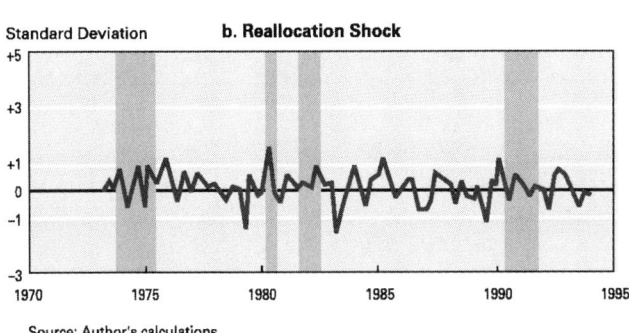

Source: Author's calculations.

almost any sensible model we write down will have enough nonlinearities, due to the natural asymmetry in both financial and labor market constraints, to "invent" reallocation shocks whenever the linear nature of VARs faces an intricate nonlinear response.

I wonder whether such a fragile decomposition is worth it. We may be better off sticking to shocks we can actually see, like oil prices, interest rates, liquidity, fiscal policy, capital flows, and so on.[9] All of these shocks will have "aggregate" and "reallocation" components, and exactly how they interact may be idiosyncratic enough that not much may be learned from pseudo-canonical decompositions and labels.

---

conclusion that reallocation shocks are not likely to be responsible for a substantial fraction of aggregate employment fluctuations, but they seem to account for an important fraction of gross flows fluctuations, especially job creation.

[9] See Davis and Haltiwanger (1997) for a shift in this direction. This is also a merit of the current paper.

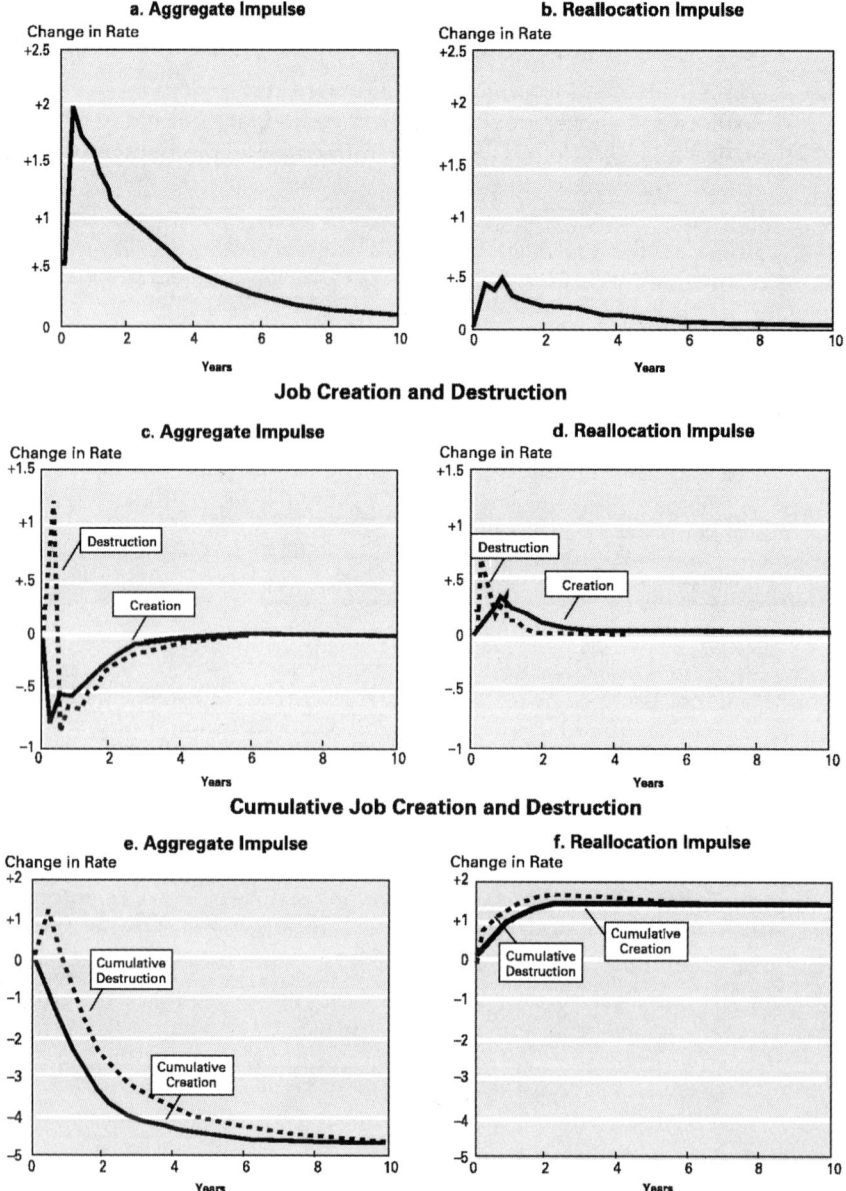

Figure 3
Impulse Responses Using Model-Generated Data

Source: VAR used in Figure 1, using model-generated data. See the text.

Conclusion

Let me summarize my views on this paper and the reallocation literature:

- This paper provides a useful organization of existing and new facts on job flows. Further investigation of a few of the correlations found, especially those between price dispersion and reallocation, seems warranted and may prove rewarding.
- Reallocation shocks per se, real or invented, are not likely to have played a large role in U.S. net manufacturing employment fluctuations over the last 30 years.
- The story may be quite different for *gross* flows and their accumulation. Furthermore, the change in the churn rate caused by these reallocation shocks may have important welfare costs or benefits not captured in unemployment.
- Having said this, I have lost some of my belief in the usefulness of a canonical decomposition in terms of aggregate and reallocation shocks. Realistic microeconomic frictions and heterogeneity will transform almost any observed shock into a complex and highly variable mix of both "canonical shocks."
- This is not to say that we should not look at the cyclical aspect of the reallocation *process*. On the contrary, the reallocation process seems to interact and correlate in important ways with the business cycle. This observation makes an analysis of the churn central to the modern study of economic fluctuations and their cost. I find it difficult to consider questions such as: What is the natural rate of unemployment? or What are the cost and incidence of recessions? without thinking about the reallocation process and its obstacles.

References

Caballero, Ricardo J. and Mohamad L. Hammour. 1994. "The Cleansing Effect of Recessions." *The American Economic Review*, 84, pp. 1350–68.
_____. 1996. "On the Timing and Efficiency of Creative Destruction." *Quarterly Journal of Economics*, 111(3), pp. 805–52.
_____. 1998. "Improper Churn: Social Costs and Macroeconomic Consequences." Mimeo, MIT, June.
Caballero, Ricardo J., Eduardo M.R.A. Engel, and John C. Haltiwanger. 1997. "Aggregate Employment Dynamics: Building from Microeconomic Evidence." *The American Economic Review*, 87(1), pp. 115–37.
Cooper, Russell W. and John C. Haltiwanger. 1993. "The Aggregate Implications of Machine Replacement: Theory and Evidence." *The American Economic Review*, 83(3), pp. 360–82.
Davis, Steven J., and John C. Haltiwanger. 1990. "Gross Job Creation and Destruction: Microeconomic Evidence and Macroeconomic Implications." *NBER Macroeconomics Annual*, 5, pp. 123–68.
_____. 1992. "Gross Job Creation, Gross Job Destruction and Employment Reallocation." *Quarterly Journal of Economics*, 107, pp. 819–64.
_____. 1996. "Driving Forces and Employment Fluctuations." Typescript, September.
_____. 1997. "Sectoral Job Creation and Destruction Responses to Oil Price Changes and Other Shocks." Mimeo, May.
Davis, Steven J., John C. Haltiwanger, and Scott Schuh. 1996. *Job Creation and Destruction*. Cambridge, MA: The MIT Press.
Hall, Robert E. 1991. "Labor Demand, Labor Supply, and Employment Volatility." In *NBER Macroeconomics Annual*, 6, pp. 17–46.

Discussion

Steven J. Davis*

The main ambition of Scott Schuh and Robert Triest's paper is to develop new evidence that helps us understand the relationship between reallocation activity and aggregate business cycle fluctuations. In my remarks on their paper, I first outline why that objective is a worthy one. I then offer a few suggestions intended to help the paper achieve that ambition.

Why Study Factor Reallocation Activity to Understand Business Cycles?

Market economies experience high rates of job creation and job destruction in almost every time period and sector.[1] Each year, many businesses expand and many others contract. New businesses constantly enter, while others abruptly exit or gradually disappear. Amid the turbulence of business growth and decline, jobs, workers, and capital are continually reallocated among competing activities, organizations, and locations.

Research in this general area has mushroomed in the past 20 years. The economics profession is now armed with some well-documented empirical regularities regarding the reallocation process and many intriguing facts. The past decade has also seen major strides in the theoretical analysis of how reallocation activity relates to business cycle fluctuations and longer-term growth. Davis and Haltiwanger (1998b),

---

*Professor of Economics, University of Chicago.
[1] For a compilation of the evidence that underlies this claim, see Davis and Haltiwanger (1998b). My comments borrow liberally from that paper.

Mortensen and Pissarides (1998), and Hall (1998) review empirical and theoretical research in this area.

Much of the reallocation process, and much of our interest in it, center on the labor market. The creation and destruction of jobs require workers to switch employers and to shuffle between employment and joblessness. Along the way, some workers suffer long unemployment spells or sharp declines in earnings; some retire early or temporarily leave the labor force to work at home or upgrade skills; some switch occupation or industry; some change residence to secure a new job, migrating short or long distances, often with considerable disruption to the lives and jobs of family members.

The workers who participate in this process differ greatly in the bundle of skills, capabilities, and career goals that they bring to the labor market; likewise, jobs differ greatly in the skill requirements, effort, and diligence that they demand from workers. The diversity of workers and jobs, and their large flows, underscore the truly breathtaking scale and complexity of the search, assignment, and reallocation processes carried out by the labor market and supporting institutions. The matching process and the prospect of match termination also influence the nature of ongoing employment relationships and the patterns of investment by both workers and firms.

On the macroeconomic level, the extent to which the reallocation and matching process operates smoothly determines, in large measure, the difference between successful and unsuccessful economic performance. The persistently high unemployment rates in France, Spain, and several other Western European countries over the past two decades point to the enormous costs of a partial breakdown in the reallocation and matching process.[2] The recent and ongoing transition to market-oriented economies in Eastern Europe and the former Soviet Union brought tremendous shifts in the industrial structure of employment and in the ownership and operation of business enterprises. Large differences in output movements, unemployment rates, private-sector expansion, and other performance indicators in formerly statist economies suggest that the efficiency of the restructuring and reallocation process varies greatly.[3] A different line of research focused on the U.S. economy shows that job reallocation from less to more productive plants plays a major role in longer-term productivity gains.[4]

How does this evidence and research on reallocation activity fit into

---

[2] Recent work on this topic includes Caballero and Hammour (1998), Cabrales and Hopenhayn (1997), Ljungqvist and Sargent (1998), Machin and Manning (1998), Millard and Mortensen (1997), and Nickell and Layard (1998).

[3] See Blanchard (1997) and Davis and Haltiwanger (1998b, section 8).

[4] Davis and Haltiwanger (1998b, section 7) and Foster, Haltiwanger, and Krizan (1998) review work in this area.

contemporary thinking about business cycles? I suspect that most policymakers and researchers acknowledge an occasional role for reallocation activity in business cycle fluctuations. It seems fair to say, however, that in their thinking about business cycles, most policymakers and researchers assign a secondary and modest role to the shocks that trigger fluctuations in reallocation activity and to the frictions involved in the reallocation process.

In any case, most formal models of business cycle phenomena certainly downplay the role of factor reallocation. Prevailing theories of the business cycle stress the role of aggregate shocks that induce broadly similar outcomes among households and among workers. See, for example, the fine collection of essays in Cooley (1995). These theories abstract from mobility costs and other frictions associated with the reallocation of jobs, workers, and capital. For the most part, they also abstract from heterogeneity on the household and firm sides of the economy. Because they abstract from reallocation frictions and heterogeneity, these theories of the business cycle are silent about the behavior of job, worker, and capital flows. For the same reason, they deliver rather stunted interpretations of unemployment fluctuations, capacity utilization, and related phenomena.

This state of affairs in thinking about business cycles shows some signs of change. Recent research on labor market flows, in particular, has greatly stimulated attention on the role of reallocation frictions and heterogeneity in aggregate economic fluctuations. Several facts about labor market flows contribute to this stimulus. I mention only a few. First, cyclical increases in unemployment predominantly reflect an increase in the number of workers who experience permanent job separations (for example, Table 5 in Davis and Haltiwanger 1998a). Second, postwar U.S. recessions are characterized by an increase in the number of workers who flow through the unemployment pool (Chapter 6 in Davis, Haltiwanger, and Schuh 1996). Third, recessions often coincide with sharp spikes in job destruction activity for major sectors of the economy (Davis and Haltiwanger 1998b, section 3.7). This burst of job destruction largely reflects permanent employment declines at the affected establishments (Davis and Haltiwanger 1998b, section 3.3). Fourth, job loss often leads to repeated spells of unemployment before the displaced worker settles into a new stable employment relationship. As a consequence, cyclical increases in job destruction lead to persistent increases in the aggregate unemployment rate (Hall 1995). These facts, and many others, point to an intimate relationship between aggregate fluctuations and the intensity of reallocation activity, as reflected in labor market flows.

When we follow the lead of these facts and build models that incorporate reallocation frictions and heterogeneity among production units, two central implications become evident: (i) aggregate shocks influence the intensity of reallocation activity, and (ii) shocks to the structure of factor demand can drive fluctuations in the economic aggregates that occupy the attention of business cycle researchers. The precise nature and strength of these influences depend on the details of the economic environment. Which details matter most, and why, are important questions on the business cycle research agenda.

Models with reallocation frictions also help to address some well-recognized shortcomings in prevailing theories of the business cycle. Standard equilibrium business cycle models generate little amplification of shocks for standard specifications of technology and preferences (Campbell 1994, Table 3). Standard models also fail to explain the persistence properties of aggregate fluctuations (Cogley and Nasson 1995; Rotemberg and Woodford 1996). As emphasized by Hall (1998), the introduction of labor market frictions improves the performance of standard models along both of these dimensions. Thus, further development of models that incorporate frictions in the reallocation of labor (and capital) promises to advance our understanding of business cycle behavior, even if we adopt a narrow definition of the subject that encompasses only the persistence and co-movement properties of aggregate output, employment, productivity, consumption, investment, and interest rates.

Which brings us back to the main ambition of the paper by Schuh and Triest: Careful descriptions of time variation in reallocation activity are essential guideposts for the development and evaluation of business cycle theories that explore the implications of reallocation frictions. Descriptive studies also lay the groundwork for structural analyses that interpret the data through the lens of an explicit theoretical model.

Describing Cyclical Variation in Reallocation Activity

Choosing an Index of Reallocation Intensity

Schuh and Triest treat the job reallocation rate—that is, the sum of creation and destruction rates—as equivalent to the intensity of reallocation activity. This position seems natural enough, especially given the terminology, and is harmless in many contexts. In a time-series context, however, the job reallocation rate is a questionable index of reallocation intensity. Job reallocation rises with simultaneous creation and destruction, but it also rises with the absolute value of the net employment change. For example, an economy with a 5 percent creation rate and no destruction has a 5 percent reallocation rate, whereas an economy with no creation and no destruction has a 0 percent reallocation rate. The first economy does not obviously involve more reallocation activity than the second. Another way to make the same point is to observe that the following two statements are equivalent: (i) the job reallocation rate and the net employment growth rate are negatively correlated over time; and

DISCUSSION

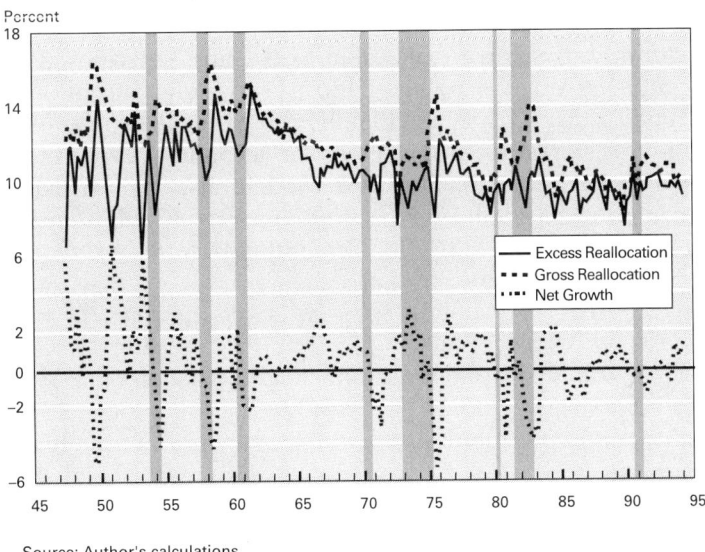

Figure 1
Quarterly U.S. Manufacturing Job Flows,
1st Quarter 1947 to 4th Quarter 1993

Source: Author's calculations.

(ii) the variance of the destruction rate exceeds the variance of the creation rate. It is not obvious that we want to treat statement (ii) as synonymous with the claim that reallocation intensity fluctuates countercyclically.

A closely related measure circumvents these difficulties: *Excess* job reallocation equals job reallocation minus the absolute value of the net employment change. Excess reallocation represents that part of job reallocation over and above the amount required to accommodate the net employment change. It is, in fact, an index of simultaneous creation and destruction. In the example above, the excess job reallocation rate is zero for both economies.

Does the distinction between job reallocation and excess reallocation matter much for the investigation by Schuh and Triest? A cursory investigation suggests an affirmative answer. Consider the quarterly job flow rates plotted in Figure 1 for the U.S. manufacturing sector from 1947 to 1993. The time-series behavior of the excess reallocation rate and the job reallocation rate differ substantially. In particular, the recessionary spikes in the job reallocation rate during the 1970s and 1980s are absent from the excess reallocation rate. Regressing the job reallocation rate on the net employment growth rate (and an intercept term) yields a slope coefficient of −0.17 with a standard error of 0.06. By this metric, countercyclic variation in reallocation intensity seems confirmed, although the regression coefficient is not especially large. However, a regression of the excess reallocation rate on the net growth rate yields a statistically insignificant coefficient of −0.08 (standard error of 0.06). I do not conclude from this regression that reallocation intensity is acyclical, because my simple bivariate specification ignores important matters of timing,[5] but it is fair to conclude that the choice between indexes matters. My previous remarks explain why excess reallocation is a better index of reallocation intensity.

Plant-Level Job Growth Regressions

The paper by Schuh and Triest is (over)stuffed with multi-way tabulations, multi-way frequency distributions, and time-series plots of frequency distribution components. In many instances, these statistical objects fail to convey a clear message and are difficult to digest. Frequency distributions and cross-tabulations are extremely useful tools for summarizing patterns in the data, but they lose much of their appeal when they do not elicit important patterns in a clear, easily digested form.

Plant-level job growth regressions offer an alternative descriptive tool that easily accommodates three (or many more) dimensions of data variation at the same time. Let me elaborate a bit on a regression approach to describing cyclical variation in reallocation activity.

Suppose we group plant-level observations into cells defined by employer characteristics like size and age and by time characteristics like calendar year or a business cycle indicator. Within each cell, we can calculate the job reallocation rate or the excess reallocation rate. We can then regress cell-level reallocation rates on cell characteristics to characterize the patterns of variation in the data.[6] We could, for example, characterize how the relationship between employer size and reallocation varies over the business cycle. In the same way, we can regress cell-level net job growth rates on cell characteristics to characterize the variation in net job growth behavior.

Once we adopt a cell-based regression approach, we will be tempted to define the cells ever more narrowly in order to more fully characterize conditional patterns of covariation in the data. Pursuing this idea to its limit, the cell-based approach leads to regressions of the plant-level absolute growth rate and net growth rate on plant-level characteristics.

---

[5] In fact, the excess reallocation rate is significantly negatively related to the sum of the current and four lagged net growth rates.
[6] See Dunne, Roberts, and Samuelson (1989) for a cell-based regression approach to plant-level entry and exit behavior.

DISCUSSION

The appropriate growth rate measure for this purpose equals the change in employment between period $t-1$ and t, divided by the simple average of employment in $t-1$ and t. This growth rate measure is symmetric about zero, lies in the closed interval $[-2, 2]$ and facilitates an integrated treatment of births and deaths.[7] It is identical to the log difference up to a second-order Taylor series expansion.

Figure 2, drawn from Davis and Haltiwanger (1998b), illustrates the approach. Using pooled data in the LRD for 1978, 1983, and 1988, we regressed plant-level growth rate observations on a battery of employer characteristics. In particular, the regression specification contains year effects, 4-digit industry effects, ownership-type effects, state effects, a quartic in the log of plant size interacted with detailed plant age categories, a quartic in plant-level energy intensity, a quartic in wages per worker, percentiles of the plant-level distribution of capital per worker (that is, 100 dummy variables), and a measure of plant-level product specialization.[8] Based on the regressions, and for selected employer characteristics, the figure plots (i) the predicted variation in the net employment growth rate and (ii) the difference between the predicted absolute growth rate and the absolute value of the predicted net growth rate. This difference yields the predicted excess reallocation rate as a function of employer characteristics. Each curve in the figure traces out the fitted relationship from the 5th to the 95th percentile of the variable on the horizontal axis.[9] In tracing out the curves, we evaluate all other variables at sample medians.

Several strong patterns emerge clearly from this figure. In particular, conditional on an extensive set of controls for other employer characteristics:

1. Net job growth declines as energy intensity increases.
2. Excess reallocation rises with energy intensity but only over the lower half of the energy intensity distribution.
3. Net growth declines with plant-level wages.
4. Excess reallocation declines with plant-level wages.
5. Net growth declines as capital intensity increases.
6. Excess reallocation rises with capital intensity.

Effects 1 to 6 are large, but in many cases they would be difficult to discern in simple cross-tabulations. For example, the figure shows a strong

---

[7] The job reallocation rate can be written as the size-weighted frequency distribution of the plant-level absolute growth rates (Davis and Haltiwanger 1998b, section 2.3). Hence, we should weight the regression observations by plant size, because larger plants account for a larger amount of job reallocation at any given growth rate.

[8] See section 4.2 in Davis and Haltiwanger (1998b) for precise variable definitions.

[9] The product specialization variable is grouped into seven ordered categories. Category 7 corresponds to complete specialization in a single 5-digit product classification. For the other variables, the line atop the horizontal axes depicts selected percentiles of its distribution in the sample.

Figure 2
Growth Rate and Excess Reallocation, by Employer Characteristics

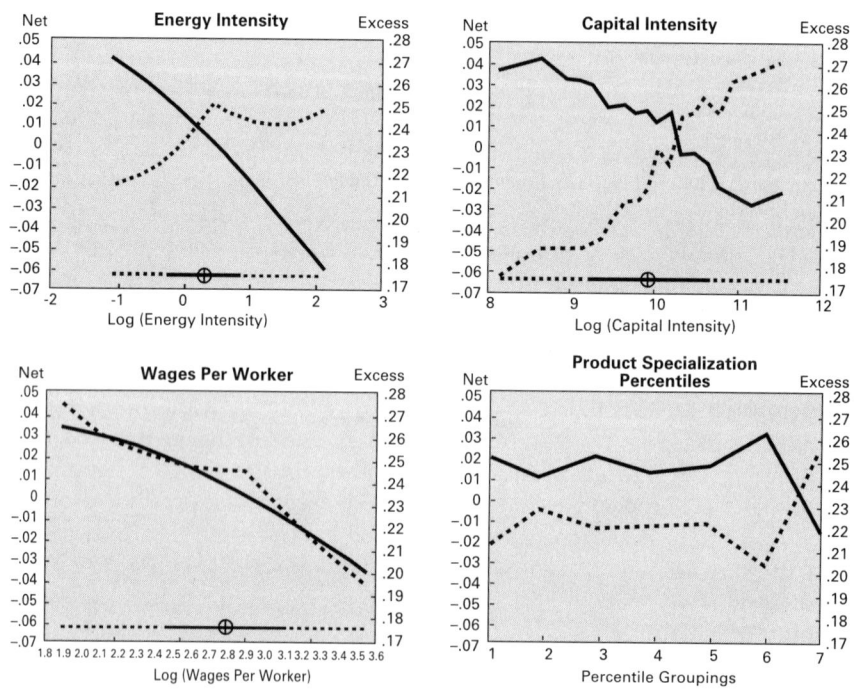

1. The solid line is the predicted variation in the net employment growth rate.
2. The dashed line is the difference between the predicted absolute growth rate and the absolute value of the predicted net growth rate (the predicted excess reallocation rate).
3. The horizontal lines above the horizontal axes depict the 5th, 25th, 50th (circle), 75th, and 95th percentiles.

Source: Davis and Haltiwanger (1998b).

positive relationship between capital intensity and excess job reallocation conditional on other employer characteristics (notably, size and wage level), but a simple cross-tabulation in Table 3.6 of Davis, Haltiwanger, and Schuh (1996) shows the opposite pattern.

The regression approach is easily adapted to the goals of the paper by Schuh and Triest. They seek to characterize cyclical variation in reallocation activity. I encourage them to pursue this goal by addressing the following sort of question: How do the curves in the attached figure (and analogous curves for other employer characteristics) shift over the business cycle? Schuh and Triest have at their disposal all the data required to answer this question. The regression method outlined above is simple and flexible, and it delivers transparent messages. It is also easily adapted to other issues taken up by Schuh and Triest, such as the relationship between a plant's current growth rate behavior and its past growth rate intensity. I hope that Schuh and Triest pursue this line of investigation. I would view the results with great interest, and I suspect others would as well.

References

Blanchard, Olivier. 1997. *The Economics of Post-Communist Transition.* Oxford: Clarendon Press.
Caballero, Ricardo and Mohamad Hammour. 1998. "Jobless Growth: Appropriability, Factor Substitution, and Unemployment." *Carnegie-Rochester Conference Series on Public Policy,* forthcoming.
Cabrales, Antonio and Hugo A. Hopenhayn. 1997. "Labor Market Flexibility and Aggregate Employment Volatility." *Carnegie-Rochester Conference Series on Public Policy,* 46, June, pp. 189–228.
Campbell, John. 1994. "Inspecting the Mechanism: An Analytical Approach to the Stochastic Growth Model." *Journal of Monetary Economics,* 33, June, pp. 563–606.
Cogley, Timothy and James M. Nasson. 1995. "Output Dynamics in Real Business Cycle Models." *The American Economic Review,* 85(3), June, pp. 492–511.
Cooley, Thomas, F. 1995. *Frontiers of Business Cycle Research.* Princeton, NJ: Princeton University Press.
Davis, Steven J. and John Haltiwanger. 1998a. "Measuring Gross Worker and Job Flows." Forthcoming in M. Manser and R. Topel, eds., *Labor Statistics Measurement Issues.* Chicago, IL: University of Chicago Press.
———. 1998b. "Gross Job Flows." Prepared for the *The Handbook of Labor Economics,* David Card and Orley Ashenfelter, eds. Amsterdam: North-Holland.
Davis, Steven J., John Haltiwanger, and Scott Schuh. 1996. *Job Creation and Destruction.* Cambridge, MA: The MIT Press.
Dunne, Timothy, Mark Roberts, and Larry Samuelson. 1989. "The Growth and Failure of U.S. Manufacturing Plants." *Quarterly Journal of Economics,* 104(4), pp. 671–98.
Foster, Lucia, John Haltiwanger, and C. J. Krizan. 1998. "Aggregate Productivity Growth: Lessons from Microeconomic Evidence." Working Paper, February.
Hall, Robert E. 1995. "Lost Jobs." *Brookings Papers on Economic Activity, 1: 1995,* pp. 221–73.
———. 1998. "Labor-Market Frictions and Employment Fluctuations." NBER Working Paper no. 6501.
Ljungqvist, Lars and Thomas Sargent. 1998. "The European Unemployment Dilemma." *Journal of Political Economy,* 106, no. 3 (June), pp. 514–50.
Machin, Stephen and Alan Manning. 1998. "The Causes and Consequences of Long-Term Unemployment in Europe." Prepared for *The Handbook of Labor Economics,* David Card and Orley Ashenfelter, eds. Amsterdam: North Holland.
Millard, Stephen P. and Dale T. Mortensen. 1997. "The Unemployment and Welfare Effects of Labour Market Policy: A Comparison of the USA and UK." In Dennis J. Snower and Guillermo de la Dehesa, eds., *Unemployment Policy: Government Options for the Labour Market.* New York: Cambridge University Press.
Mortensen, Dale T. and Christopher Pissarides. 1998. "New Developments in Models of Search in the Labor Market." Prepared for *The Handbook of Labor Economics,* David Card and Orley Ashenfelter, eds. Amsterdam: North-Holland.
Nickell, Stephen J. and Richard Layard. 1998. "Labour Market Institutions and Economic Performance." Prepared for *The Handbook of Labor Economics,* David Card and Orley Ashenfelter, eds. Amsterdam: North-Holland.
Rotemberg, Julio and Michael Woodford. 1996. "Forecastable Movements in Output, Hours and Consumption." *The American Economic Review,* 86, March, pp. 71–89.

Policy Implications:
A Panel Discussion

The New Financial World:
Policy Shortcomings and Remedies

Henry Kaufman[*]

This conference on "Beyond Shocks: What Causes Business Cycles?" has opened up for discussion the very important subject of the linkages between behavior of the financial markets and developments in the economy. Because not enough focus has been cast on this subject, I especially welcome the opportunity to present to you my views on the changes in the financial markets, how they have affected financial and economic behavior, and the consequences of these new behavioral patterns for official policy.

Structural Changes in Finance Influencing the Business Cycle

Securitization

The shift to marketable from nonmarketable assets brought about by securitization has stretched credit creation. It tends to sustain borrowers longer in economic expansion and probably to expose them more in contractions. It also has had the important side effect of removing the illusion of price stability for nonmarketable assets. Some of the new securitized instruments have therefore magnified the volatility of financial asset prices.

Consequently, the nature of financial assets has changed over the past two decades, in large part as a result of the growing process of securitization. Indeed, a good case can be made that securitization is the central feature of modern financial markets. It permits the transformation

---

[*]President, Henry Kaufman & Company, Inc.

of credit from a set of loans lodged on the books of a traditional financial institution, such as a bank, a thrift, or an insurance company, into an obligation that can be sold in the open credit market, where in normal times it can be traded and priced continuously.

Globalization of Markets

The consequence of internationalization of the financial markets is that they are linked as never before, although admittedly not perfectly. Over the past 10 years or so, during which time globalization of finance has evolved rapidly, the bond markets of the main industrial countries have moved together well over 70 percent of the time, regardless of significant differences in economic fundamentals among them. Often, the case for the decoupling of individual markets may be strong, but decoupling is the exceptional event these days, occurring principally when one or another country is a victim of financial duress.

This internationalization of financial markets has broad significance. Foreign investors are opportunists. They plow funds into a country and, if risk perceptions change, they attempt to leave quickly, as we have seen recently in Asia and earlier in Latin America. More and more they represent large multinational institutions or immense pools of entrepreneurially managed money. They have a presence in all markets. They respond to the drumbeat of a more homogenized outpouring of financial analysis, views, and forecasts. They all have access to the same information technology, which lets decisionmakers be located virtually anywhere and still be up to the second on new developments.

Performance-Driven, Highly Leveraged Investing

Performance-driven investors often deploy considerable leverage in their activities. Leverage greatly magnifies the profitability of successful investments, but naturally also magnifies losses. Greater use of leverage usually has the side effect of generating a sharp increase in the volume of transactions in the marketplace. More often than not, a heavy volume of transactions is associated with greater volatility of financial asset prices.

The composition of financial institutions themselves is undergoing significant change. The relative weight of traditional commercial banks, savings and loans, and insurance companies has diminished. Instead a new breed of institutional participant has come to the fore. These institutions are distinguished by their emphasis on short-term investment performance, a heavy use of leverage, and an ability to move in and out of markets, whether equities, bonds, currencies, or commodities, wherever the operators believe the returns will be the highest. Included in their number are the often highly publicized hedge funds. But hedge funds are not the only or even the main practitioners of this approach. A similar investment and trading approach is conducted within hedge-fund-like departments of the most prominent banks, securities firms, and a few insurance companies, as well. Even the corporate treasuries of a number of nonfinancial corporations are engaged in this activity.

Derivatives

Not long ago advocates of financial derivatives maintained that they were primarily "risk management" products. The usually unspoken assumption was that derivatives were essentially risk-reducing in their overall effect on the financial positions of end-users—in other words, tools for hedging risks that already existed. In the aftermath of a string of large and highly publicized losses incurred by a number of financial institutions and nonfinancial corporations, this rather simplistic view is no longer tenable.

However, all agree that financial derivatives—whether in the form of futures, forwards, swaps, options, or securities embodying derivatives—cannot be looked at in isolation. They are only one part of the far-reaching structural changes in our financial markets that I have been describing. It is the interaction of all of these component elements that tends to nurture the various financial risks that investors, companies, and financial institutions seek either to profit from or to hedge against. At the same time, derivatives are a catalyst and increasingly an instigator of further evolution of the financial markets.

Indexation

Indexation is the practice of passively seeking to replicate the behavior of a broad index of either the stock or the bond market, rather than actively manage portfolios to try to achieve superior returns. Ironically, the more that financial resources are invested passively, then the greater will be the impact on asset prices of the active portfolio managers who do seek superior returns. Thus, what may make a good deal of sense to an individual investor or a single institution—that is, to avoid the risk of underperformance by settling for the average return of a market index—collectively increases the probability that market values will lurch from one extreme to another.

New Risk-Takers

In America, many of the newcomers to investing in assets that carry with them the risk of capital loss have never experienced an extended bear market. How they will react when one inevitably unfolds is not quantifiable, but there is at least a reasonable likelihood that they will cut back their new investments and scale back their consumption of goods and services. Thus, the "wealth effect" will be an increasingly important element in the business cycle.

These American households are taking more market risk in their investments than ever before. The portion of household financial assets held in the form of deposits and money funds that provide certainty of capital has dwindled to barely 15 percent. In the meantime, holdings of assets with capital values that vary from day to day and over the financial cycle have increased dramatically. Much of this surge is the result of the mutual fund phenomenon. As recently as the end of 1984, the combined total of equity and bond mutual funds in the United States amounted to only a little over $100 billion, less than 2 percent of total financial net worth of households. Since then, mutual funds have mushroomed and now amount to over $3 trillion, not counting the $1 trillion in money market funds that substitute for conventional bank deposits. Of that total of equity and bond mutual funds, some $2 trillion is owned directly by households, representing almost 10 percent of household financial net worth.

Illusion of Liquidity

In a world of securitized financial markets, market participants are often mesmerized by what I have referred to as the "illusion of liquidity": the assumption that anything can be bought and sold at any moment and that open credit markets will always be open. But the functioning of secondary markets in existing debt and equity instruments and access to fresh amounts of credit have always been and always will be discontinuous. When the credit quality of companies or governments is strong, modern financial markets are ready, willing, and eager to provide financing. Secondary markets are prepared to handle even sizable trades with relatively modest impact on the going price of the security. But what is commonly overlooked is how precarious this blissful market state really is. When companies or even governments run into financial difficulty and their credit standing is open to question, a sharp discontinuity in the functioning of markets is likely to occur. Almost instantaneously, bid-offer spreads widen out, dealers cut back the amounts they are willing to buy or sell, and security prices undergo abrupt and sharp movements. Credit availability evaporates. Borrowers are flung back into an uncomfortably old-fashioned world in which they are totally dependent on their bankers for support—and may or may not get it.

Quantification of Risk

There is a belief, strongly held in some quarters, that financial risks are knowable, can be calculated with mathematical precision by massaging historical data, and can be diversified. These are fallacies. History is a useful starting point for assessing risk, but only a starting point. Most instances of sudden deterioration in the credit standing of a corporate or government borrower are not predictable. They reflect submerged weaknesses in underlying economic or financial structures that are not captured by the available data. And the likelihood of contagion is high, as we have seen dramatically in the past year in Asia.

Slowdown of Government Debt, and Commensurate Pickup of Private Debt

One of the most notable changes in the financial markets has been the slowdown in the growth of U.S. government debt. The U.S. federal government budget has moved into surplus, and Canada's will probably also register a surplus. The pursuit of the Maastricht criteria has meant that nearly all the Continental European governments have managed to bring down their deficits, although for how long we cannot say. Only Japan stands apart, as economic recession stunts revenue collection and fiscal stimulus programs swell government expenditures.

At the same time, however, business corporations are again putting a substantial volume of debt on their balance sheets, especially in the United States. Up to this point, the increases are not of the same relative magnitude as in the leveraging binge of the 1980s, when vast amounts were raised to finance mergers, acquisitions, leveraged buy-outs, and risky real estate ventures. In the aftermath of the collapse of a good number of these deals, many credits went sour, and lenders lost sizable sums as they discovered they had fewer protections than they had been led to believe. The consequence was a period of massive restructuring of corporate balance sheets and much more prudent lending and investing standards.

However, in the past three or four years, considerable backsliding has occurred. Short-term borrowings have increased at a rapid pace, long-term debt issuance has rebounded, while new equity issuance has fallen far short of the magnitude of issues that were retired or bought back by corporations. Since 1994, the rise in corporate liabilities has exceeded the total increase in equity, the sum of retained earnings and net new share issuance, by an incredible $850 billion. By comparison, in the 1991-93 period, the net increase in liabilities was $100 billion *less* than the total increase in equity.

The latest surge in corporate liabilities has partly been used to finance an impressive burst of capital expenditure, the most distinctive feature of the current business expansion. But increasingly, we find that large sums are being raised for some of the same purposes that caused trouble in the 1980s: financial engineering, mergers and acquisitions, and share buy-backs. Thus, while corporate profits were rising sharply, corporate credit quality was not improving commensurably.

Today, the marketplace treats worries such as these as remote. The general view is that plenty of time remains to sell off holdings of low-quality bonds before economic and financial circumstances deteriorate. The lesson I take from the experience of the 1980s, and from other troubled periods in the more distant past, is that such a belief commonly precedes the emergence of financial excesses.

Problems for Monetary Policy

These changes in the structure of the financial markets will continue to have profound influence on the way the economy interacts with the financial system, and therefore they pose some tricky problems for the conduct of monetary policy. The first problem is that a more open, deregulated, securitized, and global financial system will help keep debtors in the game longer than in times past. Securitization is a force for liberality in granting credit. Consider the recent case of South Korea. Here was a country that had made commendable progress toward transforming itself into a First World country. It was undeniably an export powerhouse. The government did not run a large budget deficit. Outstanding external debt of the government was moderate. Credit ratings were extremely high. (As late as October 1997, Korea had a higher credit rating than IBM!) So the bankers—Japanese, European, and American—were willing to lend large amounts for short-term maturities, assuming that they could securitize those credits at will. Never did they give much weight to the possibility that the borrowers might be confronted with a liquidity crisis that would slam the door shut on access to the purportedly "open" credit markets.

Moreover, the rapid development of financial derivatives also perpetuates a more relaxed attitude toward granting credit. Higher-rated corporations can arbitrage their credit standing to lower their cost of funds by issuing long-term, fixed-rate debt and then swapping the proceeds against the obligation to pay at a floating rate. Lower-rated corporations, which ordinarily would be squeezed out of the bond market as the credit cycle matures, are able to lock in long-term yields by borrowing short and swapping into the long-term maturity obligation. The bankers, who are in the middle, view their role as relatively risk-free.

The upshot is that it will tend to take relatively steep increases in the level of short-term interest rates for the central bank to engineer an end to a period of possibly excessive economic expansion that may put upward pressure on the rate of inflation. This is exactly the position in which the Bank of England now finds itself. It has imposed the highest short-term interest rates of any advanced industrial country; yet, the U.K. economy still manages to chug along at a brisk pace, further tightening already taut labor markets and imparting an upward tilt to wage and price inflation. At some point the Federal Reserve may face a similar dilemma as the possibly transitory factors holding down the U.S. rate of inflation—namely, a high value of the U.S. dollar in the foreign currency markets, weak economic activity in Asia that keeps many product markets highly competitive, and low commodity prices—are reversed.

A second problem for monetary policy is that the structural changes in the financial markets make conventional methods for anchoring monetary policy obsolete. Monetary targeting has been the initial casualty. The Federal Reserve continues to set target ranges for the rate of growth of several definitions of the money supply, but it goes to great lengths to assert that it does not take the targets very seriously because old relationships between money and the rest of the economy have become entirely unreliable. That is true also for measures of credit. Securitization is associated with a diminished role of depository institutions in the intermediation of credit flows, and so debt aggregates are just as unreliable as monetary aggregates. Paradoxically, while private sector institutions are relying increasingly on mathematical models in the quantification of risk, the central bank is shying away from a quantitiative approach to conducting monetary policy.

What are the choices? There are not many to choose from. A central bank can do as the Bank of England has done and condition policy on meeting an intermediate-term inflation target. Or a central bank can set an inflation target and try to attain it by pursuing a formal monetary conditions rule, along the lines of the way the Bank of Canada is operating. Or it can do as the Federal Reserve has been doing, setting a loose and unquantified objective of 'reasonable price stability' and using discretionary policy changes in pursuit of that goal.

But in each case the objective is cast solely in terms of the price indexes for goods and services. It explicitly leaves out any room for taking into account inflation (or deflation) of asset prices. But financial well-being depends on much more than merely attaining a low and stable rate of inflation. The proof of that is the case of the United States in the 1920s and that of Japan in the 1980s and 1990s. Both would meet any reasonable definition of price stability, but both suffered horrendous economic consequences from excessive asset price inflation followed by asset price collapses. Surely monetary policy should be not indifferent to such potentialities.

Wealth effects are now recognized to be powerful influences on the evolution of the economy. Not too many years ago, the Federal Reserve, along with most other central banks, was somewhat skeptical about the potency of wealth effects. But today it is conceded that more and more households recognize how their financial net worth is affected by movements in asset values and adjust their expenditures on goods, services, and housing accordingly. Business corporations modify their investment decisions in part in response to what is happening to their share prices. Business formation is subtly influenced by the level of the stock market, too, because a strong market allows individuals to take risks that they would not be inclined to take if the level of equity prices were substantially lower. International capital flows, and thus the value of the dollar, are also affected by the value of financial assets—and expectations for future asset price movements. Thus, these effects have become an important transmission belt from the financial sector to the real economy and necessarily a valid consideration for monetary policy.

However, at present no central bank has a mandate to explicitly take financial asset prices into consideration in the formation of monetary policy. Nevertheless, the financial bubbling in the American financial market is an untenable situation. The way events are unfolding now, one of several events will topple the exuberance. One is a more noticeable profit squeeze than is now beginning to emerge. Another would be a further sharp deterioration in the Japanese economy, which would weaken Japanese financial institutions even further. With these institutions so closely linked globally, financial problems are bound to occur elsewhere. Still another problem will confront us if by an unlikely chance both Japan and Europe stage strong economic recoveries. This would end the surge of foreign funds to the United States and it would also increase inflationary pressures.

From my perspective, it is not a question of whether any one or more of these will happen, but rather when, and from what level of the market. In the immediate aftermath of such an event, the central bank will then try to counter the sharp declines in asset prices by easing monetary policy significantly. Thus today's euphoria in the stock market will be followed by a sharp stock market setback, and in this carnage long government bonds may very well fall to a yield of 4 percent. After that, I suspect a more definitive monetary strategy incorporating financial behavior is likely to be formulated.

THE REFORMS NEEDED INTERNATIONALLY

While financial excesses and their hurtful economic consequences can never be fully eliminated, I do believe they can be limited by improved supervision and regulation of financial institutions and markets. The modern, globalized financial structure is based on innovation and risk-taking. Formal regulations and barriers to financial activities have been lowered, and over time they will come down further. Paradoxically, however, in a more deregulated, freewheeling financial environment, the need for better supervision of the financial institutions and markets is actually *increased*. Equally important, there has to be more intensive and more informed market discipline of risk exposures, and that requires more information about what those exposures are. Oversight, whether by official institutions or by the market itself, has been uneven at best and usually tardy, with far too little information-sharing among official organizations and far too little dialogue with private lenders and investors. Furthermore, in many of the emerging markets, formal regulatory mechanisms have been weak, and informal supervision and oversight have been practically nonexistent.

The essential ingredient in an improved global financial architecture is the establishment of a new institution, alongside a reorganized International Monetary Fund (IMF) and World Bank, to overcome the inadequacies of current national and international structures for supervising and regulating financial institutions and markets. To deal with the growing potential for market excesses, I have recommended many times over the years establishment of a Board of Overseers of Major Institutions and Markets, to put teeth into the system. This Board would have the following mandate:

1. It would set forth a code of conduct for market participants, to encourage reasonable financial behavior.

2. It would supervise risk-taking, not only by banks and other financial institutions that have always been regulated and supervised, but also by new participants in the global markets.

3. It would be empowered by member governments to harmonize minimum capital requirements; to establish uniform trading, reporting, and disclosure standards; and to monitor the performance of institutions and markets under its purview.

Eventually, this new international regulatory body would rate the credit quality of market participants under its authority. Institutions that failed to abide by the standards would be sanctioned. Lending to banks in countries that chose to remain outside the new system would be subject to higher capital requirements and limitations on maturities. Also, nonmember countries would be limited in their ability to sell new securities in the equity, bond, and money markets of members. The new Board would not enact specific regulations to control flows of capital internationally but it would visibly raise the bar to take advantage of the benefits of open capital markets. That will dramatically reduce risks in the system, although it will not eliminate them entirely.

At the same time this new financial supervisory and regulatory entity is established, the IMF needs to be reorganized so as to perform competently a more targeted set of core functions. The new IMF, like today's IMF, would be responsible for organizing and partially funding emergency lending operations to protect the safety and soundness of the global system when member governments face intense balance-of-payment problems and are shut off from normal sources of external financing. It would continue to have the responsibility for setting policy conditions that borrowers must follow to qualify for emergency loans.

In contrast to present IMF practices, however, it would have the responsibility of anticipating problems and pressing member governments to take timely preventative actions. It would be responsible for rating the economic and financial strength of its members. It would evaluate their monetary and fiscal policies as well as the structures of their economies. Where it detected deficiencies that could lead to excessive dependence on inflows of short-term capital from abroad or compromise the health of the domestic banking system, it would demand early remedial actions. If the member governments refused to act, the reorganized IMF would make the reduced credit rating public. Since that would, of course, have the effect of dramatically shrinking the recalcitrant country's access to the open credit markets, it would represent a powerful incentive for the member to cooperate. Rating the creditworthiness of sovereigns is a tough job, but an appropriately staffed IMF would have a far better chance of doing the job effectively than the private credit rating agencies, which are handicapped by a lack of the kind of detailed and timely information that the IMF would be able to get.

Finally, the G-7 also needs to be restructured to take account of the coming European Monetary Union and its common currency, the euro. It is imperative for the new European Central Bank and those of the United States and Japan to begin a dialogue on how to better harmonize their monetary policies. Each has to be prepared to recognize and take into account the global dimensions of what they do. If their actions end up creating an overabundance of global liquidity, either global inflation or excessive growth of global credit becomes a threat. If they end up with an insufficiency of global liquidity, economic growth may be jeopardized. It is probably too much to ask that this effort at better harmonization explicitly incorporate the goal of minimizing the huge swings in currency rates that have plagued the international monetary system in recent years. But at least a systematic attempt ought to be made to discuss the implications of outsized currency movements for the global trading system. Existing forums, such as the Bank for International Settlements (BIS) in Basle, Switzerland, are fine but too informal to achieve that systematic approach.

Conclusion

Why is it that official policy responses seem to lag so much the structural changes in the financial markets? There are a number of reasons. One is that officials often underestimate the potency of a structural change. By the time it is obvious that something of importance has taken place, the development has triggered a series of market adjustments that are not readily brought under the official regulatory framework. A second is that structural changes do not always fall within the neat categories that delineate the various existing official institutions. For example, when financial derivatives emerged as a major element in modern financial markets, there was considerable uncertainty over where they would fit within the official regulatory apparatus. That uneasiness as to who should oversee financial derivatives has persisted, even as the market has been buffeted by several mishaps in recent years. A third reason why official policy responses lag behind structural changes in the financial markets is that at the early stages of a development, the impact of the changes on financial and economic behavior is difficult to quantify. To illustrate, the rapid increase in the public's investments in the equity market through the use of mutual funds was well-documented. But it took quite a long time before U.S. financial officials appreciated how this phenomenon might generate a significant wealth effect for many millions of households. Now that the wealth-effect addiction has spread widely, policymakers are beginning to understand that the level of consumer expenditures on goods, services, and housing is intimately related to the strength of the stock market—and that considerable withdrawal pains might be felt, were the stock market to set back dramatically.

Internationally, official policy responses to structural changes in the financial markets are handicapped by similar and other shortcomings. Vested interests in the official international financial institutions that may need to be reformed feel threatened by the unknown outcome of reform and tend to be vocal in their opposition. Moreover, the unwillingness to give up national sovereignty remains, even though financial markets and the economy are integrating globally. It seems, for instance, that the U.S. government is a reluctant proponent of a major overhaul of the current official international financial institutions. It may be that this is out of concern that any thoroughgoing reform might require the United States to yield some of its dominance over these institutions. If true, this would be short-sighted leadership, since no permanent benefit can be gained from being the dominant participant in an institution whose authority and credibility are being eroded by structural changes in the marketplace.

Finally, developing countries are said to be opposed to reform of official international financial institutions because they are afraid that improved scrutiny of financial institutions and markets would jeopardize their access to funds in the private markets. For instance, they may be concerned about the consequences of being impelled to improve transparency in their domestic banking system or otherwise bring to light financial problems that might otherwise have been kept out of sight. This is a terrible misconception. Retaining access to credit for less than creditworthy institutions will only exaggerate the financial and economic cycle, as Asian nations have painfully found out. What is in their interest is to reduce the extremes in financial cycles, because in so doing they would help produce a steadier and less interruptible flow of private funds. Financial excesses eventually impoverish the marginal borrower and, for a while at least, mainly go to strengthen the bargaining position of the strongest participants in the credit system—namely, the governments, financial institutions, and business corporations of the major industrial countries of North America and Europe. That is certainly the clear message that comes out of the financial wreckage in Asia. Unfortunately, this narrow advantage is only of transitory benefit, since ultimately we all are losers as financial difficulties fan out from their origins. Thus, it is worth pondering whether the risks are already rising in our financial markets and whether we can avoid damage to our own economy in the absence of adequate official remedial actions to respond to the financial excesses that may now be percolating beneath the surface.

A View of Recessions, from the Automotive Industry

Martin B. Zimmerman*

I would like to talk about the issues that have arisen over the past day and a half from the perspective of a large industry, the automobile industry. We learned from Peter Temin's paper that we may have caused the Great Depression. So it is certainly worth looking at the impact of a recession on the auto industry, and then at the recommendations for policy we in the industry would make, based on our experience.

Recession in the Automobile Industry

First, just a little description. I cannot think of an industry more cyclical or more dependent on the business cycle than the auto industry. A good year in the industry is sales of 15 million units. We are now selling above that, at a rate of a little over 15 and one-half million. That is a good year. A severe recession year is 13 million units. So a drop from 15 million to 13 million, a little over 15 percent, is really the difference between decent performance and severe losses, with a lot of job reallocation or job destruction, I might add.

One way to think about our response to a recession is this: In a normal year, as I said, we sell 15 million units. With roughly 100 million households in the United States, a typical household is in the market for a new vehicle once every six and one-half years or so, on average. However, this is a postponable purchase, and if the household decides to hold on to that car for an extra year, then instead of selling 15 million units, we will sell about 13 million units. So the question is, what induces

---

*Chief Economist and Executive Director for Governmental Relations and Corporate Economics, Ford Motor Company.

a household to hold on to that vehicle a little longer? Over time, clearly, there is a secular trend, because we are making better cars and they last longer. But in the cyclical sense the question is, what induces the household to hold on a little longer? Households with incomes over $75,000 enter the automobile market once every four years, on average, households with incomes below $35,000 about once every eight years, for the overall average of once every six and one-half years. So the market is very income dependent. And clearly, if income declines in all income categories, they all enter the market less frequently, and you get people holding on an extra year or so.

THE ROLE OF SHOCKS

Now, when we look back at previous recessions and try to find out, much as the papers at this conference have done, what caused that falloff in sales or what caused people to hold on to that car, in the immortal words of the movie *Casablanca*, you "round up the usual suspects," and the usual suspects around here are higher interest rates and shocks. There is no getting around it. Every time that we have observed a precipitous, or I should say large, decline in sales, it has been associated with an increase in interest rates. But an increase in interest rates alone typically is not enough to do it. You need that shock. We could trace back through, certainly since the first post-World War II recession, and a shock has always been there. So in terms of the title of this conference, "Beyond Shocks: What Causes Business Cycles?", it is very difficult for me to get beyond the shock. The shock is typically associated with that fall in sales. Higher interest rates clearly work to make the financing of a car more expensive; the opportunity cost of capital is higher, and as a result that slows down purchases. But the kind of precipitous decline that we see in recessions really is not associated with the interest rate level, by and large; it is associated with that shock. And more often than not in recent history, the decline has been associated with an oil shock, which also has a relative price effect on autos, since autos use oil intensively.

The key question for me, working in a business firm during a recession, is whether that recession was forecastable. Well, if it was due to a shock, a shock by definition is not forecastable. Now, I have tried that line out on my management several times, and I have never succeeded. I am perhaps in somewhat the same position as the Fed appears to be, according to the papers given yesterday. The two conclusions I took away from the history highlighted in those papers are that either the Fed is irrelevant or the Fed does the wrong thing. Well, when I tell my management that while I am here to forecast, to tell you what the economy is going to do, I cannot forecast shocks, it does not go over well. But that does not mean that I am irrelevant. That is because other factors influence that recession. The shock might not be forecastable, but when a shock occurs, it does not necessarily mean that we are going to have a recession.

The Importance of a Robust Economy

Typically, what we see before recessions is some degree of vulnerability. In some sense the probability of a decline goes up, and that is where an economist can make a contribution in terms of saying, yes, things are happening and some vulnerability is present. The shock might be some totally unforecastable event, but when it occurs we will be more vulnerable. And that is an important point to bear in mind. We have tended to focus on the shock; we look at a recession, we see a shock that drives down the economy, and we know that shocks are not forecastable. But in fact, all shocks do not lead to recessions. Christopher Sims mentioned yesterday that one of the faults in our methodology is that we go and look for the recession that we can associate with a shock, even though a lot of shocks do not result in a recession.

And what if we were able to distinguish why that was the case? Just as a "thought experiment," I asked Franco Modigliani this morning, "If we were to have an oil shock today, would that cause a recession?" Well, it is arguable. Clearly it would depend on the extent of the oil shock. But the fundamental robustness of the economy right now, the fundamentally low inflation rate right now, could lead you to argue that we could absorb that kind of shock. You could say that Asia was a shock, certainly, to the U.S. economy. But do we have a recession? The jury is still out on whether we will have one, I guess, but the argument would be that the precursors, or the state of the economy, did not lead to it. At the time of the stock market crash in 1987, if you go back and look at the newspapers of that day, they were plotting the behavior of the economy against the behavior of the economy in 1929. Had I known at the time that because of the change in the structure of car financing, we were not going to get a Great Depression, I would really have made some play on that! But clearly, we have got to pay attention to those events. And that is where, for a business anyway, the skill and art and science come in. Shocks occur randomly. But, depending on the state of the economy, our job is to forecast whether or not they will result in a recession.

The 1990 Recession as an Example

I would like to illustrate these points by looking back at the 1990 recession. I understand that in the context of the post-1914 period, it is a small recession and not necessarily typical. However, it does illustrate some of the points I want to make. I went back and I looked at what the Blue Chip economic forecasters, that collection of industry and bank economists, were saying in 1990. In June of 1990 before the invasion of Kuwait, to summarize one of their forecasts, they had a few lines that said, "Once again, the consensus reaffirms that as a whole the economy will not slip into a recession either this year or next." Well, that clearly proved to be wrong. And, following on my argument that it is the shock, they should not be held responsible. Moreover, we should give them credit, because they were forecasting a slowdown. The economy grew in 1989 at a rate of 3 percent, or at least so we thought at the time, and in mid 1990 Blue Chip was forecasting a slowdown to 1.9 percent and then growth of a little over 2 percent in 1991. Two percent growth is closer to zero than 3 percent, so the economy was more vulnerable to shock, and the shock then came.

The other bit of evidence from that period that I believe emphasizes the shock, and it came home very clearly to me at the time, working in the automobile industry, was the precipitous fall after the invasion of Kuwait, which does lead you to associate the decline with a shock. If you recall, the invasion of Kuwait occurred in early August, and then the consumer sentiment index, measured by the University of Michigan, took a precipitous drop. I hesitate to say it was a record, although it may have been, in terms of both the absolute decline and the percentage decline in sentiment associated with that event. Then auto industry sales fell off. They had been slowing, and they fell off in August, bounced back in September, but then in October, November, they started to fall. And with the war beginning in January, sales took a huge dive down, and in February, when the land war began, they stayed down. So as a result, I associate that whole event with that shock.

I went back and tried to get data on our dealer retail orders at that time. Unfortunately, we had thrown them out as part of the new efficiency. So there has been some job destruction there, because we used to have people collecting these things. But I recall the abrupt falloff in orders. We schedule our plants based on dealer orders, and right after Thanksgiving, when President Bush announced the January deadline for the war, those orders just came down. It is typical for us to reschedule production once a month, on a three-month rolling basis. Our orders were so sparse at the time, the question was whether we were going to shut down, and we were doing our scheduling on a weekly basis. And in fact our scheduling meeting was chaired by the chairman of the company, which is a very unusual thing. He normally does not get involved. So, the whole sense was that this was a very abrupt thing, it was a shock. Of course, I was up there saying it was not forecastable! But where does that leave us for the questions of policy? That is where I think this whole conference is aimed, ultimately.

The Role of Monetary Policy

The question, as I said before, is how vulnerable the economy is. And that relates to the conduct of monetary policy. We heard yesterday the notion that the recessions that followed the oil shocks of the '80s, anyway, were a result of the expansionary monetary policy, inappropriate monetary policy of the '70s. Well, we have also seen in other shocks that interest rates were raised, not willy-nilly, but because of an inflationary buildup. This would suggest to me that the essence of getting policy right is as follows: You are not going to prevent that shock, but you can make the period just before the shock better, so that we are less vulnerable. Then even if we are hit with a shock, the impact on the economy will be smaller.

The second issue is that we also have the period after the shock. And the question is, after the proximate cause hits and after the implications play out, how fast do we get out? And there you will find the argument for the proper role of policy. In the most recent recession, I would argue that interest rates came down very slowly. In one period, interest rates were coming down at about the rate of decline in inflation expectations, also recorded by the University of Michigan consumer survey. As a result, the real interest rate was not changing. And then a period followed in which nominal rates were actually stable. We were going from a high level of interest rates down to a low level. We were just getting there too slowly, I think. That is, of course, arguable, but the point I make is correct, which is that the periods before and after the shock are crucial for policy, even if you accept the notion that we are not going to be able to do much about those shocks.

One sidelight on policy and recession concerns the data flow: how much information is coming into the Fed and what the Fed sees happening. Auto sales are recorded by the U.S. Bureau of Economic Analysis (BEA), but in the recession I discussed earlier, we affected the BEA numbers. The BEA recorded a more moderate decline in production than was actually taking place. The reason was the two kinds of auto sales: sales to fleet, and sales to customers, retail customers. In the early stages of a falloff (and this is looking at our own data, but I suspect you would have also seen this at GM and Chrysler), you do not know how long this decline is going to last or what the effect is going to be, and you do not want to shut down your plants. But your orders are very thin. We pulled ahead orders we knew we were going to deliver to the fleets, by that I mean Hertz, Budget, the rental car companies. So if you look at the numbers, you will see that, on a year-over-year basis, the retail numbers fell off sharply in August, then came back a bit, and then went down again. We overdid it on the fleets. In fact, in retrospect we realized that what we were doing with the fleets was inventorying cars in a novel way. We gave them to the rental companies, took them back four months later, and found that new car sales were affected by it. So we did not change the overall level of demand out there, we inventoried and paid for it later. But when you looked at the data, the falloff did not look as precipitous. However, the chairman of the company at the time would call me up and say, you have got to get the message to the Fed, you have got to get the message to the Fed, that things are deteriorating faster than we are showing. I tried my best.

In conclusion, then, if you do accept this argument that, at the end of the day, shocks are what cause the tip-over, then the essence of policy is to make the economy as good as possible, both before and after the shock.

Emerging Economies and the Business Cycle

Agustin G. Carstens*

I will try to address the topic of this conference from the point of view of emerging economies. I believe that Mexico is a good example, and I would guess that I have a comparative advantage from that perspective, do I not?

Business Cycles in Emerging Economies

When analyzing time series of the GDPs of emerging economies, first we find that there appears to be a relatively close synchronization with industrialized countries' cycles. An old saying in Mexico, attributed to our last dictator of the nineteenth century, is that when the United States gets a cold, Mexico gets pneumonia. I think the saying is still valid, and it describes this aspect of the synchronization between emerging market economies and industrialized countries.

A second finding is that the time series of GDP for emerging economies exhibit greater volatility, as measured by the standard deviations of such series. In addition, there is a crucial difference between the depths of recessions in emerging economies and in industrial ones. While in the 1970-95 period the typical recession in industrialized countries registered a reduction in GDP of approximately 2 percent, in Latin America the average fall in GDP during a recession amounted to 8 percent. So at least in Latin America, instead of the typical expansion/recession cycle common in industrialized countries, the business cycle has more extreme values of crisis and recovery. Therefore, macroeconomic policies in emerging markets are focused on avoiding a possible

---

*Director General of Economic Research, Central Bank of Mexico.

crisis or attempting to reestablish credibility after one, instead of trying to fine-tune or smooth out the business cycle.

We also find an excess of volatility in GDP in emerging economies. A salient feature of emerging markets is that, on average, they are relatively more prone to be affected by large variations in their terms of trade. Therefore, shocks in terms of trade are likely to be a major source of economic fluctuations. In many emerging countries, export bases are characterized by a high concentration in a relatively small number of commodities whose world prices are very volatile. Also, their fiscal revenues tend to be largely dependent on the prices of the main export commodities, and so the health of their public finances as well is vulnerable to major changes in the world prices of export goods.

THE ROLE OF CAPITAL FLOWS

Over the past decade, tighter integration of international financial markets and positive expectations of future growth and profitability in emerging market countries have triggered a sharp increase in capital flows to those economies. In particular, in the 1978-81 and 1990-94 periods, countries in a variety of cyclical situations and with different macroeconomic policies experienced a simultaneous surge in new capital inflows. The problem has been that those capital inflows have not always been stable and permanent. Particular conditions in the recipient countries have triggered the massive capital outflows common to recent experience in Asia and in Mexico. But factors external to the emerging markets, such as higher interest rates in industrialized countries, can also contribute to capital outflows.

The massive capital inflows have entailed major risks for those recipient countries with a predetermined exchange-rate system. The macroeconomic developments that result from a significant inflow of foreign capital, namely, real currency appreciation and increasing current account deficits, may eventually be conducive to a run on the domestic currency of the recipient country. And if the domestic financial system is weak, the interest rate increases required to support exchange rates in episodes of capital outflow can hardly take place, because they would generate a crisis in the financial system. In this sense, a weak financial system imposes major constraints on what monetary policy can do to defend a predetermined exchange rate system under stress.

OTHER IMPORTANT INFLUENCES

Collapses of exchange-rate regimes and of local financial systems have unveiled deep recessions in several emerging market economies. Capital outflows have been involved in all of these episodes, but it is hard to claim that they were the sole factor responsible for the downturns in economic activity. In most cases, policy mismanagement or external developments have been contributing factors. Foreign capital has played the role of catalyst in emerging market crises, speeding up the collapses of regimes and substantially reducing the degree of freedom of action that the local authorities once had. When crises take place, the authorities suffer a complete loss of credibility. Macroeconomic policies, instead of fulfilling their output-supporting role, have to be adjusted so that the credibility of the authorities is restored. This is why, in contrast to industrial countries' experience, fiscal and monetary policies are usually pro-cyclical in developing countries.

It could also be argued that some of the volatility that we see in emerging market economies has been policy-induced. Some decisions on fiscal, monetary, and exchange-rate policies have in themselves represented significant destabilizing policy shocks to these economies. Some of the policy mistakes can be attributed to the fact that many emerging market economies still lack the appropriate institutional arrangements. In addition, policy mistakes can arise when authorities implement a policy mix forced onto a specific short-term objective, disregarding its sustainability in the medium and the long term. A typical example is the adoption of a strict exchange-rate stabilization program. This type of program tends to deliver a sharp decrease in inflation, but oftentimes at the cost of unsustainable real exchange-rate appreciation and external sector deficits. In this situation, the exchange-rate regime tends to collapse and the previous gains in the abatement of inflation are not sustained. A typical side effect is that such devaluations are contractionary.

In addition, the adoption of a predetermined exchange-rate regime encourages external borrowing by providing an implicit exchange-rate guarantee, and it leads to excessive exposure to foreign exchange risk in both the financial and the corporate sectors. Lax banking regulation and inadequate financial supervision lead to a sharp deterioration in the quality of banks' loan portfolios. This set of mistakes has proved to be at the source of recent balance-of-payments and banking crises around the world. In summary, terms of trade shocks, capital flows instability, and policy mistakes can be considered the salient factors that induce more GDP volatility in emerging economies than in industrialized ones. The identification of these factors is useful, since it provides us with the elements for the creation of a strategy that could prevent, or at least mitigate, recessions in emerging economies.

A STRATEGY TO REDUCE VOLATILITY

The question then is, what are the policy options to reduce volatility in emerging market economies? First, emerging countries should seek to reduce the vulnerability of their economies to significant changes in the international prices of their export commodities. One policy option in this regard is to diversify export bases and productive systems by adopting more open trade and investment regimes. In many emerging countries, much can be done in terms of eliminating trade barriers that introduce the anti-export bias usually associated with protectionist measures. Emerging countries should also explore the possibility of developing strategies based on a more intense use of hedging instruments against commodity price fluctuations. Similarly, the creation of commodity stabilization funds can contribute to smoothing the revenue effect of those price fluctuations. With regard to the sensitivity of current revenues to commodity price fluctuations, as in all exporting countries, local authorities should engage in aggressive programs to fortify other sources of revenues. This might require basic tax reform and a campaign to combat tax evasion.

Most emerging market economies should also consider the role that market-determined interest rates and increased exchange-rate flexibility can play as shock absorbers. In Mexico's experience, the adoption of a flexible exchange-rate regime has substantially contributed to reducing speculative pressures in financial markets. This flexible exchange rate has served several purposes. First, it has provided us with an additional adjustment variable with which to absorb temporary shocks, such as the recent turmoil in financial markets triggered by the Asian crisis. Second, a flexible exchange rate facilitates adjustment of the real exchange rate toward its equilibrium level whenever an exogenous shock warrants a new level for the exchange rate, without affecting the credibility of the monetary authority. And third, the floating exchange-rate regime and the free determination of interest rates have discouraged short-term capital flows, because of the large losses that can be incurred by investors in the short run. Since the adoption of this regime, the nature of capital flows to Mexico has shifted from mainly short-term to long-term in nature. To give you an idea, before the crisis of 1990 to 1994, foreigners had over $34 billion in short-term investments in Mexico. As of today, they have less than $2 billion. That reduction can be attributed to the floating exchange-rate regime.

Although shock-prone economies can benefit from deep financial markets and flexible exchange rates, it is of paramount importance that policymakers ensure that financial institutions are sufficiently robust to withstand successfully major changes in the macroeconomic environment. More flexibility in financial markets cannot substitute for actions to strengthen the financial system through better prudential regulation and supervision. Emerging countries can also obtain benefits from reforming their institutions in such a way that their vulnerability to economic shocks and their propensity to commit policy mistakes would be reduced. In addition to improving the regulation and supervision of the financial system, action can be taken to achieve better coordination between fiscal and monetary policies. When there is a lack of coordination among the different aspects of economic policy, the monetary authority's actions may generate unnecessary disturbances to economic activity.

When talking about the role of policy mistakes as a source of economic instability, a particular case in point is one where the objectives of an institution are not correctly specified. In this sense, some positive institutional reforms can be introduced to diminish the vulnerability of the economy. Granting autonomy to the central bank and assigning to it the sole object of sustainable price stability is a step in the right direction. This institutional change may also reduce some of the time-inconsistency problems in policymaking that I mentioned before. Particularly relevant for the emerging countries is the need to seek greater flexibility in the labor markets. Overregulated labor markets create negative incentives for the adoption of new technologies and improvements in the quality of human capital. In addition, overregulated labor markets prevent the kind of wage flexibility that is so desperately needed to deal with external shocks.

Over the past decade, the emerging countries have made significant progress regarding structural change, through adjustments to the legal and regulatory frameworks of the economy as well as by continuing the process of divestiture of government-controlled enterprises. Further efforts in this regard can also be of much help in reducing the negative effect of economic shocks on real economic activity. Finally, emerging market economies should devise mechanisms and develop institutions with the purpose of reducing their dependency on foreign savings. Clear examples in this regard are reforms to social security schemes and pension funds.

THE EFFECTS OF INTERNATIONAL POLICY

Michael Mussa*

The thunder and lightning outside remind me of the earliest childhood experience of which I have a definitive memory, one that I share with General Colin Powell, I learned when I read his autobiography three years ago. Crawling around on the dining-room floor, key in hand, I stuck the key into the electrical socket. Shocks are meaningful! And provided they are not too large, they are memorable and a cause for learning.

AN ASSESSMENT OF PRESENTED PAPERS

We are asked in this panel to respond to what has been said earlier in the conference, and to assess whether the causes of recession are identifiable and debate whether any policies could prevent or mitigate (and, I would also add, exacerbate) recessions. So let me turn to the content of the conference, pretty much in reverse order.

On the Schuh and Triest analysis and discussions by Caballero and Davis of labor force reallocation in business cycles, this is an important and interesting phenomenon. And labor market reallocation within business cycles is worth studying in greater detail. However, I remain skeptical that labor reallocation is itself an independent cause of most U.S. business cycles - recognizing, of course, that what we describe as aggregate shocks do have significant reallocative consequences and that understanding those consequences is important for understanding how aggregate shocks generate their business cycle effects. With respect to policy implications, though, I would focus more on the issue of how, in the United States, the economy may be affected by the prevalence or

---

*Economic Counsellor and Director of Research, International Monetary Fund.

absence of large-scale redistributive shocks, and on the effect this may have had on the NAIRU.

One of the interesting things about the 1990s is that we have had a fairly long period, not of spectacularly rapid growth, but of fairly slow and stable growth, which has allowed unemployment rates to come down quite uniformly across the nation and across industries. And this may be a factor that is enabling us to achieve a lower aggregate level of unemployment without an acceleration of inflation. In Western Europe, I think we see a different phenomenon, which Davis alluded to: It is not the business cycle that is a source of concern there but the lack of flexibility in European labor markets, which has produced persistent increases in unemployment to very high levels. That is an important policy problem, even if it is not a cyclical issue.

With respect to the discussion of real business cycles, as indicated earlier I remain highly skeptical, to put it mildly, of the relevance of shifts in total factor productivity as a primary explanatory variable for U.S. business cycle movement. Indeed, I think the notion that adverse downward movements in total technology cause recessions is just plain silly. This is the theory according to which the 1930s should be known not as the Great Depression but as the Great Vacation.

Turning to the Temin paper and the discussion of it, I very much agree with Temin that we need to acknowledge that recessions in the United States, both prewar and postwar, have a multiplicity of causes. There is no single universal cause, although I would agree with Romer that Temin underplays a bit the role that monetary policy has played in some of our postwar recessions and also in our expansions, which are still more complex phenomena that have a multiplicity of economic causes. And it is not really possible, and in many cases not useful, to try and separate causes out as 50 percent this and 30 percent that. Both necessary and sufficient causes exist, and we cannot always isolate and separate them.

Concerning Bordo, Bergman, and Jonung and the discussion of their paper, I think important things are to be learned from looking at the pre-World War I cyclical experience and the interwar cyclical experience, although I would buy into Cooper's caution that the data are not that good and we probably do not want to emphasize too much the quantitative similarities in business cycle movements, in view of the fact that we are looking at economies that are very, very different in their economic structure now from what they were a century ago. My grandfather, who was born in 1855, witnessed the siege of Paris by the Prussians in 1871. That was a time in which the U.S. and the French and U.K. economies were very different from what they are now, and I would regard any similarity in business cycle movements more as a fortuitous accident than as necessarily an enduring feature of our economic systems.

Turning finally to the Sims paper, here I actually draw more comfort from what is reported and how I interpret it in terms of the way I view business cycles, with monetary policy able to play, at least potentially, a relatively large role in avoiding major business cycle downturns. Sims himself finds, according to his policy simulations, that if the Fed had pursued the alternative policy of the postwar period during the interwar period, the level of industrial production would have been 18 percent higher in 1939 and about 10 percent higher over the preceding decade than it actually was. That is certainly worthwhile having as a consequence of better monetary policy! Moreover, Sims emphasizes that his analysis does not take into account what the role of monetary policy would have been in avoiding the effects of widespread bank failures, which Bernanke and others have shown both interfere with the direct functioning of the economic and financial system and have an enormous negative impact on confidence, as we are seeing now in Japan as well.

And third, looking at Sims's results, I think that there is something bizarre in the interwar results that probably biases downward his estimates of the interest rate mechanism for monetary policy. If you look at his Figure 2, you will see a negative relationship between innovation in currency and the movement of industrial production at the 12-month to 48-month horizon. Why is that? Well, in the '20s and '30s when people went to the bank to draw out currency and put it in the mattress, that type of innovation was associated with negative movements in industrial production. However, it does not follow that the indirect channel of monetary action to stimulate increases in the supply of currency, by cutting the discount rate or engaging in open market operations, would, through that indirect mechanism of expanding currency, have a negative effect on industrial production.

So my suspicion, from the Sims paper correctly looked at, is that a properly conducted monetary policy, including its quasi-fiscal component in providing support to weak banks, could have offset at least one-third to perhaps one-half of the loss of industrial production experienced during the 1930s. And if we add to that the operation of automatic fiscal stabilizers and prompt and forceful discretionary fiscal action in the face of a major economic downturn, then I think it is plausible to conclude that one-half of the Great Depression and perhaps even three-quarters might have been avoided by more forceful policy action in those circumstances. But I think it is important to recognize, and this shows up also in the Bordo paper, that the interwar period was one of exceptionally large shocks. I do not think there is much reason to doubt that it is a real phenomenon. And one needs to be careful about assuming that policy possesses the capacity to offset, virtually immediately, even very large shocks in the economic system. I think Zimmerman made this point as well.

IMPLICATIONS FOR POLICY

Finally, I would like to turn to a couple of concluding issues with respect to economic policies. When I was in the Reagan Administration, I used to believe that you should try to relate what it was you were trying to tell the President to one of his favorite movies. The President was really into movies, and if you could tie it into a movie, then he would get the point. So when we were trying to persuade the Germans and the Japanese to get their economies moving in the mid 1980s I said, "Well, the right movie here is *My Fair Lady*, in the scene at Ascot race track, when Eliza finally blurts out, as her horse is falling behind the pack, 'Move your bloomin' arse!'" That was the message needed at that time.

The Effectiveness of Domestic Monetary Policy

In the present discussion, I would point to two movies: first, the Academy Award winner for Jack Nicholson and Helen Hunt, *As Good As It Gets*, because for U.S. monetary policy over the past decade or so, it is, in my judgment, as good as it gets. "As good as it gets" also means better than one can normally expect it to be. Now I want to emphasize that I share Zimmerman's view that maybe the Fed should not have tightened quite so much in 1989 and particularly should have eased a little more rapidly in 1991. Maybe the Fed was a little too expansionary in '85 and '86 and that came back to haunt us in '87 and '88. I think they should have tightened by at least 25 basis points more a year ago: It would have slowed the economy a little bit, and meant a little bit less of a dilemma now. But those are really quibbles in what has been, by any standard of judgment in any period, really a remarkable record of monetary policy management. It has combined very good management with very good luck.

And I think it is unreasonable to expect that policy on average is going to be quite that good. Sometimes the economy is going to zig when you think it is going to zag, and you are just going to be caught on the wrong foot. Moreover, in some circumstances clearly the right thing for monetary policy to do is, if not create a recession, then at least seriously raise the risk that a recession will occur. That is what the Federal Reserve was doing when it began to retighten monetary policy in the spring of 1988 to resist rising inflationary pressures. Clearly, if policy was tightened through 1989, the expectation was that the economy would slow quite significantly. A slow economy, one that is growing at a little over 1 percent per year, is a candidate for recession, even if you had not had the shock that happened with the invasion of Kuwait. It had to be done in those circumstances, and that was a good recession, not a bad recession. The monetary authority, in its conduct of monetary policy, cannot reasonably be expected to avoid all recessions. The principal objective is to avoid big recessions.

A Defense of International Policy

And here is where the second movie, *Titanic*, comes in. In thinking about the causes of the disaster that was the Great Depression, we should also ask, "What caused the sinking of the Titanic?" Well, the simple answer is the exogenous shock; an iceberg sank the Titanic. But the story is really not quite that simple. Errors were made in the design and manufacture of the Titanic, and there were certainly errors in the way in which the captain managed the ship: the failure of the lookouts to have binoculars, the excessive speed, the inadequate supply of lifeboats, the inadequate deployment of those lifeboats at a sufficiently early time, the failure of the California to recognize the distress signals—all of those things contributed ultimately to the magnitude of the disaster.

And I think business cycle disasters like the Great Depression are of that kind. There was an iceberg, but other things probably contributed to the magnitude of the disaster. However, some believe that the real disaster in the North Atlantic on that cold April morning was not that the Titanic sank, at a loss of 1,500 lives. It was instead that 800 were saved. Think of it. If we had had a policy of no rescues, we would have sent a message, a clear message that ocean safety has to be of paramount concern, to passengers, crews, and ocean shipping lines alike!

I say this only partly in jest, because of those who wave the bloody flag of "Moral Hazard" every time the international community steps forward and says, here we face an actual or potential disaster and here is an occasion in which it is relevant to provide support. Now moral hazard is a real phenomenon, and it is a regrettable phenomenon. And when national governments intervene to provide hundreds of billions of dollars of taxpayers' money as a gift to bail out the savings and loan industry or a trillion dollars to finance the reconstruction of East Germany, or when every time a transportation strike occurs in France the government bows before it and gives the workers what they want, well, we encourage a lot of behavior that we should not be encouraging. And there is always a concern that international financial support sponsored by the International Monetary Fund and others may have such adverse incentive effects. But that does not and should not stop rescue efforts in all circumstances.

We need to recognize that international financial support through the IMF is not a gift, it is a loan. The Mexicans have now repaid more than half their loan and have paid a quite handsome interest rate premium to the government of the United States. They repaid an important part of the loan to the Fund and continue to service that loan fully, as I am certain they will in the future. It is not a gift; the subsidy element is quite small.

Moreover, I think it simply silly to believe that a primary reason motivating capital inflow into Mexico was the expectation that a crisis would occur and an international financial support package would follow. That was not on the radar screen at that time.

I believe the same is true for Korea; despite the experience in Mexico, people were pumping money into the Korean banks because they believed Korea was a strong economy and they believed that if a problem were to occur, the Korean government would bail them out. It was not on the radar screen that the Korean government would not have enough reserves to carry out the bailout itself. Now, the bailout by the Korean government and the expectation of it were a source of moral hazard. But I assert that there was no widespread expectation that the Koreans would not be able to fulfill their guarantee of Korean banks and that international financial support would be called upon.

I draw a distinction here with Russia, because in the case of Russia the perception in the international financial community undoubtedly is that Russia is too important to fail. It is Indonesia, or potential Indonesia, with 10,000 nuclear warheads. And accordingly, there exists a perception that Western governments through the IMF or other means will be prepared to provide financial support to Russia to avoid a crisis, in a way that simply would not be done or even contemplated for other countries in similar circumstances. It was mentioned in the panel discussion yesterday.

There is no doubt in my mind that the problem of moral hazard does exist in the case of Russia: The issue remains what to do about it. If further support is provided, and that issue is being actively discussed, it will undoubtedly be associated with further significant actions by the Russian government. Those actions will probably need enactment by the Duma in advance of disbursement of most of the additional funds to address the critical problem, which is not the exchange rate but the fiscal situation in Russia. Nevertheless, residual doubts necessarily will remain about the effects of that package. And an element of moral hazard will be associated with any international support package. It will provide further evidence to those who believe Russia is "too important to fail."

So what? Moral hazard is with us in many private sector and public sector operations. And in each specific instance, a decision has to be made about whether the moral hazard problem is sufficiently important to outweigh the other relative considerations in making a key policy decision. Sometimes it will be, sometimes it will not. That decision needs to be carefully weighed and carefully decided. In my view, it was the right thing to rescue the 800 who survived the sinking of the Titanic.

About the Authors ...

SUSANTO BASU is Associate Professor of Economics at the University of Michigan. Basu has also been Visiting Assistant Professor of Economics at Harvard University and National Fellow at the Hoover Institution, Stanford University. He is a Faculty Research Fellow at the National Bureau of Economic Research. His most recent articles include "Why Is Productivity Procyclical? Why Do We Care?" (with John G. Fernald), forthcoming in the NBER volume *New Directions in Productivity Research*, and "Appropriate Technology and Growth" (with David N. Weil), also forthcoming. Basu earned his A.B. and his Ph.D. at Harvard University.

U. MICHAEL BERGMAN is Associate Professor in the Department of Economics at Lund University in Sweden. He has also been visiting researcher at Copenhagen Business School, as well as Visiting Professor at Arizona State University and Visiting Scholar at the University of California at Los Angeles. His fields of research are macroeconomics and international finance. Bergman has published several articles on the business cycle, and his forthcoming articles include "Economic Expansions and Fiscal Contractions: International Evidence and the 1982 Danish Stabilization" (with Michael Hutchison). Bergman earned his B.A. in economics and social science and his Ph.D. in economics from Lund University, where his 1992 dissertation topic was "Essays on Economic Fluctuations."

MARK BILS is Associate Professor of Economics at the University of Rochester. He has also held teaching positions at the University of Chicago, the Massachusetts Institute of Technology, and the University of Rochester. He spent a year as National Fellow at the Hoover Institution. Bils is a Research Associate with the NBER Economic Fluctuations Group, and Associate Editor of the *Journal of Monetary Economics*. His research interests include cyclical fluctuations in the labor market; cyclical patterns in productivity, pricing, and inventories; human capital and growth; and growth in quality of goods. Bils received his B.A. from Ohio State University and his Ph.D. from M.I.T., both in economics.

MICHAEL D. BORDO is Professor in the Department of Economics at Rutgers University and Director of its Center for Monetary and Financial History. He has held teaching positions at the University of South Carolina and Carleton University in Ottawa, and he has also taught at Carnegie Mellon, Erasmus University in Rotterdam, and Lund University in Sweden. Bordo is on the board of editors of several economic journals and journals of economic history, and he has published widely. His most recent book is *The Defining Moment: The Great Depression and the American Economy in the Twentieth Century* (with Claudia Goldin and Eugene White). Bordo earned his B.A. in economics and political science at McGill University, his M.Sc. in economics at the London School of Economics, and his Ph.D. at the University of Chicago.

RICARDO J. CABALLERO is Professor of Economics at the Massachusetts Institute of Technology. He has also taught at Columbia University, and he has been Visiting Scholar and Consultant at the International Monetary Fund, the

Inter-American Development Bank, the Federal Reserve Board, and the World Bank. Caballero has been awarded a number of grants and fellowships to support his work. Currently he is Associate/Co-Editor of the *Journal of Monetary Economics* and Associate Editor of *Cuadernos de Economia*. He has published numerous journal articles, most recently "Aggregate Employment Dynamics: Building from Microeconomics" (with Eric M. Engen and John C. Haltiwanger). Caballero earned his B.S. in economics at Pontificia Universidad Catolica de Chile and his Ph.D. in economics at M.I.T.

AGUSTIN G. CARSTENS is Director General of the Department of Economic Research at the Central Bank of Mexico. He has been affiliated with the Banco de Mexico for most of his professional career, serving from 1989 to 1993 as Treasurer in charge of the open-market operations unit, the foreign exchange division, and the management of international reserves. He has published a number of articles on privatization, foreign exchange markets, and other macroeconomic issues in Latin America. These include the recent "One Year of Solitude: Some Pilgrim's Tales about Mexico's 1994-1995 Crisis," in *The American Economic Review*. Carstens earned his B.A. from the Instituto Tecnologico de Mexico and his Ph.D. in economics from the University of Chicago.

LAWRENCE J. CHRISTIANO is Professor of Economics at Northwestern University and a Consultant to the Federal Reserve Banks of Cleveland and Chicago. He has been a Consultant to the Board of Governors of the Federal Reserve System, the International Monetary Fund, and the Federal Reserve Bank of Minneapolis. His principal fields of interest include macroeconomics and applied time series analysis. His most recent articles include "Monetary Policy Shocks: What Have We Learned and to What End?" (with Martin Eichenbaum and Charles Evans) and "Habit Persistence and Asset Returns in an Exchange Economy" (with Michele Boldrin and Jonas Fisher). Christiano received his B.A. and M.A. at the University of Minnesota, his M.Sc. in econometrics/mathematical economics at the London School of Economics, and his Ph.D. in economics at Columbia University.

THOMAS F. COOLEY is Professor of Economics at the University of Rochester and Fred H. Gowen Professor of Economics at Rochester's Simon School of Business. He is also Director of the Bradley Policy Research Center there. He has taught at the University of Pennsylvania, the University of California at Santa Barbara, and Tufts University. Cooley has published papers in many scholarly journals, and the Princeton University Press recently published his book, *Frontiers of Business Cycle Research*. He is the coordinating editor of *The Review of Economic Dynamics* and a member of the editorial board of the *Journal of Monetary Economics*. Cooley earned his B.S. at Rensselaer Polytechnic Institute, his M.A. and Ph.D. at the University of Pennsylvania. Cooley also was awarded a Doctorem Honoris Causa by the Stockholm School of Economics.

RICHARD N. COOPER is Maurits C. Boas Professor of International Economics at Harvard University. He served as Chairman of the National Intelligence Council between 1995 and 1997. He has also been Professor of Economics and Provost at Yale University. Cooper served as Under-Secretary of State for

Economic Affairs, Deputy Assistant Secretary of State for International Monetary Affairs, and Senior Staff Economist at the President's Council of Economic Advisers. He was also Chairman of the Board of the Boston Fed. Cooper was an undergraduate at Oberlin College and received an M.Sc. (Econ) from the London School of Economics and a Ph.D. from Harvard. He is a trustee of Oberlin College. Among his numerous publications are the books *Can Nations Agree?* and *Environment and Resource Policies for the World Economy*, as well as over three hundred articles.

STEVEN J. DAVIS is Professor of Economics at the University of Chicago Graduate School of Business. He is also the President of Chicago Economics and Finance Experts (CEFE), a firm that provides expert assistance to firms engaged in international commerce in North and South America. His past affiliations include positions at the University of Maryland, the Massachusetts Institute of Technology, the Federal Reserve Bank of Chicago, and the Hoover Institution. Davis has published in leading academic and policy journals, and his most recent work includes the book *Job Creation and Destruction* and "Gross Job Flows" for the *Handbook of Labor Economics*. He received his Ph.D. in economics from Brown University in 1986.

RUDIGER DORNBUSCH is Ford Professor of Economics and International Management at the Massachusetts Institute of Technology, where he has taught since 1975. Dornbusch's research interests include exchange rate issues, high inflation, and currency crises, as well as stabilization policy. He has written many books, including most recently *Financial Opening: Policy Lessons for Korea* (edited with Yung Chul Park) and *Reform, Recovery and Growth* (edited with Sebastian Edwards). Dornbusch has written extensively for economic journals and is also a contributor to *BusinessWeek*. He earned his Licence es Sciences Politiques at the University of Geneva, and his Ph.D. in economics at the University of Chicago.

BENJAMIN M. FRIEDMAN is the William Joseph Maier Professor of Political Economy at Harvard University. Before joining the Harvard faculty in 1972, he worked with Morgan Stanley & Co., investment bankers. He has also worked in consulting or other capacities with the Board of Governors of the Federal Reserve System and the Federal Reserve Banks of New York and Boston. Friedman's best known book is *Day of Reckoning: The Consequences of American Economic Policy Under Reagan and After*, which received the George S. Eccles Prize, awarded annually by Columbia University for excellence in writing about economics. He has published several other books and is the author of many journal articles on monetary economics, macroeconomics, and monetary and fiscal policy. Friedman received his A.B., A.M., and Ph.D. in economics from Harvard University. He received an M.Sc. in economics and politics from King's College, Cambridge, where he was a Marshall Scholar.

JEFFREY C. FUHRER is Vice President and Economist at the Federal Reserve Bank of Boston. He is a graduate of Princeton and earned his Ph.D. at Harvard. He began his career at the Board of Governors of the Federal Reserve System, where he was a Senior Economist, and moved to the Boston Fed in 1992. Fuhrer is the author of numerous journal articles on monetary policy, interest rates, and inflation. His most recent articles include "Monetary Policy When Interest Rates Are Bounded at Zero" (with Brian Madigan) and "Towards a Compact, Empirically Verified Rational Expectations Model for Monetary Policy Analysis."

LARS JONUNG is a Professor at the Stockholm School of Economics. His research is focused on stabilization policies, monetary history, and the history of Swedish economic thought. He was Economic Advisor to the Skandinaviska Enskilda Banken from 1989 through 1991 and Chief Economic Advisor to Prime Minister Carl Bildt from 1992 to 1994. He has published several books, including *The Political Economy of Price Controls: The Swedish Experience 1970-1985*. Jonung has also edited several volumes in *The Stockholm School of Economics Revisited*.

HENRY KAUFMAN is President of Henry Kaufman & Company, Inc., a firm specializing in investment management and economic and financial consulting. Earlier he was a Managing Director with Salomon Brothers Inc., where he was in charge of the four research departments. In 1987 Kaufman was awarded the first George S. Eccles Prize for his book *Interest Rates, the Markets, and the New Financial World*. He is Chairman of the Board of Trustees, Institute of International Education; Chairman of the Board of Overseers, Stern School of Business, New York University; and a member of the International Capital Markets Advisory Committee of the Federal Reserve Bank of New York. Kaufman received his B.A. from New York University, an M.S. in finance from Columbia University, and his Ph.D. from N.Y.U.'s Graduate School of Business Administration. He also holds honorary degrees from N.Y.U. and Yeshiva University.

MICHAEL MUSSA is the Economic Counsellor and Director of the Department of Research at the International Monetary Fund, a position he has held since 1991. He is responsible for advising the Management and Executive Board of the Fund on broad issues of economic policy, and he supervises the activities of the Research Department. Before joining the IMF, Mussa was a long-time member of the faculty at the Graduate School of Business of the University of Chicago, where he held the William H. Abbott Professorship of International Business. From 1971 to 1976, he served on the faculty of the Department of Economics at the University of Rochester; during this period he also served as a visiting faculty member at the City University of New York, the London School of Economics, and the Graduate Institute of International Studies in Geneva. Mussa was a member of the U.S. Council of Economic Advisers from 1986 to 1988.

MAURICE OBSTFELD is the Class of 1958 Professor of Economics at the University of California at Berkeley. His interests are in international finance and macroeconomics, areas in which he has published a number of research articles. He received his Ph.D. from M.I.T., later teaching at Columbia, the University of Pennsylvania, and Harvard before moving to Berkeley. Obstfeld has served as a consultant for the International Monetary Fund, the World Bank, the European Commission, and several central banks. His most recent book, coauthored with Kenneth Rogoff, is *Foundations of International Macroeconomics*. He is also coauthor (with Paul Krugman) of *International Economics: Theory and Policy*, which has been translated into seven languages. Obstfeld is a Research Associate of the National

Bureau of Economic Research, a Research Fellow of the Centre for Economic Policy Research, and a Fellow of the Econometric Society.

AVINASH PERSAUD is Global Head of Currency & Commodity Research at J.P. Morgan, where he is responsible for currency recommendations to clients and to in-house traders. Persaud is also a member of the Global Management Committee of Morgan's FX & Commodity Division. He was formerly a Director of Currency Research at the Union Bank of Switzerland. Persaud is the originator of a number of prize-winning analytical tools, including the J. P. Morgan Global Risk Appetite Index, which received an Amex Bank Award for International Economics in 1994. His latest tool, "The Event Risk Indicator," is web-based and real-time, designed to warn investors of a coming currency crash. He is a graduate in International Economics of the London School of Economics.

CHRISTINA D. ROMER is the Class of 1957 — Garff B. Wilson Professor of Economics at the University of California at Berkeley, where she has taught since 1988. Before that, she taught at the Woodrow Wilson School at Princeton University. Romer is currently a Research Associate with the National Bureau of Economic Research. She also serves on the research advisory board for the Committee for Economic Development and the editorial board of *The Review of Economics and Statistics*. She recently coedited (with David H. Romer) the book *Reducing Inflation: Motivation and Strategy*. Romer has written extensively on the business cycle and has a forthcoming article in the *Journal of Economic History*, "Why Did Prices Rise in the 1930s?" Romer earned her B.A. at the College of William and Mary and her Ph.D. from the Massachusetts Institute of Technology, both in economics.

PAUL A. SAMUELSON is Institute Professor Emeritus at the Massachusetts Institute of Technology. He was awarded the Alfred Nobel Memorial Prize in Economic Science in 1970 and has received more than thirty honorary degrees from universities in the United States and abroad. Samuelson was an undergraduate at the University of Chicago and earned his M.A. and Ph.D. at Harvard University. His textbook *Economics* has sold more than three million copies and has been published in over twenty languages. Volumes 6 and 7 of his collected papers are now in preparation. Samuelson has served as consultant or advisor to the U.S. Treasury, the Council of Economic Advisers, the Board of Governors of the Federal Reserve System, and the Congressional Budget Office, as well as many other public and research organizations.

SCOTT SCHUH is an Economist at the Federal Reserve Bank of Boston. Previously, he was an economist at the Board of Governors of the Federal Reserve System, and he has also taught at Johns Hopkins University. Schuh does research on labor markets, investment, and monetary policy, with an emphasis on understanding the macroeconomic implications of microeconomic heterogeneity. His recent publications include the book *Job Creation and Destruction* and the chapter "Small Business and Job Creation: Dissecting the Myth and Reassessing the Facts" in the book *Labor Markets, Employment Policy, and Job Creation* (both with Steven J. Davis and John Haltiwanger). Schuh received his B.A. from California State University, Sacramento, and his M.A. and Ph.D. from Johns Hopkins University.

CHRISTOPHER A. SIMS is Henry Ford II Professor of Economics at Yale University and a Visiting Scholar at the Federal Reserve Bank of New York. He has taught at Harvard University, the University of Minnesota, and the Massachusetts Institute of Technology. Sims's areas of research interest include econometric theory for dynamic models and macroeconomic theory and policy. He is currently a member of the Editorial Board of the *Proceedings of the National Academy of Sciences*, Associate Editor for *Journal of Business and Economic Statistics*, and Senior Advisor to the Brookings Panel on Economic Activity. He has published widely; his most recent article (with Tao Zha) is "Bayesian Methods for Dynamic Multivariate Models." Sims earned his B.A. in mathematics at Harvard College, did graduate work at the University of California at Berkeley, and received his Ph.D. in economics from Harvard University.

PETER TEMIN is Elisha Gray II Professor of Economics at the Massachusetts Institute of Technology, where he has held the positions of Department Head, Professor of Economics, and Associate Professor of Economic History in the Economics Department. He spent a year as Pitt Professor of American History and Institutions, University of Cambridge, and he has also been Assistant Professor of Industrial History at M.I.T.'s Sloan School of Management. Temin is the author of many books, including the forthcoming *Learning by Doing in Markets, Firms, and Nations* (with Naomi R. Lamoreaux and Daniel M. G. Raff). His earlier books include *Lessons from the Great Depression* and *Did Monetary Forces Cause the Great Depression?* He has also written many articles for economic journals. Temin earned his B.A. at Swarthmore College and his Ph.D. at M.I.T., both in economics.

ROBERT K. TRIEST is an Economist at the Federal Reserve Bank of Boston. He has taught at Johns Hopkins University and at the University of California at Davis, where he was an Associate Professor. His research has focused primarily on public finance and labor economics. Recent publications include "Has Poverty Gotten Worse?" in the *Journal of Economic Perspectives*; the book *Social Security Reform: Links to Saving, Investment, and Growth* (coedited with Steven Sass); and "Regional Differences in Family Poverty," in the *New England Economic Review*. Triest received his B.A. from Vassar College and his Ph.D. from the University of Wisconsin at Madison.

MARTIN B. ZIMMERMAN is Chief Economist and Executive Director for governmental relations and corporate economics for Ford Motor Company. Before joining Ford, he was a Professor and Chairman of the Business Economics Department at the University of Michigan's Graduate School of Business Administration. He also taught at the Massachusetts Institute of Technology. In September 1985 Zimmerman interrupted his assignment at the University of Michigan to serve for a year as a Senior Economist on the President's Council of Economic Advisers. He also served on the Advisory Council of the National Aeronautics and Space Administration. He has written many articles, including "Market Incentives for the Safe Operation of Commercial Aviation," (with Severin Borenstein), and "Regulatory Treatment of Abandoned Property: Incentive Effects and Policy Issues." Zimmerman earned his B.A. from Dartmouth College and his Ph.D. in economics from M.I.T.

Conference Participants

Daniel S. Ahearn, *Capital Market Strategies*
Liz Alderman, *Bridge News*
David Altig, *Federal Reserve Bank of Cleveland*
Wayne D. Angell, *Bear, Stearns & Company*
Paul Atkinson, *Organisation de Cooperation et de Développement Economiques*
Susanto Basu, *University of Michigan*
Steven Beckner, *Market News Service*
U. Michael Bergman, *Lund University*
John Berry, *The Washington Post*
Mark Bils, *University of Rochester*
Michael D. Bordo, *Rutgers University*
Frederick Breimyer, *State Street Bank and Trust Company*
Roger E. Brinner, *The Parthenon Group*
Frank Browne, *European Monetary Institute*
Lynn E. Browne, *Federal Reserve Bank of Boston*
Ricardo J. Caballero, *Massachusetts Institute of Technology*
Agustin G. Carstens, *Central Bank of Mexico*
Robert H. Chandross, *Republic National Bank of New York*
Lawrence J. Christiano, *Northwestern University*
Arthur D. Clarke, *Arthur D. Clarke & Company*
Isabelle Clary, *Reuters*
Edwin N. Clift, *Merrill Merchants Bank*
Laura Cohn, *Bloomberg News*
Paul M. Connolly, *Federal Reserve Bank of Boston*
Thomas F. Cooley, *University of Rochester*
Richard N. Cooper, *Harvard University*
E. Gerald Corrigan, *Goldman, Sachs & Company*
Allan Crawford, *Bank of Canada*
Steven J. Davis, *University of Chicago*
J. Dewey Daane, *Vanderbilt University*
Guy Dixon, *Dow Jones Newswires*
Rudiger Dornbusch, *Massachusetts Institute of Technology*
Malcolm Edey, *Reserve Bank of Australia*
Charles Evans, *Federal Reserve Bank of Chicago*
Benjamin M. Friedman, *Harvard University*
Jeffrey C. Fuhrer, *Federal Reserve Bank of Boston*
Lars Jonung, *Stockholm School of Economics*
John Judd, *Federal Reserve Bank of San Francisco*
James Kahn, *Federal Reserve Bank of New York*
Jane Katz, *Federal Reserve Bank of Boston*
Henry Kaufman, *Henry Kaufman & Co., Inc.*
Byung Hwa Kim, *The Bank of Korea*
Michael Klein, *Federal Reserve Bank of Boston*

SPENCER KRANE, *Board of Governors of the Federal Reserve System*
THOMAS K. LAVELLE, *Federal Reserve Bank of Boston*
CHUAN TECK LEE, *Monetary Authority of Singapore*
SHEPARD LEE, *The Lee Auto Malls*
JANE SNEDDON LITTLE, *Federal Reserve Bank of Boston*
ROBERT H. MCGUCKIN, *The Conference Board, Inc.*
STEPHEN K. MCNEES, *Cambridge, MA*
CATHY E. MINEHAN, *Federal Reserve Bank of Boston*
FRANCO MODIGLIANI, *Massachusetts Institute of Technology*
MICHAEL MUSSA, *International Monetary Fund*
JAMES J. NORTON, *Graphic Communications International Union*
MAURICE OBSTFELD, *University of California, Berkeley*
DIMITRI B. PAPADIMITRIOU, *The Jerome Levy Economics Institute*
NICHOLAS S. PERNA, *Fleet Financial Group*
AVINASH PERSAUD, *J.P. Morgan Co., Inc.*
JOAN POSKANZER, *Federal Reserve Bank of Boston*
CHRISTINA D. ROMER, *University of California, Berkeley*
PAUL A. SAMUELSON, *Massachusetts Institute of Technology*
SCOTT SCHUH, *Federal Reserve Bank of Boston*
CHRISTOPHER A. SIMS, *Yale University*
ALLEN SINAI, *Primark Decision Economics*
NEAL M. SOSS, *Credit Suisse First Boston*
WILLIAM O. TAYLOR, *Globe Newspaper Company*
PETER TEMIN, *Massachusetts Institute of Technology*
ROBERT K. TRIEST, *Federal Reserve Bank of Boston*
NANCY WENTZLER, *Office of the Comptroller of the Currency*
WILLIAM WREAN, *Sacajawea & Company*
WILLIAM WREAN, JR., *Sacajawea & Company*
DAVID WYSS, *Standard & Poor's DRI*
GERHARD ZIEBARTH, *Deutsche Bundesbank*
MARTIN B. ZIMMERMAN, *Ford Motor Company*

THE FEDERAL RESERVE BANK OF BOSTON CONFERENCE SERIES

No. 1	Controlling Monetary Aggregates	June 1969
No. 2	The International Adjustment Mechanism	October 1969
No. 3	Financing State and Local Governments in the Seventies (out of print)	June 1970
No. 4	Housing and Monetary Policy (out of print)	October 1970
No. 5	Consumer Spending and Monetary Policy: The Linkages	June 1971
No. 6	Canadian–United States Financial Relationships (out of print)	September 1971
No. 7	Financing Public Schools (out of print)	January 1972
No. 8	Policies for a More Competitive Financial System	June 1972
No. 9	Controlling Monetary Aggregates II: The Implementation	September 1972
No. 10	Issues in Federal Debt Management	June 1973
No. 11	Credit Allocation Techniques and Monetary Policy	September 1973
No. 12	International Aspects of Stabilization Policies (out of print)	June 1974
No. 13	The Economics of a National Electronic Funds Transfer System	October 1974
No. 14	New Mortgage Designs for Stable Housing in an Inflationary Environment	January 1975
No. 15	New England and the Energy Crisis (out of print)	October 1975
No. 16	Funding Pensions: Issues and Implications for Financial Markets	October 1976
No. 17	Minority Business Development	November 1976
No. 18	Key Issues in International Banking	October 1977
No. 19	After the Phillips Curve: Persistence of High Inflation and High Unemployment	June 1978
No. 20	Managed Exchange-Rate Flexibility: The Recent Experience	October 1978
No. 21	The Regulation of Financial Institutions	October 1979
No. 22	The Decline in Productivity Growth	June 1980
No. 23	Controlling Monetary Aggregates III	October 1980
No. 24	The Future of the Thrift Industry	October 1981
No. 25	Saving and Government Policy	October 1982
No. 26	The Political Economy of Monetary Policy: National and International Aspects	July 1983
No. 27	The Economics of Large Government Deficits	October 1983
No. 28	The International Monetary System: Forty Years After Bretton Woods	May 1984

No. 29	Economic Consequences of Tax Simplification	October 1985
No. 30	Lessons from the Income Maintenance Experiments	September 1986
No. 31	The Merger Boom	October 1987
No. 32	International Payments Imbalances in the 1980s	October 1988
No. 33	Are the Distinctions between Equity and Debt Disappearing?	October 1989
No. 34	Is There a Shortfall in Public Capital Investment?	June 1990
No. 35	The Financial Condition and Regulation of Insurance Companies	June 1991
No. 36	Real Estate and the Credit Crunch	September 1992
No. 37	Safeguarding the Banking System in an Environment of Financial Cycles	November 1993
No. 38	Goals, Guidelines, and Constraints Facing Monetary Policymakers	June 1994
No. 39	Is Bank Lending Important for the Transmission of Monetary Policy?	June 1995
No. 40	Technology and Growth	June 1996
No. 41	Social Security Reform: Links to Saving, Investment, and Growth	June 1997
No. 42	Beyond Shocks: What Causes Business Cycles?	June 1998

Copies of individual volumes in the conference series may be obtained without charge by writing to the Research Library—D, Federal Reserve Bank of Boston, P.O. Box 2076, Boston, MA 02106-2076. The fax number is (617) 973-4221, and the e-mail address is boston.library@bos.frb.org. A $10.00 payment (check drawn on a branch of a U.S. bank) will be required for 10 or more volumes or 10 or more copies of the same volume.

Materials may be reprinted from the conference volumes if the source is credited in full, unless it is otherwise noted at the beginning of a paper or discussion. Please send information about any reprinting of materials to the Editor, *New England Economic Review*, Federal Reserve Bank of Boston.